Managed Care
Answer Book

Fifth Edition

Managed Care Answer Book

Fifth Edition

Sheryl Tatar Dacso, JD, DrPH
Clifford C. Dacso, MD, MBA

A PANEL PUBLICATION
ASPEN PUBLISHERS, INC.

Copyright © 2002 by Panel Publishers
A Division of Aspen Publishers, Inc.
A Wolters Kluwer Company
www.panelpublishers.com

ISBN 0-7355-2106-9

Printed in the United States of America

1 2 3 4 5 6 7 8 9 0

About Panel Publishers

Panel Publishers—including the former Little, Brown and Company's Professional Division, Wiley Law Publications, the Bureau of Business Practice, Summers Press, Harcourt Professional Publishing, and Loislaw—is a leading publisher of authoritative and timely treatises, practice manuals, information services, and journals written by specialists to assist attorneys, financial and tax advisors, and other business professionals. Our mission is to provide practical, solution-based how-to information keyed to the latest legislative, judicial, and regulatory developments.

We offer publications in the areas of compensation and benefits, pensions, personal financial planning, payroll, employment, family law, taxation, estate planning, and elder law.

Other Panel products on related issues include:

Books and Manuals
COBRA Handbook
Employee Benefits Answer Book
Flexible Benefits Answer Book
Health Insurance Answer Book
Mandated Benefits Compliance Guide
The Pension Answer Book
Quick Reference to COBRA Compliance
Quick Reference to HIPAA Compliance

Periodicals and Electronic Titles
Compensation and Benefits Management
COBRA Advisory
Flexible Benefits
Medical Benefits
Managed Care Quarterly
Managing Employee Health Benefits
Panel Employee Benefits Library on CD-ROM

PANEL PUBLISHERS
A Division of Aspen Publishers, Inc.
Practical Solutions for Legal and Business Professionals
www.panelpublishers.com

SUBSCRIPTION NOTICE

This Panel product is updated on a periodic basis with supplements to reflect important changes in the subject matter. If you purchased this product directly from Panel, we have already recorded your subscription for the update service.

If, however, you purchased this product from a bookstore and wish to receive future updates and revised or related volumes billed separately with a 30-day examination review, please contact our Customer Service Department at 1-800-234-1660, or send your name, company name (if applicable), address, and the title of the product to:

Panel Publishers
A Division of Aspen Publishers, Inc.
7201 McKinney Circle
Frederick, MD 21704

To Matthew, studying medicine at the University of Texas Medical Branch; Mara, a second year student in the Ecology of Health department at McGill University; and Rebecca, hacking her way through high school; as well as their grandmother, Ruth Tatar, we once again dedicate this work.

About the Authors

Clifford C. Dacso, MD, MBA, is the John S. Dunn Sr. Research Chair in General Internal Medicine at the Baylor College of Medicine and The Methodist Hospital in Houston, Texas. At Baylor he is Professor and Vice-Chair for Strategic Development in the Department of Medicine and is the recipient of several awards for teaching excellence. He is on the Board of Carondelet Health System and the Tucson Heart Hospital. Dr. Dacso holds Bachelor's and Master's degrees from the University of Pennsylvania, a Doctor of Medicine degree, residency, and Infectious Diseases fellowship from Baylor College of Medicine, a Master's degree in Public Health from the University of Texas, and an MBA from Pepperdine University. He is President of eMedicalResearch, Inc., an innovative information management company specializing in health care issues.

Sheryl Tatar Dacso, JD, DrPH, is the Principal of Dacso & Associates, an innovative law and consulting group in Houston, Texas. Specializing in HIPAA, medical group organization and contracting, and rural managed care, Dr. Dacso has brought together a consortium of the finest minds in the health care law field. In addition to a law degree from South Texas College of Law, she holds doctoral and master's degrees from the University of Texas Health Science Center in Houston. During the course of her career, Dr. Dacso has held virtually every type of position in the health law field from in-house counsel to practice leader in health law for a major law firm. She has been highly active in the political process at both the state and national level. Additionally, she has held academic positions at two medical schools and the University of Houston Institute of Law and Medicine. Dr. Dacso consults nationally and is highly sought after as a speaker and commentator.

Contributors

Matthew M. Dacso is a graduate of McGill University of Montreal, PQ, Canada. His chapter was researched in Buenos Aires under the direction of Dr. Adolfo Rubinstein and Dr. Alejandro Razé. Mr. Dacso wishes to express his gratitude to Drs. Rubinstein and Razé, and colleagues at the Hospital Italiano, as well as to Dr. Stephen Spann, Professor and Chairman of Family and Community Medicine at Baylor College of Medicine in Houston, who helped arrange the study.

Jennie E. Tucker is a graduate of the University of Michigan who currently consults for DiamondCluster International in Chicago. She performed the research on which her chapter is based while studying in Buenos Aires. She wishes to express her gratitude and appreciation to Dr. Adolfo Rubinstein and Dr. Alejandro Razé of the Hospital Italiano for their guidance and support during the research project.

Acknowledgments

Clifford Dacso wishes to acknowledge the continuing support of the John S. Dunn, Sr. Foundation and its medical director, Dr. Lloyd Gregory. The Dunn Research Chair in General Medicine has proven to be a life raft in these turbulent academic times and when it comes with the support of Dr. Gregory, it is doubly valuable. The Department of Medicine at Baylor College of Medicine and its Chair, Dr. Andrew I. Schafer, provide just the right amount of challenge and yeast to allow a long job like this to continue. This year, three philanthropists and their charitable foundations provided academic support and guidance. To Morrie Abramson, Chairman of the Board of the University of Houston, Edward O. (Ted) Gaylord, and Selby Sullivan we express our thanks for the support and our gratitude for the friendship.

Sheryl Dacso acknowledges the friendship and support of colleagues at the law firm of Jenkens and Gilchrist, PC, as well as the support of the firm in the writing and collection of data. Ms. Zelma Rosado again provided administrative support as well as interesting fiction to account for the hours spent writing.

The international portions of this book are based on continuing contact with the Eisenhower Exchange Foundation of which we both are Fellows. Ambassador Adrian Basoura provides sound leadership that allows Fellows to study and influence political developments both in the United States and abroad.

Both Clifford and Sheryl acknowledge Dancy Burns, our *non pareil* editor at Aspen Publishers. She cajoles and caresses and, when that fails, holds over our heads the immutable deadline of the coming of her new baby. Dancy is a wonderful person, and we thank her for guiding us through the publication of this book year after year.

Preface

Although managed care and its permutations formed the medical business theme of the last 15 years, the industry has evolved beyond its original parameter. It has grown into a complex system of financing, service providing, and regulation. As costs were squeezed out of the health care system, the Clinton health care plan wove through the political process, and the Internet took hold, managed care and managed cost remained the dominant themes. In fact, managed care was successful in wringing out certain inefficiencies from the health care system, reducing length of stays, and replacing a priestly profession with a business-oriented one. Despite the reduction in real dollars in physicians' incomes, costs continue to rise and, for the most part, outcomes do not improve. What then are the drivers of health care provision and systems that operate in the opening of the 21st century and beyond? The following are trends that are discussed throughout the Fifth Edition:

Commercialization of health care delivery: The ascendancy of for-profit health care reached its apex with Columbia/HCA in hospital services and physician practice management corporations such as PhyCor on the physician side. Their abrupt decline and fall heralded the dramatic decentralization of health care in the wake of the failed Clinton plan. With the dramatic exception of Tenet and a few other national systems, even the Catholic hospitals are, at best, approaching regionalization. Forays of provider the drive into smaller and more profitable health care systems and physician groups has emerged as an important factor in determining cost and quality.

Change in disease patterns: The bubble of the baby boomers courses through the nation's demographics, compelling radical alterations in Medicare and long-term disease management. Where chronically ill people will be cared for, how their last days will be spent, and who will pay are key questions in the future of health care.

Indigent care: Care of the economically disadvantaged has always been a challenge to the health care economy. Heart disease, hypertension, HIV/AIDS, drug addiction, trauma, and depression disproportionately affect the medically underserved, but the health care of the economically disadvantaged is still largely in hospital-based public systems. Add the impact of undocumented patients to that creaking system, and revolution is no longer just optional.

Development of new medical technology: When the managed care revolution began in the 1980s, medical technology was reeling from the introduction of the CAT scan and the role that technology played in substituting for traditional hands-on work of the physician. At that time, cutting cost, the major motivator of the managed care industry, came abruptly in conflict with the development of technology. An initial attempt on the part of the industry was to interpose a physician's evaluation of "medical necessity" between the practicing physician and the patient. Another ploy was to label innovation as experimentation. This latter exercise resulted in dramatic verdicts and an amazing amount of bad press. Despite this obvious failing in managed care, many companies persisted in huge "utilization review" departments that never denied claims but did require enormous expense and caused bad feelings toward managed care.

Physician workforce and supply: Nowhere has the ebb and flow of the medical marketplace been as well demonstrated as in the physician supply and demand analysis. Who can forget the national crisis faced by the Johnson Administration in the mid-1960s over the critical physician shortage? That analysis resulted in a virtual doubling of the size of medical school graduating classes over eight years and the creation of two new disciplines: physician assistants and nurse practitioners. Far from increasing access to health care, the increase in the number of physicians fueled the rise in health care costs with the growth of specialization and its resulting cost.

Role of the environment and society: Until recently, little was known or written about the role of society in the health of the individual. Even with the advance of population sciences, it is impossible to extrapolate epidemiological data to the level of the individual.

Further, epidemiological data is rapidly accumulating to show the importance of the social milieu in the determination of health—a factor never considered in the design of health systems. Research in this area can be expected to contribute to the next leap forward in health care.

Communications and information systems: Despite the Internet revolution and the subsequent "dot bomb," communications in the health care arena are occupying more time and money than ever before. The transformation of data into information and subsequently into judgment requires an elaborate information structure that is revolutionizing the way people relate to their health care systems. The electronic medical record, the bellwether of the future in health care information technology, is still a dream for the future, awaiting solid and reproducible voice recognition technology.

Patients' rights and health plan liability: The concept of patients' rights never entered into the initial formulation of managed care. Patients were "lives" to be managed and had no rights other than those conferred by the canons of medical ethics. As patients became consumers, they became more litigious and demanded a set of legal entitlements, an area still in development.

Change in health care professionals' demographics and roles: When managed care began to grow as a way of delivering medical care to a population, physicians were predominantly male and white. In 2001, almost one-half of medical school graduates are women and, in some schools, the majority is made up of formerly minority populations.

The decline of the hospital: Hospital bed occupancy achieved its zenith immediately prior to the institution of DRG prospective payment for health care in 1982. That such a dramatic reduction in the length of stay for medical care resulted merely from a change in the payment mechanism should have served as a harbinger of the severe excess of medical beds. Nonetheless, acute care hospital beds continued to be built now resulting in an enormous excess capacity that is dragging on attempts at cost saving.

Consumerism and prevention: Consumerism is a concept distinct from patients' rights. Consumerism is a new force in health care and is allied with the wide dissemination of information about health care. Patients are no longer passive receptacles of medical orders;

they are active in decision-making and are increasingly demanding. How to serve information up to patients to allow them to make the right choices is a major challenge. Allied with the dissemination of information comes a desire to avoid being a patient. People are seeking to avoid the scourge of chronic disease they see in their parents.

Variation in health care services: Evidence has accumulated over the past ten years that not all medicine is alike. Across the country, there exists enormous variation in health care services and procedures that cannot be accounted for by mere differences in the health of the populations. Many factors influence this variation including socioeconomic stratum, norms of the medical community, payment capability, and individual comparison shopping. Further analysis of variation in care delivery will tease out very helpful information such as best practices and the value of outcomes measurements.

Legal structure of health care: As the complexity of the health care transaction deepened, laws that regulated the relationships between a patient and a physician were no longer adequate to assure the rights and define the obligations of the myriad parties. Indeed, health law as a discipline is not much older than the rise of managed care. As necessary as it is now, it was inconceivable 20 years ago that the Supreme Court and the Congress would be acting to assure the rights of the individual versus the health care colossus.

Population demographics: The hackneyed image of the gerbil passing through the python is often invoked to describe the cohort born between 1946 and 1964. The first wave of this group is hitting the Medicare shore in the very near future. Not only is this generation big, it is educated and entitled. What its characteristics are and what its health care needs will be the single most influential issue in health care for the next decade.

Complementary and alternative medicine: Coupled with the dissemination of information has come the recognition on the part of the health care consumer that the promise of eternal youth and freedom from sickness has not been fulfilled (as if it had ever been made!) The requirement on the part of the health care consumer that so-called complementary practices be included in benefit plans has caused wide consternation. Although many of these procedures have utility, they have, for the most part, not been subject to the scientific rigor that characterizes mainstream Western medicine. The evaluation and promulgation of information about complementary medicine will form a major focus of the health care debates to come.

Pharmaceuticals and prescription drugs: Arguments concerning the price and availability of ethical pharmaceuticals have reached alarming volume and are likely to continue. The inability of the market to reach equilibrium on this important issue will define a boundary of health care costs for the foreseeable future.

As managed care has achieved iconic status, the real debate about this industry that occupies one seventh of the nation's gross domestic product is becoming more obscure. The nation has awakened to the reality that we observed several years ago that despite a huge amount of our national treasure devoted to the health sector, our population has little to show for it. America's infant mortality rate is far above that of economies far less robust. In conventional measures of wellness, we have received little value for our expense. In spite of this, the American medical system remains the envy of the world in terms of competence, technology, and sophistication. The research and clinical care enterprises continue to be the engines that power drug development, new interventions, and new descriptions of illness and the paths to prevent them. The future holds the challenge of balancing the availability and quality of American medicine with the need for a greater reach into our communities. It is the aim of this book to tease out the threads of the health care themes and define the fences around specific influences to allow thoughtful and accurate planning.

The questions in this book should be used as a guide and an index. We have tried to anticipate the type of questions that a sophisticated student of the health care business would ask. We have benefited from criticism and suggestions by friends and readers, but all error and omissions are ours alone.

Sheryl Tatar Dacso
Clifford C. Dacso

Houston, Texas
and Spruce Head Island, Maine
March 2002

How to Use This Book

Managed Care Answer Book, Fifth Edition is designed for professionals who need quick and authoritative answers to help them navigate the maze of managed care issues. This book uses straightforward language and avoids technical jargon whenever possible, but it also provides professionals with the tools to become conversant in the idiom of managed care. Citations to authority are provided as research aids for those who wish to pursue particular items in greater detail.

Format. The question-and-answer format breaks down complex subject areas into concise units. Introductory text provides an overview of the subject that is covered in detail in the questions and answers. Extensive cross-referencing facilitates locating information. Questions are numbered consecutively within each chapter (e.g., Q 1:1, Q 1:2, Q 1:3).

List of Questions. The detailed List of Questions that follows the Table of Contents helps the reader locate areas of immediate interest. A series of subheadings helps to organize questions by topic within each chapter.

Tables, Charts, and Figures. Included throughout the book are numerous tables, charts, and figures that illustrate material in the text.

Index. An index is provided as a further aid to locating specific information. All references in the index are to question numbers rather than page numbers.

Glossary. A comprehensive glossary is included for easy reference to terms used in the book. A list of acronyms is also provided.

Table of Contents

CHAPTER **5**

CHAPTER **10**

CHAPTER 11

List of Questions

Chapter 1 Introduction and Review of Trends in Managed Care

Overview

The National Debate

Managed Care's Effect

Managed Care and the Physician

Table of Contents

Chapter 2   Health Care in a Global Economy

The Global Health Care Economy

Public Health Issues in a Global Economy

Table of Contents

Chapter 3 Evolution and Revolution in Product Design

Historical Overview

Managed Care Organizations and Products

Health Maintenance Organizations

Preferred Provider Organizations

Point-of-Service and Other Mixed Plans

Community Health Plans and Rural Community Health Systems

Chapter 4 Employer Benefit Plans and Purchasing Organizations

Overview

Table of Contents

Table of Contents

Chapter 6 Managed Care Organizations and Health Care Networks

Introduction

Independent Practice Associations

Fully Integrated Systems

Community-Based Organizations

Legal Issues

Integrated Credentialing and Corporate Compliance

Strategies for Success and Unwinding Failures

Chapter 7 Government Programs

Table of Contents

Table of Contents

Table of Contents

Table of Contents

Corporate Practice of Medicine

Credentialing and Peer Review

Table of Contents

Emergency Medical Treatment and Active Labor Act

ERISA

Table of Contents

Table of Contents

Managed Care Answer Book

Table of Contents

Chapter 9 Medical Care Management

Overview

Utilization Management

Case Management

Hospital-Based Case Management

Table of Contents

Managed Care Organization Case Management

Measuring Case Management Performance

Medical Management

Legal and Regulatory Issues

Table of Contents

Demand Management

Chapter 10 Trends in Quality Management and Consumer Rights

Overview

Table of Contents

Licensing and Certification

State and Federal Requirements

Chapter 11 Managed Care Contracting and Negotiation Strategies

Fundamentals of Contracts

Table of Contents

Direct Contracting

Risk Contracting in the Public Sector

Medicaid Risk Contracts

Medicare + Choice Risk Contracts

Regulatory Issues

Fundamentals of Negotiation

Negotiation Strategies in Managed Care Contracting

Chapter 12 Alternative Dispute Resolution

Overview

Arbitration

Mediation

Table of Contents

Health Care Disputes

Managed Care Disputes

ADR and ERISA Plans

Government Rules

Bad Deals and Salvage Strategies

Table of Contents

Health Plans and Managed Care Information

Health Database Organizations and Community Health Information Networks

Role of Government

Confidentiality of Information

Electronic Medical Records

Telehealth and Telemedicine

Disease Management and Information Technology

Interactive Health Communication

Chapter 14 The Future of Managed Care

Trends

Hospitals and Physician Groups

Table of Contents

Chapter 1

Introduction and Review of Trends in Managed Care

When the first edition of *Managed Care Answer Book* was published, the concept of managed care was new, confusing, and, it appeared, more than slightly dangerous. The authors advocated managed care and its potential benefits, such as decreasing variation within the system of health care delivery and providing measures for success. Subsequent editions covered the Health Care Security Act of 1994, now inextricably intertwined with former President Bill Clinton and Senator Hillary Clinton and emblematic of the failure of big government to repair what is fundamentally a business problem. Since then, many of the objectives of the Health Care Security Act have been achieved using more subtle legislative reforms such as the Health Insurance Portability and Accountability Act of 1996 (HIPAA) and the Balanced Budget Act of 1997 (BBA). Most states have implemented sweeping reforms affecting managed care through legislation, rule making, and case law.

The deterioration of several large long-term health care companies and significant reductions in the valuation of the managed care, hospital, physician practice management (PPM), and home health sectors continue unabated.[1] Consolidation in the health care industry continues as predicted, and the economic pressures on the industry continue to expand. Health maintenance organizations (HMOs) report reductions in membership, and providers report reduced compensation. A report by the California Medical Association suggests that health plans are beginning to experience the same financial pressures that physicians and hospitals have experienced for years.[2] Many health plans may be forced to seek the protection of the bankruptcy courts through receivership or reorganization proceedings.

The Medicare, Medicaid, and SCHIP Balanced Budget Refinement Act of 1999 (BBRA) did little to correct the BBA's impact on providers despite efforts to restore funds previously eliminated or reduced. As the Medicare + Choice program is implemented across the country, many managed care plans have ceased further enrollment or expansion, and many are leaving markets considered unprofitable. These markets tend to be those where a Medicare risk program is most desired by the community. The accelerating withdrawal of commercial managed care organizations (MCOs) from the Medicare market is likely to provide a fierce reaction from those who have become accustomed to "value-adds" such as prescription benefits.

It appears that a patients' bill of rights will continue to be debated but never enacted by Congress, given the politics of the 2002 election year.

Managed care trends include the following:

- Reemergence of medical care inflation as the "managed care miracle" ceases to be a subject of polite conversation
- Continued financial pressure on health care payments as the effects of the BBA are amplified by the recession
- Increasing pressure on managed care companies to offer unprofitable Medicare products
- Switch from defined benefit to defined contribution employer-based health care plans, making the consumer a careful shopper
- Increasing focus on quality and outcomes in response to the Institute of Medicine's report on medi-

cal errors and the widespread perception that medical decision making is not reproducible

- Change in disease management from the step-check method of utilization review restrictions on medical practice to decision support for the consumer
- Rise of e-health

Overview

Q 1:1   What is managed care?

Broadly speaking, managed care is a system of delivering health care that combines financing or insurance functions with the management of the delivery of health care services. Usually, it involves a party other than the physician and the patient in the process of determining the type, nature, and extent of medical care delivered. The managed care concept generally combines a financing mechanism and a delivery system under the control and direction of a single management entity. Some forms of indemnity insurance that limit benefits using various methods based on cost and utilization may fall under this rubric, but such a system is not truly managed. Limitations on benefits serve to limit access nonselectively. A managed care system may limit benefits to its customers but will actively manage those limitations by assessing their outcomes. A managed care system actively manages both the medical and financial aspects of a patient's care.

Beyond this general description, the phrase *managed care* has become laden with economic, moral, and ethical overtones. In some political circles, it has become synonymous with denying medical care to people in need solely on the basis of economic and profit considerations. From the perspective of nurses, physicians, and other health care professionals, it has come to mean the depersonalization of medical care by putting a disinterested intermediary between the patient and the caregiver. To these health care professionals, managed care is symbolized by the transmutation of a general practitioner to a primary care physician (PCP) and a nurse practitioner to a health care provider.

Managed care is most often associated with the HMO, which is really one of the many forms of managed care. Other systems, such as early forms of preferred provider organizations (PPOs), merely negotiated discounts with physicians and hospitals in return for volume considerations in pricing and prompt payment. These systems managed costs rather than care, and their financial success was emblematic of the vast amount of fat in the medical care system. Later generations of managed care began to focus more on actual care management with an emphasis on outcome measures as indicators of success.

Defining managed care is difficult because it is an evolving concept that embraces disparate organizations. The sharp distinctions that once existed between different types of plans have become clouded as plans have adopted various features of other plans. The characteristics most common to managed care include (1) arrangements with selected providers who furnish a package of services to enrollees; (2) explicit criteria for selection of providers; (3) quality assurance, utilization review, and outcome measures; (4) financial or program coverage incentives or penalties to encourage use of selected providers; (5) provider risk-sharing arrangements; and (6) management of providers to ensure that enrollees or members receive appropriate care from the most cost-efficient mix of providers.

Q 1:2 How did managed care evolve?

To understand the evolution of managed care, it is important to understand the evolution of the U.S. system of insurance and health care. In the early 1900s, the American health care system could best be characterized as a system in which "a random patient with a random disease consulting a doctor chosen at random had better than a 50-50 chance of benefiting from the encounter."[3] By the 1940s, however, modern medicine emerged with great improvements in the training of physicians and the use of new therapies such as penicillin. With these advances came increases in health care costs.

Efforts to pay for health care services also have roots in early American history. The important historic events that influenced the evolution of managed care are chronicled in appendix 1-A at the end of this chapter.

Early Forms of Insurance. Commercial health insurance initially covered only accidents by paying a weekly indemnity in the event the insured was injured in an accident. In the late 1800s, similar policies extended coverage to include wage replacement for disability resulting from specified diseases, and eventually from all diseases. These policies were initially sold to individual wage earners; however, expenses associated with sales and other costs prompted the development of group policies for employees of a business.

Before World War I and until 1920, there was a major effort to enact compulsory health insurance in the United States. Although workers' compensation reform was enacted in almost all states, efforts to require health insurance failed because of the political clout of the American Medical Association (AMA). World War I ended that progressive era in health care reform and with it any consideration of compulsory health insurance.

Industry-specific hospital associations developed in response to the needs of certain high-risk industries, including railroad, construction, mining, and timber, extending a program initiated by the American Federation of Labor (AFL). These industries fostered the development of comprehensive health care services for employees and their dependents. These associations ceased to operate after World War II but served as the precursors to a new health care system that became known as the HMO because many of them were prepaid.

Rise of Commercial Insurance. During the Great Depression (1931–1939), new systems evolved, including the precursor to Blue Shield, in which a group of schoolteachers in Dallas, Texas, contracted with Baylor University Hospital for health care services on a prepaid basis. Each teacher paid $1.50 per semester, which guaranteed three weeks of hospital care in semiprivate rooms with no extra charges for operating rooms, laboratory services, or routine drugs and dressings. Similar plans had been created in Rockville, Illinois (1912); Grinnell, Iowa (1921); and Brattleboro, Vermont (1927).[4]

In a surprising move in the late 1930s, the AMA, in reaction to the rapid expansion of Blue Shield, approved the concept of a periodic payment plan for physician services, provided that the plan was physician controlled and community based. These plans, which became known as the Blue Cross plans, were launched in California, Michigan, and New York in 1939 as a combination direct service and indemnity product open to participation by all physicians. The reason for the dramatic shift in AMA policy was to forestall competition in the market by other plans and possible government intervention. Eventually, Blue Cross and Blue Shield began cooperating in their marketing and administration in most of the states in which they were operating and, until recently, were not-for-profits.

At the same time, commercial insurance carriers began to market hospital and surgical insurance policies, although indemnity surgical insurance had been added to disability policies as early as 1903. The earlier policies covered hospital room and board. Surgical benefits were introduced later. The major difference between these commercial indemnity policies and those offered through plans such as Blue Cross/Blue Shield and other fraternal or industrial organizations was the absence of any promise to deliver actual hospital or medical services. The commercial indemnity insurers had little interest in when the patient sought care or which physician provided that care. In fact, the insurance companies formed a relationship only with the insured, through the policy purchased. The insured patient paid the physician and was "indemnified" for the out-of-pocket payment from the insurance company.

Early Government Initiatives. Although a comprehensive national health benefit program was the focus of a bitter legislative battle in 1948 that gave rise to *socialized medicine* as a term of opprobrium, success glimmered first in the Johnson Administration. In the 1960s, after three failed efforts to adopt a national health insurance system for all Americans, the federal government focused on the two most vulnerable populations without access to private health insurance — the poor and the elderly. Despite strong opposition from the AMA, in 1965 Medicare was enacted for the elderly as an expansion of Social Security and Medicaid was enacted for the poor as a joint federal and state entitlement program. These programs are discussed in more detail in chapter 7.

Early Managed Care. Managed care evolved from traditional health care, which lacked organized systems to manage care. The delivery models that are currently referred to as managed care developed from two very different forms of organizations: (1) the county medical society-sponsored medical care foundations and (2) the group- and staff-model prepaid group practice organizations. Group- and staff-model HMOs had their roots in the 1930s with the advent of the Kaiser Health Plan during World War II, which used a clinic-based system. The foundation form came later. Other organizations developed, including Kaiser Permanente, the Group Health Cooperative of Puget Sound, the Health Insurance Plan of Greater New York, Group Health Inc. in Minneapolis, and the Group Health Association of Washington, D.C., which were pioneers of the MCOs referred to as group- and staff-model HMOs.[5]

The evolution of managed care and MCOs began in the early twentieth century and continues in the twenty-first. Appendix 1-A includes a timeline of important events in the development of managed care and MCOs. Most important was the enactment of the HMO Act in 1973, which paved the way for HMO growth, which accelerated in the 1980s and 1990s with the conversion of many nonprofit health plans and insurers to publicly held companies with access to capital.

Some early managed care systems contained cost by providing global care and putting the providers at risk. They emphasized preventive as well as crisis-oriented intervention. Others merely negotiated discounts with physicians and hospitals in return for volume considerations in pricing. These systems could well be called managed cost, not managed care. Later generations of MCOs increasingly emphasized outcome measures as indicators of success. These organizations are discussed in more detail in chapters 9 and 10.

Q 1:3   What role has managed care played in health care reform?

Managed care has been a component of every major effort to reform health care. Even before President Clinton proposed the Health

Care Security Act in 1994, managed care had been a platform for health care reform, in both the public and private sectors.

Managed Care and Health Care Policy. Beginning in 1969, after enactment of Medicare and Medicaid, there was a dramatic shift in government focus from expansion of health care to a strategy of cost containment. In developing health care policy during the turbulent period from 1969 through 1980, six programs were identified as necessary to control costs:[6]

1. Reform of provider reimbursement to involve providers in the economics of health care to a much greater extent than just "getting paid";
2. Redesign of insurance benefits to place greater emphasis on primary care and reduce incentives for use of expensive specialty and acute-care services;
3. Expansion of prepaid group practice programs and other organized systems that encourage efficiency;
4. Greater use of peer review programs to improve quality and manage utilization;
5. Adoption of area-wide planning to make the most efficient use of health care resources; and
6. Enhanced use of preventive medicine and health education.

These policies became the bases for regulatory reform instead of legislative reform.

In a country where national policy favors competition, health care policy was not immune. The politics surrounding health care reform became extremely complex and highly partisan. During this period the AMA lost much of its younger membership and had to redefine itself as the representative organization of physician interests, and other professional organizations, such as the American Group Practice Association (AGPA) and the American Association of Medical Colleges (AAMC), began to assert their political influence. AGPA represented the growing number of physicians working in groups. AAMC represented the interests of academic medicine.

Managed Care in Legislation. With the enactment of the HMO Act of 1973 [Pub L No 93-222], the HMO model became a necessity in the package of products offered by any private insurer, partly because the Act required all employers with at least 25 employees to offer an HMO option to their employees. During the 1970s and 1980s, new managed health care companies, such as U.S. HealthCare, United HealthCare, and HealthCare Compare, joined the older HMO prototypes, such as Kaiser Permanente Medical Care and the Harvard Community Health Plan, to overtake the more traditional insurance carriers, such as TransAmerica, Allstate, and New England Mutual. To survive, insurers such as CIGNA and Blue Cross/Blue Shield had to restructure their operations to remain competitive as managed care plans.

Managed Care and the Courts. Managed care reform was also being advanced through court decisions. In response to the early use of the cooperative model for organizing and financing health care services (see appendix 1-A for reference to Dr. Michael A. Shadid, in 1927, 1934, and 1947, and the Group Health Association (GHA) in 1937), the AMA and several local medical societies took an aggressive approach in 1938 that led to one of the earliest antitrust actions against a trade association by a grand jury based on violations of Sherman antitrust laws. The case set a precedent and resulted in a U.S. Supreme Court decision upholding fines against the AMA and the District of Columbia Medical Society for anticompetitive conduct involving GHA. This decision is important because it opened the health care industry to managed care; however, the mechanisms by which providers participated in managed care were still subject to scrutiny. In the landmark case of *Arizona v. Maricopa Medical Society* [457 US 332 (1982)], a county medical society was found to be in violation of federal antitrust laws because of well-intentioned efforts to set minimum fees for managed care contracting. This case was the first of many cases in which antitrust laws were used to "manage" the managed care movement.

Managed Care and Payment Reform. In 1983, in an effort to contain costs, the Health Care Financing Administration (HCFA), now the Centers for Medicare and Medicaid Services (CMS), instituted a prospective payment system (PPS) approach to reimbursing hospitals using diagnosis-related groups (DRGs) to determine the amount of payment. The theory behind PPS was that paying hospitals a fixed amount would provide an incentive for them to treat patients in a more cost-effective manner. To ensure that quality standards were maintained and to prevent underutilization, professional review organizations (PROs) monitored the care. This program had the greatest single impact on the cost of hospital care because it changed the entire focus of health care delivery and use of acute-care services. In 1989 and 1990, the government began to explore models of payment reform intended to limit physician payments, culminating in a new payment system, the Resource-Based Relative Value Scale (RBRVS), developed by Dr. William C. Hsiao of the Harvard School of Public Health.

Q 1:4 Did early efforts to manage care reduce the dramatic escalation in the cost of health care?

No. Despite the increased penetration of managed care in the U.S. health insurance market, managed care did nothing to prevent the health care financial crisis that occurred in the early 1990s. This crisis occurred because of two important factors: escalating health care costs and growing unavailability of affordable health care. The crisis threatened U.S. competitiveness in world markets and greatly affected the U.S. economy because so much of its gross domestic product (GDP) was spent on health care. In the 1990s, on a per capita basis, the United States spent 40 percent more than Canada for health care, 90 percent more than Germany, and 125 percent more than Japan.[7] Despite these high expenditures, the U.S. ranking in infant mortality and life expectancy rates was not enhanced. In fact, in 2002, it is estimated that 46.5 million Americans are uninsured. One third of the uninsured have incomes below the poverty level in 2002 ($18,100 annually for a family of four), and 27 percent of the uninsured are under the age of 19.[8]

Q 1:5 How is managed care distinguished from other health care financing arrangements?

Managed care arrangements should have many of the characteristics outlined in Q 1:1. Managed care systems can be distinguished from the systems of fiscal intermediaries, whose primary function is to channel a payer's funds to the health care provider. These intermediaries may perform utilization review and quality control functions but do not manage or assume risk for an enrollee. A managed care provider takes at least some of the risk for the patient's health care. Rather than simply approving or denying coverage based on a benefit plan, the health care manager intervenes to provide what it considers appropriate medical care for the minimum cost.

This distinction becomes critical as the labels for care delivery proliferate. Even traditional insurance companies may vend to a self-insured employer a product called a third-party intermediary, whereby they perform no insurance function; they merely process claims and do precertification and other clerical tasks. The self-insured employer holds the risk.

In analyzing the structure-function relationships of an MCO, it is useful to follow the money. It is also useful to follow the risk because the party that holds the risk has the most at stake in the successful management of the care of the patient.

Q 1:6   What has been driving the growth of managed care?

Managed care growth has been fueled by demands for cost control, accountability, access, and quality. Medical costs have always been irritants for patients and payers. Nevertheless, physicians were historically at the top of the nation's most respected list. Hospitals, by virtue of their voluntary, nonprofit nature, were considered public treasures, regarded with pride. It is difficult to remember in this age of profit-making hospital consortia that community fundraisers were commonly directed at building hospital wings and that broad-ranging federal legislation (the Hill-Burton Act) tried to put a hospital in every community as recently as 50 years ago.

The turning point in the public perception of the medical profession may have occurred when the ethical prohibition against physician advertising was lifted. The notion of physician advertising was so contrary to patients' perception of the doctor's priestly role that the medical profession immediately lost much of its credibility and respect. The increase in medical malpractice litigation then was also symptomatic of the widely held feeling that if medicine cost so much, it had to be perfect and that advertising was some form of implied guarantee. Similarly, a notion grew that medicine was simply too dear and hospitals and physicians made too much money. Malpractice litigation was viewed as a way to spread the wealth. The medical profession was increasingly seen as avaricious and unresponsive to the needs of the public. The feeling was, "If they want to act like a business, we'll simply have to treat them like a business." This reaction included increased regulation and price competition.

Managed care has been viewed as an answer to the problems of increasing price, decreasing access, and uncertain quality. Cost-conscious employers or payers can better estimate at the beginning

Figure 1-1.   **National Health Expenditures, 1990–2008 (projected)**

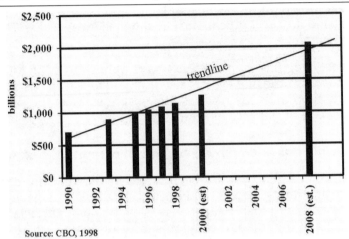

Source: CBO, 1998

of the fiscal year what their medical costs will be at the end. Patients, on the other hand, feel insulated from medical price increases and catastrophic expenses that could completely deplete their assets.

Providing medical care is expensive. Figure 1-1 shows U.S. health care expenditures over time. Although medical care expenditures have continued to grow, the rate of growth has decelerated. Initially, there was explosive growth in the number of HMOs, which eventually moderated, only to pick up again as government programs increasingly mandated care management. Determining the current number of HMOs is difficult primarily because of the large numbers of mergers and acquisitions that now mark the industry. More significant than the absolute number of HMOs is the number of enrollees, which continues to increase (see Figure 1-2).

Q 1:7   What are the challenges to the continued growth of managed care?

The continued growth and future viability of managed care will be affected by several events in the industry. Historically strong and successful MCOs such as Kaiser Permanente have had to divest holdings in many states because of significant losses of hundreds of millions of dollars. Oxford Health Plans, a Connecticut-based for-profit

Figure 1-2.   Total HMO Enrollment and Growth Rate: January 1988 to January 1998

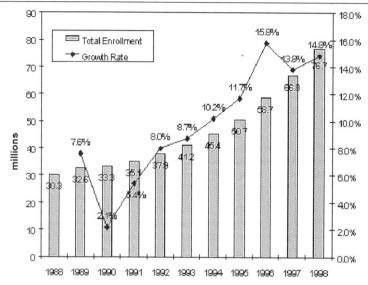

Source: Interstudy Publications http://www.hmodata.com/dir82pr.html

managed care company serving the New York area, experienced significant losses when its stock was first traded on the stock exchange despite positive predictions. A number of MCOs have filed for bankruptcy. Many large companies, such as FPA (once a darling of Wall Street), have used the bankruptcy courts to get out of untenable financial circumstances created by insolvent positions in managed care. These filings for creditor protection have rippled through the health care industry, with many participating physician groups declaring bankruptcy along with the primary MCO with which they contracted. For these and other reasons, for-profit managed care is no longer attractive to speculators, and access to capital is becoming more difficult. Further, the federal and state governments are adopting more stringent consumer-protection legislation and rules, which have the effect of reducing profitability.

Despite the government's effort to move eligible populations into managed care, many for-profit HMOs are not participating because of the reduced payments and regulatory burden of compliance. As discussed in more detail in chapter 7, M + C payment rates are lower than predicted. With the early profits gone from the Medicare managed care market, many HMOs are terminating participation in M + C plans. The same is occurring in the Medicaid managed care market, with many health plans choosing not to bid for the state contracts owing, in part, to the reduced contract rates and the cost of "value-added" services.

With the federal government funding almost 40 percent of total health care expenditures in the United States (over $540 billion in 1998[9]), ongoing congressional and presidential debates on containing federal spending for health care will push the issue of reforming the system to the front line of health care policy decisions. The federal tax subsidies for private health insurance coverage total over $600 billion—money that could be available to the federal and state governments for more universal health care coverage.[10] As discussed in chapter 2, when the total GDP relating to health care in the United Kingdom (where health care access is universal and coverage is mostly equal) is the same as the amount associated only with government programs and tax subsidies for private insurance programs in the United States, the issues of access, coverage, and cost become much more telling of the differences in management of care and cost between these two countries. Health care is much more expensive and much less available under the current U.S. system.

Despite the consolidation of providers and payers in the marketplace, and the trends that have contributed to the growth of managed care, health insurance premium costs have increased. According to data from Watson Wyatt Worldwide, premium rates increased 5 to 7 percent in 1998 and 1999, with point-of-service (POS) plan rates up almost 9 percent in 1999. Data for 2001 show the trend continuing. As premiums rise, employers will find it difficult to maintain health insurance coverage for their employees. Alternatively, employers will ask their employees to contribute a larger percentage of the premium cost. Figure 1-3 shows the differences in premium costs between various types of health plans.

Q 1:8   What are the most recent significant issues and trends affecting health plans and providers?

A number of changes in the health care industry have affected health plans and providers that participate in managed care arrange-

Figure 1-3.   Average Actual Premium Cost Increases in 2001

Indemnity	9.6%
PPO	9.1%
POS	9.6%
HMO	10.5%
Overall	10.3%

Source: Watson Wyatt Worldwide, Employers Facing More Double-Digit Increases in Health Care Benefit Costs, http://www.watsonwyatt.com/news/article.asp?ArticleID = 8034.

ments. These changes are all associated with an increased level of financial distress and uncertainty in the managed care industry. Important trends include (1) increased merger and consolidation activity among health plans throughout the country, (2) withdrawal of health plans from certain markets, (3) continued regulatory and administrative pressures, and (4) increased legal liability.

Liability Reform. As discussed in detail in chapter 8, the managed care industry has become a target for litigation and liability reform. The Employee Retirement Income Security Act of 1974 (ERISA) and its preemption of state law have been substantially limited by state legislative initiatives and judicial challenges.

Many states have passed legislation permitting liability lawsuits against insurers and HMOs on the basis of their utilization decisions. For example, Texas, Missouri, and Georgia have enacted statutes that hold health plans liable for medical malpractice without impinging on ERISA,[11] and several other states are considering similar bills.

Policymakers at the national level have considered legislative changes that would increase MCOs' exposure to civil liability for withholding coverage or failing to deliver needed care. These changes were contentiously debated as part of the patient-protection bills introduced in the 105th and 106th Congresses.[12] Leading proposals from both political parties have included provisions that would reduce barriers to lawsuits against plans for withholding coverage or failing to deliver needed care. Specifically, these provisions sought to undo a degree of legal immunity conferred by ERISA, as it has been interpreted by the federal courts.[13]

Recent court decisions have eroded ERISA preemption, leaving providers and plans more vulnerable to liability for administrative decisions.[14] For example, courts sometimes allow health plans to be held vicariously liable for medical malpractice committed by affiliated physicians and even for negligently selecting and monitoring their medical personnel.[15]

Finally, the former tobacco litigation lawyers have targeted HMOs and MCOs using novel theories of liability based on the Americans with Disabilities Act (ADA), the Racketeer Influenced and Corrupt Organizations Act (RICO), and antitrust laws (see chapter 8).

Reimbursement Reform and the Balanced Budget Act of 1997 and the Medicare, Medicaid, Balanced Budget Refinement Act of 1999. On November 29, 1999, President Clinton signed a massive federal government spending bill [HR 3194, 106th Cong (1999)] that included a financial package for Medicare providers [HR 3426, 106th Cong (1999)] totaling $16 billion over five years and $27 billion over ten years. Besides HMOs, hospitals were the biggest winners. They will receive about $7.2 billion over five years, according to the Congressional Budget Office (CBO). Skilled nursing facilities will receive $2.1 billion over five years, and home health agencies will receive $1.3 billion over five years. Although the law contains some provisions affecting physicians, those provisions do not increase Medicare payments. The law will help rural areas indirectly, because rural providers often own home health agencies and skilled nursing facilities. Rural areas will also benefit from bonus payments for M + C plans entering underserved areas. This issue is discussed in more detail in chapter 7.

Medicare Solvency. There has never been consensus on the status of the Medicare trust. Debates constantly occur between the parties, between the Office of Management and Budget (OMB) and CBO, and even within CMS as to whether there is a surplus. The OMB said categorically in 2002 that there is no Medicare surplus. Further, the OMB states:

> Currently, there is no comprehensive measure of Medicare's solvency that takes into account SMI [supplementary medical insurance] finances, as well as HI [hospital insurance]. This seriously underestimates the magnitude of the Medicare financial problem. The Medicare Trustees acknowledged this disconnect in their 2001 Trustees report. They stated that: "Although

this report focuses on the financial status of the HI Trust Fund, it is important to recognize the financial challenges facing the Medicare program as a whole and the need for integrated solutions." As the Trustees report begins to show, on a combined basis Medicare spending will grow from 2.2 percent of GDP in 2000 to 4.5 percent in 2030 and 8.5 percent in 2075. Sources of dedicated Medicare financing will rise at a slower rate, from 1.8 percent of GDP in 2000, to 2.2 percent in 2030, and 2.5 percent in 2075. The gap in Medicare financing will therefore grow from 0.4 percent of GDP in 2000 to six percent of GDP in 2075.

[See http://www.whitehouse.gov/omb/budget/fy2002/bud13.html.]

Q 1:9   What are the policy issues associated with trends in liability in managed care?

No industry has experienced more change in the past few years than the health care industry. No segment of the health care industry has experienced as much scrutiny over the past five years as the managed care industry. HMOs, PPOs, preferred provider arrangements (PPAs), POS plans, and other MCOs are encountering direct liability exposure in lawsuits initiated against them by plan enrollees and affiliated physicians. The regulation of MCOs has become a focus of federal and state lawmakers who seek to make insurers and HMOs legally accountable to the public while protecting consumers' rights. Each year, new legislation, new regulations, and new case law outcomes have an impact on various aspects of managed care. The reasons for this increased focus on managed care are myriad but all cut across a very fundamental tension in health care: social policy versus the law.

In trying to balance social policy and the law, several issues must be considered: (1) increasing the provider's responsibility for quality and cost while limiting third-party authority to intervene in medical decision making; (2) containing costs while assuring quality; (3) balancing a decentralized, competitive, and incentive-based system against a system that regulates, centralizes, and attempts to control through regulatory oversight; (4) the belief that for most medical decisions there is a "right way" (medicine as science) versus the reality that there is much uncertainty in medicine and physicians must rely on professional judgment in patient care decisions (medicine as art); and (5) addressing the need for innovation in response to the demands of health care reform while recognizing that there are constraints in the law that restrict such innovations.

As discussed in Q 1:8, the combination of legislative reforms opening the way for suing MCOs for their decisions and the use of existing federal and state laws to leverage liability claims in court are significant issues. Consumers, trial lawyers, and physicians appear to be on one side, with employers, the insurance industry, and their trade associations on the other.

Proponents of liability reform assert that (1) freeing up access to legal remedies will compensate patients who suffer physical or financial injury as a result of decisions made negligently, in bad faith, or in breach of contractual obligations; (2) legal checks on managed care practices will sound a warning to health plans about the limits of public tolerance, thereby improving the quality of care; and (3) clearing avenues to suits against plans will correct a stark deficiency in health plans' accountability compared with that of physicians and hospitals. Opponents assert that (1) liability proponents overestimate the role of health plans in medical decision making and idealize the potential for litigation to influence quality of care and (2) the collateral consequences of expanded liability will be premium increases, reductions in benefits, and even market exit of affordable health insurance. Employers add that premium increases, plus the fear of direct liability, will prompt them to trim benefit packages or terminate coverage altogether.[16]

Q 1:10 What are the major factors that will affect the future of managed care?

Among the major factors that will affect the future of managed care are employer benefit plans, demographics, the physician workforce, financial constraints, tax incentives, and legal, regulatory, and legislative changes.

Employer Benefit Plans. As the major purchasers of health care benefits, employers have great influence over benefits coverage and plan structure (copayments, premiums, and network products). Many employers pay either the full cost or a fixed percentage of the premium of any health plan offered. This allows fee-for-service plans to have the greatest level of employer subsidy. Unless employees are given responsibility for paying more of their health insurance premium, they have little incentive to select the lower-cost plans.[17] As employers become more active consumers of health care plans, their use of incentives to encourage employees to use low-cost plans has been effective. In times of full employment, such as 1997–1999, competition for the workforce increases and there is concomitant upward pressure on benefits. This situation is somewhat analogous to the rise of health insurance itself following World War II.

Demographics. Most managed care arrangements require a specific mix of providers. There are also strictures governing the population of Medicare HMOs. In view of the American preference for choice, significant incentives are needed to influence consumer behavior. This preference is much more pronounced among the elderly, whose level of attachment to a health plan often is directly related to location of hospitals, drug stores, and clinics. Although many managed care arrangements use economic incentives (copayments and deductibles) to influence choice, many also include POS features and other "opt-outs" to allow for more freedom of choice, balanced with higher out-of-pocket charges for using non-network providers. These issues are discussed in detail in chapters 3 and 4. In addition, rural and inner-city populations have special needs. Many MCOs are unable to provide adequate coverage for them as a result of the sparseness of providers. These issues are discussed in detail in chapters 5 and 6.

Physician Workforce. Managed care depends on an adequate supply of PCPs who can manage a patient's care and ensure that patients receive only medically necessary services (however loosely or strictly that term is construed). These PCPs (family practice, general internal medicine, and general pediatrics) are conventionally thought to be in short supply because of the historical focus of medical education and training on subspecialization. The reality of physician supply is always a subject of debate in the literature. The physician density in the United States is one of the highest in the world; it is the distribution of physicians (and therfore access to care) that is the crux of the problem rather than actual numbers of physicians. On the other hand, there is thought to be an oversupply of many types of specialists, who are finding it increasingly difficult to survive without being associated with a managed care plan. A fascinating turnaround heralded in early 2002 is the suggestion that there may be a shortage of specialists. The medical manpower market is indeed evolving and uncertain, as shown below:

1. Obstetrician-gynecologists were at one time demanding to be considered PCPs for women. Heretofore, they had universally been considered specialists. Some, however, now find that, although managed care plans encourage them to provide primary care, they feel uncomfortable in that role. Data also suggest that specialists serving as PCPs may utilize resources at a higher rate when they practice outside their specialties. The converse is also true: Specialists may utilize resources more appropriately within their specialties and have superior outcomes when compared to generalists. An obstetrician can be a PCP and accept pitifully low rates, or be a specialist and depend on PCPs for referrals. The choice must be governed by what is best for the doctor's patients.

2. Publicly held management corporations are consolidating physicians' practices and contracting as units. They are also consolidating into large corporations capable of executing nationwide contracts for care. Hospital-based primary care groups, constructed originally as defensive measures, are suffering from a lack of profitability and demonstrated contribution to the profit margin.

3. Physicians' incomes are declining. The median income for physicians fell 3.8 percent in 1993, even among PCPs, and has stayed relatively steady since that time. Similarly, Medicare payments to PCPs fell in 1995 on a relative value unit (RVU) basis and now show some sign of increasing for the specialist. The drop was most spectacular for PCPs in 2000 and continues in 2002 with more Medicare fee reductions.

4. Medical schools are considering decreases in class sizes and are consolidating. Funding for postgraduate training is generally limited to the first specialty board. Similarly, there is strong support for eliminating funding for training of international medical graduates, who now form the core of house staff in many inner-city institutions. A bold experiment by the CMS pays some New York hospitals *not* to train physicians.

Financial Constraints. Many managed care arrangements are capital intensive. In developing an integrated delivery system (see chapter 6), the costs of the physical plant (offices and facilities), network development, and provider contracting may be prohibitive because the payment for services has become constricted. This situation has stimulated significant activity in mergers and acquisitions of PPM organizations. Information technology (see chapter 15) has emerged as perhaps the single most avid consumer of capital in the health care business as payers and providers alike seek to control the information flow and garner knowledge about enrollees. HIPAA is beginning to bite as a consumer of capital resources for information technology.

Tax Incentives. The current tax structure does little to motivate employers to control health insurance costs because such expenses are tax-deductible to the employer and are not taxed to the employee. The net result is a federal subsidy of the purchase of health insurance, with the most expensive plans (i.e., fee-for-service plans) receiving the greatest subsidies. Medical savings accounts (MSAs) allow individuals to deduct amounts paid into an MSA during the taxable year, up to specific limits. The influence of MSAs remains to be seen as a new administration takes office and one of its greatest proponents, Representative Bill Archer of Texas, retires. The extended Archer MSA is set to expire in December 2002 unless extended by the 107th Congress.

Legal and Regulatory Issues. As discussed in detail in chapter 8, there are many legal barriers at the state and federal levels to achieving health care reform through managed care, including ERISA and state insurance regulations. In addition, the specter of medical malpractice liability becomes more acute in a managed care environment because of the competing interests of the patient and physician and of the physician and the MCO. Even employers risk liability exposure for administrative errors and omissions not subject to ERISA preemption.

Legislative Issues. MCOs are critical of the numerous antimanaged care laws and regulations currently in existence, which pose barriers to the growth of managed care in the health care industry. Although there is a wide range of opinion as to the most significant anti-managed care legislation, the following are commonly thought to be barriers to the growth of managed care: (1) networking legislation (e.g., "any willing provider" laws), (2) utilization review regulation, and (3) state benefit mandates. Efforts by the states and an abortive effort by Congress in the summer of 1998 have been directed toward securing "patients' rights." This issue continues to be on the agenda of the 107th Congress. Other sentinel legislative enactments include managed care liability legislation and, most recently in Texas, a physician collective bargaining bill that was signed into law in June 1999. [Texas Ins Code, Article 29.01-29.14]

Q 1:11 What are the likely effects of managed care liability reform?

Managed care liability reform will affect health plans, employers, consumers, and providers in a number of ways.

Increased Premium Costs. Some health plans will increase their premium costs to include the increased cost of insurance and administration associated with managing risk.

Liberalized Access and Coverage Determinations. Other health plans might reduce their exposure (but still incur premium increases) by liberalizing standards for access and coverage.

Modification in Utilization Review Decision Making. The threat of litigation is also likely to cause plans to pay greater attention to the process of making coverage decisions. There will likely be (1) increased emphasis on documentation of decision making; (2) greater use of attorneys and risk managers at every stage of business operations; and (3) increased use of external review to shelter responsibility for denials in an expert, economically disinterested party.

Increased Use of Alternative Dispute Resolution. Mandatory arbitration is well established for medical malpractice claims but has been used less often in managed care disputes relating to coverage and utilization determinations. Alternative dispute resolution can reduce litigation expense and exposure to punitive damages; properly conducted, it can also increase access to compensation for injured plaintiffs. (For more information on alternative dispute resolution, see chapter 14.)

Increased Emphasis on Disclosure. Increased liability can be expected to affect the availability and quality of information shared among purchasers, health plans, and consumers. ERISA specifies several areas of mandatory disclosure, and courts have read additional information requirements into its fiduciary duty provisions.[18] State courts are also imposing disclosure requirements through non-ERISA fiduciary law.[19] This issue played an important role in *Herdrich v. Pegram* [530 US (2000)], which is discussed in chapter 8.

Modification in Contracting. Increased liability exposure may alter the content of contracts between employers and health plans and between health plans and providers. Modifications will likely include the following:

- Greater specificity about coverage definitions and decision-making functions (e.g., unbundling catchall terms such as *medical necessity* into specific examples of clinical scenarios and developing detailed protocols for determining when treatments are experimental)

- More specific contract language allocating responsibility for utilization review activities between the employers, plans, and providers—the main parties to managed care contracts

- Greater specificity in purchasing agreements, with detailed disclosures at the time of enrollment to place consumers on notice about the managed care features in their health benefit plans and policies in response to lawsuits whose decisions turned on the element of disclosure and discrepancies between health plans' marketing materials and formal plan documents.[20]

Spillover Liability Exposure. Because managed care plans often function as intermediary organizations, with many of the risk management functions delegated to other organizations and entities that make up the complex set of relationships in managed care, any liberalization in the law to allow lawsuits against health plans will likely spill over into other functions and affect other entities, including providers.

Providers that own insurance or HMO companies that control plan functions and provide health services may have enhanced liability exposure. Conflict of interest and breach of fiduciary duty under ERISA were theories raised in the respondent's arguments before the U.S. Supreme Court in *Herdrich*.

The physician groups and networks that formed or expanded to accept risk (and the freedom to manage it) from health plans now find themselves in litigation with patients or enrollees under theories based on conflict of interest because of the financial incentives inherent in prepaid, capitated arrangements, which are the reverse of the conventional financial incentives of health plans and physicians and potentially transform their advocacy role.[21] In short, the risk-bearing provider group introduces yet another locus of sensitive coverage decisions that sits outside the conventional health plan.

Q 1:12   What types of MCOs are experiencing the largest growth?

HMOs were thought to be the ascendant MCOs, and provider-sponsored organizations (PSO) were viewed as a major force in managed care. Since the passage of the BBA and the ability of MCOs to contract directly with CMS for Medicare patients, the solvency requirements for a federal waiver have proved daunting. At one time it was thought that PSOs would emerge as a viable solution to the high transactional friction of payment for medical care because these organizations would be designed for direct payer contracting. Their failure to gain acceptance in this role can be interpreted as a recognition on the part of physician groups that they were ill equipped to assume that degree of risk and that the rates were too low. PSOs could achieve a competitive advantage over health plans by allowing physicians and other providers to develop the long-term relationships they need to develop optimal work processes and efficiencies. Long-term, stable direct contracts with employers would allow these organizations a chance to develop. By contrast, most health plans contract for relatively short periods with physicians and providers, making it difficult to integrate networks enough to achieve the greatest efficiencies.

Employers were looking to HMO plans as an easy way to reduce health care expenditures. It appears, however, that other forms of managed care, such as PPOs, are retaking the market. It was expected that PPO enrollment would decline as a result of a demonstrated inability to effect dramatic cost reductions, but PPOs have piggybacked on the growth of managed care and have grown at the same rate as HMOs. In 1998, 40 percent of patients enrolled in plans were in PPOs, up from 35 percent the year before. HMO enrollment experienced a small decline.

In April 1999 *Internal Medicine World Report* published the results of a survey conducted by William M. Mercer, Inc., that found that the number of employees enrolled in HMOs in 1998 had declined from 50 percent to 47 percent. This change was noted as significant because it was the first time HMO enrollment had decreased. The report went on to say that the percentage of those enrolled in less restrictive PPOs increased from 35 percent to 40 percent. This increase was coupled with a 6 percent increase in health care costs, which had been flat or showing only modest increases in the preceding five years. Figure 1-4 shows HMO industry growth for commercial or group products. Of course, since the definitions of managed care products change, the numbers shown are approximations.

The National Debate

Q 1:13 What are the issues in the national debate about health care?

The national debate about the U.S. health care system continues to be one of cost and access. The United States has the most expensive health care system in the world, exceeding the cost in all other countries by more than half,[22] yet the number of people without insurance continues to increase.[23]

Although low inflation and managed care have slowed the growth of spending, it is anticipated that health care expenditures will begin to rise again and may even double over the next decade.[24] From the federal government's perspective, there have been two dominant trends: (1) the rate of growth in health care spending has slowed, and (2) the government's share of health care spending has increased. In 1997, the growth rate was the slowest in the more than 35 years for which there are data on medical spending; however, spending by federal, state, and local governments rose in 1997 to $507 billion, or 46 percent of the total, an increase from 40 percent in 1990. Private resources financed 54 percent of personal health services ($585 billion) in 1997, down from 60 percent in 1990.[25]

Q 1:14 What are the national economic drivers of managed care?

There is a widespread desire on the part of industry, government, and even the medical profession to reduce the growth of health care spending as a percentage of the GDP. Some forms of managed care still hold out that promise, although the tightly restrictive, so-called lock-in HMOs are clearly declining to nonexistence.

Figure 1-4.   Number of HMOs, 1976-1997

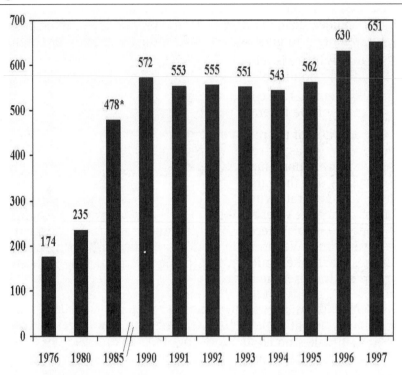

* Increase partially due to change in reporting

Source: National Center for Health Statistics. Health, United States, 1998. Hyattsville, MD, 1998

Both the actual dollar amount and the proportion of the GDP spent on health care in the United States are the largest in the world, but the perceived value returned is not thought to be great enough to justify the expense. This discrepancy becomes far more dramatic when compared with health care expenditures of other industrialized nations, which spend a much lower percentage of their GDP on health care (see chapter 2). Nonetheless, the expense continues to grow. The drive to lower the cost, or at least lower the rate of increase in cost, has several bases:

1. Medical care and medical care providers are perceived as too opulent, although that perception is now fading as doctors

are becoming, once again, the patients' champions against the HMOs.

2. Despite enormous successes, the medical care establishment is thought to give too little value for the money expended.

3. Medical care is felt to be a fungible commodity, although the rise of "boutique" medicine is a countervailing trend.

4. Entitlements are consuming what is seen as a disproportionate share of the federal budget.

The question of the relative contribution of health care to the nation's economy has far-reaching implications. The question of value received is even more important for health care policy. Conventional wisdom says that the value of health care as perceived by the payers is not commensurate with the cost. But who is being asked? For the millions of eligible veterans who receive first dollar health care from the Department of Veterans Affairs and pay nothing, the value received is infinite. Veterans argue that they paid for their health care in advance with their military service, and it is incontrovertible that some were promised health care for life if they developd a service-connected disability. In terms of dollar outlay, the eligible veteran's return is highly satisfactory. An even more obvious example of value received is indigent health care (where it is available). In this setting, the patient makes no contribution to his or her health care and yet is often afforded high-quality care by practitioners who are held to the same standard as those delivering compensated care.

A single segment of the population that is least satisfied with its health care has yet to be identified. The call for reform emanates from the magnates and the politicians. It certainly emanates from workers whose health benefits are tied to their employment and from those who feel they have significant out-of-pocket expenses despite health insurance. The call also emanates from the advocates for the uninsured and those who must rely on indigent health care systems. From a social point of view, the advocates' claim of poor value for patients who utilize indigent health care systems is understandable. From a purely national economic perspective, it is inexplicable because these patients receive care at no monetary cost to themselves.

Q 1:15 What has happened to health care costs overall?

As early as the post–World War II era, health care costs began to skyrocket, increasing 82 percent from 1948 to 1958. These increases were attributed to increased utilization and an absolute increase in the price of medical care. By 1960, medical prices were rising at over three times the rate of the general price index. At that time, the focus of attention was on the insurers rather than the providers.

Enactment of Medicare and Medicaid in 1965 has had the greatest impact on health care costs. The demands for health services resulting from government funding, along with a perceived limited supply of services, fueled the crisis in health care discussed above. Between June 1965 and July 1967, physicians' fees increased an average of 6.5 percent each year compared with an average annual increase of just below 3 percent during the previous five years. Hospital costs increased even more dramatically, with average annual increases of 14.8 percent for the four years between March 1966 and March 1970. In fact, the average patient day expense rose 38 percent in the three years between 1965 and 1968. Finally, national health expenditures increased an average of 12.3 percent per year between 1960 and 1970. During the previous five years, the average annual increase was 8.9 percent. As a percentage of GDP, national health expenditures rose from 5.9 percent in 1966 (where it had been constant for three years) to 7.3 percent in 1970, an increase of more than twice the increase during any comparable period.

There is no question that the decline in the rate of growth of health care costs promised by the Health Care Security Act of 1994 and delivered by macroeconomic forces and the resolve of purchasers had occurred to the point of putting enormous cost pressure on the system. The rebound of health care costs is the inevitable result of trying to reconcile minimal utilization with a demanding and needy population and a for-profit investor-based structure. Figure 1-5 shows the consumer price index for medical care compared with the CPI for all other items. Health care costs over time show a steady decline, however, when the CPI deflator is applied.

Q 1:16 How is the consumer price index for medical care calculated?

Medical care is one of the major groups of items in the CPI. It consists of medical care commodities and medical care services. Medical care services, the dominant component of medical care, are organized into two expenditure categories (ECs): professional medical services and hospital and related services. (An additional expen-

Figure 1-5.   CPI versus CPI for Medical Care, 1950–1999

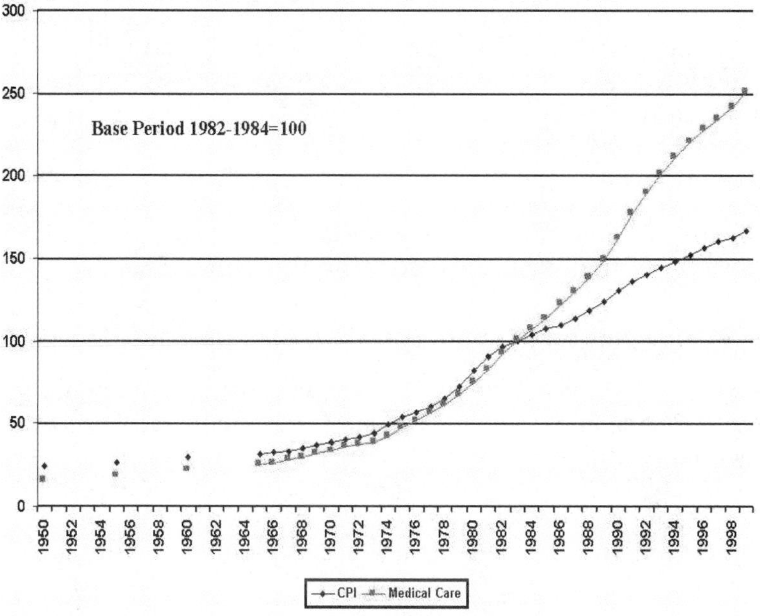

Base Period 1982-1984=100

Source: Bureau of Labor Statistics August, 1999

diture category for health insurance is part of medical care services but is not published separately.) Medical care commodities comprise prescription drugs and nonprescription medical equipment and supplies.

The base period weight for each CPI item is the out-of-pocket expenditures households incurred for that item in a three-year base period. Weights for the medical care CPI reflect household expenditures for health insurance premiums and for out-of-pocket medical expenses (those not covered by health insurance). The CPI does not include employer-paid health insurance premiums or government-paid health care such as Medicare Part A; these amounts are considered part of consumers' incomes and not their expenditures. Consequently, the share of medical care in the CPI is smaller than its share of the GDP and other national accounts measures.

Q 1:17 What has happened to the relationship between the CPI for health care and the CPI for all goods and services?

The curve for the CPI for medical care continues to diverge from the CPI for all goods and services and to increase at a greater rate. Figure 1-5 shows the relationship of the two indices.

Q 1:18 How is the health care dollar generated and spent?

Figure 1-6 shows the most recent CMS data on the generation and disposition of the health care dollar in the United States.

Q 1:19 How has health care spending changed over time?

Figure 1-7 shows changes in personal health care spending between 1996 and 2000. The most prominent, and therefore most politically charged, item is the money spent on personal drug prescriptions. In 2000, William Mercer estimated that drug costs increased 17.5 percent over the previous year's costs.[26] At the time of this writing, prescription drug benefits are a major political issue and their fate is unclear.

Q 1:20 What is contributing to the increase in health care expenditures?

In the early 1990s, American society demanded cost containment. At the same time, however, the population demanded freedom of choice in health care providers and access to health care services, which come at a cost and run contrary to the mechanisms necessary to contain expenses. In fact, it is this schizophrenic behavior by society that caused the rate of growth in national health care costs to accelerate from 4 percent in 1996 to 6 percent in 1997 to 7 percent in 1998. Health care expenditures represented 13.2 percent of the GDP in 2000 and by 2002 are expected to represent more than 16 percent of the GDP as a result of high-priced pharmaceuticals, technological advances, and increased use of outpatient services.[27]

In addition, the concurrence of freezing the Medicare DRG reimbursement rate to hospitals in 1998 and repealing the Boren Amendment (which required state Medicaid programs to pay "reasonable rates" for hospital and nursing home care) has caused hospitals to increase prices to the private sector. This means that tradi-

Figure 1-6. The Nation's Health Dollar, 2000

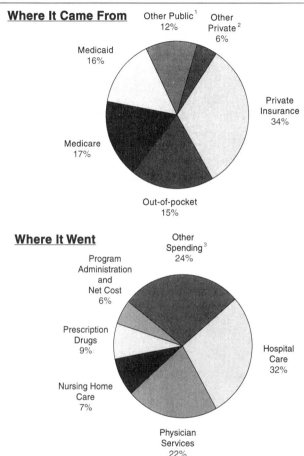

Where It Came From

Other Public[1] 12%
Other Private[2] 6%
Medicaid 16%
Private Insurance 34%
Medicare 17%
Out-of-pocket 15%

Where It Went

Other Spending[3] 24%
Program Administration and Net Cost 6%
Prescription Drugs 9%
Hospital Care 32%
Nursing Home Care 7%
Physician Services 22%

[1] "Other Public" includes programs such as workers' compensation, public health activity, Department of Defense, Department of Veterans Affairs, Indian health services, and state and local hospital, and school health.

[2] "Other Private" includes industrial inplant, privately funded construction, and non-patient revenues, including philanthropy.

[3] "Other Spending" includes dentist services, other professional services, home health, durable medical products, over-the-counter medicines and sundries, public health, research, and construction.

Note: Numbers shown may not add to 100.0 because of rounding.

Source: Health Care Financing Administration, Office of the Actuary, National Health Statistics Group, 2001.

Figure 1-7.   Percentage Change in Medical Prices from Same Period a Year Ago: 1996–2000

Indicator	CY 1996	CY 1997	CY 1998	CY 1999	1997 Q3	1997 Q4	1998 Q1	1998 Q2	1998 Q3	1998 Q4	1999 Q1	1999 Q2	1999 Q3	1999 Q4	2000 Q1	2000 Q2
Consumer Price Indexes, All Urban Consumers[1]	*Annual Percentage Change*				*Percentage Change from Same Period of Previous Year*											
Medical Care Services[2]	3.7	2.9	3.2	3.3	2.7	2.8	2.9	3.1	3.5	3.4	3.4	3.3	3.3	3.4	3.7	4.2
Professional Services	3.7	3.4	3.2	3.1	3.4	3.1	3.0	3.1	3.3	3.3	3.2	3.1	3.1	3.1	3.5	3.7
Physicians' Services	3.6	3.0	3.0	2.9	3.0	2.7	2.6	2.7	3.2	3.3	3.1	2.9	2.7	2.7	3.4	3.8
Dental Services	4.7	4.7	4.2	4.7	4.4	4.1	4.1	4.1	4.3	4.4	4.8	4.8	4.6	4.5	4.6	4.7
Hospital and Related Services	4.5	3.3	3.3	4.2	2.9	3.0	3.0	3.0	3.6	3.4	3.9	4.0	4.1	4.7	4.9	5.7
Hospital Services (12/96 = 100)	—	—	3.2	4.2	—	—	2.9	3.0	3.6	3.3	3.9	3.9	4.2	4.6	4.9	5.8
Inpatient Hospital Services (12/96 = 100)	—	—	2.6	3.8	—	—	2.3	2.3	2.9	2.8	3.5	3.6	3.7	4.2	4.5	5.3
Outpatient Hospital Services (12/86 = 100)	5.1	4.6	3.7	5.5	4.1	4.4	3.3	3.5	4.0	3.9	4.8	5.0	5.8	6.4	6.7	7.1
Nursing Home Services (12/96 = 100)	—	—	4.6	4.2	—	—	4.4	4.8	4.8	4.5	4.3	4.0	3.9	4.5	4.2	4.7
Medical Care Commodities	2.9	2.3	3.0	4.0	2.1	1.9	2.0	2.6	3.5	4.0	4.0	3.8	4.2	4.0	3.9	3.4
Prescription Drugs	3.3	2.6	3.8	5.7	2.4	1.9	2.3	3.1	4.4	5.2	5.5	5.6	5.8	6.0	5.4	4.6
Nonprescription Drugs & Medical Supplies (1986 = 100)	1.9	1.6	1.6	0.5	1.5	1.7	1.4	1.6	1.5	1.7	0.9	0.3	0.9	0.0	0.7	0.9
Internal and Respiratory Over-the-Counter Drugs	1.9	1.7	1.3	0.3	1.6	1.3	0.5	1.3	1.8	1.7	0.9	0.2	0.4	-0.3	0.4	0.7
Nonprescription Medical Equipment and Supplies	1.7	1.4	2.0	1.0	1.4	2.5	3.2	2.0	1.0	1.7	0.8	0.6	2.0	0.7	1.2	1.1

Indicator	CY 1996	CY 1997	CY 1998	CY 1999	1997 Q3	1997 Q4	1998 Q1	1998 Q2	1998 Q3	1998 Q4	1999 Q1	1999 Q2	1999 Q3	1999 Q4	2000 Q1	2000 Q2
Consumer Price Indexes, All Urban Consumers[1]	Annual Percentage Change				Percentage Change from Same Period of Previous Year											
Producer Price Indexes[3]																
Industry Groupings[4]																
Health Services (12/94 = 100)	2.2	1.4	1.5	2.0	1.5	1.0	1.3	1.4	1.6	1.9	2.1	1.9	2.0	2.1	2.3	2.3
Offices and Clinics of Doctors of Medicine (12/93 = 100)	0.7	1.3	2.1	2.2	1.6	1.2	1.8	2.1	2.0	2.5	2.3	2.1	2.3	2.1	2.0	1.9
Medicare Treatments (12/93 = 100)	-3.7	0.3	4.4	2.4	0.3	0.3	4.4	4.4	4.4	4.4	2.4	2.4	2.4	2.4		
Non-Medicare Treatments (12/93 = 100)	1.8	1.7	1.6	2.2	2.0	1.5	1.3	1.6	1.5	2.1	2.4	2.2	2.3	1.9		
Hospitals (12/92 = 100)	2.4	0.8	0.7	1.7	0.8	0.1	0.4	0.5	0.8	1.3	1.7	1.6	1.7	1.9	2.0	2.1
General Medical and Surgical Hospitals (12/92 = 100)	2.4	1.0	0.8	1.7	1.2	0.6	0.7	0.8	0.7	1.2	1.6	1.5	1.8	1.9	2.0	2.2
Inpatient Treatments (12/92 = 100)	2.3	0.9	0.7	1.7	1.4	0.5	0.7	0.8	0.4	1.0	1.5	1.4	1.7	2.0	2.1	2.3
Medicare Patients (12/92 = 100)	3.3	0.6	-0.7	0.6	1.2	-1.0	-1.0	-1.0	-1.0	0.4	0.4	0.4	0.4	1.3	1.3	1.3
Medicaid Patients (12/92 = 100)	2.2	-1.1	-0.7	0.7	-0.5	-0.9	0.2	0.5	-1.6	-1.6	0.1	0.0	1.2	1.6	2.1	2.4
All Other Patients (12/92 = 100)	1.8	1.7	1.9	2.5	2.2	1.9	1.9	2.0	1.8	2.1	2.5	2.4	2.6	2.6	2.6	2.9
Outpatient Treatments (12/92 = 100)	2.6	1.0	1.0	1.8	0.5	0.5	0.5	0.8	1.3	1.5	1.8	1.7	2.0	1.6	1.7	1.7
Medicare Patients (12/92 = 100)	1.7	2.6	2.4	3.9	2.9	1.8	1.9	2.0	2.0	3.5	4.7	4.0	4.1	2.9	1.9	1.8
Medicaid Patients (12/92 = 100)	-0.2	-1.1	0.9	2.4	-0.8	0.8	0.4	0.3	0.3	2.5	2.5	3.1	3.3	0.9	0.9	0.3
All Other Patients (12/92 = 100)	3.0	1.0	0.8	1.3	0.3	0.3	0.3	0.6	1.3	1.1	1.3	1.2	1.4	1.4	1.7	1.8
Skilled and Intermediate Care Facilities (12/94 = 100)	6.1	4.3	4.3	3.8	4.3	4.1	3.9	4.1	4.5	4.6	4.2	3.9	3.5	3.6	5.1	4.6
Public Payers (12/94 = 100)	6.5	4.4	4.3	3.3	4.6	4.4	4.2	4.0	4.5	4.7	3.9	3.8	2.9	2.6	4.6	4.1

Figure 1-7. Percentage Change in Medical Prices from Same Period a Year Ago: 1996–2000 (Cont'd)

Indicator	CY 1996	CY 1997	CY 1998	CY 1999	1997 Q3	1997 Q4	1998 Q1	1998 Q2	1998 Q3	1998 Q4	1999 Q1	1999 Q2	1999 Q3	1999 Q4	2000 Q1	2000 Q2
Consumer Price Indexes, All Urban Consumers[1]																
	Annual Percentage Change				Percentage Change from Same Period of Previous Year											
Private Payers (12/94 = 100)	5.9	4.1	4.2	4.7	4.0	3.6	3.6	4.4	4.4	4.3	4.5	4.0	4.7	5.5	6.2	5.6
Medical Laboratories (6/94 = 100)	1.3	0.8	0.3	–0.5	0.9	0.9	0.4	0.3	0.2	0.2	0.0	–0.3	–0.9	–0.8	0.2	0.8
Home Health Care Services (12/96 = 100)	—	—	2.8	0.9	—	—	4.0	2.9	2.4	1.8	0.5	0.3	0.7	2.0	4.3	3.2
Medicare Payers (12/96 = 100)	—	—	1.4	0.4	—	—	1.6	2.3	0.6	1.1	–0.1	–0.2	0.9	1.1	6.5	7.2
Non-Medicare Payers (12/96 = 100)	—	—	2.7	0.8	—	—	2.5	3.1	3.3	1.7	0.4	0.1	0.3	2.5	3.2	1.0
Commodity Groupings																
Drugs and Pharmaceuticals	1.8	2.1	10.7	3.7	1.9	2.7	5.4	12.0	12.8	12.5	8.0	2.4	2.3	2.2	3.2	2.7
Ethical (Prescription) Preparations	3.3	3.1	18.1	3.7	2.5	3.6	8.9	20.5	21.7	21.2	11.9	1.5	1.4	1.1	3.4	3.0
Proprietary (Over-the-Counter) Preparations	–0.8	–0.1	–0.1	0.8	0.6	0.4	–0.7	0.2	0.1	–0.1	0.3	1.0	1.0	1.0	1.0	1.1
Medical, Surgical, and Personal Aid Devices	1.3	0.0	0.2	0.9	0.4	0.3	0.3	–0.1	0.0	0.6	0.6	1.3	0.9	0.7	0.9	0.6
Personal Aid Equipment	4.2	0.7	2.2	2.7	–0.6	0.6	1.2	2.5	3.2	2.0	3.1	2.5	2.6	2.6	0.8	2.5
Medical Instruments and Equipment (6/82 = 100)	1.4	–1.5	–1.1	–0.5	–0.9	–1.7	–0.7	–1.4	–1.5	–0.7	0.0	0.2	–0.8	–1.3	–1.1	–0.9
Surgical Appliances and Supplies (6/83 = 100)	1.4	1.2	1.1	1.7	1.5	2.2	1.4	0.7	1.1	1.3	0.6	1.8	2.1	2.3	2.7	2.3
Ophthalmic Goods (12/83 = 100)	–1.6	–0.4	–0.1	–0.2	–0.3	0.0	–1.0	–0.7	0.2	1.0	1.0	0.4	–0.5	–1.8	–1.1	–1.2
Dental Equipment and Supplies (6/85 = 100)	2.5	3.9	3.2	5.8	4.1	3.8	2.0	3.0	3.6	4.0	4.0	6.6	6.5	6.1	6.2	1.91

[1] Unless otherwise noted, base year is 1982–84 = 100[2]

[2] Includes the net cost of private health insurance, not shown separately.

[3] Unless otherwise noted, base year is 1982 = 100. Producer price indexes are classified by industry (price changes received for the industry's output sold outside the industry) and commodity (price changes by similarity of end use or material composition).

[4] Further detail for Producer Price Industry groupings, such as types of physician practices, hospital DRG groupings, etc., are available from BLS.

Notes: Q designates quarter of year. Quarterly data are not seasonally adjusted.

Source: U.S. Department of Labor, Bureau of Labor Statistics: CPI Detailed Report and Producer Price Indexes. Washington. U.S. Government Printing Office. Monthly reports for January 1996–September 2000.

tional insurance companies (and self-insured employers) will bear the brunt of this price inflation. HMOs will be less affected because they negotiate provider charges and can hold down price inflation.

Q 1:21   What market forces affect health care cost inflation?

Several important, yet ambiguous, market forces affect health care cost inflation:

1. Managed care, by judicious contracting, selection of populations, and risk management, brought a reduction in health care expenditures for some of its customers; however, the methods used to achieve cost containment generally are not favored by American society and the reductions have not been endurable.

2. Employers (and purchasing coalitions) have worked to hold down price increases following the lead of large purchasers such as the California Public Employees Retirement System (CPERS). They have also used objective measures of value and customer satisfaction in making their purchasing decisions. The restrictions required to achieve this constraint, however, are becoming increasingly socially unacceptable.

3. Individual consumers are price sensitive when shopping for health plans but are less sensitive to cost when accessing health care services. Employees demand instant access with accountability when their employer is paying for their health care benefits.

4. Consumer groups oppose restrictions necessary to hold down cost.

5. Lawyers and politicians seek increased regulation of managed care.

6. Physicians are pressuring patients to challenge HMO restrictions, yet they seek to organize into unions and other collective bargaining organizations to negotiate with managed care plans.

7. Health plans are forced to spend more money to cover losses associated with increased regulation and financial losses and therefore have no choice but to increase premiums.

8. Pharmaceutical companies are marketing directly to consumers, attempting to bypass managed care and thereby create

demand. At the same time they purport to manage demand using pharmacy benefit managers that they own. The divestiture of Medco by Merck in 2002 may signal a change in that strategy.

9. Federal and state governments continue to mandate new benefits while adding new administrative requirements, particularly to Medicaid and SCHIP.

Q 1:22 What is the impact of the rise in the cost of coverage on the availability of employee and dependent health insurance coverage?

Health insurance coverage for dependents is shifting from defined benefits to defined contributions, with more responsibility for premium increases passed on to the employee.

Q 1:23 What will be the effect of the Medicare, Medicaid, and SCHIP Balanced Budget Refinement Act of 1999 on Medicare Part B?

The BBRA (as incorporated into Public Law 106-113, the appropriations bill for the District of Columbia for fiscal year 2000, enacted on November 29, 1999) included a number of provisions affecting the supplementary medical insurance (SMI) program, more commonly known as Medicare Part B. As its name implies, the BBRA primarily modified and refined some of the provisions enacted in the BBA. [Pub L No 105-33] The more important SMI provisions, from an actuarial standpoint, are described in the following paragraphs.[28] This topic is discussed in much more detail in chapter 7.

The BBA required the Secretary of Health and Human Services (HHS) to develop and implement a PPS for outpatient hospital services. The law required that the Secretary determine the aggregate amount payable under the PPS in 1999 (the base period) based on (1) the total amount that would have been paid in the absence of the PPS and (2) the total amount of copayments estimated to be paid for outpatient services in 1999 under the PPS. This aggregate amount was then to be used to establish the conversion factor used to determine the outpatient fee schedule under the PPS. The BBA specified that coinsurance amounts under the PPS would be 20 percent of the median charges; however, using median rather than mean charges would result in aggregate payments to hospitals being lower than they would be in the absence of the PPS. The BBRA clarified that it was the intent of Congress to have aggregate payments to hospitals be budget neutral for 1999. Hence, based on the BBRA, the SMI program will make up the difference in hospital payments that occurs when median charges rather than mean charges are used to set coinsurance amounts for the PPS rates.

The BBA extended through calendar year 1999 two provisions that would otherwise have expired at the end of fiscal year 1998: the 10 percent reduction in payments for hospital outpatient capital, and the 5.8 percent reduction for outpatient services paid on a cost basis. The BBRA extends these reductions beyond 1999, until such time as the outpatient PPS is implemented.

The BBA allowed the Secretary of HHS to establish adjustments to the outpatient PPS, when implemented, in a budget-neutral manner, as deemed necessary to ensure equitable payments. The BBRA specifically establishes "transitional corridors" until January 1, 2004, for the PPS to limit payment losses experienced by individual hospitals under the PPS. A formula is established so that hospitals receive additional payments for outpatient services rendered if the amount they receive under the PPS in relation to their costs is less than their 1996 payment-to-cost ratio. These transitional payments are to have no effect on beneficiary copayments and are not subject to the budget neutrality constraint. The BBRA then specifies how to determine the transitional payments.

The BBA directed that under the outpatient PPS, when implemented, the beneficiary copayments were to be 20 percent of national median charges. It froze these rates until such time as the copayments represent 20 percent of the total fee schedule amount. The BBRA caps beneficiary copayments under the outpatient PPS (when implemented) to the dollar amount of the hospital insurance (HI) inpatient deductible, with the SMI program paying the difference to the hospital between the limited copayment amount and the otherwise applicable copayment amount.

Prior to the BBRA, direct medical education payments to teaching hospitals were based on hospital-specific per resident amounts, based on inflation-adjusted 1984 costs. There were therefore wide variations in per resident payment amounts. The BBRA increases per resident payment amounts for hospitals below 70 percent of a geographically adjusted national average to 70 percent of that average. For hospitals above 140 percent of a geographically adjusted national average, payments were frozen in fiscal years 2001 and 2002, and increased by the consumer price index minus two percentage points in fiscal years 2003 through 2005. Hospitals with per resident payment amounts between 70 percent and 140 percent of a geographically adjusted national average continue to receive pre-BBRA payment amounts.

The BBA required development and implementation of a PPS for home health services, effective for cost reporting periods beginning on or after October 1, 1999. It also required a 15 percent reduction in home health payment limits, with or without the implementation of a PPS. An emergency appropriations act prior to BBRA delayed the 15 percent reduction until October 1, 2000, with or without the implementation of a PPS. The BBRA delays the 15 percent reduction further, until one year after implementation of a PPS; requires the Secretary of HHS to report within six months of implementation on the need for the 15 percent or other reduction; and eliminates the 15 percent reduction if a PPS is not implemented at all.

The BBA established a sustainable growth rate (SGR) mechanism to balance the need to control total Medicare spending with the need to ensure adequate payment for physicians' services; however, the formula provided by the BBA resulted in wide, unintended fluctuations in payments to physicians from year to year. The BBRA stabilizes the formula used for updating physician payment rates, and moves the SGR target for total physician spending, which is used to adjust inflation updates, from a fiscal-year to a calendar-year basis, beginning in 2000. It also modifies the calculation of the update adjustment factor, and provides for special adjustments for 2001 through 2005.

Prior to the BBA, there were two annual per beneficiary limits of $900 each for physical therapy and occupational therapy furnished by independent practitioners of therapy. The BBA established broader limits, covering all outpatient SMI therapy services, except those furnished in hospital outpatient departments. Specifically, the BBA established a $1,500 per beneficiary annual cap for all outpatient physical therapy and speech pathology services, and a $1,500 per beneficiary annual cap for all outpatient occupational therapy services. The BBA also required the Secretary of HHS to report to

Congress by January 1, 2001, recommending a revised policy for therapy services based on classification of individuals by diagnostic category and prior use of services, in place of dollar limitations. The BBRA suspends the annual payment limits imposed by the BBA for calendar years 2000 and 2001. During this suspension, the Secretary is to conduct focused medical reviews of therapy claims. The latest reports on the BBA and BBRA can be found on the CMS Web site (www.cms.gov).

Prior to the BBRA, composite rates of reimbursement for dialysis services for end-stage renal disease patients were $126 for hospital-based providers and $122 for freestanding facilities. The rate did not increase each year. For services furnished in calendar year 2000, the BBRA increases the composite rates by 1.2 percent over the rates for calendar year 1999, and increases the composite rates for services furnished in calendar year 2001 by 1.2 percent over the rates for calendar year 2000.

Prior to the BBRA, SMI paid for the laboratory test component of Pap smears under the clinical laboratory fee schedule. There was no minimum payment amount. The BBRA established a minimum payment amount of $14.60 for tests furnished in calendar year 2000, with updates to that amount for subsequent years.

Prior to the BBRA, SMI covered drugs used to provide immuno-suppressive therapy for 36 months following a Medicare-covered organ transplant. The BBRA increased the number of months of coverage by eight months, from 36 to 44 months, for calendar year 2000, for individuals who exhaust their 36 months of coverage during that year. For individuals who exhaust their 36 months of coverage during calendar year 2001, at least eight more months will be covered. (The Secretary of HHS must specify what the increase, if any, beyond eight months will be.) For beneficiaries who exhaust the 36-month period in calendar years 2002, 2003, and 2004, the number of additional covered months may be more or less than eight. Again, the Secretary must specify what the increase will be for each of these years. The Secretary must determine the additional months in such a way that the estimated cost of these months is no more than $150 million.

Prior to January 1, 2000, M + C payments were adjusted using only demographic factors. The BBA required implementation of a new risk adjustment method, based on health status, effective January 1, 2000, and the Secretary of HHS announced a five-year transition to the new method. The payments were to be based on a blend of the old and new methods, with the new method accounting for 10, 30, 55, 80, and 100 percent of the blend for calendar years 2000 through 2004, respectively. The BBRA changed the transition schedule by providing that the new method will account for 10 percent of the blend in 2000 and 2001 and no more than 20 percent of the blend in 2002.

The BBRA provided for an increase in the national per capita M + C growth percentage for fiscal year 2002 by reducing the update factor for the year by 0.3 percentage point, rather than the previously scheduled 0.5 percentage point.

Q 1:24   What effect will BBRA have on the HI trust?

For PPS hospitals, the BBA reduced the teaching adjustment for indirect medical education payments to 6 percent for fiscal year 2000 and 5.5 percent for fiscal year 2001 and later. The BBRA increased indirect medical education payments to teaching hospitals by setting the adjustment at 6.5 percent for fiscal year 2000, 6.25 percent for fiscal year 2001, and 5.5 percent for fiscal year 2002 and later.

The BBA required development and implementation of a PPS for home health services, effective for cost reporting periods beginning on or after October 1, 1999. It also required a 15 percent reduction in home health payment limits, with or without the implementation of a PPS. (Congress realized it might not be possible to develop and implement the system by October 1, 1999. Indeed, such a system was not in place by that date.) An emergency appropriations act prior to BBRA delayed the 15 percent reduction until October 1, 2000, with or without the implementation of a prospective payment system. The BBRA delays the 15 percent reduction further, until one year after implementation of a PPS; requires the Secretary of HHS to report within six months of implementation on the need for the 15 percent or other reduction; and eliminates the 15 percent reduction if a PPS is not implemented at all.

The BBA reduced the annual update in daily payment rates for hospice care from the hospital market basket percentage increase to the hospital market basket percentage increase minus 1 percentage point, for each of fiscal years 1998 through 2002. The BBRA increases the payment update by 0.5 percentage point for fiscal year 2001 and 0.75 percentage point for fiscal year 2002.

Q 1:25   What is the status of the HI trust?

The Medicare trustees report of 2001 contains the following assessment of the HI Trust:[30]

- The financial outlook for the HI program, as shown in this annual report, presents a mixed picture. In the short range (2001–2010), the financial status of the HI trust fund is favorable and continues to improve. Over the full long-range projection period, however, use of improved assumptions indicates a greater actuarial deficit than previously projected.

- The HI trust fund meets the Trustees' test of short-range financial adequacy for only the second time since 1991. HI income exceeded program expenditures by $36.1 billion in calendar year 2000—the third consecutive trust fund surplus. Income increased significantly as a result of robust economic growth, and expenditures increased by only 0.4 percent from their 1999 level. This slow growth was due to continuing implementation of the Balanced Budget Act of 1997 (including a further transfer of home health care costs to the Supplementary Medical Insurance (SMI) program), low increases in health care costs generally, additional efforts to combat fraud and abuse in the Medicare program, and a reduction in the utilization of home health and skilled nursing facility services.

- Under the intermediate assumptions, the HI trust fund is estimated to be depleted in 2029—a significant improvement over last year's estimate of 2025. Income from all sources is projected to continue to exceed expenditures for the next 20 years under the Trustees' intermediate assumptions. Thereafter, income would fall short of expenditures, but by drawing down on trust fund assets, the program could continue to pay benefits for another 8 years.

- Projected HI tax income would meet only a declining share of expenditures under present law. Tax income is expected to equal 112 percent of expenditures in 2001 but would fall short of expenditures by a rapidly growing margin after 2015. Tax revenues would represent 68 percent of costs in 2029 (when the fund is estimated to be depleted) and only 32 percent 75 years from now.

- The HI trust fund fails by a wide margin to meet the Trustees' long-range test of close actuarial balance. Specifically, an actuarial imbalance of 1.97 percent of taxable payroll is projected. To bring the HI program into actuarial balance over the next 75 years, either outlays would have to be reduced by 37 percent or income increased by 60 percent (or some combination of the two) throughout the 75-year period.

- The long-range cost projections shown in this report are much higher than projected in the 2000 annual report because of a revision to the long-range Medicare expenditure growth rate assumptions. The change was recommended by the 2000 Medicare Technical Review Panel, an independent, expert group of actuaries and economists convened by the Trustees to review the Medicare projections. Reflecting an expected continuing impact of advances in medical technology on health care costs—both in Medicare and the health sector as a whole—per beneficiary HI expenditures are now assumed to increase in the long range at the rate of per capita GDP growth plus 1 percentage point. This assumption change is primarily responsible for the increase of 0.76 percent of taxable payroll in the 75-year actuarial deficit compared to last year's estimate.

- The future operations of the HI trust fund will be very sensitive to future economic, demographic, and health-cost trends and could differ substantially from the intermediate projections. Under the Trustees' "low cost" assumptions, for example, HI assets would increase steadily throughout the projection. Under the "high cost" alternative, however, assets would be depleted in 2016.

- There are expected to be 3.7 workers per HI beneficiary when the baby boom generation begins to reach age 65 in 2010. Then the worker/beneficiary ratio is expected to swiftly decline to 2.3 in 2030 as the last of the baby boomers reaches age 65. The ratio is expected to continue declining thereafter (but more gradually) as life expectancy continues to lengthen and birth rates remain at roughly the same level as during the last 2 decades.

- In the long range, HI expenditures are projected to grow rapidly as a fraction of workers' earnings, from 2.7 percent in 2000 to 10.7 percent in 2075. As a fraction of the Gross Domestic Product (GDP), expenditures would grow somewhat more slowly, from 1.3 percent in 2000 to 4.7 percent in 2075. Expenditure growth results from increases in both the number of beneficiaries and the average cost of health services per beneficiary.

- Although this report focuses on the financial status of the HI trust fund, it is important to recognize the financial challenges facing the Medicare program as a whole and the need for integrated solutions. Combined HI and SMI expenditures as a percent of GDP are projected to increase rapidly, from 2.24 percent in 2000 to 5.03 percent in 2035 and then to 8.49 percent in 2075.

- Despite the improvement in the short-range financial outlook for the HI trust fund, we should determine effective solutions to the remaining long-range problems. The development of further reforms should occur in the relatively near future, since the sooner solutions are enacted, the more flexible and gradual they can be. At the same time, however, solutions determined and implemented today will likely need adjustment over time. We believe that solutions can and must be found to ensure the financial integrity of the HI program in the long term. Effective and decisive action is necessary to build upon the strong steps taken in recent reforms.

Q 1:26 Why were Medicare HMOs created?

When Medicare HMOs were created, they were presented as a way for the federal government to control the costs of providing health care while increasing the benefit options available to Medicare beneficiaries. Initially, Medicare HMOs were greeted with enthusiasm by both beneficiaries and payers and increased rapidly in number, peaking at 346 in 1998. As enchantment faded, however, the number of HMOs providing services for Medicare recipients dropped precipitously, reaching 262 in April 2000, with a pronounced downward slope. Similarly, enrollment growth in 1995 was 36.2 percent, but reached a mere 4.8 percent in 1999. In 1999, 99 M + C programs either closed their doors or reduced their service areas. As the July 3, 2000, date approached for notifying Medicare about changes in coverage and benefits, more HMOs headed for the exit.

Q 1:27   How can Medicare beneficiaries in managed care programs return to indemnity Medicare?

Beginning in 2002 Medicare beneficiaries can elect plans only during the annual election period in November, once during the open enrollment period (January through June), or at any time during a special election period. In 2003, the open enrollment period will be reduced in length and will last from January through March. In general, at all other times during the year, a Medicare beneficiary cannot enroll in a new plan and cannot disenroll to original Medicare. Beneficiaries are able to make plan changes in some circumstances, such as when they move or when their plan terminates its contract.

Q 1:28   Why are managed care corporations leaving the Medicare market?

The initial premise for Medicare managed care was that the HMO miracle could be replicated in a senior product. That is, the decrease in medical cost inflation, which was attributed to HMOs and their control of costs, could be transferred to a population other than normal commercial payers. The premise was that HMOs could be paid less than the adjusted average per capita cost and they would be able to supply augmented services, including a pharmacy benefit, merely by restricting choice and using other standard HMO tools. The HMOs suffered from a rapid influx of sick Medicare patients who immediately taxed the system. In addition, the requirements of the capital markets made fewer dollars available for patient care. The result was a squeeze on rates, withdrawals of providers, and rapid egress of commercial managed care companies from the Medicare market.

Managed Care's Effect

Q 1:29   How has managed care affected the health care industry?

Although managed care has certainly affected provider reimbursement and the growth of medical expenditures, it is not clear that this has occurred by virtue of management. Whether there has been a Hawthorne effect (a distortion of research results caused by the response of subjects to the special attention given to them by researchers) because of the enormous scrutiny of health care costs is yet to be determined. One of the major problems in assessing the effect of managed care on the health care industry is the influence of the addition of administrative costs and profits to the mix. Administrative costs and profits were not factors many years ago, when the baseline data were being accumulated and health care was voluntary, not for profit. For example, one analysis shows that 15 percent of the premium dollars in a prepaid, capitated system go to administrative costs, and this figure does not include corporate profits.

Despite possible alternative explanations, it appears that, at least in some markets, managed care has reduced costs. This savings has occurred, however, at the expense of traditional characteristics of the health care system:

1. Hospitals will continue to close as the market for beds consolidates, leaving certain communities vulnerable. As a reaction to this, however, rural networks have begun to form and exert power.

2. The cost of health care services as an absolute figure will continue to increase in the inpatient and ambulatory care settings.

3. The poor and uninsured require the presence of safety-net institutions, which are required to compete on unfamiliar terrain and under significant financial constraints with limited resources. Public providers who took their lead from managed care in the private sector and formed HMOs and other vehicles to compete for government-sponsored programs are now finding it difficult to survive as health plans. Many are abandoning this bold experiment and returning to their core services.

4. "Value competition" is difficult for the general public to understand. The emergence of "direct to consumer" advertising

by pharmaceutical houses seems to have galvanized a return to finding ways to publicize success. The impact of the *U.S. News and World Report* ratings of hospitals in the market has even caused analyses of that rating to be published in respected medical journals.

5. Vigilance regarding antitrust violations is required as large health care conglomerates emerge. Antitrust considerations seem to be assiduously observed by regulators.

6. Continued analysis is required to maintain initial cost reductions squeezed out by reengineering.

Q 1:30 How are patients affected by managed care?

In traditional, or fee-for-service, plans, an encounter between a covered individual and the health care system is compensated by the payer. If the encounter represents a covered benefit of the patient's plan, the indemnity payer pays the bill subject to deductibles or other contractual reductions in benefit. If the patient does not have insurance coverage, or the encounter is not a covered benefit, he or she is liable for the bill. The patient chooses the physician or hospital to provide the service based on his or her own criteria, which may include reputation, proximity, perception of quality, amenities, religious or ethnic considerations, or even decor. Fee-for-service medicine is not highly price sensitive.

Managed care, on the other hand, generally presents the patient with a list of physicians from which to pick the one who will supply a covered benefit. Often, once a physician has been chosen, it is difficult to change, even if the patient is dissatisfied. Many managed care plans stipulate times during which patients can change physicians. Perhaps under the influence of Medicare, this principle of locking in provider choice has started to break. Now, the ability to change providers is viewed as a competitive advantage, further weakening the bond between patient and physician.

Depending on the plan, the patient may be required to see a PCP who will be responsible for making all assessments and determinations as to medical needs. Patients generally are restricted in their ability to see specialists; referrals must be initiated by the PCP. Newer plans are entering the market with expanded choice and decreased restrictions. In recent experiments with defined populations, self-referral to specialists has not been restricted and the results have not been an economic catastrophe.[31] The universal applicability of these findings has not been shown.

Choice is often mentioned as a strong reason for patients to resist managed care. In this context, choice generally is taken to mean that patients can choose their physician for whatever reason they want. Thus, if a patient chooses to see an orthopedist for back pain (regardless of whether the back pain is caused by an orthopedic problem), that is considered exercising choice. If a patient is required to see a PCP who treats the back pain himself or herself (successfully or unsuccessfully), that is restriction of choice. Responding to this perceived need for choice, managed care plans try to have a large number of geographic, ethnic, and professional choices available. Choice is a valuable marketing tool. Left largely unsaid and unwritten is that the consumer has few data points on which to make an informed choice. Quality and outcome measures are available at some time, but they often do not address the issue of consumer satisfaction.

After choice, the patient is likely to be most struck by the way managed care pays for medical services. The patient is likely to have a fixed copayment or fee for every visit, regardless of its complexity, and will probably not need to file insurance papers or be responsible for any other payment. Hospitalizations are likely to be covered entirely, with the exception of amenities such as a television or a private room. As patients become more responsible for the costs of their health care, the cost burden of medical service utilization will increase. Prevention visits such as immunizations, Pap smears, and mammograms are likely to be covered benefits, with a copayment.

When switching from an indemnity, fee-for-service system to managed care, patients are often required to change physicians to one who is "on the list" of the managed care company. In the past, this would have been viewed as unacceptable. Patients developed long-term relationships with physicians who may have delivered their babies, treated their parents, and then delivered their children's babies. Medical complexity, modern mores, physician specialization, advertising, litigation, and other factors have conspired to render this relationship anachronistic, particularly in the urban environment. Thus, patients are not likely to miss someone with whom they never had meaningful contact. Interesting studies performed during the rise of managed care showed that a patient's loyalty to a physician is not strong and can be subverted by a relatively small financial disincentive. As plans proliferate and more physicians participate in more plans, patients may be able to change payers without changing physicians.

An unintended consequence of managed care has been the re-emergence of primary care as a respected discipline among physicians and health educators. Pediatrics and family medicine have been joined at the primary care level by general internal medicine, which is garnering a respectable percentage of the best graduates of medical schools. This has not been accompanied by an increase in those physicians' salaries when compared with physicians who perform procedures.

Q 1:31 How has managed care affected graduate medical education?

Academic health centers (AHCs) are unique institutions that combine the missions of education, research, and clinical care. They traditionally provide public access to the most sophisticated, and often the most expensive, health care. Because of their structure and functions, they often have access to a broad variety of funds, both public and private, and thus have been able to shift costs adroitly to cover shortfalls in areas of low funding. As funding for research constricts, along with payment for health care, the AHCs are finding themselves under enormous pressure. In markets in which there is intense competition and a broad variety of skills, this pressure is especially intense. Blumenthal and Meyer[32] identify several clinical strategies:

- Increasing sales of clinical services (patient care services and management services) to private purchasers
- Reducing costs of clinical services
- Increasing sales of clinical services to government payers
- Increasing sales of nonclinical services in private markets such as research and teaching

Other strategies for the AHCs include developing international markets, becoming the provider of last resort for complex cases, and assuming a leadership role in quality and outcome measures and research.

AHCs play a major role in the nation's health care delivery system, and special accommodations may be needed to allow them to survive in a market in which the majority of their services are no longer unique.

The AHC's travails are beginning to attract attention from payers, who recognize that managed care has stripped out much of the general work on which teaching programs were founded, leaving them to offer only highly specialized or indigent care. Clinical research is suffering in the new environment as a result of the AHC's inability to cost-shift and shortened length of stays in the hospital.[33]

Q 1:32   How is the general public affected by managed care?

It has become clear that Americans will not accept the current growth of health care as a proportion of the GDP. Organized medicine was told 20 years ago to police itself with regard to pricing. It did not. Therefore, the promised external controls have been initiated in the form of DRGs, relative value-based payments, and strict utilization review and control. Managed care promises to place price controls in the market. That is, managed care promises to reduce cost (or at least slow its growth) by the application of market forces, rather than by statutory price control. Market forces, however, reward efficiency and profitability. The "invisible hand" of the market does not care about the infirm or the poor. Market forces need to be allowed to act judiciously.

Competition among managed care strategies tends to emphasize generic relationships and benefits, not the maintenance of an individual patient-physician affiliation. That relationship may turn out to be dispensable in the face of the need for monetary savings.

Q 1:33   How is the health care workplace affected by managed care?

Over the past five years, health care organizations have reorganized, reengineered, and restructured. Cost-cutting solutions have resulted in downsizing, layoffs, and reductions in non-nursing personnel. The high cost of technology has forced many employers to decide between the investment cost of acquiring "personnel-replacing" equipment and keeping the personnel.

On a more positive note, employers are focusing more on work teams that are recognized and given incentives for high performance. The reengineering movement has changed how employers manage and deliver health care services. The U.S. Bureau of Labor Statistics predicts a 50.2 percent increase in health and allied services employees between 1996 and 2006.[34]

Q 1:34   How have policymakers responded to managed care?

Many of the changes being forced on the health care delivery system as a way to control cost and improve quality are encountering barriers in the form of existing federal and state laws. Some argue that federal antitrust laws, traditional state insurance laws and regulations, and newer rules such as "any willing provider" laws may pose barriers to the evolving relationships in the industry (see chapter 8). Others are concerned that these new systems are developing outside existing laws and regulations, thereby posing a threat to consumers and providers. Common issues that arise in the public policy debates related to managed care include the following:

- ERISA preemption of state laws
- Medical liability reform
- Role of local, state, and federal government in health care reform
- Accountability
- Quality assurance
- Access to care
- Antitrust and competition
- Privacy and confidentiality
- Provision of "safety nets" for vulnerable populations
- Graduate medical education

Managed Care and the Physician

Q 1:35   How do physicians perceive managed care?

Physicians' attitudes toward managed care range from rage and resistance to enthusiastic acceptance. As might be expected, the majority fall in the middle.

Some physicians are strongly opposed to any form of managed care. The reasons for this are complex and partially rooted in the ethos of professionals trained to be conservative and skeptical. Physicians have long opposed any government intrusion in health care, even before the enactment of Medicare in 1965. To understand physicians' attitudes regarding managed care, it is instructive to examine the way they are trained. From the very first, physicians are taught that they are to be the "captains of the ship" and accountable for anything happening to their patients. As any manager knows, accountability has to be married to authority and control in order to be effective. Managed care inserted a nonphysician into the sacred physician-patient relationship, a person who had no firsthand clinical knowledge of the management of the patient and whose only function was to restrict access to care the physician deemed necessary. Thus, an antagonistic relationship was created. Of late, physicians have moved into senior leadership positions in MCOs, and opportunities exist for them to control the full gamut of care. Therefore, they are being re-enfranchised and tensions have decreased. Nonetheless, the restrictions of managed care are real, particularly for specialist physicians.

Under managed care, most major procedures and many minor ones must be precertified. Precertification is commonly done by algorithm and is not under the direct control of the ordering physician. Capitation can put a perverse incentive on the physician-patient relationship, whereby the physician can be rewarded for doing less.

Specialist and primary care physicians may have their natural alliance altered as traditional referral patterns and practice patterns are distorted by managed care. The aging population and the demand for choice, however, are creating more demand for specialty physician services. In fact, there is an entirely new category of specialist, called the hospitalist (see Q 1:39).

Q 1:36   How has managed care affected the way physicians practice?

Medical practice styles in the United States have always varied. Physicians have practiced under the strict salaried arrangement of government medicine in the military, the Department of Veterans Affairs, the public health service, the prison health service, and elsewhere. The group practice of medicine, with responsibilities, assets, and liabilities shared among members, dates back to the end of the nineteenth century with the founding of the Mayo Clinic. Some physicians practice wholly within an academic institution and see patients only in a teaching setting. Of course, the traditional model of American medical practice is the solo practitioner.

Managed care has added a new practice style to the repertoire, but the physician's role varies. In truth, however, the contemporary physician's professional life remains highly scrutinized, reviewed, and regulated. With managed care, the physician's cherished autonomy has eroded substantially under the influence of utilization review and sharp constraints on benefits paid. Virtually all payers have discovered that the physician is responsible for setting the cost of illness and have thus closely managed this aspect of medical practice.

Cost management has had the effect of changing the relationship between physicians and patients because it has introduced the payer into the process of disease prevention and treatment. Whereas once diagnosis and treatment decisions were made by the patient and physician and the bill was submitted to the payer, now the payer is placed in a decision-making role. Physicians are therefore in an awkward position. The physician's responsibility, legally and ethically, is only to the patient. Yet the payer in a managed care system will exercise discretion as to the dollars it will commit to an individual therapeutic decision. Thus, the physician is required to defend his or her therapeutic plan to any number of intermediaries who do not have the same fiduciary responsibility. As discussed in chapter 8, the Wickline decision in California has rendered this relationship even more complex. The implication of this decision is that, regardless of the payer's decision, the physician has the obligation to render full and complete medical care, even if the physician or hospital will not be paid for it.

Physicians are therefore feeling under siege. They are being publicly pilloried for avarice and at the same time being beggared by Medicare and some managed care providers. The outcome of this conflict is not easy to predict, yet clearly the advent of managed care will radically alter the physician-patient relationship. One of the consequences that is already being felt is the loosening of the bonds between the PCP and the patient. Many managed care systems that tightly control physician time have already begun restricting the physician-patient encounter by setting performance standards and providing service on a first-come, first-served basis (rationing by queue). How that restrictive style of management will influence a new generation of physicians regarding their obligations to their patients is unknown. Another consequence of managed care is the reduction in time donated by physicians for charity care as a result of economic constraints. As discussed in Q 1:39, one of the outgrowths of evolving physician-patient and physician-physician relationships is the development of new specialists such as the hospitalist, whose practice is to attend inpatients covered under managed care plans.

Physicians must become more informed about the business aspects of their medical practice if they are to survive. The perceived need for knowledge has fostered the development of many academic programs geared toward educating physician executives and medical directors.

Q 1:37 How has managed care affected physician-patient relationships?

Although managed care insulates the individual patient from the act of paying the physician, it also reduces the direct accountability of the physician. When patients pay fees for service, they contract directly for those services, know their costs, and feel connected to the outcome. This is communicated to the physician in a direct way by the continuation or discontinuation of the patient as a customer. In a managed care setting, regardless of the management paradigm, the physician and the patient do not have a direct financial bond. The financial relationship exists between the physician and the payer; the patient is no longer the customer. This is not to say that the patient has no influence over the distribution of his or her dollars, but the accountability of the physician has been diluted for issues such as "customer service." The more restrictive the managed care setting, the more likely this is. In a highly managed staff-model HMO in which physicians are essentially employees, patients are less able to vote with their feet. All such managed care systems try to build in safeguards for patient satisfaction, but these are externally imposed management tools, not the mutual accountability of a physician-patient relationship in which the latter has actively chosen the former. As discussed in Q 1:39, the rise of the hospitalist movement has raised controversial questions relating to the principles underlying the physician-patient relationship.

Information concerning physician satisfaction is anecdotal; yet it seems the change in practice style from an individual fee-for-service practice to an HMO is substantial. Younger physicians have grown up with the idea of managed care, and it seems likely that they would adapt to managed care more easily.

Q 1:38   How has the physician's role evolved under managed care?

Many managed care plans require a physician to serve as a gate-keeper, interposed between the patient and specialty medical care. This is a role for which physicians received no training in the past, although it is certainly an integral part of contemporary medical education. Medical education trains the physician to provide the most medical care possible for the patient. For that reason, physicians find themselves in an awkward position when they are asked to deny patients medical care. For example, a PCP detects a precancerous skin lesion and treats it appropriately with liquid nitrogen. A dermatologist would have done the same thing in exactly the same manner. Suppose, however, that the patient feels uncomfortable about the ability of the PCP to treat this lesion and requests a consultation. In the gatekeeper role, the physician must resist this request. In the fee-for-service role, the physician may have encouraged the referral both from a medical and a business perspective and might have been rewarded with a return referral from the specialist. Now, the reward system is likely to discourage referral. In some managed care programs, referral may actually cost the PCP real money. Much of this confusion is alleviated in an integrated delivery system. As discussed in chapter 6, integration aligns the incentives of all providers to create the most favorable outcome for the patient.

Q 1:39   What is a hospitalist?

A hospitalist is a physician who spends at least 25 percent of his or her time acting as the physician-of-record for patients admitted or transferred by the PCP to the hospital. The hospitalist movement has developed over the past decade, beginning with programs existing in some form during the 1990s at Henry Ford Health System, Penn State/Geisinger Medical Center, Park Nicollet, and Emory University Crawford Long Hospital.[35] Not to be confused with such hospital-based physicians as infectious disease or critical care practitioners, the hospitalist concept revolves around economic necessity and clinical practice. Groups and programs that use hospitalists impose mandatory transfers of care from the patient's PCP to the physician in the hospital. Detractors challenge the discontinuity this imposes on patient care. Others commend the concept for its efficiency and quality of care attributes. Hospitalists have organized under the banner of the National Association of Inpatient Physicians.

Q 1:40   What is the role of the medical director in an HCO?

Most HMOs are required to have a full-time medical director. This person must be a physician and is responsible for a variety of functions, depending on the HMO. These responsibilities include the following:

- Responsibility for quality of care, which may take the form of directing quality improvement activities and credentialing (see chapters 8, 9, 10)
- Responsibility for the medical staff, which may include network design, peer review, and the appeal process
- Responsibility for medical care, which includes designing and implementing pathways and protocols, overseeing the review process, and functioning as a patient advocate in the review process
- Education, which includes educating fellow physicians and health care professionals about health care delivery in the HCO and educating patients regarding preventive care, access, and responsibilities
- Relationship with governance, which means that the medical director is the physician to whom the board or owners of the HCO should look for guidance regarding the impact of financial decisions on the quality of care

Typically, the HCO medical director has a license to practice medicine in the jurisdiction where the HCO operates.

Q 1:41   To whom should the medical director report?

The answer to this question is more a function of opinion and local preference. Two principles should be operative in the medical director's reporting relationships:

1. The medical director has primary responsibility as a physician to ensure the care of the patients under management by the MCO. Any reporting arrangement that interferes with that duty is unsatisfactory.

2. The medical director cannot be pressured to violate an obligation to the patients cared for by the MCO.

Care of the Indigent and Underinsured

Q 1:42   How does managed care affect the indigent, uninsured, and underinsured populations?

Managed care, for all its faults, has increased the attention of the country's health care establishment on PCPs and primary care delivery. Although there are many arguments about the extent of the abilities of the PCP in the care of the complex and hospitalized patient, there is no disagreement with the notion that PCPs are needed and are now lacking in the inner city. Data show less use of preventive services in low-income areas as well as lower rates of interventions for atherosclerotic disease and higher limb amputation rates for peripheral vascular disease and complications of diabetes. Figure 1-8 shows the projected increase in numbers of medically uninsured. Figure 1-9 shows the cost of uncompensated care as a proportion of total care costs. The trend is expected to continue and will be compounded by the fact that there are now fewer plans participating in publicly funded programs.

Managed care, in that it is a technique capable of managing the health of a population, is ideally suited to address these issues, but that intervention must be funded. The American College of Physicians, in a seminal report,[36] identified major interventions that will have an impact on inner-city and urban health and must be strongly considered by the managed care community:

1. Leverage all appropriate government and institutional resources to produce an adequate number of PCPs and other providers who are willing to practice in underserved inner-city areas.

2. Create incentives to change medical school recruitment and education and residency training. Medical school recruitment

Figure 1-8.   Medically Uninsured

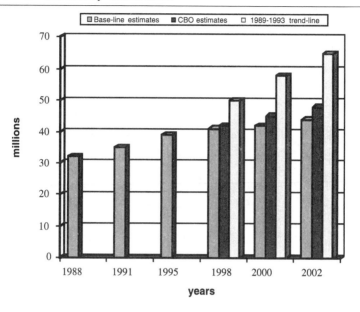

Figure 1-9.   Uncompensated Care Costs

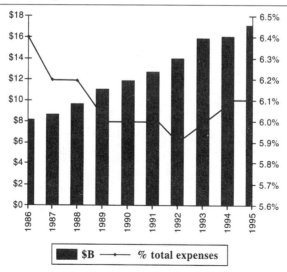

Source: Medical Benefits 14:9, 1997

policies, curricula, and clerkship programs must be retooled to address the health needs of inner-city residents.

3. Provide substantial fiscal incentives to attract individual providers to inner-city locations.

4. Deploy financial incentives and technical assistance to safety-net providers who are being squeezed by reductions in public funding and competition for insured patients that have been brought on by the changing health care marketplace.

5. During a transitional period, require MCOs to contract with essential community providers (e.g., those who serve low-income populations, such as community health centers) if the MCOs are serving persons in underserved, inner-city locations and are financed in whole or in part by federal funds.

6. Have an objective representative of the public (e.g., the state attorney general or an insurance commissioner) carefully scrutinize in advance all mergers, acquisitions, and conversions involving nonprofit hospitals and insurance plans to evaluate the potential effects on the community served by these nonprofit organizations. Community participation and vigilance are necessary to ensure that charitable resources remain dedicated to maintaining the well-being of the community.

It is incontrovertible that inner-city hospitals rely on Medicaid payments wholly or in part. In many communities managed care is viewed as a way of cutting the overall cost of Medicaid. For the inner-city public hospital, however, the siphoning off of Medicaid normal deliveries and well-child examinations by managed care leaves the hospital with only the severely ill and complex cases. Further, since disproportionate share payments (DSP) are paid on the basis of discharges, an efficient public sector HMO has the effect of saving money on the MCO side and losing revenue on the DSH side.

The American College of Physicians has the following recommendations for regulation regarding federal waivers for Medicaid:

1. Require MCOs to provide special services that are essential in inner-city environments, such as primary care services that are geographically accessible (providing transportation when necessary), after-hours availability of primary and urgent care, outreach services, and self-care education. MCOs must

have linguistic and cultural competence and must be able to coordinate interaction with other social services, such as nutrition programs. Capitation rates would reflect the additional cost of providing specialized services and the savings from reduced emergency department and other hospital costs.

2. Restrict direct marketing and encourage enrollment and education through independent brokers to eliminate "cherry picking" and to provide objective information, thereby enabling enrollees to choose the health plans that meet their health care needs.

3. Provide case management for persons with HIV infection, AIDS, and other serious illnesses.

4. Include risk adjustment mechanisms to protect plans with a higher than expected number of patients who have HIV infection, AIDS, and other costly diseases and conditions.

Further, the medical model is insufficient to answer the questions of health care for the poor and underinsured inner-city resident. The results of a study conducted by the Center for Studying Health System Change, however, suggest that the expansion of Medicaid managed care may be adversely affecting patient access.[37]

Q 1:43   How do surveys define *uninsured*?

Two definitions that are important to consider when interpreting estimates of the uninsured are the definitions of *health insurance* and *uninsured.*

How is *uninsured* defined? Are respondents categorized as uninsured if they do not have insurance at a particular point in time, during the entire study period, or during a portion of the study period? What is defined as *health insurance*? Is single service coverage such as a dental or vision plan considered health insurance? Or is only comprehensive medical coverage considered health insurance?

The following is an example of how two national surveys differ in this measurement area:

The Current Population Survey (CPS) considers respondents to be insured if they

1. Have Department of Veterans Affairs health care;

2. Are categorically eligible for Medicaid, regardless of enrollment status;

3. Are children of adults covered by Medicaid; or

4. Have single service or supplemental coverage (e.g., dental or vision plans).

The Medical Expenditure Panel Survey considers respondents insured only if they have comprehensive physician and hospital coverage or coverage by Medicaid.

Q 1:44 What would be the impact of extending HMO-type coverage to the medically uninsured population?

Bogard and colleagues[38] examined this question by comparing a population newly enrolled in an HMO with previously uninsured low-income persons newly enrolled in a similar plan. There were no differences in the utilization of services that are of major concern to organizations bearing financial risk: hospital days, hospital admissions, laboratory or pharmacy utilization, and radiology services. Previously uninsured persons did have a higher frequency of outpatient visits than the control population, perhaps related to their poorer overall health. Both the control and the study populations exhibited what is commonly known as the start-up effect, in which a population with previous low rates of utilization exhibits a higher rate on entry into an HMO. This is generally felt to be a result of pent-up demand and not a characteristic of the population.

Thus, HMOs, with their defined services and the ability to predict costs based on population dynamics, may well serve to care for the indigent, uninsured, and underinsured population. Bogard et al. affirm this and note:

> As many physicians move into managed care practices where they may no longer control patient access and billing, the charity care that many physicians have traditionally provided to the uninsured by reducing or waiving fees may become more difficult to accomplish. In addition, the movement of many states toward contracting with managed care systems for Medicaid service delivery, driven by the desire to control Medicaid costs, has the potential for additional untoward effects on the uninsured. Public health delivery systems currently use Medicaid dollars to fund not only care for Medicaid recipients, but also to fund care for the medically indigent. If the expanding num-

ber of HMOs engaging in Medicaid contracts do not provide care for the medically indigent, access to services for the uninsured individuals may decline.

Managed Care and Medical Ethics

Q 1:45 How does managed care affect traditional medical ethics?

The fundamental principle of the ethical practice of medicine relies on the relationship between the individual patient and the individual physician. On that mutual accountability rests the canon of ethics of the profession. When medicine consisted only of that relationship, all ethical questions of life and death, confidentiality and disclosure, and consent and autonomy were resolved according to the values and ethics of the two participants. Physicians made the assumptions that their patients would be responsive and comply with instructions; patients assumed their physicians would be educated, compassionate, and not venal. Managed care increases the interests of a third party in the physician-patient relationship. That third party is not bound by the same canon of ethics as the physician, and thus, ethical conflicts inevitably occur.

Q 1:46 How has the change in payment methodology affected the ethical relationship between physician and patient?

Before the end of the nineteenth century, payment for medical services was largely an issue between the patient and the physician. Hospitals were rarely used except in large cities and by the poor. Medical care was generally rendered in the home, and the physician billed the patient. The introduction of third parties into medical care, which began with union- and organization-sponsored medical care, meant a profound change for medicine. Nonetheless, third parties were, for the most part, benevolent. They viewed their role as that of financing medical care and were reluctant to enter into decisions concerning the delivery of that care. The view of the community supported this idea of the autonomy of the physician-patient axis. Because most hospitals were community supported, they were viewed as benevolent servants, as were physicians. A third party, bound by different ethics and with different motivations, is often at odds with the binary physician-patient relationship.

Q 1:47   How can managed care be reconciled with ethical medical practice?

Managed care has the potential to reverse some of the excesses of the medical care system. With alignment of incentives, the physician has no reason to perform unnecessary or questionable procedures and has no stake in a bad outcome either. With proper alignment, the physician is most successful when the patient has the best result. Unfortunately, such accountability is rare in current MCOs. Accountability was one of the principles of the proposed Clinton health plan that failed. The amount of the health care dollar now going to monitoring physicians' activities under free-market managed care is really quite astounding.

The physician has a fiduciary obligation to the patient to provide the most expert care, regardless of payment capability. This has been affirmed by the medical profession and the courts many times over. The medical care system, however, has no interest in beggaring its providers. Moreover, physicians must never be placed in a position that is adversarial to their patients' interests. The challenge in analyzing extant payment mechanisms is to order the intellectual, moral, ethical, and financial incentives in a way that ensures the finest use of the appropriate medical care and preventive services for each individual in a compassionate and caring physician-patient relationship.

Q 1:48   What are a physician's ethical obligations relating to continuity of care under managed care?

One of the problems with employer-based health care and many HMOs and PPOs is the effect of an employer's change of health care providers on a patient's health and well-being because of discontinuity of care. Such changes can be particularly problematic for patients with chronic health conditions. Ethical questions may also arise: Do the physician's duties to the patient end when the patient is switched from one health plan to another? How diligently should the physician try to maintain the physician-patient relationship with patients who are involuntarily removed from their plan? What should physicians as a group do to advocate for greater stability, longer continuity of care, and better coordination of care? How essential are continuity of care and coordination of care to the ethical principle of beneficence?

Some managed care systems have applied their organizational and technological expertise toward improving continuity of care and coordination of care, but problems persist in many organizations. Physicians have used their associations to lobby for laws that support the physician-patient relationship. The AMA has published ethical guidelines and policy statements in these areas.

Some states have tried to address these issues in the context of consumer protection and continuity of care. Measures that have been implemented in several states include (1) providing specific transition periods before a physician becomes an out-of-network provider and (2) expanding freedom of choice and patient protection laws to allow patient choice and continuity of care even for providers who are out of network.

Q 1:49   What are a physician's ethical obligations with respect to patient disclosure?

The issue of disclosure and not withholding from a patient information relating to options, even if not covered under a patient's health benefit plan, has been a controversial part of managed care. Until recently, many managed care contracts had "gag clauses" preventing participating physicians from advising patients of their therapeutic options when such options were not covered under the insured's policy. Over the years, managed care companies have instituted three types of gag clauses.[39] One type forbids physicians from disclosing to patients information about treatments not covered by the plan. A second type prohibits physicians from disclosing any other specific limitations of the plan. A third type forbids physicians from making any negative general comments about the plan. The most common type of gag clause is the first. Prior to the new laws,[40] this type of gag order was present in nearly every physician contract. Managed care companies point out that physicians have rarely been censured for violating these clauses, but the severity of the potential punishment serves as a powerful deterrent and interferes with physician-patient communication and quality of patient care.

Medicare has imposed prohibitions on such clauses, and many states have passed laws that prohibit such language in provider contracts. Beyond an ethical duty, some states are imposing legal duties on insurance companies to disclose information regarding benefits, provisions, and restrictions of managed care plans to prospective enrollees, as well as criteria for selection of plan providers. In some states physicians are also being accorded some protection, as insurance companies are being required to disclose to physicians the criteria for selection and termination of providers, criteria for the makeup of the plan's network, and, in the case of physicians terminated from the plan, the reasons for termination and an opportunity for appeal. Patient protection acts, whose purpose is to require MCOs to disclose to patients the benefits and limitations of their plan, have been passed in several states, and legislation is pending in many others.

From an ethical perspective, the following queries may arise: Does the patient's right to informed consent entail an obligation on the part of the physician to disclose all legitimate treatments, regardless of whether they are covered by the plan? Does signing a gag order forbidding such disclosure exempt the physician from this responsibility? If the physician believes the plan does not serve the patient's needs, should the physician convey this concern to the patient? If the plan contains financial disincentives to treat and other conflicts of interest that might adversely affect the quality of the patient's care, does the patient's right to informed consent imply a duty of the physician to convey such information?

With respect to the issue of disclosure, the AMA Council on Ethics and Judicial Affairs issued an opinion in 1997 stating that "physicians must assure disclosure of any financial inducements that may tend to limit the diagnostic and therapeutic alternatives that are offered to patients or that may tend to limit patients' overall access to care." Based on a recent case out of Illinois, however, *Neade v. Portes* [No 87445 (Ill Oct 26, 2000)], the AMA opined that, although physicians may have an ethical duty to inform patients of managed care financial incentives to limit care, that should not translate to a legal obligation.[41]

Q 1:50   Does a physician actually have a fiduciary duty to a patient with respect to the delivery of health care?

There has been considerable discussion, but little consensus, as to the physician's fiduciary responsibility to patients in the managed care setting. In some cases the patient insists on a frivolous test or treatment. In other cases the patient needs a legitimate service, such as mammography, physical therapy, mental health referral, or medications, but the service is not available in the managed care plan. In some cases the patient can pay out of pocket, but often the patient cannot do this without shifting resources away from some other area of need. The reasonable limits of a physician's duty to a patient are not well defined outside of recent court decisions. Many recent cases focus on a physician's duty of care, and many plaintiffs' attorneys are seeking to hold physicians to a higher standard of care when there are financial incentives associated with certain medical decisions. These issues are discussed in detail in chapter 8.

Sometimes, physicians get caught between their patients' demands for certain tests or therapies and what is truly medically indicated for that patient. Physicians are constantly challenged by patients seeking necessary and unnecessary care and treatment. The physician's duty to the patient is to provide care that meets the following two criteria. First, the care it must have been shown to help others in a similar condition, or it must fall within the standard of care. Second, provision of this care should not preclude treatment of other patients with a significantly greater likelihood of benefit. When patients demand tests or treatments with no proven clinical benefits, physicians should decline, not because the test or treatment is not covered by the plan, but because it does not meet the criteria of beneficence and justice stated here, and because patient autonomy should never be allowed to override physician integrity.[42]

Most managed care companies allow physicians to appeal on behalf of patients for tests and treatments not covered by the plan, and many physicians report that this process works effectively. Many others, however, report frustration at the degree of paperwork, the time spent playing "telephone tag," and the intrusion on the physician-patient relationship. Such a process has become known as rationing by exhaustion. The "hassle factor," not clinical judgment, often becomes the basis for whether a patient receives a particular test or treatment.

Who benefits from rationing by exhaustion? To the extent that rationing by exhaustion encourages cost-effective medicine, prevents resources from being wasted on patients who do not need them, and enables resources to be available for those who do, then patients are the beneficiaries. But when the appeal process is so time-consuming that physicians are deterred from making legitimate appeals, or so clinically flawed that such appeals are routinely rejected, the one who stands to lose is the patient, as well as the conscientious physician who wants to do what is best for the patient.

Q 1:51 Can managed care be delivered in an ethical manner?

Yes. The context in which managed care applies to the physician-patient relationship, however, must be analyzed to determine the scope and limits of the physician's role in providing care to patients in managed care settings. Whether or not the relationship is, or the level at which it becomes, fiduciary in nature will require further review. At the heart of the debate is the duty of the physician to advise, and the patient's right to have sufficient information to make an informed decision regarding acceptance or refusal of medical care. Finally, a physician's duty of care may require continuity of care even in the absence of payment.

Holleman et al. have reported that "managed care systems have the potential to correct many of the deficiencies of the fee-for-service system, most notably: the inability of that system to discipline itself to practice cost-effective medicine; the exclusion of large sectors of the population based on inability to pay; the incentive to overtreat; the failure to inform patients about conflicts of interest and financial incentives to overtreat; and the development of an expensive, disjointed specialist-dominated system. But such improvements by managed care systems will provide only marginal benefits unless they can learn how to be cost-effective without themselves sacrificing fiduciary responsibilities, informed consent, and continuity of care."[43]

References

1. Bank of America, Healthcare Industry Review and Outlook, 1999 Third Quarter 1999.

2. Managed Care Information Center (MCIC), CMA Warning to Consumers: 1998–99 HMO Profits Down; Consider Before Choosing, www.themcic.com (extracted July 5, 2000).

3. Richard Harris, *A Sacred Trust* (New York: New American Library, 1966).

4. Franz Goldman, *Voluntary Medical Care Insurance in the United States* (Dallas: National Center for Policy Analysis, Nov. 1988).

5. H. Luft and M. Greenlick, "Contributions of Group and Staff-Model HMOs to American Medicine, *Milbank Q.*, 74(4) Dec. 1996, 445–467.

6. W.J. McNerney, "Health Care Financing and Delivery in the Decade Ahead," *JAMA*, 222:2254, 1972.

7. L. Kirkland, "A Labor Leader's View of Insurance Reform," *Health Affairs*, 10(4):3, 1991.

8. Kaiser Commission on the Uninsured, Uninsured in America, 2d ed. (Kaiser Family Foundation, 2000).

9. S. Smith, M. Freeland, S. Heffler, and D. McKusick, "The Next Ten Years of Health Spending: What Does the Future Hold?" *Health Affairs*, 17(5):128–140, 1998.

10. D.L. Trostorff, "The State of Managed Care," *TIPS on Managed Care*, May–June 1999, at 5–6.

11. Tex. Civ. Prac. & Rem. Code Ann. §§ 88.001–88.003; Mo. Rev. Stat. §§ 538.205–538.30; Ga. H.B. 732 (1999).

12. A. Mitchell, "Senate Approves Republican Plan for Health Care," *N.Y. Times*, July 16, 1999, at A1; C.M. Cropper, "In Texas, a Laboratory Test of the Effects of Suing HMOs," *N.Y. Times*, Sept. 13, 1998, at C1; A. Goldstein and J. Eilperin, "Partisan House Swiftly Passes GOP Patients' Rights Bill," *Wash. Post*, July 25, 1998, at A4.

13. M.A. Chirba-Martin and T.A. Brennan, "The Critical Role of ERISA in State Health Care Reform," *Health Affairs*, Spring II): 142–156, 1994; W.K. Mariner, "State Regulation of Managed Care and the Employee Retirement Income Security Act," *New Eng. J. Med.*, 335:1986–1990, 1996.

14. New York State Conference of Blue Cross & Blue Shield Plans v. Travelers Ins. Co., 514 U.S. 645 (1995); DeBuono v. NYSA-ILA Med. & Clinical Serv. Fund, 117 S. Ct. 1747 (1997). For further evidence of this recent trend outside the health insurance context, see California Div. of Labor Standards Enforcement v. Dillingham Constr., 117 S. Ct. 832 (1997).

15. Dukes v. U.S. Healthcare, 57 F.3d 350 (3d Cir. 1995), *cert. denied*, 116 S. Ct. 564 (1995); Dunn v. Praiss, 606 A.2d 862 (N.J. Super. Ct. App. Div. 1992); PacifiCare of Okla. v. Burrage, 59 F.3d 151 (10th Cir. 1995); Prihoda v. Shpritz, 914 F. Supp. 133 (D. Md. 1996).

16. M.A. Hofmann, "Self-Insurers Taking Aim at Managed Care Legislation," *Bus. Ins.* February 15, 1999, at 17.

17. *OECD Health Data 1998: A Comparative Analysis of 29 Countries* (Paris: Organization for Economic Cooperation and Development, 1998); P. Taulbee and C.E. Cordero, "Employers Are Experimenting with Managed Competition," *Bus. & Health,* Mar. 10, 1992, at 26–38.

18. 29 USC §§ 1021–1022; 29 CFR §§ 2520.102-5, 2560.503-1; Shea v. Esensten, 107 F.3d 625 (8th Cir. 1997); Drolet v. Healthsource, Inc., 968 F. Supp. 757 (D.N.H. 1997). *But see* Weiss v. CIGNA Healthcare, Inc., 972 F. Supp. 748 (S.D.N.Y. 1997); and Ehlmann v. Kaiser Found. Health Plan, 20 F. Supp. 2d 1008 (N.D. Tex. 1998).

19. Neade v. Portes, Ill. Sup. Ct. No. 87445 (Oct. 26, 2000); 1999 WL 179338 (Ill. App. Ct. Mar. 31, 1999).

20. For self-funded plans, see Engalla v. Permanente Med. Group Inc., 37 Cal. App. 4th 497 (Ct. App. 1995); Sarchett v. Blue Shield of Cal., 729 P.2d 267 (Cal. 1987); Williams v. HealthAmerica, 535 N.E.2d 717 (Ohio Ct. App. 1987). For insured plans, see Warner v. Lincoln Nat'l Corp., No. 96932 (Idaho Dist. Ct. July 23, 1994).

21. W.M. Sage, "Physicians as Advocates," *Houston L. Rev.,* 35: 1529–1630, 1999.

22. According to the U.S. Bureau of the Census, in 1997 43.4 million people, or 16.1 percent of the population, were uninsured. *See Current Population Reports, Health Insurance Coverage, 1997 and 1998* (Washington, D.C.: Government Printing Office, 1997, 1998).

23. *See* Bank of America, *supra* note 1.

24. J.K. Iglehart, "The American Health Care System—Expenditures," *New Eng. J. Med.,* 340:70, 1999.

25. This report can be accessed at http://www.aahp.org.

26. B. Bos, 15th Annual Mercer/Foster Higgins Survey (Chicago: Mercer, 2000).

27. K.S. Abramowitz, "HMOs: Pricing Cycle Has Finally Turned," *Managing Employee Benefits*, 7(2):72, 1999.

28. *See* http://www.hcfa.gov/pubforms/tr/smi2000/SECIIA.htm (last accessed July 4, 2000).

29. HCFA, 2000 Annual Report of the Board of Trustees of the Federal Hospital Insurance Trust Fund (corrected Apr. 20, 2000), http://www.hcfa.gov/pubforms/tr/hi2000/toc.htm (last accessed July 4, 2000).

30. HCFA, 2001 Annual Report of the Board of Trustees of the Federal Hospital Insurance Trust Fund.

31. T.G. Ferris, "Leaving Gatekeeping Behind—Effects of Opening Access to Specialists for Adults in a Health Maintenance Organization," *New Engl. J. Med.*, 345:1312–1317, 2001.

32. D. Blumenthal and G.S. Meyer, "Academic Health Centers in a Changing Environment," *Health Affairs*, 15(2):200–215, 1996.

33. R. Rettig, "Are Patients a Scarce Resource for Academic Clinical Research?" *Health Affairs*, 19(6):195, 2000.

34. U.S. Bureau of Labor Statistics, http://stats.bls.gov/asp/oep/niome/empior.asp.

35. J.L. Lenow, "The Implications of the Hospitalist Medicine," *Health Pol'y Newsl.*, Jan. 1999, at 3.

36. American College of Physicians, "Inner City Health Care," *Annals Internal Med.*, 27:485–490, 1997.

37. Center for Studying Health System Change, Issue Brief No. 19 (Mar. 23 1999), reported in *On Managed Care*, 4:5, May 1999.

38. H.Y. Bogard, D.P. Ritzwoller, N. Calogne, et al., "Extending Health Maintenance Organization Insurance to the Uninsured," *JAMA*, 277:1067–1072, 1997.

39. T.E. Miller, "Managed Care Regulation: In the Laboratory of the States," *JAMA*, 278:1102–1109, 1997.

40. P. Wynn, "When Your Plan Tells You What Not to Say," *Managed Care*, June 1995:33–34.

41. Sarah A. Klein, *Am. Med. News*, Mar. 20, 2000.

42. D.J. Doukas, M. Fetters, M.T. Ruffin, and L.B. McCullough, "Ethical Considerations in the Provision of Controversial Screening Tests," *Archives Fam. Med.*, 6:486–490, 1997.

43. W.L. Holleman, M.C. Holleman, and J.G. Moy, "Continuity of Care, Informed Consent, and Fiduciary Responsibilities in For-Profit Managed Care Systems," *Archives Fam. Med.*, 9:21–25, 2000.

Appendix 1-A

Managed Care: A Timeline*

1646—Colonial legislature of Virginia enacts laws related to "immoderate and excessive rates and prices exacted by practitioners in Physick and Chyrgery."

1787—Earliest forms of insurance found in fraternal societies and lodges that begin to appear in the United States are funded by membership dues and are used to provide aid to members and their families in times of need. One of these fraternal societies, La Société Française de Bienfaisance Mutuelle, established in 1851, becomes the French Hospital in San Francisco, California.

1798—Congress establishes the U.S. Marine Hospital Services and institutes a prepaid program under which 20 cents per month per seaman is paid into a fund to finance new hospitals. This system evolves into the U.S. Public Health Service and is cited as the first prepaid medical program in the United States.

1847—Earliest forms of commercial health insurance, called indemnity insurance, are developed in the United States with the Massachusetts Health Insurance Company of Boston (1847), the Franklin Health Assurance Company of Massachusetts (1850), and the Travelers Insurance Company (1863), which introduced general accident

*Adapted from the Internet posting of John Short, Phase II Consulting; at http://www.phase-ii.com/html/history.htm; the *1997 Health Care Almanac and Yearbook,* compiled by Daniel Moskowitz, Faulkner & Gray, Inc., and Kennett L. Simmons, Ph.D., from his doctoral dissertation, "Managed Health Care: Right Idea—Wrong Rules," presented to the Faculty of the Graduate School of the University of Texas at Austin, University of Texas at Austin, Aug. 1992.

insurance. Early policies provide for the payment of a weekly indemnity in the event the insured is injured in an accident.

1882—Employee mutual benefit associations begin to offer organized medical services during times of disabling illness or accident. Early plans include Macy Mutual Aid Association (1885) and the Wabash Employees Hospital Association of Decatur, Illinois (1882).

1887—The earliest medical group practice is traced to the Mayo Clinic in Rochester, Minnesota, when Dr. William N. Mayo, joined by his sons Charles and William, Jr., forms a partnership with a specialty in general surgery.

1895–1919 (WWI)—Much progress is made in health care technology and public health. In 1906, the Pure Food and Drug Act is passed, and in 1912, the Children's Bureau is established within the Department of Labor, a precursor to the Department of Health and Human Services (HHS). Efforts undertaken by the American Association for Labor Legislation (AALL) are successful in securing enactment of workers' compensation laws, but unsuccessful in obtaining compulsory health insurance, which is being established in Germany, Austria, Hungary, Norway, Great Britain, Russia, and the Netherlands.

1910—First prepaid group practice begins as Drs. Thomas Curran and James Yocum of Western Clinic, Tacoma, Washington, contract with a lumber company to provide medical services for 50 cents per member per month. By 1924, over 60 percent of the clinic's business is from its prepaid contracts. Dr. Bridge, also of Tacoma, begins the Bridge Company, a chain of prepaid group clinics throughout the Washington-Oregon area. The first group health insurance policy is issued, covering employees of Montgomery Ward.

1917—Early medical society opposition to managed care begins. Pierce County Medical Service Bureau is organized by private practice physicians to limit competition from prepaid plans.

1920s—American Medical Association (AMA) adopts a resolution at its annual session stating its opposition to the institution of any plan or system of compulsory insurance against illness or other plan of compulsory insurance in which medical services are provided, controlled, or regulated by any state or federal government. Four of the highest risk industries—railroad, timber, mining, and construction—expand beyond the workers' compensation programs to develop hospital associations to provide comprehensive health care services for members and their dependents. Some of these industries "self-insure" for injury and disease not covered by workers' compensation laws. These self-insured programs use payroll deductions to cover the costs of the program.

1927—Dr. Michael A. Shadid (known as the Crusading Doctor) forms the Community Hospital Association and initiates a cooperative program of prepaid health care using his group practice and a new hospital financed by membership dues to deliver medical services to residents of Elk City, Oklahoma. Elk City residents are in favor of the idea, but the local medical community is outraged. This opposition typifies tensions between private and group practice.

1929—The Great Depression decreases philanthropic support for hospitals; patient fees become a major funding source. Patients begin to face debt as a result of inflation, and hospitals experience declining bed use income. The need for protection from the financial consequences of illness becomes apparent. At the same time, prepaid hospitalization coverage begins with a group of 1,250 Dallas schoolteachers contracting with Baylor University Hospital in Texas. In that same year, the Ross-Loos fee-for-service clinic establishes a prepaid program for the Los Angeles water and power departments.

1930s—More trade union health plans begin to include health benefits with union membership beginning in the 1930s. One of the first unions to provide medical services to members is the International Typographical Union, which establishes a printer's home and tuberculosis sanitarium in Colorado Springs, Colorado, in 1892 to care for sick and aged members. In 1913, the International Ladies Garment Workers Union opens a medical clinic in New York, which is, initially, limited to physical examination services. Early insurance plans by unions initially focus on life insurance and disability insurance instead of health insurance.

1931—Drs. Ross and Loos are expelled from the Los Angeles County Medical Society for operating group clinics. This escalating tension between private and group practice lays the foundation for national control.

1932—Committee on the Costs of Medical Care Report is published in *Medical Care for the American People*. The Report is the result of a five-year study funded by several large foundations. The

Report recommends that consumers make payments into a common fund for the purpose of contracting with physicians and private clinics to provide medical services. The AMA publishes a strong statement opposing prepaid medical care. This action leads to the development of Blue Cross because the medical community thinks health insurance is more palatable than prepaid medical care.

1933—King County Medical Society charges Dr. Curran (Western Clinic, 1917) with "practicing in two counties" and suspends him from membership. He sells his interest in the State Clinic (Seattle) and continues with the Western Clinic (Tacoma), where his medical society membership is restored.

1934—The group practice model survives despite opposition. The Farmer's Union assumes sponsorship of Dr. Shadid's project (see 1927). Community Hospital becomes the Farmer's Union Cooperative Association.

1937—Group Health Association (GHA) of Washington, D.C., is begun in response to the problem of mortgage default resulting from large medical expenses. This represents the first HMO established in an urban area. Henry Kaiser becomes aware of Dr. Sidney Garfield's prepaid medical care plan among construction workers in Southern California. He asks Garfield to start a similar program for the Grand Coulee Dam construction site. The Permanente Health Plan begins.

1939—The first Blue Shield plan is established as a statewide program by the California Medical Association to cover home and office visits as well as physician hospital visits as a mixture of direct service and indemnity product open to every physician in the local society, and requiring open access to physicians by subscribers.

1940—By this time, the key elements of private health insurance have been established, with 9 percent of the civilian population covered by some form of private insurance for health care. The industry accommodates the primacy of physicians during this period. Efforts to nationalize health care are successfully defeated, despite general public support, through the political efforts of the AMA.

1941—A four-year battle between GHA and the District of Columbia Medical Society (DCMS) ends when the U.S. Supreme Court indicts the AMA and DCMS for restraint of trade in its efforts to block GHA's development. A pattern of defeat of organized medical opposition to prepaid medical care becomes apparent.

1944—New York City Mayor Fiorello La Guardia establishes the New York Health Insurance Plan, a community-based, prepaid medical care plan for city employees.

1945—Congress enacts the McCarran-Ferguson Act, supported by the insurance industry, which insulates the business of insurance from federal antitrust laws "to the extent such business is not regulated by state laws."

1947—Dr. Michael Shadid settles an antitrust suit against county and state medical societies out of court; he is awarded $300,000 in damages.

1950—Over 100 rural group health plans are in existence. Operational HMOs increase to approximately 20.[1] From 1940 to 1950 the St. Louis Teamsters, Appalachian United Mine Workers, and Detroit United Auto Workers establish prepaid group health care programs.

1954—San Joaquin Foundation for Medical Care is formed in California. Physicians agree to accept peer review, and a fixed fee schedule and to risk financial loss in this model of an independent practice association.

1956—Group Health Mutual Insurance, a traditional insurer, builds a clinical facility along with its new headquarters. In this way, Group Health Plan, the largest HMO in Minneapolis-St. Paul, begins.

1965—Social Security is expanded to include medical insurance for the elderly (Medicare) and poor (Medicaid).[2]

1970—Number of HMOs jumps to 37 in 14 states. Total U.S. health expenditures are $85 billion.[3] The Nixon Administration endorses HMOs as the new national health strategy.[4]

1971—HMO Office is established within the Department of Health, Education and Welfare (DHEW) Office of the Administrator, Health Services and Mental Health Administration, in May. This is followed by the establishment of the Health Maintenance Organization Service and the Office of Prepaid Health Care in October.[5] The American Managed Care and Review Association (AMCRA) is also founded.[6]

1973—The Health Maintenance Organization Act is signed by President Nixon in December. The Act provides "assistance and encouragement for the establishment and expansion of health maintenance organizations, health care resources, and the establishment of a Quality Health Care Commission" stimulating industry growth.[7]

1974–1980—The federal government invests $190 million in a new HMO.[8]

1975—183 HMOs are in existence in 32 states; 297 future HMOs are in planning.[9]

1976—HMO Act Amendment liberalizes requirements, brings widespread acceptance of federal qualification.[10]

1978—National Industry Council for HMO development is established to further HMO growth. Kaiser has 3.5 million members or nearly 50 percent of U.S. total.[11]

1980—236 HMOs are serving 9.1 million members.[12]

1981—Federal financial assistance reaches its objectives and is terminated. Federal efforts to encourage private investment begin.[13] The Omnibus Budget Reconciliation Act gives the states greater flexibility to contract with HMOs for their Medicaid programs. Medicaid enrollments increase 58 percent from 1981 to 1982, concentrating in older and larger HMOs.

1982—Network model gains popularity; 39 states plus the District of Columbia and Guam have HMOs. Plans are concentrated in urban areas. The Tax Equity and Fiscal Responsibility Act encourages further Medicare enrollments in HMOs.[14]

1983—Federal government begins paying hospitals a flat fee for Medicare patients, based on diagnosis rather than the length of hospitalization.[15]

Dec. 1983–June 1985—Number of national firms nearly doubles, representing 59 percent of all enrollment in HMOs.

1984–1985—HMO enrollment increases 25 percent. Total number of HMOs increases 29 percent to 393.[16]

1985–1986—Independent practice association model surges in popularity. Private sector support for managed care increases. Excluding Kaiser, investor-owned HMOs dominate the industry. Competition surges. Premium wars produce widespread losses.[17]

1987—662 operational HMOs. By December 1987, the number is 650, half of which are national firms; 25.5 percent of U.S. members are now in group practice plans. Maxicare declares losses of $255.9 million.

1988—75 percent of all HMO members are enrolled in plans with more than 50,000 members; 71 plans terminate. U.S. national health expenditures are $540 billion.[18] Congress passes and then, in an unprecedented move under tremendous political pressure from the elderly, repeals the Medicare Catastrophic Coverage Act of 1988.

1989—Maxicare files for bankruptcy.[19]

1990—Total enrollment in HMOs is up over 220 percent since 1984. Competitive emphasis is cost containment and measurable differences in quality of care.[20] Positive gross incomes are reported by 90 percent of HMOs, and industry-wide earnings are $1.39 billion before taxes on $45.61 billion in revenue.[21]

1991–1992—These years represent a period of slow growth and even decline for the managed care industry. Total number of HMOs begins to fall as economic stagnation is the order of the day not only in the health care industry but also in the economy as a whole.[22]

1992—Total number of operational HMOs has dropped to 546; however, enrollee numbers have grown to 41.4 million. Nearly one in five insured individuals is enrolled in an HMO. The number of start-up plans increases from three plans in 1991 to 12 plans in 1992.[23]

1994—More than 650 of the nation's hospitals are involved in mergers or acquisitions, with health care mergers among physicians' groups, HMOs, laboratories, and other providers totaling $22 billion.[24] Total revenues for all HMOs climb to $82.5 billion.[25]

1995—Ten major U.S. corporations form the first nationwide health care purchasing cooperative in the country.[26] By the end of the year, the number of HMOs has grown once again to 628. HMO enrollment numbers increase to approximately 52 million people. Approximately 8.5 million enrollees, 24 percent of the Medicaid population, are served by managed care plans nationwide.[27]

1996—Another backlash against managed care begins. Approximately 1,100 bills are considered in 46 states to regulate managed care quality and administration. Many states pass laws to ban HMO gag rules and ensure coverage of emergency services.[28] Despite the backlash, about 30 percent of the insured population, some 60 million people, are covered by HMOs.[29] PPO enrollment shows similar gains, reaching an estimated 91 million people.[30] Congress enacts HIPAA, which represents the first major reform of health insurance benefits since ERISA and the Consolidated Omnibus Budget Reconciliation Act of 1986.

1997—The BBA is enacted. The BBA includes sweeping reforms relating to Medicare, Medicaid, and the emergence of PSOs, which are eligible to contract directly with CMS to provide coverage to Medicare beneficiaries. As part of the BBA, an advisory committee is constituted. President Clinton appoints a three-member advisory panel to draft a bill of rights for health care consumers and investigate HMO practices. As of April 1997, legislators in 49 states have introduced 800 proposals to regulate managed care in 1997 alone.[31]

1998—Despite the proposed patients' bill of rights and other patient protection measures proposed during the 105th Congress, no legislation relating to health care is adopted in 1998. The final safe harbor rules are issued in the Federal Register for Stark I, which prohibits physician self-referral.

1999—Patient protection is, again, a hot issue in Congress, and most states have adopted various managed care reform legislation targeting liability, utilization review, mandated benefits, and confidentiality. Physician union activity gains momentum as a physician collective bargaining bill passes in Texas and the AMA board of governors authorizes the association to begin representing physicians in collective bargaining.

References

1. Robert G. Shouldice, *Medical Group Practice and Health Maintenance Organizations* (New York: Information Resources Press 1997) 28.
2. *1997 Healthcare Almanac and Yearbook* (New York: Faulkner & Gray) C-19.
3. N. Kraus, M. Porter, and P. Ball, *The Interstudy Edge: Managed Care, a Decade in Review, 1980–1990,* Daniel Moskowitz (ed.) (Minneapolis: Interstudy 1991).
4. *Id.*

5. Shouldice, *supra* note 1, at 35.

6. Kraus et al., *supra* note 3.

7. Shouldice, *supra* note 1, at 36.

8. Kraus et al., *supra* note 3.

9. *Id.*

10. *Id.*

11. *Id.*

12. *Id.*

13. *Id.*

14. *Id.*

15. *1997 Healthcare Almanac and Yearbook, supra* note 2, at C-21.

16. Kraus et al., *supra* note 3.

17. *Id.*

18. *Id.*

19. *Id.*

20. *Id.*

21. *HMO Industry Profile* (Group Health Association of America 1992) vi.

22. *The Guide to the Managed Care Industry* (HCIA Inc. and Coopers & Lybrand 1996) ix.

23. *1993 Directory of HMOs* (Group Health Association of America Inc.) 9.

24. *The Guide to the Managed Care Industry, supra* note 22, at ix.

25. *Id.* at xi.

26. *1997 Healthcare Almanac and Yearbook, supra* note 3, at C-23.

27. *The Interstudy Competitive Edge,* HMO Industry Report 6.2 (Minneapolis: Interstudy 1996) 2.

28. *Bangor Daily News,* Apr. 10, 1997.

29. A. Pham, *Boston Globe,* Mar. 30, 1997.

30. J. Ziegler, *Bus. & Health,* Aug. 1996.

31. *Bangor Daily News,* Apr. 10, 1997.

Chapter 2

Health Care in a Global Economy*

The issues associated with financing and delivering health care take on more importance as health status becomes not only an essential feature of a country's stability but also a critical component of its economy. Authorities in international health such as the World Bank and the World Health Organization (WHO) have identified strategies for reform in countries with statutory financing systems and public delivery systems differ substantially from the strategies being considered in the United States. In the most developed countries (excluding the United States), reform strategies include decentralizing management responsibilities and developing public-private partnerships to offer a private market program to those who can afford market prices while maintaining statutory programs as a safety net for the medically indigent. For all countries, including the United States, the strategies appear to focus resources on primary care, prevention, and health education instead of on the more costly curative interventions. Of the countries reviewed in this chapter, none seek to replicate the U.S. health care system.

E-commerce and the global communcation of health care information are also discussed in this chapter. Pri-

* This chapter was prepared by Dr. Clifford Dacso and Dr. Sheryl Tatar Dacso, who both served as Eisenhower Exchange Fellows in Hungary and the Czech Republic during the spring of 1999, studying health care systems in Central and Eastern Europe, and by Mr. Matthew M. Dacso and Ms. Jennie E. Tucker, based on their research in Buenos Aires, Argentina, during the summer of 1999.

vacy and security of health information have become international issues, resulting in the promulgation of rules and principles for e-commerce among nations.

The Global Health Care Economy

Q 2:1   How does health care spending in the United States compare with health care spending in other industrialized nations?

The World Bank has released data on the percentage of gross domestic product (GDP) devoted to health care throughout the world. Reports have also been developed by the Organization for Economic Cooperation and Development (OECD) (see Q 2:13) showing the resource allocation to a country's health care system. As shown in Table 2-1, the United States spends disproportionately large sums on health care in comparison to other OECD countries.

Q 2:2   Is there a correlation between resources devoted to health care spending and distribution of wealth among countries?

Yes. Although only 16 percent of the world's population live in high-income countries, they consume 89 percent of the world's health care resources. The most recent data available from the World Bank are shown in Table 2-2. The disparity between spending and population is exacerbated by the distribution and variety of diseases.

Public Health Issues in a Global Economy

Q 2:3   Has globalization affected health status around the world?

Yes. Globalization—the ease of travel and of communication—has improved health status. Highly developed countries benefit from

**Table 2-1.   Health Spending as Percent of GDP by
Sources of Funds, 1998**

	Total Health Spending (1)	Public Spending (2)	Private Collective Spending (3)	Out-of-Pocket Spending (4)
Australia	8.6	6.0	1.2	1.4
Austria	8.0	5.8	0.9	1.3
Canada	9.3	6.5	1.3	1.5
Czech Republic	7.1	6.5	0.0	0.6
Denmark	8.3	6.8	0.1	1.4
Finland	6.9	5.3	0.2	1.4
France	9.4	7.3	1.1	1.0
Germany	10.3	7.8	1.2	1.3
Iceland	8.4	7.0	0.1	1.3
Ireland	6.8	5.2	0.8	0.8
Italy	8.2	5.5	0.8	1.9
Japan	7.4	5.8	0.3	1.3
Korea	5.1	2.4	0.6	2.1
Mexico	5.3	2.6	0.1	2.6
Netherlands	8.7	6.0	2.0	0.7
New Zealand	8.1	6.3	0.5	1.3
Norway	9.4	7.1	0.2	2.1
United Kingdom	6.8	5.7	0.3	0.8
United States	12.9	5.8	5.1	2.0
Average of above countries (5)	8.2	5.9	0.9	1.4

Source: OECD Health Data 2001.
Notes:
1. Total expenditure on health includes public and private spending.
2. Public expenditure includes government tax-funded and social security programmes.
3. Private collective spending includes private voluntary, private mandatory social insurance (group contracts and/or employer-subsidised programmes), plus charity and direct employer benefits.
4. Out-of-pocket spending comprises over-the-counter and cost-sharing (co-payment, co-insurance).
5. Unweighted average.

improved health status in other countries given the pattern of disease and its epidemiology. The ability to affect health status in developing countries can have a significant effect on the general health status of the international community. With globalization, however, has come the increase in world obesity, tobacco consumption, HIV and AIDS, and a host of other maladies.

Table 2-2.   Global Distribution of Income, Health Spending,
and Population, 1994

	Gross Domestic Product (%)	Health Spending (%)	Population (%)
Distribution by Income Group			
High income	82	89	16
Low income	18	11	84
Distribution Among Low- and Middle-Income Countries			
East Asia and Pacific	24	17	35
Europe and Central Asia	19	18	11
Latin America and Caribbean	35	42	29
Middle East and North Africa	8	9	7
South Asia	9	8	26
Sub-Saharan Africa	5	6	12

Source: World Bank Health, Nutrition, and Population Database (as modified).[1]

Q 2:4   What effect have telemedicine and the Internet had on health status and disease?

As discussed in detail in chapter 15, the developments and advances in telecommunication technology represent one of the most important opportunities for improving health status on an international basis. The ability to use telecommunication and the Internet to access health care information, products, and services also represents one of the biggest challenges for regulators who seek to protect their citizens from unregulated products and services.

Q 2:5   What indicators are used internationally to define health status and disease?

A widely used indicator of public health is life expectancy at birth. Table 2-3 shows the changes in life expectancy at birth in various countries over the last century.

Q 2:6   What are the reasons for longer life expectancy in developing and developed countries?

The reasons for longer life expectancy are many and generally include better sanitation, nutrition, immunization, and control of in-

Table 2-3. Life Expectancy at Birth, in Selected Countries, Around 1910 and 1998

	Around 1910		1998	
Country	Males	Females	Males	Females
Australia	56	60	75	81
Chile	29	33	72	78
England and Wales	49	53	75	80
Italy	46	47	75	81
Japan	43	43	77	83
New Zealand*	60	63	74	80
Norway	56	59	75	81
Sweden	57	59	76	81
United States+	49	53	73	80

* Excluding Maoris.

\+ States only, includes DC.

Source: World Health Organization, *Making a Difference in People's Lives: Achievements and Challenges* (Geneva: WHO 1999) 2; see http://www.who.int/whr/1999/en/report.htm.

fectious diseases. Even in the developed countries of the OECD, however, there is wide variation in premature deaths. These data are shown in Table 2-4.

The reasons for the disparities in the data are varied but may include the traditional causes of a high mortality rate (poverty, low education levels, poor sanitation, and inadequate public health care) and differences in tobacco consumption, environmental pollution, and infectious diseases. In parts of Africa, HIV and AIDS have had a dramatic effect on mortality rates in young and middle-aged populations.

The fertility rate in several Western economies has been persistently below the replacement rate, and China has an official policy restricting couples to one child. Increased income is correlated with fertility decline; however, there is good reason to believe that the emergence of health care intervention has an independent effect on the reduction in the fertility rate.

Thus, the determinants of health and disease throughout the world are not a result of changes in a single sector. In fact, WHO has analyzed the relative contributions of different sectors to health. It concluded:

Table 2-4.   Premature Deaths in OECD Countries from 1960 to 1995

	Females				Males			
	Annual Rate of Decline			Level in 1995	Annual Rate of Decline			Level in 1995
	1960–1980	1980–1990	1990–1995	1995	1960–1980	1980–1990	1990–1995	1995
Australia	2.3	2.6	3.0	3103	1.6	3.2	3.5	5193
Austria	2.8	3.4	3.0	3248	2.0	3.5	2.5	6321
Belgium	2.3	2.8	1.9	3526	1.9	2.9	1.9	6259
Canada	2.5	2.7	2.2	3284	1.9	2.9	3.1	5451
Czech Republic	0.9	2.2	3.1	4233	0.1	1.0	3.9	8935
Denmark	1.6	0.8	1.8	4058	1.0	0.9	2.2	6217
Finland	3.4	0.8	3.9	2856	2.2	1.7	4.0	5271
France	2.5	2.7	2.2	3092	1.4	2.0	2.1	6661
Germany	3.5	2.3	1.7	3337	2.7	1.9	1.0	6505
Greece	2.5	3.0	2.7	3165	1.2	2.2	0.4	6317
Hungary	1.8	0.9	1.7	6334	0.4	0.6	0.1	14519
Iceland	2.6	0.3	5.6	2520	1.0	3.4	6.2	3928
Ireland	2.6	2.7	3.6	3444	1.5	2.9	2.7	5795
Italy	3.8	3.5	1.5	3144	2.5	2.9	2.3	5951
Japan	5.3	3.1	2.1	2399	4.2	2.4	2.0	4443
Korea				3251				7403
Luxembourg	0.8	3.2	6.4	3015	0.9	1.7	3.1	6303
Mexico	3.0	5.5	7.5	5872	1.6	5.1	6.6	9945
Netherlands	2.0	1.2	1.4	3262	1.2	1.9	2.2	5139
New Zealand	1.1	2.7	0.4	4775	1.1	2.2	0.2	7342
Norway	2.3	0.7	1.9	3070	1.3	1.7	4.3	4968
Poland			2.1	5361			2.1	12103
Portugal	4.5	3.5	3.4	4117	2.8	2.8	1.4	9234
Spain	3.8	2.4	2.9	3056	2.5	0.7	1.8	6940
Sweden	2.3	4.6	3.5	2631	1.3	2.2	4.0	4305
Switzerland	2.7	1.5	2.2	2948	2.2	1.3	2.4	5527
United Kingdom	1.5	2.6	2.3	3616	1.5	2.6	2.6	5690
United States	2.1	1.7	1.0	4591	1.6	1.6	0.9	8401
OECD average	2.6	2.3	2.8		1.7	2.2	2.6	

Source: *OECD Health Data, 1998: A Comparative Analysis of Twenty-nine Countries* (Paris: OECD 1998).

Hungry children easily acquire diseases, and easily die from diseases they do acquire. Dwellings without sanitation provide fertile environments for transmission of intestinal infections. Air dense with particulates or acids destroys lungs and lives. Hopeless life circumstances thrust young girls (and boys) into prostitution with its attendant risks of violence and sexually transmitted diseases including HIV/AIDS. Manufacturers of tobacco and alcohol benefit enormously from advertising and promotion that spreads addiction. Rapid growth in vehicular traffic—often with untrained drivers on unsafe roads—generates a rising toll of injury. Poorly designed irrigation projects create breeding grounds for vectors of disease. The list could be much extended, and it could be rephrased in terms of factors favorable to health, but the point is clear: determinants of health are truly multisectoral.[2]

Q 2:7   What major factors influence variations in life expectancy among different countries?

An assessment commissioned for WHO's 1997 Ad Hoc Committee on Health Research estimated the percentage of deaths associated with certain risk factors by region and globally. It concluded that in 1990, the following risks contributed to global mortality rates in the following percentages:[3]

- Tobacco use, 6.0 percent
- Hypertension, 5.8 percent
- Inadequate water and sanitation, 5.3 percent
- Risky sexual activity, 2.2 percent
- Alcohol use, 1.5 percent

Underlying most specific risks are more general determinants of health—income and education levels. Income and education influence risk (and being able to utilize health services effectively). For example, poorer societies may forgo expensive mechanisms for cleaning polluted air or water from factories, and poorer households lack the resources to purchase indoor sanitation or piped water. Poorly educated individuals may fail to observe basic hygiene or may neglect appropriate weaning practices for their children, and they are increasingly the population that smokes. The effects of education and income are indeed real and quantitatively important, even though only about half of health improvements in developing countries from 1960 to 1990 result from these factors.[4]

Another measure of disease burden is the amount of morbidity that disease causes. This is shown in Figure 2-1.[5] A recurring theme is that health status and income are very closely related.

The efficacy of interventions is commonly measured in quality-adjusted life-years (QALY). WHO has proposed that the burden of disease worldwide be measured in disease-adjusted life-years (DALYs). One DALY is equal to one year of health lost, with a standardized, long-lived population—Japan—used as the basis for comparison. To compare one population with another, a "stan-

**Figure 2-1.   Disability Burden from Noncommunicable Diseases in
Low- and Middle-Income Countries: 1998**

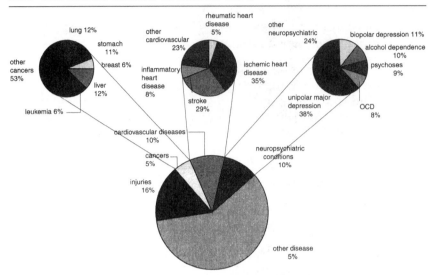

dard DALY" was created by the World Bank and WHO and is becoming more widely used.[6]

Q 2:8   What is the importance of demographics for health care worldwide?

Demography is the study of a population's characteristics, such as birth and death rates and age and sex distribution. The demographics of a country are important to health assessment and health care planning. Since the middle of the twentieth century, there has been a gradual decline in fertility rates around the world. The only exception is Africa, but there is evidence that a decline has begun in Africa too. The net effect of a decline in the birth rate is stabilization of the percentage of the younger population; as these people traverse their fertile years, the trend is perpetuated. As a result, there is a gradual aging of the population, with the effect on illness distribution that naturally follows.

Research performed by WHO, the Asia Development Bank, and others confirms the link between demography and income in a population. Estimates of the contribution of health to economic growth range as high as 30 percent for the United Kingdom between the mid-eighteenth century and the end of the twentieth century.[7]

Q 2:9 Is there a demonstrable link between the economic status of a country and its health?

There are strong data to suggest that there is a link between a country's economic status and its public health status. In recent years, WHO Member States in the Region of the Americas expressed interest in improving the understanding of links between investments in health, economic growth, and poverty reduction. In response, a joint Pan American Health Organization (PAHO)/Inter-American Development Bank (IADB)/United Nations European Community Latin American Center (UNECLAC) study has been initiated, aiming at elucidating relations between investments in health, economic growth, and household productivity. Preliminary data from Latin American and Caribbean countries show that growth in GDP is statistically associated with life expectancy, as has been found in other studies for a wider sample of countries.

Life expectancy at birth, alone, is one of the strongest explanatory variables of growth in GDP. Estimates based on data from Mexico throw some light on the time frame in which health affects economic indicators. High life expectancy at birth for males and females has an economic impact over the next five years. The impact of male life expectancy on the economy is greater than that of female life expectancy, probably because of the higher level of economic activity among males. The results suggest that for any additional year of life expectancy there will be an additional 1 percent increase in GDP 15 years later. Similar findings were observed for schooling; a child whose mother lives until he or she grows to adulthood is more likely to continue with school than one who does not have that support. In this case, the correlation between female life expectancy and schooling is greater than that between male life expectancy and schooling, probably because of the larger role that women play in childrearing.

This work implies that the relationship between health improvement variables and economic growth is sufficiently significant in the long term to justify sustained national commitment to investing in health. Continued work by the Pan American Health Organization and its collaborators should further elucidate these links at both the household level and the national level.[8]

Health Care Reform Around the World

Q 2:10   How do health care systems differ around the world?

Chapter 1 discusses the evolution of the U.S. health care system, which developed as a competitive, privatized, insurance-based model in which access is not universal. The U.S. model differs from most other countries' health care systems, which developed as more socialized, government-sponsored systems with the fundamental principle of universal access. Each society approaches the problem of caring for the sick with the overlay of its own cultural values and norms. L. Payer emphasized that, even in economically developed countries, cultural issues determine a person's response to illness and even the definition of illness itself.[9]

Q 2:11   What are the major issues affecting health care reform in developing countries?

In developing countries, the issues associated with health care reform are far more basic and focused on public health than they are in developed countries. For example, in Pakistan, a very poor country, there are approximately 133 million people for whom the country spends less than 1 percent of its gross national product (GNP) on health care.[10] Access is affected by the high patient-to-physician ratio. There are approximately 2,000 people to each practicing physician. Government programs focus on the two thirds of the population that are impoverished, who must pay the equivalent of $6 for a "health card" that covers only basic health services and does not cover maternal, preventive, emergency, or specialty care, or drugs, which must be purchased out of pocket. The very poor may receive care at publicly funded district hospitals, which are staffed by physicians who may also practice privately during the evenings to supplement their incomes. The remaining third of the population are encouraged to find private insurance carriers or pay out of pocket for their health care. Hospitals are largely unregulated as to quality and standards; however, physicians are generally well trained, having gone to school in the United States or the United Kingdom.

Q 2:12   What is driving health care reform in the former Warsaw Pact countries?

Health care reform in former Warsaw Pact countries such as Hungary and the Czech Republic is being driven primarily by anticipated accession into the European Union (EU). Hungary and the Czech Republic formally entered the North Atlantic Treaty Organization (NATO) in 1999. With their entry into NATO and their status as members of the OECD, these countries are attempting to harmonize a large body of laws and systems to comply with EU standards. Included in these standards are a host of health care reforms. The general reforms are in the areas of professional education and training, health care systems, individual rights, and financial systems.

Q 2:13   What is the Organization for Economic Cooperation and Development?

The OECD is a 29-member community that studies markets and provides for common processes and data gathering. It is a voluntary organization with broad-range interests devoted to promoting market economies. The OECD proposes regulatory, environmental, and societal guidelines. According to Article I of the OECD Convention signed in Paris in 1960, the OECD promotes policies designed

1. To achieve the highest sustainable economic growth and employment and a rising standard of living in member countries, while maintaining financial stability, and thus to contribute to the development of the world economy;
2. To contribute to sound economic expansion in member countries, as well as in nonmember countries in the process of economic development; and
3. To contribute to the expansion of world trade on a multilateral, nondiscriminatory basis in accordance with international obligations.

Q 2:14   What is the status of health care in candidate countries for the European Union?

The report of the EU Commission Staff Working Paper on Health and Enlargement states that

[D]espite recent improvements, the health status in most Candidate Countries is lower than in the EU despite recent improvements, and some threats to health are increasing. For the statistically most reliable health indicators (life expectancy and infant mortality) most Candidate Countries are lagging behind the EU. Infant mortality is higher than in the EU but differences are narrowing. The higher incidence of some chronic diseases appears to be related to the increased prevalence of risk factors such as smoking, unbalanced diets, life style and environmental pollution. Furthermore the abuse of both legal and illegal drugs is a growing phenomenon. The resources for health and health care are scarce with the share of GDP devoted to the health sector in the Candidate Countries at 4.5% in comparison to 8.5% of GDP in the EU. Furthermore the decrease in the GDP and the emphasis placed on other priorities in the transition phase is likely to squeeze spending on health and health care. Health care reforms are progressing in the Candidate Countries. The process is supported by an important number of co-operation programmes from the European Commission, international organizations, Member States and third countries. Some of the Community's public health programmes are already open to the Candidate Countries who are progressively taking part in them. Mutual awareness of policies, priorities and concerns are indispensable in defining and implementing accession strategies in the field of health. The knowledge and experience gained on the ways and means to tackle health issues by the Candidate Countries in the last few years should also be shared with the Community.[11]

The following health-related issues have been identified as deserving particular attention in relation to accession preparations:[12]

- Lack of clear, modern public health policies equal to the challenges facing the health system and the relatively low priority given to this sector

- Increasing incidence of communicable diseases and decline in vaccination coverage

- Increase in drug use

- Need for better emergency care facilities

- Low social and economic status of health professionals and consequent potential pressures on migration, resulting in a crippling exodus or unwarranted influx

- Relative lack of appropriate and sufficient involvement of the civil society in health issues and paucity of relevant institutions and associations

- Continued negative impact on health of poor environmental conditions

Q 2:15 What is being done to further accession of candidate countries into the European Union?

To ensure that health care conditions conducive to a smooth transition to an enlarged EU community are in place, the following options are being considered:[13]

1. Encourage all the candidate countries to participate in each community public health program.

2. Assess and encourage the improvement of the expertise and facilities related to surveillance of communicable diseases, and encourage early participation in the community network on disease surveillance and control.

3. Organize regular meetings on specific health-related accession topics between member states and individual candidate countries to identify priorities for cooperation, and exchange information on establishing priorities related to resource allocation and investment allocations.

4. Promote participation of experts from the candidate countries in the commission expert groups, whenever possible.

5. Facilitate cross-border cooperation.

6. Develop health research, including on accession-related health issues, and exchange of experience on the use of information systems and technologies related to health care.

7. Further promote participation of experts from the candidate countries in the community health and health care research activities, notably in the "quality of life and management of living resources" and "creating a user-friendly information society" programs.

8. Foster exchanges and links between nongovernment organizations in the member states and the candidate countries active in the field of health.

From this summary, it is clear that the challenges faced in the harmonization process by the candidate nations are indeed formidable. For the same commitment to outcome to be maintained across the entire EU—along with access to care—some form of standardization of care is inevitable.

An emerging problem is that of the Roma, colloquially called gypsies. The Open Society Institute commissioned a study in 2001 on Roma and public services in Romania, Bulgaria, Macedonia, and the Czech Republic. The report, *On the Margins* by Ina Zoon, is a call to action to improve Roma access to social protection, health care, and housing. It underscores the effects of bad policies and direct and indirect discrimination on the further marginalization of the Roma. Such policies are creating a permanent underclass of Roma—a human and societal problem that will overburden these transitional economies if left unaddressed.

Q 2:16　Are there any principles universal to health care reform in developing economies?

Yes. Investigation in several countries by the authors demonstrates that the reports and forms published and unpublished provide only a partial insight into a society's health care reform efforts. Factors that need to be taken into account include the following:

- Prevalence and severity of illnesses
- Dominant illness activity (e.g., HIV and AIDS in sub-Saharan Africa)
- Economic foundation of the health care system
- Effect and influence of the academic community
- Structure of the physician organization
- Presence of an "underground" health care economy
- Availability of technology
- Societal priorities and traditions
- Training and accessibility of medical and paramedical personnel
- Status of health care professionals in the society
- Salary and compensation structure of health care professionals
- Utilization and quality monitoring of health care

- Membership or affiliation in a standards-setting body
- Health care infrastructure
- Public health commitment to prevention, immunization, nutrition, and infectious disease control
- Stability of the government and its health ministry

Q 2:17   What major health care reforms should countries seeking to enhance their health care financing and delivery systems undertake?

For countries with central financing systems and public delivery systems, the World Bank and WHO agree that critical strategies for reforming the health sector's performance and attracting outside investment include (1) decentralizing management responsibilities; (2) developing public-private partnerships to enable private insurance and private providers to serve those able to afford market prices; and (3) creating safety-net programs for the uninsured or needy. For all countries, including the United States, reform strategies call for shifting resources from costly curative care to public health-focused primary care, including prevention and health education.[14]

Q 2:18   What factors influence reform in the global health care industry?

Factors that influence reform in health care financing, delivery, and public policy include history and culture, current domestic and international political and economic trends, and the opinions, demands, expectations, and influences of major stakeholders. According to Sir Duncan Nichol, the principles underpinning health care systems development include effectiveness, efficiency, equity, access, appropriateness, and partnership.[15] Other factors needed to support reform in the health care system include the following:

- A growing economy
- A strong, stable, and competent central government capable of proposing attainable reforms and managing the reform agenda
- An informed and supportive public
- Consensus among a majority of the stakeholders

Q 2:19 Other than government reform, what factors are affecting managed care penetration in markets outside the United States?

Private businesses are seeking to expand their markets from the United States into other countries, mainly in response to anticipated market saturation in the United States. The president of the Association of Latin American Pre-paid Health Plans noted the relation between market saturation and exportation: "By the year 2000, it is estimated [that] 80% of the total U.S. population will be insured by some sort of MCO [managed care organization]. Since 70% of all American MCOs are for-profit enterprises, new markets are needed to sustain growth and return on investment."[16] At this writing, data are not available as to whether that percentage of coverage was achieved. The collapse of the Argentine economy in 2002 may stall corporate medical penetration into contiguous areas of South America.

Privatization efforts in many countries such as Hungary, the Czech Republic, and Argentina are viewed as an opportunity to use government health and social security systems as a platform to develop insurance products for purchasers who can afford private health insurance. Economic globalization and removal of trade barriers through the General Agreement on Tariffs and Trade (GATT), the North American Free Trade Agreement (NAFTA), and the Common Market of the South have enhanced investment in managed care by outside companies and venture capital firms.

Q 2:20 What is the potential effect of privatization on health care and public health programs in countries outside the United States?

Like the United States, countries experimenting with privatization are concerned about reduced access to health care services for vulnerable populations, and reduced spending for clinical services as a result of increased spending for administration and pressures to return a profit on investment. The introduction of copayments has created barriers to accessing care, and the result is increased use of public clinics and hospitals. In fact, public hospitals in Argentina are experiencing an increase in patients covered by privatized social security funds. The private administration of public funds may introduce the worst of the U.S. free-economy system to fragile foreign economies that are already underfunded.

Q 2:21   Are any aspects of the U.S. health care system attractive to other countries?

In doing the research for *The Compass Report on Health Care,* a resource tool for global investment, Dr. Elias Mossialos of the London School of Economics and Political Science reported that most countries were not interested in replicating the U.S. system of health care and its approach to managed care. Instead, there was interest in U.S. expertise, technology, management tools, systems, and capital.[17]

International Support for Health Care Reform

Q 2:22   What role does the U.S. Agency for International Development play in global health care reform?

The U.S. Agency for International Development is one of the largest sources of international assistance to countries seeking to reform their national health care systems and improve health status. The proposed USAID budget for 2002 is over $7 billion, of which close to $1.46 billion is earmarked for global health policy reform, health care financing, and health care delivery.[18] Under a matching program, most countries use USAID funds to obtain technical assistance from the private sector to assist them in areas such as child survival, AIDS and HIV prevention, prevention of other infectious diseases, maternal health, and health promotion.

Q 2:23   What other organizations contribute to improving global health care?

There is a trend toward international cooperation in addressing health care issues, partially enabled by telecommunications and the Internet. For example, WHO and the World Bank collaborate in co-sponsoring global conferences on health policy reform and dissemination of reform strategies. Additional efforts have been undertaken by the following organizations:

1. WHO provides targets for national health reforms with its *Health for All* goals and monitors the performance of member nations and changes in world patterns of epidemiology.

2. The World Bank provides funding to improve population health status in developing countries.

3. The American Red Cross hosts international collaborative meetings among multilateral agencies such as UNICEF, WHO, and USAID.

4. Multilateral lenders such as the Asian Development Bank, the EU's PHARE, and the InterAmerican Development Bank are increasing their support for health care reform in developing nations.

5. The U.K. Department for International Development is funding health care reforms in developing countries in coordination with USAID.

6. Medecins sans Frontieres (Doctors Without Borders) and other nonprofit, nongovernment organizations such as the International Red Cross are actively involved in assisting other countries in addressing their health care issues.

7. The EU has developed regulations and cooperative agreements for health care in member countries.

8. Some U.S. managed care organizations, such as Aetna, United Health Care, and Kaiser Permanente, have been marketing their technical expertise on an international basis.

Special Issues for U.S. and Canadian Health Care

Q 2:24 What has been the experience of the Canadian health care system?

Beginning in 1957, the Canadian health care system was nationalized, with the federal government providing direct cash transfers to provinces that agreed to operate a universal hospitalization scheme with first-dollar coverage. Medical insurance was added in 1968. By 1971, Canada's health care system operated in the ten provinces and two northern territories using 12 nonprofit Medicare plans. Each plan offered universal first-dollar coverage of necessary medical and hospital services, including, long-term care for all provincial residents. There was public, nonprofit administration; portability of benefits among the provinces; no restriction on choice of physician; and pharmaceutical coverage for senior citizens. In essence, the Canadian system relied solely on public funding and private delivery of health care.

In response to inflationary pressures and caps on fee increases, coupled with the rapid growth in physician supply for urban areas, medical incomes declined. Physicians therefore began charging patients fees outside the negotiated fee schedule. In 1984, the Canadian government responded with the Canadian Health Act, which consolidated its various health insurance programs and reduced federal transfers of funds to provinces that allowed hospitals and doctors to charge patients fees beyond the negotiated rates. In the early 1990s, as a result of escalating cost and reduced financial resources, Canada's federal government reduced its financial commitment to the provincially administered health insurance plans. The plans reduced their spending on hospitals; this resulted in system cuts for inpatient care, expanded community services, and the consolidation of hospitals under regional authorities in nine of the ten provinces. Provincial governments are seeking to respond to the public's concern over these economic constrictions by integrating services across the continuum of care. The Canadian Health Act applies only to physician and hospital services, leaving open opportunities for developing approaches to integrating other services.

Q 2:25   What are some of the more controversial issues developing between the United States and Canada with respect to cross-border health care delivery?

One of the dramatic effects of the difference between the U.S. and Canadian health care systems is the migration of patients across the border for health care services, supplies, and drugs. Because of long waiting periods in Canada for certain health care services, it is not unusual for Canadians to seek health care services in the United States if they can pay for the services. In fact, some Canadians purchase private U.S. health insurance for such purposes. Many U.S. senior citizens are known to travel across the border into Canada for drugs that would cost far more if they were purchased in the United States. This practice has raised concerns on both sides, with U.S. policymakers questioning the appropriateness of U.S. prescriptions being filled by Canadian pharmacies, and Canadian insurers questioning the potential liability exposure of such practices.

According to the Canadian malpractice insurance provider, Canadian Medical Protective Association, Canadian physicians who treat patients from the United States, particularly patients who travel to Canada to take advantage of lower-cost prescription pharmaceuticals, are exposing themselves to U.S. lawsuits that may not be covered by their liability insurance policies.[19] The provincial medical associations suggest having Canadian doctors obtain from out-of-country patients a signed special consent form that requires legal disputes to be resolved in Canada. For claims that arise as a result of a Canadian physician's use of the Internet, however, the liability carrier says it cannot insure such claims.

E-Commerce and Global Communication of Health Information

Q 2:26   What steps have been taken to protect electronic communications of confidential information on a global basis?

The United States has only recently developed standards for electronic communication of confidential medical information, but the EU has developed comprehensive privacy legislation that encompasses the communication of health care data. The EU legislation, called the Directive on Data Protection, became effective on October 25, 1998. It requires that transfers of personal data take place only to non-EU countries that provide an "adequate" level of privacy protection. For purposes of applying the directive and applicable safe harbors, "personal data" and "personal information" are data about an identified or identifiable individual that are within the scope of the directive, received by a U.S. organization from the EU, and recorded in any form.

The Electronic Privacy Information Council (www.epic.org) said in its 2002 report: "Many countries are moving to enact laws to guarantee freedom from government and corporate surveillance and intrusion. However, technological developments, law enforcement demands, and business efforts to exploit personal information continue to pose new threats to privacy and anonymity in today's society."

Q 2:27 Are the privacy standards in the United States and the European Union different?

Yes. Although the United States and the EU share the goal of enhancing privacy protection for their citizens, they have different approaches to privacy. The United States uses a sectoral approach that relies on a mix of legislation, regulation, and self-regulation. Many U.S. organizations have expressed uncertainty about the impact of the EU-required "adequacy standard" on personal data transfers from the EU to the United States.

Q 2:28 How is the United States reconciling the difference in privacy standards for purposes of global commerce?

In an effort to "harmonize" the EU privacy directive with U.S. standards for international commerce, the U.S. Department of Commerce (DOC) issued a series of questions and answers (DOC principles) as guidance for U.S. companies that receive personal data from the EU to facilitate compliance with the EU privacy directive.[20] These DOC Principles were developed in consultation with industry and the general public to facilitate trade and commerce between the United States and the EU. They are intended for use solely by U.S. organizations receiving personal data from the EU for the purpose of qualifying for the safe harbor of the UE privacy directive and the presumption of "adequacy" created by the safe harbor.

The EU Commission and member states will use the flexibility of Article 26 and any discretion regarding enforcement to avoid disrupting data flows to U.S. organizations during the implementation phase of the safe harbor. This will give U.S. organizations an opportunity to decide whether to enter the safe harbor and (if necessary) to update their information practices. The DOC encourages U.S. organizations to enter the safe harbor as soon as possible to enhance privacy protection and because participation in the safe harbor provides greater certainty that data flows will continue without interruption.

Protecting the privacy of confidential information, including health care information, involves the following requirements, as set forth in the EU privacy directive:

1. *Notice.* An organization must inform individuals about the purposes for which it collects and uses information about them, how to contact the organization with any inquiries or complaints, the types of third parties to which it discloses the information, and the choices and means the organization offers individuals for limiting information use and disclosure. This notice must be provided in clear and conspicuous language when individuals are first asked to provide personal information to the organization or as soon thereafter as is practicable, but in any event, it must be provided before the organization uses the information for a purpose other than that for which it was originally collected or processed by the transferring organization or before it discloses the information for the first time to a third party.[21]

2. *Security.* Organizations creating, maintaining, using, or disseminating personal information must take reasonable precautions to protect it from loss, misuse, and unauthorized access, disclosure, alteration, and destruction.

3. *Data integrity.* Consistent with the DOC principles, personal information must be relevant for the purposes for which it is to be used. An organization cannot process personal information in a way that is incompatible with the purposes for which it has been collected or subsequently authorized by the individual. To the extent necessary for those purposes, an organization should take reasonable steps to ensure that data are reliable for their intended use, accurate, complete, and current.

4. *Access.* Individuals must have access to personal information about them that an organization holds and must be able to correct, amend, or delete that information if it is inaccurate, except when the burden or expense of providing access would be disproportionate to the risks to the individual's privacy in the case in question, or when the rights of persons other than the individual would be violated.

5. *Enforcement.* Effective privacy protection must include mechanisms for ensuring compliance with the safe harbor principles, recourse for individuals to whom the data relate affected by noncompliance with the safe harbor principles, and consequences for the organization when the safe harbor principles are not followed. At a minimum, such mechanisms must include (a) readily available and affordable independent re-

course mechanisms by which each individual's complaints and disputes are investigated and resolved by reference to the safe harbor principles and damages awarded when the applicable law or private sector initiatives so provide; (b) follow-up procedures for verifying that the attestations and assertions businesses make about their privacy practices are true and that privacy practices have been implemented as presented; and (c) obligations to remedy problems arising out of failure to comply with the safe harbor principles by organizations announcing their adherence to them and consequences for such organizations. Sanctions must be sufficiently rigorous to ensure compliance by organizations.

Q 2:29 Must an organization always provide explicit choice with respect to sensitive data?

No. One of the DOC principles provides that the individual whose personal information is the subject of potential dissemination must have a choice as to the manner in which and as to whom the information is to be transmitted as well as a choice as to its intended use. Such choice is not required in cases in which the processing is (1) in the vital interests of the data subject or another person; (2) necessary for the establishment of legal claims or defenses; (3) required to provide medical care or diagnosis; (4) carried out in the course of legitimate activities by a foundation, association, or any other non-profit-seeking body with a political, philosophical, religious, or trade union aim and on condition that the processing relates solely to the members of the body or to the persons who have regular contact with it in connection with its purposes and that the data are not disclosed to a third party without the consent of the data subjects; (5) necessary to carry out the organization's obligations in the field of employment law; or (6) related to data that are manifestly made public by the individual.

Q 2:30 Are Internet service providers, telecommunications carriers, and other organizations liable under the safe harbor principles of the European privacy directive when on behalf of another organization they merely transmit, route, switch, or cache information that may violate their terms?

No. Like the EU Directive on Data Protection itself, the safe harbor does not create secondary liability. To the extent that an organization is acting as a mere conduit for data transmitted by third parties and does not determine the purposes and means of processing those personal data, it is not liable.

Q 2:31 How do companies that commit to cooperate with European data protection authorities make those commitments, and how are they implemented?

Under the safe harbor of the European privacy directive, U.S. organizations receiving personal data from the EU must commit to employ effective mechanisms for ensuring compliance with the safe harbor principles. As set out in the enforcement principle, these mechanisms must include (a) recourse for individuals to whom the data relate, (b) follow-up procedures for verifying that the attestations and assertions they have made about their privacy practices are true, and (c) obligations to remedy problems arising out of failure to comply with the safe harbor principles and consequences for that failure. An organization can satisfy points (a) and (c) of the enforcement principle if it adheres to the requirements established by the DOC for cooperating with the data protection agencies (DPA). An organization can commit to cooperate with the DPAs by declaring in its safe harbor certification to the DOC that the organization

1. Elects to satisfy the requirement in points (a) and (c) of the safe harbor enforcement principle by committing to cooperate with the DPAs;
2. Will cooperate with the DPAs in the investigation and resolution of complaints brought under the safe harbor; and
3. Will comply with any advice given by the DPAs when the DPAs take the view that the organization needs to take specific action to comply with the safe harbor principles, including remedial or compensatory measures for the benefit of individuals affected by any noncompliance with the principles, and will provide the DPAs with written confirmation that such action has been taken.

The cooperation of the DPAs will be provided in the form of information and advice given in the following way:

1. The advice of the DPAs will be delivered through an informal panel of DPAs established at the European level. This will, *inter alia*, help ensure a harmonized and coherent approach.

2. The panel will provide advice to the U.S. organizations concerned on unresolved complaints from individuals about the handling of personal information that has been transferred from the EU under the safe harbor arrangements. This advice will be designed to ensure that the safe harbor principles are being correctly applied and will include any remedies for the individual or individuals concerned that the DPAs consider appropriate.

3. The panel will provide such advice in response to referrals from the organizations concerned and to complaints received directly from individuals against organizations that have committed to cooperate with the DPAs for safe harbor purposes, while encouraging, and, if necessary, helping such individuals in the first instance to use the in-house complaint-handling arrangements that the organization may offer.

4. Advice will be issued only after both sides in a dispute have had a reasonable opportunity to comment and provide any evidence they wish. The panel will seek to deliver advice as quickly as this requirement for due process allows. As a general rule, the panel will aim to provide advice within 60 days after receiving a complaint or referral and more quickly if possible.

5. The panel will make public the results of its consideration of complaints submitted to it, if it sees fit.

6. The delivery of advice through the panel will not give rise to any liability for the panel or for individual DPAs.

As noted in the previous list, organizations choosing this option for dispute resolution must undertake to comply with the advice of the DPAs. If an organization fails to comply within 25 days of the delivery of the advice and has offered no satisfactory explanation for the delay, the panel of DPAs will give notice of its intention either to submit the matter to the Federal Trade Commission (FTC) or another U.S. federal or state body with statutory powers to take enforcement action in cases of deception or misrepresentation, or to conclude that the agreement to cooperate has been seriously breached and must therefore be considered null and void. In the latter case, the panel will inform the DOC (or its designee) so that the list of safe harbor participants can be duly amended. Any failure to fulfill the undertaking to cooperate with the DPAs, as well as failures to comply with the safe harbor principles, will be actionable as a deceptive practice under Section 5 of the FTC Act or other similar statute.

Organizations choosing this option for dispute resolution will be required to pay an annual fee, which will be designed to cover the operating costs of the panel, and they may additionally be asked to meet any necessary translation expenses arising out of the panel's consideration of referrals or complaints against them. The annual fee will not exceed $500 and will be less for smaller companies. The option of cooperating with the DPAs will be available to organizations joining the safe harbor during a three-year period.

Q 2:32 How does an organization self-certify that it adheres to the safe harbor principles?

Safe harbor benefits are ensured from the date on which an organization self-certifies to the DOC or its nominee its adherence to the safe harbor principles in accordance with the guidance set forth here. To self-certify for the safe harbor, organizations can provide the DOC (or its designee) with a letter, signed by a corporate officer on behalf of the organization that is joining the safe harbor, that contains at least the following information:

- Name of the organization, mailing address, e-mail address, telephone number, and fax number
- Description of the activities of the organization with respect to personal information received from the EU
- Description of the organization's privacy policy for such personal information, including the following:
  — Where the privacy policy is available for viewing by the public
  — Its effective date of implementation
  — Contact office for the handling of complaints, access requests, and any other issues arising under the safe harbor
  — Specific statutory body that has jurisdiction to hear any claims against the organization regarding possible unfair or deceptive practices and violations of laws or regulations governing privacy (and that is listed in the annex to the DOC principles)

— Name of any privacy programs in which the organization is a member

— Method of verification (e.g., in-house, third party)

— Independent recourse mechanism that is available to investigate unresolved complaints

Q 2:33   How do organizations provide follow-up procedures for verifying that the attestations and assertions they make about their safe harbor privacy practices are true and that those privacy practices have been implemented as represented and in accordance with the safe harbor principles?

To meet the verification requirements of the enforcement principle, an organization can verify such attestations and assertions either through self-assessment or outside compliance reviews. Under the self-assessment approach, the verification would have to indicate that an organization's published privacy policy regarding personal information received from the EU is accurate, comprehensive, prominently displayed, completely implemented, and accessible. The organization would also need to indicate that its privacy policy conforms to the safe harbor principles; that individuals are informed of any in-house arrangements for handling complaints and of the independent mechanisms through which they can pursue complaints; that it has in place procedures for training employees in implementation and for disciplining them for failure to follow the policy; and that it has in place internal procedures for periodically conducting objective reviews of compliance with the foregoing. A statement verifying the self-assessment should be signed by a corporate officer or other authorized representative of the organization at least once a year and made available on request by individuals or in the context of an investigation or a complaint about noncompliance. Organizations should retain their records on the implementation of their safe harbor privacy practices and make them available on request in the context of an investigation or a complaint about noncompliance to the independent body responsible for investigating complaints or to the agency with unfair and deceptive practices jurisdiction.

An outside compliance review needs to demonstrate that the organization's privacy policy regarding personal information received from the EU conforms to the safe harbor principles, that it is being complied with, and that individuals are informed of the mechanisms through which they can pursue complaints. The methods of review can include, without limitation, auditing, random reviews, use of "decoys," or use of technology tools as appropriate. A statement verifying that an outside compliance review has been successfully completed should be signed either by the reviewer or by the corporate officer or other authorized representative of the organization at least once a year and made available on request by individuals or in the context of an investigation or a complaint about compliance.

Q 2:34 Is the right of access absolute?

No. Under the safe harbor principles of the EU Directive on Data, the right of access is fundamental to privacy protection. In particular, it allows individuals to verify the accuracy of information held about them. Nonetheless, the obligation of an organization to provide access to the personal information it holds about an individual is subject to the principle of proportionality or reasonableness and has to be tempered in certain instances. Indeed, the Explanatory Memorandum to the 1980 OECD Privacy Guidelines makes clear that an organization's access obligation is not absolute. It does not require the exceedingly thorough search mandated, for example, by a subpoena, nor access to all the different forms in which the information may be maintained by the organization.

Experience has shown that in responding to individuals' access requests, organizations should first be guided by the concerns that led to the requests in the first place. For example, if an access request is vague or broad in scope, an organization may engage the individual in a dialogue so as to understand the motivation for the request and to locate responsive information. The organization might inquire about which parts of the organization the individual interacted with and about the nature of the information (or its use) that is the subject of the access request. Individuals do not, however, have to justify requests for access to their own data.

Expense and burden are important factors and should be taken into account, but they are not controlling in determining whether providing access is reasonable. For example, if the information is used for decisions that will significantly affect the individual (e.g., the denial or grant of important benefits, such as insurance, a mortgage, or a job), the organization would have to disclose that information even if it is relatively difficult or expensive to provide. If the information requested is not sensitive or not used for decisions that will significantly affect the individual (e.g., nonsensitive marketing data that will be used to determine whether to send the individual a catalog), but is readily available and inexpensive to provide, an organization would have to provide access to factual information that the organization stores about the individual. The information concerned could include facts obtained from the individual, facts gathered in the course of a transaction, or facts obtained from others that pertain to the individual.

Consistent with the fundamental nature of access, organizations should always make good-faith efforts to provide access. For example, when certain information needs to be protected and can readily be separated from other information subject to an access request, the organization should redact the protected information and make the other information available. If an organization determines that access should be denied in any particular instance, it should provide the individual requesting access with an explanation of why it has made that determination and a contact point for any further inquiries.

Q 2:35 **What is confidential commercial information, and can organizations deny access to safeguard it?**

Confidential commercial information (as that term is used in the Federal Rules of Civil Procedure on discovery) is information that an organization has taken steps to protect from disclosure, when disclosure would help a competitor in the market. The particular computer program an organization uses, such as a modeling program or the details of that program may be confidential commercial information. When confidential commercial information can readily be separated from other information subject to an access request, the organization should redact the confidential commercial information and make the nonconfidential information available. Organizations can deny or limit access to the extent that granting it would reveal its own confidential commercial information as defined here, such as marketing inferences or classifications generated by the organization, or the confidential commercial information of another when such information is subject to a contractual obligation of confidentiality in circumstances in which such an obligation of confidentiality would normally be undertaken or imposed.

Q 2:36   In providing access, can an organization disclose to individuals personal information about them derived from its databases, or is access to the database itself required?

Access can be provided in the form of disclosure by an organization to the individual and does not require access by the individual to an organization's database.

Q 2:37   Does an organization have to restructure its databases to be able to provide access?

Access needs to be provided only to the extent that an organization stores the information. The access principle does not itself create any obligation to retain, maintain, reorganize, or restructure personal information files.

Q 2:38   In what other circumstances can an organization deny individuals access to their personal information?

Such circumstances are limited, and any reasons for denying access must be specific. An organization can refuse to provide access to information to the extent that disclosure is likely to interfere with the safeguarding of important countervailing public interests, such as national security, defense, or public security. In addition, when personal information is processed solely for research or statistical purposes, access can be denied. Other reasons for denying or limiting access are as follows:

- Interference with execution or enforcement of the law, including the prevention, investigation, or detection of offenses or the right to a fair trial
- Interference with private causes of action, including the prevention, investigation, or detection of legal claims or the right to a fair trial
- Disclosure of personal information pertaining to other individuals in cases in which such references cannot be redacted
- Breaching a legal or other professional privilege or obligation

- Breaching the necessary confidentiality of future or ongoing negotiations, such as those involving the acquisition of publicly quoted companies
- Prejudicing employee security investigations or grievance proceedings
- Prejudicing the confidentiality that may be necessary for limited periods in connection with employee succession planning and corporate reorganizations
- Prejudicing the confidentiality that may be necessary in connection with monitoring, inspection, or regulatory functions connected with sound economic or financial management
- Any circumstances in which the burden or cost of providing access would be disproportionate or the legitimate rights or interests of others would be violated

An organization that claims an exception has the burden of demonstrating its applicability (as is normally the case). The reasons for denying or limiting access and a contact point for further inquiries should be given to individuals.

Q 2:39 Can an organization charge a fee to cover the cost of providing access?

Yes. The 1980 OECD Privacy Guidelines recognize that organizations can charge a fee, provided that it is not excessive. Thus, organizations can charge a reasonable fee for access. Charging a fee may be useful in discouraging repetitive and vexatious requests. Organizations that are in the business of selling publicly available information can charge the organization's customary fee in responding to requests for access. Individuals may alternatively seek access to their information from the organization that originally compiled the data. Access cannot be refused on cost grounds if the individual offers to pay the costs.

Q 2:40 Is an organization required to provide access to personal information derived from public records?

Public records are records kept by government agencies or entities at any level that are open to consultation by the public in general. It is not necessary to apply the access principle to such information as long as it is not combined with other personal information, apart from when small amounts of non-public record information are used for indexing or organizing public record information. Any conditions for consultation established by the relevant jurisdiction, however, are to be respected. When public record information is combined with non-public record information (other than as specifically noted here), an organization must provide access to all such information if it is not subject to other permitted exceptions.

Q 2:41 Does the access principle have to be applied to publicly available personal information?

As with public record information, it is not necessary to provide access to information that is already publicly available to the public at large, as long as it is not combined with information that is not publicly available.

Q 2:42 How can an organization protect itself against repetitious, vexatious, or fraudulent requests for access?

An organization does not have to respond to such requests for access. Organizations can charge a reasonable fee and can set reasonable limits on the number of times within a given period that access requests from a particular individual will be met. In setting such limitations, an organization should consider such factors as the frequency with which information is updated, the purpose for which the data are used, and the nature of the information.

Regarding fraudulent requests, an organization is not required to provide access unless it is supplied with sufficient information to allow it to confirm the identity of the person making the request.

Q 2:43 Is there a time frame within which responses must be provided to access requests?

Yes. Organizations should respond without excessive delay and within a reasonable time period. This requirement can be satisfied in different ways, as the explanatory memorandum to the 1980 OECD Privacy Guidelines states. For example, a data controller who provides information to data subjects at regular intervals may be exempted from obligations to respond at once to individual requests.

Q 2:44 Is the transfer from the European Union to the United States of personal information collected in the context of the employment relationship covered by the safe harbor?

Yes. When a company in the EU transfers personal information about its employees (past or present) that it collected in the context of the employment relationship, to a parent, affiliate, or unaffiliated service provider in the United States participating in the safe harbor, the transfer enjoys the benefits of the safe harbor. In such cases, the collection of the information and its processing prior to transfer will have been subject to the national laws of the EU country where it was collected, and any conditions for or restrictions on its transfer according to those laws will have to be respected. The safe harbor principles are relevant only when individually identified records are transferred or accessed. Statistical reporting relying on aggregate employment data and the use of anonymous or pseudonymous data does not raise privacy concerns.

Q 2:45 How do the notice and choice principles apply to such information?

A U.S. organization that has received employee information from the EU under the safe harbor can disclose it to third parties or use it for different purposes only in accordance with the notice and choice principles. For example, when an organization intends to use personal information collected through the employment relationship for non-employment-related purposes, such as marketing communications, the U.S. organization must provide the affected individuals with choice before doing so, unless they have already authorized the use of the information for such purposes. Moreover, such choices must not be used to restrict employment opportunities or to take any punitive action against such employees. Certain generally applicable conditions for transfer from some EU member states may preclude other uses of such information even after transfer outside the EU, and such conditions will have to be respected. In addition, employers should make reasonable efforts to accommodate employee privacy preferences. This could include, for example, restricting access to the data, anonymizing certain data, or assigning codes or pseudonyms when the actual names are not required for the management purpose at hand. To the extent and for the period necessary to avoid prejudicing the legitimate interests of the organization in making promotions, appointments, or other similar employment decisions, an organization does not need to offer notice and choice.

Q 2:46   How does the access principle apply?

The DOC principles on access provide guidance on reasons that may justify denying or limiting access on requests in the human resources context. Of course, employers in Europe must comply with local regulations and ensure that European employees have access to such information as is required by law in their home countries, regardless of the location of data processing and storage. The safe harbor requires that an organization processing such data in the United States will cooperate in providing such access either directly or through the European employer.

Q 2:47   How will enforcement be handled for employee data under the safe harbor principles?

Insofar as information is used only in the context of the employment relationship, primary responsibility for the data vis-à-vis the employee remains with the company in the EU. It follows that when European employees make complaints about violations of their data protection rights and are not satisfied with the results of internal review, complaint, and appeal procedures (or any applicable grievance procedures under a contract with a trade union), they should be directed to the state or national data protection or labor authority in the jurisdiction where they work. This approach also includes cases in which the alleged mishandling of their personal information has taken place in the United States and is the responsibility of the U.S. organization that has received the information from the employer, and not responsibility of the employer, and thus involves an alleged breach of the safe harbor principles, rather than of national laws implementing the EU Directive on Data. This will be the most efficient way to address the often overlapping rights and obligations imposed by local labor law and labor agreements as well as data protection law.

A U.S. organization participating in the safe harbor that uses European human resources data transferred from Europe in the context of the employment relationship and that wants such transfers to be covered by the safe harbor arrangement must therefore commit to cooperate in investigations by and to comply with the advice of competent European authorities in such cases. The DPAs that have agreed to cooperate in this way will notify the European Commission and the U.S. DOC. If a U.S. organization participating in the safe harbor wants to transfer human resources data from a member state when the DPA has not so agreed, it must satisfy the DOC principles.

Q 2:48   When data are transferred from the European Union to the United States only for processing purposes, will a contract be required, regardless of participation by the processor in the safe harbor?

Yes. Data controllers in Europe are always required to enter into a contract when a transfer for mere processing is made, whether the processing operation is carried out inside or outside the EU. The purpose of the contract is to protect the interests of the data controller (i.e., the person or body who determines the purposes and means of processing), who retains full responsibility for the data vis-à-vis the individuals concerned. The contract thus specifies the processing to be carried out and any measures necessary to ensure that the data are kept secure.

A U.S. organization participating in the safe harbor and receiving personal information from the EU merely for processing thus does not have to apply the safe harbor principles to this information, because the controller in the EU remains responsible for it vis-à-vis the individual in accordance with the relevant EU provisions (which may be more stringent than the equivalent safe harbor principles). Because adequate protection is provided by safe harbor participants, contracts with safe harbor participants for mere processing do not require prior authorization (or such authorization will be granted automatically by the member states) as would be required for contracts with recipients not participating in the safe harbor or otherwise not providing adequate protection.

Q 2:49   How should the dispute resolution requirements of the enforcement principle be implemented, and how will an organization's persistent failure to comply with the principle be handled?

The enforcement principle sets out the requirements for safe harbor enforcement. The enforcement mechanisms can take different forms, but they must meet the enforcement principle's requirements.

Organizations can satisfy the requirements through the following: (1) compliance with private sector-developed privacy programs that incorporate the safe harbor principles into their rules and that include effective enforcement mechanisms of the type described in the enforcement principle; (2) compliance with legal or regulatory supervisory authorities that provide for handling of individual complaints and dispute resolution; or (3) commitment to cooperate with DPAs in the European Community or their authorized representatives, provided those DPAs agree. This list is intended to be illustrative and not limiting. The private sector can design other mechanisms to provide enforcement, as long as they meet the requirements of the enforcement principle and the DOC principles. The enforcement principle's requirements are additional to the requirement set forth in paragraph 3 of the introduction to the principles that self-regulatory efforts must be enforceable under Section 5 of the FTC Act or similar statute.

Recourse Mechanisms. Consumers should be encouraged to raise any complaints they may have with the relevant organization before proceeding to independent recourse mechanisms. Whether a recourse mechanism is independent is a factual question that can be demonstrated in a number of ways, for example, by transparent composition and financing or a proven track record. As required by the enforcement principle, the recourse available to individuals must be readily available and affordable. Dispute resolution bodies should look into each complaint received from individuals unless it is obviously unfounded or frivolous. This does not preclude the establishment of eligibility requirements by the organization operating the recourse mechanism, but such requirements should be transparent and justified (e.g., to exclude complaints that fall outside the scope of the program or are for consideration in another forum), and should not have the effect of undermining the commitment to look into legitimate complaints. In addition, recourse mechanisms should provide individuals with full and readily available information about how the dispute resolution procedure works when they file a complaint. Such information should include notice about the mechanism's privacy practices, in conformity with the safe harbor principles.[22] They should also cooperate in the development of tools such as standard complaint forms to facilitate the complaint resolution process.

Remedies and Sanctions. The result of any remedies provided by the dispute resolution body should be that the effects of noncompliance are reversed or corrected by the organization, insofar as feasible, and that future processing by the organization will be in conformity with the principles and, where appropriate, that processing of the personal data of the individual who has brought the complaint will cease. Sanctions need to be rigorous enough to ensure compliance by the organization with the principles. A range of sanctions of varying degrees of severity will allow dispute resolution bodies to respond appropriately to varying degrees of noncompliance. Sanctions should include both publicity for findings of noncompliance and the requirement to delete data in certain circumstances.[23] Other sanctions could include suspension and removal of a seal, compensation for individuals for losses incurred as a result of noncompliance, and injunctive orders. Private sector dispute resolution bodies and self-regulatory bodies must notify safe harbor organizations failing to comply with their rulings to courts or the government body with applicable jurisdiction or to the courts as appropriate, and to notify the DOC (or its designee).

FTC Action. The FTC has committed to reviewing on a priority basis referrals received from privacy self-regulatory organizations, such as BBBOnline and TRUSTe, and from EU member countries alleging noncompliance with the safe harbor principles to determine whether Section 5 of the FTC Act (prohibiting unfair or deceptive acts or practices in commerce) has been violated. If the FTC concludes that it has reason to believe that Section 5 of the FTC Act has been violated, it can resolve the matter by seeking an administrative cease and desist order prohibiting the challenged practices or by filing a complaint in a federal district court, which if successful could result in a federal court order to the same effect. The FTC can obtain civil penalties for violations of an administrative cease and desist order and can pursue civil or criminal contempt for violation of a federal court order. The FTC will notify the DOC of any such actions it takes. The DOC encourages other government bodies to notify it of the final disposition of any such referrals or other rulings determining adherence to the safe harbor principles.

Persistent Failure to Comply. If an organization persistently fails to comply with the principles, it is no longer entitled to benefit from the safe harbor. Persistent failure to comply arises when an organization that has self-certified to the DOC (or its designee) refuses to comply with a final determination by any self-regulatory or government body or when such a body determines that an organization frequently fails to comply with the principles to the point at which

its claim to comply is no longer credible. In these cases, the organization must promptly notify the DOC (or its designee) of such facts.
Failure to do so may be actionable under the False Statements Act.
[18 USC § 1001] The DOC (or its designee) will indicate on the public
list it maintains of organizations self-certifying adherence to the safe
harbor principles any notification it receives of persistent failure to
comply, whether it is received from the organization itself, from a
self-regulatory body, or from a government body, but only after first
providing 30 days' notice and an opportunity to respond to the organization that has failed to comply. Accordingly, the public list maintained by the DOC (or its designee) will make clear which organizations are assured and which organizations are no longer assured of
safe harbor benefits. An organization applying to participate in a self-
regulatory body for the purposes of requalifying for the safe harbor
must provide that body with full information about its prior participation in the safe harbor.

Q 2:50   **If personal data are collected in the European Union and
transferred to the United States for pharmaceutical
research or other purposes, do the laws of member states
or the safe harbor principles apply?**

Laws of the member states apply to the collection of the personal
data and to any processing that takes place prior to the transfer to
the United States. The safe harbor principles apply to the data once
they have been transferred to the United States. Data used for pharmaceutical research and other purposes should be made anonymous
when appropriate.

Q 2:51   **If personal data are collected for one research study and
transferred to a U.S. organization in the safe harbor, can
the organization use the data for a new scientific
research activity?**

Yes, as long as appropriate notice and choice have been provided
in the first instance. Such a notice should provide information about
any future specific uses of the data, such as periodic follow-up, related studies, or marketing. It is understood that not all future uses
of the data can be specified, because a new research use could arise
from new insights on the original data, new medical discoveries and
advances, and public health and regulatory developments. When ap-

propriate, the notice should therefore include an explanation that personal data may be used in future medical and pharmaceutical research activities that are unanticipated. If the use is not consistent with the general research purposes for which the data were originally collected, or to which the individual has consented subsequently, new consent must be obtained.

Q 2:52 What happens to an individual's data if a participant decides to withdraw from a clinical trial voluntarily or at the request of the sponsor?

Participants may decide to withdraw or may be asked to withdraw from a clinical trial at any time. Any data collected previous to withdrawal can still be processed along with other data collected as part of the clinical trial if this is made clear to the participant in the notice given at the time he or she agreed to participate.

Q 2:53 Are similar transfers allowed to parties other than regulators, such as locations within the same company and other researchers?

Yes, but the practice must be consistent with the principles of notice and choice. Pharmaceutical and medical device companies are allowed to provide personal data from clinical trials conducted in the EU to regulators in the United States for regulatory and supervision purposes.

Q 2:54 Will participants in such clinical trials (referred to as "blinded" studies) have access to the data on their treatment during the trial?

To ensure objectivity in many clinical trials, participants, and often investigators as well, cannot be given access to information about which treatment each participant may be receiving. Doing so would jeopardize the validity of the research study and results. Therefore, access does not have to be provided to a participant if this restriction has been explained when the participant entered the trial and the disclosure of such information would jeopardize the integrity of the research effort. Agreement to participate in the trial under these conditions is a reasonable forgoing of the right of access. Following the conclusion of the trial and analysis of the results, participants should have access to their data if they request it. They should seek it primarily from the physician or other health care provider from whom they received treatment within the clinical trial, or secondarily from the sponsoring company.

Q 2:55   Does a pharmaceutical or medical device firm have to apply the safe harbor principles with respect to notice, choice, onward transfer, and access in its product safety and efficacy monitoring activities, including the reporting of adverse events and the tracking of patients or subjects using certain medicines or medical devices (e.g., a pacemaker)?

No, such a firm does not have to apply the safe harbor principles for those situations to the extent that adherence to the principles interferes with compliance with regulatory requirements. This is true both with respect to reports by, for example, health care providers and to pharmaceutical and medical device companies, and with respect to reports by pharmaceutical and medical device companies to government agencies such as the Food and Drug Administration.

Q 2:56   Does a transfer from the European Union to the United States of coded data constitute a transfer of personal data that is subject to the safe harbor principles?

No. Invariably, research data are uniquely key-coded at their origin by the principal investigator so as not to reveal the identity of individual data subjects. Pharmaceutical companies sponsoring such research do not receive the key. The unique key-code is held only by the researcher so that he or she can identify the research subject under special circumstances (e.g., if follow-up medical attention is required). Transfer of coded data therefore does not constitute a transfer of personal data subject to the safe harbor principles.

References

1. G. Schieber and A. Maeda, "Health Care Financing and Delivery in Developing Countries," *Health Affairs*, 18(3):194, 1999.

2. World Health Organization, *World Health Reports 1999: Making a Difference* (Geneva: WHO 1999) 6.

3. *Investing in Health Research and Development: Report of the Ad Hoc Committee on Health Research Relating to Future Intervention Options* (Geneva: WHO 1996).

4. Id.

5. Id.

6. *The Global Burden of Disease: A Comprehensive Assessment of Mortality and Disability from Diseases, Injuries, and Risk Factors in 1990 and Projected to 2020*, C.J.L. Murray and A.D. Lopez, eds., Global Burden of Disease and Injury Series, vol. I (Cambridge: Harvard School of Public Health on behalf of WHO and the World Bank 1996).

7. D.T. Jamison, L.J. Lau, and J. Wang, "Health's Contribution to Economic Growth, 1965–90," *Health, Health Policy and Economic Outcomes* (Geneva: WHO Director-General's Transition Team 1998; Health and Development Satellite Final Report) 61–80.

8. WHO Regional Office for the Americas/Pan American Health Organization, *World Health Reports, supra* note 2, at 9.

9. L. Payer, *Medicine & Culture* (New York: Holt 1988).

10. Over 30 percent of the country's GNP is spent on the military.

11. Commission Staff Working Paper on Health and Enlargement (EU 1999); *see* http://europa.eu.int/comm/dg05/phealth/sec99>713/workpaper_en.pdf.

12. Id.

13. Id.

14. Id. at 5.

15. Id. at 7.

16. K. Stocker, H. Waitzkin, and C. Iriart, "The Exportation of Managed Care to Latin America," *New Eng. J. Med.*, 340(14): 1131–1136, 1999.

17. Id. at 10.

18. *See* http://www.usaid.gov/pubs/cbj2002/request.html.

19. *See* "Canadian Physicians Warned of Liability in Treating Patients from United States," BNA 11(23) Bureau of National Affairs, Inc., Washington, D.C., June 9, 2000.

20. This guidance is published by the U.S. Department of Commerce as Principles and FAQs at http://www.ita.doc.gov/td/ecom/menu.html.

21. It is not necessary to provide notice or choice when disclosure is made to a third party that is acting as an agent to perform tasks on behalf of and under the instructions of the organization. The onward transfer principle, on the other hand, does apply to such disclosures. Onward transfer principles apply to the further transmission of confidential information to a third party and require that there be some assurance that the third party will adhere to the same principles as the party receiving the information at its primary source of communication.

22. Dispute resolution bodies are not required to conform with the enforcement principle. They may also derogate from the principles when they encounter conflicting obligations or explicit authorizations in the performance of their specific tasks. This issue is discussed further in chapter 14.

23. Dispute resolution bodies have discretion about the circumstances in which they use these sanctions. The sensitivity of the data concerned is one factor to be taken into consideration in deciding whether deletion of data should be required, as is whether an organization has collected, used, or disclosed information in blatant contravention of the principles.

Chapter 3

Evolution and Revolution in Product Design

The origin of "health insurance" is murky. Twentieth century health insurance likely originated from the desire of labor leaders like Samuel Gompers to provide health and preventive medicine benefits for union members. Almost contemporaneously, European Jewish immigrants of the late nineteenth century established *landsmanshaftn,* organizations to provide the mutual support of a village in a new land. The modern concept of health insurance originated when the Blue Cross system developed as a health care finance mechanism between hospitals and school teachers in Dallas, Texas, in 1929. Blue Cross covered a preset amount of hospitalization costs. Blue Shield was developed following the same plan to cover ambulatory (nonhospital) medical care. The Blue Cross/Blue Shield plans were developed to complement the traditional fee-for-service method of paying for health care. Under this method, a physician would charge a patient directly for services rendered and the patient would pay the physician. The Blue Cross/Blue Shield plans were early "indemnity plans." Later, providers would submit claims information to the insurers as a convenience for their patients. For insured patients in the fee-for-service system, two contracts were created, one between the doctor and the patient and one between the patient and the insurance company.

Reforms at the state and federal levels have driven product diversification in health care. Passage of the

Health Insurance Portability and Accountability Act of 1996 (HIPAA) and the Balanced Budget Act of 1997 (BBA) has motivated insurers, employers, providers, and consumers to develop innovative managed care products, as employers seek to control health care costs (see chapter 4) and the federal and state governments seek to introduce managed care models into Medicare and Medicaid (see chapter 7).

The failure of the Health Security Act to achieve popularity dramatically shifted the federal approach from comprehensive reform to piecemeal adjustment. Health care reform shifted to the states, with particular emphasis on financing and regulatory mechanisms. Although the BBA prescribed health maintenance organizations (HMOs), as the remedy for Medicare expense, the health care industry spoke at the end of the twentieth century and into the twenty-first by withdrawing HMOs from the Medicare system.

Over the past ten years, most states have passed some form of health insurance reform for small businesses, but the skewed distribution of health care expenditures remains and contributes to adverse selection, a major barrier to expanding coverage and improving performance in small-group and individual insurance markets. This chapter focuses on the types of health care products that are available and the effect of recent public and private health care reforms on the design of health plans.

Historical Overview

Q 3:1 What were the important early events in the development of health insurance products and benefits?

In addition to the need to spread risk for health care, insurance developed as a result of several historical economic forces.

The scarcity of workers during World War II forced companies to offer benefits, including health insurance, to compete. Health insurance premiums paid by employers were tax deductible to the employer, thus rendering a dollar spent on health insurance more valuable.

The rise of labor unions solidified health insurance as a benefit when the Supreme Court upheld the notion that benefits were a legitimate part of labor-management bargaining. [Taft-Hartley Act, LMRA; 29 USC §§ 141–197]

The increase in the costs of health care led private insurers, rapidly followed by Blue Cross/Blue Shield in the 1950s, to offer "major medical" coverage with a deductible.

Increasing competition for increasing benefits led to a large gap between the insured and uninsured populations' abilities to pay for health care. In July 1966, Title XVIII of the Social Security Amendments of 1965 [42 USC §§ 1395–1395ccc] was made operational, creating Medicare. Title XIX of the same act created the federal-state partnership for the poor called Medicaid.

After the Blue Cross/Blue Shield plans were developed, traditional insurers noted their community rating practices and realized that they could enter the market and attract healthier community members with rates lower than the community rates. By introducing screening to identify healthier individuals, and offering lower rates to younger individuals, these companies were able to lure lower-risk populations to their health plans. This left the Blue Cross/Blue Shield plans with the highest-risk and costliest population to insure. Eventually the Blue Cross/Blue Shield plans also began using risk-segregation policies and charged higher-risk groups higher premiums.

Under both the fee-for-service system of health care delivery, in which private indemnity insurers charge premiums and pay the bills, and the Medicare-Medicaid system, in which taxes largely fund the programs and the government pays the bills, the relationship between the patient and the doctor remains distinct. Both physician and patient are insulated from the cost of various medical procedures, and fees for services are paid without significant oversight by the payers. When more services are performed by a physician under a fee-for-service system, the result is greater total fees.

From 1960 to 1990, per capita medical costs in the United States rose almost 1,000 percent, which was four times the rate of inflation. As a consequence, a different way of paying for health care came to prominence. "Managed care," which had been in existence as long as indemnity health insurance plans, became the health plan of choice among U.S. employers seeking to reduce the premiums paid for their employees' health care. The central idea of managed care was to create an efficient health system that would manage cost by managing care. Of necessity, managed care interposed a regulator or decision maker between the physician and the patient—quite distinct from fee-for-service medicine.

Managed care has affected Medicare as well as private health care. In 1983, Congress changed the payment system for Medicare Part A from a fee-for-service, retroactive payment system to a prospective payment system, which fixes the amount that the federal government will pay based on a patient's initial diagnosis, not on the costs actually expended. [Pub L 98-369] Medical diagnoses are grouped according to the medical resources usually consumed to treat them, and from that grouping a fixed amount that will be paid by Medicare for each diagnosis is determined. Although this system, called DRG (diagnosis-related group) payment, is applicable only to the acute-care hospital setting, it is clearly an example of shifting the risk of the cost of health care from the payer (in this case, Medicare) to the provider, which is an important element of *traditional* managed care.

In the early 1990s, with the election of President Clinton, the Health Security Act was proffered as a model of universal coverage with a standard benefit package. It accomplished this by requiring employers to provide health insurance for employees and their families. Most employees and all the self-insured or uninsured would choose health plans through mandatory regional health alliances, also known as health insurance purchasing cooperatives (HIPCs). These health alliances were to provide usable information about different plans to consumers and would monitor the quality of care provided. Costs would be controlled by competition, with federally enforced premium limits as a backstop. States were to have substantial discretion in implementing the plan. Although the Health Security Act was not enacted, Congress has since made incremental reforms in health care coverage. Most important was the Kennedy-Kassebaum bill (HIPAA) [Pub L No 104-191], which, in addition to mandating insurance portability and accountability, led to the enactment of laws in the areas of fraud and abuse, disposition of assets for Medicaid eligibility, tax preferences for long-term care insurance, and state insurance pools for medically uninsurable persons. HIPAA is discussed in more detail in this chapter and in chapter 5.

The BBA [Pub L No 105-33] was another large piece of health care legislation that accomplished much of the political agenda of the framers of the Health Security Act. Its major long-lasting features were

1. Creation of the Children's Health Insurance Program (CHIP), which extends the benefits of sponsored health insurance to poor children who do not qualify for Medicaid;
2. Significant fraud and abuse provisions;
3. Changes in payments for medical education; and
4. Creation of Medicare Part C for managed care.

In recognition of the major shifts in health care and the true burden that the BBA placed on hospitals and providers, in 1999 Congress passed the Balanced Budget Refinement Act, which was incorporated into Public Law 106-113. The BBRA restored some of the cuts made in payments for special and severely ill patients, refined payments for graduate medical education, and added some money for providers. These changes are discussed in more detail in chapter 7.

Q 3:2   Has managed care reduced health care costs?

Yes. Managed care has made an impact on controlling health care cost increases until now. However, the cost of premiums for health benefits is expected to increase over the next few years. There was a brief time in the mid-1990s that the *slope* of the increase in medical costs declined. Costs, however, increased in those years, as they have in all recent and subsequent years. In fact, the slope of the increase has become steeper as the artificial caps created by draconian controls on reimbursement have been breached. This topic is discussed in greater detail in chapter 1.

Q 3:3   What is driving health benefit plan reform?

Health benefit plan reform is being driven by the varying demands of purchasers (employers and business coalitions) for accountability, lower prices, improved access, and consistent quality. It is also being affected by the increased competition between health plans, HMOs, and insurers, which are engaged in premium wars that affect provider reimbursement when premiums are reduced.

There was less price competition among managed care organizations (MCOs) in 2000 and 2001. The almost manic price competition of the mid-1990s led to egregious declines in quality of care and in access to care. The result of those declines has been a decrease in utilization controls and with it an increase in prices. Premium increases were in the 8 to 12 percent range in 2000 and 2001 and are expected to maintain that pace through 2002 in the face of a stagnating economy. The impact of the World Trade Center atrocity on the economy is not clear at this writing, but there is likely to be a significant impact on industrial revenues and hence on health care premiums. In response to the market, providers are organizing networks to increase market share and negotiate leverage in the face of decreased revenues. Consumers drive health care market trends when they choose their health plans. The increasing power of the providers decreases the ability of MCOs to institute utilization controls.

The drivers of health reform in the coming few years will be the flight to quality and the attempt to portray a given health care system as the provider of that quality. Next, the progressive inability of corporations to provide lifetime health care will shift more of the burden to the end-user. At that time, the payment transaction and the service transaction will begin to occur between the same two parties.[1]

The impact of information technology on managed care cannot be underestimated; however, those who believed that the electronic medical record would revolutionize the uniquely personal medical transaction remain disappointed, as do their investors. Similarly, telemedicine has yet to achieve its promise of infinite access and minimum cost, although it has found some niches such as prison systems, rural networks, and boutique teleconsultation.

Q 3:4   Is there a role for "managed competition" in the private sector?

Uwe Reinhardt suggests that health plans that use managed care methods such as negotiated fees, utilization review, and case management actually engage in a form of "regulation" and are therefore private regulators of health care services.[2] Managed competition, on the other hand, refers to a regulatory system that helps consumers pick their own private health care plan (or regulator) from a menu of competing plans (regulators). The organization that establishes the rules of competition among the different health plans can be a government agency, a private employer, a health purchasing group, or a consumer cooperative. Although the concept of managed competition was tarnished during debate on the ill-fated Health Security Act, it has been used successfully by a few U.S. corporations and some state agencies such as the California Public Employees Retirement System (CalPERS) to manage choice rather than manage cost. Managed competition has yet to find a niche among health care options. The present iteration of managed competition tries to strike a balance between medical and social needs.

Q 3:5   What is the condition of private health insurance in the United States today?

The U.S. health insurance industry is in turmoil. The trend toward consolidation in the health care payer market has accelerated. Some large insurers have consolidated to become even larger insurance companies, such as Aetna, which acquired U.S. Healthcare, Foundation Health Systems, PacifiCare, United HealthCare and WellPoint Health Networks, NylCare, and Prudential. Others have left the market entirely. HMO enrollment has been flat for the past several years, with growth in managed care limited to the hybrid products and preferred provider organizations (PPOs) (see Figure 3-1).

The organizational paradigm of managed care, which has historically been a multiproduct, multimarket health plan, is in a state of transformation. Vertically integrated ownership relationships are be-

Figure 3-1   HMO Enrollment Growth, 1990–2004

Managed Care Industry - Growth in Total HMO Enrollment, 1990-2004 (In Millions)

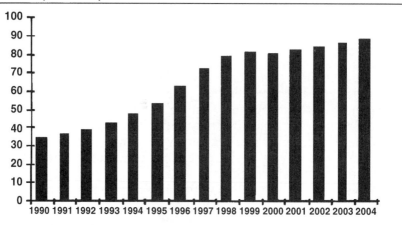

Economic: Industry and Bank of America.

Note: Data for 2001–2004 are estimated.

ing abandoned in favor of contractual relationships, and more horizontal relationships are developing between indemnity carriers, Blue Cross plans, HMOs, and specialty plans. Managed care products are moving away from local organization relationships to national, full-service corporations. Several important transitions are apparent:

Increased Downstream Integration with Purchasers. The best example of the increasingly dominant role of the health care purchaser in accessing health care services can be seen in the prototype public program under the Federal Employees Health Benefits Program (FEHBP), which owns no health plans but contracts with private plans offering indemnity, PPO, HMO, and point-of-service (POS) products.[3] Some large employers are looking to commercial carriers to provide administrative services management of their self-insured products using the networks, contracted provider rates, utilization management systems, and quality oversight tools developed for the carrier's fully insured products.

Upstream Integration by Providers. Some of the largest and most successful MCOs originated as a result of upstream integration with providers. Examples of such plans are Humana, PacifiCare, and United Healthcare Inc. Large provider organizations have assumed global capitation and, with it, have undertaken many of the functions commonly performed by health plans such as utilization management, claims management, and quality management, to name a few. Medical groups have assumed greater responsibility and accountability for the quality of care, including patient satisfaction and preventive care services.

Network Diversification. Until recently, most plans offered limited choices of networks based on the type of managed care plan. As health insurance products evolve from discrete HMO or PPO models to more flexible arrangements that allow multiple options under a single managed care plan, the type and scope of the network have changed. Health plans now have options of using a single major network or diversifying among several networks that service different segments of their product.

Plan Consolidation. Health plan consolidation continues despite increased enrollment in managed care plans. Consolidations result from the need for health plans to achieve economies of scale, the growth of multistate operations in response to the needs of multistate employers, the need to increase market share, the demand for capital to invest in health care system development, and the need for management expertise. The dual market forces of competition and consolidation have led to horizontal and vertical integration of managed care products.

Benefit Diversification. The benefit packages offered by health plans have become much more diverse. Health plans are more willing to tailor benefits to suit large corporate purchasers, public employee programs, and other public programs. The ability to offer benefit diversity requires administrative capabilities in actuarial estimation, benefit pricing, and cross-marketing. Plans that remain attached to a uniform benefit design and community-rated pricing structure will be at a distinct disadvantage. Benefit plan design is discussed in more detail in chapter 5.

Channel Diversification. Historically, health plans used secure distribution channels for marketing their products to purchasers. The distribution channel was geared to the particular beneficiary market. Marketing to Medicare beneficiaries was individualized, whereas marketing to small employers required the use of local agents or brokers. Large corporate purchasers used competitive bidding, consultants, and other avenues to obtain detailed benefit and performance packages. Because of these differences in customers, health plans must become knowledgeable in and market to all market segments through diversification in the distribution channels for their products.

Geographic Market Diversification. The trend is for health plans to combine local market penetration with geographic diversification. The health plan with national breadth and shallow depth, or the plan with local depth but little geographic breadth, will not remain competitive.

Managed Care Product Expansion and Diversification. Managed care expansion is evidenced by increases in enrollment in network-based plans and continuing consolidation among health care plans in the market, and has been driven by public and private sector concerns about rising health care costs and by increased demand for high-quality, cost-effective health services. It is clear that HMO and PPO arrangements are better suited than fee-for-service plans to respond to these and other concerns. Managed care shifts the risk of "insuring" a population away from the purchaser and onto the HMO or providers. Cost-plus businesses can no longer "pass through" costs as they could in indemnity arrangements. There has also been a dramatic shift to health care networks. Just as important, many employers are signing multiyear contracts with MCOs, fixing their risk and costs for health care in the market.

Plan and Provider Integration. Horizontal product integration has developed in response to employer and consumer demand for choice and flexibility among a broader range of managed care products from a single source. Many HMOs have supplemented their delivery systems with POS options, which operate as a fee-for-service arrangement at the point of service. These POS products are becoming very popular among consumers.

Public-private partnerships, an example of plan and provider integration, have developed in response to government's need to increase access to care for indigent populations. The success of managed care in the private sector has curtailed the practice of cost shifting from public programs to the private market. Consequently, government-sponsored plans have experienced double-digit increases in spending. Now, at least 49 out of the 50 states contract with private organizations such as HMOs, partially capitated health plans, and primary care case managers to provide health care to Medicaid recipients. This is discussed in greater detail in chapter 7.

Q 3:6 What are the major trends predicted for health plans into 2002?

The health care environment is evolving in both design of coverage and delivery of care. The trends are being driven by customer demand and medical technology. At the heart of the evolution is access to information technology and its influence on the design of health benefit plans. Consumers will be watching for developments in these areas:

- Prescription drug benefits: The 107th Congress is in deep debate about prescription drug benefits for Medicare recipients. This has become a rallying cry for interest groups but is also a major social concern. By 1998, the last year for which figures are available, 31.5 percent of Medicare recipients were spending greater than 5 percent of their income on prescription drugs.

- Preventive medicine: The ability to prevent diseases has long been known to be a great money saver, in addition to being good medicine. The ability of medical practice to accurately define medical risk is the first step to increased prevention capabilities. This is occurring in connection with the human genome identification.

- Complementary medicine: The National Institutes of Health has created an institute to study complementary and alternative medicine, thus legitimizing the discipline. In some studies, up to 80 percent of patients are utilizing some form of complementary or alternative medicine.

- Access to care: Access has become less of a problem for managed care as the networks are easing restrictions on provider choice. Developments to watch include the growth of point-of-service programs.

- New technology: In addition to the aforementioned human genome project completion, technological innovations in minimally invasive surgery, noninvasive imaging, implantable devices, and transplants promise to enhance the quality and reach of medicine.

- Quality and outcomes: New and more sophisticated measures in quality and outcomes promise to deliver to the consumer the means of enhancing the value of the purchase that they will increasingly make with their own money.

- Ratings and rankings: The major challenge in the next year for rating physicians and hospitals will be the quality and dissemination of information. A recent study by the Commonwealth Fund[4] demonstrated that a large number of physician directory and information services provided inaccurate or inadequate information. Thus, it is crucial that ratings and rankings be judged critically.

As purchasers of health benefits become more sophisticated, they will make their decisions based on value and accountability, rather than price only.

Q 3:7   How does public policy deal with the issues discussed in Question 3:6?

As in other industries that have been subject to increased market competition, one public policy response has been to attempt to legislate safeguards and protections for vulnerable populations. The increase in competition, consolidation, and integration in response to managed care has increased regulatory and legislative activity, which includes a number of anti-managed care proposals, such as "any willing provider" laws, patient protection acts, direct access laws, mandated benefits (including maternity stays, emergency services, and POS options), disclosure requirements, gag rule legislation, limits on provider payment mechanisms, and unitary drug pricing. The patient protection fervor that was sweeping Congress has subsided because of the terrorist attacks of September 11, 2001; however, it can be expected to reappear when Congress resumes business as usual. Patient protection legislation is discussed in more detail in chapter 6.

Of course, the events of September 11 have derailed all public policy decisions on health care at the national level. Revenue considerations at the state level can be expected to drive limited expansions in Medicaid and CHIP. Finally, the focus on bioterrorism does not affect issues surrounding the provision of individual health care.

Q 3:8   What managed care arrangements are most commonly used in the private sector?

The managed care arrangements most commonly used in the private sector are managed indemnity, PPOs, HMOs, POS options, and direct contracting arrangements. These arrangements are discussed in the following sections.

Managed Care Organizations and Products

Q 3:9   What is managed care?

To the public, managed care has come to mean a lock-in HMO, which is a system by which the physician and the patient are locked into a payment mechanism that gives complete control to unseen bureaucrats who are interested only in the bottom line. These bureaucrats accomplish their ends by gagging physicians and restricting the access of patients to the care they need—all in the name of profits that are transferred to Wall Street. In reality, managed care is merely a payment mechanism that creates a triangular relationship between the physician, patient, and payer and has no normative value.

Q 3:10   What are the most common types of managed care products and organizations?

HMOs and PPOs were the earliest forms of managed care. Other common structures include exclusive provider organizations (EPOs), independent practice associations (IPAs), and POS plans. The differences between these products are disappearing as new health plans that combine various features of these plans are created. In fact, as managed care has become a mature industry, the term has lost its distinction. It is now construed to mean a payment mechanism that attempts to exercise some prescriptive authority over the medical care a person receives.

Health Maintenance Organizations

Q 3:11　What is a health maintenance organization?

An HMO is an organized health care system that is responsible for both the financing and the delivery of health care services to an enrolled population. The HMO is the most common form of managed care product. Many HMOs were established in 1973 under the Federal HMO Act [Pub L No 93-222], sponsored by Senator Kennedy and signed into law by President Nixon. All HMOs share one very important feature: the health care providers cannot bill patients directly for services rendered and must seek all reimbursement from the HMO.

Today's HMO is an integrated health care financing and delivery system responsible not only for collecting and disbursing funds but also for delivering and managing care to participants and reporting outcomes to government authorities. Many modern HMOs are large group models that exist as autonomous health care systems with their own delivery system and insurance product; others are sponsored by major insurance companies as a product line. Some of the larger proprietary HMOs are integrating the insurance product with the provider delivery system. It is important to note, however, that in the 2002 market, an HMO can be anything as long as it manages care according to state guidelines.

Q 3:12　What are the traditional HMO models?

There are five general models of HMOs, which differ based on the relationship between the HMO and the providers. As HMO product development continues to expand and include hybrid structures (see discussion of POS plans at Q 3:23), it is becoming increasingly difficult to classify a product under a single HMO model. The traditional HMO models are the following:

Staff Model. In a staff model HMO, the physicians are employed by the HMO to provide covered services to health plan enrollees. They are usually paid a salary, as well as a bonus or incentive based on performance and productivity. Some health plans subcontract for services that the employed physicians are unable to provide.

Group Practice Model. The group practice model HMO contracts with an organized group of physicians who are not direct employees of the HMO, but who agree to provide basic health care services to the HMO's members in exchange for payment, usually on a capitation basis. Physicians are generally employed by the group and usually share facilities, staff, records, and equipment. There are two categories of group practice models: a captive group and an independent group practice. A captive group appears independent and may have a management services arrangement with the HMO; it depends significantly on the HMO contracts for patients. An example of this type of group is the Permanente Medical Group under the Kaiser Foundation Health Plan. An independent group practice involves a truly independent group that may be the owner or sponsor of its own HMO. In addition to providing services under contract to the HMO, the group provides services to other HMOs and plans. An example of this type of group is the Geisinger Health Plan of Danville, Pennsylvania. Both types of group practice models have certain characteristics of a staff model. On the positive side, group models have (1) a closed panel (all physicians who participate are members of the group), (2) a high degree of integration receptive to utilization management controls, and (3) lower capital requirements. On the negative side, group models offer a more limited choice of providers and locations.

Network Model. In this model, a network contracts with more than one group practice to provide primary care and specialty physician services to the HMO's members. The network may be a multispecialty or primary care network. This model is somewhat like the group practice model. An example of the network model is the Health Insurance Plan (HIP) of Greater New York, which contracts with many multispecialty physician group practices in the New York area. In contrast to the group practice and staff models, the network model may use either open or closed panels. The broader base of participating groups overcomes many of the disadvantages associated with limitations in choice of providers or geographic scope of services.

Individual or Independent Practice Association Model. The IPA model HMO contracts with an association of physicians (the IPA) to provide services to its members. As discussed in more detail in chapter 6, IPAs are a form of integrated delivery system in which physicians are members of the IPA for purposes of the HMO contract but retain their practices separately from each other. Most IPA models are open to providers who meet the plan's and the IPA's criteria for participation. Some IPAs are primary care providers who subcontract with specialists; others may be either multispecialty or specialist only. Most HMOs compensate IPAs on a full medical capitation basis. Individual IPA physicians are paid on either a capitation or fee-for-service basis. These differing approaches to payment are discussed in chapter 13.

Direct Contract Model. The direct-service contract/network HMO model is the most basic model. Under it, an HMO contracts directly with individual providers to provide services to the HMO's patients, on either a capitation or a discounted fee-for-service basis. This arrangement is similar to IPA model plans, except that there is no separate legal entity involved in the contract; rather, each individual physician has a contract with the HMO. Physicians are compensated on either a capitation or fee-for-service basis. Primary care capitation with controlled referrals to specialists who are paid by the plan on a fee-for-service basis has the practical effect of achieving the referral benefits of an IPA without sacrificing the HMO's contracting leverage; however, there is more administrative burden on the HMO for the provider contracts and for utilization and quality management oversight.

In reality, there are no bright lines that distinguish the offerings of the various managed care companies. That is why the term *HMO penetration* to describe market share has lost most of its meaning.

Q 3:13   How do for-profit and nonprofit HMOs differ?

Nonprofit HMOs have their roots in the early days of HMO development, before the enabling legislation of "federal qualification." Organizations such as Kaiser Permanente and Group Health of Puget Sound were configured to be managed either by physicians or by the community the HMO served.

For-profit HMOs grew rapidly because of their access to capital markets and the growth promised to investors. The growth came with the understanding that the for-profit model would deliver efficiencies in such a quantity that investors would receive adequate return with no compromise in the quality of care.

For-profit HMOs fall into two general categories: partnerships and corporations. Many for-profit HMOs are operated by holding companies, so they can incorporate. Incorporation is an advantage because many states do not levy general income tax on corporations.

The federal government has actively supported the for-profit HMO sector. First, the Tax Equity and Fiscal Responsibility Act of 1982 (TEFRA) enables Medicare and Medicaid beneficiaries to enroll in a for-profit or a nonprofit HMO if the HMO federally qualified. Second, a 1982 change in federal HMO regulations allows the Secretary of Health and Human Services to "waive all or part of the amount of funds repayable to the Secretary when an HMO converts to for-profit."

The Minnesota Department of Health offers this helpful contrast between for-profit and nonprofit HMOs:[5]

Possible Advantages to Permitting For-Profit HMOs
For-profit entities may be more efficient. For-profits may instill greater cost consciousness and operate in a more cost-effective manner.
It has been argued that for-profit institutions will make the delivery of health care more efficient because they are purportedly able to generate otherwise unavailable capital through equity financing, to offer more attractive employee incentives and operate with a simpler corporate and administrative structure. When providers share in an organization's profits, they are thought to provide care in a more cost conscious manner. Although the literature dealing with HMOs is voluminous, there is little empirical analysis, and no studies have assessed the efficiency of for-profits versus nonprofits. There is no conceptual reason, however, to believe that for-profits should achieve greater economies of scale than nonprofits.

Profit-making facilities are thought to attract more capable managers, leading to lower administrative costs and other managerial efficiencies.
For-profit HMOs may be able to attract better managers because they can offer more attractive employee incentives than nonprofits. For-profit HMOs are in a good position to reward management for outstanding achievement through financial in-

centives. They are not faced with the prohibitions faced by the nonprofits and may establish profit-sharing plans and incentive stock option plans.

Because they can issue stock, investor-owned institutions are thought to have access to capital at lower costs. The ease in generating capital can lead to expanding to new locations and markets.

The most compelling force driving nonprofit HMOs to convert to for-profit status is their need to acquire capital to maintain operations and expand into new locations. The need to acquire capital occurs in new HMOs that face extensive start-up costs, as well as in mature plans that are growing and acquiring more sophisticated plant (e.g., laboratories) and expanded facilities (e.g., owned hospitals). As Leonard Schaeffer, past president of Group Health in Minnesota said, "Capital markets are only interested in for-profit entities. It is not our desire to become for-profit that drives us in this direction. It is our determination to compete."[6]

Although nonprofit HMOs have obtained capital from the sale of tax-exempt state bonds, this source has been limited because many state bonding authority enabling statutes do not include nonprofit HMOs as eligible participants. Therefore, HMOs in need of capital have found the private capital markets attractive and are assuming a for-profit status in order to compete for available funds.

For-profits can stimulate growth and competition.

For-profit HMOs will likely play an increasing role in the HMO industry as a result of the development of new for-profit entities as well as the conversion of nonprofits to for-profit. Such conversions are seen by health care officials as a trend toward more fierce competition among health care insurers as a means of survival, a way of raising capital and a response to pressures from the government, business, and labor to hold down health care costs.

Possible Disadvantages to Permitting For-Profit HMOs

The profit-maximizing philosophy may lead to decreases in the quality of care.

There is an ongoing controversy concerning the quality of care provided in prepaid plans. In addition, there is concern that the economic incentive[s] faced by for-profit HMOs tend to drive them to provide fewer rather than more services, in order to contain costs and make a profit.

For-profit HMOs may be less willing to serve the disadvantaged.

Some observers question the willingness of for-profit HMOs to serve the disadvantaged. Recent changes in federal and state laws allow Medicare- and Medicaid-eligible elderly and low-income individuals to receive health care services in HMOs.

It is not entirely clear that a for-profit HMO will necessarily behave efficiently.

Future growth of the for-profit sector will depend on its ability to compete on both cost and quality. The Schlessinger data provide[ ] some insights in[to] the cost comparisons between for-profits and nonprofits. These data show for-profits to be more costly. For-profits had a higher cost per inpatient day ($538 vs. $495), higher average total ambulatory cost ($364 vs. $330), and higher average inpatient cost per enrollee ($214 vs. $196). In addition, for-profits averaged higher revenues per enrollee ($695 vs. $654). It is impossible to discern from these data the causes for the higher costs (e.g., higher utilization; higher capital costs; newer, more expensive facilities; different patient mix; greater use of ancillary services; or inefficient operations). However, this does force a careful evaluation of the consequences of the profit motive in HMOs and the significance for the payers of health care.

Q 3:14   How have Medical service payment arrangements changed under HMO plans?

Payment arrangements for medical services have undergone major changes in the past quarter century so as to invalidate older assessments of physicians and the profit motive. That physicians are concerned about reimbursement is not surprising. Recent data show that physicians are more concerned about receiving adequate payment for services from managed care and Medicaid than they are about receiving adequate payment for services from Medicare,[7] as shown in Table 3-1. Further, physicians' perception of the seriousness of the problem varies by medical specialty, as shown in Table 3-2.

Q 3:15   What have been the major factors increasing HMO premium costs?

Several answers present themselves:

- Increasing drug costs. By all estimates, drug costs have increased dramatically. From 1993 to 2000, the drug costs for CalPERS, often a bellwether, increased 120 percent.

Table 3-1   **Physicians' Assessment of Seriousness of Problem with Reimbursement Levels, by Type of Payer, 1994 and 1999**

Type of Payer	Number of Respondents		Percent of Respondents Who Said Reimbursement Was a "Very Serious" Problem		Percentage-point Change, 1994–1999
	1994	1999[a]	1994	1999	
PPO and other private FFS	913	535	16.0%	25.3%[b]	9.3[c]
FFS Medicare	983	567	48.0	45.0	−3.0
FFS Medicaid	485	236	60.0	58.6[b]	−1.4
HMO/other capitated plan	506	449	33.0	66.0[b]	33.0[c]

Sources: Physician Payment Review Commission (PPRC) 1994 Survey of Physicians; and Medicare Payment Advisory Commission, 1999 Survey of Physicians.

Notes: 1994 numbers are as published in Table 1-4 of the report on the 1994 PPRC survey. 1999 percentages are weighted to account for oversampling of selected specialties. Missing values are excluded from all calculations. Analysis is limited to physicians spending at least 10 percent of their patient care time with the given type of patient. PPO is preferred provider organization. FFS is fee-for-service. HMO is health maintenance organization.

[a] Approximately half of the 1999 sample received an alternative set of questions and thus are excluded from this exhibit.

[b] Percentage differs from percentage for FFS Medicare patients at 0.05 significance level or better (no tests conducted for 1994).

[c] Change from 1994 to 1999 is different from zero at 0.05 significance level or better.

- Aging population.
- Increasing technology costs.
- Need of for-profit HMOs to show a profit and pay dividends.

As a consequence of these and other influences, many employers have increased the percentage of the premium that the employee must pay. Others have eliminated health insurance contributions for part-time employees, initiated defined contribution plans whereby the employee is provided a quantum of money to purchase his or her own health plan, or shifted to cheaper plans.[8] Several health plans do not offer drug coverage or have dramatically increased co-payment amounts.

Table 3-2   Seriousness of Physicians' Problems with Reimbursement
Levels, by Type of Payer and Type of Physician, 1999

| Type of Physicians | Percent of Respondents Who Said Reimbursement Was a "Very Serious" Problem | | | |
	PPO and Other Private FFS	FFS Medicare	FFS Medicaid	HMO/Other Capitated Plan
Proceduralists	18.3%	32.3%[a]	52.2%	75.8%[a]
Surgeons	34.5[a]	59.0[a]	71.6[a]	72.5
Nonproceduralists	21.9	40.5[a]	54.1	59.1[a]
Ophthalmologists	34.3	57.8	59.4	75.3
Orthopedic surgeons	47.2[a]	78.2[a]	83.9	83.0
Cardiothoracic surgeons	45.2	63.1	66.7	67.3
All physicians	25.3	45.0	58.6	66.0

Source: Medicare Payment Advisory Commission, 1999 Survey of Physicians.
Notes: Missing values are excluded from all calculations. Percentages are weighted to account for oversampling of selected specialties. Analysis is limited to physicians spending at least 10 percent of their patient care time with the given type of patient. PPO is preferred provider organization. FFS is fee-for-service. HMO is health maintenance organization.
[a] Percentage differs from other physician groups at 0.05 significance level or better.

There are several studies indicating higher mortality and morbidity for those with a higher risk of health care costs.[9]

Q 3:16   What has been the effect of HMOs on hospital use?

When prepayment became the dominant mode of hospital reimbursement, it had a profound impact on length of stay in the hospital. This effect has been noticed in many other economies, most recently in Italy, where average length of stay was halved years after the institution of a prospective payment mechanism.[10]

Although the Italian study did not examine quality of care, other studies have. It does not appear that the mere fact of belonging to an HMO impedes quality of care in the hospital. Some studies have suggested that because the barrier to seeking primary care is lower for HMO enrollees, illnesses such as appendicitis are diagnosed earlier. Others suggest that HMO patients are less likely to have surgery for heart disease than their fee-for-service counterparts. The HMO in these studies, however, is the lock-in variety, which has little currency today. Interpretation of HMO data requires an in-depth knowledge of the exact nature of the product and of what is allowed or restricted in the specific plan.

Q 3:17　How have clinical practice guidelines affected HMOs?

The proliferation of national clinical practice guidelines (CPGs) has exceeded the ability of physicians to incorporate them. As respected a source as the online information service MD Consults lists guidelines from 50 societies and professional groups. Medscape lists eight separate guidelines for a primary care physician's management of asthma. Clearly, this blizzard of guidelines has transcended the boundaries of clinical utility. The use of guidelines by HMOs remains a thorny issue, because mandating the use of guidelines blurs the lines between payer and provider and opens HMOs to issues regarding practice of medicine.

Arnold J. Rosoff has discussed the legal aspect of evidence-based medicine.[11] He addresses the issue of guidelines as follows:

> Proposals for federal certification of clinical practice guidelines, including not only my own freestanding proposal but also those contained in the Clinton, Chafee, and other federal health care reform proposals, have been "around" for over five years without attracting substantial attention or support. This is true despite the growing acceptance and use of CPGs [clinical practice guidelines] during this period. If anything, the continuing proliferation of CPGs makes it more advisable that some mechanism be devised to introduce guidelines more prominently into the legal process and help courts decide which guidelines should be regarded as authoritative. . . .
> . . . If the general principles and specific elements can be fashioned into a national framework for the certification of clinical practice guidelines and a rationalized approach to their use in the courts, I believe the expanded use of CPGs it will enable will bring substantial benefits to our health care system. While there will always be a need and a place for professional medical judgment, we should make maximum use of available empirical evidence as to what works and doesn't work, synthesizing that data into carefully analyzed, widely disseminated guidelines to assist physicians to properly apply their clinical judgment. Benefits will flow to the legal system as well, making possible more accurate, efficient, and affordable resolution of

disputes about the quality and appropriateness of health care provided.[12]

Preferred Provider Organizations

Q 3:18   What is a preferred provider organization?

PPOs are entities through which employer health benefit plans and health insurance carriers contract to purchase health care services for covered beneficiaries from a selected group of participating providers. Most PPOs agree to abide by utilization management and other procedures implemented by the PPO plan sponsor, and providers agree to accept the terms of the PPO's reimbursement structure and payment levels. In return, PPOs often limit the size of their provider panel and provide incentives for the covered individuals to use participating providers instead of other providers.

Unlike HMO enrollees, PPO enrollees are not absolutely restricted to the provider panel and may go outside the PPO provided they bear greater financial responsibility. A PPO does not take the place of the traditional fee-for-service provider (as does a staff model HMO; see Q 3:12) and does not rely on capitated payments to providers. Instead, a PPO contracts with individual providers and groups to create a network of providers. Members of a PPO can choose any physician they wish for medical care, but if they choose a provider in the PPO network, their copayments (predetermined fixed amounts paid per visit, regardless of treatment received) are significantly reduced. This provides the incentive to stay in the PPO network. No federal statutes govern PPOs, but many states regulate their operations.

PPO models have matured as the rigid HMO models have declined, and the lines continue to blur. A useful definition of PPO is provided by the Commonwealth Fund:

> The term PPO encompasses a very broad spectrum of organizations. Many experts on PPO operations assert that the purpose of PPOs is to provide lower-cost health care and wide choice of providers—not to "manage" care per se. PPOs can be generally categorized into those that operate as "wholesale" or leased organizations; those that have a network and provide some medical management activities; and those that integrate both

insurance and network organizations. Wholesale entities lease their network to a payer customer (insurer, self-insured employer, or third-party administrator), and do not bear insurance risk. PPOs are paid a fixed rate per member per month to cover network administration costs. Their customers bear insurance risk. PPO network providers are also paid on a fee-for-service basis. Unlike health maintenance organizations (HMOs), wholesale PPOs generally do not have enrollment data or claims data—two major sources of data for performance measurement. The integrated PPO model does bear risk through its insurance functions.[13]

Q 3:19   What are the common PPO models?

There are three basic PPO models:

Gatekeeper. In the gatekeeper plan, a patient must choose a primary care provider from the PPO network. This primary care provider handles most of the patient's health care needs and must authorize any referrals to specialists or other providers. If the patient "self-refers" without authorization, the cost savings of the PPO will not apply.

Open Panel. The open panel plan allows a patient to see different primary care physicians and to self-refer within the PPO network. The financial penalties for seeking medical care outside the PPO network are much greater in this model than in the gatekeeper model.

Exclusive Provider. The exclusive provider plan shifts onto the patient all the costs of seeking medical care out of network, and in this respect is very similar to an HMO plan.

Q 3:20   What are the basic characteristics of a PPO?

The common features of a PPO include the following:

Preferred Provider Panel. PPOs have contracts with the insurer, plan, or employer group that stipulate that they will abide by the utilization and quality requirements and accept as payment in full (except for copayments, etc.) the amounts under either a fee schedule or a discount off standard charges. Recent legislation in many states has imposed additional criteria on the selection and deselection of providers to be included or not included in the panel. This arrangement is discussed in more detail in chapter 6.

Negotiated Rates. PPOs attempt to obtain provider agreement to negotiated fees that will allow them to be cost competitive in obtaining subscribers to the PPO's plan. In addition to discounts on charges and negotiated fee schedules, some PPOs develop per diem, DRG, or bundled rates that include both medical and facility reimbursement.

Prompt Payment. Many PPOs offer prompt payment of claims in return for providers' price or charge discounts. Some PPOs will pay claims in as little as 15 days in return for a larger discount from charges.

Utilization Management. Most PPOs use a variety of utilization management techniques as a means of controlling cost, utilization, and quality.

Consumer Choice. One of the key features of a PPO is the preservation of consumer choice in selecting health care providers, which is a fundamental difference from HMO plans. Most PPO plans use increased cost sharing by the enrollee through higher copayments or deductibles if the enrollee goes outside the panel of preferred providers.

Q 3:21   Is there a difference between a preferred provider organization and a preferred provider arrangement?

No. Whether called a PPO or PPA, the structure is generally the same. PPOs contract with selected providers in a community to provide services to covered individuals. These providers may include hospitals, physicians, IPAs, or physician-hospital organizations (PHOs). Most PPO participation agreements require providers to accept the PPO's payment as payment in full for covered services (less deductibles, copayments, and other costs for which the enrollee is responsible). Most often, PPOs negotiate on a basis of discounted fee-for-service charges, all-inclusive per diem rates, or payments based on DRGs.

Q 3:22   What is the major difference between a PPO and an HMO?

The major difference between an HMO and a PPO is the PPO patient's ability to choose nonparticipating providers for covered services (subject to higher deductibles and copayments). PPOs developed in response to the perception that HMOs limit a patient's choice of a personal health care provider. This freedom of choice issue resulted in a strategy of establishing contractual relationships with preferred providers who agree to certain discounts in return for volume guarantees and prompt payment. Employees are offered financial incentives such as reduced or no copayments or deductibles for using preferred providers. Like HMOs, PPOs were intended to control health care costs through strict utilization controls. With the advent of POS options, the lines have blurred, making national enrollment data and epidemiologic studies difficult and sometimes unreliable.

Point-of-Service and Other Mixed Plans

Q 3:23   What is a point-of-service plan?

A POS plan is a combination of an HMO and an indemnity insurance plan, allowing full coverage within the network of providers and partial coverage outside the network. A patient must choose one primary care physician and may pay a higher monthly rate to the POS plan if the physician is not in the HMO network. Another version of the POS plan creates "tiers" of providers, which are rated by cost effectiveness and quality of patient outcomes. A patient may choose a provider from any tier and owes a monthly premium set to that tier. These plans are hybrids containing features of both PPOs and HMOs. Those evolving from the PPOs are often referred to as capitated and primary care PPOs; those evolving from HMOs are referred to as open-access or point-of-service HMOs.

Under POS plans, primary care physicians are reimbursed through capitation payments (fixed per-member per-month (PMPM) payments) or other performance-based reimbursement methods. Often, some amount is withheld from physician compensation and is paid contingent on achievement of utilization or cost targets. (This financial arrangement has irked consumer groups and regulators alike and has given rise to some components of the so-called patient protection legislation.) The primary care physician acts as a gatekeeper for referral and institutional medical services. If services are not authorized by the primary care physician or are delivered by nonparticipating providers, coverage is significantly reduced (e.g., from 100 percent to 60 percent). Traditional HMOs may offer a similar option through an out-of-plan benefits rider.

Q 3:24 What are the characteristics of an open-access or point-of-service HMO?

Because the limited choice of providers is viewed by some potential members as unappealing, many HMOs provide some level of indemnity-type coverage. HMO members covered under these types of plans may decide whether to use HMO benefits or indemnity-style benefits for each instance of care. That is, the member can choose at the point of service. Some states require entities that offer POS plans to have both HMO and insurance licensure.

Q 3:25 What are the characteristics of a capitated and primary care PPO?

This hybrid of traditional HMO and PPO models has the following basic characteristics:

1. Primary care physicians are reimbursed through capitation.
2. Provider withholds are commonly used to ensure utilization compliance.
3. Primary care physicians serve as gatekeepers to the system.
4. Members assume greater financial risk for services provided outside the network or plan.

Q 3:26 Is there a role for managed indemnity products?

Yes. Many traditional insurers and self-insured indemnity plans have sought the cost containment measures of managed care as an overlay to their traditional indemnity product. Managed care overlays that may be used include the following:

General Utilization Management. These plans include many of the features of PPOs such as provider panel selection criteria, authorization, and prospective and retrospective reviews. Plans can also contract for value-added products for their members that may produce added compliance leading to better outcomes. Such products have been launched commercially for chronic diseases such as diabetes, heart failure, and obstructive lung disease. Well-managed operations have been profitable while providing services to patients and savings to the plans.

Specialty Utilization Management. These plans often overlay specialty carve-out services such as mental health, vision, and dental care. Requiring surgical second opinions is also a common method of controlling utilization, although its actual utility in overall cost containment has never been convincingly demonstrated. Further, carving out services leads to fragmentation in the continuum of care as different organizations not accustomed to communicating are asked to focus on the management of a single patient. Carving out services is one of the greatest irritations to physicians, who are forced to provide referrals to services or practitioners they do not know. Although data are not available, authorities in the field believe that carve-out strategies are on the wane as full-risk capitation is maturing.

Catastrophic or Large Case Management. Services are available to help employers and insurers manage catastrophic or large cases regardless of specialty. These case management services include screening to identify catastrophic cases, negotiation of services and reimbursement with the appropriate treating providers, development of treatment protocols, and ongoing case and care management.

Workers' Compensation Utilization Management. General and specialty utilization management and catastrophic or large case management are being applied in workers' compensation claims to achieve the savings and capabilities of managed care.

Community Health Plans and Rural Community Health Systems

Q 3:27   What is a community health plan?

A community health plan (CHP) was originally conceived as an organization that would bring physicians, hospitals, and community leaders together in the design and management of a risk-bearing organization and local health care delivery system. CHPs allow communities to capture local health care dollars, deliver the scope of locally available medical services (which will depend on resources within the community), and retain control over medical decision making.

The initial CHP models originated in Washington and Oregon, where they were used in both public and private sector delivery systems. CHPs were developed in response to large, urban, integrated delivery systems entering rural markets and removing both patients and health care dollars from the rural community, destroying not only the local health care infrastructure but also the community's economic base. By keeping the dollars and clinical management at the local level, communities could use the savings generated by CHPs to invest in the local health care system and in health-improvement initiatives.

CHPs are designed to deliver the scope of locally available health services, with emphasis on primary and preventive care. Services not available in the community, such as subspecialty or tertiary care, are to be externally contracted. Each CHP is to include the full array of locally available physicians and health care providers, including, but not limited to, nonprofit and for-profit hospitals, mid-level practitioners, and rural health clinics. Physician and facility participation in the local CHP should be voluntary and nonexclusive.

Q 3:28   What is the Rural Community Health System of Texas?

The Rural Community Health System (RCHS) of Texas is a unique rural organization that was developed as a second-generation model to build on the fundamental principles of the CHP to enable the development of a statewide organization that could aggregate rural communities and their local health care providers. The primary purpose of the RCHS is to allow rural health care providers to organize under a statewide network. Through that network, the RCHS can offer or sponsor different insurance products for government and commercial insurance.

The RCHS was initially created as a result of legislation authorizing new law under the Texas Insurance Code to enable the development of a nonprofit, statewide risk-bearing entity that could contract with locally developed rural community health networks, individual health care practitioners and institutions, or other health care organizations and entities, as discussed in more detail in chapter 6.

Subsequent legislation in 1999 and 2001 enabled the RCHS to distance itself from the HMO model and to function as a statewide network for other HMOs and insurance companies as well as offer under its own statute a unique form of insurance product, the EPO. The EPO model is discussed in more detail in chapter 6.

The RCHS is authorized by state law to

1. Establish a statewide rural health network that is inclusive of health care providers;

2. Operate only in areas designated as "rural";

3. Sponsor insured program alternatives for under- and uninsured citizens of rural Texas through its own chapter of the Texas Insurance Code;

4. Develop and pilot an indemnity insured EPO model for Medicaid in a designated rural area; and

5. Be included as one of the contracted providers in the event the state expands its 1915b waiver program.

Q 3:29 What is unique about the RCHS of Texas?

The RCHS of Texas is governed by its own chapter of the Texas Insurance Code, Chapter 20C, and is regulated by the Texas Department of Insurance (TDI). To achieve its goals of preserving local control over medical care while keeping dollars in local rural communities, the RCHS will establish a statewide network and sponsor indemnity insurance programs for county indigent, working uninsured, and other government programs such as Medicaid and Medicare, along with other local, state, and federal initiatives.

The RCHS is rural-focused, cooperative, and supportive of frontier and rural communities in managing the cost and delivery of health care services while fostering appropriate, natural linkages and referral patterns among primary and tertiary health care providers in urban, semi-urban, and other rural communities.

Q 3:30 What is the structure of the RCHS of Texas?

The RCHS of Texas is a quasi-governmental, nonprofit corporation established under the Texas Nonprofit Corporations Act. Its 18-member board represents rural hospitals, rural physicians, and rural community leaders from all over the state. Each category of board member comes from one of six regions of the state to ensure geographic representation of all rural communities.

Q 3:31   Must an RCHS be set up as a quasi-governmental entity?

No. The RCHS of Texas is organized under state statute. It is not a state agency. An RCHS could be structured as a private organization in states where the laws are flexible and allow EPOs as an insurance option. As a quasi-governmental entity, an RCHS can receive the benefits available under state law to public entities but will be subject to open meetings and open records laws, with certain exceptions. By designating an RCHS as quasi-governmental, certain liability protections will be afforded to its members by virtue of their status as state political subdivisions.

Q 3:32   Who can participate in the RCHS of Texas?

Nonprofit and for-profit hospitals can participate in the RCHS of Texas, as can other allied health professionals, rural health clinics, and federally qualified health centers. Physician and facility participation in the RCHS is voluntary and nonexclusive.

Q 3:33   How will the RCHS of Texas interface with medical schools and teaching facilities in rural areas?

Rural hospitals and physicians currently refer tertiary and many subspecialty services to medical schools and teaching centers. The RCHS of Texas does not change these relationships. The RCHS will continue to contract with medical schools and teaching facilities, as well as children's hospitals and other specialty and tertiary care centers, to provide services that are not available in the rural community.

Q 3:34   Is the RCHS of Texas an insurance company or HMO?

When originally organized, the RCHS of Texas was authorized to obtain a certificate of authority from the TDI in anticipation of the continued roll-out of Medicaid managed care into rural areas. For many reasons, including the cost to hold an insurance or HMO license, the RCHS can sponsor and enable health care funding models for fully insured products for Medicaid, uninsured, and other eligible populations. The RCHS will sponsor these programs in rural communities under arrangement with certain licensed insurers, reinsurers, and other program partners. These strategic relationships will allow the RCHS to preserve the rural providers' control over their patient relationships while bringing new sources of funding to these communities.

Q 3:35 How will the RCHS of Texas address antitrust issues, particularly in the rural environment?

The RCHS of Texas is cooperative in structure. There is no physician or hospital exclusivity, and for government payers, reimbursement is at government-set rates. In addition, since it is authorized under the Texas Insurance Code, federal antitrust regulation may be preempted under the "state action" doctrine or because RCHS engages in the "business of insurance," which is exempt from antitrust regulation pursuant to the McCarren-Ferguson Act (see chapter 8). Therefore, antitrust issues are not really a concern.

Q 3:36 Who holds the insurance risk in the RCHS of Texas?

An issuing carrier will license the RCHS product and will bear all insurance risk. Other vendors will be contracted to provide the other essential functions of the program, including, but not limited to, care coordination and quality or outcome management, claims administration, and data capture and management. The RCHS is authorized to obtain licensure as an HMO or other regulated risk-bearing entity, or it can develop a relationship with a risk-bearing entity.

Q 3:37 How can provider-sponsored HMOs, including those developed by hospital districts and medical schools, participate in an RCHS?

An RCHS is organized to be very flexible and inclusive in its structure and operation. Provider-sponsored HMOs can participate in an RCHS system in several ways. An RCHS could contract with a provider-sponsored HMO and its network to take risk for certain services on a carve-out basis. As such, an HMO could contract directly with an RCHS to deliver services in a rural community. Other HMOs may offer services in rural areas and contract with local physicians and hospitals.

Q 3:38   Is the RCHS model applicable only to the Medicaid managed care program?

No. An RCHS may offer or sponsor products for other government and private health insurance programs, including Medicare and the Civilian Health and Medical Program of the United States (CHAMPUS), as well as individual and small-business health insurance programs.

Q 3:39   How are tertiary services included in an RCHS?

Each local community network delivers the range of locally available health services, with emphasis on primary and preventive care. Services not available in the community, such as subspecialty or tertiary care, are externally contracted.

Q 3:40   How does the RCHS model address the surplus of facilities, physicians, and other health care providers in the community?

Most rural communities are medically underserved. To the extent there are adequate numbers of facilities, physicians, and other health care providers in the contracted community, this is an advantage to an RCHS because it reduces the dependency on urban and semi-urban providers.

Q 3:41   Can urban health care systems participate in an RCHS?

Yes. Again, the RCHS model does not exclude other HMOs or health care systems from operating in rural areas. An urban hospital system could establish its own rural network, or partner or contract with an RCHS to develop a rural delivery system.

Q 3:42   Is legislation needed to establish an RCHS?

No. The RCHS model can function as a private, community-based initiative. The purpose of having specific legislation is to allow rural hospital districts, hospital authorities, and other taxpayer-supported hospitals to collectively finance, organize, and establish a risk-bearing entity. In rural areas, few hospital districts could muster adequate financial resources or population bases to form a system on their own.

Legislation passed in many states allows individual hospital districts to establish HMOs. They cannot, however, jointly establish one HMO, although they can contract with each other for services. Further, legislation allows for intergovernmental transfer of public funds (e.g., disproportionate share funds) between RCHS members so that these monies can be used to capitalize an RCHS. (State and federal regulations allow disproportionate share monies to be used for this purpose within specified guidelines.) In fact, establishment of an RCHS helps to solve one of a state's thorniest managed care Medicaid issues: out-of-county liability.

Medical Savings Accounts

Q 3:43   What is a medical savings account?

One development in health insurance is the medical savings account (MSA), a pilot program created by the HIPAA. The premise behind the MSA was to take the bulk of the financial risk, and premium payments, away from the managed care and indemnity insurers and allow individuals to save money, tax free, in a savings account for use for medical expenses.

Individuals or their employers purchase major-medical policies, medical insurance policies with no coverage for medical expenses until the amount paid by the patient exceeds a predetermined maximum amount, such as $2,500 per year. These policies have extremely high deductibles and correspondingly low monthly premiums. Participants deposit the money that they would have spent on higher premiums in the MSA. This money accrues through monthly deposits and interest and can be spent only for medical care. The major-medical policy comes into force after the deductible is met or after the account becomes depleted.

MSAs do not incorporate any of the cost-controlling aspects of MCOs. Instead, they depend on competition between providers for patients (who are assumed to be more cost conscious about spending their own money) to encourage efficient health care delivery and discourage unnecessary expense.

MSAs operate as flexible spending accounts (FSAs) in that employees may submit eligible health care claims for reimbursement from their accounts. MSAs differ from FSAs in that any MSA balance remaining at year-end may be carried over or taken out in cash by the employee, whereas FSAs have a "use it or lose it" rule.

Prior to the passage of the Health Reform Act of 1996 (which included HIPAA), federal tax law required taxation of MSAs and FSAs. With the passage of the Health Reform Act, Congress made tax-free MSAs available on a test basis to aid small businesses, the self-employed, and the uninsured. Enrollment under the pilot MSA project is capped at 750,000 account holders of tax-exempt MSAs. Under the HIPAA pilot program, to be eligible for an MSA, a person must be self-employed or work for a small business (i.e., a business with fewer than 50 employees).

Q 3:44   Is there an insurance market for MSAs?

It was anticipated that many traditional insurers would compete for the MSAs. The plans offered were expected to be high-deductible, loosely managed health care products marketed to the small-group and individual markets. Although MSAs are less interesting to most standard HMOs, Congress's intent was to entice federally qualified HMOs to offer MSAs for the Medicare population. The Medicare + Choice program includes a category for MSAs as a qualifying Medicare + Choice plan. A model for integrating MSAs into an HMO model is discussed in chapter 7.

There are inconsistencies between managed care and MSAs. For example, capitation fees are not tax deductible medical expenses under rules. This means that HMOs would have to perform the administrative task of calculating discounts from in-network providers separately from out-of-network, nonqualified charges. In addition, MSAs appear to discourage early and ongoing preventive care, an underpinning of the managed care philosophy, in favor of waiting for a health care problem to develop before accessing health care services. Finally, although MSAs do not specifically address pharmacy benefits, nothing precludes using an MSA to buy medicine. Medicare + Choice is foundering on that issue.

In 1998, only about 50,000 people availed themselves of the MSA option. As a consequence, it is difficult to assess the pilot project.

Q 3:45 What are the concerns in the industry about implementing MSAs?

Large employers and MCOs have been cautious about MSAs. MSAs represent a significant change in the health care benefit system because they allow the individual user of health care services to control medical dollars without oversight. Supporters of MSAs claim that MSAs create economic incentives for employees to ensure that the medical services they receive are necessary and priced competitively. Placing choice within the control of the consumer has been touted as a significant feature of the Health Reform Act. Unfortunately, the savings potential of the MSA is subject to the "20/80 rule," which is that 20 percent of plan participants usually account for 80 percent of total medical claims. Unfortunately, MSAs do not provide adequate incentives to conserve for that small portion of individuals who account for most of the cost. This lack of incentives also makes MSAs vulnerable to adverse selection and exploitation.

Other concerns raised about MSAs include (1) the ability of plan participants to make prudent decisions regarding their health care needs and (2) the ability of plan participants to negotiate price and monitor the charges for health care services. Organizations may funnel healthy individuals from the broader insurance pool to the MSA model. This has the unexpected consequence of adverse selection and imbalanced utilization rates. The consequence to the employer may be higher premiums for its general product.

Those who have evaluated various models for MSA programs have considered marrying the MSA method of funding an individual's ability to purchase a policy with an HMO plan. This would allow the individual to access a network of providers and not have to negotiate separately with the providers. There are already MSA plans that provide access to PPOs. Therefore, MSAs should be able to link up with HMOs to achieve the cost savings and efficiencies of managed care.

Q 3:46 How can an MSA work with an HMO?

Under a typical MSA arrangement, the patient pays the doctor and then bills the MSA. One option would be to foster the "no claim, copay" situation in which the MSA pays out in a manner similar to the manner in which a credit union does, with the ability to use a debit card at the point of service. For the MSA-HMO arrangement to work, managed care networks would have to think of themselves as "retail" health care delivery outlets. This approach would allow HMOs to negotiate "wholesale" prices for provider access and then sell it back to participants at higher, but still discounted, "retail" prices. This would require disclosure for ERISA plans pursuant to Department of Labor rules.

In an example of how the MSA-HMO scenario would work, Howard Tarre describes an arrangement whereby an HMO sells the participant a plan with a large deductible to be drawn against the MSA, with 100 percent coverage after the deductible is met.[14] For example, if the deductible is set at $2,000, the participant places $1,000 in the MSA, leaving individual exposure of $1,000 as an out-of-pocket expense until the deductible is met. This exposure is the risk portion of the MSA-HMO arrangement.

The participant receives a provider list that is the same as the provider list for other HMO products. Incentives are created to encourage the participant to go through a referral to access specialty services by setting lower prices for the services. When the participant sees a primary care physician, using a card-swipe system, his or her MSA is debited for the cost of the service that is not paid to the physician, who is still paid on a capitation basis by the HMO. The physician is paid a small "copayment" to ensure participant cooperation with the card-swipe system. When the participant goes to a specialist for consultation, the same card-swipe method is used to debit the MSA for the consultation, and the deductible is treated as a charge to the participant. If the charges for the services ultimately exceed the amount of the deductible (e.g., $1,000), the participant is billed the difference and the catastrophic coverage portion of the HMO plan covers the remainder of the expenses for the rest of the year.

Essentially, this MSA approach requires the participant to "self-insure" up to the amount of the deductible, using the MSA to defray the costs in reaching that deductible amount. In addition, there is a financial incentive to go through the referring primary care physician to obtain the deep discount for the services of specialists in lieu of directly accessing specialists.

Q 3:47 Is the MSA model appropriate for Medicare enrollees?

There is much to be learned from the private sector's experience with the consumer choice model. In fact, the MSA approach to allowing Medicare-eligible individuals to purchase coverage directly from qualified HMOs using MSA dollars is consistent with a consumer choice model. Caution is advised in view of the susceptibility of the Medicare-eligible population and the political sensitivity of the Medicare program. Various managed care models for Medicare are discussed in chapter 7.

Q 3:48   What is the current status of the MSA?

The MSA pilot project was intended to last only through 2001. Although MSAs were not under active discussion at the time of this writing, the Bush Administration's intent has been to expand MSAs beyond the current limits and to make them permanent. Because of the similarities of the tax advantages of MSAs and individual retirement accounts (IRAs), there are enormous tax consequences to expanding MSAs making them permanent. Other issues include adverse selection, lowered deductibles, and lack of utilization controls.

Special Programs, Practitioners, and Products

Q 3:49   What is a private label health product?

A private label health product is a product offered by an organization that develops its own managed care products, options, and services, and then contracts with various vendors, including licensed insurers, to support the insurance, claims, and other administrative and marketing functions required of a health plan. One of the companies offering "designer" private label plans using the vendor model is Celsus Health Group, a consulting and management company based in Dallas, Texas. Celsus is developing private label strategies for several community-based providers that want to offer a private label product.

Q 3:50   What is required to establish a private label health plan?

To establish a private label health plan, the entity must establish the plan's goals, as well as identify the services the plan will require on an outsourced, vendor basis. Most private label plans are built around provider organizations that "rent" licenses and insurance services from commercial carriers; however, there is significant flexibility in the design of these plans, and some of the more innovative organizations are developing their insurance capabilities on a "design" basis. To develop a private label plan, the following considerations are applicable:

Goals. The goals of most private label plans are to (1) control relationships with payers, (2) gain a larger share of the premium dollar, and (3) create marketable products. To do these things, the organization must have a cooperative, long-term, and win-win partnership with hospitals, physicians, and vendors.

Organization Requirements. To have a successful private label plan, there must be (1) a partnership between the hospitals and physicians, (2) transaction processing systems, (3) the ability to manage risk, (4) the ability to accept risk, (5) managed care expertise, (6) vendor partners, and (7) compliance programs.

Infrastructure Requirements. The infrastructure requirements to manage and maintain a private label plan include (1) actuarial services, (2) benefit administration and services, (3) third-party administration, (4) medical management, (5) marketing, (6) risk management, (7) wrap-network access, and (8) legal and compliance programs.

Key Services (by Product). Some of the more critical support functions required to support a private label product for all plans include (1) reinsurance (self-funded and provider), (2) indemnity (individual, small group, and large group), (3) HMO, with and without POS (commercial, Medicare, and Medicaid), and (4) workers' compensation.

Drivers of Change in Managed Care Products

Q 3:51   How can economic, political, and consumer issues be expected to influence health plan design?

Rising premiums coupled with a less robust economy can reasonably be expected to put pressure on the consumer to pay more of the cost of health care. This will likely take the form of defined contribution plans and MSAs. Uwe Reinhardt has commented that consumers will have to comparison-shop and that they do not have the information required to make intelligent choices:

> Imagine going blindfolded into Macy's and being told to buy shirts. You pick a shirt, they say, "We'll send you a bill later," then you drive home. Now, you understand how health care is bought. If you wanted to get prices on health care, you couldn't get [them]. Prices for drugs, you can't get them. Imagine unleashing people into a market where they don't know what they're buying and don't know the price of what they're buying. I can't imagine American consumers saying, "I feel empowered." They'll hate their doctors and their hospitals, and there could be a big backlash if MSAs became widespread.[15]

References

1. Robert B. Teague, M.D., personal communication.

2. Uwe E. Reinhardt, "Managed Competition in Health Care: Are Private Employers Up to the Task?" *Managing Employee Benefits*, 7(2):1–9, Winter 1999.

3. S.M. Butler and R.E. Moffit, "The FEHBP as a Model for a New Medicare Program," *Health Aff.*, 14(4):47–61.

4. http://www.cmwf.org/programs/quality/ stone_mdinternet 503.pdf

5. *See* http://www.health.state.mn.us/divs/hpsc/hep/issbrief/ hmo96.htm (last accessed Sept. 30, 2001).

6. Dan Ermann, "Health Maintenance Organizations: The Future of the For-profit Plan," *J. Amb. Care. Mgmt.*, 9(2): 72–88, 1986.

7. Julie A. Schoenman, Kevin J. Hayes, and C. Michael Cheng, "Medicare Physician Payment Changes: Impact on Physicians and Beneficiaries," *Health Aff.*, 20:2, 2001.

8. Laura Cohn and Pamela L. Moore, "Managed Care Takes to the Sickbed," *Bus. Wk.*, May 15, 2000.

9. M.P. Doescher, P. Franks, J.S. Banthin, et al., "Supplemental Insurance and Mortality in Elderly Americans," *Archives Fam. Med.*, 9:251–257, March 2000.

10. U.L. Aparo, Luca Lorenzoni, Roberto Da Cas et al., "An Analysis of Hospital Productivity," *Casemix Q.,* 1:3, 1999.

11. A.J. Rosoff, "Evidence: Its Meanings in Health Care and in Law," *J. Health Pol., Pol'y & L.,* 26:2, Apr. 2001. Copyright 2001, Duke University Press. All rights reserved; posted with permission.

12. A.J. Rosoff, "Evidence-Based Medicine and the Law: The Courts Confront Clinical Practice Guidelines," *Health Pol., Pol'y & L.*

13. L. Greenberg, "Perspectives on PPO Performance Measurement from Consumers, PPO Leaders, and Employers," Commonwealth Fund Publication #409, Sept. 2000.

14. H. Tarre, "The MSA-Risk HMO: What Looks at First Like Oil and Water Might Really Be Milk and Honey," *Managing Employee Health Benefits,* 5(4):59–63, Summer 1997.

15. *See* http://www.ama-assn.org/sci-pubs/amnews/pick_01/ bisb1001.htm (last accessed Nov. 14, 2001)

Chapter 4

Employer Benefit Plans and Purchasing Organizations

Employers have aligned themselves with managed care to achieve greater cost savings and administrative efficiencies than possible in fee-for-service medicine. Managed care in general and health maintenance organizations in particular offer employers the certainty of knowing their cost exposure. That is, a purchaser of an HMO product shifts the responsibility of allocating medical care to another entity that is also assuming the risk for it.

Recently, employee and political concerns over the quality and accountability of managed care plans have made health care purchasers wary of their relationships with plans. Although employees appreciate the cost savings attendant to HMO care, they resist the restrictions in choice and other burdens associated with a managed care product, and this resistance is daily becoming more vocal. Health care purchasers, both employer and government, are looking to reduce cost and improve access through managed care arrangements and will continue to do so as the burden of payment shifts increasingly to employees.

Most states allow purchasers to form voluntary purchasing groups or coalitions and allow providers to engage in direct contracting with employers or government programs without an insurance company or licensed HMO in the picture. Employers in 28 states and at the federal level are being pulled into political battles over proportionate liability extended to managed care plans, the most threatening of which does away with protections afforded large employers that self-insure company health plans under the Employee Retirement Income Security Act of 1974. This political climate, coupled with almost certain double-digit spending increases for employers, makes direct contracting between employers and physicians and providers a strategy for businesses to explore.

The increase in employer spending for health care raises a number of difficult issues. Among these are the pretax nature of health insurance premiums versus the direct expense of a medical benefit payment; defined benefits versus defined contributions, including the differential exposure to medical costs among employees; and employer responsibility for the health of employees.

This chapter addresses how some employers have responded to the changes in the health care system and the regulations affecting employer benefits.

Overview

Q 4:1 What have been employers' experiences with offering HMOs to their employees?

A June 27, 1997, article by William M. Mercer, Inc., based on a survey of employers, predicted that 40 percent of workers would enroll in HMOs.[1] This has turned out to be true, but only because the definition of HMO has changed. The "HMO heavy" model is decreasing in popularity as an option for insured people outside of Medicaid. HMOs are being transformed into preferred provider organization (PPO) and point-of-service (POS) models but are still being called HMOs. Therefore, it is impossible to compare data on enrollment longitudinally using the rubric *HMO*. Nevertheless, employers still offer options called HMOs and benefits managers still contract with them.

Q 4:2 What criteria do employers use in selecting and evaluating HMOs?

Employers use the following criteria in selecting and evaluating HMOs:

- Access
- Current cost or premiums
- Member satisfaction
- Financial strength
- Reputation of networks
- Ease of doing business
- Outcomes of care
- Prevention and wellness focus
- Accreditation by the National Committee for Quality Assurance
- Historical cost trends
- Ability to improve health status
- Physician turnover
- Physician credentialing
- Reports based on the Health Plan Employer and Data Information Set
- Workers' compensation and time loss

From the employer's perspective, the most effective managed care plans control cost and utilization. They tightly control the cost, use, and appropriateness of services rendered by network providers. They select providers who provide cost-effective care and use benefit design provisions (see Q 4:5) to encourage use of network benefits.

They place utilization controls on both in-network and out-of-network services and use a gatekeeper physician paid on a capitated or discounted fee-for-service basis to control access to the network. They give the physician incentives based on plan performance and employ a common carrier for administration to allow pooling of data and experience.

Q 4:3 What have been providers' responses to the criteria employers use in selecting and evaluating HMOs?

One response by providers and plans has been to offer a greater variety of options from which employers and employees can choose their health care benefits. Single plans with multiple products have evolved in response to the employer's desire to control premium cost and the employee's desire to have choice.

Double-digit percentage premium increases are expected in 2002, along with a broadening of the menu of health plans to encourage more cost sharing with employees. Further, employers are increasingly not offering retiree health insurance to new hires. It is reasonable to expect that retirees will be asked to contribute to the cost of their health care.

Q 4:4 What are employers doing to influence change in the health care system?

By exercising their purchasing power over health insurers, private sector employers, purchasing coalitions, and other private sector organizations have played a key role in health care system change. Their purchasing strategies have influenced shifts from open-ended, fee-for-service arrangements to managed care products on a capitated basis. Employers' purchasing decisions are based on employees' satisfaction with a plan and on premium cost. Employers and other large purchasers of health care benefits are using a number of strategies to reduce premium cost and improve the value and quality of the products they offer to employees, including the following:

- Providing incentives to employees and retirees to select managed care options and requiring employees to share in the cost
- Negotiating for lower increases in premiums
- Introducing competitive bidding for plan contracts

- Setting standards for quality, access, and performance
- Contracting directly with providers through independent practice associations (IPAs), exclusive provider organizations (EPOs) where allowed by state law, and independent consolidators of insurance business
- Demanding greater accountability from providers and plans (e.g., requiring accreditation)

Some employers have adopted a system under which they provide a defined contribution toward the cost of health insurance to each employee. The amount of the contribution may be equal for all employees or may be based on the cost of the available health plans. The two model public sector purchasers, the Federal Employees Health Benefits Program (FEHBP) and the California Public Employees' Retirement System (CPERS), have implemented this approach.

Benefit Plan Design

Q 4:5   What factors are considered in designing a health benefit plan?

The first step in designing a health benefit plan is to establish a schedule of benefits. How providers' allowable charges will be determined is considered next. These charges can be based on fee schedules or negotiated rates. Often, no balance billing is allowed. Once the allowable charges are determined and accepted as eligible expenses covered by the plan, benefit design provisions, including the following, are considered:

Deductible. Commonly, a flat dollar amount will be paid before benefits are paid. This amount is deducted from covered charges and generally runs on an annual basis.

Coinsurance. Often some percentage of the covered charges is borne by the patient and the rest by the benefit plan.

Copayment. Sometimes a flat dollar amount is paid directly to the provider at the time services are rendered for office visits or prescription drugs.

Out-of-Pocket Maximum. There is often a dollar limit on the total amount of covered charges paid by an individual or family. After that point, the cost sharing ends, and the plan pays for covered charges in full. The intent is to limit the employee's liability for catastrophic care.

Per-Confinement Deductible. A flat dollar amount may be applied to each hospital confinement, including outpatient surgery. This provision has been used most recently by HMOs to share the first dollar coverage costs.

Percentage-of-Pay Cost Sharing. Some percentage of an employee's salary (e.g., 1 percent) determines the premium contribution, deductible, or coinsurance. The out-of-pocket maximum can also be capped as a percentage of pay. These percentages may vary, depending on whether services are provided in network or out of network. This approach creates some administrative difficulties and requires considerable accuracy on the part of the claims administrator. The advantage of this approach is that lower-paid employees view it as equitable, and cost sharing becomes more tied to economic means.

Annual and Lifetime Maximums. Benefit limits are commonly fixed on either an annual or lifetime basis. The limits are often different for different benefits (e.g., dental, psychiatric, or podiatric care). Limits can be made on the basis of a total dollar amount, the number of visits, or each admission.

Penalty Provisions. Benefits may be reduced for failure to comply with plan requirements.

Incentives. Higher levels of benefits for compliance with plan requirements (e.g., using preferred providers or obtaining preadmission testing) can result in greater voluntary compliance with plan requirements by employees.

Q 4:6   How do managed care organizations get into trouble?

The failed managed care organization (MCO) is the benefit manager's nightmare, since continuity of care, pricing and budget certainty, quality of care, and hospital networks are disrupted by the need to change providers quickly. A number of problems are common to MCOs, including undercapitalization of new plans, predatory pricing, overpricing of services, unrealistic financial projections, uncontrolled growth and overextended management, incurred but not reported (IBNR) liabilities, failure to reconcile accounts receivable and membership, use of improper underwriting criteria, not understanding reports, difficulty tracking medical costs and utilization, and educating and dealing with noncompliant providers.[2]

Undercapitalization. New plans are at increased risk for uncontrolled losses that can range into the millions of dollars even in the first year. This risk can be minimized at the outset by using an experienced actuary or financial consultant to estimate losses before the break-even point under multiple scenarios. Plans may fail on the basis of undercapitalization, which is an important reason for the underwriting and solvency requirements of insurance and HMO laws and regulations in most states.

Predatory Pricing. Some plans use artificially low premium pricing to enter and capture a market share position. This is a high-risk strategy that must be factored into the plan's capitalization requirements. The key to survival, and, ultimately, to success, is to sustain the losses as long as possible and outlast the competition. Unfortunately, this approach can precipitate price wars among plans that often never recoup their losses.

Overpricing. Overpricing may be a reaction to a previous price war among plans. It can also reflect other problems, such as excessive overhead, failure to control utilization and medical costs, adverse selection, or just pure greed.

Unrealistic Financial Projections. The two most common errors made in financial projections are overestimating enrollment and underestimating medical expenses. Many factors contribute to these problems, which can be minimized through the effective and appropriate purchase of reinsurance for the plan.

Uncontrolled Growth. The uncontrolled, rapid growth of a managed care plan can be a mixed blessing. It has the potential of outstripping the plan's resources and may result in poor quality, inadequate management, and reversal in the market as a result of client dissatisfaction. A plan should anticipate its growth and attempt to plan for controlled growth. The converse, low subscription in a competitive market, can also occur and does not lessen the plan's liabilities for contracted services.

Incurred but Not Reported Liabilities. Of critical importance to the sustained solvency of a plan is its ability to anticipate accrued IBNR claims. Some plans have difficulty capturing IBNR data, particularly during times of expansion. This problem has accounted for many health plan failures and is often associated with serious claims: processing problems and inadequate utilization controls.

Failure to Reconcile Accounts Receivable. The liability of the plan for items under risk requires as accurate a membership count as possible. Most plans undergo changes in membership on a monthly basis. Government programs such as Medicaid and Medicare may have many members leaving the rolls on a monthly basis. This problem has contributed to the reluctance of MCOs to inaugurate Medicare + Choice plans and to withdraw from markets where these plans exist. Other government programs, such as the FEHBP, are chronically late in reporting membership changes.

Improper Underwriting Criteria. Strict underwriting criteria are important to a plan's ability to project its costs based on enrollment. This area is subject to reform by federal and state health insurance legislation.

Not Understanding Reports. Not all plan managers fully understand the information that is or should be contained in the reports prepared for the plan. For example, reports of disenrollment rates may be misleadingly high if they include members who changed status or coverage but continue with the same plan under a different group. Management should be involved in developing the formats of these reports and the information to be included in them.

Difficulty Tracking Medical Costs and Utilization. Tracking medical costs and utilization is critically important for avoiding serious financial problems and spurious reports of poor performance. Most plans base their utilization and quality programs on medical cost and utilization information reports. Errors in reporting or lags in the timing of such reports can have serious consequences.

Noncompliant Providers. A plan's success or failure can hinge on the knowledge and capability of its provider panel. Effective orientation of new providers and their office staff as to plan policies and procedures is an important first step, along with continuing education and effective programs of quality and utilization improvement. The more difficult task is dealing effectively with noncompliant providers.

Since most states having "any willing provider" laws, these laws will have to be taken into consideration in the selection and deselection process. This issue is discussed in more detail in chapter 8.

Q 4:7   What are the challenges facing employers in meeting employee demands for health benefits?

The present health care system tends to place employers and employees at odds with each other. Employers are concerned with health care cost management. Employees want open access and choice in their health plans. The challenge is to design a benefit strategy that addresses this fundamental conflict. A complicating factor is that a small percentage of the employee population usually accounts for a large percentage of health care costs.

Satisfaction is hard to judge, but it appears that most people are reasonably satisfied with their health plans and their doctors; this could change as consumerism takes hold as a movement.

Q 4:8   How can employers achieve cost control while preserving some level of employee satisfaction?

Benefits for using network providers need to exceed those for using non-network providers by enough of a margin to encourage the use of the former. Cost sharing is appropriate to discourage high utilization. Another way to encourage network use is to require that specific types of services be provided in network in order to be covered. Generally, these are the more costly procedures, such as organ transplants, mental health care, chemical dependency treatment, heart surgery, and high-risk obstetrical procedures.

Another technique is to use an HMO plan, with the out-of-plan benefits structured as a comprehensive medical plan with annual deductibles and 80 percent employer and 20 percent employee co-insurance. Another is to use higher copayments for office visits when the patient goes outside the plan. Employee cost increases with the use of out-of-plan services. This is attractive to employees who live in areas that are outside the network but who still have access to providers whose services will be covered at some level.

In a PPO, the incentives could be much like those used in the open-ended HMO. PPOs offer greater design flexibility because cost sharing is usually based on a percentage of cost rather than on co-payments. Usually, hospitals and physicians in a PPO have agreed to specific rates, and employees pay coinsurance as a percentage of the total rate.

An unanticipated effect of managed care that is not well quantified is out-of-pocket payment to providers for services that are difficult to obtain in the network. It appears that this occurs more frequently in obstetrics and gynecology and in mental health care.

Q 4:9   What are some of the challenges faced by employers in designing benefit plans?

Areas that pose a challenge in benefit plan design include the following:

Uniformity of Plans and Benefits. One of the major problems with any benefit program is achieving parity or uniformity, particularly when the employer does business in many parts of the country or has employees who live in different communities, even if they work in the same location. The mobile workforce has posed some interesting challenges for benefit plan design, particularly in compliance with the mandates of the Health Insurance Portability and Accountability Act of 1996. Minor inconsistencies in plan design can occur even when benefits are managed by a single carrier. Other inconsistencies occur because of competitive factors. For example, one carrier may refuse to participate if its products are not offered in each area where the employer does business.

Managed Mental Health Care. Some employers are responding to the costs associated with mental health care services by entering into exclusive provider arrangements or by carving out mental health and chemical dependency benefits from the medical benefits and contracting these out separately. When a single organization is made the gatekeeper for mental health care services, the organization is usually responsible for initially assessing the patient's needs, referring the patient to an appropriate provider, certifying the need for inpatient care, and reviewing emergency admissions within 24 hours to determine the appropriate course of treatment and the need for hospitalization.

Flexible Compensation. Managed care plans and flexible compensation are compatible. A fully flexible compensation program allows employees to choose how they will use employer contributions and their own salaries to purchase benefits. It defines the employer's cost while providing employees with choices for their benefit dollars. An employer may offer one or several medical plans under a flexible program. The fundamental issue is whether one medical plan can meet the needs of all employees and still allow for cost containment. Employee needs may vary, depending on whether there are employees who have dual coverage, whether there are high- and low-compensation employees in the same workplace, and so on. This will affect the choice of a plan. A pure HMO offers a less costly alternative than a POS plan, but HMOs are not available in all geographic locations. Since new health care benefit and financing arrangements will continue to evolve, an employer may want to design a variety of medical benefit options that offer choices among provider delivery systems, varying the degree of freedom of choice, or may introduce cost-sharing alternatives.

Multiple Options. Many carriers offer multiple-option plans with a lock-in or POS arrangement. These plans depend on network availability and can take many different forms. The following are some common delivery system combinations:

Plan Option	System	Alternative Systems*
Dual	Indemnity	HMO
	Indemnity	PPO
	HMO	PPO
	HMO	EPO
	Workers' compensation PPO	PPO (medical)
Triple	Indemnity	HMO or PPO
	PPO	EPO or indemnity
Multiple	Indemnity	PPO (standard and 50% copayment for out-of-network care: HMO look-alike)
Indemnity	HMO (standard and POS)	PPO
	Indemnity	PPO (ancillary-specific services, e.g., dental and vision)
	PPO	Workers' compensation PPO Indemnity
	PPO	EPO Workers' compensation PPO

* Not all EPOs are designed to be HMO alternative products, as was originally the case. EPOs may emerge as strategic hybrid products in more highly competitive markets.

Pricing Plans. Pricing managed care plans may be based on actual cost or actuarial value. Actual cost is based on claims experience (also used for experience rating). Actuarial value represents each option as if all employees were participating. How the plans are priced can contribute significantly to plan enrollment, depending on employer subsidy levels. Clearly, employers need more flexibility in pooling the experience of their medical plans and pricing plans based on their value to the employee. This means that the plans have to be sufficiently flexible to allow employers to charge employees on the basis of plan design value, and employees should be able to select a plan based on a number of factors, both subjective and objective.

Q 4:10 Why do employers purchase health care through managed care products?

The reasons for this vary, depending on an employer's size, industry, culture, financial viability, and history. There is also an enormous difference between the way public and private employers purchase health care. For public entities, the dollars invested in health care are tax dollars. Therefore, public entities are subject to strict, sometimes cumbersome rules regarding the purchase of care. Other employers may collectively bargain for the type of health benefits they will provide. Although each employer may look at purchasing health benefits differently, certain common elements have moved many employers to use managed care.

Cost. Health care costs have recently been growing at a rate exceeding twice the growth rate of the gross domestic product (GDP). Of all the strategies that employers have used to combat this problem, managed care seems to have had the most success. The transferring of risk from the employer to the MCO and/or to providers has been very appealing to employers. Through 1996, managed care stabilized employer costs. Since then, there has been an increase in costs with a rapid increase in premiums.

Accountability. Unlike other products and services that employers procure, health care benefits have been rather difficult to gauge in terms of the quality of the services provided. Mechanisms for judging the quality of care are in their infancy. In addition, most medical providers are reluctant to provide information on their performance to their customers, partly because of the complex nature of their specialty, partly because customers have never asked (or known how to ask), and partly because of economic self-interest, as well as confidentiality and medical liability. Without information to judge the quality of care, purchasers can focus only on the cost aspect of the product, not on its value. What managed care companies have capitalized on is their willingness to be held accountable for their results in managing care for a population of patients and employers. For a fixed fee, they take the risk for providing a wide spectrum of health care services. In addition, they are willing to be rated for performance and customer service. Increasingly, HMOs have been willing to sign multiyear contracts and have a series of performance standards built into their contracts that put them at financial risk if they are unable to deliver on service standards for items as diverse as appointment scheduling, telephone response, member satisfaction, immunization rates, and even improved health status of a given population.

Value. Employers define value in health care benefits as appropriate medical care delivered in an appropriate setting at competitive, predictable pricing. Creating value begins by choosing a benefit plan design that covers medical procedures but does not encourage overutilization of medical services. Managed care actively manages the utilization of medical services by comparing actual and proposed medical services against clinical benchmarks. Next, the managed care company negotiates competitive financial arrangements with a series of service providers. These negotiations have transformed the provider industry from a cost-plus business to one that has by necessity become more price sensitive and cost effective. These negotiations and contractual arrangements link the providers and employers by shifting and sharing risk. With the advent of multiyear contracts between the parties, pricing for the employer has become not only competitive but also more predictable. Standard performance measures, such as HEDIS, provide employers with tools to evaluate and negotiate for health services on behalf of their employees. Although the definition of value may vary slightly among employers, the overall trend of purchasing health benefits on criteria other than price alone is significant.

Q 4:11 How else can employers reduce the cost of health care?

Typically, an employer periodically reviews the scope of its benefits package. It may modify the level of deductibles, coinsurance amounts, lifetime benefit levels, specific services covered, and other aspects of a benefits package. If the employer is not large enough to negotiate or modify its own plan design, it may take its plan specifications to a benefits broker or agent to find competing products with plan designs close to what it wants.

Once the appropriate level of benefits is attained, the employer may look at specific cost management services to help "manage the delivery of care." These services typically include second opinion services on elective surgery, hospital preadmission reviews, case management programs, hospital bill audits, and other programs aimed primarily at the overutilization of health services. Some employers have reviewed whether the financing of their health benefits should be done on a fully insured, partially insured, or self-funded basis.

In addition, the employer may decide to increase the employee's responsibility for the premium. More employers are doing this, particularly for dependent care. Although most large employers offer their employees several health plan options, the trend is toward limiting health plan offerings to achieve administrative and volume efficiencies, particularly among small employers. The clear trend is to avoid restricting services or access to care but rather to shift the financial burden to the employee.

Q 4:12 Have PPOs been successful in managing costs for employers?

The answer depends on the type of PPO. Some early PPOs negotiated contracts for a certain percentage off the provider's retail prices. These arrangements simply encouraged providers to raise their retail rates. Other set rates were negotiated without utilization controls; the result was the overutilization of certain medical tests and procedures by the providers. The most effective PPOs have combined negotiated pricing with utilization review or comparative practice or peer benchmarking reviews. This information, especially if it is shared with the purchasers of the services, is a powerful cost management tool.

The newer generation of PPOs may use some of the economic disincentives and controls used by HMOs. For example, many PPO arrangements are using gatekeeper physicians to control specialty referrals and are transferring some of the financial risk to providers. With these changes, the distinction between a PPO and an HMO becomes less clear. In fact, with the double-digit rise in premiums expected for 2002, employers have ceded control of the market to consumers, expecting them to make decisions that are in their best interests using their own money.

Q 4:13 How common are POS arrangements in employee benefit plans?

The POS arrangement is a rapidly growing managed care hybrid and is becoming increasingly popular among plans and provider organizations such as IPAs and physician-hospital organizations (PHOs). POS plans encourage the use of contracted managed care networks while allowing freedom of choice; that is, they pay a reduced percentage for out-of-network services.

Under a POS plan, employees are not locked into a specific plan or provider panel for the entire plan year but can choose among certain health care plans at the time they seek health care services. When employees require medical care for themselves or a dependant, they can choose a provider from within the managed care network or from outside the network. Care in a POS network is tightly managed using gatekeeper physicians, and employees enjoy lower deductibles or copayments and a larger scope of benefits. For a higher premium, health care coverage can extend beyond the closed provider network.

Q 4:14 What types of incentives are used in a POS plan?

The deductible and copayment structures differ among the various plan options accessed under a POS arrangement. A typical plan may include a core benefit, a 10 percent copayment for office visits, and low or no payment for inpatient and outpatient services. Individuals who opt out of the provider network pay significant deductibles and coinsurance, perhaps a 40 percent copayment with 60 percent coverage out of network compared to a 10 percent copayment with 90 percent coverage for network providers.

Q 4:15 Why would an employer offer a POS plan?

The primary reason for an employer to offer a POS plan is to allow its employees to maintain some freedom of choice in the selection of health care providers. POS plans can also serve as a transition step for an employer that wants to move from an indemnity plan to an HMO. This strategy can be highly successful. Because POS plans cover out-of-network providers, albeit with higher patient copayments, workers are less likely to feel that they are being forced to relinquish their established doctor-patient relationships. At the same time, they are very likely to forgo those relationships and to choose network providers. A 1999 Milliman & Robertson report demonstrates that 90 percent of POS claims are for network providers.[3] Finally, an employer might offer a POS plan if travel time to network providers is a significant issue.

Although POS plans can be cost effective for employers, employers that already offer an HMO option should not expect automatic savings from adding a POS option. POS plans are likely to attract older and sicker employees (because they are more likely to have long-standing relationships with their caregivers), and the benefit design can greatly affect the plan's ability to deliver savings. Milliman & Robertson found that a POS plan within an HMO benefit design could either increase or decrease claim costs by 10 percent, depending on the HMO's selection of benefit designs.[4]

The apparent industry trend toward loose networks and unfettered access to subspecialty services has dangers. Consumers are attempting to navigate the waters of an increasingly complicated medical system without a guide. David Lawrence[5] offers an intelligent solution that emphasizes the role of a primary care physician to help manage care, not to block access to needed services.

Health Care Purchasing Coalitions

Q 4:16 What is the primary role of an employer health care purchasing coalition?

The primary role of an employer health care purchasing coalition is to focus on alternative delivery systems, benefit design, data analysis, health education, planning, legislative activities, and competitive promotion. Some coalitions have even sponsored the development of PPOs and HMOs; others have supported bringing in outside HMOs to establish local programs. More than 20 states have adopted legislation to help establish some form of purchasing cooperative, recognizing the value of aggregating small-employer groups into purchasing cooperatives in order to obtain the benefits available to larger employers. Although most states allow purchasing cooperatives to restrict choice, some states, including California, Minnesota, and Kentucky, have designed pools to expand the choice of health plans.

The idea of cooperatives is not new in industry, although it is a novel concept for health care. Major purchasing organizations such as CalPERS (for California state employees) and the Cleveland, Ohio-based Council of Smaller Enterprises have been models for the development of alliances. In view of the complicating unknown of ERISA preemption, many states have initiated legislation to authorize the formation of organizations variously referred to as alliances, health insurance purchasing cooperatives, or employer coalitions. Features of a coalition or cooperative usually include premium rates based on risk pooling among a large number of employers; rates guaranteed for a fixed period of time; risk sharing with physicians and hospitals; and performance levels based on medical outcomes, patient satisfaction, and service levels.

Q 4:17   How do purchasing coalitions help to control health care costs?

One important way purchasing coalitions help to control costs is by obtaining negotiated discounts for insurance or provider rates using the leverage of numbers. A coalition of 100,000 lives has much greater bargaining power than an individual employer with 50 to 500 employees. Some coalitions provide their members with information on health care issues to use in altering their benefit programs. Others support legislation that is beneficial to employers. Many are mixed-model coalitions containing health care purchasers, providers, and others. A few, however, are purchaser-only organizations.

Health care purchasing coalitions have also banded together to create for even more purchasing power and to standardize plan analysis. The National Business Coalition on Health (NBCH; www.nbch. org), an umbrella group of state and local employee coalitions involved in group purchasing efforts and the quest for value and accountability in the health care system, has developed a tool, Standardized Health Plan RFI/RFP Toolkit Version 2.0, that allows purchasers to evaluate plans in a systematized fashion.

Purchasing coalitions have been leaders in measuring quality and outcomes and in using these measures as a basis for making health care purchasing decisions.

Q 4:18   How effective have purchasing coalitions been in managing health care costs?

Results have varied depending on the market and the coalition. Certain alliances are run by state governments; others are employer sponsored. Many of the state alliances are aimed at the uninsured and the small-employer market. Several employer coalitions target ERISA-protected employers.

The most successful purchasing coalitions are located in urban markets such as Denver, Houston, Minneapolis, Orlando, and Memphis. The Pacific Business Group on Health has been successful in obtaining significant reductions in HMO premiums for its members, who have agreed to a common evaluation tool for the managed care plans. New efforts in smaller markets, in states such as Iowa, Kansas, Alabama, and Virginia, sometimes group-purchase managed care products or may directly contract with physicians and hospitals for services and bypass the MCO.

Q 4:19   Have any model purchasing coalitions been successful?

Several purchasing coalitions have reported not only significant reductions in the cost of health plan premiums but also increased levels of employee satisfaction with the managed care plans available. The Washington Business Group on Health (www.wbgh.com) has staked out a leadership position in demanding quality and accountability from health plans. The Houston Healthcare Purchasing Organization (www.hhpo.com) claims members have experienced a 30 percent reduction in cost by using its contracted services rather than paying on a fee-for-service basis. Payment for contracted services may be an improvement over direct payment, but the savings so achieved do not approach the price reductions possible in more tightly managed (and thus more restrictive) environments.

Q 4:20 How else can purchasing coalitions affect health care?

Purchasing coalitions have influenced the way medicine is practiced. A study by the Memphis coalition focused on the level of cesarean sections performed at area hospitals. The data were used to reduce these procedures by almost 30 percent. The Ozarks business coalition was instrumental in helping to bring primary care physicians into rural Missouri. The Orlando coalitions utilized a common hospital database analysis program to evaluate care in Florida institutions. Coalitions of employer purchasers are breaking new ground with their concept of value-based purchasing.

Q 4:21 What is the Leapfrog Group?

The Leapfrog Group is a coalition of Fortune 500 companies with a mission "to trigger giant leaps forward in patient safety, as well as the overall quality, customer service, and affordability of health care." Consisting of more than 90 public and private organizations that provide health care benefits and representing approximately 28 million health care consumers in all 50 states, the Leapfrog Group works with medical experts throughout the United States to identify problems and propose solutions that it believes will improve hospital systems that could break down and harm patients. It provides important information and solutions for consumers and health care providers.

The Leapfrog Group conducted a survey of 900 hospitals in June 2001 regarding the three initial safety leaps:

1. *Computerized physician order entry.* Physician order entry in hospitals should be computerized because adverse drug events are a major area of concern and opportunity for improvement in health care practice.

2. *Intensive care unit (ICU) physician staffing.* Hospital ICU care should be "managed by a physician certified (or eligible for certification) in critical care medicine, who: (1) is present during daytime hours and provides clinical care exclusively in the ICU and, (2) at other times, returns more than 95 percent of ICU pages within five minutes (unless the paging system can designate low-urgency pages), and can rely on an 'effector' (physician or physician extender) who is in the hospital and

able to reach ICU patients within 5 minutes in more than 95 percent of cases." Intensivists in only about 10 percent of ICUs in the United States currently meet these standards per Leapfrog Group reports.

3. *Evidence-based hospital referral.* Elective treatment should be guided by providers to hospitals and clinical teams with superior outcomes if valid comparative quality measurement systems exist; if not, such guidance should be based on scientific evidence of volume-outcome relationships.

Hospitals that fulfill the computerized physician order entry standard will

1. Require physicians to enter medication orders via computers linked to prescribing error prevention software;

2. Demonstrate that their computerized physician order entry system can intercept at least 50 percent of common serious prescribing errors, utilizing test cases and a testing protocol specified by the Institute for Safe Medication Practices;

3. Require documented acknowledgment by the prescribing physician of the interception prior to any override; and

4. Post the test case interception rate on a Leapfrog-designated Web site.

Hospitals that satisfy the evidence-based hospital referral standard will meet these favorable hospital volume characteristics:

1. Coronary artery bypass with an annual volume of 500 or more;

2. Coronary angioplasty with an annual volume of 400 or more;

3. Carotid endarterectomy with an annual volume of 100 or more;

4. Abdominal aortic aneurysm repair with an annual volume of 30;

5. Esophageal cancer surgery with an annual volume of 100;

6. Delivery with expected birth weights under 1,500 grams or gestation age under 32 weeks for a regional neonatal ICU with average daily census of 15 or more; and

Table 4-1. Benefits Expected from Leapfrog Group's Safety Initiatives

Safety Initiative	Potential Benefit with Full Implementation
CPOE	522,000 serious medication errors avoided
EHR	
Five high-risk procedures	2,581 lives saved
High-risk deliveries	1,863 lives saved
IPS	53,850 lives saved

CPOE—Computerized physician order entry
HER—Evidence-based hospital referral
IPS—ICU physician staffing

7. Delivery with prenatal diagnosis of major congenital anomalies for a regional neonatal ICU with average daily census of 15 or more.

Leapfrog Group purchasers will continue to share results from these surveys with enrollees and the general public as part of its goal of initiating breakthroughs in the safety of health care in the United States.[6]

Research sponsored by the Business Roundtable suggests enormous benefits can be expected from adopting the Leapfrog Group's standard. These benefits are outlined in Table 4-1.[7]

The Leapfrog Group published rankings of 241 hospitals and their accomplishment of the three Leapfrog Group standards in January 2002. The American Hospital Association is promulgating its own standards. The Leapfrog Group standards are not accepted by the hospital industry. Only five hospitals in Texas participated in the Survey of Standards, and only one, a major university teaching hospital, was able to meet one of the standards (ICU staffing). Nonetheless, this effort by the Leapfrog Group is rippling through the industry.

Q 4:22 How many employer health care purchasing coalitions currently exist in the United States?

The NBCH estimates that there are over 150 employer health care purchasing coalitions in the United States. As of January 2002, the NBCH had nearly 85 members, representing over 11,000 employers and 21 million employees and dependents. These members come from small markets, such as Madison, Wisconsin, and large metropolitan areas, such as Houston, Texas. Some coalitions have organized on a statewide basis, such as the Pacific Business Group on Health in California.

Q 4:23 Who joins a business health care coalition?

Coalition membership varies by market and coalition mission. For example, the coalition in Detroit, Michigan, includes employers, labor unions, and providers. Coalition membership in other markets is usually dominated by large employers. Several coalitions target only small businesses.

Many coalitions have two classes of membership. Corporate members (often the employers) are the purchasers of health care. Associate members are usually providers of some form of health care service, such as managed care companies, hospitals, physician groups, and pharmaceutical companies. Associate members do not always have the right to sit on the coalition's board or to vote on certain issues, particularly if there might be a conflict of interest.

Q 4:24 How are business health care coalitions structured?

The answer varies with the coalition market and mission. Most business health care coalitions started as Internal Revenue Code (IRC) Section 501(c)(3) tax-exempt nonprofit organizations that served educational and research purposes by allowing educational information to be shared among members and the community. More recently, however, several new legal structures have evolved as coalitions have assumed a more active role as group purchasing agents or organizations, or as they enter into direct contracts for certain medical services. Some coalitions have developed joint ventures with their members. Others have developed a legal cooperative structure. Several statewide coalitions have obtained Code Section 501(c)(6) tax-exempt trade association status and focus on lobbying and political action at the state level. Most recently, primarily because of reluctance by the IRS to grant business health care coalitions tax-exempt status, more coalitions have become for-profit ventures, usually "owned" by their business members, or they have created management services companies to operate the nonprofit organization.

Small-Employer Purchasing Groups

Q 4:25   What problems do small employers or self-employed individuals face in obtaining insurance?

One business sector that is not adequately served by the insurance industry is the small employer or self-employed individual. Affordable coverage is often unavailable to small employers, which are most vulnerable to adverse selection, escalating premium rates, and strict exclusions for preexisting conditions. Coverage may be unavailable for people who are expected to have high levels of health expenditures either because of their health status or the type of work they do. Other concerns include differences in premiums paid by consumers in the individual or small-group market versus those paid by consumers in the large-group market. Interruption or loss of coverage because of changes in employment status or location is also an issue.

Q 4:26   How can small businesses and the self-employed be protected in the small-group insurance market?

Most small-group insurers handpick their insureds to avoid significant risk. To improve the functioning of the insurance market for small groups and individuals, the Prospective Payment Review Commission (PPRC) has made the following suggestions, several of which have been incorporated into the Health Insurance Portability and Accountability Act of 1996 (HIPAA).

Market Rules and Rating Restrictions. Market rules should be developed to reduce risk selection by limiting insurers' ability to exclude groups and to promote continuity of coverage by reducing incentives for both the groups and insurers to change their insurance contracts. These rules, which are similar to those included in the National Association of Insurance Commissioners (NAIC) model laws, include:

Guaranteed issue. All insurers that sell policies in the small-group market should offer those same policies to all small employers, regardless of the health condition of their employees. Insurers should also limit the length of any exclusion (e.g., six months) for pre-existing conditions.

Guaranteed renewability. The small employer must have the option to renew its health plan except in limited circumstances (e.g., nonpayment of premiums or insurer's withdrawal from the market). Premium increases should be limited to a certain percentage over the increases in that insurer's rate for new business.

Portability. Insurers must waive the preexisting condition exclusion for a person who was previously covered as recently as 30 to 90 days earlier.

Market restrictions. Health plans must not use selective marketing practices aimed at attracting less risky employers.

Rating restrictions. There should be some form of community rating or rating restrictions. NAIC's model laws proposed limiting the difference between the lowest and highest premium rates charged to different premium classes to 20 percent and the variation within a premium class to 25 percent. Under this model, premium risk classes are based on certain characteristics, excluding health status, race, and sex.

Risk Adjustment and Reinsurance. Insurers will argue that the foregoing rules and rating reforms will put them at increased financial risk because the premiums will no longer reflect the expected risk of each insured group. To prevent this, payments to plans should be adjusted to reflect the risk of their enrollees and further reduce the incentives for risk selection. The use of risk adjusters with reinsurance should help. In a voluntary market, employers or purchasing groups could use risk adjusters to modify the published premiums seen by their enrollees. Alternatively, a state could create a pool through which all health plans transfer money, based on differences in risk profiles. In its model laws, NAIC offers states several reinsurance approaches, including prospective reinsurance on a voluntary or mandatory basis.

Purchasing Groups. The availability of purchasing groups is one of the major innovations in the insurance market. Purchasing groups are being formed by some states or employers to obtain the same advantages as large employers, trade associations, and unions. In theory, purchasing pools can provide both the administrative economies and risk pooling associated with larger groups. In practice, however, the inclusion of a higher-cost employer will affect the premiums of all group members.

Q 4:27 What efforts have the states made to facilitate reform in the small group market?

Many states have adopted rules designed to reform the small-group insurance market. State reforms enacted since 1990 include the following:

NAIC rating limits premiums charged to small groups to a ratio of 2:1 for experience, health status, or duration of coverage.

Tight rating bands limit use of experience, health status, or duration in setting premium rates for small groups.

Community rating prohibits the use of experience, health status, or duration in setting premium rates for small groups. Some also prohibit use of demographic factors.

NAIC renewal requires carriers to renew coverage, with only specific exceptions (e.g., failure to pay premiums).

Guaranteed issue requires carriers to offer coverage to small groups regardless of their health status or claims experience. Many laws that require guaranteed issue also establish either voluntary or mandatory carrier participation in a reinsurance program to spread the cost of covering high-risk groups among small-group carriers in a state.

Reinsurance establishes a program to help carriers bear the risk of accepting all groups. Under a voluntary program, carriers may elect to opt out of the reinsurance program and become a "risk-assuming carrier" (not subject to reinsurance assessments). Under a mandatory program, however, all carriers must participate in the reinsurance program and are subject to assessments for losses in the program.

Preexisting-condition coverage is specified. Carriers must limit preexisting-condition waiting periods and must credit waiting periods satisfied under previous coverage (for portability purposes).

These specifications include limitations on waiting periods, credit for coverage of a qualified medical condition in determining the waiting period, or continuous coverage to avoid gaps in coverage.

Group size is defined by each state. At least 44 states have passed some rules relating to determining the size of a small group. Most of these rules include guaranteed renewability (43 out of 44 states), guaranteed portability for previously insured people shifting between employers (41 of 44 states), and guaranteed issue of insurance to any small group that applies (38 of 44 states). In almost each case, the reforms are limited to businesses below some maximum size, usually between 25 and 50 employees. Many states also set a threshold of two or three employees. All 44 states have included some limit on premium pricing in the form of rating restrictions, modified community rating, or full community rating. Some have restricted the use of health status and other factors in rating rules.

Among the 44 states that have enacted insurance reforms, about 30 have incorporated risk-adjustment mechanisms or reinsurance pools. About 10 states mandate participation in reinsurance pools, although some exempt Blue Cross/Blue Shield plans. As of September 1999, 27 states had enacted NAIC's Small Group Health Insurance Premium Rates and Coverage Renewability Model Act or similar legislation, with related legislation adopted in 21 states.

At least 21 states have passed legislation to create or enable private or state-run purchasing groups. These initiatives vary widely from allowing voluntary purchasing pools to eliminating restrictions on private sector groups joining together to seek coverage. Others seek to create state-sponsored noncompeting alliances with fixed geographic areas and explicit responsibilities for managing insurance markets.

Several pieces of legislation before the 107th Congress address the need of small businesses to maintain their health insurance (e.g., H.R. 2082).

Employer-Sponsored and Employer-Designed Plans

Q 4:28 What does developing an employer-sponsored and employer-designed plan entail?

Some employers are taking an aggressive approach to designing health care benefits and delivery systems. The process is time consuming and expensive, but the result is a custom-made product that fits the employer's unique situation.

Before embarking on a particular design, an employer needs to have some idea of its historical health care expenditures per employee, preferably broken down by category of medical service, such as inpatient and outpatient hospitalization, office visits, diagnostic x-ray and laboratory studies, drugs and injections, surgery charges, anesthesia, and radiation treatment and chemotherapy. With this information in hand, the employer is in a position to begin planning. A number of factors must be considered in planning, including the involvement of union representatives, if applicable. Issues to be addressed include (1) how the provider network will be developed and governed, (2) how primary care and specialty physicians will be paid, (3) how selective hospital contracting will be, (4) how emergency services will be handled, (5) what type of ancillary providers will be included in the contracting activities, and (6) which employee benefit incentives or disincentives will be utilized.[8]

Q 4:29 Do employers ever intervene in the administration of benefit plans?

Yes. It is not uncommon for employers, whether self-funded or fully insured, to intervene in the administration of benefit plans on a "special needs" basis. For example, sometimes special dispensation will be granted for a company employee who seeks an experimental treatment that would not otherwise be covered by the employer's plan. Alternatively, an employer may waive an annual or lifetime cap on services for a longtime employee whose child suffers from a chronic illness.

Such ad hoc intervention may be initiated by both small and large employers. Smaller employers may intervene because of the immediacy of management-employee relations, or because of the relatively large impact special determinations are likely to have on future premiums. Large employers' tendency to intervene usually arises from familiar relationships between the firm's human resources managers and the plan's benefits administration personnel.

Q 4:30 Can an employer become liable for health plan determinations that adversely affect its employees?

Yes. Litigation against employer-purchasers for decisions about health benefits is virtually nonexistent. The selection activities discussed above, however, may make employers, which often have "deep pockets," potentially attractive defendants in personal injury suits.

For example, employer audits at the point of plan selection or an ongoing role in quality assurance may provide the basis for allegations of corporate negligence.[9] Courts may also regard an employer's power to offer final appeals as evidence of a level of control sufficient to support a vicarious liability claim.[10] Similarly, granting special dispensation for particular individuals or treatments may be deemed the exercise of a level of discretion that would subject the employer to close scrutiny under tort, contract, trust, and employment law.

If employers are indeed playing active roles, and potentially negligent or discriminatory ones, there are certainly strong policy arguments for ensuring that they are not shielded from liability, especially when they exert the same kind of control over clinical decisions for which many now seek to hold health plans accountable.

Q 4:31   What are the basic elements of an employer-designed benefit plan?

The following elements are part of an employer-designed health benefit plan:

Employee Incentives and Disincentives. Incentives can be used to direct patients to primary care physicians or community hospitals and must be carefully crafted in the benefit plan. Disincentives are used to discourage the random and unmanageable utilization of specialists and tertiary care hospitals.

Coinsurance Differentials. Employers commonly adjust the difference between how much of the cost is borne by the employer and how much is carried by the employee. Employers have found that it takes as much as a 30 percent benefit difference to influence employee choice.

Deductibles. Another way to influence employee choice is through deductibles. This approach has less impact on the employee's choice because it is a one-time annual payment. Another method is to charge a separate deductible for certain types of services or inpatient admissions.

Employee's Maximum Out-of-Pocket Expenses. Another technique is to manipulate the employee's out-of-pocket maximum, differentiating between in-plan and out-of-plan providers or services. Some employers do not place a cap on employee out-of-pocket expenses for nonparticipating providers.

Benefit Carve-Outs. Benefit carve-outs are often used with centers of excellence programs for which high-cost, high-technology services are required, such as cardiac procedures or transplants. If the employee goes to the participating provider for these services, the employer may waive the normal deductible, coinsurance, and out-of-pocket maximum and pay 100 percent of the agreed contracted rate for the services. Noncovered expenses or expenses in excess of the threshold amount are borne entirely by the patient.

Q 4:32 How should employers evaluate plans and providers?

It is becoming increasingly common for employers that do direct contracting to use requests for proposals (RFPs) for plan or provider selection. The information obtained from these proposals allows the employer to measure the plans' or providers' programs and services against one another. Factors considered include the scope of services, price, payment method, and manageability of the system. The less the employer has to do to oversee the delivery system, the more attractive the system.

Q 4:33 In what types of products are employers interested?

Not all employers buy the same employee benefits. Different products are available in different bundles. Employers buy indemnity insurance, transitional PPO or HMO managed cost products, self-funded discounted fee-for-service products, and directly contracted products (purchasing cooperatives, provider networks, and so on). Employers are interested in choice (provider access), cost effectiveness (provider discounts and risk sharing), and quality and outcomes in the delivery of health care.

As discussed in chapter 5, there are differences among employers, based on their size and whether they are self-funded, that affect their purchasing decisions with respect to health plans. For example, small employers (1 to 50 lives) base their purchasing decisions almost exclusively on price and rely extensively on brokers and agents, although some states allow for purchasing coalitions among small employers. Purchasing decisions of medium-sized employers (50 to 500 lives) are more variable. Price is still significant, as is network composition. As an employer gets into the range of 500 to 2,000 lives or more, far more options are available. These employers value price, but quality and member services are important.

Q 4:34 If a request for proposal is used, what information should be obtained?

An RFP is usually a lengthy document that seeks a broad array of information about a provider network or plan. Types of information typically obtained as part of the process include (1) identifying information (name of provider, address, tax identification number, license, ownership structure); (2) management information (chief executive officer, chief financial officer, medical director or chief of staff, quality management director); (3) type of services (primary care, tertiary care, teaching institution); (4) accommodations (number of licensed beds, room rates); (5) service area (based on inpatient volume); (6) quality management capabilities; (7) hospital services inventory (ICU, psychiatric unit, home health, emergency, ancillaries, clinical); (8) relationships with other providers; and (9) professional liability (insurance levels, coverage, carriers, claims history).

Some employers engage in in-depth, on-site evaluations during the network selection process. According to Towers Perrin of New York, the important issues in credentialing a health plan or provider network include the following:[11]

1. Is the network constructed and managed to offer a full range of medical services and to provide enough access to care efficiently for the needs of the employees? Are the providers credentialed according to NCQA standards?

2. Is there a documented quality management process in place? If the network is not NCQA accredited, is it striving to achieve that accreditation or some other external quality validation?

3. Is there a member-oriented program staffed by well-trained and properly motivated individuals? Are service levels monitored, and is historical performance documented?

4. Is the medical management staff properly trained, and do staff members follow a well-documented, consistent process in the course of medical reviews? Is there an external peer review process in place for appeals?

5. Is there a professional staff responsible for communicating with providers? Is there a documented program for routine field visits?

6. Can the network produce standard utilization, cost, and quality management reports? Can the network provide all HEDIS measurements?

7. Is the network financially viable? Is the overall medical loss ratio adequate to sustain the program?

Financial bids can differ from one RFP to another. This allows for flexibility in the bidding process. Historical rates of price increases for hospital services may be valuable in determining the hospital's cost and pricing structure. Common diagnosis-related groups (DRGs) and per diem rates are often requested.

Q 4:35   Are there successful employer-sponsored models?

Several innovative products have been developed by employer or business coalitions. One example of a successful employer-sponsored model is the Buyers Health Care Action Group of Minneapolis, Minnesota. The group entered into a direct contract with provider-sponsored health care systems in January 1997. The RFP developed by the group requires the same level of benefits, quality, outcomes, and data collection for all of the plans. This standard removes from the employers the responsibility for deciding which plan to offer their employees. Instead, employees are given a list of provider-sponsored plans approved by the group so that the employees can decide which plan to choose. Elements considered by the group in selecting approved PSOs include plan cost, network coverage, perceived quality of providers, and total quality management. The overall goal is to foster competition among the PSO plans.

Other models are the association health plans (AHPs). The underlying principle is that for insurance to be effective, risk has to spread among a large number of purchasers. There are several pieces of legislation favoring the establishment of AHPs wending their way through the 107th Congress. They have in common these features:

1. Small businesses, through bona fide trade and professional associations, would be able to negotiate agreements with insurance providers, which larger companies and labor unions currently do.

2. Small businesses would have the flexibility to choose the coverage they want, including uniform benefits across state lines.

3. AHPs would be registered as ERISA plans with the Department of Labor and be subject to state oversight.

Direct Contracting

Q 4:36   What is direct contracting?

Direct contracting is a strategy by which physicians and other providers of health services contract directly with employers as payers for those services to deliver health and medical services to their employees. Under such an arrangement, an employer agrees to mandate the use of, or to provide financial incentives to employees to use, specific physicians and providers while the physicians and providers are given incentives through a prepaid or other financial arrangement. If the contracting arrangement involves prepayment, most states require it to be made through an HMO that is regulated under state law. More often than not, however, direct contracting arrangements are not structured through HMOs, but instead involve an insurer or similar company acting as a third-party administrator (TPA), or providing administrative services only. These issues are discussed in greater detail in chapter 13. Although this activity is often regulated too, it generally does not require the same stringent financial security as an HMO.

Q 4:37   Why is there an increased interest in direct contracting?

Perhaps the best reason for increased employer interest in direct contracting is the political and economic climate. Health care costs are rising once more; some experts say in the double digits. Congress approved limited direct contracting in Medicare in the Balanced Budget Act of 1997. Employers are looking for economic certainty. In addition, limitations are arising in the traditional relationship between employers and managed care companies that make direct contracting an appealing alternative strategy for many employers. These limitations include the following.

Lack of Control. The employer, when it contracts with an HMO, places the responsibility for the medical care of its employees in the hands of a third party that has accepted this responsibility in return for financial rewards dictated by contractual obligations. Although the employer may have dictated the terms and characteristics of the health plan at the time of the negotiation, its actual day-to-day control is limited. Nonetheless, the employer's contracting department, usually human resources, is the focus of employee discontent (if it is present) with the health plan.

Lack of Flexibility. For health plans, contractual terms are usually established annually at the time of contract renewal. Thus, alterations in an employer's financial status, employee relations, or business standing cannot be reflected in the health plan in a meaningful time frame.

Lack of Accountability. Once again, the relationship between the employer and the health plan is dictated contractually. The employer, however, is more directly accountable for its employees' health than the health plan is as a result of day-to-day contact.

Lack of Trust. This problem stems from the fundamental lack of alignment between the participants in the employer-plan-provider triangle.

Q 4:38   What are the trends in direct contracting?

Consultants suggest that two approaches are gaining momentum for employers that are trying to control health care costs. The first trend is to self-insure for health care rather than purchase fully insured plans. This allows employers to take the risk and pay for health care as costs are incurred. Employers can buy stop-loss insurance to minimize their financial risk. Stop-loss insurance is intended to protect against catastrophic events and kicks in once a certain level of cost has been reached. The second trend is direct contracting by employers either on their own or as part of a purchasing group. These employers or groups contract with fully capitated provider networks for health care services.

Employers today are more concerned about receiving value for their capital investment than they were in years past. In the previous decade, cost was the benchmark by which employers chose health plans for their employees. As long as increased cost was accompanied by an increase in quality or accountability, employers were happy. Today, employers want value for their health care investment dollar—value expressed in quality outcomes rather than in goals or cost-saving strategies, and in predictable, reasonable pricing rather than in the least costly physician, provider, or health plan.

From a service quality standpoint, many employers are becoming increasingly dissatisfied with their managed care plans. Companies are asking for increased control in the development, administration, and credentialing of contracted physician networks. Many are also upset over the lack of flexibility in plan offerings by HMO and PPO plans. Still others are weary of their lack of control or input into plan modifications, claims adjudication, or the complaint resolution process. Indeed, the latter concern is the catalyst that sparked state medical association efforts over "patient protection" and proportionate liability for denial of medically necessary treatment by HMOs.

Perhaps the greatest employer concern is the power of HMOs in the negotiating process and in the delivery of care. In some instances, HMOs download risk to physician and provider organizations without a perceived equitable sharing of the resultant rewards. There is also widespread perception that HMOs are unreasonably and unfairly profiting at the expense of employers and consumers alike. Finally, employers are most concerned about the lack of willingness on the part of HMOs and PPOs to share data on quality of care or internal operating costs and procedures, even with employers offering blanket confidentiality agreements.

Q 4:39   Why are physicians and providers interested in direct contracting?

On the physician and provider side, direct contracting is a valuable strategic asset and a means to increase reimbursement by, in most cases, cutting out the intermediary. If physician, provider, and purchaser are happy, a direct-contracting relationship with a large company can assure a physician practice or hospital system a solid income and bring them closer to the patients they serve—the company employees and their families.

Physicians and providers, like many employers, believe that managed care plans—especially HMOs—are too profitable at the expense of providing care. Many physicians and providers believe that HMOs merely manage cash, not care.

Physicians and providers believe that they must regain "ground" lost to HMOs. Some believe they have become nothing more than vendors in today's health care delivery system. Like many employers, physicians and providers believe that managed care plans do not share any "savings" with employers or providers. In fact, physicians and providers believe that direct contracting may enable them to align their incentives with the downward reimbursement trends occurring in both the public and private markets. Direct contracting allows physicians and providers to align their financial gains with the provision of care in their local communities, rather than gain significant advantages from keeping patients out of their offices and hospitals.

Finally, as public programs such as Medicare and Medicaid explore new means to achieve financial savings and push responsibility for funding and control to the states, physicians and providers believe that direct contracting is a better means of interacting with government purchasers than serving as mere providers under contract to selected HMOs. Quality and reimbursement concerns in many state Medicaid programs may give physicians and providers the competitive edge they need to compete effectively with managed care for such business.[12]

Q 4:40   What types of employers should consider direct contracting?

Any employer that sponsors its own health care plan or plans is a candidate for direct contracting. Typically, major employers (e.g., Delta Airlines, American Airlines, Dow Chemical, U.S. West, Mobil Oil, Weyerhauser, Brown and Root, International Paper) have the size and number of employees to achieve the administrative efficiencies and quality outcomes they seek. On the other hand, many small companies are finding ways to contract collectively and directly through purchasing coalitions and cooperatives.

Direct contracting and its value and accountability underpinnings have also been the springboard for several business, physician, provider, and health care vendor industry coalitions, the purpose of which is to study the outcomes and accountability of the members of the health care industry. Some of the more prominent groups include the Foundation for Accountability, the North Central Texas HEDIS Coalition, the Washington Business Group on Health, and a new institute founded by Sean Sullivan of the National Business Group on Health and the National Association of Managed Care Physicians.

Q 4:41 For which services do employers typically contract?

Employers typically contract for targeted medical and health services such as acute-care hospital services, laboratories, home health and skilled nursing care, physician services, prenatal and maternity care, prescription drug benefits, and mental health programs. Employers also contract for management services with TPAs, which function as aggregators of health care services without themselves becoming providers.

Q 4:42 What direct-contracting models do employers use most often?

Each marketplace has its own unique direct-contracting model based on politics, physician and provider demographics, managed care market penetration, and employer size and participation in group purchasing arrangements. The six models most often used by employers are the following:

Single Service, or Carve-Out, Model. In this model, coalitions use their collective purchasing power to consider such programs as prescription drug benefits, mental health care services, utilization review, outpatient laboratory work, drug testing, and specialty and postacute care. Coalitions in Kalamazoo, Michigan; Nashville, Tennessee; and Tampa, Florida, are examples of this approach. Employers receive value for their collective union by receiving lower unit prices for these services.

Group Purchasing and Evaluation of HMO Services. In this model, a single RFP is offered to competitive bidding by interested HMOs. Coalitions usually use a product satisfaction or patient satisfaction tool in the selection process. The results of these surveys are used in the rate negotiations and are usually published and shown to the employees and to the managed care plans. This approach is best employed in mature managed care markets. As a result, it is most widely used in California by the Pacific Business Group on Health. It is also popular in the midwestern market, and is employed in Missouri by the Gateway Purchasers for Health. To some extent, the "Big 10" coalition of employers, including Sears and American Express, used this model when it created a single RFP for collective employer bargaining in 1995. In that case, employee benefits consulting giant William M. Mercer, Inc., designed and implemented the study and the model.

Employer-Provider Cooperative Model. Under this model, a group of employers in a community band together, design a plan, and invite providers to bid. This approach has been successful in some markets where there are a few dominant employers.

Provider-Sponsored Network Model. Several coalitions have increasingly contracted directly with individuals and networks of physicians and providers. This model has been employed in Denver, Colorado; Madison, Wisconsin; Memphis, Tennessee; and Houston, Texas. The Houston Healthcare Purchasing Organization (HHPO) contracts directly with over 55 hospitals and 4,500 physicians in the Houston and surrounding market. Denver's model uses a competitive pricing approach, but the HHPO prices its physician and provider contracts on a uniform basis. This means that the service and unit price provided in an out-of-medical center hospital is the same as that provided in a medical center facility. The hospital pricing is based on DRGs; thus, the overall control and responsibility for utilization is with the physicians and the providers rather than with a TPA. Physician contracts are structured similarly, except that they are negotiated on a fixed-fee basis. The HHPO does not have a common plan design or claims payer, and employees maintain that responsibility. The HHPO maintains responsibility for negotiating contracts, repricing resultant claims, and administering the quality analysis reviews of network physicians and providers. As part of their contract with the HHPO, network physicians and providers have agreed to submit UP 92 (Uniform Billing Code of 1992) data to the HHPO for quality and analysis review for all patients, not simply HHPO patients. None of the HHPO contracts are currently capitation based because Texas requires that a prepaid contract be administered solely through HMOs or corporations.

Contracts Between One Medical Group or One Hospital, and One Employer. This type of relationship is best where the provider is a multispecialty group or IPA offering a large number of services. Such an arrangement will reduce the employer's overall administrative burden and costs associated with contracting multiple provider relationships. Medical groups that offer fewer, less comprehensive services are at a competitive disadvantage with one employer or employer group, but may seek to align competitively with employers as a mechanism to achieve certain business objectives. For these medical groups, independence is the primary motivation, and simplicity is the primary motivation for the employer. For larger medical groups, this type of arrangement allows for hiring or contracting new physicians (depending on the state) to "fill in the gaps" and attract other business arrangements.

Contracts Between Several Medical Groups and Hospital Facilities and One Employer. This approach, similar to the HHPO model, involves an agreement between several medical groups and hospital facilities and one very large employer. In some states, the physicians or physician groups and hospitals may form a PHO or enter into some other joint venture arrangement. This approach provides the employer with the same incentives as the single service, or carve-out, model, with an additional diminution of unit prices.

Q 4:43   What risks do providers think are associated with direct-contracting arrangements?

Many physicians and hospitals are concerned that entering into direct-contracting relationships with employers will damage, perhaps to their economic detriment, their relationships with managed care plans. Some providers even believe that vindictive HMOs may alter their patient flow, renegotiate their financial incentives, or worse, terminate their relationship. These concerns should not prevent physicians and providers from exploring direct-contracting relationships.

Hospitals may have the most to lose, since their capital base is derived completely from factors beyond their control: physician referral patterns, HMO contracting patterns, demographics, and technological innovation. For hospitals, loss of managed care business may be damaging, and even "life threatening." Because of favorable congressional activity on the provider-sponsored network issue in Medicare, however, hospitals especially should not be deterred from direct-contracting relationships. In fact, in a well-penetrated market, or in markets with sophisticated purchasers, managed care plans, physicians, and providers may all benefit from collaboration and sharing product offerings.

Retiree Health Benefits

Q 4:44 What are the major issues confronting employers that provide retiree health benefits?

As part of their retirement plans, most employers offer coverage of Medicare supplemental insurance. As a result of Financial Accounting Standard 106 (FAS 106) and the increasing number of retirees, however, employers are looking for ways to control the health care costs of retirees. FAS 106 changed employer expenditures for employee benefits from defined benefits to defined contributions and therefore requires employers to account for the expenditures in the year they are incurred rather than in the year the benefits are accessed. Some employers have cut back on benefits offered to retirees; others have eliminated them entirely. Still other employers are attempting to shift the cost of Medicare supplemental health care coverage to retirees.

Q 4:45 What are the advantages of Medicare managed care products to employers faced with these retirement benefit issues?

Many employers have embraced Medicare risk plans as an acceptable option for their retirees. Most Medicare HMOs offer standard Medicare and enhanced benefits at little or no additional cost and offer coverage of services covered by supplemental insurance policies. Many include drug benefits as well. The strong trend in 2000 and 2001 was for MCOs providing Medicare services to exit that market. Nevertheless, by enrolling employees in a Medicare HMO, employers obtain the following benefits:

Reduction in FAS 106 Liability. With lower monthly premiums and claims costs, companies can achieve a reduction in retiree medical expenses of up to 75 percent or more in the per person FAS 106 liability.

Lower Premiums or Claims Liability. Medicare HMOs usually reduce an employer's premium cost per retiree per month by half, yet benefits are likely to be enhanced or, at a minimum, remain the same.

Continuous Health Care for Employees and Retirees. Medicare HMOs allow employers to continue to offer medical benefits to retirees. Former employees get the benefits they believe they have earned, and current employees can look forward to retiree health benefits.

Retirees reap the following benefits:

Coordinated, Quality Health Care. Retirees obtain medical benefits and services far beyond those received under traditional Medicare. With M + C plans, retirees can look forward to an expanded choice of products.

Low Out-of-Pocket Costs. For most HMOs, the only costs to retirees are insignificant copayments for physician office visits or for prescription drugs.

No Paperwork. There is virtually no paperwork involved in handling claims for benefits under a Medicare HMO.

Q 4:46   What are the issues raised with respect to retiree benefits under the Balanced Budget Act of 1997?

The BBA made dramatic changes to the Medicare system. One of the major problems for employers with retiree health care liabilities is the decision on the part of the Health Care Financing Administration (HCFA), how the Center for Medicare and Medicaid Services (CMMS), to make no provisions for educating retirees who receive corporate benefits about the new choices, benefits, and information under the M + C program. After evaluating Medicare managed care against traditional Medicare benefits, employers must scrutinize the M + C program for their Medicare-eligible employees. Although eligible Medicaid beneficiaries can choose from any available M + C option available to individuals, employers are not required to offer M + C options as part of their group program for retirees.

It is too early to predict the effect of the M + C program on retiree health benefits. Employers will want to evaluate each M + C option against traditional Medicare before adding it to their retiree health care programs. The biggest challenge, however, will be in educating the retirees as to the choices available under Medicare as a result of the BBA.

References

1. W.M. Mercer, Inc., "Employers Predict Growth in HMO Enrollment," *Med. Benefits,* 14(4): 1997.

2. P.R. Kongstvedt, "Common Operational Problems in Managed Health Care Plans," in *Essentials of Managed Health Care,* P.R. Kongstvedt, ed. (Gaithersburg, MD: Aspen Publishers, 1995), 280–288.

3. Thomas R. Wortman, *Research Report: Pricing Considerations for POS and PPO Products* (Radner, PA: Milliman & Robertson, 1999).

4. D.F. Ogden et al., Milliman & Robertson, Inc., Mar. 14, 1995.

5. D. Lawrence, "Gatekeeping Reconsidered." *New Eng. J. Med.,* 345:1341–1342, 2001.

6. *See* http://www.leapfroggroup.org/.

7. The Leapfrog Group, *Patient Safety Standards: The Potential Benefits of Universal Adoption* (Business Roundtable, Nov. 2000).

8. C.E. Dowd, "Employer Strategies for Designing a Health Care System," in *The Integrated Health Care Delivery Systems Manual,* A. Fine, ed. (Washington, DC: Thompson Publishing Group 1993), 48.

9. *See* Pedroza v. Bryant, 101 Wash. 2d 226 (1984); McClellan v. HMO, 604 A.2d 1053 (Pa. 1992); Harrell v. Total Health Care, Inc., 781 S.W.2d 58 (Mo. 1989).

10. Vicarious liability is the liability of a person or organization for the negligence of a third party. Bing v. Thunig, 2 N.Y.2d

656 (1957). Typically, the third party is an employee; however, courts have extended the doctrine to include an independent contractor. Jackson v. Power, 743 P.2d 1376 (Alaska 1987).

11. P.R. Kongsvedt, "The Employer's View of Managed Health Care," in *The Managed Health Care Handbook,* 3d ed. (Gaithersburg, MD: Aspen Publishers 1996) 588.

12. E.P. Gee and A. Fine, "The Direct Approach," *Health Syst. Rev.,* Mar./Apr. 1997, 70–74.

Chapter 5

Benefit Plan Design and Administration in Managed Care

Most Americans get their health care through an array of private coverage arrangements referred to as *health insurance.* As most know, this is a misnomer, since many of these arrangements do not perform an insurance function but rather serve as third-party administrators (TPAs) for self-insured plans.

Health insurance is governed by complex state and federal requirements that affect the design of benefit plans offered by insurers, managed care organizations (MCOs), and employers. These state and federal requirements also affect the duration and scope of health plan coverage. One of the most important laws affecting health insurance is the Health Insurance Portability and Accountability Act of 1996, which applies to all forms of health plans, including self-funded plans.

Most employers with fewer than 500 employees offer only one type of medical plan, whereas employers with more than 500 employees are more likely to offer a mix of plan types, ranging from traditional indemnity to full capitation (with or without point-of-service (POS) options). More than half of all medium-sized and large firms (and many small firms) self-insure. For these large employers, the Employee Retirement Income Security Act (ERISA) of 1974 continues to play an important role in the development and administration of health care benefit plans. ERISA can be expected to become increasingly important as self-insurance grows in popularity. When an employer self-insures for health care, it can either administer its own plan or contract out under an administrative-services-only arrangement to a TPA or insurance company.

With the emergence of so many variations of managed care plans from which to choose, purchasing health maintenance organization (HMO) and related POS plans has become an interesting mix of art and science and is far more complex than would appear on the surface. For many employers, HMO and POS plans are the only medical plan offerings; for others, they are merely a component of a broad array of benefit plans that range from managed indemnity and preferred provider plans to risk-based models. These complexities have led many large employers, especially those that are geographically dispersed, to rely on health and welfare consultants and brokers to guide them through selecting and dealing with these plans. By conducting various objective and subjective studies, a purchaser or its consultant can determine what best suits the needs of its organization and its employees and begin the processes of plan evaluation, negotiation, selection, employee premium (contribution) setting, and implementation.

Organizations have purchased HMO and POS services primarily to reduce costs in their medical benefit programs. History, however, has taught many purchasers that if they do not negotiate for and implement these services properly within the context of all their medical plans, they can increase aggregate medical costs and create significant long-term employee relations problems. The good news is that in today's competitive environment, employers can be more proactive in dealing with HMOs and insurers. This chapter seeks to describe the determinants of successfully selecting, negotiating, and implementing an HMO or POS plan and how to evaluate the adequacy of the benefits being offered.

Overview of Health Insurance

Q 5:1 What is health insurance?

Health insurance is a policy or plan that allows an individual or organization to finance health care coverage by paying a fixed monthly premium in return for access to health care services. Insurance also provides a way for risks of a population to be shifted and spread across a larger group.

The most common ways in which health care coverage is arranged are (1) indemnity or third-party reimbursement, (2) employer self-insurance, and (3) HMOs.

Indemnity or Third-Party Reimbursement. Simply put, indemnity health insurance is a system in which, in return for the payment of premiums, one party agrees to reimburse another for certain medical costs as those costs are incurred. The system is defined by the insurer's payment for services either directly or through reimbursement to the patient. Under this approach, the insurer bears the risk and can lose money if the amount of reimbursement it must provide (including administrative costs) exceeds its income from premiums, investment, and other sources. As discussed in chapter 1, this form of health insurance started in the 1920s, but did not expand substantially until the 1940s with the emergence of Blue Cross and Blue Shield plans.

Employer Self-Insurance. Many employers offer some form of health insurance or other employee benefit covering the employee and the employee's family. For many reasons, employers have self-insured for their employees' health coverage, with over half of all insured employees covered through a self-insured plan. Under self-insurance, the employer defines the benefits to be provided and then pays for those benefits. The self-insured employer may purchase some form of stop-loss or excess coverage from a commercial insurer to protect itself from higher than projected costs. In essence, however, the self-insured employer functions as the insurer, using other commercial insurers or TPAs to administer the self-insured program.

Indemnity, Service, and Assignment. Insurers and employers can use two basic forms of contractual payment arrangements: indemnity or service benefit. Under an indemnity plan, the insured is reimbursed for covered health benefits. The patient pays the bill and submits the receipt for reimbursement from the insurance company. No relationship is created between the insurer and the provider. Under a service plan, the insurer agrees to pay the provider directly for part of the covered services. The provider submits the bill to the insurer rather than to the patient and charges the patient a deductible or copayment as permitted under the insurance policy. Over time, most indemnity insurers began to behave like service plans by accepting "assignment" of the payment from the insured individual. Under this method, the provider bills on behalf of the patient and is entitled to receive payment. Medicare uses this method for its Part B program.

Health Maintenance Organizations. An HMO differs from a third-party indemnity plan in an important way. Instead of agreeing to reimburse the insured for health care costs, the HMO provides or arranges for the provision of certain defined health services in return for a fixed monthly premium. Members are not billed except for co-payments as permitted under the policy. These organizations are discussed in more detail in chapter 3.

Hybrid Managed Care Plans. Driven by the need to lower the costs of health care, traditional insurers and self-insuring employers have tried to adopt characteristics of HMOs by involving those who deliver medical care. POS plans, risk-impact preferred provider organizations (PPOs), and gatekeeper models are a few of these hybrids and are discussed in more detail in chapter 3. Most recently, triple option plans have evolved. These plans allow an individual to enroll in an HMO but to go outside the HMO to a group of PPOs selected by the sponsoring company or insurer in return for the payment of a relatively low copayment and deductible. The copayment and deductible increase significantly if the individual chooses to go outside the PPO network entirely, where care is reimbursed using an indemnity approach.

Q 5:2 How is health insurance sold?

The pricing and marketing of health insurance coverage form a critical component of any health benefit product, because success or profitability depends on such factors as the targeted population, the choice of individual versus group policies, and the underwriting criteria. Another important factor is whether the policy is experience or community rated.

Adverse Selection. One of the concerns of marketing insurance is adverse selection. The concept behind adverse selection is that certain people will select certain types of policies based on their medical conditions and the likelihood of requiring covered services. From the perspective of the organization providing health care coverage, that means that older and sicker people are more likely than younger and healthier people to purchase insurance. Adverse selection will result in the organization's having a higher than average cost.

Group or Individual Coverage. In marketing health insurance, one of the basic decisions is whether to offer group (employers, unions, religious organizations, professional associations) or individual coverage. An advantage of group coverage is its ability to limit the problem of adverse selection.

Underwriting Criteria. Health insurance is either medically underwritten or not. Medical underwriting means that the insurer examines the medical background of each individual to be covered and decides on an individual basis whether to cover the insured entirely, partially, or not at all. Both conventional insurers and HMOs use medical underwriting in selling individual health coverage. It is also used when covering small groups of ten or fewer. It is being used more with larger groups because of the increasing costs of health care.

Experience Rating and Community Rating. Insurers, including HMOs, can also set premiums for group coverage using either community rating or experience rating:

1. *Community rating.* Under community rating, a group is charged a premium per covered employee (or per coverage unit) based on the average cost to the insurer or HMO of covering people in that geographic region. The premium may change from year to year as medical inflation or overall cost experience in the region changes, but remains constant for any given year for groups covered by that insurer or HMO in that geographic area.

2. *Experience rating.* Experience rating makes the current year's premium dependent, in part, on a particular group's past experience. Therefore, a group that had a high cost one year would be charged a higher premium in the following year. Many commercial insurers in the United States have used various forms of experience rating, whereas Blue Cross and Blue Shield plans traditionally have avoided using experience rating in favor of community rating. In fact, in the case of federally qualified HMOs, only community rating is permitted.

Federal Regulation of Health Coverage

Overview

Q 5:3 What mechanisms are used by the federal government to regulate health coverage?

As discussed in chapter 7, the federal government directly regulates public programs such as Medicare and Medicaid, CHAMPUS, and the Federal Employees Health Benefits Program (FEHBP). The federal government also regulates private health coverage through both direct statutory intervention and indirect methods such as income tax treatment. The major means of federal regulation are federal tax laws, ERISA, the Health Maintenance Organization Act of 1973, and a variety of other regulations affecting insurance and insurance coverage.

Federal Taxes

Q 5:4 What are the tax incentives behind private health coverage?

The federal tax laws play an important role in shaping private health coverage. The tax treatment of employer payments for health coverage is largely responsible for the dominant role of employer-sponsored health coverage in the United States. Under 26 U.S.C. Sections 104 through 106 (Supp. 1990), health insurance premiums or benefits paid by an employer on behalf of an employee or qualifying dependent of that employee are excluded from income for purposes of federal taxation. These payments are also not taxable to the employer because they qualify as a business expense. [26 USC § 162 (West Supp 1992)] Another option available to employers is to use a cafeteria plan under Section 125 of the Internal Revenue Code (IRC), which gives the employees a choice of how to allocate certain funds for benefits. Subject to certain limitations, employees can choose among the different offers and the value of the benefits chosen by the employee are not counted as income for purposes of federal (and state) taxation. [26 USC § 125 (Supp 1990)] For self-employed individuals, the Code allows a 25 percent deduction of the cost of health insurance.

The Code also dovetails into the continuation of coverage requirements of the Consolidated Omnibus Budget Reconciliation Act of 1986 (COBRA) and HIPAA. The right to continuation coverage is a right to purchase such coverage and is subject to the nature of the event that ended the previous coverage. For example, loss of coverage allows up to 18 months' continuation unless the termination is for gross misconduct. The incentive to offer COBRA continuation coverage is the avoidance of an excessive excise tax. In addition, some organizations that provide health benefits are exempt from federal income tax. These include nonprofit insurers and HMOs exempt under Code Section 501(c)(4).

ERISA

Q 5:5 What is the Employee Retirement Income Security Act?

ERISA directly regulates private pension plans and provides important substantive rights to employees covered by employer-sponsored pension and other welfare benefit plans. [29 USC § 1002(1) et seq] This means that all fringe benefits, including medical, surgical, or hospital care benefits, are subject to ERISA.

ERISA covers almost all benefit programs of almost all employers or employee organizations. Although the majority of the statute is devoted to pension benefits, health plans (whether through purchased insurance or self-insurance) are directly ruled by parts of ERISA. The most important feature of ERISA is its preemption clause, which is discussed in chapter 8.

Q 5:6 What are the essential features of an ERISA plan?

ERISA Section 402 requires that every qualified benefit plan, including health plans, be maintained pursuant to a written plan document that allows employees to determine their rights and obligations under the plan. [See HR Rep No 1280, at 297 (1974), *reprinted in* 1974 USCCAN 5038, 5077–78] Nevertheless, no written plan document or funding mechanism need exist for there to be a plan for ERISA purposes.

Plan assets must be held in trust by one or more trustees (unless exemptions apply). This imposes a fiduciary duty on plan trustees to administer the plan in a manner consistent with ERISA and the plan document. ERISA Section 404(a)(1)(D) provides that the plan's fiduciaries must discharge their duties in accordance with the plan document and instruments insofar as they are consistent with ERISA.[1]

The plan must establish, maintain, and inform participants and beneficiaries of the procedures for presenting claims, the bases of claim denials, and the procedures for appeal of denials. The benefits to which a participant is entitled are specifically limited to those set forth in the written plan, and no claim by a participant or beneficiary can be made for a benefit not provided by the terms of the written plan. There is always a risk, however, that certain terms in the written plan will be deemed ambiguous and will subject the plan to interpretation under rules of contract construction recognized in the courts, which generally construe contracts against the insurer and in favor of the insured.

The plan must contain benefit provisions as required by ERISA. The only substantive requirement applicable to an ERISA plan is the obligation that the plan comply with the continuation of benefit provisions of COBRA.

Failure to meet any of these requirements will not cause the plan to cease being subject to ERISA, but may subject the plan sponsor or administrator to the various penalties under ERISA. The following issues should be considered in welfare benefit plan administration:

- Integration with the plan document through consistent terms and consistent relationships
- TPA's duties and responsibilities
- Designation of the TPA as fiduciary
- Parties to the agreement
- Reporting obligations and issues
- No prohibited transactions or illegal instructions
- Claims procedures for benefits denials consistent with the plan
- Representations and warranties
- Insurance coverage
- Restrictive covenants
- Communication of plans to the TPA

Q 5:7   What ERISA issues should be considered in drafting an administrative services agreement?

Several important contractual and liability issues relating to ERISA compliance should be included in an administrative services agreement.

Contractual Issues

1. Who are the parties and what are their responsibilities?
2. How will payment be made?
3. What is the claims process?
4. How will disputed claims be handled?
5. Will the payer or patient take financial responsibility in the event that the bill is not paid?
6. How will the TPA be paid for its services? Are there any third-party matters?

Liability Issues

1. Does the agreement affect professional judgment in patient care or provider selection?
2. Who is the TPA, and what is its legal structure and its financial status?
3. Is there adequate insurance coverage for risks and responsibilities?

Other legal and regulatory aspects of ERISA plans as they relate to managed care are discussed in chapter 8.

Q 5:8 What is the purpose of ERISA?

ERISA was intended to remedy problems of pension fraud and mismanagement, such as inadequate funding and poor investment of pension plans. It was enacted based on the recognition that employee benefit plans were becoming increasingly interstate and thus affected interstate commerce, and it applies broadly to employee benefit plans, including those that offer medical care benefits. Congress recognized that disclosure needed to be made to employees and safeguards provided for the establishment, operation, and administration of employee benefit plans. ERISA therefore provides national fiduciary standards for employee health and welfare plans, including disclosure and filing requirements, fiduciary responsibilities, plan administrator responsibilities, beneficiary remedies, sanctions, enforcement, and federal preemption of state laws. [29 USC §§ 1001–1461] Through amendment by COBRA, ERISA requires continuation of health plan coverage for specified periods following separation from employment.

Q 5:9 Which agencies are responsible for administering ERISA?

ERISA is administered by the Department of Labor (DOL) through implementing regulations at 29 C.F.R. Sections 2510.3 through 2500.408b-2 and through advisory opinion letters issued in response to specific inquiries on ERISA-related matters. The IRS enforces the tax aspects of ERISA and is the initial recipient of the government reporting form required to be filed under ERISA.

Q 5:10 How is an ERISA health benefit plan created?

ERISA health benefit plans do not have to be in writing. The existence of an ERISA plan is determined by a "surrounding circumstances" test. That is, an ERISA plan exists if, from the surrounding circumstances, a reasonable person could ascertain the intended benefits, beneficiaries, source of funding, and procedures for receiving benefits. [Donovan v. Dillingham, 688 F 2d 1367 (11th Cir 1982)] Therefore, mere conduct absent intent can result in the creation of a plan. Once a plan is deemed to exist, the formal obligations on employers and plan fiduciaries apply. These obligations include preparing and distributing a summary plan description (SPD) to plan participants, filing reports with the DOL and IRS, and having the plan's books and records independently audited. [29 USC §§ 1021–1024]

Q 5:11   Do all ERISA health and welfare benefit plans have to be the same?

No. An employer can design ERISA health and welfare plans with much discretion. Employers can choose to provide limited coverage for certain conditions or levels of care. Employers can amend their plans over time, even if this results in harm to a beneficiary. For example, in *McGann v. H&H Music Co.* [946 F 2d 401 (5th Cir 1991)], an employer was allowed to amend its benefit plan to limit coverage for AIDS.

In fact, employers have the ability, through ERISA, to take advantage of the cost-containment capabilities of managed care because they can design their benefit plans liberally. For example, plan design can include coverage definitions, utilization management, quality assurance, case management, and effective claim grievance procedures.

Q 5:12   How flexible is ERISA in allowing changes to health care plans?

With the health care system evolving and prospects for health care reform increasing locally and, perhaps, nationally, it is likely that many ERISA plans will need to be modified in response to those changes. ERISA plans should be easily modified prospectively without violating any fiduciary duty in view of the express exemption of welfare benefit plans from ERISA's vesting provisions. [ERISA §§ 201, 301]

Q 5:13   How does ERISA apply to participant contributions?

Most employer-sponsored health benefit plans require that employees contribute some portion of the premiums. It is therefore important to know at what point those contributions become plan assets, subject to the various fiduciary requirements of ERISA. Under final DOL regulations, the assets of a plan are defined to include amounts paid by a participant or beneficiary or withheld by an employer from a participant's wages for contribution to a plan. [DOL Reg § 2510.3-102]

Q 5:14   How does ERISA apply to employer contributions?

Health plans are not subject to the funding requirements that apply to pension plans. Therefore, health plans can be funded on a pay-as-you-go basis. If the plans are funded or have plan assets other than insurance policies, they have obligations that an unfunded plan would not have, such as maintaining plan assets in trust subject to all prohibited transaction rules. [ERISA §§ 403(a), 406] Funded plans with fewer than 100 participants would not be exempt from the requirements that Form 5500 be filed each year and that the SPD and any summary of material modifications be filed with the DOL. [DOL Reg § 2520.104-20] Under current rules, funded plans with 100 or more participants are not subject to the financial statement and audit requirements of ERISA. [DOL Reg § 2520.104-44]

Q 5:15   Why should a benefit plan have coordination of benefits?

Coordination of benefits (COB) is necessary to avoid a windfall to an individual when there is a potential for duplicate health care coverage under more than one benefit plan. To avoid duplication of coverage, plans pay benefits or provide services in a sequence determined by which plan is the primary payer and which is the secondary payer.

COB situations include the following: (1) both husband and wife are employed and each is covered as a dependent on the other's health plan; (2) a covered employee or dependent has coverage through a union or professional association in addition to coverage provided by the employer; (3) an employee holds two jobs and has health coverage from each employer, or an employee with coverage under a current employer still maintains coverage under the health plan of a prior employer; (4) a covered dependent child, still covered under a parent's plan, is employed and covered by the health plan of his or her own employer; (5) a child whose parents are divorced is covered under the plans of both parents, or of one or both natural parents and a stepparent; (6) a covered employee or dependent has injuries that are also covered by one or more automobile insurance policies; and (7) a covered employee or dependent is also entitled to Medicare benefits.

A discussion of the COB rules is beyond the scope of this chapter.

Q 5:16 What are the Medicare secondary rules?

When an individual is covered under an employer's health benefit plan but is otherwise qualified for coverage under Medicare (e.g., end-stage renal disease, general eligibility for elderly), Medicare is always the secondary payer. If there are COBRA benefits, the rules become a little more complicated. Employers of at least one employee must report to a Medicare and Medicaid data bank specified identifying information with respect to individuals who elect coverage under the employer's health plan over Medicare benefits. [COBRA 1993 § 13581]

Q 5:17 What is a qualified medical child support order?

Under ERISA Section 609(a), a qualified medical child support order (QMCSO) is an order requiring a participant's child to be provided coverage under a plan even if the child does not otherwise meet the plan's requirements for coverage. Under ERISA Section 609(c), adopted children are entitled to be treated exactly as they would be if they had been born to the participant or beneficiary, regardless of whether the adoption is final.

Q 5:18 What effect does ERISA have on multiple employer welfare arrangements?

Under ERISA Section 514(b)(6)(A), if a multiple employer welfare arrangement (MEWA) is fully insured, state insurance law can regulate the arrangement to require the maintenance of specified levels of reserves and contributions, which must be met and can be enforced under state law. For any other MEWA, state insurance law can apply to the extent not inconsistent with ERISA Section 514.

Being subject to state regulation does not, however, exempt a MEWA otherwise subject to ERISA from ERISA's requirements.

Q 5:19   Are there any exemptions to ERISA preemption?

Yes. Congress granted one exemption to ERISA preemption for Hawaii's requirement that all employers offer health insurance as part of its state health care reform legislation. The U.S. Supreme Court had ruled that state regulation of employer benefits was invalid, but Congress passed special legislation to allow Hawaii an exemption, in part because its law predated ERISA.

Q 5:20   Does ERISA preemption impede health care reform at the state level?

Many states take the position that ERISA impedes health care reform and stifles innovation in areas such as universal coverage and cost containment to the extent any of their initiatives involves employment-based insurance. Large businesses and employer groups believe that ERISA preemption serves an important purpose by allowing large multistate employers to offer identical benefit packages to all their workers and spares them the burden of complying with different and potentially burdensome state regulations.

Q 5:21   When does ERISA preempt state law?

ERISA is deemed to preempt state common law and statutes in many situations. For example, state statutes regulating TPAs may be preempted by ERISA. Liability under tort and contract is discussed in chapter 8.

Q 5:22   Is there an alternative to litigation for addressing ERISA preemption?

One alternative would be for the federal government to make broader use of its regulatory powers by allowing federal agencies to grant specific ERISA exemptions to test different reform strategies, conditioning them on explicit congressional objectives and state capacity, and making them renewable if specific performance objectives were met. Another option would be to amend ERISA to allow states to proceed with reforms while protecting the interests of large multistate firms through predetermined standards.

Health Insurance Portability and Accountability Act of 1996

Q 5:23   What is the effect of HIPAA on state insurance laws?

State laws regulating the business of insurance cannot be inconsistent with the requirements of HIPAA. In general, HIPAA supersedes any state law that establishes, implements, or continues in effect standards or requirements concerning preexisting-condition exclusions that differ from HIPAA's standards and requirements. To avoid ERISA preemption of state insurance laws through the HIPAA-specific amendments, states must adopt consistent laws that do the following:

- Reduce the six-month look-back period used to determine pre-existing conditions
- Reduce the 12-month (18-month for late enrollees) look-back exclusion
- Increase the break-in coverage time to more than 63 days
- Increase the time parents have to enroll newborns or children adopted or placed for adoption to more than 30 days
- Prohibit preexisting-condition exclusions
- Require additional special enrollment periods
- Reduce the maximum waiting period allowed

HIPAA requires special open enrollment periods for people who lose other coverage. It also requires group health plans that offer dependent coverage to allow participants at least 30 days to enroll new dependents following marriage, birth, adoption, or placement for adoption.

Q 5:24   What is the impact of HIPAA on COBRA?

HIPAA affects COBRA by amending certain provisions that have an impact on COBRA administration. The three COBRA provisions

affected by HIPAA are (1) disability extension, (2) definition of qualified beneficiary, and (3) maximum coverage period. These changes
became effective on January 1, 1997, regardless of when the qualifying event occurred.

Under COBRA, if an employee terminates employment or reduces
his or her hours, an eligible individual can continue coverage for up
to 18 months. Before HIPAA, an individual's 18-month maximum
coverage was extended to 29 months if he or she was disabled at
the time of the qualifying event. Employees and their spouses and
children eligible for COBRA are qualifying beneficiaries if they were
covered by the plan on the day before the qualifying event. HIPAA
expands the definition to include children born to or adopted by a
covered employee during a period of COBRA coverage.

Q 5:25   What are the penalties for noncompliance with HIPAA?

If an employer or group health plan fails to comply with HIPAA,
penalties can be imposed under ERISA, the CODE, or the Public
Health Service Act (PHSA). The DOL, which is the agency responsible for enforcing ERISA, can impose a $100-per-day penalty for each
participant the plan administrator fails to notify of his or her HIPAA
rights. [ERISA § 734(g)] A participant or beneficiary can sue for
HIPAA violations under ERISA and the court can award civil penalties, including attorneys' fees.

The PHSA penalties apply to state and local government employers that fail to comply with HIPAA. The Centers for Medicare and
Medicaid Services (CMMS), formerly the Health Care Financing Administration (HCFA), can impose a $100-per-day penalty for each
individual to whom a failure to comply with HIPAA applies. [42 USC
§ 300gg-61; CMS Reg § 146.180(d)(7)]

The IRS can impose excise taxes on liable parties who fail to comply with HIPAA. The parties subject to such penalties include (1)
multiemployer plans, (2) MEWAs, and (3) employers. The excise tax
is $100 per day during the noncompliance period for each individual
affected by a HIPAA violation. [IRC § 4980D(b)(1)] These penalties
may be corrected and avoided retroactively if a HIPAA violation is
(1) a result of reasonable cause and not willful neglect or (2) corrected within 30 days beginning on the day any of the persons liable

for the excise tax knew or should have known that the violation occurred. [IRC § 4980D(c)(2)]

Health Maintenance Organization Act of 1973

Q 5:26   How does the Health Maintenance Organization Act affect health coverage?

The term *health maintenance organization*, or HMO, was first used by Dr. Paul Ellwood to describe a prepaid group health care arrangement. The Health Maintenance Organization Act [42 USC §§ 300e–300e-17] was passed in 1973 to authorize grants, loans, and loan guarantees for start-up HMOs. The HMO Act defines a qualified HMO as an HMO that meets certain requirements relating to benefits, deductibles, and copayments, and uses community rating. The Act prohibits financial discrimination against employees who select HMOs and preempts state laws that inhibit HMOs from forming and operating.

The net effect of the HMO Act is not entirely clear, since many HMOs have developed and not sought federal qualification because the provisions for qualification are onerous. Federal qualification is no longer a prerequisite to Medicare or Medicaid contracting, and the Act's requirement that a federally qualified HMO be offered by employers offering health benefits was eliminated in 1995.

Other Federal Laws

Q 5:27   What other federal laws directly affect employment-related health insurance?

Health benefits are included in the National Labor Relations Act as a mandatory subject of collective bargaining. Other federal laws relating to discrimination in employment include Title VII of the Civil Rights Act of 1964, the Pregnancy Discrimination Act, the Age Discrimination in Employment Act, and the Americans with Disabilities Act.

Title VII and the Pregnancy Discrimination Act. Title VII of the Civil Rights Act of 1964 [42 USC §§ 2000e–2000e-17] prohibits discrimination in the compensation, terms, conditions, or privileges of employment because of an individual's race, color, religion, sex, or national origin. The effect on health coverage is to prohibit employers from discriminating against a protected class. For example, an employer cannot prohibit coverage for treatment of uterine cancer, found only in women, or sickle cell anemia, found primarily in blacks. Title VII has been found not to apply to exclusions for HIV and AIDS, which do not affect a protected class for purposes of Title VII discrimination. The Pregnancy Discrimination Act amended Title VII to protect women affected by pregnancy, childbirth, or related medical conditions.

Age Discrimination in Employment Act. The ADEA bars discrimination in the compensation, terms, conditions, or privileges of employment on the basis of age. [29 USC § 621 et seq (Supp 1992)] Like Title VII, it extends to health benefits and coverage. The ADEA does, however, allow the employer to observe the terms of a bona fide employee benefit plan that has different provisions based on age as long as the plan "is not a subterfuge to evade the purposes of this chapter." [29 USC § 623(f) (Supp 1992)]

Americans with Disabilities Act. One of the more recent antidiscrimination laws affecting health coverage is the ADA [Pub L No 101-336], which expands the Rehabilitation Act of 1973 [29 USC §§ 701–796 (1985)], which prohibits discrimination against the disabled by the federal government or by recipients of federal contracts or grants. The ADA prohibits discrimination in the compensation, terms, conditions, or privileges of employment. The term *disability* is interpreted broadly, although a U.S. Court of Appeals decision deemed an otherwise disabled individual under treatment (epileptic on medication) no longer disabled for purposes of applying the ADA. [See also McKay v Toupta Motor Mfg, USA, Inc., 110 F 3d 369, 371 (6th Cir 1997)] The ADA is discussed in chapter 8.

McCarran-Ferguson Act. The McCarran-Ferguson Act limits the application of antitrust laws to insurance and the states' right to regulate the business of insurance without federal interference. [15 USC § 1011] To be exempt from antitrust scrutiny, the action must be part of the business of insurance regulated by the state and not an activity that is otherwise anticompetitive. Antitrust and insurance laws are discussed in chapter 8.

Mental Health Parity Act of 1996. The Mental Health Parity Act of 1996 (MHPA) does not require employers to offer mental health benefits, but if they do, it requires parity with respect to how annual and aggregate lifetime benefits are applied to certain mental health benefits. MHPA requirements do not apply to a plan sponsored by a small employer (2 to 50 employees), nor do they apply if the cost of the plan would increase by at least 1 percent. MHPA requirements apply to group health plans for plan years beginning on or after January 1, 1998, and they ceased to apply to benefits for services furnished on or after September 30, 2001. Under MHPA, group plans, insurance companies, and HMOs that offer mental health benefits cannot set annual or aggregate lifetime benefits that are lower than limits for medical and surgical benefits. [See ERISA § 712(a)(1), (2), 42 USC § 300gg-5(a)(1), (2)] These provisions do not apply to benefits for substance abuse or chemical dependency.

Q 5:28 What recent federal health reforms affect coverage under managed care arrangements?

Since the passage of HIPAA, the federal government has considered a number of regulations affecting health care coverage. Rather than focusing on access to coverage, however, recent federal actions and enactments have focused on the nature of the coverage:

- Newborns' and Mothers' Health Protection Act of 1996, [Pub L No 104-204], which limits "drive through" deliveries by requiring health plans to cover at least 48 hours of hospitalization for vaginal deliveries and at least 96 hours for cesarean section deliveries

- Minimum hospital stays for mastectomies

- Prohibition of "gag clauses" in Medicare and Medicaid health plans

- Patients' bill of rights for health plans that contract with Medicare, Medicaid, and FEHBP

The patients' bill of rights has attracted the most recent attention. It was originally designed to define the circumstances under which an injured patient could bring a lawsuit against an MCO on the theory that the MCO was practicing medicine. Debate in the 107th

Congress casts serious doubt on whether this simple but controversial theme can survive unobscured by amendments and debate.

State Regulation of Health Coverage

Q 5:29 How do the states regulate health coverage?

The states influence health care coverage much more than the federal government because they directly regulate the provision of health care services through licensing, professional discipline, and malpractice law. The states also influence health care coverage through direct regulation of the business of insurance, state tax laws, and state regulation of risk-bearing and risk-sharing activities.

Q 5:30 How do the states influence health coverage through taxation?

Forty-five states have a state income tax, and most state income tax laws conform to federal income tax law. Determination of the income tax owed by insurance companies, however, is complicated because of the treatment of the insurer's reserves. Reserves against future losses are a predictable expense that is incurred in one year but must be paid in another. Consequently, most states do not try to apply their income tax statutes to insurance companies; instead, they impose a premium tax on the insurer, charging a set percentage (around 2 percent) on all premiums paid in the state.

Until the Tax Reform Act of 1986, nonprofit health plans, like Blue Cross and Blue Shield, did not have to pay premium taxes. After 1986, however, most states have made them liable for state tax if they are for-profit entities. Self-insuring employers do not pay premium tax on their benefit payments, and these payments are deductible business expenses.

Q 5:31 What are the major areas regulated by states as part of the business of insurance?

State insurance regulations vary from one state to another but have certain features in common. This uniformity has been accomplished, in part, by the advisory efforts of the National Association of Insurance Commissioners (NAIC), a trade association of state insurance officials. The areas most commonly regulated include solvency, coverage and benefits, and consumer rights.

Most states require an insurer to have a state license to sell insurance in the state. To be licensed, the insurer must meet stringent financial regulations intended to ensure solvency. Contribution to state reserve funds, requirements for internal financial reserves, and minimum capital levels are some of the means used to ensure financial solvency. States also oversee the relationships between insurer and insured by imposing various content and marketing standards on the insurer. Some states even regulate the prices charged for health insurance policy premiums.

States also regulate health insurance by requiring health insurers to include certain mandated benefits in their policies. The most common mandates include alcoholism treatment, mammography screening, mental health care, drug abuse treatment, and automatic enrollment of newborns. More recent requirements address consumer issues, such as "freedom of choice" and "any willing provider" laws. These are particularly applicable to the regulation of HMOs and PPOs.

Plan Design and Administration

Q 5:32 What items contribute most to the cost of a health plan?

The following items contribute most to the cost of a health plan:

1. *Pharmaceuticals.* Research and technology in the drug industry have resulted in effective, but costly, new drugs. New drugs that enhance the quality of life but are not medically necessary have also been developed.

2. *New technologies.* New technologies that improve care and the quality of life are being developed. Employers and plans will be challenged to make coverage decisions on the basis of the benefits versus the cost of these technologies.

3. *Aging population.* The aging "baby boomers" are a sophisticated group accustomed to accessing health services when they want them. Consumer demand and expectations from this group will likely increase cost.

4. *Provider cost shifting.* Providers who are caring for an increasing number of uninsured or underinsured people will require higher levels of reimbursement from private payers to continue to deliver care to these other groups. This will increase premiums, making them less affordable to small employers, who will then drop their health insurance plans, thereby increasing the uninsured and underinsured population and creating a vicious circle.

Q 5:33   What aspects of a health plan can be used to contain costs?

A number of plan design features can be used to control costs without compromising quality.

Coordination of Benefits. COB provisions avoid duplicate payments for the same services by apportioning responsibility for payment among several plans.

Subrogation. Subrogation clauses allow a plan to step into the shoes of a participant or beneficiary injured by a third party and recover the amount applicable to the medical benefits paid out for the injury. These provisions are usually set out in the written plan, and the right to subrogate is perfected by notice of the plan's subrogation rights to the third party. Some plans require the participant or beneficiary to execute a subrogation agreement as a condition of receiving benefits.

Benefit Limitations. Based on *McGann v. H&H Music Co.* [946 F 2d 401 (5th Cir 1991), *cert denied sub nom* Greenberg v H&H Music Co No 91-1283, *cert denied,* 506 US 981 (1992)], an employer can reduce the lifetime benefits available under a health plan without violating ERISA. In this case, the employer reduced its lifetime AIDS-related benefit from $1 million to $5,000 after learning the plaintiff had AIDS. The plaintiff sued the employer, the insurance company, and the administrator for violating ERISA Section 510. Because the plan expressly provided for termination or amendment at any time, there was no evidence of a promise not to reduce the $1 million lifetime benefit, and the action appeared to be in the interest of the fiscal viability of the company and not an act of retaliation against the employee, the court found no violation. It is important to note, however, that this case was decided before the ADA became effective.

Limitations and Exclusions Based on "Experimental" Procedures. The use of this method to contain costs must be balanced against the emotional issues that are often involved. In addition, the different medical standards that may apply to the definition of *experimental* must be considered. It is important to specify and define terms such as *experimental* and *investigational* very carefully. Use of specific language defining the scope of the limitation or exclusion is critical to a successful defense, because the greater the degree of specificity, the more the court is restricted from finding the limitation or exclusion ambiguous and construing it against the plan. When a plan provides that certain procedures or treatments are experimental, the plan should (1) specify when or how that treatment will be deemed experimental,[2] (2) be specifically exclusive as to noncovered experimental treatments and procedures, or (3) provide its own specific barometer as to how and/or when a treatment or procedure is no longer considered experimental under the terms of the plan.

Copayments and Deductibles. Making sure that plan participants share some of the expense is a critical feature of most health benefit plans. It is often used in managed care arrangements to create strong incentives and disincentives for use of certain panels of providers.

Q 5:34 What are the likely trends in administration of health benefit plans?

According to an article by Booz-Allen & Hamilton consultants Gary Ahlquist, David Knott, and Philip Lathrop, "When Consumers Rule: The Next Revolution in U.S. Healthcare,"[3] before long, employee health plans will mimic employee retirement plans by using a defined contribution model that gives employees more choice and more control over their health care while saving employers millions of dollars. Under this system, employees will explore and purchase health care plans through Internet superstores, using employer-provided defined contributions. Consumers will pick a plan that fits their needs and allows them to decide what they want to pay in premiums, deductibles, and copayments. The more risk consumers take on themselves, the smaller their premiums will be.

A Booz-Allen & Hamilton survey of *Fortune* magazine's 100 best companies to work for found all respondents anticipating health care cost increases above the rate of inflation during 2002. All but a few anticipate a shift to defined contribution systems, which would save them millions of dollars in administrative costs by taking them out of the selection and retailing process. Two thirds of employers said they are convinced that defined contribution plans are in the offing, but they are unwilling to be the first to make the change because of the risk of alienating employees in a tight labor market.

The defined contribution system will lead to big changes not only for employers and employees but also for health care providers. Ahlquist, Knott, and Lathrop say insurers need to prepare now for more informed consumers by exploring potential niches in manufacturing and underwriting, distribution and sales, information aggregation, transaction processing, and e-commerce. Large insurers may also want to forward-integrate by acquiring or forming alliances with major benefits managers or outsourcers. The authors say e-commerce players should also begin staking out their distinctive roles, since they will be at the center of the new, consumer-driven system.

Q 5:35 How does HIPAA affect plan design and administration?

HIPAA's primary purpose was to increase the availability of and access to health insurance for individuals by limiting an insurer's ability to deny coverage for preexisting conditions and restricting discrimination against prospective or current enrollees based on health status. The guarantee issue and guarantee renewal provisions of HIPAA apply to both the group insurance market and the group-to-individual insurance market. HIPAA requires states to impose restrictions on insurers that "gamed" the system by segmenting insurance risk pools and imposing preexisting-condition limitations on individuals or groups on the basis of health status.

States are given three implementation choices: (1) pass laws consistent with or stronger than the federal floor specified in HIPAA and use state agencies to enforce them; (2) create an acceptable alternative mechanism for eligible persons in the individual market and enforce it through state agencies; or (3) decline to pass new laws or strengthen existing laws, and leave enforcement to the federal government. In states that already require all private insurers to guarantee issue to eligible individuals, enforcement rests with the state, and no state-level reform is needed. In other states, if an insurer offers at least two products under a guaranteed offering that is overseen by the state, no additional law is required. Finally, if there are acceptable alternatives available in a state to ensure access to individual market coverage for eligible persons, no additional law is required. In many states, however, this alternative is met through the use of state-sponsored high-risk pools for eligible persons.

Q 5:36 What should a company consider when it decides to self-administer its health care plan?

A properly self-administered benefit plan can reduce administrative expenses, improve employee relations, and contain costs. It can also have distinct disadvantages, particularly when there are staff cuts, which are commonly followed by increased claims for health care services postponed during employment. This increased volume of claims can stress the human resources department or financial office of an organization, where the administration is most likely to be conducted.

When considering a self-administered program, a company must be sure that it has adequate resources to process the claims, such as a good computer system, good reference materials, good medical and claims consultants, legal counsel, and adequate office space with trained employees. Going to a self-administered plan may cost more initially, and the organization loses the insurer or TPA as a buffer between it and the employee. Employee relations then become an important factor in an effective self-administered program.

Q 5:37 What should a company consider in a TPA or insurer to administer its plan?

It is important to obtain enough information to make an informed selection of a TPA or insurer. The entire organization should be reviewed. Insurance companies have many more resources at their disposal than TPAs. TPAs, however, can have greater flexibility and adaptability in meeting a plan sponsor's needs. In particular, if a plan sponsor intends to get involved in direct contracting, there will be a greater need for the plan sponsor to be in control, and a large organization may be unable to accommodate that need. John Garner outlines several important considerations when using a TPA:[4]

Recruiting. Some TPAs use experienced examiners; others rely on trainees. Each method affects productivity and has distinct advantages and disadvantages.

Training. Some TPAs have formal training programs; others have on-the-job training.

Online versus Batch Edits. Many computer systems are fully online with real-time updates; others rely on batch edits done in overnight processing. Although there are delays associated with batch edits, the more comprehensive edits are best done in batch processing.

Turnaround Goal. A plan sponsor should be sure that the TPA's turnaround goals are consistent with its own. Turnaround time affects cash flow and employee relations.

Production Levels. Production expectations for examiners can vary, although high productivity goals can reduce processing costs at the possible expense of accuracy.

Reasonable and Customary Charges. The determination of reasonable and customary (R&C) charges for specific procedures differs from one geographic area to another. TPAs usually purchase data from organizations such as the Health Insurance Association of America or use a conversion factor for different procedures to determine an allowance for each. Important questions to ask include the following:

1. How frequently are R&C data updated?
2. What have the savings been?
3. How long are R&C data retained?
4. If an old claim is received, are current R&C data applied? (This may encourage late filing.)
5. How are claims involving multiple surgeries handled?
6. Does the system automatically calculate R&C charges for multiple surgeries, or must the examiner make a manual calculation?

Customer Service. Claims offices may have a separate unit that handles telephone calls from employees or may combine customer service and claims examination into one position. The more direct the customer's communication with the examiner, the more likely the examiner will be effective. A separate customer service unit, however, is an effective way to ensure positive employee relations.

Location. The availability of toll-free telephone numbers makes it possible to process claims from anywhere; however, some plan sponsors may prefer utilizing companies within the same time zone.

Regulatory Compliance. Many states regulate the activities of claims management and claims adjudication by licensing organizations that function as TPAs. Evidence of compliance with state law is essential.

Q 5:38   What should be considered when conducting a TPA audit?

A TPA audit is an effective way to find out whether corporate goals, including cost containment, are being met by those administering the company's benefit plans. This means that the employee health care program is being administered in accordance with the coverage available, corporate intent, and employee needs as efficiently and cost effectively as possible. Areas relating to performance should also be included in the scope of the audit. The type of data and reports available as compared to those that are needed is another audit consideration. The lack of good statistical data or an ongoing reporting system prevents interim reviews of performance costs and problems.

Another important consideration is cost control of claims administration and its effect on the payment of claims. Sometimes the method of claim settlement (whether by the claim or by the hour) will affect not only the quality of the claim service but also the amount being paid for the claims. When considering or initiating an audit, a clear understanding of the sample size, type of evaluation, and presentation of audit results will be needed. There are several factors to be considered:

1. What is intended to be accomplished by the audit? Is it part of an overall management audit process, or was it necessitated by staff changes, financial considerations, or plan structural revision?

2. To whom is the report to be addressed? The administrator? The plan sponsor? The union?

3. What method is to be used for the audit? Personal interview? Review of policies and procedures and management control? Employee survey, in-depth file review, or a combination?

4. Who will establish the audit parameters? How will the review be evaluated?

5. Will only closed claims be reviewed, or both open and closed claims? Older claims often do not reveal current problems, whereas current claims do not reflect historical trends.

Q 5:39 What are the most common types of TPA audits?

There are generally two types of audits: management audits and claim audits.

Management Audits. The objective of a management audit is to confirm that implementation of the TPA is appropriate to the employee health plan or program. The administration should be consistent with the coverage, corporate intent, and employee needs while minimizing inefficiency and improper payment. These audits are generally audits against a written set of goals and responsibilities. The steps in this type of audit are (1) meeting with the administrator's senior staff to confirm goals and responsibilities and clarify areas of concern or possible misunderstanding; (2) reviewing the administrator's structure, philosophy, staffing, position requirements, and clinical and statistical support; (3) reviewing policy and procedure manuals and outcomes; and (4) reviewing steps in the claims or servicing process. As noted by Arthur Parry and John Fortin, a good management audit requires factual information with statistical measures.[5] They suggest the following questions in fact gathering:

1. How often is the administrator understaffed?

2. How long have such understaffings existed?

3. How often are unqualified claims personnel used?

4. How often are procedures changed without documentation?

5. How often is software "down"? How often are computer runs unavailable?

6. How frequently are supervisor reports made or required?

7. How frequently are coverage verifications made or required?

8. How often are provider verifications conducted?

Other factors to consider are actual claims handling by employees, morale, management competence, and commitment.

Claim Audits. Most claim audits begin with a review of the historical claim reports by both the employer and the administrator to identify (1) how large the program is (based on time, dollars, or claims); (2) the distribution of major claims or groups of claims; (3) divisions within the employer group of large subsets (by location, department, employee age, or date of hire); (4) problem areas (age of claimants, date of hire, functional area, geographical area); (5) claims that require a lower level of analysis (e.g., medical only with no wage-loss payment); (6) patterns in the data that require special analysis; and (7) gaps in the data that may require special runs or special handling of individual files in order to provide a particular type of analysis.

Following the historical review, the complete claim file should be included in the audit sample. According to Parry and Fortin, a claim audit should cover the following areas:[6]

- Applicability, including verification of coverage, limits, date of loss, eligibility of individual, expense, and injury

- Process, including the method of reporting, timeliness of process, investigation, adherence to claim standards, dealing with physicians and other providers promptly, contact with employee, and contact with employer

- Reporting, including reports of individual claims, statistical reporting to the employer, special reports as required by the claims, and coding claims of active versus retired employees

- Reserving, including the nature of the reserving process; when the initial reserve is established, by whom, and how it is reviewed; and how and when it is charged

- Payment, including timeliness, method, type of accounting and banking used, check register availability, controls in place, and number of signatures involved

- Authorization, including authorities and requirements for investigating, reserving, reporting, approving and making payments, and need identification and verification

- Offset verification, including the use of other parties for payment within employee benefit payment programs, such as payments by employees (deductibles), payments by other payers (copayments), reinsurers, and even third parties under subrogation; verification that all parties have been correctly involved is important

- Litigation, including controls or flags to ensure prompt involvement of the employer and appropriate handling of all situations that may become lawsuits

- Auditing third-party payer bills, including assessment of the controls, reviews, and analyses in place as to reasonable and customary charges, double billing, inaccurate billing, and discounts from network providers

- Utilization review (usually conducted as a separate audit), including looking at the linkage to the utilization review process, particularly preadmission certification, concurrent review, and large-case management

- Employee handling, including employee requests, concerns, rehabilitation, training, and overall attitude

- Documentation, including showing that the entire claims process is based on orderly, clear file documentation that will allow an auditor to trace the file process without gaps in information

Q 5:40 What is benefits administration, and how does it differ from claims administration?

Benefits administration is the administrative aspect of the delivery of health care benefits to members of an MCO. It focuses on the role of the MCO in the delivery of services under a health benefit plan. Benefits administration generally includes member eligibility verification, benefit interpretation, provider claim for services adjudication and payment, provider support and system file maintenance, member reimbursement for services, COB and third-party liability recognition and collection, capitation accounting and payment, liability accrual estimation, authorization of services, and verification and statistical reporting of utilization and internal productivity.

Claims administration is the administrative aspect of the processing and adjudication of filed claims for payment under the applicable benefit plan. Although claims administration overlaps in many respects with benefits administration, its primary focus is on the provider's compliance with claims filing and payment processes. The effectiveness of the claims department can make the difference between financial success and failure along the entire chain of payment. For this reason, most MCOs pay close attention to their claims and benefits administration responsibilities.

Q 5:41 Is there a role for TPAs in MCO benefits administration?

Yes, there is a role for TPAs in MCO benefits administration. The criteria to consider in selecting a TPA to perform external benefit administration on behalf of MCOs are similar to those to be considered in selecting a TPA to administer a self-insured plan (see Q 5:37), but there are some differences. Because most TPAs work with indemnity-type plans, the prepaid, reporting, and preauthorization requirements of MCOs may be unfamiliar to many TPAs.

Q 5:42 What should a company consider in selecting a TPA to handle benefits administration?

If an organization intends to use a TPA to handle benefits administration, it should evaluate the TPA in several areas:

Productivity. There should be a mechanism to evaluate and monitor the productivity of the TPA in administering the claims. Evaluation can be based on a review of dollars spent, dollars per provider type, dollars collected or avoided through COB, dollars and claims per processor, claims denied and reasons for denial, and claim payment lag analysis.

Membership System Interface. There should be a method for interfacing the TPA's benefits administration computer and the membership files of the MCO.

Authorization System Interface. There should be an effective authorization system for out-of-area or out-of-plan services. This allows the MCO to have better control over the frequency and expense of these services and estimate liability for expenses incurred but not reported.

Q 5:43 How does managed care affect the administration of health benefit plans?

Historically, employers relied on insurance companies, TPAs, and utilization review committees to administer the health care services delivery system under fee-for-service arrangements with some level of utilization review and discounts on pricing. Most managed care plans are administered to encourage employee and provider compliance with plan restrictions:

1. Benefit differentials can include penalties for noncompliance with such requirements as preadmission certification before nonemergency hospitalization.

2. Limitations on provider selection had been a common feature in most managed care plans but are being challenged in several states under "any willing provider" statutes. In addition, restricting providers has been one of the most damaging aspects of modern managed care. The POS product is designed to circumvent this restriction while placing an increased financial burden on the beneficiary.

3. Use of copayments and deductibles places certain financial responsibilities on those using the services of the managed care providers.

4. Periodic reapproval of extended treatments controls costs and manages care.

Liability Issues in Administration

Q 5:44   What types of activities in managed care plan administration can create liability for either the administrator or the employer?

Plan Administration Liability. Even under indemnity arrangements, in which the patient is not directed to a particular provider, the plan administrator is liable for improper administration activities relating to the plan, such as attempts to recover improperly granted claims from the payee, improper denials of claims, improper or no notification to the plan participants of rights under the plan, civil monetary penalties for failure to file Form 5500 with the IRS and/or DOL, and COBRA penalties for failure to give COBRA notices.

Employer (Plan Sponsor) Liability. There is potential liability for unintended benefits if plan documents do not clearly specify the plan benefits or if plan assets are not properly kept in trust.

Shared Liability (Administrator and Sponsor). The plan sponsor and/or administrator of plans that use an HMO are at risk for liability. This liability commonly relates to employee dissatisfaction with the selection of providers, improper selection and supervision of providers or the HMO, and access to and level of care decisions. These issues are discussed in chapter 8.

Many states are holding health plans and their medical directors legally accountable for coverage decisions. For example, in an Arizona case, a medical director's coverage determination was determined to be the "practice of medicine" rather than a "determination of coverage"; this brought the matter under the jurisdiction of the Arizona Board of Medical Examiners. [Murphy et al v Board of Medical Examiners, 949 P 2d 530 (Ariz Ct App 1997)]

Q 5:45   How does ERISA preemption affect liability issues in managed care?

ERISA offers substantial protection to managed care plans through its preemption of state laws and claims "insofar as they relate to any employee benefit plan." [See 29 USC § 1144(a)] ERISA preemption has been successfully used to avoid liability in bad-faith cases,[7] to overcome application of state "any willing provider" laws,[8] and to avoid liability under state common law contract and tort claims.[9] Thus, plan participants and their beneficiaries, in suing for any plan benefits, must do so under ERISA; this limits their claims to the benefits sued for and—in the discretion of the court—attorneys' fees.

Businesses argue that another important benefit of ERISA preemption is that it allows ERISA's standard of review in contract claims for benefits to be used instead of state standards of review. Under ERISA, the claimant has the burden of proof in challenging any rights claimed under the benefit plan agreement. In state law challenges under a contract theory of liability, the burden of proof is on the insurer rather than on the insured.

ERISA also gives an MCO broad discretion in interpreting a plan's benefits provisions. A court can review the interpretation of coverage *de novo* only if the fiduciary has a conflict (such as an economic stake in the outcome). Such conflicts rarely exist when an MCO administers a self-funded plan or when an MCO is functioning in a utilization review capacity, even though the MCO's compensation may be tied, in some ways, to its interpretation of coverage.

With respect to the application of ERISA preemption to negligence claims, the courts are divided concerning claims brought against MCOs on a vicarious liability theory. Some courts have held that ERISA expressly preempts such claims.[10] Others have reached a contrary conclusion.[11]

Q 5:46   For purposes of managed care arrangements, who is a fiduciary under ERISA?

All managed care arrangements have the potential to make the entity determining the care a fiduciary under ERISA and thus potentially liable for decisions that are in breach of the fiduciary duty. TPAs and even MCOs have been deemed fiduciaries in certain cases.

Q 5:47   Can an MCO be an ERISA fiduciary?

Under appropriate circumstances, an MCO can be an ERISA fiduciary to an ERISA plan for a variety of purposes. For example, if an employer or plan sponsor retains no discretion over the administration of a plan and payment of benefits, the MCO will be deemed the fiduciary of the plan. [See Gelardi v Pritak Computer Corp., 761 F 2d 1323, 1325 (9th Cir 1985)] If the responsibilities are divided between multiple parties such as a PPO and a TPA, each may be deemed a fiduciary for ERISA purposes in connection with its particular responsibilities. To the extent the employer uses a closed-panel structure and imposes utilization management procedures on the provision of benefits, the employer is a fiduciary with respect to the selection of providers, the cost-containment mechanisms, and their subsequent implementation.

Evaluating Health Benefits and Plans

Q 5:48   What self-study is required of an employer prior to evaluating a managed care plan offering?

In determining if and how a benefit plan offering would meet a purchaser's needs, a purchaser should understand several fundamental issues:

- Overall compensation and benefits philosophy
- Number and types of medical plans currently offered (including retiree medical plans)
- Age and sex demographics of the workforce (by medical plan, including retirees)
- Historical medical costs and trends for all plans (including employee contributions to cost)
- Plan costs versus regional costs and costs for organizations in the same industry
- Geographic distribution of current and future workforce and the percentage of workforce in markets with adequate managed care plan penetration

Q 5:49 What external information should an employer be capturing as part of the plan evaluation process?

A great deal of information is available from both the state HMO regulatory agencies and HMOs themselves. The following categories of questions are offered as a starting point for each managed care plan under consideration.

Q 5:50 What characteristics of ownership are important in the benefit plan evaluation process?

Several important ownership characteristics of the benefit plan should be considered before entering into any business arrangement:

- Recognition and track record nationally or regionally. Virtually all national news and business magazines have ranked HMOs and managed care products. With the fury of mergers and acquisitions in the insurance and HMO market and the rapid turnover in management, these rankings are, regrettably, of little use in making a purchase decision, since the published data lag behind the reality of the health plan.
- Financial stability (ratings by companies such as A.M. Best, Moody's, and Dun and Bradstreet). The most up-to-date data are usually available from the state insurance commission.
- Years of operation in markets under consideration

- Profit status (for-profit or nonprofit). It is critical to obtain current information on the status of MCOs, since the trend is to convert to for-profit status.
- Management team and management systems
- Stable versus "in transition"
- Medical director's role in management and in improving quality and outcomes. It is generally accepted that the medical director should be a critical part of the management team; however, this is often not the case. Although it is difficult to assess the degree of participation of the medical director, certain clues can be gleaned from the organizational structure:
  —Is the medical director part of the executive committee of the health plan?
  —Does clinical decision making regarding care delivery, pathways, and criteria emanate from the medical director's line of authority?
  —Is the medical director involved in credentialing, care management, and case review?
- Management information system (MIS) utilized, number of months in place, and tenure of MIS director. MIS is a moving target in all health services. The HMO should have an MIS strategy that is responsive to changes in the environment and amenable to innovation as the technology shifts.
- Customer services team structure and tenure of key staff. As all managed care becomes similar in pricing, the value-added services loom large to differentiate products.
- System for handling physician and medical staff issues. This is often called "provider relations" and is critical in ensuring continuity between the payer, the plan, and the medical care system.
- Financial and utilization data (two years minimum)

Q 5:51 What type of financial data should be reviewed?

Data availability and trends are important indicators of a health plan's performance. Such data include the following:

- Premium trend (preferably three years). Data regarding the premium trend are complex and have to be analyzed in the context of the secular trend of premiums, as well as in the context of the change in premiums in the local market. When comparing premiums, it is critical to compare plans that are alike. That is, value-added services differ among health plans. After a five-year decline, HMO premiums are increasing nationwide in recognition of the underpricing of HMO products and poor market performance of HMOs in general.

- Underwriting restrictions (i.e., thresholds of employer size to "experience rate" versus "community rate"). Some size restrictions are established by payers (as in a cap for Medicaid patients in certain markets), whereas others are terms of the HMO's certificate of authority issued by the state. It should not be assumed that the geographic area covered by an HMO is congruent with the service area desired by the purchaser. Service area characteristics of the certificate of authority should be carefully determined in the contracting process.

- Net after-tax profit or loss

- Equity per member

- Ratio of assets to liabilities

- Medical loss ratio (MLR) (total claims divided by total revenues). The medical loss ratio is a proxy for how much the HMO projects spending on the actual care of the patient. This ratio has become the moral touchstone for HMO performance in that a low MLR can indicate overly aggressive profits or a restrictive access policy.

- Claims coverage (total current assets divided by average monthly claim costs). All HMOs are required to have the financial security necessary to pay claims for their patients in the event of a default or serious financial reversal. The claims coverage trend can be used as an element of the assessment of the exposure of the HMO.

- Membership levels and composition (e.g., commercial, Medicare, Medicaid)

- Net worth as a percentage of annual revenues

- Prior year IBNR (incurred but not reported) estimate per member versus actual claim costs. IBNR is the bane of the HMO industry. It is particularly critical in a young HMO that has not yet achieved a steady state in claims. When valuing an HMO, IBNR is an important measure.

The financial data produced by a health plan or state agency may not relate directly to the dollar amount of premiums proposed to an employer. An employer must, nonetheless, evaluate the market as to competitive rates as well as the employer's historical cost data. Depending on the situation, a health plan may be designed to be a more competitive bid if it is understood that the plan is under a competitive bid or, conversely, that it could get the business (exclusively) if it meets both price and performance conditions set out by the purchaser.

Q 5:52 What type of utilization data is collected by health plans and HMOs?

The utilization data and a health plan's ability to capture such data are of critical importance to the evaluation of a benefit plan. Such data should include the following:

- Hospital days and discharges per 1,000 members (all cases—maternity, psychiatric and substance abuse, medical and surgical, etc.). In assessing hospital days per 1,000 members, two features must be kept in mind:
  - The case mix. This represents the type and severity of illness cared for in the enrolled population. Variations in the case mix can dramatically affect cost of care.
  - Demographic adjustment. Hospitalization rates vary by age and sex, particularly with Medicare.
- Standard of the community
- Hospital cost per day (all cases—maternity, psychiatric and substance abuse, medical and surgical, etc.). Hospital costs are a complex variable, depending on the costs of the community and labor and professional costs. On the other hand, all other things being equal (including outcomes), this metric can be useful in comparing the cost or efficacy of several plans. When comparing plans, it is critical to be certain that all things are indeed equal, including value-added services.
- Physician visits per 1,000 (primary care and all physicians)
- Pharmacy (outpatient) utilization and cost per member per month, and generic substitution rate
- Delivery system
- Number and type of providers in the market. The distribution and quality of providers may be the critical feature of an HMO network structure.

- Current directory of providers (subjectively review general de-sirability and name recognition of the major hospitals and medical groups)
- Primary care physician (PCP) to member ratio (both target and actual rates)
- Percentage of PCPs and all physicians who are board certified
- Percentage of PCPs accepting new patients
- Payment mechanisms for physicians (percentage under capitation, fee-for-service, etc.), including bonus pool arrangements for hospitalization, specialty referral, and pharmacy benefits
- Pharmacy network providers
- Pharmacy benefit program (description, formulary, and incentive arrangements with physicians)
- Process for members accessing specialist care
- Utilization and case management program documentation and clinical practice guidelines utilized
- Centers of excellence contracted nationwide for high-cost procedures
- Out-of-area network coverage and description (subcontracted national networks)
- Member services, including the following:
  —Appointment waiting time (routine and urgent care)
  —Member satisfaction survey results (grievance rate per 1,000, overall satisfaction rate, and percentage that would recommend the plan to others)
  —Claims turnaround time
- Disenrollment rates
- Client (employer) services
- Extent of on-site support during enrollment periods
- Process for handling transitional members (those in process of receiving medical treatment who are changing plans)
- Provision of inventory control and distribution (year-long enrollment materials, directories, etc.). This is a major consideration for purchasers with numerous employee locations
- Process and timing of handling enrollment tapes, invoicing, reconciliation, and so forth

- Limits on retroactive membership count and related premium adjustments

Q 5:53 What are the particular areas in which a purchaser can have some level of control in negotiating with a health plan?

The areas in which a purchaser can exercise some degree of control in obtaining the most value for its health care dollar are the following:

- Negotiating HMO premiums and negotiating funding approaches (fully insured, self-insured, etc.)
- Negotiating benefit packages (HMO-specific); analyzing and determining appropriate employee premium contributions
- Establishing streamlined administrative services and performance requirements (including refunds if complaints exceed prenegotiated levels per 1,000 members)
- Telephone response times from customer service
- Limiting the amount, nature, and timing of any marketing efforts to employees

When an employer has significant leverage with an HMO (i.e., over 10 percent of the lives in a market), the employer can typically influence other things, including which providers to add or delete (for its specific program), negotiating shared savings arrangements, and placing limitations on annual rate increases. Rate negotiation usually is the primary focus of the purchasing process. Arming itself with information such as that suggested in the foregoing questions can be a key determinant for the purchaser that would like to obtain the most favorable rate for its medical benefit program.

Q 5:54 When offering multiple plans, why is it important to establish a strategy for consistent plan design across all plans and corresponding employee contribution levels?

Establishing a level playing field for all the benefit packages offered by different plans, or at least understanding the dollar value of those differences, is an important step in successfully offering multiple plans. An employee's selection of a medical plan will depend primarily on how much the plan costs him or her each pay period, the benefit coverage (deductibles, office visit costs, etc.), and the perceived quality and adequacy of participating providers. The employees' plan selection pattern is a major determinant in the financial health of the entire medical program. It will also determine, on another level, if the employer or the HMO wins in the "risk game." In an ideal world, a "win-win" results when the HMO profits, not by stealing healthier and lower-cost members, but by efficiently managing the level of risk for which it is responsible (and for which it is commensurately paid).

To the extent an employer has in place an overall benefits strategy or clearly stated philosophy, the process of steering employees through employer-employee premium contribution rates and/or the leveling of the benefit packages across all plans can begin. For example, the benefits philosophy might be stated as follows: "It is the organization's position to offer employees a choice of plans" or "It is the organization's intent to move everyone into the lowest cost plan." With this fundamental understanding, one can begin the evaluation process.

In the 1980s, many employers learned first hand the meaning of the term *adverse selection*. Adverse selection, in this context, is a phenomenon whereby younger and supposedly healthier employees (who typically earn less than their older colleagues) select an HMO (or other fully insured plan) based mostly on a lower (even if only marginally) premium cost to them, causing their employer's self-insured plan to lose the most desirable risks and therefore cause a disproportionate rise in the cost of that plan. Unfortunately, many employers that intend to lower overall costs by offering a second, "less expensive" plan actually exacerbate the cost spiral. The general principle of insurance involves the spreading of risk among the largest possible number of people. When an employer subdivides the risk pool by offering multiple plans in the name of "freedom of choice," it runs an increased risk of creating adverse selection and raising the aggregate cost of its medical programs, especially if there is a self-insured plan in place. Unabated, this trend causes more and more people to flee the self-insured plan (which may be politically untouchable) and creates what is known in the actuarial business as the "death spiral." The employer may eventually terminate the self-insured plan, leading to painful employee relations.

Whether negotiating the total premium with an HMO or establishing internal employee-employer contribution rates, the "base benefit plan" must be priced along with the actuarial cost differences of the benefits across different plans. Different benefits (e.g., vision, prescription drug) cost different amounts and often attract different categories of employees. For example, a 20-year-old male may be more interested in coverage for prescription glasses and contact lenses (low actuarial cost) than in a generous hospitalization benefit (high actuarial cost). Employers that require employees to pay the cost of the differences beyond the base benefit package have tended to be more successful in reducing adverse selection. Armed with an understanding of the benefit cost differences among plans—for example, Base Plan A, 1.00, and Plan B, 1.05—an employer wanting to "level the playing field" may want to ensure that employees pay 5 percent more for Plan B, regardless of the total premium negotiated with the HMO (assume there are no other age and sex selection considerations).

The following table illustrates the relative cost weights by employee age and dependent coverage categories, based on a composite premium of 1.00. The table shows the extent of variation in costs among different age segments and coverage types.

Specimen Age Factors by Coverage Tier: Three Tier Rates

Employee Age Segment	Employee Only	Employee Plus Spouse or Child	Employee Plus Family
15–24	0.630	1.199	2.256
25–29	0.815	1.586	2.629
30–34	0.975	1.792	2.851
35–39	0.985	1.811	2.859
40–44	1.022	1.858	2.911
45–49	1.101	2.037	3.089
50–54	1.337	2.365	3.420
55–59	1.649	2.923	3.971
60–64	1.871	3.265	4.320
65+	2.030	3.611	4.667

When these factors are adjusted using actual employer data and geographic cost factors, the employer has a basis for adjusting the employee contribution levels internally (and negotiating or adjusting total premiums with an HMO rather than accepting their "off-the-shelf" community rates) to reflect either historical or actual enrollment patterns.

Q 5:55   How does one evaluate a plan's ability to meet the geographic requirements for an employee and retiree population?

Employers can use any one of several commercial software products on the market to map employees, doctor's offices, and hospitals by zip codes. For example, Map Lynx can graph provider locations and employee residences on a printed map and give the analyst a thumbnail sketch of geographic desirability.

For large and/or multisite employers, more sophisticated tools can be employed. For example, GeoNetworks, produced by GeoAccess Inc. of Overland Park, Kansas, is a managed care-specific software package, typically leased by major consulting houses, large provider organizations, and managed care vendors. An employer can produce a simple ASCII file containing the addresses and zip codes of its employees (with other optional data elements, such as coverage type, sex, and active or retiree) for an HMO or other managed care plan and have it match the covered population against its database of PCPs and hospitals. Some of the typical reports and specifications that can be requested include the following:

- Percentage of employees within eight miles (driving distance) of two PCPs (Ten or more miles to one physician may be more appropriate for certain rural settings, and two PCPs within five miles may be suitable for large metropolitan areas.)

- Percentage of employees within ten miles of a full-service acute-care hospital (30+ miles for rural areas)

- Maps showing employees without desired access (with attached summaries listing county, city, and zip codes)

Many plans, unless it is requested, will not differentiate types of PCPs in their reports, which may be relevant to a given population mix. Several special reports may be requested, but the employer must provide the necessary demographic data (e.g., employee sex, family status, active or retiree):

- Geographic distance of employees with family coverage to pediatricians

- Geographic distance of single female employees and employees with two-party and family coverage to obstetrician-gynecologists

- Geographic distance of all employees to adult medicine providers

- Maps showing employees without desired access according to the preceding categories

In all cases, one must be certain that the physicians included in the analyses have practices that are open to new patients, and that if there are limitations on the types and ages of patients, those are clearly shown. In addition to mapping software reports, certain internal reports that may provide previews of potential problems, especially those dealing with hospital-based physicians, can be requested. For example, a list of all specialists sorted by participating hospital and medical specialty will indicate the holes in coverage of various specialties in the most commonly used hospitals, with particular emphasis on the hospital-based physician specialties (radiology, anesthesiology, pathology, and emergency medicine). Many employee complaints arise out of a lack of in-network coverage within a hospital, which may cause an employee to have to pay higher out-of-pocket costs to these specialists despite having complied with the plan by selecting in-network surgeons and facilities. Having this information can provide a basis for causing the HMO to fill its coverage holes before problems occur.

Q 5:56 What are the major administrative challenges for an employer offering managed care plans?

The major administrative challenges for an employer offering managed care plans are the following:

- Conducting the enrollment process (with the added complexity of dependent enrollment and assignment to PCPs)

- Reconciling membership counts (adds and deletes) and associated dollar disbursements

- Dealing with questions and complaints

- Acting as a medical ombudsman (i.e., dealing with denials of payment for common outpatient services not preauthorized by a PCP, and denied coverage for "experimental" treatments)
- Conducting rate renegotiations (planning and execution)

Many of the larger, more geographically dispersed employers rely on consultants and specialty brokers to "manage" various or all aspects of their HMO relationships. Often these consultants and brokers are paid an hourly fee to perform these services, especially services involving only premium rate analysis and negotiation. Others are paid on a percentage-of-premium basis, especially for full service contracts. The payment approach for these services must be considered carefully, much as an individual investor might hire a fee-only financial advisor versus a commissioned advisor, or vice versa. In general, an employer's administrative workload should be somewhat less demanding with an HMO versus a self-funded indemnity plan; however, an HMO plan needs to be monitored throughout the year. Utilization and cost data should be provided regularly so that rate renegotiations can be done with plenty of lead time before the employer's open enrollment period. Furthermore, it is important to keep track of complaints, especially those relating to providers, so that corrective action (i.e., termination from the employer's network) can be taken on contract renewal or sooner. Customer service and claims service complaints should also be documented, and can be utilized in the renewal process, as well as in documenting performance requirements.

References

1. Under ERISA § 502(a)(1)(B), 29 USC § 1132(a)(1)(B), a plan participant or beneficiary can sue in federal or state court to recover plan benefits, enforce rights under a plan, or clarify rights to future benefits under a plan, regardless of the amount in controversy. *See also* ERISA § 502(e)(1), (f), 29 USC § 1132(e)(1), (f).

2. Heasley v. Belden & Blake Corp., 16 Employee Benefits Case (BNA) 2649, 2659 (3d Cir 1993).

3. Booz-Allen & Hamilton. Contact: Stacy Roose, 212-484-7486.

4. J.C. Garner, "Who Should Administer Your Health Plan," *Strategy and Business* (Mar 2, 2000), in *Driving Down Health Care Costs: Strategies and Solutions* (New York: Panel Publishers 1993) 213–223.

5. A.E. Parry and J.D. Fortin, "Auditing Third Party Administrators," in *Driving Down Health Care Costs: Strategies and Solutions* (New York: Panel Publishers 1993) 224–232.

6. Id. at 231.

7. *See* O'Reilly v. Cuelleers, 912 F.2d 1383, 1389 (11th Cir. 1990); Pilot Life Ins. Co. v. Dedeaux, 481 U.S. 41 (1987).

8. *See* Cigna HealthCare of La v. Louisiana, No. 94-885 (M.D. La. Apr. 17, 1995). *But see* Stuart Circle Hosp. Corp. v. Aetna Health Management, 995 F.2d 504 (4th Cir. 1993), *cert. denied,* 114 S. Ct. 579 (1994) (holding), ERISA preemption did not apply.

9. *See* Sandler v. New York News Inc., 721 F. Supp. 506, 512 (S.D.N.Y. 1989).

10. Dukes v. US Healthcare Sys. of Pa., Inc., 848 F. Supp. 39 (E.D. Pa. 1994); Altieri v. Cigna Dental Health Plan, 753 F. Supp. 61 (D. Conn. 1990); Holmes v. Pacific Mut. Life Ins. Co., 706 F. Supp. 733 (C.D. Cal. 1989); Rollo v. Maxicare of La., Inc., 695 F. Supp. 245 (E.D. La. 1988).

11. Smith v. HMO Great Lakes, 852 F. Supp. 669 (N.D. Ill. 1994); Elsesser v. Hospital of the Phil. College of Osteopathic Med., 795 F. Supp. 142 (E.D. Pa. 1992); Independence HMO v. Smith, 733 F. Supp. 983 (E.D. Pa. 1990).

Chapter 6

Managed Care Organizations and Health Care Networks

Health care providers have been organizing into groups for decades, beginning with the medical group practice structure, which, in most states, is a creature of statutes that allow the use of different business structures, such as limited partnerships, limited liability companies, limited liability partnerships, and professional corporations. The original purpose of these structures was to permit licensed practitioners to institutionalize their delivery of health care services without violating state prohibitions against the corporate practice of medicine and to receive some of the tax benefits primarily available to legal structures such as corporations.

The federal HMO Act, enacted in 1973, offered incentives for the creation and expansion of health maintenance organizations (HMOs) and the introduction of payment through capitation. As health care delivery moved from traditional fee-for-service systems to managed care prepaid and capitated systems, physicians and other health care providers organized into "contracting" organizations. The independent practice association (IPA) emerged as one of the early provider organizations to respond to economic trends associated with managed care. The IPA structure was quickly followed by a number of other legal and organizational entities intended to give providers options for contracting as a single entity rather than as individual practitioners. These organizations included the physician-hospital organization (PHO), the integrated or organized delivery system (IDS or ODS), and the nonprofit health corporation that could function as either an IPA or a group practice.

The life cycle of managed care organizations (MCOs) has followed managed care trends. The original MCOs, such as IPAs that became affiliated with management services organizations (MSOs) and then incorporated into IDSs during the late 1980s and into the mid-1990s, have completed a life cycle and are now less integrated and have looser affiliations. In addition to this return of IPAs to freestanding status, new models of virtual provider organizations now rely on electronic commerce and the Internet as a platform for payer contracting, claims processing, and credentialing of online provider networks.

With cost containment as a goal, complete vertical integration is no longer the structure of choice. It is being replaced by less resource-intensive, innovative models that use horizontal, functional, and virtual integration techniques to create organizations that can contract as a single entity and share risk and reward from payer contracts.

There is no one successful form of MCO. This chapter discusses the elements associated with success and failure of provider organizations. With the poor response from the provider industry to the availability of the provider-sponsored organization proposed under the Medicare + Choice (M + C) provisions of the Balanced Budget Act of 1997 (BBA) , the integrator of the future is expected to operate through telecommunications and the Internet. This issue is discussed in chapter 15.

This chapter uses a number of terms to describe health care structures that may appear to overlap or refer to the same or similar entities. This is far from fact, since organizations come in all different sizes, compositions, forms of governance, and contractual arrangements. Some provider organizations, referred to generically as networks, are organized by vertical relationships (e.g., hospitals and physicians) or by horizontal relationships (e.g., independent hospitals with other independent hospitals). These distinctions are discussed in detail in the antitrust section of chapter 8. These networks are easily distinguished from the more structured and integrated delivery systems, which are legally and functionally organized and are often characterized by common ownership or control over governance, financing, and other system support for affiliated entities. These more structured organizations may include one or more hospitals, long-term care and intermediate care facilities, home health and ancillary health care organizations, health plans, and medical practices that are staffed by physicians who are either contracted or employed.

This chapter is intended to draw subtle distinctions between these organizations in the context of their role in the managed care "food chain" as a contracting entity to a health plan, as a sponsor of a health plan, or as a member of a network that includes other health care providers that come together to contract collectively and "downstream" of a health plan. The process of coming together to create a relationship among these providers is referred to as provider integration. To the extent the integration is successful, the end-product can be an integrated provider organization that reflects a broad range of different legal and organizational characteristics depending on (1) the degree to which integration occurs, (2) the purpose of integration, and (3) the manner in which the integrated organization operates.

Introduction

Q 6:1   What is an integrated delivery system?

The traditional IDS is a health care delivery system that consists of a parent holding company that owns or controls subsidiary organizations that provide separate health care services. A common example of an IDS is the medical foundation, which is generally structured under a state's nonprofit corporation statutes as an entity that may have as its corporate member a hospital or health care system that qualifies as a provider of care and can employ or contract with physicians to provide medical care to the foundation's patients. In states that strongly prohibit the corporate practice of medicine, such as Texas and California, the foundation model allows a clinic to control the managed care contracts and contract with either physicians or medical groups for medical services. In states without strict corporate practice restrictions, the foundation can employ physicians.

Integration occurs along several tracks in the health care delivery system and includes clinical integration, physician-system integration, and functional integration. Clinical integration involves the coordination of patient care services across the continuum of care, including the application of treatment protocols, consolidated services, and outcomes tracking and measurement. System integration involves the legal and economic association of the system with its physicians. Functional integration focuses on the administrative coordination of services and management throughout the system in areas such as marketing, finance, quality and utilization management, and outcomes measures over a continuum.

Key characteristics of an integrated system include (1) shared vision; (2) collaborative environment; (3) risk identification processes;

(4) integrated information systems (for tracking clinical and financial information); (5) system-wide case management; (6) wellness and prevention services; and (7) infrastructure and support systems.

Another type of provider integration is the affiliation of physicians or a medical group with a hospital. This can occur either through the facilitation efforts of MSO or through a provider structure such as a PHO. The PHO is similar to the IPA, except that the hospital or institutional provider is included in the contracting entity and participates in managed care contracts with the physicians. In some communities, hospitals and physician groups are organizing integrated health care organizations (IHOs), which achieve the vertical integration of hospitals with medical practices. The characteristics of an IHO include (1) the use of a single organization owning the medical practice, the hospital, and ancillary services; (2) global contracting by the IHO for both medical and hospital services with payers; (3) a single governing body; (4) single management; (5) employed or independent contracting physicians; (6) common consolidated capital and operating budgets; (7) a common data and information management system; and (8) a common business focus.

Q 6:2   Why do health care providers form provider organizations?

As health plans began to evolve into models that integrated the financing and delivery of health care, hospitals and physicians felt pressure to form or join integrated networks made up of other health care providers who would be contracted to a particular health plan. Payers (health plans, employers, etc.) found it more convenient to contract with existing networks than to negotiate with individual providers.

Health care providers have been forming organizations engaged in health care in response to a changing economic market, the legal system, and expansion of managed health care benefit products that place greater emphasis on lower cost, higher value, greater access, and improved quality of care. With many states enacting legislation designed to control costs and increase access, market forces are driving health care providers into organizations that can accommodate coordinated care and shared reimbursement. To compete effectively in the various types of managed health care benefit products being developed by employers, insurers, and others, health care providers have been arranging themselves into various legal and operational structures that would allow them to accept and share economic risk.

The successful provider organization had to be able to accept capitation and share economic risk, attract payers, and maintain a high level of quality of care.

Essentially, the events that drove provider integration included the following:

- Increase in managed care contracting and need to accept risk in return for increased volume
- Increasing demand for efficiency in cost and service
- Increasing number of legal and regulatory restraints inherent in the health care industry
- Increasing competition among providers under managed care
- Administrative complexity of managed care
- Need for and access to capital
- Changes in lifestyle preferences among physicians
- Increased accountability

Q 6:3   What are the advantages and disadvantages of provider integration?

The major advantage of provider integration is the ability to operate more efficiently than traditional, fragmented health care systems. Networks allow fixed costs to be spread over a larger base and reduce duplication of services. Because integrated systems can support infrastructure services such as quality management and peer review, these networks can respond effectively to changes in the industry.

Provider networks sometimes fail because their participants do not adopt a collective approach to health care delivery. This is due, in part, to a general lack of trust between independent parties. Many providers are unable to shed their need for autonomy and control, and eventually undermine the advantages inherent in a group arrangement. In addition, development of provider networks is costly and time-consuming, and there are many barriers to the process.

Q 6:4   What are the barriers to achieving effective integration?

These issues are often barriers to achieving effective integration:

- Use of separate versus interdependent provider organizations
- Selection and form of information systems
- Short-term focus on cost containment without long-term goals

grams that promote preventive care in place? Are physicians involved and committed to program goals?

Strategy and Governance

Physician Participation. Physician involvement is necessary not only in routine decision making but also in planning and implementing strategies for effective physician networks. In addition, strong relationships between primary care physicians and specialists are vital.

Are both primary care physicians and specialists represented in governance? Are appropriate primary care networks and specialist affiliations in place? Are they organized to accept risk and manage patient care? Are physicians actively involved in developing and implementing these strategies?

Strategic Planning: Mission and Vision. Like any business, an integrated system needs a strategic plan that includes a mission and vision incorporating physician goals and objectives.

Are physicians actively involved in developing strategic initiatives? Does the plan contain specific and measurable goals to gauge organizational performance over time?

Managed Care and Contracting. Although risk contracting has yet to materialize in many markets, it continues to be attractive to payers. Systems organized to accept and manage risk have a competitive advantage.

Does the system have a contracting initiative in place? Does the initiative have the support and commitment of physicians? Is it structured so as not to limit opportunities for patient growth (an important issue for systems that sponsor health plans)?

Operations, Financial Management, and Cost Control

Clinic or Practice Operations. Inefficient operations—from patient scheduling to billing—can contribute to poor productivity and unnecessary cost.

Has an operational assessment been conducted to identify areas needing improvement? Have all practice sites been reviewed? Have recommendations for improvement been implemented? Have other opportunities for improvement been explored, including standardization and consolidation of practices with excess capacity?

Facilities and Capital Improvement. When systems acquire established physician practices, they often find themselves owning facilities of widely varying quality and there is a temptation to invest heavily in facility upgrades.

Have upgrades been analyzed to determine whether they will yield a direct return? Are all existing facilities necessary? Are there opportunities for facility consolidation?

Staffing. Converting independent practice staff to hospital employment often results in new costs, since hospital salaries and benefits are typically more generous. When these additional costs are allocated back to the practice, once-profitable practices may end up in the red. Too many people are an obvious expense, but so are too few. Benchmarks should be established to optimize staffing. Importantly, less costly staff and providers, such as physician assistants and nurse practitioners, may be able to minimize costs and help raise productivity.

Have staffing needs been analyzed to determine whether the number of staff is appropriate? Are staffing ratios consistent throughout the system? Are mid-level providers involved in the delivery system?

Accounts Receivable Management. When a system acquires independent practices, it often acquires a variety of billing and collections systems with a variety of performance levels. The transition from practice control to system control can be costly, especially since payers have become more rigid in claims management.

Have sufficient resources been directed toward consolidating and standardizing billing practices? Are systems in place to minimize accounts receivable days outstanding? Does the billing staff receive guidance on individual payer requirements for copayments, deductibles, preauthorizations, and referrals? Are delinquent accounts pursued beyond the time they might be viewed as write-offs by the hospital?

Coding and Compliance. Appropriate coding and documentation are critical for reimbursement and regulatory compliance. As government scrutiny of integrated systems continues to increase, larger matters of compliance must be addressed. Physicians and staff are central to optimizing reimbursement and minimizing denials and compliance risks.

Do physicians and staff receive ongoing training in proper coding procedures? Is the training specific to individual specialties? Are all providers audited regularly? Are organizational relationships in compliance with relevant rules and regulations? Are compliance programs implemented and observed throughout the system?

Information Systems. Physicians generally make minimal investments in practice management systems, typically only to handle billing. As a result, integrated systems are often tempted to initiate information system upgrades after practice acquisition.

Are the upgrades cost effective and appropriate to individual practice settings? Have opportunities been explored to consolidate information-related functions, both to minimize cost and improve efficiency? Will upgrading yield data relevant to physician practice management?

Utilization Management. Moving from fee-for-service to risk-based reimbursement requires changes in physician behavior. As reimbursement continues to decline, utilization costs must be understood.

Has the system taken advantage of advances in utilization and disease management, outcomes measurement, and medical informatics to improve quality, productivity, and cost efficiency? Is there a formulary management system in place? Are clinical teams in place to develop programs and educate physicians?

Q 6:7 What are the important governance issues associated with developing an integrated provider organization?

Whenever separate individuals or organizations are merged into a single organization, there are inherent conflicts of interest, often associated with control. One of the most important steps in the provider integration process is to define, design, and develop the governing body of the newly integrated organization to view the organization as a new, unified, and unique entity rather than an organization made up of multiple parts. In determining a governance structure, an organization must consider four key issues: (1) control, (2) structure, (3) function, and (4) composition.

The objectives of the governance structure should be to facilitate effective decision making and ensure representation of interests.

Sometimes the desire of the parties to maintain equal representation on the governing board and on all committees can undermine effective integration. The use of supermajority voting or reserved voting rights may be considered less objectionable than having unequal board representation; however, these strategies generally protect the minority stakeholder and can paralyze the board from effective decision making and action. Too often, effective integration strategies fail because the group dynamics are not addressed or resolved at the organizational stage, even if the documentation is perfect and the economics of the arrangement are ideal.

Q 6:8   What are some of the major problems associated with establishing an IDS?

In addition to the governance issues, the most common problems encountered in the development and operation of an IDS include (1) access to capital, (2) moving money around the system, (3) system-wide credentialing and accreditation, and (4) managed care contracting.

When organizations are integrated or affiliated, there must be a careful planning process and anticipation of potential problems. In some cases, problems affect the parties equally and they can respond collectively. In other cases, problems affect one of the parties and the situation can adversely affect the other parties. The structure and documents should anticipate a number of potential problems, such as changes in the law, and should allow for midcourse adjustment in the structure and relationships, including the ability to terminate and unwind the relationship.

Q 6:9   What are the capital requirements for establishing a successful IDS?

The capital requirements for establishing a successful IDS depend on its structure and activities. To be a meaningful business organization, the IDS must be capitalized sufficiently to allow it to undertake the operations and functions associated with managed care contracting. These include organizing the providers, the management information systems, and the infrastructure and obtaining qualified IDS management. At a minimum, there should be senior management in executive, operations, marketing, and financial areas. Organizations can approach satisfying their infrastructure requirements through either "make" or "buy" strategies; that is, they can develop their capabilities internally or acquire what they need from external vendors.

Capitalization estimates range from as little as $100,000 to form and operate the entity to over $1 million to fully fund a start-up business. The capitalization should cover anticipated operating losses associated with start-up operations, including losses on managed care contracts.

Capital comes from four primary sources: (1) equity investment by participating providers; (2) funds borrowed from a lender or participating providers; (3) charging participating providers a participation fee and changing payers a network access fee; and (4) exchanging equity interest in the IDS for venture capital funding. Since networks do not represent a valuable investment to third-party investors, the most common source of capital is the participating providers.

Unfortunately, continued access to capital can become a serious barrier to the success of any IDS or other provider organization, particularly if there is economic risk involved in the contractual arrangements.

Q 6:10   What role are employers and businesses playing in the trend toward integration of health care providers?

As discussed in chapters 3 and 4, this trend is being driven by the increasing demands being placed on the health care delivery system by those responsible for paying for health care services. As businesses seek to control health care expenses, as business communities develop coalitions, and as federal and state governments focus on legislating health care reform, several common themes appear in these proposed plans: cost control, access, and quality. The provider models developed in response to these demands seek to redefine managed care, which was previously described as something someone from the outside imposed on providers.

Q 6:11   What are the different types of integration and reengineering?

Attorney Gerald R. Peters describes two basic types of integration from a business perspective: structural integration and operational integration.[2]

Structural Integration. Structural integration is the consolidation of separate businesses into either a single organization or a group of affiliated organizations under common ownership and control. For example, a hospital and physician group practice create a holding company and transfer control over their respective organizations to the new company. PHOs and IPAs are not structurally integrated; they are structures ancillary to the participants' existing but separate businesses. Structural integration does not require that the participants operate as a single enterprise.

Operational Integration. Operational integration is the consolidation of previously separate business operations such as planning, staffing, and operational systems. Peters outlines the following characteristics of operational integration:[3] (1) operating all lines of business (hospital, medical practice, ancillary services) under a consolidated budget; (2) unified governance and management responsibilities to coordinate all lines of business; (3) coordination and compatibility of all operating systems (e.g., accounting, billing, collections, and data processing); (4) shared vision and common goals; (5) unified strategic planning and marketing; and (6) single-payer contracting.

Reengineering a health care organization becomes part of the integration process. As described in *Remaking Healthcare in America,* the primary objective of reengineering is to develop an "organized delivery system" out of a system of individual providers, or a merged system of systems.[4] Before an organization can become truly organized, it must first become functionally integrated across institutions and then integrated with its physicians. Only when the system-physician integration occurs can there be clinical integration.

Functional integration involves coordination across operating units of the health system. Physician integration occurs when physicians become economically tied to the system and are actively involved in key management and decision-making roles. Clinical integration is the goal and, like the quality improvement process, is never perfected. It is achieved through the development of a "seamless" process of patient care, which requires a high level of communication among caregivers, excellent information system technology, and the ability to utilize standardized protocols in key clinical areas. The focus becomes patient care.

Q 6:12   What are the traditional integration vehicles for provider organizations?

Historically, the preferred provider organization (PPO), IPA, PHO, and MSO were the predominant organizations used in the development of networks as provider organization models. It is helpful to differentiate the models that represent the integration of physicians or other licensed individual providers (such as the IPA or single and multispecialty medical group practice arrangements) from the models that include hospitals (such as the PHO and the medical foundation model). The provider-based PPO was one of the earliest models to bring together providers in order to obtain payer contracts on an indemnity or discounted fee-for-service basis. The MSO is often used to facilitate and integrate these various provider organizations, or may be the entity that brings a network of providers to a payer relationship.

Q 6:13   What models should providers seeking to develop a fully integrated delivery system consider?

Because integration occurs at a number of levels, one must distinguish between strategies that involve the development of entry models such as IPAs, PHOs, and PPOs and strategies that have actually achieved the more effective level of integration as a provider organization. Between the entry models and the more integrated models, there are transitional models designed to allow the system to evolve to the next higher level. From the perspective of the hospital and physician seeking integration, there are several models to consider.

Entry Model. The most common entry models are structures such as the following:

- A physician office management service bureau, which usually involves a hospital's department providing or arranging for the provision of basic office services such as billing, collection, information systems, and group purchasing
- A group without walls (GWW), which brings together a number of previously independently practicing physicians in a common legal or operational structure
- The "open" PHO, which establishes a contracting vehicle with shared governance between the hospital and physicians to engage jointly in managed care contracting

Transitional Model. The common characteristic of a transitional model is its use of a selection and monitoring process to ensure that the appropriate mix of providers is maintained in response to the needs of prospective payers. A PHO that uses stringent selection and deselection criteria for its participating providers and maintains a specific size and composition (referred to as a closed PHO) will be far more competitive than an open PHO. The MSO is often an important part of the transitional model, because it can facilitate the selective integration process, provide access to capital during the start-up and transition periods, and directly manage the managed care contracting on behalf of the provider organization.

Integrated Model. Although many IPAs, closed PHOs, and MSO-managed groups can function almost as effectively as a foundation model, staff model, or equity model, the latter structures are still more efficient. The major distinction between the foundation model and the staff model is the manner in which the physicians relate to the entity and are paid. In a foundation model, the relationship between the foundation and the physicians is contractual. This continues, to some degree, the inherent conflict between and the adverse interests of the parties to the system. The staff model places the physicians in an employment relationship with the clinic or entity. This model may not be available in states that prohibit the corporate practice of medicine. The equity model has several advantages over the other two models, the most important being its ability to recruit and retain physicians because of the ownership opportunity, allowing both "voice" and "equity." Another advantage is its focus on the physician rather than the hospital. The equity model reflects the acceptance of a hospital as a cost center rather than a revenue center and structures its contracts accordingly. The disadvantage of the equity model is that it is the most capital-intensive model because it often involves acquisition of physician practices.

An approach to integrating physicians into a health care delivery system without acquiring their practices involves contractual agreements between hospitals and physician groups around various practice settings and arrangements. These agreements can take the form of MSO-based models that are either owned by hospitals or by physician-hospital joint ventures. Other arrangements involve the use of outpatient clinics, rural health clinics, or federally qualified health centers, which can be hospital owned or controlled, or physician owned or controlled. As discussed in chapter 8, jointly owned clinics pose problems under federal and state antireferral and anti-kickback laws.

Q 6:14   What role do physicians play in an integration strategy?

A discussion of provider integration cannot be complete without focusing on the alternative forms of physician integration. The organization of physicians into groups is key to the success of any integration strategy except the staff model, in which all physicians are employed by the entity. The general forms of physician organizations include the following:

1. *Independent practice association.* The IPA is a practitioner-controlled legal entity that acts as a vehicle for managed care contracting on behalf of its members, who are generally independent practitioners. Except for risk sharing in managed care contracting, there is little sharing of economic risk or practice.

2. *Medical group practice.* Some medical groups begin their integration process through more loosely structured arrangements, such as those involving individual practitioners and group practices with shared overhead arrangements. The progress toward integration of physicians into group practices can be further facilitated by MSOs, which provide business management and contract administration services to individual or group practices. An example of a partially integrated practice is the GWW, a form of partially integrated medical group practice (PIMG) that involves physicians who maintain separate practice sites but come together to form a single professional organization. They share economic risk but treat overhead, profit, and loss as if they were still in separate practices. A PIMG can mature into a fully integrated medical group practice (FIMG), which is characterized by more complete operational and economic integration in a single, more powerful organization. Characteristics of an FIMG include centralized governance and control; centralized medical records and operational policies and procedures; uniform and consolidated managed care contracting with all participants as providers; formal quality assurance and utilization management programs; and income allocation systems that reward according to group as well as individual performance.

Physicians remain key to the success of any IDS. The most successful IDSs are those that align physician interests and behavior with the strategic and operational goals of the system. Important considerations include compensation arrangements, employment versus independent contractor status, and credentialing and peer review.

Compensation Arrangements. Of critical importance to this alignment is physician compensation. Compensation programs that reward cost-effective behavior have been shown to have an effect on costs. Both base compensation—which can be discounted fee-for-service compensation, resource-based relative value scale (RBRVS) compensation, or capitation-based compensation—and incentive compensation have been shown to be effective in influencing behavior. Performance criteria on which incentive compensation is often based include the following:

- Cost effectiveness
- Quality of care
- Market share
- Patient satisfaction
- Number of subscribers served
- Productivity
- Practice costs

Employment or Contractual Relationships. Whether to establish relationships with physicians as employees or independent contractors will be determined by several factors. The first is whether the physicians can be legally employed by the entity. This is subject to individual state corporate practice of medicine laws, as discussed in chapter 8 and this chapter. Most IDSs want to establish independent contracts with their participating providers because of legal and financial liability considerations. Recent cases, however, have relied on IRS audit guidelines to find an employer-employee relationship for purposes of holding the IDS legally accountable for its physician providers. These criteria are set forth in appendix 6-A.

Credentialing and Peer Review. The process of credentialing and periodically reviewing the performance of physicians is a critical component of any IDS. This is discussed in more detail in Qs 6:45 to 6:52.

Q 6:15   What are the common structural choices for provider integration?

The fundamental structural choices for provider integration include IPAs, GWWs, consolidated medical group practices, MSOs, PHOs, medical foundations, and fully integrated systems. Table 6-1

Table 6-1. Managed Care Organizational Models

Structural Models	General Characteristics	Major Advantages and Disadvantages	Legal Concerns
IPA	• Separate entity • Simple governance • Market flexibility • Separate physician practices	• Access to managed care contracts • Physician independence • Medical staff competition • Cost of operations	• ERISA/pensions • Antitrust • Credentialing • Utilization review • Insurance regulations
PHO	• Separate entity or contractual • Joint governance • Open or closed panel • Unified product(s) • Integrated services	• Enhanced marketability • Physician options • Communications to physicians • Cost of operations • Need for contract expertise	• Antitrust • Business of insurance • Contracts • Credentialing • Liability • Fraud and abuse • Illegal remuneration
MSO	• Separate entity • Full services to medical practices • Asset purchase • Practice management • Paid on fixed fee or percentage basis	• Recruitment vehicle • Economies of scale • Central management • Equity opportunity • Lack of control • Unilateral management • Competition • Need for management expertise	• Corporate practice of medicine • Fraud and abuse • Stark II • ERISA/pensions • Taxes • Restrictive covenant • Licenses
GWW	• Combined practices • Central management • Pooled revenue and expenses	• Multiple sites • Shared overhead and risks • Lessened efficiency • Not full integration	• Antitrust • Fraud and abuse • ERISA/pensions • Stark II ancillaries
Fully integrated system	• Truly integrated services • Employed physicians or nonprofit models (foundation or Texas 5.01(a) nonprofit medical corporation)	• Economies of scale • Aligned interests • Recruitment vehicle • Start-up costs • Physician sensitivity to control	• Corporate practice of medicine • Antitrust • ERISA/pension • Stark II • Fraud and abuse • Tax-exempt status

outlines the general characteristics, major advantages and disadvantages, and typical legal concerns of some of these structures.

Independent Practice Associations

Q 6:16 What is an independent practice association?

The IPA is the simplest form of physician organization. It is an organization composed of individual practitioners who partially integrate their practices through sharing risk in managed care contracting. An IPA contracts with payers to arrange for the provision of medical services and with individual physicians to provide services under the payer contracts arranged by the IPA. Because the IPA is nominally capitalized, it is attractive to physicians who have no prior experience with managed care or practicing as a group.

Developed in the 1980s, the IPA offers a vehicle for physicians and other health care professionals to participate in managed care contracting as an effective alternative to the full-time multispecialty group practice. IPAs perform a dual function in managed care: they can facilitate direct fee-for-service contracting through messenger arrangements, and they can act as an integrated group for purposes of accepting economic risk through capitation. IPAs commonly contract with HMOs and managed care plans to deliver the services desired by the HMO or the plan for its members or subscribers on either a capitated or other risk basis. The IPA in turn contracts with individual providers to provide the services, either on a capitated or fee-for-service basis.

Examples of various IPA structures are shown in Figures 6-1 and 6-2. Figure 6-1 represents a standard IPA structure and its contractual relationships with other providers (e.g., hospitals) and payers. Figure 6-2 represents a second-generation IPA that accommodates fee-for-service and risk-taking providers through shared-risk arrangements. To the extent the IPA can legally assume full or global risk, it may assume management functions such as utilization management, quality assurance, and credentialing from the payer, as well as administration of the risk pools on behalf of its "downstream" contractors.

Figure 6-1.   Standard IPA Physician Shareholders

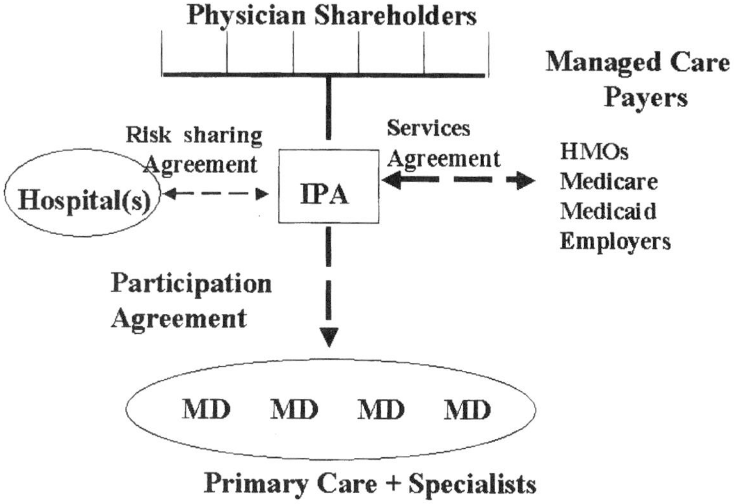

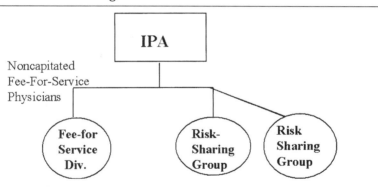

Figure 6-2.   Risk-Sharing IPA

Q 6:17   What dictates the form an IPA takes?

The form an IPA takes is usually dictated by the local market, the role (if any) of the hospital in associating with the IPA, and the number and practice specialties of physicians choosing to participate. These can be hospital affiliated or can be part of a network of IPAs under the umbrella of a larger IPA. The contemporary IPA often functions as a part-time group practice for physician participation in various managed care arrangements.

Q 6:18 What are the general characteristics of an IPA?

Most IPAs are organized as corporations made up of individual or small groups of physicians. Some are set up as not-for-profit corporations, and others are organized as professional corporations, partnerships, or associations. Common characteristics of most IPAs include the following:

1. They are partially integrated and are physician owned or sponsored.
2. Contracts are on a fee-for-service or capitated basis.
3. Physicians remain independent competitors.
4. Contracting physicians may be owners or members, but this is not a requirement.

Most IPAs have a simple and efficient method of governance, flexibility in the increasingly competitive and dynamic managed care market, equal distribution of economic benefits and burdens, and minimal income tax liability.

According to a report of the Managed Care Information Center (MCIC), the average IPA in the United States

1. Includes about 460 physicians;
2. Offers 17 types of specialty physician services;
3. Employs 35.8 nonphysician employees;
4. Has about 14.5 managed care contracts; and
5. Has just under four contracts under negotiation with MCOs.

The MCIC also found that among the IPAs in the United States,

1. 60 percent offer three to five services to their physicians;
2. Quality management is the service they most commonly offer to their physicians;
3. Pediatrics is the specialty most frequently offered;
4. 60.1 percent are "for profit";
5. Less than half (45.6 percent) have or are affiliated with an MSO;

Table 6-2.   MCIC Report on IPA Size

Number of Physicians	% of Total IPAs
< 100	28.20%
100–199	22.60%
200–399	24.00%
400–599	9.50%
600+	15.90%

Note: Percentage may not add up to 100 because of rounding.

Source: *Inside IPAs: An Analysis of Growth Trends, Services and Managed Care Contracts* (Managed Care Information Center, 2000).

6. 87.5 percent are 100 percent owned by physicians;

7. 32.3 percent are seeking contracts outside their service areas; and

8. 75.8 percent get their revenue from only one source. (Managed care was the only source of revenue for 95.7 percent of these IPAs.)

As shown in Table 6-2, most of the nation's IPAs surveyed by MCIC had fewer than 400 physicians.

According to the MCIC, the nine types of services an IPA generally offers to its physicians are authorizations, claims, credentialing, finance, group purchasing, marketing, quality management, referrals, and utilization management. Data show about 25 percent of IPAs offer five of these nine services; 19.18 percent offer four services; and about 15 percent offer three services.

Quality management is the service offered most often; it is offered by more than 82 percent of the IPAs responding. Credentialing ranks second at 78.62 percent and utilization management ranks third at just under 78 percent.

Q 6:19   What are the advantages of the IPA structure?

The IPA is a flexible model that does not compromise practice autonomy. The IPA is attractive to HMOs and other MCOs because it can provide a large panel of participating providers and accept payment on a capitated basis over a broad geographic area. Most

IPAs also perform peer review, quality assurance, utilization management, and review of outcomes data, which are required by most HMOs and MCOs.

For physicians, the advantage of an IPA structure is that they can maintain practice autonomy while participating on a capitated or fee-for-service payment basis. For physicians who are willing to accept capitation, the IPA can capitate their services through its provider agreements. For physicians who do not want to accept capitation payments, the IPA can accept capitation and pay the participating physicians on a fee-for-service basis. An IPA also has more leverage in negotiations with hospitals and payers.

Q 6:20   What are the disadvantages of the IPA structure?

Physician practices under the IPA structure, like practices under any of the less than fully integrated models, do not benefit from group efficiencies, and therefore practice expenses are not significantly reduced. Except for IPA contracts, the physicians remain independent competitors. This not only can be divisive but also subjects the IPA to antitrust risks. Further, the presence of an IPA in a hospital that has an existing PPO may cause divisiveness among the medical staff because it will directly compete with the physicians associated with the PPO. Other potential concerns with the IPA model are its operational expenses, which, coupled with its members' financial exposure under capitated contracting and the increased liability exposure associated with improper credentialing of participating providers, may be too much for physicians, who are generally risk averse. Depending on the legal structure, the participating providers may have problems protecting the qualified status of their pension plans in view of the IRS's application of the affiliated service group rules; and depending on the degree to which the IPA is economically integrated, there may be antitrust problems (see chapter 8).

Q 6:21   How can an IPA enhance its value to providers and payers?

Where possible, an IPA should attempt to secure exclusive contractual agreements with physicians. This reduces the effect of HMOs playing one IPA off against another by using different reimbursement rates to attract common physician participants. IPAs should use incentives to increase physician loyalty such as risk pool surplus participation or equity positions in the IPA or affiliated MSO. Smaller boards, and an expedited process for discipline and termination of physicians, allow an IPA to make decisions efficiently and effectively. Finally, the IPA should have access to capital to meet funding requirements that may arise in risk contracting arrangements. As discussed in chapter 13, many IPAs that go into risk arrangements are often ill-prepared to manage the economic risk.

Q 6:22   How does a hospital-affiliated IPA differ from a physician-sponsored PPO?

During the early days of managed care, when most plans offered a PPO option using discounted fee-for-service products, hospitals and their medical staffs developed PPOs. Typically, these PPOs were made up of staff members of the hospital. The PPO's ability to participate effectively in the more modern managed care plans and products is substantially limited by its loose, inefficient structure. In addition, its lack of sufficient integration makes it an easy target for antitrust challenges.

The hospital-affiliated IPA developed as an effective alternative for more selective physician participation in managed care contracting, particularly in capitated arrangements. Some hospitals have both PPO and IPA models in place. The presence of these two arrangements in the same hospital may result in competition between the PPO and the IPA for the same physician services component of a managed care contract. The preferred approach is one that has the hospital affiliated with a single physician organization under an arrangement that is flexible enough to allow for a broad range of managed care contracting options for both the hospital and its affiliated physicians.

Groups Without Walls

Q 6:23   What is a group without walls?

A GWW is a form of group medical practice that has taken one step toward structural integration of multiple individual practices under a single medical practice organization. It is a partially integrated medical group organization that consolidates the staffing, billing, and collection functions under a single organization that has a single provider identification and tax number but leaves each individual practice in its original location, with the same staff, the same patient records, and often the same practice style. Some physicians also attempt to retain their individual professional revenues and expenses. Physician compensation can be structured as either (1) practice revenues less local office expenses, less a proportional share of central office expenses, or (2) pooled revenues less expenses at all sites. Of these two options, the latter more clearly reflects integration.

Q 6:24   What is the difference between a group without walls and a traditional medical group practice?

A GWW represents a level of integration among independent group practices without full merging of the separate practices. The major distinction is the degree of integration among the physicians' medical practices and with the medical practice organization with respect to risk sharing; pooling of revenues and expenses; and common central services, billing, and collection. These areas may appear the same, but they are functionally quite different.

Q 6:25   What are the advantages of a group without walls?

The GWW structure provides many of the benefits of a fully integrated group practice, such as cost efficiencies and pooled working capital, with limited up-front capital investment and without mandating relocation to a single site. It also gives the physician greater autonomy and allows primary care and specialty physicians to achieve the benefits of a multispecialty group practice. This structure enhances managed care opportunities because (1) some contracts are available only to large physician groups; (2) multiple sites may be attractive to managed care payers; and (3) the financial risk may be spread among several physicians. The GWW provides physicians with increased leverage in negotiating with hospitals and payers for inpatient risk pools. The group practice attribute also facilitates the sale of physician practices on retirement.

Q 6:26   What are the disadvantages of a group without walls?

The GWW model affords no integration between hospitals and the physicians of the GWW except to the extent an MSO is involved.

In addition, many GWWs have experienced a high level of physician dissatisfaction, which has been attributed to the compensation structure and absence of physician commitment to a group practice philosophy. There is also the risk that regulators will view this arrangement as a sham and will deem that the referral and compensation arrangements violate antireferral laws. This problem, along with the inability to centralize ancillary services on behalf of its members consistent with the extension of the Stark Amendment, makes the GWW structure potentially unworkable under current Medicare reimbursement regulations.[5]

Multiple independent practice sites hamper efficiencies of scale, and therefore the group may not be competitive with more fully integrated practices. Additionally, because of the multiple scattered sites, governance and decision-making bodies may be disjointed and in conflict. Finally, some physicians will not adjust to a group practice style of medicine, and therefore the GWW model must provide for the departure of incompatible physicians.

Medical Group Practices

Q 6:27   What are the general characteristics of a medical group practice?

A fully integrated medical group practice formally consolidates physicians into a single cohesive entity. The entity has a single tax and provider number, and all revenue and expenses flow through the group practice. All professional staff are employed by the practice, although if there is a management arrangement with an MSO, the MSO may employ the lay administrative staff. Generally, there is a group compensation system, which may be fixed or production based. These models can be either primary care or specialty practice, although some are multispecialty. Today, the integrated medical practice usually has the following characteristics:

- Single legal entity
- Single tax and provider number
- All revenue and expenses generated by the physicians flow through the group practice

- All employees—including physicians, allied health professionals, and lay administrative staff—are employed by the group
- Group compensation system
- Single specialty or multispecialty
- Single site or multisite

Q 6:28   What are the advantages of a medical group practice?

Full integration guarantees physician oversight and involvement in practice decisions while maximizing the ability to contract, compete, and gain access to capital. A greater degree of integration also increases the financial advantages achieved through economies of scale. The integrated medical group is usually able to consolidate most of the administrative responsibilities of physician practices such as marketing, contracting, billing and collection, purchasing, and human resources. Because the physicians' interests are aligned, much of the conflict and confusion otherwise present are eliminated. The consolidation of the groups with the ability to spread managed care risk for capitated contracts among all physicians in a medical group makes them attractive to HMOs and other MCOs. An integrated medical group practice also eliminates capital obstacles for new physicians in practice start-up, management, recruitment, and retention.

It is easier to grow and consolidate organizations that already have centralized structures and multiple providers. This makes the merger and consolidation of multiple groups into a larger single group much easier than trying to form a large group from many individuals. These larger organizations obtain leverage in the marketplace and have improved access to managed care contracts.

The integrated medical group eliminates a number of legal barriers that confront other forms of physician or provider organizations such as IPAs and PHOs, including antitrust, fraud and abuse, and Stark problems. (See chapter 8 for more details on each of these legal issues.)

Q 6:29   What are the disadvantages of a medical group practice?

The most obvious disadvantage is the loss of autonomy physicians may feel, which could cause them to refuse to devote maximum effort to the group. Moreover, as a result of the level of detail involved, full integration requires greater start-up time and costs, as well as greater capital outlay if a practice acquisition strategy is involved. Large physician organizations tend to have less flexibility to respond to market pressures than smaller groups, which may leave them unable to reduce their overhead in a timely manner and result in economic instability. There are legal and tax issues associated with "buy-in/buy-out" situations involving new or retiring physicians. Finally, developing fair compensation formulas for the practicing physicians is always a challenge.

Management Services Organizations and Physician Practice Management Companies

Q 6:30   What is a management services organization?

An MSO is a business that provides management services to physicians and physician groups. It can be hospital affiliated, physician owned, jointly owned, or investor owned. Most MSOs own the facilities, equipment, and supplies used in the medical practices they manage. MSOs developed out of the perceived need for separating business and management functions from the medical practice. The MSO can provide a broad range of services, facilities, equipment, and support to a variety of provider entities such as individual physicians, medical groups, IPAs, PHOs, medical foundations, and related entities on a contract basis. Often, the MSO also functions as an administrator of managed care contracts on behalf of its managed entities.

The MSO may acquire the tangible assets of a medical practice or acquire new assets and then lease the assets to the medical practice under a management services agreement (MSA). The physicians remain the providers of care, operate all clinical aspects of the practice, and own the medical records and any HMO or PPO contracts. Physician bonding can be achieved through asset purchase payout over time, deferred compensation, and restrictive covenants. Figure 6-3 shows the general structure of a freestanding MSO. Figure 6-4 shows a hospital-affiliated structure. Figure 6-5 depicts a joint venture MSO.

Figure 6-3.   Freestanding MSO

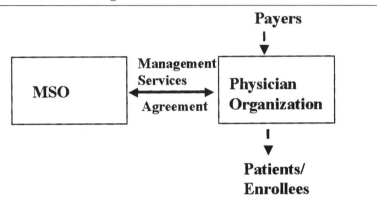

Figure 6-4.   Hospital-Affiliated MSO

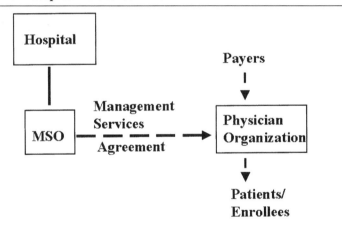

Q 6:31   What is a physician practice management company, and how does it differ from an MSO?

A physician practice management company (PPMC) is a form of MSO that has institutionalized the acquisition and ownership of assets necessary to the practice of medicine, incorporates the management services, and generally offers as an incentive to the managed group an ownership position in the PPMC. These entities have

Figure 6-5.   Joint Venture MSO

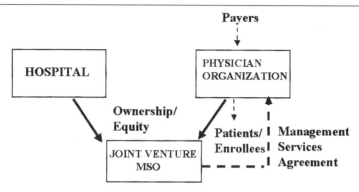

been around since the early 1990s. Most PPMCs were initially structured to be publicly held companies. Despite initial successes in the market, by late 1998 the collective stock prices of PPMCs had gone down by 75 percent and many of the largest PPMCs were no longer in existence.[6] The PPMC free-fall continued throughout 2000 and 2001, but there is a suggestion of a rebound in the surviving companies as of 2002.

PPMCs were originally designed to acquire the tangible assets of the medical practice and lease them back to the practice as part of an MSA. Sometimes PPMCs acquire new assets and lease them to the practice. Occasionally, PPMCs provide support services to other organizations, such as hospitals. Some PPMCs focus on specialty care networks, and others concentrate on primary care practices. A PPMC is not a provider of health care services, but it often affiliates with physician groups, negotiating and even executing managed care contracts on behalf of the contracted groups. This model has generally failed to succeed in the market and very few remain economically viable. The basic PPMC models include the following:

1. *Risk joint venture PPMC.* This model requires the least investment by the PPMC and the least loss of assets by physicians because it sets up a local organization to manage risk contracts and then seeks out IPAs or physician groups that have capitated or risk contracts. These PPMCs manage capitated contracts in return for a management fee.

2. *Independent medical group PPMC.* This model involves a PPMC serving as a parent company of local or regional MSOs. These MSOs purchase assets of local physician groups and leave the practice intact, with the PPMC having a management contract with the independent physician group.

3. *Captive physician group PPMC.* This form of PPMC forms the physician organization and either directly or indirectly owns the practice entity while providing management services either through an owned or controlled MSO or directly.

Q 6:32 What services are generally provided by an MSO?

An MSO can provide a broad range of services to support a medical practice. These services generally fall into the categories of billing, practice management, network administration, and medical outcome management.

The MSO bills and collects for medical services on the physicians' behalf and may negotiate and administer managed care contracts on behalf of the physicians as attorney-in-fact. Nonclinical employees of the medical practice may become employees of the MSO, adding employee benefits and taxes to the MSOs responsibilities.

Q 6:33 What are the general characteristics of an MSO or PPMC?

Most MSOs and PPMCs are separate legal entities that furnish all equipment, supplies, practice sites, personnel, and administrative support services required by physician practices. Compensation typically is based on a fixed fee or percentage of gross revenue. The physicians remain the providers of care, and the MSO bills and collects on the physicians' behalf.

Physician bonding is achieved through asset purchase payout over time, deferred compensation, and restrictive covenants. The physicians own and operate clinical aspects, own the medical records, and hold the HMO and PPO contracts. The MSO may negotiate and execute managed care contracts on behalf of a hospital and physicians as attorney-in-fact and maintains exclusive management for the physician organization or has the right of first refusal to capitalize and manage new clinic sites. The MSO may be owned solely by a hospital or jointly by physicians, HMOs, entrepreneurs, and so on.

The MSO is a taxable entity (a general or membership corporation or a general or limited partnership).

Q 6:34 What are the advantages of an MSO or PPMC?

The principal benefit to each physician in an MSO setting is the ability to retain his or her practice autonomy while eliminating management headaches. Additionally, physicians who are managed by a common MSO or PPMC can benefit from reduced overhead resulting from economies of scale, the MSO's or PPMC's management expertise, and increased access to capital and managed care plans. The MSO or PPMC allows the physicians to recover the equity from their medical practices by selling the tangible assets to the MSO or PPMC and to assign liability by transferring overhead and practice responsibilities to a business that specializes in practice management. For physicians who practice in a state where the corporate practice of medicine is prohibited, MSOs offer unlicensed entities the ability to participate in the management and revenues of a medical practice as long as clinically related decision making is not affected. Even in states that do not prohibit the corporate practice of medicine, MSOs are a viable alternative to selling one's practice to a hospital or other entity and becoming an employee of someone else's business.

The MSO can bring added value to a physician practice through centralized marketing and management services and the collective purchasing power of its several managed entities. A MSO offers one-stop shopping to patients, flexibility in the range of services and number of physicians, and a vehicle for physician recruitment, network development, and practice acquisition.

PPMCs are in a position to bring a greater degree of governance control over physician organizations, but this has not been proven in the marketplace. In fact, as PPMCs became larger and acquired more physicians, governance control appeared to break down or was ignored entirely at the clinical level. Most PPMCs are now trying to restructure to bring physicians together using computer technology for governance and utilization control of medical management.

Q 6:35 What are the disadvantages of an MSO or PPMC?

Because of the regulatory restrictions on PPMC or MSO activities that preclude its control of patients and referrals, there is a financial risk associated with the potential for a runaway medical group that either is recruited from under the contracted medical group or terminates the contract with the PPMC or MSO and enters into direct competition with it. In view of the significant capital investment required of most PPMC or MSO operations, these risks can be significant to the PPMC's or MSO's economic viability.

An PPMC or MSO offers limited opportunity for the operational integration of providers who are not already in one group practice. Because physicians continue to practice separately, their economic interests are not necessarily aligned and they potentially could compete against each other.

The removal of control over the management of the practice from the physicians may be perceived as a loss of control and autonomy, even if the physicians retain ownership of the MSO. An inherent conflict of duties may arise when physicians as owners of the MSO have different objectives than they would as the owners of their own medical group. The bureaucracy in a business organization such as an MSO increases as it takes on the management of more than one group.

Finally, there is still much uncertainty as to the future of the practice management industry. To date, there are few success stories involving PPMCs. In fact, very few PPMCs are finding start-up capital, and companies that are publicly held have taken a huge hit since 1998 as evidenced by significant losses in share value.

Q 6:36 How does an MSO facilitate provider integration?

An MSO facilitates the integration of providers and associated delivery systems by funding the development or start-up of a physician group practice. By facilitating physician integration, an MSO can coordinate functions with a hospital to allow for the possible development of either a network or an IDS.

Physician-Hospital Organizations

Q 6:37 What is a physician-hospital organization?

A PHO is a form of joint venture managed care contracting organization that has the following characteristics:

1. It functions as a negotiating vehicle for managed care contracts on behalf of hospitals and physicians.
2. It may perform utilization review, management, and credentialing functions.
3. Usually it does not assume direct contract responsibility for services.

Q 6:38 How has the PHO evolved?

The PHO evolved from the earlier PPO structures as an organization that can offer to HMOs and managed care contractors both inpatient hospital and professional health care services on a risk basis. A PHO is similar to an IPA for contracting purposes, but it represents a slightly broader group of providers. The PHO brings together the hospital, physicians, and possibly other ancillary providers, with shared governance among all, and may have either open or closed physician membership.

PHOs arose because hospitals struggled to develop new sources of revenues and improve their relationships with physicians on their medical staffs. The PHO was the first form of IDS, and in the late 1980s and early 1990s it was estimated that over 90 percent of the hospitals in the country had organized some form of PHO. The formation of the PHO allowed hospitals and physicians to organize and have stronger negotiating power with MCOs.

The most common structure for a PHO includes a hospital organization and a physician organization; however, there are many different levels of integration. Some PHOs are structured as a mere contractual arrangement between a hospital and its affiliated physicians (or affiliated physician organization or IPA). Others take the form of a separately organized legal entity made up of equal ownership and representation by the hospital and its affiliated physicians (or physician organization or affiliated IPA). The latter description is the most commonly used because of the legal and operational realities of managed care contracting. PHOs can be organized as for-profit business corporations or nonprofit (usually taxable) entities. Figure 6-6 shows the generic PHO structure.

Most PHOs have joint hospital-physician ownership or board membership and may be capable of contracting on a risk basis for inpatient hospital and professional services (depending on the vari-

Figure 6-6. Physician-Hospital Organization

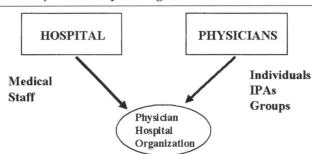

ous state laws relating to risk-bearing activities). PHOs may be open or closed membership organizations. Open membership permits all physicians with basic credentials to participate. Closed membership is typically chosen if a sufficient number of primary care physicians are members. Physician participation may be through an IPA structure, separate physician organization, or independent contractors. Common characteristics of a PHO include the following:

- Hospital-dominated, nonprofit organization
- Funded for the most part by the hospital member
- Typically supported by the hospital's MSO

The PHO operates as a contract broker and facilitates negotiations with payers by bringing a complete package of providers to the negotiating table subject to limitations imposed by antitrust reviews of PHOs (see chapter 8).

According to a study conducted by the MCIC, almost two thirds of the nation's PHOs are located in only 15 states. In addition, none of these states are in the Mountain or Pacific regions of the nation. The top five states ranked according to total number of PHOs are Texas, 86; Illinois, 63; Pennsylvania, 54; Ohio, 48; and Georgia, 44.[7]

Q 6:39   What are the advantages of a PHO?

A PHO integrates the physicians with the hospital in a separate legal and contracting entity. This creates negotiating leverage for both the hospital and the physicians. Hospitals and physicians can share both ownership and control of the legal entity with less up-front capital investment. Because of the separation of the PHO from the more adversarial, traditional hospital-physician relationship, the PHO can arrange for managed care and HMO contracting on behalf of its hospital and physician members. PHOs can receive compensation under a variety of methods, ranging from fee-for-service and discounted fee-for-service compensation to compensation on a capitation, case rate, or per diem rate basis, as well as a variety of other risk-shifting payment mechanisms. These arrangements are subject to the insurance law considerations discussed in chapter 8.

A PHO builds teamwork and trust by means of shared decision making, and this enables the providers to present themselves to payers as a single voice. Shared resources and contracting efforts often improve cost effectiveness and lessen physicians' contracting hassles. There is flexibility in the PHO model, although it increases its participants' awareness of joint cost-control measures and patient care concerns in managed care settings.

Q 6:40   What are the disadvantages of a PHO?

Experience has now shown a high failure rate for hospital-owned and -controlled MSOs and PHOs. In fact, it has been estimated that between 30 and 40 percent of largely controlled MSOs and PHOs go out of business after two or three years. This is due, in part, to the lack of trust physicians have in the sponsoring hospitals and, in part, to the many legal barriers to the effective operation of the model.

The PHO model produces only a partial integration of the hospital and physicians. This increases the risk of antitrust scrutiny. Until recently, it was possible to establish minimum reimbursement rates in contract negotiations. Because of increased scrutiny by the Federal Trade Commission (FTC) under its antitrust enforcement role, many PHOs have lost some leverage and economies of scale in price negotiation terms. This issue is discussed in greater detail in chapter 8.

In addition, because of state laws that regulate the business of insurance and require licensure of HMOs, many PHOs are limited to discounted fee-for-service or direct contracting arrangements on a global fee basis. Capitated arrangements require careful structuring of the PHO contracting arrangement to avoid having the PHO function as an unlicensed insurance company or HMO.

Most PHO provider panels are not selective enough to exclude inefficient providers. The difficulty of excluding practitioners with whom they have practiced for years causes most PHO participants to be overly inclusive, thereby diminishing the ability to control cost through effective utilization.

Like many managed care provider organizations, the PHO may have high overhead because some system is required for tracking utilization, costs, and patient outcomes. The PHO must have expertise in contract negotiations and management.

Fully Integrated Systems

Q 6:41   What is a fully integrated health care delivery system?

Broadly defined, a fully integrated health care delivery system is a network or group of affiliated organizations that provides or arranges to provide a coordinated continuum of services to a defined patient population and is willing to be clinically and financially accountable for the outcomes and health status of the population served. At a minimum, the IDS provides hospital, physician, and related ancillary services. More sophisticated systems coordinate care to patients and may also provide home health, hospice, skilled nursing, preventive medicine, mental health, rehabilitation, long-term care, and other programs representing the full continuum of care. An IDS may be a single organization or a group of affiliated entities under common control or management. The affiliated groups are organized into a comprehensive delivery system that can offer a variety of provider arrangements to payers and other health plans, including HMOs, and to employers under direct contract. This represents the integration of alternative structures into a health care delivery system that can be responsive to a variety of managed care arrangements, including both capitated and discounted fee-for-service health plans.

Most integrated health care delivery systems are provider organizations that do not include the insurance component. Comprehensive systems such as Kaiser, which includes the Kaiser hospitals, the Permanente Medical Group, and the Kaiser Health Plan, are now the trend. Some of the large insurers are using both the MSO and direct acquisition of medical practices to integrate providers with health plans and products in response to health care reform pressures.

Community-Based Organizations

Q 6.42 How does the community fit into the organized delivery system?

Studies have highlighted the importance of local, community-based partnerships as a means of identifying community health needs that can be addressed through innovative community health plans. As discussed in chapter 3, these organizations can evolve into cooperatives or, as in Texas, a state-wide rural health network.

Based on findings from a study conducted by the Community Care Network Demonstration (CCND) under the auspices of the American Hospital Association's Hospital Research and Educational Trust, the Catholic Hospital Association of the United States, and the Voluntary Hospital Association, Inc., with grant support from the Duke Endowment and the Kellogg Foundation, three governance issues emerged: (1) managing jurisdiction issues among partner organizations, (2) defining and incorporating community accountability into the governance process, and (3) coping with the competing demands of partnership growth and development.[8]

Q 6:43 What is a community-based organization and what is its role in health care delivery?

A community-based organization (CBO) is an innovative systems approach to addressing health care needs, delivery, and financing from the local community perspective. The model works well in rural communities and has applicability to any size community that is trying to build infrastructure and manage shrinking resources. Building on the strength and history of the local community the CBO continues the commitment to the local community while incorporating a more diverse representation on its governing board. Its success is based on its ability to integrate physicians, provide low-cost, high-quality care, and govern itself aggressively in a demanding market.

The development of a CBO should incorporate five important aims into its strategic vision: (1) health, (2) cost containment, (3) progress, (4) respect, and (5) collaboration. Using these goals, the CBO should be much more nimble than its competitors in accommodating change, integrating different perspectives, and responding to local community needs.

As discussed in more detail in chapter 3, one example of an organization that relies on local CBOs is the Rural Community Health System of Texas (RCHST), which is a nonprofit, statewide network that supports the development of local community health networks, or PSOs, such as medical foundations. It may also contract directly with individual physicians, hospitals, rural health clinics, and other providers in the community. The RCHST provides centralized administrative, financial, and technical support to locally organized systems. The local CBOs retain oversight of the local delivery system, including quality and utilization management. By establishing one umbrella organization, this model avoids duplication of administrative costs in the rural health care delivery system. Further, this arrangement allows rural communities to share costs associated with administrative simplification under the Health Insurance Portability and Accountability Act of 1996 (HIPAA).

Legal Issues

Q 6:44 What are the major legal issues associated with the development of integrated health care delivery systems and networks?

The legal issues associated with the development of an integrated network of provider arrangements depend on the type and extent of responsibilities that the integrated entity takes on. The legal and regulatory considerations associated with the activities of the various integration models include (1) antitrust; (2) licensing and corporate practice of medicine issues; (3) personnel and benefit issues; (4) employment law; (5) choice of legal entity; (6) state certificate of need or rate-setting laws; (7) insurance law and HMO regulation; (8) illegal remuneration laws; (9) Medicare and Medicaid rules; (10) self-referral prohibitions; and (11) tax exemptions. In certain religious organizations, canon law will apply to the IDS. Confidentiality considerations and general contract law will also apply to IDS arrangements. If the IDS employs its providers, employment law will also apply. Of course, liability issues will exist regardless of the form or structure of the IDS. These legal issues are addressed in more detail in chapter 8. The 11 items listed in this paragraph apply most often to the development and operation of networks or PSOs, and each is considered briefly in the following discussion.

Antitrust. Federal and state antitrust laws regulate competition and, in general, prohibit certain "unreasonable" restraints on trade. Any antitrust analysis should include assessing the risks of both developing a network that involves merger of providers and operating it without creating market dominance and incurring antitrust risk associated with such a market position. Issues to be considered in analyzing the antitrust risk of a network or PSO include the following:

1. Does the formation of the network create too much market dominance or power?

2. Are the physician relationships exclusive? If so, are other competitor organizations foreclosed from effectively competing because the physicians are tied to a particular organization?

3. Does the network agreement preclude its members or participants from dealing with its competitors?

4. Does the network payer contract tie the purchase of a separate service (e.g., hospital services) to the one being sought by the payer (physician services)?

5. Have the physicians and hospital engaged in any illegal pricing discussions prior to actual formation?

6. Has the merger of participating providers been done in compliance with antitrust statutes, including premerger guidelines?

Licensing and Corporate Practice of Medicine. Whenever an organization seeks to employ or contract with a licensed professional or institution or seeks to engage in a regulated activity, it is important to determine whether any licensing laws apply or whether the corporate practice of the licensed activity is prohibited. Because the scope of the corporate practice doctrine varies among the states, it is important to analyze each state's laws as part of developing a network. For example, if a state has a strong corporate practice of medicine doctrine, it is likely that absent specific exceptions in the law, a true network will not be possible (unless it is owned by physicians and licensed as a medical practice entity). Under such circumstances, an MSO can be used to coordinate the institutional and licensed professionals to obtain efficiencies through contract and operation rather than structure.

Personnel and Benefit Issues. In addition to standard employer liability issues for "employed" providers, two key benefit law concepts could affect network participants and their employees. The first concerns the tax treatment of each participant's employee benefits plan on the basis that the entity's structure does not discriminate against non-highly compensated employees in favor of highly compensated employees. The second benefit law concept focuses on the application of nondiscrimination tests to organizations related by common ownership or control, or on the basis of the services provided in determining whether they should be treated as a single employer.[9]

Employment Law. The relationship between a provider organization and its providers may be subject to laws regulating the employer-employee relationship, including federal or state tax and compensation laws. Although most IDSs or networks structure their agreements with providers as independent contractor agreements, because of the government's interest in collecting payroll taxes these arrangements may be subject to IRS scrutiny. In determining whether an individual is an employee, the IRS uses a multifactor test (see appendix 6-A). The key factors focus on control and direction by one party over the other. In the network context, these factors include (1) the degree to which the provider has become integrated into the operation of the network; (2) the nature, regularity, and continuity of the provider's work for the network; (3) the authority reserved by the network to require compliance with its general policies; (4) the availability of employee benefits to the physician; and (5) the network's ability to hire and fire the physician.[10]

Choice of Legal Entity. Although a corporate structure is most common, the choice of entity depends on many factors of a business and tax nature, as well as regulatory considerations. Partnerships allow flexibility in operations and pass through taxable income and losses. Corporations, limited liability partnerships, and limited liability companies allow limited liability for owners, centralized management, and ease of transfer of ownership interests. Nonprofit corporations may be preferred because of tax-exemption issues. States also regulate the types of entities that can contract on a risk basis for medical or health care services. For example, a state department of insurance may restrict a provider to accepting risk only for its own services and preclude "downstream" subcontracting for covered services. Other states may allow a provider organization to control a risk contract for both institutional and professional services. A thorough review of a state's HMO and insurance regulations is essential to the development of a network.

State Certificate of Need or Rate-setting Laws. Many states have certificate of need (CON) laws that govern the establishment and expansion of health care facilities and services in order to manage health care resources and control costs. Although most of these laws apply to expenditures relating to facilities and expensive equipment, some extend to new services. Most CON laws exempt physician services. West Virginia is the only state that has retained a law that prohibits a hospital from discounting below its reported costs. Hospitals are required to report costs to the state on an annual basis. These costs become the floor for any change in charge that the hospital may make. To discount below the reported cost will result in penalties to the hospital.

Insurance Law and HMO Regulation. State insurance laws will determine whether a risk-sharing organization such as a PSO or network can enter into a particular risk-sharing arrangement, the nature and extent of the risk it can bear, and whether the organization will require HMO or insurance licensure. Most HMO statutes define HMOs as any person who undertakes to arrange for the provision of health care services to subscribers and enrollees, or to pay for or reimburse any part of the cost of such services, in return for a prepaid or periodic charge paid by or on behalf of such subscribers or enrollees. Absent an exception for certain types of provider organizations that are allowed to accept business risk for services they provide as licensed providers, HMO licensure may be required.

Illegal Remuneration Laws. A network should be organized with careful attention to state and federal illegal remuneration laws, which prohibit the payment or receipt of anything of value to induce, or in return for, referrals of patients. There are no safe harbors applicable to the purchase of a physician's practice by a hospital, another physician group, or a network in which the physician is to remain in the practice. Important issues in the analysis of network formation include valuation of the assets and the nature of the assets to be purchased. The essential consideration is that there can be no "hidden" payment for an asset. In fact, good will, ongoing business value, and payments for exclusivity or noncompetition could be suspect as inducements for future referrals.

Medicare and Medicaid Rules. Medicare and Medicaid rules pertinent to network arrangements include reassignment rules and physician incentive plan rules:

1. Reassignment rules prohibit a physician from reassigning payment to another entity except where payment is made to the physician's employer under a contract or if the service is being provided in a hospital or rural primary care facility. Therefore, in a practice acquisition by a network, the physician's Medicare or Medicaid accounts receivable may not be assignable to the network as part of the acquisition. If the physician is an independent contractor rather than an employee, he or she may not be able to assign the right to receive payment to the network for the services provided.

2. Physician incentive plan rules apply to managed care arrangements that make a specific payment of any kind to a physician or physician group as an inducement to reduce or limit medically necessary services. These rules require an entity that operates a physician incentive plan that places physicians at substantial financial risk to conduct annual beneficiary surveys, disclose information about the plan to regulatory authorities and beneficiaries, and ensure that all physicians subject to such plans have specified stop-loss protection.

Self-Referral Prohibitions. Federal and many state laws prohibit a physician from referring a patient to an entity for "designated health services" when the physician or a member of the physician's family has a financial relationship with the entity. Financial relationship can mean ownership or compensation arrangements.

Tax Exemptions. When a tax-exempt institution is involved in the development of a network or PSO, there are compelling reasons to seek tax-exempt status for it. Most important is the avoidance of inurement to the exempt institution that is seeking to develop and participate in the network. The more difficult issue is the ability of the network to obtain a tax exemption from the IRS given the strict guidelines it uses to determine whether such organizations serve an exempt purpose.[11]

Integrated Credentialing and Corporate Compliance

Q 6:45   What is the relevance of the Health Care Quality Improvement Act to the selection and deselection of providers in an IDS?

In organizing an IDS or MCO, the organizers should determine whether the benefits of the protection offered by the Health Care Quality Improvement Act (HCQIA), including antitrust immunity and access to the National Practitioner Data Bank (NPDB), outweigh its drawbacks, which include mandatory reporting to the NPDB of adverse credentialing decisions based on clinical competence or conduct, and compliance with the requirements of the statutorily defined due process. Due process, at a minimum, means that the entity must offer the affected provider notice of the reasons for the adverse action and an opportunity to respond to or rebut those reasons. A debate continues among attorneys and other interested parties as to whether an IDS should afford due process to providers who are not selected or who are deselected from participation in the IDS and whether HCQIA even applies to entities such as an IDS.

Q 6:46   Are the credentialing materials used by an IDS discoverable?

The discoverability of confidential credentialing information has been the subject of many treatises and court decisions. The most common request is from plaintiffs' attorneys requesting information in malpractice suits and from physician plaintiffs in antitrust suits. In the absence of a statutory privilege protecting against the discovery of such information, a few courts have allowed discovery of peer review documents. [See, e.g., Kenney v Superior Court of Cal, 255 Cal App 2d 106 (Ct App 1967)] Most courts, however, have tended to restrict discovery by the malpractice plaintiff, reasoning that the harm to the peer review process outweighs the advantages to the plaintiff, who has other means for obtaining the information. Courts have been more liberal in granting discovery requests by physician plaintiffs, reasoning that there is a due process right to the information pertaining to the physician's own case and a greater need for information pertaining to general practices of the peer review committee.

Q 6:47   What are the advantages of centralizing and integrating the credentialing and peer review process system-wide?

With the development of IDSs (hospitals, clinics, and physician organizations), some of which include licensed health plans (insurance or HMO plans), an increasing level of redundancy is inherent in the credentialing and peer review process. Accreditation organizations such as the National Committee on Quality Assurance (NCQA), the Joint Commission on Accreditation of Healthcare Organizations (JCACHO), and the Utilization Review Accreditation Commission place much emphasis on the credentialing and peer review program as part of the overall measurement of quality and outcomes of a network or health plan. The centralization of the credentialing process in health care organizations has increased over the past few years, but few IDSs have achieved true centralization of the credentialing function and fewer have attempted to integrate credentialing and peer review activities within the IDS. One of the major hospitals affiliated with a major teaching program in Houston, Texas, has implemented such a model, which offers several advantages:

1. By eliminating redundancy of effort, the process becomes easier to administer and understand.

2. Centralizing and integrating the credentialing functions reduce the potential for inconsistent credentialing decisions. This is an important risk management consideration.

3. By centralizing the credentialing process within the IDS, the risk that one system entity will take unfair action against a practitioner is minimized.

4. By eliminating redundancy of effort, the process consumes less time and money and takes advantage of existing resources and capacity.

5. The potential for sharing information among the IDS entities improves the quality of information on which credentialing decisions are made and outcomes are measured.

6. A well-organized, centralized, and professional credentialing office is likely to be delegated credentialing functions by other provider organizations and payers.

Q 6:48 What is the difference between a centralized and an integrated credentialing program?

Centralized credentialing involves the consolidation of the application and verification activities for multiple organizations into a central clearinghouse. The process respects the separate oversight and decision making of each organization, which retains its own standards for review, appraisal, and decision making, even though these organizations may be related entities. A credentialing program can be centralized but not integrated, or can be centralized and integrated.

Integrated credentialing involves both the consolidation and the integration of the review and appraisal process beyond a clearinghouse function within a health care system. Such consolidation allows a single credentialing process and standard to be used by related organizations within the same health care system. Parts of a credentialing program may be integrated even though other parts may not even be centralized.

Q 6:49 What are the goals of a centralized and integrated credentialing program?

The goals of a centralized and integrated credentialing program for an IDS should be to

1. Provide an accurate base of information for assessment of the qualifications of physicians and other clinical personnel;
2. Assure a fair and understandable process to those administering the credentialing program as well as to the applicants subject to the process;
3. Serve as a clearinghouse for information received from the many sources inside and outside the IDS;
4. Protect the confidentiality of the peer review process to the fullest extent possible under applicable state and federal law;
5. Provide immunity from suit for those administering the process to the fullest extent allowed by law;
6. Respect the differences among the IDS entities and ensure that each entity meets its unique fiduciary, licensing, certification, and accreditation requirements;

Figure 6-7.　Integrated Credentialing

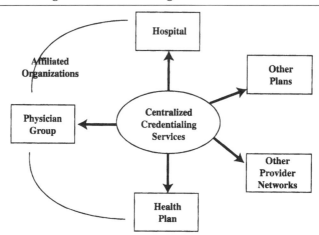

7. Improve IDS system-wide risk management and loss control through an effective credentialing and peer review program; and

8. Be efficient, cost effective, and integrated, both functionally and organizationally, with each IDS entity.

Q 6:50　What is the functional design of a centralized and integrated credentialing program?

Figure 6-7 depicts the model for integrated credentialing. Figure 6-8 represents the current credentialing process for most IDS entities. It reflects a decentralized process with no integration of functions. Each IDS entity has a separate verification and review process. The differences between centralizing the credentialing process and integrating the credentialing function within a health care system range from having centralized verification of primary source information to achieving coordinated qualitative appraisal, reappraisal, and peer review.

Q 6:51　What efforts have been taken to standardize credentialing for provider organizations?

One of the more complicated issues involved in the formation and operation of provider organizations involved in managed care

Figure 6-8. Unintegrated Credentialing

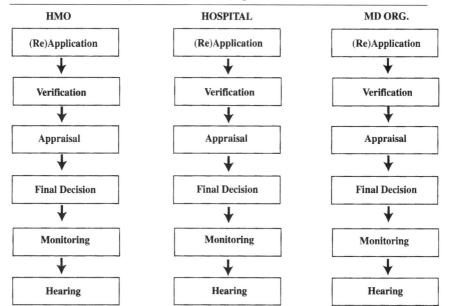

contracting is the process of credentialing the participating providers. Redundancy and cost have posed barriers to a system that should be able to establish common standards and procedures. Credentialing has been identified as the single greatest barrier to accreditation for PPOs and similar organizations. In a novel move, three of the major accreditation organizations announced in July 2000 the initiation of discussions focused on standardizing credentialing criteria. Presently, each of the three major accreditation organizations in managed care, JCAHO, NCQA, and URAC, has its own standards for credentialing providers as part of its accreditation process.

In a separate but equally important move, the Dallas Business Group on Health proposed a common form for physician credentialing designed to save time and money for physicians and health plans. This method has been endorsed by key groups in Texas, including Aetna U.S. Healthcare, the state Medicaid program, and the Texas Association of Health Plans. The common form is intended to replace the separate forms now used by different health plans and hospitals to obtain background information on physicians before granting or renewing their privileges to see patients and seeks a wide range of information ranging from education, type of practice, licensure, and training to office hours, languages spoken, facility affiliations, and malpractice claims history. The new form, which is in two parts and 24 pages long, can be found at the Texas Medical Association Web site (http://www.texmed.org/documents/application.doc).

Q 6:52 What are the most challenging legal issues facing a centralized and integrated credentialing program?

Protecting the confidentiality of the information being accessed by the IDS and maintaining all statutory protections from discovery are the most challenging legal issues facing a centralized and integrated credentialing program. For an IDS that includes two hospitals, a home health company, a physician organization, and an HMO, the regulations and disclosure requirements relating to credentialing and peer review will differ among these organizations. Some are subject to extensive regulatory oversight; others are not. Some must meet accreditation standards involving credentialing that might be inconsistent with the credentialing and peer review standards of accrediting organizations of other component entities within the IDS. For example, JCAHO and NCQA standards are inconsistent in some respects. These distinctions are discussed in chapter 10.

Strategies for Success and Unwinding Failures

Q 6:53 What are the critical elements for a successful provider organization?

The critical elements of a successful provider organization fall into three major categories: financial resources, management resources, and physician resources.

Financial Resources. The ultimate measure of success for any business entity is the financial viability to support ongoing operations. Achieving this goal involves adequate capitalization and capital resources, and an adequate reserve base.

Management Resources. The administration of the organization is critical to its success and relates to the shepherding of financial resources. Critical issues include (1) the size and range of providers in sufficient numbers to develop leverage with payers and employers; (2) time and resources dedicated to strategic planning, allowing strategic instead of reactive change to market conditions; (3) competent financial management using cost-based accounting; (4) knowledgeable and competent professional management; (5) appropriate organizational structure; and (6) physician-led clinical strategies, quality assurance, and utilization review.

Physician Resources. Key to the success of any provider organization are the physicians. A successful provider organization (1) places clinically respected physicians in leadership roles; (2) encourages broad physician participation in group decisions; (3) uses fair compensation criteria; (4) has a physician-focused management style; (5) dedicates resources to educating physicians on management issues and managed care in general; and (6) has a strong governance structure, legally, operationally, and clinically.

Q 6:54   What makes a provider organization fail?

The absence of any of the features listed in Q 6:53 most commonly leads to an organization's failure. Factors most often contributing to the operational and financial difficulties of any provider organization, including an IDS, include failure to obtain anticipated rate increases, poor management of capitation (particularly Medicare), decreased physician productivity, and increased overhead expenses.

Failure in Organizational Objectives. Most IDSs were organized in response to certain economic and business pressures with objectives that have since lost their viability. Others formed for no real business reason except to have the same type of organization as the competition. IDSs were often organized under unrealistic financial projections that never materialized. These systems were usually based on anticipated physician performance that was not realized. Some of the problems in achieving organizational objectives were based on inadequate management systems, and others were attributed to poor information systems. Some systems have large and ungainly networks that cannot be managed effectively. Others are unable to gain a good market position and end up with a disproportionate share of unfunded and underfunded patients.

Failure in Financial Management. Poor financial performance is difficult to correct in an IDS because there are so many potential sources of financial distress. Inability to manage the risk inherent in managed care arrangements is often a key factor. There are many others, including those outside the control of the IDS, such as delayed payments by payers. Other problems may be inherent in the compensation structure. Experience has shown that physicians on fixed salaries do not perform as well as physicians who are compensated on an incentive basis. In fact, many systems paid a high price for a medical practice that could not improve on, or even maintain, its historical performance. Excessive overhead is another area that is difficult to control because of the costly infrastructure requirements for an IDS. Sometimes an IDS has underpriced its services in the market or is undercompensated because of deep discounts for the services it provides. Poor collection procedures coupled with increasing operating costs can quickly turn an IDS into an economically distressed organization.

Increased Regulatory Burdens. As discussed in chapter 8, an IDS as an MCO is subject to numerous legal and regulatory requirements. The cost of compliance can be unpredictable for the organization and contribute significantly to economic and organizational instability. An IDS that is a nonprofit, tax-exempt organization may have extensive limitations on how it can expend funds and manage its affairs. Regulation of incentive and referral relationships within an IDS can impede its ability to be competitive. Finally, there is always the risk of antitrust scrutiny.

Q 6:55 What are the options available to a failing IDS?

The decision to unwind an IDS is usually made when the organization is no longer economically viable and the parties are no longer able to maintain the necessary contractual and working relationships. Since 1998, a number of practice management companies and health care systems have experienced serious financial losses, resulting in their pursuing an exit strategy. The process of unwinding the organization and terminating the multitude of relationships is a challenging one. There is no single approach to unwinding an IDS because each model has its own forms of affiliations and relationships that vary according to the state law, organizational and governance structures, and related factors. Options available to a failing

IDS include (1) restructuring, (2) termination of IDS contracts, and (3) bankruptcy.

Restructuring. Most restructurings of relationships between hospitals, health systems, and medical groups include modification of financial terms with the goal of better aligning financial incentives and eliminating or reducing operating losses. In their haste to acquire and attract physicians and medical groups, many systems developed overly optimistic compensation structures without consideration of available future funds, leaving few options for renegotiation. Some restructuring methodologies go beyond compensation and include returning some portion of the operations to the medical group, along with the risk associated with that portion of the operating costs.

Termination of IDS Contracts. Complete termination of affiliations between hospitals or health systems and physicians is becoming more common. Termination rarely occurs by mutual agreement or on an amicable basis and is often associated with threats of litigation, bankruptcy, or medical disintegration. The negotiations are usually tied to the terms of the initial transaction. For example, stock for practice assets transactions will differ from acquisitions of tangible assets from the physician. The process of terminating and unwinding an IDS is complicated because of regulatory factors that affect the ability of the parties to structure an arm's-length, fair market value separation agreement. Because of the applicability of tax and federal and state fraud and abuse laws to the unwinding process, the following items will affect any negotiation:[12]

- Price of repurchased assets
- Debt allocation and reallocation
- Resolving breach of contract claims
- Ownership of medical records
- Ownership of business records
- Responsibility for office space leases
- Ownership and valuation of accounts receivable
- Continuation of billing and other administration services
- Ownership and valuation of furniture and equipment
- Ownership and valuation of HMO and payer contracts
- Content and timing of notices to patients

- Content and timing of notices to payers
- Nature and scope of releases of liability
- Financial considerations for early termination of contractual obligations
- Resolution of noncompete and nonsolicitation issues
- Continuation of the medical group as an entity

Bankruptcy. Bankruptcy can be used to unwind an IDS in the absence of an internally negotiated dissolution. Asset transfers associated with contractual agreements between the parties to the IDS are not sufficient to address the interests of third-party creditors. Creditor and other liability issues associated with asset reallocation in the unwinding process may leave the parties with no choice but to seek the protection of a bankruptcy court in order to unwind an unsuccessful IDS. Bankruptcy provides an effective means of unwinding an IDS over objections of third parties while preserving the going concern value of the organization and its assets. Bankruptcy is described in more detail in chapter 8.

Q 6:56   What is the advantage of using bankruptcy as the vehicle for unwinding an IDS?

One of the primary advantages of unwinding an IDS through the bankruptcy courts is the ability to sell all or substantially all IDS assets free and clear of liens, interests, and claims over the objection of third parties. This places the debtors in a powerful negotiating position with creditors of the IDS. Another advantage to this legal process is that the Bankruptcy Code allows a debtor to "reject, assume or assign" its contracts, which include the participating provider contracts. In addition, the unwinding aspect can be imposed on dissenting creditors, which include the doctor groups under contract with the IDS.

Q 6:57   What can doctors and other contracted participants in an IDS do in anticipation of and during a bankruptcy?

Clauses in contracts that provide for termination on the commencement of a bankruptcy proceeding are generally unenforceable; thus, the participating providers will not be able to terminate their contracts unilaterally. Nothing, however, prohibits the termination of a contract on the triggering of some other, prebankruptcy provision such as unfavorable financial ratios or other economic "red flags" indicating financial distress. These provisions should be part of the contract and are discussed in detail in chapter 13.

Future Provider Organizations

Q 6:58   What will be the likely forms of provider organizations in the future?

As managed care moves away from risk-based models and complex, capital-intensive legal structures, the likely forms of provider organizations in the future will rely on the Internet for contracting and network administration. Several companies have initiated strategies using the "virtual" IPA, such as doctorandpatient.com and Vivius. Both attempt to integrate the provider network with the payer and plan options. Some seek to offer benefit options directly to enrollees.

The Vivius concept involves a prepaid provider network. It differs from some forms of capitation in that providers are not at risk for any outside services. The provider panel (physicians, hospitals, pharmacy, emergency room, surgery center, and home health) offers its services for a specific per-member per-month (PMPM) rate that is adjusted based on the age and sex of the enrollee and on the enrollee's copayment choices. Physicians and other providers establish their own rates by entering, on the Vivius Web site, a targeted percentage of Medicare fees they want their PMPM rates to achieve. The Web site algorithm then establishes the targeted age-, sex-, and copayment-adjusted PMPM prices for the provider. Providers are free to change any of the prices at any time, but must honor the price selected by enrollees before the change. The rate includes only professional services directly provided by the physicians plus some office supplies. All physicians include a list of their recommended panel of specialists and hospitals. The physician panel includes 18 of the most commonly used specialists. Physicians outside those specialties are covered through a traditional wraparound insurance policy. Enrollees will go on the Web site and select a full complement of 18 specialties, a hospital, and selected other providers. If they do not make a choice for a particular specialty, their personal physician's recommendation will be used.

One feature of the Vivius model is that enrollees will be able to identify cost differences between providers during the selection process. They will also be able to review what the physicians report about their qualifications. Physicians must also respond to a standard set of questions posed by Vivius, including questions about any felony convictions and whether their medical license has ever been revoked. Enrollees will select five copayment choices for physician, hospital, pharmacy, emergency room, and outpatient facility. The PMPM rates for the selected physician panel (adjusted by the copayment selections) and the wraparound policy will add up to a premium.

The doctorandpatient.com Web site operates differently from managed care companies in that it does not take a percentage of savings from the discounts given by its provider network. It is not a PPO; rather, it is designed to change the way managed care operates today. Via the Internet, doctorandpatient.com creates a direct relationship between the patient, purchasers of medical services, and providers of health care and has developed one of the nation's first Internet medical provider networks (IMPNs). This network is represented to create two important advantages for medical providers. First, physicians and hospitals will be able to offer all their discounted fee-for-service payers a single "best rate" that individual medical providers, not payers, control. This rate is intended to allow efficient claims administration and revenue enhancement. Second, the IMPN will allow medical providers to market their services to qualified cash-paying patients seeking care through the Internet. A patient will be able to access doctorandpatient.com's consumer portal for free. Patients may pay a small access fee if they choose to purchase medical services from an IMPN participating medical provider.

References

1. Used with permission of the Medical Group Management Association. *See* http://www.mgma.com/consulting/ipstool. cfm.

2. *Healthcare Integration: A Legal Manual for Constructing Integrated Organizations* (Washington, DC: The Focus Series, National Health Lawyers Association, 1995) 4–5.

3. Id. at 6.

4. Stephen M. Shortell, Robin R. Gillies, et al., *Remaking Health Care in America: Building Organized Delivery Systems* (San Francisco: Jossey-Bass, 1996).

5. 42 USC § 1395nn, Medicare § 1877.

6. U.E. Reinhardt, "The Rise and Fall of the Physician Practice Management Industry," *Health Affairs,* Jan./Feb. 2000:42–55.

7. *See* http://www.themcic.com/company/press/pr112000.htm.

8. For more information, see B.J. Weiner and J.A. Alexander, "The Challenges of Governing Public-Private Community Health Partnerships," *Health Care Mgmt. Rev.,* 23(2):39–55, 1998.

9. The nondiscrimination rules associated with such benefit plans exceed the scope of this book and are the subject of Cynthia M. Combe, *Employee Benefits Answer Book* (New York: Panel Publishers, 2000).

10. *Employment Status—Employee v. Independent Contractor,* Tax Mgmt. (BNA), 391-2d:A-78 to A-79 (1993).

11. One of the earliest determinations for an integrated health organization was IRS Exemption Ruling Friendly Hills Healthcare Network, TNT 93:40-113, Jan. 29, 1993, wherein the IRS set out certain safe harbors for avoiding the possibility of physicians having too much control over or receiving too much benefit from the organization. The specific safe harbors address board composition, committee structure, compensation, medical staff, nondiscrimination among patients, emergency services, and other community benefit requirements. The IRS will allow covenants not to compete and, in one case, actually required this covenant as part of a transaction.

12. Derek F. Covert and Alan S. Gassman, "The Honeymoon's Over: Divorcing, Separating or Restructuring the Troubled Physician Ownership Organization," presented at the Ameri-

can Health Lawyers Association Annual Meeting, June 27–30, 1999, Chicago.

Appendix 6-A

Factors Used by the IRS to Evaluate Employment Status

1. The hiring party requires the provider to comply with instructions about where, when, and how the work is to be performed.
2. The hiring party provides some form of training for the provider.The provider's services are integrated into the hiring party's business operations.
3. The provider personally provides the services.
4. The hiring party hires, supervises, and pays assistants to help the provider.
5. The provider and the hiring party have a continuing relationship.
6. The hiring party establishes or sets hours of work.
7. The provider is required to work substantially full time.
8. Work takes place on the premises of the hiring party or the hiring party provides free office space to the provider.
9. The provider is required to perform services in the order or sequence set by the hiring party.
10. The provider is required to submit regular or written reports.
11. The provider is paid by the hour, week, or month as opposed to being paid by the job or on a straight commission.
12. The hiring party pays for (or reimburses the provider for) the provider's business and/or travel expenses.
13. The hiring party furnishes medical equipment and supplies and other "significant tools" to the provider.
14. The provider is dependent on the hiring party for facilities at which to perform services (except where the provider has a financial interest in the facilities).

15. The provider has no ability to realize a profit or suffer a loss as a result of his or her services.

16. The provider may not work for more than one entity at a time.

17. The provider's services are not marketed to the general public on a regular and consistent basis.

18. The provider does not have a private practice or business outside of and independent of or from the hiring party.

19. The hiring party has the right to discharge or terminate the provider at any time, without cause, for failure to obey instructions.

20. The provider has the right to end his or her work relationship at any time without incurring liability.

Chapter 7

Government Programs

Simplification of government has been the theme of the Bush Administration. In June 2001, the Secretary of Health and Human Services (SHHS) renamed the Health Care Financing Administration (HCFA) the Centers for Medicare and Medicaid Services (CMS). CMS is made up of three centers of service: a center for beneficiary choices, focusing on Medicare's health maintenance organization (HMO) operations; a center for Medicare management to oversee fee-for-service operations; and a center for Medicaid and state operations.

By the end of 2001, Congress had made progress on an extensive set of administrative reforms of Medicare, beginning with the passage of the Medicare Regulatory and Contracting Reform Act of 2001 (H.R. 3391) by the House of Representatives in December 2001 and the introduction in the Senate of the Medicare Appeals, Regulatory, and Contracting Improvement Act of 2001 (S. 1738), which is in committee at the time of this writing.

Since Medicare and Medicaid began in the mid-1960s, the government has become the major source of health care funding in the United States. Efforts have been ongoing since then to reform these programs to improve access and coverage, control expenditures, and enhance quality. To control the spiraling costs of both programs, the federal government favors managed care solutions. Of all the reforms affecting health care over the past six years, the two most significant are the Balanced Budget Act of 1997 (BBA) [Pub L No 105-33] and the Health Insurance Portability and Accountability Act of 1996 (HIPAA) [Pub L No 104-191]. The BBA reformed the Medicare and Medicaid programs and established the State Children's Health Insurance Program (SCHIP). HIPAA was an omnibus bill that made a number of changes affecting health coverage portability and health information privacy and security. HIPAA is discussed in detail in chapter 8.

The government's managed care initiative, Medicare + Choice (M + C), initially resulted in the withdrawal of most health plans from the senior market. Following passage of the Medicare, Medicaid, and SCHIP Benefits Improvement and Protection Act of 2000 (BIPA), which included an increase in premiums for M + C plans, some M + C plans are returning to the market; however, their benefit packages have been greatly reduced, with most eliminating drug benefits. This has made the government's effort to offer a Medicare prescription drug benefit plan a high priority for seniors.

Unfortunately, the events of September 11, 2001, redirected congressional attention from health care to homeland security and preparedness for bioterrorism. Most congressional funding initiatives since then have been directed at these efforts.

Overview

Q 7:1 What are the major government-sponsored payer programs?

The major government-sponsored payer programs include Medicare and Medicaid. The Social Security Amendments of 1965 established Medicare, a health insurance program primarily for aged persons, to complement the retirement, survivors, and disability insurance benefits available under Title II of the Social Security Act of 1935 (as amended). Medicare provides health insurance to people who are 65 years old or older, people who are disabled, and people with permanent kidney failure. When Medicare began on July 1, 1966, there were 19.1 million people enrolled in the program. By the end of 1966, 3.7 million people had received at least some health care services covered by Medicare. In 2001, about 40.1 million people were enrolled in one or both parts of the Medicare program.

Medicaid provides basic medical assistance for certain individuals and families with low incomes and limited resources. The program, which became law in 1965, is a jointly funded cooperative venture between the federal and state governments. [42 USC §§ 1396–1396u(j), 430–456] Within broad guidelines set by the federal government, each state establishes its own eligibility standards; determines the type, amount, duration, and scope of services covered; sets rates of payment for services rendered; and administers its own program. Thus, the Medicaid program varies considerably from state to state, as well as within each state over time. Medicaid is the largest program providing medical and health-related services to America's poorest people. The Medicaid statute requires each state to include certain categories of eligible recipients and permits each state to include other categories of eligible recipients.

In addition the federal government sponsors the Federal Employees Health Benefits Program (FEHBP), which is authorized under the Federal Employees Health Benefits Act [5 USC § 8901] and administered by the Office of Personnel Management. FEHBP covers about 9 million federal workers, retirees, and dependents (see Q 7:82).

Finally, the Civilian Health and Medical Program of the Uniformed Services (CHAMPUS) covers approximately 6 million military retirees and family members of active-duty military personnel. It is administered by the Department of Defense (DOD), which also administers the Military Health Services System, which is made up of Army, Navy, and Air Force military treatment facilities (see Q7:82).

Q 7:2　What is the relationship between Medicare and Medicaid?

Medicare beneficiaries who meet low-income eligibility criteria or who have medical conditions eligible for coverage may also receive Medicaid benefits. For those who are eligible for full Medicaid coverage, the Medicare portion of their coverage is supplemented by services available under the state's Medicaid program, such as hearing aids, prescription drugs, eyeglasses, and nursing facility care beyond the 100 days covered by Medicare. Medicaid, however, has always been the payer of "last resort." As discussed in detail in Q 7:8, certain categories of Medicaid beneficiaries, such as qualified Medicare beneficiaries (QMBs) and specified low-income Medicare beneficiaries (SLMB), are eligible for coverage under both Medicare and Medicaid.

Structurally, Medicare and Medicaid have little in common, except that both are administered by CMS (formerly HCFA). Medicare is a federally funded and administered program, whereas the administration of Medicaid is shared by the state and federal governments. This sharing has created some tension with respect to apportionment of payments.

As a result of the BBA, states have received capped allocations for each of the five years from 1998 through 2002 to cover all or some of the Medicare supplemental medical insurance (MSMI) premiums for eligible individuals whose incomes are above 120 percent and less than 175 percent of the federal poverty level (FPL). These individuals are known as qualifying individuals (QIs). Unlike QMBs and SLMBs, who may be eligible for Medicaid benefits in addition to their QMB or SLMB benefits, QIs cannot be otherwise eligible for medical assistance under a state plan. Payment of QI benefits is 100 percent federally funded, up to the state's allocation.

Medicaid and Managed Care

Q 7:3   What is Medicaid?

Medicaid, which is authorized under Title XIX of the Social Security Act, is a joint federal-state program supplying health care coverage to low-income, aged, and disabled recipients. Medicaid was established to serve the poor, but rather than being a federally mandated and federally funded program, it relies on the states to set eligibility limits. As a result, there is a wide variation in Medicaid benefits from state to state.

Although Medicaid and Medicare were both enacted as part of President Lyndon B. Johnson's Great Society, Medicaid was actually a creature of Congress. In fact, it was Wilbur Mills (D-AR) who favored the expansion of the Kerr-Mills Act to establish a federal-state model for Medicaid. This was the model favored by the American Medical Association (AMA) for Medicare.

Q 7:4   How is Medicaid financed?

Medicaid is financed jointly through state appropriations and federal financial participation (FFP), the latter at a rate that varies from state to state. Under the Medicaid statute, the federal government is required to pay each state a percentage of the state's expenditures for medical services under its Medicaid plan. This percentage is called the federal medical assistance percentage (FMAP) (see Q 7:5). [42 USC § 1396b(a); 42 CFR § 433.10] Each state must pay not less than 40 percent of the nonfederal share of expenditures under the state plan. [42 USC § 1396a(a)(2); 42 CFR § 433.53] In addition, the state plan must guarantee that lack of adequate state funds from local sources will not result in lowering the amount, duration, scope, or quality of care and services available under the plan.

Q 7:5   How is the FMAP calculated?

The FMAP is determined annually by a formula that compares a state's average per capita income level with the national income average. The formula used to calculate the enhanced FMAP is clearly specified in the Medicaid statute. If a state chooses to expand Medicaid with the SCHIP funds, the state allocation is paid out through an "enhanced" FMAP. The maximum enhanced FMAP is 85 percent. The state will receive the enhanced FMAP until the state's SCHIP funds run out. If there are still Medicaid expenses, the state match reverts to the regular FMAP. Because of a fear of using up the SCHIP funds, states may choose to be conservative when expanding Medicaid eligibility. For example, a state may choose to expand Medicaid eligibility to 185 percent of the FPL, instead of the maximum 200 percent. The enhanced FMAP is equal to the sum of 70 percent of a state's current FMAP plus 30 percentage points. Therefore, if a state's current FMAP is 50 percent, its enhanced FMAP will be 65 percent. States with a higher per capita income level are reimbursed a smaller share of their costs. By law, the FMAP cannot be lower than 50 percent or higher than 85 percent. In 1997, the FMAPs varied from 50 percent (for 13 states and the District of Columbia) to 77.2 percent (for Mississippi), with the average federal share among all states being 57 percent.

The federal government reimburses states for 100 percent of the cost of services provided through facilities of the American Indian Health Service and shares in each state's expenditures for administration of its Medicaid program. For all states, most administrative costs are matched at 50 percent, with higher matching rates for certain activities such as development of mechanized claims processing systems. Federal payments to the states for medical assistance have no set limit (cap); rather, the federal government matches (at FMAP rates) state expenditures for the mandatory Medicaid services plus the optional services that the state decides to cover for eligible recipients and matches (at the appropriate administrative rate) necessary and proper administrative costs.

Q 7:6 How are Medicaid services paid for?

Medicaid is a vendor program. States can pay providers of Medicaid services directly or pay for Medicaid services through a variety of allowable prepayment arrangements, such as HMOs. Within federally imposed limits, states have broad discretion in determining payment methodology and rates for services. Generally, payment rates must be sufficient to enlist sufficient numbers of providers to ensure availability of covered services comparable to those available to the general population within the same geographic area. Providers participating in Medicaid must accept Medicaid payment rates as payment in full. No balance billing is permitted, although states can impose nominal deductibles, coinsurance, or copayments on some Medicaid recipients for certain services.

States must make additional payments to qualified hospitals that provide inpatient services to a disproportionate number of Medicaid beneficiaries and/or to other low-income or uninsured persons under what is called a disproportionate share hospital (DSH) adjustment. The use of DSH adjustments had increased Medicare expenditures, which were brought back in line with the enactment of the BBA.

Q 7:7 Who is covered by Medicaid?

Medicaid eligibility is complex. Following is the latest list of eligibility criteria from CMS:

> States have some discretion in determining which groups their Medicaid programs will cover and the financial criteria for Medicaid eligibility. To be eligible for Federal funds, States are required to provide Medicaid coverage for most individuals who receive Federally assisted income maintenance payments, as well as for related groups not receiving cash payments. Some examples of the mandatory Medicaid eligibility groups are:
>
> - low income families with children, as described in Section 1931 of the Social Security Act, who meet certain of the eligibility requirements in the State's AFDC plan in effect on July 16, 1996;
> - Supplemental Security Income (SSI) recipients (or in States using more restrictive criteria—aged, blind, and disabled individuals who meet criteria which are more restrictive than those of the SSI program and which were in place in the State's approved Medicaid plan as of January 1, 1972);
> - infants born to Medicaid-eligible pregnant women. Medicaid eligibility must continue throughout the first year of life so long as the infant remains in the mother's household and she remains eligible, or would be eligible if she were still pregnant;
> - children under age 6 and pregnant women whose family income is at or below 133 percent of the Federal poverty

level. (The minimum mandatory income level for pregnant women and infants in certain States may be higher than 133 percent, if as of certain dates the State had established a higher percentage for covering those groups.) States are required to extend Medicaid eligibility until age 19 to all children born after September 30, 1983 (or such earlier date as the State may choose) in families with incomes at or below the Federal poverty level. This phases in coverage, so that by the year 2002, all poor children under age 19 will be covered. Once eligibility is established, pregnant women remain eligible for Medicaid through the end of the calendar month in which the 60th day after the end of the pregnancy falls, regardless of any change in family income. States are not required to have a resource test for these poverty level related groups. However, any resource test imposed can be no more restrictive than that of the AFDC program for infants and children and the SSI program for pregnant women;

- recipients of adoption assistance and foster care under Title IV-E of the Social Security Act;

- certain Medicare beneficiaries; and

- special protected groups who may keep Medicaid for a period of time. Examples are: persons who lose SSI payments due to earnings from work or increased Social Security benefits; and families who are provided 6 to 12 months of Medicaid coverage following loss of eligibility under Section 1931 due to earnings, or 4 months of Medicaid coverage following loss of eligibility under Section 1931 due to an increase in child or spousal support.

States also have the option to provide Medicaid coverage for other "categorically needy" groups. These optional groups share characteristics of the mandatory groups, but the eligibility criteria are somewhat more liberally defined. Examples of the optional groups that States may cover as categorically needy (and for which they will receive Federal matching funds) under the Medicaid program are:

- infants up to age one and pregnant women not covered under the mandatory rules whose family income is below 185 percent of the Federal poverty level (the percentage to be set by each State);

- optional targeted low income children;

- certain aged, blind, or disabled adults who have incomes above those requiring mandatory coverage, but below the Federal poverty level;

- children under age 21 who meet income and resources requirements for AFDC, but who otherwise are not eligible for AFDC;

- institutionalized individuals with income and resources below specified limits;

- persons who would be eligible if institutionalized but are receiving care under home and community-based services waivers;

- recipients of State supplementary payments; and

- TB-infected persons who would be financially eligible for Medicaid at the SSI level (only for TB-related ambulatory services and TB drugs)

- low-income, uninsured women screened and diagnosed through a Center's for Disease Control and Prevention's Breast and Cervical Cancer Early Detection Program and determined to be in need of treatment for breast or cervical cancer.

Medically Needy Eligibility Groups

The option to have a "medically needy" program allows States to extend Medicaid eligibility to additional qualified persons who may have too much income to qualify under the mandatory or optional categorically needy groups. This option allows them to "spend down" to Medicaid eligibility by incurring medical and/or remedial care expenses to offset their excess income, thereby reducing it to a level below the maximum allowed by that State's Medicaid plan. States may also allow families to establish eligibility as medically needy by paying monthly premiums to the State in an amount equal to the difference between family income (reduced by unpaid expenses, if any, incurred for medical care in previous months) and the income eligibility standard.

Eligibility for the medically needy program does not have to be as extensive as the categorically needy program. However, States which elect to include the medically needy under their plans are required to include certain children under age

18 and pregnant women who, except for income and resources, would be eligible as categorically needy. They may choose to provide coverage to other medically needy persons: aged, blind, and/or disabled persons; certain relatives of children deprived of parental support and care; and certain other financially eligible children up to age 21. In 1995, there were 40 medically needy programs which provided at least some services to recipients.

Amplification on Medicaid Eligibility

Coverage may start retroactive to any or all of the 3 months prior to application, if the individual would have been eligible during the retroactive period. Coverage generally stops at the end of the month in which a person's circumstances change. Most States have additional "State-only" programs to provide medical assistance for specified poor persons who do not qualify for the Medicaid program. No Federal funds are provided for State-only programs.

Medicaid does not provide medical assistance for all poor persons. Even under the broadest provisions of the Federal statute (except for emergency services for certain persons), the Medicaid program does not provide health care services, even for very poor persons, unless they are in one of the groups designated above. Low income is only one test for Medicaid eligibility; assets and resources are also tested against established thresholds. As noted earlier, categorically needy persons who are eligible for Medicaid may or may not also receive cash assistance from the TANF program or from the SSI program. Medically needy persons who would be categorically eligible except for income or assets may become eligible for Medicaid solely because of excessive medical expenses.

States may use more liberal income and resources methodologies to determine Medicaid eligibility for certain AFDC-related and aged, blind, and disabled individuals under sections 1902(r)(2) and 1931 of the Social Security Act. For some groups, the more liberal income methodologies cannot result in the individual's income exceeding the limits prescribed for Federal matching.

Significant changes were made in the Medicare Catastrophic Coverage Act (MCCA) of 1988 which affected Medicaid. Although much of the MCCA was repealed, the portions affecting Medicaid remain in effect. The law also accelerated Medicaid eligibility for some nursing home patients by protecting assets for the institutionalized person's spouse at home at the time of the initial eligibility determination after institutionalization. Before an institutionalized person's monthly income is used to pay for the cost of institutional care, a minimum monthly maintenance needs allowance is deducted from the institutionalized spouse's income to bring the income of the community spouse up to a moderate level.

[http://www.hcfa.gov/medicaid/meligib.htm (Mar 30, 2002)]

Eligibility for Medicaid is set by the states. The percentage of low-income parents insured by Medicaid fell by almost one quarter from 1995 to 2000, according to Census Bureau data, and the number of low-income parents who are uninsured rose by 7 percent. Twelve states have substantially expanded low-income working parents' eligibility for Medicaid since 1997, but income eligibility limits for parents in most states remain well below the poverty line, and about one third of low-income parents remain uninsured. The Center on Budget and Policy Priorities reports as follows:

> To better understand the actions states are taking to increase health insurance coverage for parents, the Center on Budget and Policy Priorities surveyed Medicaid eligibility staff in all 50 states and the District of Columbia to gather information about the eligibility rules that each state applies to families with children under Medicaid (and in a few cases, non-Medicaid public insurance programs). We asked the state officials to provide information on their policies for parents as of July 1, 2000. In some cases, the Center has learned of policy changes adopted by states since July 1, 2000; these changes are noted whenever possible. . . .
>
> - Prior to 1997, seven states had expanded Medicaid coverage for both parents and children to include families with incomes up to 100 percent of the federal poverty line or higher. These states include Delaware, Hawaii, Minnesota, Oregon, Tennessee, Vermont, and Washington.
> - Since 1997, an additional 12 states have raised income eligibility limits for parents up to or beyond 100 percent of the poverty line. These states include Arizona, California, Connecticut, the District of Columbia, Maine, Massachusetts, Missouri, New Jersey, New York, Ohio, Rhode Island, and Wisconsin.

- Nevertheless, most states provide Medicaid coverage to low-income parents only if they have income far below the poverty line.

More than half of the states provide coverage to a working parent with two children only if the parent's earnings fall below roughly $10,000 a year, an amount that leaves the family nearly $5,000 below the poverty line. In the typical (or median) state, a working parent with two children becomes ineligible for coverage when her earnings reach 69 percent of the poverty line.

In some states, the eligibility cutoff for parents is even lower. In Alabama, for example, a parent with two children is ineligible for Medicaid if her earnings exceed $3,048 a year, an amount more than $11,500 below the poverty line. By contrast, 37 states (including the District of Columbia) now provide coverage to *children* in families with income up to at least 200 percent of the poverty line.[1]

Q 7:8 What categories of persons are eligible for coverage under both Medicare and Medicaid?

There are eight categories of persons eligible for coverage under both Medicare and Medicaid. These persons are known as dual eligibles. Medicare has two basic coverages: Part A, which pays for hospitalization costs; and Part B, which pays for physician services, laboratory and x-ray services, durable medical equipment, and outpatient and other services. Dual eligibles are individuals who are entitled to Medicare Part A and/or Part B and are eligible for some form of Medicaid benefits. According to CMS, the eight categories are as follows:[2]

1. *QMBs without other Medicaid (QMB only).* These individuals are entitled to Medicare Part A, have income of 100 percent of the FPL or less and resources that do not exceed twice the limit for supplemental security income (SSI) eligibility, and are not otherwise eligible for full Medicaid. Medicaid pays their Medicare Part A premiums, if any; Medicare Part B premiums; and to the extent consistent with the state Medicaid plan, Medicare deductibles and coinsurance for Medicare services provided by Medicare providers. FFP equals the FMAP.

2. *QMBs with full Medicaid (QMB plus).* These individuals are entitled to Medicare Part A, have income of 100 percent of the FPL or less and resources that do not exceed twice the limit

for SSI eligibility, and are eligible for full Medicaid benefits. Medicaid pays their Medicare Part A premiums, if any; Medicare Part B premiums; and to the extent consistent with the state Medicaid plan, Medicare deductibles and coinsurance. It also provides full Medicaid benefits. FFP equals the FMAP.

3. *SLMBs without other Medicaid (SLMB only)*. These individuals are entitled to Medicare Part A, have income greater than 100 percent of the FPL but less than 120 percent of the FPL and resources that do not exceed twice the limit for SSI eligibility, and are not otherwise eligible for Medicaid. Medicaid pays their Medicare Part B premiums only. FFP equals the FMAP.

4. *SLMBs with full Medicaid (SLMB plus)*. These individuals are entitled to Medicare Part A, have income greater than 100 percent of the FPL but less than 120 percent of the FPL and resources that do not exceed twice the limit for SSI eligibility, and are eligible for full Medicaid benefits. Medicaid pays their Medicare Part B premiums and provides full Medicaid benefits. FFP equals the FMAP.

5. *Qualified disabled and working individuals (QDWIs)*. These individuals lost their Medicare Part A benefits because they returned to work. They are eligible to purchase Medicare Part A benefits, have income of 200 percent of the FPL or less and resources that do not exceed twice the limit for SSI eligibility, and are not otherwise eligible for Medicaid. Medicaid pays their Medicare Part A premiums only. FFP equals the FMAP.

6. *Qualifying individuals (1) (QI-1s)*. This group is effective for 1998 through 2002. There is an annual cap on the amount of money available, which may limit the number of individuals in the group. These individuals are entitled to Medicare Part A, have income of at least 120 percent of the FPL but less than 135 percent of the FPL and resources that do not exceed twice the limit for SSI eligibility, and are not otherwise eligible for Medicaid. Medicaid pays their Medicare Part B premiums only. FFP equals the FMAP at 100 percent.

7. *Qualifying individuals (2) (QI-2s)*. This group is effective for 1998 through 2002. There is an annual cap on the amount of money available, which may limit the number of individuals in the group. These individuals are entitled to Medicare Part A, have income of at least 135 percent of the FPL but less than

175 percent of the FPL and resources that do not exceed twice the limit for SSI eligibility, and are not otherwise eligible for Medicaid. Medicaid pays only a portion of their Medicare Part B premiums ($2.23 in 1999). FFP equals the FMAP at 100 percent.

8. *Medicaid-only dual eligibles (non-QMB, -SLMB, -QDWI, -QI-1, or -QI-2).* These individuals are entitled to Medicare Part A and/or Part B and are eligible for full Medicaid benefits. They are not eligible for Medicaid as a QMB, SLMB, QDWI, QI-1, or QI-2. Typically, these individuals need to spend down to qualify for Medicaid or fall into a Medicaid eligibility poverty group that exceeds the limits listed in (1) through (7) above. Medicaid provides full Medicaid benefits and pays for Medicaid services provided by Medicaid providers, but Medicaid will pay only for services also covered by Medicare if the Medicaid payment rate is higher than the amount paid by Medicare; and within this limit, will pay only to the extent necessary to pay the beneficiary's Medicare cost-sharing liability. Payment by Medicaid of Medicare Part B premiums is a state option; however, states cannot receive FFP for Medicaid services also covered by Medicare Part B for certain individuals who could have been covered under Medicare Part B had they been enrolled. FFP equals the FMAP.

Q 7:9 What benefits are covered under Medicaid?

Title XIX of the Social Security Act (Medicaid) gives states considerable flexibility within their plans with respect to coverage. As a general rule, Medicaid covers a broad range of services with nominal cost sharing by beneficiaries. The benefits extend beyond those covered by Medicare and most employer-sponsored plans. The scope of coverage varies depending on the category of eligibility. If federal matching funds are received, a state's Medicaid program must offer medical assistance for certain basic services to most categorically needy populations. These services include the following:

- Inpatient hospital services
- Outpatient hospital services
- Prenatal care
- Vaccines for children

- Physician services
- Nursing facility services for persons 21 years of age or older
- Family planning services and supplies
- Rural health clinic services
- Home health care for persons eligible for skilled nursing services
- Laboratory and x-ray services
- Pediatric and family nurse practitioner services
- Nurse-midwife services
- Federally qualified health center (FQHC) services and ambulatory services of an FQHC that would be available in other settings
- Early and periodic screening, diagnostic, and treatment (EPSDT) services for children under age 21

States can also receive federal matching funds for providing certain optional services. The most common of the 34 currently approved optional Medicaid services include the following:

- Diagnostic services
- Clinic services
- Intermediate care facilities for the mentally retarded (ICFs/MR)
- Prescribed drugs and prosthetic devices
- Optometrist services and eyeglasses
- Nursing facility services for children under age 21
- Transportation services
- Rehabilitation and physical therapy services
- Home and community-based care to certain persons with chronic impairments (this one is an option only with an approved waiver) [42 USC § 1396(a)(1); 42 CFR § 440.210]

Q 7:10   Do all people eligible for Medicaid enroll as beneficiaries?

No. Many people who are eligible for Medicaid benefits do not enroll. There are many reasons for this. Some are concerned about the social stigma. Others do not enroll because of the administrative complexity of the process. It is believed that since the enactment of the Personal Responsibility and Work Opportunity Reconciliation Act of 1996 [Pub L No 104-193], a large number of people do not take advantage of Medicaid because of difficulties entering the system.

In 1997, CHIP was established under a section of the BBA that authorized the expenditure of $24 billion over five years for low-income children not eligible for Medicaid or other government programs. A report published by the Kaiser Commission on Medicaid and the Uninsured noted that Medicaid enrollment rose by 1.1 million people, or 3.6 percent, in the year ending December 31, 1999. More than a quarter of that increase was due to the enrollment of more children in Medicaid as part of CHIP. As of October 2000, HCFA proposed new rules to allow greater access to Medicaid at a cost of $960 million over five years. States would have to spend the same amount. HCFA said the plan would give states more flexibility to determine Medicaid eligibility, potentially making tens of thousands more low-income Americans eligible for the program. Under this rule, a state could disregard part of a person's income, such as that used for food, clothing, and housing.

Finally, a study conducted by the National Academy for State Health Policy determined that increased federal flexibility, together with state policies that address the specific needs and realities of individual states, has proved to be an effective way to extend the reach of Medicaid and while recognizing the diversity of economic conditions in the states.

Q 7:11 What is the Personal Responsibility and Work Opportunity Reconciliation Act of 1996, and how does it affect Medicaid?

The Personal Responsibility and Work Opportunity Reconciliation Act of 1996, also known as the Welfare Reform Bill, changes eligibility for SSI coverage, which affects Medicaid. Legal resident aliens and other qualified aliens who entered the United States on or after August 22, 1996, are barred from participating in Medicaid for five years. Medicaid eligibility for aliens who entered before that date is at the option of the state, as is the five-year ban, with the exception of emergency care. A number of disabled children who lost their SSI as a result of the Welfare Reform Bill regained their eligibility with the passage of the BBA.

Another feature of the Welfare Reform Bill was its repeal of "open-ended" federal entitlement under Aid to Families with Dependent Children (AFDC), which was replaced by the Temporary Assistance for Needy Families (TANF). This program provides grants to states to be spent on time-limited cash assistance. TANF limits a family's lifetime cash welfare benefits to a maximum of five years and permits states to impose additional restrictions.

States are permitted to modify or simplify Medicaid eligibility standards as long as the 1996 Medicaid rules are treated as minimum standards. Consequently, some individuals will be eligible for Medicaid even though they are not eligible for TANF.[3] Other provisions of the law may result in fewer people receiving Medicaid benefits. Tightened eligibility scrutiny for coverage of disabled children under SSI could result in loss of coverage. States will not receive federal matching funds for coverage provided to legal immigrants within five years of their entering the country. Legal immigrants already on Medicaid will not lose their eligibility.[4]

Q 7:12 How are the amount and duration of Medicaid benefits determined?

Within broad federal guidelines, states determine the amount and duration of services offered under their Medicaid programs. States can place appropriate limits on a Medicaid service based on such criteria as medical necessity and utilization control. For example, states can place a reasonable limit on the number of covered physician visits or require prior authorization for services. These limits must result in a level of services sufficient to reasonably achieve the purpose of the benefits and cannot discriminate among beneficiaries based on their medical diagnosis or condition.

With certain exceptions, a state's Medicaid plan must allow recipients freedom of choice among health care providers participating in Medicaid. States may provide and pay for Medicaid services through various prepayment arrangements, such as an HMO. In general, states are required to provide comparable services to all categorically needy eligible persons. An individual is categorically needy if:

1. The family includes a dependent child who is living with a caretaker relative;

2. The family income does not exceed the 185 percent gross income test limit; and

3. The family's countable income and resources do not exceed the applicable AFDC income and resource standards (including any special needs) established in the state's Medicaid plan.

There is an important exception related to home- and community-based services waivers under which states offer an alternative health care package for persons who would otherwise be institutionalized under Medicaid. States are not limited in the scope of services they can provide under such waivers as long as they are cost effective (except that, other than as a part of respite care, they cannot provide room and board for such recipients).

Q 7:13   What mechanisms have the states used to change their Medicaid programs?

Medicaid has been a low-paying indemnity provider with a small number of physicians seeing a large number of patients. Because of its payment structures, Medicaid has had a tendency to be abused by unscrupulous physicians, pharmacists, and other health care providers. They have created Medicaid "mills" that churn patients through, generate invoices, and give rudimentary care at best. Thus, in the eyes of many, Medicaid is rather unsavory.

As Medicaid has become increasingly restrictive and a poor payer, Medicaid managed care has sparked interest in the provider community. Several pilot programs have been authorized to allow the states to try new ways of delivering medical care to Medicaid beneficiaries. The availability of managed care plans has sparked major growth in the Medicaid market.

The states accomplish changes in their Medicaid programs primarily by means of the waiver mechanism. Sections 1915 and 1115 of the Social Security Act allow the states to apply to CMS for waivers of access or eligibility requirements. The Section 1915 mechanism is primarily for defined pilot programs, and the Section 1115 mechanism is for statewide programs.

Under what is described as the "upper payment limit loophole," some states took advantage of the flexibility afforded by federal regulations in setting the maximum rates that could be paid under Medicaid. This, according to the Department of Health and Human Services (DHHS), cost taxpayers nearly $2 billion without increasing coverage or improving care. These states allowed county- and city-owned hospitals to claim higher federally matched Medicaid reimbursement rates and then allowed these facilities to use only a fraction of the federal funds, diverting the money to fund state programs not necessarily health related. According to DHHS, 17 states had amendments to their Medicaid plans approved to take advantage of the loophole; 11 other states submitted plan amendments.

The January 18, 2002, Federal Register completes changes proposed in November 2001 to close this loophole. The regulations build on reforms to Medicaid's upper payment limit requirements made in January 2001. The earlier changes allowed states to make overall payments to local government-owned or -operated hospitals of up to 150 percent of the estimated amount that would be paid under Medicare for the same services. The final changes limit such payments to 100 percent of estimated Medicare payments, which is the limit for all other hospitals. The rules became effective March 19, 2002.

Q 7:14 What are the common models of Medicaid managed care?

There are three major forms of Medicaid managed care:

1. *Primary care case management (PCCM).* This arrangement is the most loosely controlled Medicaid managed care product. It establishes a relationship between a primary care physician (PCP) and a Medicaid client in which the PCP agrees to provide gatekeeper services for a fixed fee per client per month. The contractual relationship usually exists between the state and the PCP. The primary care case manager (PCCM) approves and monitors all services provided to the client and is accessible for emergencies 24 hours a day, seven days a week.

2. *Prepaid health plans (PHP).* A state Medicaid agency can contract with a PHP for a specific range of services and limited risk, which the PHP can then contract to individual providers or clinics.

3. *HMO plans.* The state can contract with HMOs to provide the full range of services to Medicaid clients, thus bearing the en-

tire risk. In an HMO contract, all the providers are part of the same plan. The state may contract for multiple HMOs in a provider area. Another variety of risk plan is the health-insuring organization (HIO), which takes full risk as a fiscal intermediary.

The guiding principle of Medicaid managed care is to achieve cost reduction by controlling utilization and offering incentives to the providers to control patients' care. The two basic types of contracts under Medicaid are comprehensive risk contracts and noncomprehensive risk contracts. Managed care plans that are either federally qualified HMOs or state plan HMOs, and certain grandfathered PHPs, may qualify for comprehensive risk contracts. [42 CFR § 434] HMOs, which typically do not assume responsibility for the direct provision of medical services, may also qualify for comprehensive risk contracts. With certain exceptions, a state's Medicaid plan must allow recipients freedom of choice among health care providers participating in Medicaid.

Q 7:15 Has Medicaid managed care been successful in achieving federal and state objectives?

The federal and state governments have two major objectives in moving toward Medicaid managed care. The first is to save money by managing care and cost. The second is to increase access to and continuity of care. Beginning in the 1980s, HCFA applied a liberal waiver policy to allow some 40 states to make managed care mandatory in whole or in part for certain groups of beneficiaries. The BBA eliminated the waiver requirement except for dual eligibles, children with special needs, and Native Americans. It also eliminated the requirement that at least 25 percent of the members of an HMO with Medicaid beneficiaries not be Medicaid beneficiaries. Today, all states except Alaska rely on some form of managed care to serve their Medicaid populations. These states use one of the three forms of Medicaid managed care described in Q 7:14, with preference being shown for HMOs. In a study conducted by the Urban Institute, researchers examined Medicaid in 13 states (Alabama, California, Colorado, Florida, Massachusetts, Michigan, Minnesota, Mississippi, New Jersey, New York, Texas, Washington, and Wisconsin). Their initial findings revealed that Medicaid managed care, overall, has had limited success.[5] It is usually restricted to children and younger adults, with few states having extended enrollment to the more costly elderly and disabled enrollees. In addition, safety-net providers that need Medicaid revenues to survive have been given special treatment by the states to protect their status as significant traditional providers in the program, thereby impeding the ability of managed care networks to be developed free of restriction or special requirements.

Finally, many HMOs that were participating in the Medicaid managed care program are withdrawing because of low rates, high compliance requirements, and problems with administration. Private HMOs and their investors see little profit-making opportunity in the Medicaid product market. This has affected HMO penetration in small (and often rural) communities, as well as in states with low per capita payment rates.

Q 7:16   What is the role of Medicaid as a benefit program?

Today, Medicaid assists over 35 million low-income families as the safety-net health insurance program for the poor, as a "Medigap" policy for the poor elderly and disabled Medicare beneficiaries, and as a long-term care program for the disabled and elderly. Long-term care is an increasingly utilized part of Medicaid, with almost 45 percent of the total cost of care for persons using nursing facility or home health services being paid for by the program.[6]

Medicaid finances care for one in eight Americans and one in four American children, and pays for 40 percent of the nation's births and half of all nursing home care. As an entitlement program, Medicaid pays for medical services for as many as 37 million low-income people who are blind, aged, disabled, or members of families with dependent children.

Q 7:17   What are the unique challenges facing federal and state Medicaid policy makers?

Medicaid poses different challenges to regulators than does Medicare. The federal government pays for more than half of the expenditures for Medicaid eligibles. This has caused federal regulators, and in response, state regulators, to control Medicaid spending. The federal government seeks to reduce federal spending and limit its liability for Medicaid costs. States also seek to curb Medicaid spending, which usually makes up a substantial portion of state budgets. A major tension in Medicaid comes from the pressure to maintain and expand services for the poor, elderly, and disabled while containing cost.

Another challenge is the continued growth in enrollment. Medicaid now covers a larger population of poor persons than ever before. As insurance coverage for the nonelderly population has eroded (with close to 45 million uninsured Americans by some 1998–1999 estimates), Medicaid has become the major vehicle for the low-income population, particularly poor children and pregnant women. This, along with the increased number of elderly and disabled beneficiaries whose per capita costs account for a greater share of the spending increases, has escalated over the past few years. In fact, more than a third of Medicaid spending is for long-term care services.[7] But what about the working poor who earn more than the state threshold for eligibility? Should public funds be used to broaden private coverage availability for these individuals who fall through the safety net? Some states have taken the approach of using public funds to broaden private coverage through managed care. Other states have increased income thresholds so that more people will be eligible for Medicaid. The challenge continues to be where to "draw the line." Dual eligibles (beneficiaries who receive both Medicare and Medicaid benefits) are another concern.

Finally, the immigrant population has an impact on Medicaid. According to a study published in the *American Journal of Public Health,* more than one third (34.3 percent) of the 26.2 million immigrants (citizens and noncitizens) residing in the United States are uninsured—9 million people. Major findings of the study include the following:[8]

1. Immigrants have low rates of employer-sponsored health coverage. Half (51 percent) of all noncitizen immigrants who work full time are uninsured—3.34 million people.

2. Immigrants make up a small percentage (less than 5 percent) of people with government-sponsored health insurance.

3. Almost half (43.3 percent) of noncitizen immigrant children are uninsured—1 million children. If these children entered the country after 1996, they are not eligible for Medicaid or CHIP.

4. Country of origin makes a big difference. Immigrants are more likely to be insured if they are from Russia, Cuba, Europe, or Canada. Immigrants from Central America, Haiti, Vietnam, and Korea are most likely to lack coverage. In fact, over 50 percent of all immigrants from Mexico and Central America did not have health insurance.

5. Immigrants who are not citizens (62.9 percent of all immigrants) and their children are more likely to be uninsured; 43.6 percent of noncitizen immigrants are uninsured, compared with 18.5 percent of immigrants who have become U.S. citizens. (The study used data from the 1998 Current Population Survey conducted by the Census Bureau. The survey does not ask respondents if they are legal immigrants.)

Other issues of critical concern to state Medicaid commissioners include the "deconstruction" effects associated with the withdrawal of managed care organizations (MCOs) and HMOs from government program contracting because of the BBA. At a meeting held in October 2000, state Medicaid directors expressed their concern that the pattern of health care insurers withdrawing from the M + C program is spreading to Medicaid. They are studying the efforts being undertaken by Medicare to address this problem.

Q 7:18   Can CMS require cost sharing for Medicaid recipients?

States can impose nominal deductibles, coinsurance, or copayments on some Medicaid recipients for certain services. Certain Medicaid recipients, however, must be excluded from cost sharing: pregnant women, persons under age 18 or 21 (at the state's option), hospital or nursing home patients who are expected to contribute most of their income to institutional care, and categorically needy recipients enrolled in HMOs. In addition, emergency services and family planning services must be exempt from copayments for all recipients.

Cost sharing is the shifting of some of the cost of care onto the recipient of the care and can be accomplished by instituting a copayment or requiring coinsurance. Coinsurance can take the form of a separate policy that pays for deductibles or direct payment of a percentage of the cost by the beneficiaries. When cost sharing is applied, it typically is for pharmacy benefits and physician visits. Under a Section 1115 waiver, cost sharing can be implemented within the defined expansion program. Because eligibility thresholds in many states are very low, any cost sharing may represent an unacceptable barrier to care. When cost sharing is applied, the amount collected may be so low that it is less than the cost for the state to collect the revenue.

Q 7:19　What are the key issues that states face in introducing managed care to their Medicaid programs?

As mentioned throughout this section, there is wide variation in state Medicaid programs. Although there has been growth in Medicaid enrollment, overall, the managed care Medicaid programs of each state have proportionally fewer enrollees compared to states that have implemented Section 1115 waivers (Arizona, Tennessee, and Hawaii), which have the largest proportion of their eligible Medicaid population enrolled in managed care. In contrast, Texas, Louisiana, Maine, Wyoming, and Mississippi have large eligible populations with small managed care enrollment. According to a report of the Urban Institute, the following questions have been raised as part of the states' consideration of mandatory managed care for Medicaid:[9]

1. Which types of beneficiaries should be required to enroll in managed care? The Urban Institute notes that this is an important question because the eligible population influences the type and extent of savings that can be expected from managed care, as well as the challenges plans will have in serving eligible populations. The most attractive populations for MCOs are the healthiest ones, and the majority of those who are eligible for Medicaid are comparatively healthy; however, these non-disabled, nonelderly adults account for only about 32 percent of Medicaid expenditures. The opportunity for the largest savings is on the care of the populations that are the most expensive and difficult to treat (the poor elderly and the disabled, i.e., those with severe developmental disabilities, severe mental illness, or AIDS). Unfortunately, these are populations that MCOs tend to have little experience with or incentive to enroll.

2. What types of services should Medicaid managed care plans be required to provide? The Urban Institute has determined that Medicaid has historically paid for a broader range of ser-

vices than most private managed care plans. If managed care plans assume responsibility for delivering services under Medicaid but are unable to deliver them, or view them as "medically unnecessary," the move to managed care may limit beneficiary access.

3. Do states need to ensure the continued existence of traditional Medicaid providers as a part of managed care? The Urban Institute reports that states have three choices. They can enroll Medicaid eligibles in capitated plans that involve commercial, mainstream insurers; they can rely on plans that specialize in Medicare and Medicaid managed care; or they can use a combination of the two. Sometimes, the interests of the significant traditional providers such as public hospitals, neighborhood clinics, and local health departments are in conflict with the state's interest in expanding the number of providers who might participate in Medicaid.

4. How should the enrollment process work? This is one of the most difficult questions that needs to be addressed before implementing a Medicaid managed care program. The Urban Institute notes that depending on the type of waiver, enrollment in managed care may be voluntary or mandatory. In a voluntary system, beneficiaries can choose to enroll in an HMO or remain in the fee-for-service system. Mandatory enrollment, however, increases the state's obligation to provide adequate access to services. These programs give beneficiaries a period of time to select from a list of managed care plans. Some states have had difficulties getting beneficiaries to enroll in managed care plans. When beneficiaries do not choose a plan, the states automatically assign them to a plan.

5. How will the managed care plans get paid? The Urban Institute reports that once a state determines the eligible beneficiaries and covered services under its managed care program, the monthly payment rates have to be established to allow the state to realize savings from its fee-for-service Medicaid program. Typically, states expect savings in the range of 5 to 10 percent. Unfortunately, it is difficult to set appropriate capitated rates until there is sufficient enrollment in the managed care program. The problem is that there are limited incentives for health plans to enroll higher-cost patients given the limited

penetration of managed care and the effect of the disproportionate share funding to most traditional institutional providers who recover losses under the fee-for-service program.

6. How will states monitor plan performance? The Urban Institute reports that states will want to know if they are getting
value from their contract with managed care health plans.
This will require some form of program to oversee plan performance. States differ as to how they achieve this objective, but
their concerns are similar: utilization and quality of care.

Q 7:20 What has been the effect of Medicaid managed care on the quality of care for Medicaid recipients?

Quality is a nebulous value and therefore it is difficult to assess,
even in a program as large as Medicaid. Nevertheless, several systematic efforts have been made to assess quality in Medicaid programs.

Medicaid has been operating as a managed care program in Arizona since 1982. Before then, Arizona did not participate in Medicaid. The Arizona Health Care Cost Containment System (AHCCCS)
was created to enroll Arizona's poor in a managed care program. In
1989, long-term care was added through the Arizona Long Term
Care System (ALTCS). The Kaiser Foundation studied the outcomes
of AHCCCS in its 1999 study entitled "Access to Health Care: Promises and Prospects for Low-Income Americans." According to its
findings, patients enrolled in the system had the same (or better)
access to medical care as the comparison group in neighboring New
Mexico, and the quality of care given to children was better. Prenatal
care and nursing home care, however, were not as good. The Kaiser
Foundation found that AHCCCS had saved money in its lifetime, perhaps over $500 million. Yet the administrative costs of the program
are higher than those of comparable indemnity plans, largely as a
result of managing the care and providing the necessary information
system.

Concurrent with the increasing need for stronger Medicaid managed care programs has been the development of improved tools,
techniques, and strategies for delivering and monitoring managed
care programs. In 1991, DHHS began the Quality Assurance Reform
Initiative (QARI) to provide technical assistance tools and assistance
to state agencies. In 1993, DHHS produced a QARI guide, entitled

"A Health Care Quality Improvement System for Medicaid Managed Care—A Guide for States," that contained four areas of guidance: (1) a framework for quality improvement systems for Medicaid managed care programs; (2) guidelines for internal quality assurance programs of Medicaid HMOs and PHPs; (3) guidelines for clinical and health services focus areas and use of quality indicators and clinical practice guidelines; and (4) guidelines for the conduct of external quality reviews conducted under Section 1902(a)(30)(C) of the Social Security Act.

In 1995, HCFA, working in collaboration with the National Committee for Quality Assurance (NCQA) and the American Public Human Services Association, produced a Medicaid version of the Health Plan Employer Data and Information Set (HEDIS). HEDIS is a standardized quality performance measurement system used by private sector purchasers of managed care services. NCQA, under contract with HCFA, also developed "Health Care Quality Improvement Studies in Managed Care Settings: Design and Assessment—A Guide for State Medicaid Agencies." In 1997, the Agency for Health Care Policy and Research (AHCPR) produced a set of consumer survey instruments and measurement tools under the auspices of the Consumer Assessment of Health Plan Study (CAHPS). The CAHPS instruments include measures and tools specifically designed for use by state agencies. Also in 1997, the George Washington University Center for Health Policy Research published a compendium of provisions of state contracts with Medicaid MCOs. This nationwide study of Medicaid managed care contracts has provided valuable information that can be used by all state agencies in the design and management of their managed care contracts.

In the last decade, private sector group purchasers, quality oversight organizations, the managed care industry, and quality improvement experts have greatly advanced the knowledge base of how managed care can be made more effective in serving consumers, through research, program evaluations, and tests of new administrative, payment, and health care delivery systems. DHHS has attempted to incorporate the knowledge shared by these organizations, along with literature evaluating managed care, to develop specifications for state Medicaid managed care purchasing programs and expects to continue working with these organizations and the state agencies.

Q 7:21　Is Medicaid subject to HIPAA regulations?

Yes. HIPAA defines state Medicaid programs as health plans and they are therefore required to comply with HIPAA regulations. HIPAA is discussed in detail in chapter 8.

Medicare and Managed Care

Q 7:22　How does one enroll in Medicare?

Enrollment in Medicare is handled in one of two ways: either one is enrolled automatically or one has to apply.

Automatic Enrollment. If one is not yet age 65 and is already getting Social Security or Railroad Retirement benefits, it is not necessary to apply for Medicare. Enrollment is automatic for both Part A and Part B of Medicare. A Medicare card is mailed to the eligible individual about three months before that person's 65th birthday. The card contains instructions on how to disenroll from Part B.

For individuals whose eligibility comes with disability, enrollment is automatic for both Part A and Part B of Medicare beginning in the 25th month of disability. A Medicare card is mailed to the eligible individual about three months before eligibility.

Applying for Medicare. One needs to apply for Medicare if one is not receiving Social Security or Railroad Retirement benefits three months before reaching age 65, or if one requires regular dialysis or a kidney transplant. The application begins the seven-month initial enrollment period. By applying early, it is possible to avoid any delays in the start of Part B coverage. If one misses enrollment during this seven-month period, one will have to wait to enroll in the next general enrollment period. General enrollment periods are held January 1 to March 31 of each year, and Part B coverage starts the following July. Applications can be obtained from any Social Security Administration office, or if applicable, from the Railroad Retirement Board.

Q 7:23　What services are covered by Medicare?

Part A, or hospital insurance, benefits include the following:

1. Inpatient hospital care. This benefit includes coverage for the first 60 days, less a deductible ($812 in 2002), for each period

of acute illness. For days 61 to 90 in a hospital, a beneficiary must pay a daily copayment ($203 in 2002). Beyond 90 days, he or she may elect to draw on a 60-day lifetime reserve with a daily copayment ($406 in 2002).

2. Inpatient psychiatric care. There is a 190-day lifetime maximum for this benefit.

3. Skilled nursing care or rehabilitation associated with recuperation for up to 100 days following a hospitalization. There is no cost sharing for the first 20 days, but there is a daily copayment for days 21 to 100 ($96 in 1999).

4. Home health care, which refers to skilled nursing or rehabilitation benefits provided in the home and prescribed by a physician. There are no deductibles, coinsurance, limits on the number of covered days, or required prior hospitalization.

5. Hospice care for the terminally ill, ranging from home health aide services to medical supplies and limited, short-term inpatient care. Coinsurance is required for some services.

An important limitation of HI is the benefit period, which commences when the beneficiary enters a hospital and ends when there has been a break of at least 60 consecutive days since inpatient hospital or skilled nursing care was provided. There are no lifetime limits on the number of benefit periods; however, inpatient hospital care is normally limited to 90 days during a benefit period, and copayment requirements apply for days 61 through 90. If a beneficiary exhausts the 90-day inpatient benefit period, he or she can elect to use days of Medicare coverage from a nonrenewable lifetime reserve of up to 60 total additional days of inpatient hospital care.

Part B (SMI) generally pays 80 percent of physician and outpatient services after an annual $100 deductible. Coverage includes physician services; laboratory and other diagnostic tests; x-ray and other radiation therapy; outpatient services at a hospital, rehabilitation facility, or rural health clinic; home dialysis supplies and equipment; ambulance services; physical and speech therapy; mammography screening and Pap smears; and outpatient mental health services (50 percent of the approved amount only). Not covered are such items as outpatient prescription drugs, routine physical examinations, nonsurgical dental services, hearing aids, and eyeglasses. Long-term care is not a covered benefit for Medicare, although physician visits in long-term care institutions are covered. Indigent elderly may have both Medicare and Medicaid and fall into the dual eligible group.

Part C (M + C) coverage is available to beneficiaries who have both Part A and Part B coverage. To participate in Part C, beneficiaries must be entitled to HI and be enrolled in SMI, except end-stage renal disease (ESRD) patients, who must be enrolled in Part C before they get ESRD (they cannot switch to Part C after diagnosis of ESRD). The plans that will be eligible to contract for Part C include the following:

- Coordinated care plans, which include HMOs, provider-sponsored organizations (PSOs), preferred provider organizations (PPOs), and other certified public or private coordinated care plans or entities that meet approved standards
- Private, unrestricted fee-for-service plans, which allow beneficiaries to select among private providers with payment being on a "nonrisk" basis
- The medical savings account (MSA) plan, which allows beneficiaries (a limited amount over the first five years) to enroll in a plan with a high deductible (maximum for 1999 is $6,000), with the federal government paying a prescribed portion of the capitation amount into an insurance fund for each enrollee

Q 7:24 How are providers and vendors paid under Medicare?

For HI benefits, before 1983, payment to providers and vendors was on a "reasonable cost" basis. Medicare payments for most inpatient hospital services are now paid under a prospective payment system (PPS), which pays the hospital a predetermined amount based on the patient's diagnosis within a diagnosis-related group (DRG). This payment system places the hospital at some risk because it must absorb costs of care that exceed the DRG payment amount. Conversely, if the costs are less than the DRG payment amount, the hospital makes a profit. The BBA reduced DRG payments to hospitals and payments for services reimbursed on a fee-for-service basis based on reasonable costs, including payments for inpatient rehabilitation, psychiatric care, home health, hospice, and skilled nursing care coverage.

For SMI, before 1992, physicians were paid on the basis of a "reasonable charge," which was initially defined as the lowest of (1) the physician's actual charge, (2) the physician's customary charge, or (3) the prevailing charge for similar services in that location. Since 1992, physicians are paid the lower of an amount based on a resource-based relative value scale (RBRVS) formula or submitted charges. Payments for durable medical equipment and clinical laboratory services are based on a fee schedule; hospital outpatient services and home health agencies are paid on a reasonable cost basis. Payments to ambulatory surgery centers have been based on a fee schedule, but are moving toward payment based on ambulatory care groupings. The BBA provided for implementation of a PPS for these services in the future; however, implementation has been delayed because of strong opposition and problems raised by the industry.

Payments to M + C plans are based on a blend of local and national capitated rates determined according to the methodology described in Section 1853 of the Social Security Act. Actual payments to plans vary, based on characteristics of the enrolled population.

Q 7:25 What are the sources of Medicare funding?

All financial operations for Medicare are handled through two trust funds, one for Part A (HI) and one for Part B (SMI). These trust funds, which are special accounts in the U.S. Treasury, are credited with all income receipts and charged with all Medicare expenditures for benefits and administration costs. Assets not needed for the payment of costs are invested in special Treasury securities. The HI trust fund money is used only for the Part A program, and the Part B trust funds cannot be transferred for Part A use.

Part A fund revenues accrue mainly from a tax on individuals' employment earnings. The Part A trust fund also receives income from (1) cost-sharing payments by beneficiaries, (2) a portion of the income taxes levied on Social Security benefits paid to high-income beneficiaries, (3) premiums from certain persons who are not otherwise eligible and choose to enroll voluntarily, (4) general fund reimbursements for the cost of certain uninsured individuals, and (5) interest earnings on the invested assets of the trust fund.

For Part B, financing is through (1) premium payments ($54 per month in 2002), which are usually deducted from the monthly Social Security benefit checks of those who are voluntarily enrolled in the Part B plan; (2) cost-sharing payments by beneficiaries; (3) interest income on invested assets; and (4) contributions from the general revenue of the U.S. Treasury. Part B benefits may also be "bought" for persons by a third party directly paying the monthly premium on behalf of the enrollee. Beneficiary premiums are currently set at a level that covers 25 percent of the average cost for aged beneficiaries. General revenues provide most of the financing for Part B.

Part C financing is dependent on the type of plan chosen. Funding for M + C comes from the HI and SMI trust funds in proportion to the relative proportion of HI and SMI benefits to the total benefit paid by the Medicare program.

Q 7:26   What is the current status of the Medicare trust fund?

The HFCA reported in November 2000 (the most recent HI data available at the time of this writing) that Medicare Part A trust fund assets were 11.8 percent higher at the end of 1999 than at the end of 1998, and the fund will be financially solvent until 2025. The report noted that medical services prices were up 3.4 percent in the fourth quarter of 1999 compared with the same period in 1998, while hospital service prices increased 4.2 percent, compared with 3.2 percent the previous year.[10]

Q 7:27   Is cost sharing required of Medicare beneficiaries?

Yes. Beneficiaries face cost sharing in the form of premiums, deductibles, and coinsurance, as well as the cost of services and products not covered by Medicare. Unlike most private insurance, Medicare does not cap a beneficiary's out-of-pocket costs. For Parts A and B, beneficiaries are responsible for charges not covered by Medicare and for various cost-sharing aspects of both Part A and Part B. For hospital care covered under HI, the beneficiary's share includes a one-time deductible amount at the beginning of each benefit period. If inpatient care exceeds 60 days, a coinsurance payment is required through the 90th day of a benefit period. After the 90th day, Medicare pays nothing unless the beneficiary elects to use part of the lifetime reserve (which requires a copayment). For SMI, the beneficiary's payment includes an annual deductible, monthly premiums, copayments for SMI services (usually 20 percent of medically allowed charges), a deductible for blood, and payment for any services not covered by Medicare. For Part C, the beneficiary's payment share is based on the cost-sharing structure of the specific M + C plan selected because each plan will have its own requirements.

These liabilities may be paid by (1) the Medicare beneficiary, (2) a third party such as Medigap insurance purchased by the Medicare beneficiary, or (3) state medical assistance (Medicaid) if the person is eligible. The term *Medigap* means private health insurance that, within limits, pays most of the health care service charges not covered by Part A or Part B of Medicare. These policies, which must meet federally imposed standards, are offered by Blue Cross (for Part A) and Blue Shield (for Part B) and by various commercial health insurance companies.

Most elderly beneficiaries (89 percent) have supplemental coverage—separately purchased private insurance (Medigap, 37 percent), employer retiree coverage (33 percent), Medicaid (12 percent), or another type (2 percent). Since 1988, state Medicaid programs are required to pay Medicare Part B premiums and cost sharing for all qualified Medicare beneficiaries (QMBs) whose incomes are below 100 percent of the FPL and whose assets are below certain levels ($4,000 for individuals and $6,000 for couples in 1999). For those with incomes between 100 and 120 percent of the FPL, Medicaid pay Part B premiums only. Individuals must apply for Medicaid in their state to be eligible.[11]

Q 7:28 What is the trend in private health plan participation in Medicare risk contracts?

Prior to the effective date of M + C, the number of health plans signing risk contracts with HCFA had been increasing. According to various HCFA reports, an estimated 41 health plans intended to pull out of the M + C program for 2000, and another 58 plans planned to reduce their service area, affecting over 327,000 beneficiaries. States with the greatest number of Medicare beneficiaries affected by the pullouts are New York (39,000), Louisiana (34,000), Texas (32,000), Arizona (31,000), and Florida (29,000).[12] It is predicted that about 1.3 percent (79,000) of all Medicare managed care enrollees will return to traditional Medicare because Medicare managed care plans are not available in their area.

Q 7:29 How are HMOs paid under Medicare?

The Medicare capitation payment is based on the adjusted average per capita cost (AAPCC) set by the CMS Office of the Actuary. The payment to an MCO is 95 percent of the AAPCC.

The AAPCC for risk plans is calculated using the following methodology:

1. Each enrollee is assigned to a demographic class. Determinants of the class include age, sex, Medicare entitlement status, institutionalization, and Medicaid status.

2. CMS estimates the AAPCC by county, with the exception of ESRD, which is calculated at the state level. CMS goes through the following steps to calculate the AAPCC:

   a. Medicare national average calendar year per capita costs are projected for the future year under consideration.

   b. Geographic adjustment factors create a relationship between the county's costs and the national level.

   c. Expected costs are corrected for reimbursement and enrollment in eligible organizations.

   d. The remaining fee-for-service cost is reduced to the county level.

Current risk-plan payments are based on two factors. The first is the AAPCC for fee-for-service beneficiaries at the county level. These numbers may vary widely from one state to another, and from urban to rural areas. The second component is the adjusted community rate (ACR), through which risk plans determine the amount of Medicare noncovered benefits they will provide to Medicare enrollees and the premiums they can charge for those benefits. This payment methodology is intended to ensure that (1) Medicare pays no more for a beneficiary who enrolls in a risk plan than it would pay, on average, for one who stays in a fee-for-service plan; and (2) no plan makes a proportionately larger profit on its Medicare business than on its commercial business.

Q 7:30 What factors do Medicare beneficiaries consider when choosing a plan?

Although many beneficiaries consider maintaining physician relationships important, a survey published in March 2000 by the Office of the Inspector General of the DHHS reported that lower costs are more important to beneficiaries than additional benefits when choosing to join the M + C program instead of the fee-for-service program. Out of 600 M + C beneficiaries who were surveyed, 75 percent of respondents said they chose their health plan mostly because of the costs associated with joining, with 49 percent calling low costs the most important reason for selecting their plan. Respondents favored the lower copayments for doctor visits and no annual out-of-pocket deductible to meet before Medicare coverage begins. In fact, 40 percent of respondents said they would not stay in their plan without the benefit of lower costs. This reflects a change from a 1996 survey performed by Nelson et al., which reported that beneficiaries selected a plan based on costs *and* benefits.[13]

Public opinion polls and other studies show that another feature important to a Medicare beneficiary is the coverage available for most prescription drugs under Medicare risk policies. In the Nelson study, one third of respondents called their prescription drug benefit the most important reason for selecting their current plan. When additional benefits were ranked, 87 percent called prescription drugs most important, followed by regular physicals at 70 percent and vision benefits at 68 percent.[14] The Inspector General's survey is available at http://orig.hhs.gov/.

Q 7:31 What is Medigap insurance?

Medigap insurance is a Medicare supplemental insurance policy, which covers the amount for which an eligible individual is personally responsible. Medigap is private insurance that is designed to help pay Medicare cost-sharing amounts. There are ten standard Medigap policies. Each offers a different combination of benefits.

Approximately one third of fee-for-service Medicare beneficiaries purchase Medigap insurance. Another 31 percent have insurance through their former employers. Six percent of the beneficiaries have both Medigap and an employer-sponsored retirement plan. Approximately 16 percent of enrollees are dual eligibles under Medicaid and Medicare.

The best time to buy a Medigap policy is during the applicable open enrollment period. For a period of six months from the date a person is first enrolled in Medicare Part B and is age 65 or older, there is an absolute right to buy a Medigap policy of the person's choice. One cannot be turned down or charged higher premiums because of poor health if a policy is bought during this period. Once the Medigap open enrollment period ends, however, it may not be possible to buy one's policy of choice, and the Medicare beneficiary may have to accept whatever Medigap policy an insurance company is willing to sell. For a person who has Medicare Part B but is not yet age 65, the six-month Medigap open enrollment period begins when the person turns 65; however, several states (Connecticut, Maine, Massachusetts, Minnesota, New Jersey, New York, Oklahoma, Oregon, Pennsylvania, Virginia, Washington, and Wisconsin) require at least a limited Medigap open enrollment period for Medicare beneficiaries under age 65 (see Q 7:49).

According to research by the nonpartisan Employee Benefit Research Institute (EBRI), the number and percentage of elderly Medicare beneficiaries with an additional source of health insurance coverage dropped significantly from 1994 to 1998.[15] Although the decline in supplemental coverage could be due to elderly beneficiaries migrating to managed care plans as a substitute for the traditional Medigap plans, EBRI's analysis found that in 1998, enrollment in Medicare managed care plans slowed significantly, while the number of Medicare beneficiaries without an additional source of coverage increased. Those most likely to be without an additional source of coverage were older beneficiaries, minorities, the "near poor," and women. This research indicates that a growing number of elderly Americans are not insured for their share of health care costs.

Among other findings cited in the EBRI report are the following:[16]

1. The number of noninstitutionalized elderly Medicare beneficiaries increased from 30.2 million in 1994 to 31.1 million in 1998, or about 3 percent. During the same period, the number of those without an additional source of coverage increased from 6.9 million to 9.2 million, or 33 percent.

2. The data generally support the hypothesis that Medicare beneficiaries have enrolled in managed care plans as a substitute for Medigap coverage. From 1994 to 1998, total managed care enrollment in the Medicare program increased from 3.1 million to 6.6 million; however, the 3.5 million additional beneficiaries in these plans do not necessarily include all of the 2.3 million additional elderly Medicare beneficiaries without an additional source of coverage.

3. Nearly 40 percent of Medicare beneficiaries age 85 and older did not have a supplemental source of coverage in 1998, compared with slightly more than 20.7 percent of those who were

65 to 69 years old. All age groups experienced an increase in the number without an additional source of coverage.

4. In 1998, 27.1 percent of white Medicare beneficiaries did not have a supplemental source of coverage, compared with 44.7 percent of blacks, 44.6 percent of Hispanics, and 34.3 percent of beneficiaries of other races; however, the percentage of beneficiaries without additional coverage grew at a faster rate for whites than it did for both blacks and Hispanics.

5. Approximately 44 percent of elderly Medicare beneficiaries just above the FPL had no additional source of coverage in 1998, whereas only 21.8 percent of those at 400 percent or more of the FPL had no additional coverage.

6. Among male beneficiaries, 27.9 percent were without an additional source of coverage in 1998, compared with 30.9 percent of female beneficiaries.

An analysis of 273 Medicare HMOs and 559 Medicare supplemental insurance plans in 30 cities across the country, published in *Consumer Reports* in May 2000, demonstrates the significant value provided by Medicare HMOs, particularly for people looking for prescription drug coverage.[17]

Q 7:32 How much are the elderly spending out of pocket on health care?

According to a study, "Out-of-Pocket Health Care Costs Among Older Americans," published on March 6, 2000, in the *Journal of Gerontology/Social Sciences*, on average, American senior citizens spend 19 percent of their total income on out-of-pocket medical expenses each year, with those elderly who reported their health status as poor spending 29 percent.[18] According to the study, American seniors most affected by out-of-pocket costs are (1) the elderly in the lowest one-fifth income level (up to $6,720 per capita family income), who spend 32 percent of their income on out-of-pocket health care costs; (2) the elderly who reported their health status as poor, who spend 29 percent; (3) the elderly who are age 85 and up, who pay 22 percent; and (4) the elderly without a high school diploma, who spend 21 percent. The study found that prescription medicine costs make up 33.9 percent of senior citizens' out-of-pocket health care expenditures. For the elderly in the lowest two-fifths income level (below $9,384 per capita family income), prescription medicine costs account for 40 percent of total out-of-pocket health care expenses. Dental services, which are not covered by Medicare, and generally not covered by most insurance plans, accounted for 18 percent of out-of-pocket expenses.[19]

The study also found that insurance coverage affected how much out-of-pocket costs an elderly person had to pay. The elderly with private supplemental insurance spent 25 percent of their total income on out-of-pocket health care costs, while the elderly with only fee-for-service Medicare coverage spent 23 percent. The elderly participating in HMOs or employer-provided plans paid 14 percent to 16 percent of their income on out-of-pocket health care costs.[20]

Q 7:33 How has Medicare addressed the health care needs of vulnerable populations?

Medicare managed care offers the potential for improved access and enhanced care for vulnerable beneficiaries through improved coordination of care and flexibility in the management and delivery of health care services. Two groups of beneficiaries are most vulnerable to the problems of access under capitated arrangements. The first group includes those whose medical requirements make them high utilizers of more expensive specialized care or more resource-intensive care on an ongoing basis. The second vulnerable group includes those who do not know how to access the system because of medical, psychological, economic, sociological, or other factors.

Most Medicare managed care plans are not capable of adequately supporting or covering the expenses for the systems of care for these populations absent changes in payment policies and incentives; however, there are some lessons to be learned from the Medicaid managed care experience for these vulnerable populations. Most notable is the tendency for states to carve out subgroups of the Medicaid program and provide their care under specialized programs. This practice leads to an implicit risk adjustment. Another technique used in most Medicaid programs is to have the program share risk with the plan as extra protection against large or catastrophic losses. These risk-sharing approaches include various combinations of stop-loss limits on catastrophic care, partial capitation, and risk corridors.

Medicare + Choice

Q 7:34   What is Medicare + Choice?

The M + C is a program that was enacted as part of the BBA to replace traditional Medicare coverage for eligible individuals. Under M + C, Medicare beneficiaries are offered a greater variety of managed care and fee-for-service plans. These choices extend far beyond the traditional fee-for-service, "intermediary"-administered products for Medicare Parts A and B and expand beyond the private options of Medicare risk and cost HMO contracts. All plans, with the exception of MSAs, must offer the traditional benefits available under Parts A and B of Medicare and can offer supplemental benefits, which DHHS must approve and which enrollees have the option to select.

M + C dramatically changes the Medicare program by increasing plan options, changing benefit structure, and adding numerous beneficiary protections. Eligible individuals may enroll under the traditional Medicare fee-for-service system or under an M + C plan or M + C organization. An M + C organization is a public or private entity organized and licensed by a state as a risk-bearing entity (with the exception of PSOs receiving waivers) that is certified by the CMS as meeting the M + C contract requirements. [42 CFR §§ 422.2]

These M + C plans include the following:

- Coordinated care plans, including HMOs with or without point-of-service options (POS), PPOs, and PSOs
- Religious or fraternal benefit society plans, which may restrict enrollment to members of the church, convention, or other group with which the society is affiliated (Payments to such plans may be adjusted as appropriate to take into account the actuarial characteristics and experience of plan enrollees.)
- Private fee-for-service plans, which reimburse providers on a fee-for-service basis, and are authorized to charge enrolled beneficiaries up to 115 percent of the plan's payment schedule (which may be different from the Medicare fee schedule)
- MSA options (limited to 390,000 enrollees), under which beneficiaries obtain high-deductible health policies that pay for at least all Medicare-covered items and services after an enrollee meets the annual deductible of up to $6,000 (The difference

between the premiums for the high-deductible policy and the applicable M + C premium amount is placed into an account for the beneficiary to use in meeting his or her deductible expenses.)

With the enactment of the Balanced Budget Refinement Act of 1999 (BBRA) the implementation of M + C payment rate adjustments was "slowed" to more accurately reflect differences in per enrollee costs. By 2004, M + C rates will be risk adjusted based wholly on data from multiple settings.

HCFA and the National Association of Insurance Commissioners (NAIC) developed guidelines for the regulation of M + COs, which were first issued in December 1999. They are not mandatory, but are intended to clarify authority in the areas of M + C state licensure requirements, federal preemption of state-licensed M + C organizations, and financial reporting by state-licensed M + C organizations. In general, the guidelines stipulate that plans must comply with both state and federal laws that apply to M + C organizations—except in the areas of benefits, inclusion and treatment of providers, and coverage determinations where federal law preempts state law. The states are primarily responsible for determining a plan's financial solvency; CMS must ensure that a plan works only with financially sound organizations.

As part of M + C, Medicare offers preventive benefits and patient protections, as well as a far-reaching information program that includes a national toll-free phone number—1-800-MEDICARE (1-800-633-4227)—an Internet site—www.medicare.gov—and a coalition of more than 200 national and local organizations to provide beneficiaries with information.

Q 7:35 Were there any major, unexpected changes in the M + C final rules?

No. On June 29, 2000, CMS released final rules governing the operation of health plans participating in the M + C program (HCFA-1030-FC). The final rules respond to the many comments submitted on the interim final rules, published in 1998, and do not contain any major unexpected changes. One provision in the final rules assures plans that no major changes that would impact plans financially will be made during a contract year. The rules focus on increased flexibility in the program:

1. M + COs can include an in-network POS option.
2. M + COs will be allowed to charge different prices to beneficiaries within a network, and not just out of the network.
3. M + COs will be allowed to contract with providers without replicating community patterns of care as long as access to care requirements are met.

Other changes include clarification that not all providers must be located in the service area to participate, and elimination of the self-reporting requirements. These final rules were published as the July 3, 2000, deadline approached for M + C plans to announce whether they would no longer offer a Medicare managed care product, or would reduce their service areas.

The final rules also alter the phase-in for the comprehensive risk adjuster payment system. Under the BBA, the phase-in would have been 90 percent demographic/10 percent risk adjustment ratio in 2000, 70/30 in 2001, 45/55 in 2002, and 20/80 in 2003, with risk adjustment fully implemented in 2004. That schedule was adjusted by BBRA, and was changed again in the final rules. In December 2000, HCFA announced the new phase-in schedule for both the hospital-only risk adjuster and the comprehensive risk adjuster, based on agency research on the collection of encounter data and a report by the Medicare Payment Advisory Commission (MedPAC), both required by Congress.

Q 7:36 Have any fee-for-service M + C plans been approved?

Yes. On May 24, 2000, the first fee-for-service M + C plan was approved by HFCA. Offered by the Sterling Life Insurance Company (Sterling) in 17 states, the plan became available to beneficiaries beginning in July 2000 and had 17,202 enrollees as of July 2001. The plan, called Sterling Option ISM, is a combination of traditional Medicare and Medicare supplemental coverage. It also has HMO features, such as health risk assessment and disease management.

Medicare beneficiaries who choose to enroll in the private fee-for-service plan (PFFS), Sterling Option I, are not restricted to a network and can get health care services from any provider in the country who can be paid by Medicare. A PFFS is a private insurance program that charges enrollees a premium and cost-sharing amounts and lets beneficiaries choose the providers they want to see. PFFS enrollees are not restricted to a network of providers and do not need a referral to see a specialist. They can see any physician who agrees to accept the PFFS terms. Providers are paid on a fee-for-service basis by the plan and are not subject to utilization review. While providers are not required to accept PFFS members, there is no compelling reason not to if they are already accepting Medicare reimbursement.

Sterling is contacting physicians to explain its PFFS. Physicians who agree to the PFFS terms and conditions become deemed providers when providing services to Sterling Option I enrollees. By 2001, more than 1,260 physicians had become deemed providers. Physicians who do not know Sterling Option I's terms or that a patient is a Sterling Option I enrollee prior to providing medical services are treated as noncontracted providers and may collect what they normally collect under original Medicare. As part of the benefit package, Sterling pays the difference for Sterling Option I members.

In most cases, beneficiaries enrolled in the PFFS will pay less to see a doctor than they would under original fee-for-service Medicare. The Sterling Option I plan furnishes enrollees with coverage of all Medicare Part A and B services and in addition will provide worldwide emergency care and coverage of more inpatient hospital days. It does not cover prescription drugs.

An HFCA program manual published in May 2000 provides that under Sterling Option I's structure, claims for services provided to private fee-for-service beneficiaries are to be sent directly to Sterling. Any such claims will be rejected by the common working file if they are sent to intermediaries and carriers. Contractors should follow standard procedures for dealing with rejected claims. Sterling must demonstrate adequate access to health plans as a part of its M + C contract with CMS, and it plans to do so by paying rates at least equivalent to the Medicare payment rate offered in fee-for-service Medicare. That means most payments will be based on current CMS payment methodologies, and services for which payments are not already set will be covered through proxies created by CMS.[21]

Q 7:37   What has been the experience with the M + C program?

The M + C program experienced the loss or service area reductions of 99 HMOs in 1998 and 1999. As a result, many beneficiaries

Table 7-1. Medicare + Choice Enrollees Affected by Withdrawals,
1999–2002

Year	Enrollees Number	Percent*	Enrollees with No Other Medicare + Choice Plan**	
			Number	Percent***
1999	407,000	6.7	47,000	12
2000	327,000	5.2	79,000	24
2001	934,000	14.7	159,000	17
2002	536,000	9.6	92,400	17

Source: Centers for Medicare and Medicaid Service reprints.
* Percent of Medicare + Choice Enrollment in December of the prior year.
** Estimates private fee-for-service option (Sterling) in 2000. 114,000 enrollees in administering prices have access to this option.
*** Percent of affected workers.

who had enrolled in M + C programs had to return to fee-for-service Medicare.

Currently, about 6.5 million Medicare beneficiaries out of a total of nearly 40 million aged and disabled Americans have enrolled in M + C managed care plans. Original fee-for-service Medicare, currently chosen by more than 33 million beneficiaries, is available to all beneficiaries no matter where they live. According to a report published in May 2000, the M + C program saw enrollment fall by nearly 10,000 beneficiaries from April to May 2000, or a 0.1 percent decrease.[22] From 1997 to 2002, 2.2 million beneficiaries have been involuntarily disenrolled from M + C. See Table 7-1.

The termination of Medicare participation by many of the major managed care plans has had a significant effect on M + C enrollment and is one of the most pressing issues facing CMS and Congress. It is a direct result of the effects of the BBA on the Medicare payment system. Several large M + C contractors announced pullouts in multiple markets, effective January 1, 2001. Among the largest was Aetna U.S. Healthcare, which withdrew from 11 states completely and from parts of 3 others, affecting some 355,000 Medicare members. Other large pullouts include those announced by United Healthcare, affecting 56,000 Medicare beneficiaries, Foundation Health Systems Inc. (19,000), and Humana Inc. (18,000).[23]

Q 7:38   What has been the practical effect of the pullout of HMOs from the M + C program?

HMO withdrawals from the M + C program were expected to force nearly 1 million of the 6.5 million beneficiaries participating in M + C to find alternative and often more expensive coverage. Roughly 934,000 Medicare beneficiaries have been affected by the decisions by managed care plans to leave the M + C program in 2001. The majority (775,000) of those affected, however, live in areas where there are other M + C managed care plans. Texas has the largest number of beneficiaries affected by the pullouts, at 180,749, followed by Pennsylvania (89,641), Florida (87,727), Ohio (65,617), New York (64,329), Maryland (53,038), California (52,464), Connecticut (51,185), Washington (32,177), Louisiana (25,131), Arizona (24,327), and Massachusetts (21,171). A large number of the affected M + C beneficiaries were enrolled in managed care plans offered by Aetna U.S. Healthcare and CIGNA HealthCare Inc.[24]

According to a report of Weiss Ratings Inc. in Reuters, of the 90 plans remaining in the M + C program after December 31, 2000, 37 are losing money. Those losses totaled $645 million in 1999 and $82 million in the first quarter of 2000. Of those 90 plans, 34 have been rated D+ or lower based on their weak financial condition. Only 22 plans have earned a good rating of B− or better.[25]

Q 7:39   Has HFCA or CMS taken any steps to reduce withdrawals of health plans from the M + C program?

Yes. In June 2000 HCFA loosened its program policies. It issued final rules that give plans more flexibility in setting up provider networks and creating benefit options and make it a lot easier for HMOs to re-enter M + C after dropping out. In addition, HFCA made some concessions to the managed care industry's concerns about a new reimbursement method that is based partly on risk adjustment. HFCA agreed to a slower transition into the new payment scheme. It also offered a bonus to health plans if they offer coverage in areas that have no Medicare HMO plans.

At the end of 2000, Congress passed BIPA. BIPA established a new monthly minimum payment amount in 2001 for months after February. The new minimum payment is $525 for any payment area in a metropolitan statistical area within the 50 states and the District of Columbia with a population of more than 250,000; and $475 for any other area within the 50 states. Beginning in fiscal year 2002, premium rates for most U.S. counties will increase by more than five percent. The law follows two years of mass exodus of M + C managed care plans from the Medicare market and has been credited with the return of managed care plans to certain U.S. markets.

Q 7:40 Has the M + C program been effective in meeting federal objectives?

No. Although the BBA achieved much savings for the federal government, the M + C program has not achieved its intended objectives. Three studies performed by the Commonwealth Fund found the following:

1. Plans will continue to reduce both their service areas and the number of benefits they offer. One-third fewer plans offered zero premium products in 2000, while copayments rose. Prescription drug coverage fell from 73 percent to 68 percent, and a majority of those plans offered drug coverage of less than $500.[26]

2. M + C beneficiaries still may face high out-of-pocket expenses with their managed care plans. Annual expenses averaged $1,652, or 13.3 percent of beneficiary average income. Dental services accounted for the largest portion of personal expenditures at 31 percent, followed by health care provider services and prescription drug benefits at 28 percent and 25 percent, respectively.[27]

3. M + C reduces, rather than boosts, competition.[28] Although few plans left New York, Tampa-St. Petersburg, and Cleveland since the start of M + C, pullouts in surrounding areas were widespread. The new lock-in provision, which prevents beneficiaries from changing their M + C plan for one year starting in 2002, could create significant problems for evaluating plan effectiveness and could make beneficiaries feel "trapped."

Q 7:41 How must plans notify beneficiaries if they are leaving Medicare?

If a Medicare managed care plan is leaving Medicare, it sends a letter to beneficiaries about its intention to withdraw. This letter is followed by a second letter that explains the beneficiary's rights and protections and lists other health plans that are available in the beneficiary's community. CMS posts information about which managed care plans are leaving Medicare on Medicare's Web site, http://www.medicare.gov.

Q 7:42 What are a plan's continuing obligations if it leaves the M + C program?

Plans that elect not to renew M + C contracts have the following continuing obligations:

1. *Encounter data.* 42 CFR Section 422.257 requires all M + COs to submit encounter data to CMS so that it can calculate risk-adjusted payments to M + COs. CMS must have all the required historical data for each beneficiary who has been enrolled in a Medicare managed care plan. Terminating contractors must continue to submit the required inpatient encounter data for services provided to all the organization's Medicare beneficiaries enrolled during the preceding calendar year.

2. *Maintenance of records.* 42 CFR Section 422.502(d) requires M + COs to maintain and provide CMS access to books, records, and other documents relating to the operation of an M + C contract. M + C contractors are to maintain these records and allow CMS access to them for six years.

Q 7:43 What are a beneficiary's options if his or her managed care plan decides to leave Medicare in his or her area?

A Medicare beneficiary whose managed care plan has decided to discontinue coverage for Medicare can either return to the original Medicare plan, with or without a Medigap policy, in another Medicare health plan effective on January 1, 2001, or he or she can leave the managed care plan and return to the original Medicare plan, with or without a Medigap policy, if other Medicare health plans are available in the beneficiary's area, enroll in another health plan. If there are other plans available in the beneficiary's area, they are required to be open for enrollment in October, November, and December, unless they already have as many members as they are able to serve. Under this special election period, the beneficiary can choose an effective date of November 1, 2000, December 1, 2000, or January 1, 2001, as long as an enrollment form is submitted to the managed care plan before the effective date requested. Beneficiaries can also enroll in another plan before October if the plan is accepting new enrollees. If a plan is accepting new enrollees in July, August, and September, beneficiaries can enroll in the plan effective the first day of the next month as long as they enroll by the tenth of the month. If they enroll after the tenth of the month, their effective date is the first day of the second month following the month they make the election. For example, if they enroll in another plan on July 9, their enrollment is effective August 1, 2000. If they enroll on July 15, their enrollment is effective September 1, 2000. Plans are not required to accept enrollees in August and September 2000.

Beginning in 2002, beneficiaries may only elect plans during the Annual Election Period (AEP) in November, once during the Open Enrollment Period (OEP) from January through June, or at any time during a Special Election Period. In 2003, the OEP is reduced in length and lasts from January through March. In general, at all other times during the year, a Medicare beneficiary cannot enroll in a new plan and cannot disenroll to Original Medicare. Beneficiaries will be able to make plan changes in some circumstances, such as when they move or if their plan terminates its contract. Beginning in 2002 beneficiaries may only elect plans during the AEP in November, once during the OEP from January through June, or at any time during a Special Election Period. In 2003, the OEP is reduced in length and lasts from January through March. In general, at all other times during the year, a Medicare beneficiary cannot enroll in a new plan and cannot disenroll to Original Medicare. Beneficiaries will be able to make plan changes in some circumstances, such as when they move or if their plan terminates its contract.

Q 7:44 Does a beneficiary lose coverage if his or her managed care plan decides to leave Medicare?

No. Unless they choose to leave their current managed care plan, beneficiaries continue to be covered by their managed care plan until December 31, 2000. If they stay in their current managed care plan through the end of the year, they must continue to use that plan's network of providers.

Q 7:45 If a beneficiary's Medicare managed care plan is leaving Medicare at the end of the year, how does the beneficiary return to original Medicare?

If a beneficiary chooses to return to the original Medicare plan and wants to purchase a Medigap policy, Medicare recommends that he or she apply for Medigap early enough to have Medigap coverage begin at the same time the beneficiary returns to the original Medicare plan. This will be on January 1, 2001, or on whatever date the disenrollment is effective if the beneficiary chooses to disenroll before December 31, 2000. If the beneficiary chooses to disenroll during the special election period in October, November, or December, the beneficiary can choose an effective date of November 1, 2000, December 1, 2000, or January 1, 2001, as long as the disenrollment request is submitted before the effective date chosen. There are special Medigap protections for people who are in health plans leaving Medicare, but the protections are not the same for everyone.

Q 7:46 Can a beneficiary join another Medicare health plan before January 1, 2001, if his or her managed care plan is leaving the area?

Yes, if there are other Medicare health plans available in the community. Beneficiaries may be able to enroll in another health plan at any time if the plan chooses to be open to new enrollees, but these plans are required to accept new enrollees during a special election period in October, November, and December unless they already have as many members as they are able to serve. Under the rules of the special election period, a beneficiary can choose an effective date of November 1, 2000, December 1, 2000, or January 1, 2001, as long as the enrollment form is submitted to the health plan before the effective date requested. All plans must be open to accept elections from all beneficiaries from November 1, 2000, through November 30, 2000, for a January 1, 2001, effective date.

Some managed care plans have approved limits on the number of beneficiaries they can enroll (called "capacity limits"). The approved limits on elections apply to both the special election period (October 1, 2000, through December 31, 2000) and the annual election period (November 1, 2000, through November 30, 2000). If a managed care plan refuses to accept an election, it must provide a written denial.

HCFA reported in August 2000 that most Medicare eligibles who had to leave their HMOs because of market withdrawals were able to make a smooth transition to another HMO.[29]

Q 7:47   If a beneficiary has ESRD, can he or she join another Medicare health plan?

If a beneficiary has ESRD, which is permanent kidney failure, and his or her current managed care plan is leaving Medicare, he or she cannot enroll in a new managed care plan or PFFS offered by another managed care company. The beneficiary can enroll in another plan offered by his or her current managed care company if one is available.

Q 7:48   If a beneficiary only has Medicare Part B, can he or she join another Medicare health plan?

Such a beneficiary must generally be enrolled in Medicare Part A and Part B before he or she can enroll in a Medicare managed care plan or PFFS. If the beneficiary has only Medicare Part B and wants to join a new managed care plan or PFFS, he or she will have to purchase Medicare Part A. The 2002 monthly premium for Part A is $319 per month.

Q 7:49   If a beneficiary chooses to return to the original Medicare plan, can he or she purchase a Medigap policy?

In most cases, yes. When a managed care plan leaves Medicare, the beneficiary has certain rights but must apply for a Medigap policy within certain time frames. These rights apply to all beneficiaries over age 65. If the beneficiary is under age 65, these rights apply to the extent that Medigap policies are made available in the beneficiary's state to beneficiaries under age 65.

If a beneficiary voluntarily disenrolls from a managed care plan before December 31, 2000, the 63-day guaranteed issue period will end 63 days after the date on the final notification letter, or December 4, 2000. If the beneficiary remains in the plan until he or she is automatically disenrolled on December 31, the 63-day guaranteed issue period will end on March 4, 2001. If the beneficiary disenrolls any time before December 4, he or she will still have only until December 4 to apply for a Medigap policy. If the beneficiary disenrolls any time after December 4 but before coverage automatically ends on December 31, he or she will have no Medigap protections. If the beneficiary applies for a Medigap policy within one of these two guaranteed issue periods, the seller or insurer of that policy

1. Cannot deny Medigap coverage or place conditions on the policy;
2. Cannot charge more for a policy because of past or present health problems; and
3. Must cover all preexisting conditions.

Q 7:50 Can a beneficiary return to his or her previous Medigap policy?

Maybe. If a beneficiary is age 65 or older and dropped his or her Medigap policy to join a Medicare managed care plan, he or she may be able to buy the same type of Medigap policy he or she had before if

1. The Medigap policy he or she dropped is still being sold by the same insurance company;
2. This is the first time the beneficiary has ever been enrolled in any kind of Medicare managed care plan;
3. The beneficiary leaves (disenrolls from) this managed care plan within 12 months of joining the plan; and
4. The beneficiary applies for the revious policy no later than 63 days after coverage from the managed care plan terminates.

If the previous policy is no longer available, the beneficiary is still guaranteed the right to buy a Medigap policy designated A, B, C, or F and offered by insurers in his or her state. The beneficiary can use his or her right to return to the old Medigap policy any time during the first 12 months that he or she is enrolled in the managed care plan. This right also applies to those under age 65 to the extent policies are made available in the state to beneficiaries under age 65.

Q 7:51 Is there a Medigap open enrollment period for those who joined a managed care plan when they first turned age 65 and have been in it less than six months?

Yes. During the first six months an individual is both 65 years of age or older and enrolled in Medicare Part B, the individual has a

Medigap open enrollment period. During this period, an insurer cannot (1) refuse to sell any of the ten standardized Medigap policies that the insurer sells in the state, including the three called H, I, and J, which contain outpatient prescription drug coverage; (2) delay the issuance or effectiveness of the policy; or (3) discriminate in the pricing of such policy because of health status, claims experience, receipt of health care, or medical condition. If the beneficiary became entitled to Medicare Part A at age 65 within the last six months, the beneficiary may still have some time left in the Medigap open enrollment period. The time is not lost because the beneificiary decided to enroll in a Medicare managed care plan when he or she first became entitled to Medicare Part B at age 65 or older.

Q 7:52 Do beneficiaries who never used their six-month Medigap open enrollment period because they chose an HMO instead get any special protections?

Yes. Even if their Medigap open enrollment period has passed or will expire very soon, beneficiaries are guaranteed the right to buy any Medigap policy (plans A through J), including the three plans that cover outpatient prescription drugs, if they meet all of the following conditions:

1. They enrolled in a Medicare managed care plan upon first becoming eligible for Medicare at age 65.
2. They disenroll from the Medicare managed care plan within 12 months of their original enrollment date in the managed care plan.
3. They apply for the Medigap policy within 63 days of the date the managed care plan coverage ends.

Q 7:53 What should an M + CO look for in site visits with respect to its compliance plan?

In site visits, an M + CO should determine the scope and placement of the compliance function, and decide whether the compliance program will focus solely on M + C or be enterprise-wide, recognizing that this decision will have serious implications for the complexity and expense of the program.

A compliance plan document should describe how the compliance program will operate and should include all relevant documentation. The compliance plan document should also respond to the seven major components of the Sentencing Commission guidelines and include detailed policies and procedures for how the compliance program will be carried out on an ongoing basis. (See chapter 8 for more information on compliance plans and sentencing guidelines.)

A code of conduct should be developed, and signed by all staff prior to CMS's arrival. The point of a code of conduct is to influence the behavior of the front-line staff most directly accountable for compliance. It should clearly articulate the company's expectations for appropriate execution of staff duties, encourage questions and problem solving, and describe the process by which operational issues will be identified and remedied.

The compliance officer should be on the job well in advance of the site visit. Ideally, this will be an independent position, not a responsibility added to the duties of the M + C product manager, chief financial officer, or general counsel. The position should be paid comparably to other senior managers. The unique skill set this individual must have to carry out his or her responsibilities should be considered before hiring or appointing. The compliance officer has to be capable of "in the trenches" audit work; handling difficult, sensitive issues; and reporting directly to the board of directors.

Activities should be underway in at least three key areas of the compliance program: staff training, internal audits, and reporting. The compliance plan document should lay out schedules for regular staff training and internal reviews of all operational areas in M + C, and a full round of these activities should be conducted before CMS's arrival. Documentation is critical. Sign-in lists at training sessions and detailed records of audit findings of the business units should therefore be maintained.

Q 7:54 What type of information is collected by Medicare and how is it used?

Medicare collects limited information on Medicare health plans' performance and quality of care. This information is used in three ways. First, it is used to evaluate plan compliance with Medicare participation requirements. Second, it is used by regional quality improvement organizations (RQIOs) as part of the Medicare quality program previously conducted by peer review organizations (PROs). QIOs, unlike PROs, focus on quality improvement in specific clinical areas rather than on identification of individual episodes of substandard care. Third, this information is used to monitor managed care program capability.

Medicare-contracting HMOs are required to have an internal quality assessment and improvement (QAI) program. Those that receive risk-based payment are subject to additional external quality review of the care they provide. The QAI program involves the following:

- An ongoing program evidenced by a written plan describing the structure, responsibilities, types of activities, and specific quality-improvement projects for the coming year
- A committee of practicing physicians and other representative practitioners with the commitment of adequate resources, including staff, and board accountability
- An approach that stresses health outcomes, covering the entire range of care provided, and that examines the effects of provider compensation and incentive arrangements to ensure that appropriate services are provided
- A systematic, iterative process to identify problems and areas for improvement, make appropriate changes, and monitor changes over time for effectiveness
- Peer review by physicians and other health professionals of the processes of clinical care
- Systematic data collection of performance and patient outcomes, and interpretation and feedback of these data to practitioners
- Written procedures for taking appropriate action to change areas needing improvement, and a process to determine overall effectiveness of the program and individual action plans

In carrying out the QAI activities, CMS's Office of Managed Care and regional offices expect HMOs to use an integrated approach, addressing all operational areas that affect the quality of care delivered. Once CMS contracts with an MCO to provide services to Medicare beneficiaries, monitoring activities are carried out on an ongoing basis and on-site biennial reviews are conducted. (Efforts are under way to move to a system of annual review of Medicare MCOs.) CMS receives a variety of information from the MCOs, all of which is reviewed against prior plan data. By looking at appeals and reconsiderations, disenrollment patterns, QIO concerns, and member complaints, as well as financial reports, CMS staff are alerted to possible access and quality problems. If a potential problem is identified, CMS can request information from the plan and, if necessary, conduct site visits that will allow CMS to identify problems that need to be addressed by the plan.

The biennial review assesses all aspects of the plan's operations, including eligibility requirements and Medicare contracting operations (marketing materials and activities, enrollment, disenrollment, appeals and grievances, claims processing). If deficiencies are noted, the plan is requested to develop a corrective action plan. Following approval, the plan is monitored to ensure that the appropriate changes are made.

Section 1853(a)(3)(B) of the Social Security Act requires M + C organizations, as well as eligible organizations with risk-sharing contracts, to submit physician encounter data. These data are necessary to identify beneficiaries' health status, formulate the risk adjustment payment factor, and maintain the risk adjustment model over time. M + C organizations are required to collect and submit encounter data regarding physician services beginning October 1, 2000, for all physician services rendered on or after that date. CMS will use the data to implement a risk adjustment methodology that accounts for variation in per capita costs based on health status. The system is scheduled for implementation in January 2004.[30]

Q 7:55 How will information on Medicare managed care health plan quality and performance be used in the future?

Most likely, quality and performance information on Medicare managed care health plans will be used to assist beneficiaries choose a plan. Other uses will be based on both political and technical considerations, as CMS will be working cooperatively with the private sector leaders in health plan performance and quality measurement to avoid duplication of effort and potentially inconsistent results. These other uses may include (1) evaluating ongoing compliance with Medicare participation standards, (2) developing eligible criteria for a "preferred plan" designation, (3) developing payment formulas that include criteria based on performance, and (4) selective contracting.

Plans must now report information on the health care provided to Medicare beneficiaries using specially developed Medicare measures from HEDIS. Enrollees will be surveyed on their satisfaction using an instrument developed for the Medicare population as part of the AHCPR's Consumer Assessments of Health Plans Study. Finally, CMS intends to use a set of outcomes measures developed by the Foundation for Accountability, an organization composed of public and private health care purchasers and consumer groups.

Q 7:56   What are the major issues raised by the new reporting requirements for health plans?

The major issues raised by the new reporting requirements for health plans relate to the data's accuracy, completeness, standardization, and comparability across plans. Confidentiality and cost are additional concerns. The proposed uses of health plan data should be defined before reporting requirements are established. For example, data reported should be sufficient to assess the quality and accessibility of care, to determine risk adjustments for payment purposes, and to compare utilization or outcomes across plans and providers.

Accuracy. The data must be accurate. In the private sector, some employers and health plans specify in contracts the degree of accuracy and completeness of reporting required. Compliance is achieved through medical record audit.

Completeness. Many health plans have incentives to encourage reporting of complete data. These incentives can be financial or non-financial. Punitive financial incentives are most common and involve a withhold of payment pending receipt of required information. Failure to provide the information within a specified period of time may result in a penalty being assessed against the plan and providers. Others use positive financial incentives to reward the reporting of encounter data. Nonfinancial incentives relating to reported information include the feedback of reported data to the plans and providers to allow them to take advantage of such information.

Standardization. Standardization is essential to a common database. Both the format for the data and the definitions of the data elements themselves must be standardized. There are many problems in achieving standardization when each plan has its own data requirements. Between plans, there may be little standardization from the perspective of the provider that has to report the information. In an effort to improve standardization, CMS is working on a number of initiatives. The National Committee on Vital and Health Statistics (NCVHS), an advisory body to the Secretary of HHS, has developed a uniform encounter data set that defines 25 data elements but is not yet ready for implementation.[31] CMS has also developed a standardized encounter data set for use by Medicare and Medicaid called the Medicaid-Medicare Common Data Initiative (McDATA), which overlaps with the NCVHS core data set by 95 percent. The core set of encounter data was developed based on the fee-for-service claims forms used by physicians under Medicare Part B services (Form 1500) and hospitals under Medicare Part A (UB-92). States operating under Medicaid Section 1115 waivers are required to provide inpatient and ambulatory care encounter data using a subset of the McDATA elements. Another database being developed by CMS is the Medicare Transaction System (MTS), which will contain all Medicare claims data and will have the potential to incorporate encounter data from Medicare managed care in the McDATA format.[32] As discussed in chapter 15, HIPAA created a federal mandate regarding the identification, reporting, and use of health information.

Comparability. Most health data are not comparable from one plan to another because of the processes used to collect the data or the underlying populations being compared. Another problem occurs when data are collected differently in different plans. Fee-for-service claims data differ from capitated health plan encounter data. At issue are coding differences.

Aggregate versus Patient-Level Data. Aggregate data are often easier and less expensive to collect and report. Raw data, however, have more use than summary data. Patient-level data offer the greatest degree of flexibility because these data allow the development of better risk-adjusted models.

Cost. There is an inherent cost-benefit analysis associated with the collection and reporting of data. Information systems are very expensive, and collection and analysis are resource intensive. Some collectives of users have organized health information organizations, community health information systems, and other forms of cooperatives to allow the ownership, use, and cost of information collection and reporting to be shared.

Confidentiality. Issues of privacy and confidentiality always arise when patient-specific and patient-identifiable information is being collected for external use. Particularly sensitive items include mental health conditions, AIDS testing and treatment, and genetic testing. HIPAA attempts to address not only the confidentiality of this information but also its use in a nondiscriminatory manner.[33] Other barriers to information sharing arise because health plans may want to protect certain types of information as proprietary trade secrets. Capitated provider groups may not want to report encounter data to health plans to maintain their negotiating position in rate setting. NCQA recommends that health plans require all capitated providers to report encounter data.[34]

Balanced Budget Act of 1997 and Balanced Budget Refinement Act of 1999

Q 7:57   What is the Balanced Budget Act of 1997?

The BBA is a piece of federal legislation containing the most significant reforms affecting health care since enactment of Medicare and Medicaid in the mid-1960s. It includes provisions affecting Medicare, Medicaid, and CHIP. Despite BBA's intentions, its reforms resulted in hospital closures in rural markets, increased numbers of health plans pulling out of the M + C program, and economic distress in academic medicine.

As part of the BBA, the M + C program, also known as Medicare Part C, was enacted to replace traditional Medicare coverage for eligible individuals. As a consequence, Congress has struggled with lobbying pressures from rural constituencies, academic medical centers, and underserved populations, to cite a few.

Q 7:58   What was the impact of the BBA on Medicare?

The BBA set in motion significant changes toward modernizing Medicare. Its combination of constraints on provider fees, increases in beneficiary payments, and structural reforms is expected to lower program spending by $386 billion over ten years. Because certain key provisions have only recently or have not yet been phased in, the full effects on providers, beneficiaries, and taxpayers wrought by BBA will not be known for some time.

Of particular significance was BBA's creation of the M + C program, which furthered the use of a choice-based model of providing Medicare benefits. M + C expanded Medicare's managed care options to include, in addition to HMOs, health plans such as PPOs, PSOs, and PFFSs. As part of this expanded consumer choice program, BBA provisions placed a dramatic new emphasis on the development and dissemination to consumers of comparative plan information to foster quality-based plan competition. Other BBA provisions were designed to pay health plans more appropriately than Medicare had done under the previous HMO payment formula.

BBA also made historic changes to traditional Medicare. It is gradually eliminating, for the most part, cost-based reimbursement methods and replacing them with PPSs. The intent is to foster the more efficient use of services and lower growth rates in spending for traditional Medicare providers, replicating the experience for acute-care hospitals following the implementation of Medicare's PPS for hospitals, which began in the mid-1980s. BBA mandated phasing in a PPS for skilled nursing facilities (SNF), home health agencies, hospital outpatient services, and certain hospitals not already reimbursed under such arrangements.

The BBA's intent was to maintain Medicare Part B premiums at 25 percent of program costs and phase into the premium, over seven years, the cost of home health provisions. The intent was to achieve the following goals:

- To extend the life of the Medicare Part A trust fund for ten years
- To reform the structure of Medicare and expand choice through PSOs, PPOs, PFFSs, a demonstration project for MSAs, and private contracting for health care services
- To expand preventive health care benefits for mammography, Pap smears, diabetes, prostate and colorectal cancer screening, bone density measurement, and vaccines
- To increase accountability through fraud and abuse penalties and strengthen program integrity through increased disclosure of information to beneficiaries and encouragement of prudent purchasing decisions

Medicare beneficiaries were to be assured of choice through expanded options and being allowed to return to fee-for-service Medicare after trying another plan. The expanded options included PSOs, MSAs, PFFSs, private plans or HMOs, and PPOs. These M + C plans were intended to encourage expansion of managed care into rural and low-cost urban areas by doing the following:

1. Setting minimum monthly payments to $367 as of 1998 (most current rural payments are substantially lower than urban rates);

2. Gradually moving the calculation of payment from its existing formula to a 50-50 blend of national average costs and local costs;

3. Guaranteeing plans a minimum percentage increase;

4. Replacing the 50-50 Medicare/non-Medicare enrollment rule with enhanced quality and outcome measures;

5. Authorizing new competitive pricing demonstration projects; and

6. Carving out graduate medical education costs (direct and indirect) from payments over five years and making the payments directly to the teaching hospitals.

Q 7:59 What are the important provisions of the BBA that affect Medicaid?

One of the BBA's goals is to achieve approximately $13 billion in net Medicaid savings over five years with increased state flexibility and oversight of the program. BBA gives states the option of providing Medicaid services through managed care without a waiver. The requirement that states pay FQHCs on a cost basis will be eliminated over several years. States can use Medicaid payment rates to determine whether cost sharing is owed for QMBs and dual eligibles.

The BBA increases health coverage for children who are uninsured. It provides for $24 billion to be spent on children's health care, with more than 7 million of the country's uninsured children becoming eligible for coverage. CHIP entitles states to grants to expand health insurance access for eligible children. Many states have adopted appropriate legislation to provide such access and to match the federal funding through a specified formula. CHIP is discussed in more detail in Q 7:71 et seq.

Q 7:60   Are there significant consumer protection features in the BBA?

Yes. BBA includes significant consumer protections, such as monthly disenrollment through 2001, annual enrollment with a six-month disenrollment period in 2002, and annual enrollment with a three-month disenrollment in 2003 and thereafter. Other protections include the following:

1. All plans must make medically necessary care available seven days a week, 24 hours a day.
2. Plans are prohibited from restricting providers' advice to beneficiaries about medical care and treatment.
3. Plans are required to have grievance and appeal mechanisms in place to protect beneficiary rights.
4. Plans must provide coverage for care that a "prudent layperson" would consider an emergency.
5. Plans are required to safeguard the confidentiality of health information while allowing patients access to their medical records.

Q 7:61   What has been the effect of the payment reforms in the BBA?

The BBA represented the most comprehensive Medicare reform since the program's establishment in 1965. These changes included (1) expanding Medicare's coverage of preventive benefits; (2) providing additional choices for seniors through the M + C program; (3) implementing new tools to combat health care waste, fraud, and abuse; and (4) establishing initiatives to modernize and strengthen Medicare's fee-for-service payment system. New payment methods were established affecting virtually every segment of the health care industry, including managed care plans, hospitals, skilled nursing facilities, and home health agencies.

The BBA's Medicare provisions were enacted in response to rapid program spending growth that was clearly unsustainable. The reforms sought to control Medicare spending by changing the financial incentives inherent in payment methods that, prior to the BBA, did not reward providers for delivering care efficiently. Since these changes, provider groups have remained steadfast in their support of rolling back payment reforms. Others have indicated a need to wait for evidence demonstrating the need for such modifications. Calls for BBA changes came at a time when federal budget surpluses and lower-than-expected growth in Medicare outlays might have made it easier to accommodate higher Medicare payments. The BBA is expected to reduce overall Medicare spending by almost $30 billion in 2002.

Prior to the BBA, Medicare paid for hospital outpatient department services, home health care, and care in skilled nursing facilities mostly on a retrospective, cost-reimbursement basis. The BBA replaced those procedures with PPSs under which providers receive predetermined, fixed amounts. Some provider groups contend that beneficiary access to care has been adversely affected as a result of these reforms. In addition, some M + C organizations, which either are terminating their program participation or reducing their service areas, attribute these actions to reductions in Medicare payment rates and other BBA changes.

By the end of the BBA's first full year of implementation, health care providers believed that the spending reductions contained in the BBA harmed their ability to provide care to Medicare beneficiaries and that the federal government did not accurately keep track of their financial problems or pay them adequately. As discussed in chapter 1, the BBA achieved its intended result of cutting health care costs. In making those cuts, however, a number of providers and programs were significantly affected. In response to growing concern for rural providers, academic medical institutions, and other safety-net providers, Congress enacted BBRA.

Q 7:62 What is the Balanced Budget Refinement Act of 1999?

BBRA was enacted in November 1999 to increase payments to Medicare providers by approximately $11.5 billion over five years. The goals of BBRA are as follows:

- Provide hospitals with greater flexibility to participate in Medicare as critical access or sole community hospitals, and strengthen and increase flexibility for critical access hospitals

- Offer Medicare beneficiaries more flexibility through M + C by (1) authorizing incentives for health care providers to enter counties that do not currently offer managed care plans; (2)

allowing M + C beneficiaries an open enrollment period when they learn their plan is ending its contract; (3) slowing the implementation of M + C payment rates to more accurately reflect differences in per enrollee costs; and (4) allowing beneficiaries more time to enroll in M + C or Medigap plans when health plans withdraw from their market

- Ease the financial burden on hospitals that care for a disproportionate share of low-income individuals

- Ease the transition for outpatient hospitals switching to the new payment system

- Permit the Secretary of HHS to provide hospitals with (1) additional payments to cover certain high-cost cases (i.e., outlier adjustments) and (2) transitional pass-through payments (for orphan and cancer therapy drugs and new medical devices)

- Ensure the availability of home health care services

- Increase payments for medically complex skilled nursing facility patients

- Increase access to prostheses, cancer fighting drugs, and ambulance services

- Freeze the indirect medical education adjustment for one year and provide a more equitable structure for direct graduate medical education payments to teaching hospitals nationwide

- Adjust the payment system for existing long-term and psychiatric hospitals through increased improvement and bonus payments through FY 2002

- Modify the way doctors are paid for treating patients to improve the accuracy of physician payment updates and limit future fluctuations in the update factor

- Make a number of changes to the Medicaid program, including (1) increasing DSH payments for several states and the District of Columbia; (2) modifying the SCHIP allotment formula to provide states with a more stable financing system; and (3) authorizing states to create a new payment system for community health centers and rural clinics that recognizes the cost of providing health coverage in rural and underserved areas and the high volume of uninsured patients served by these health centers

Q 7:63   How does the BBRA change the BBA?

BBRA attempts to correct the unintended consequences of the BBA by modifying several components of government programs.

Medicare Part A. For PPS hospitals, BBRA freezes the Indirect Medical Education adjustment at 6 percent for FY 2001 and then reduces the adjustment to 5.5 percent in FY 2002 and subsequent years. The BBA outlined reductions in the indirect medical education adjustment from 7.7 percent to 7 percent in FY 1998; to 6.5 percent in FY 1999; to 6 percent in FY 2000; and to 5.5 percent in FY 2001 and subsequent years. Medicare provides indirect medical education payments to teaching hospitals to account for higher patient care costs incurred by facilities with medical education programs (as opposed to nonteaching hospitals). This adjustment delay is intended to help teaching hospitals adjust to the impact of the BBA. For DSHs, BBRA freezes the reduction in the DSH payment formula at its FY 2000 level of 3 percent for one year (FY 2001) and changes the reduction to 4 percent in FY 2002. In addition, BBRA requires the Secretary of HHS to collect hospital cost data on uncompensated inpatient care, including bad debt and charity care. The BBA reduced the DSH payment formula by 1 percent each year starting in FY 1998 and continuing through FY 2002. This provision is intended to ease the financial burden on hospitals that care for a disproportionate share of low-income individuals.

For PPS-exempt hospitals, such as psychiatric, long-term care, and rehabilitation facilities, the BBRA adjusts the payment system for existing long-term and psychiatric hospitals through increased improvement and bonus payments through FY 2002. Specifically, BBRA increases the amount of continuous bonus payments to eligible providers from 1 percent to 1.5 percent on October 1, 2001, and to 2 percent on October 1, 2002. The BBA established a smaller amount of bonus and relief payments for eligible PPS-exempt providers. This provision is designed to provide temporary relief to PPS-exempt hospitals until the PPS is implemented.

For skilled nursing facilities, BBRA temporarily increases the federal per diem payment by 10 percent for 12 resource utilization groups (RUGs) for medically complex patients. BBRA increased payments from April 1, 2000, through September 30, 2000, at which time the Secretary of HHS was expected to refine the case-mix measure and adjust the average rates for case mix based on data on intensity that had not been available at the inception of the PPS. The BBA required the Secretary of HHS to implement a PPS for skilled nursing facilities starting in July 1998. The PPS outlined in the BBA is based on the RUG design that HCFA developed over several years and tested through demonstration projects. The RUG system requires skilled nursing facilities to categorize their Medicare patients according to 44 hierarchical groups based on the kinds and intensities of care and services they need. The skilled nursing facility PPS provides facilities a fixed amount per day per patient (i.e., a per diem payment), with the amount of the payment determined by the RUG into which the patient is classified. BBRA increases payments for certain RUG categories so that access to skilled nursing facility services is not impaired. BBRA also (1) increases the federal per diem rate for skilled nursing facility "market baskets"; (2) permits skilled nursing facilities to receive payments based wholly on the federal per diem rate (rather than a mix of federal and facility-specific rates) if that is more advantageous to the facility; (3) permits separate billing by skilled nursing facilities for certain prosthetic devices, chemotherapy drugs, and ambulance and emergency services (because of their relatively rare occurrence and high cost); (4) permits skilled nursing facilities that participated in the Nursing Home Case Mix and Quality Demonstration Project to receive an additional payment for Medicare Part B services in the facility-specific component of their payment rates; (5) authorizes payments based on costs for certain skilled nursing facilities that treat specialized, high-cost patients; and (6) requires MedPAC to study the need for special adjustments for Alaska and Hawaii and submit a report to Congress within 18 months of enactment.

Medicare Part B. The BBA made several adjustments relating to how physicians are compensated. It modified the procedure by which doctors are paid for treating patients based on a sustainable growth rate (SGR); this is expected to improve the accuracy of updates to physician payments and limit future fluctuations in the update factor. BBRA permits the Secretary of HHS—for certain high-cost cases—to provide hospitals with additional payments for covered services for which the hospital's costs exceed a certain PPS amount (i.e., outlier adjustments) and to provide transitional pass-through payments (for orphan and cancer therapy drugs, biological devices, and new medical devices). The policy must be implemented on a cost-neutral basis.

CMS's plans to implement the hospital outpatient PPS form of reimbursement pose serious concerns. The agency's proposal (1) fails to provide adjustments for high-cost care; (2) does not provide an adequate transition to include new medical devices, drugs, and biological devices in the system; and (3) will not be updated annually to keep pace with changes in technology and medical practice. The hospital outpatient PPS was scheduled to be implemented in full and simultaneously for all services and hospitals around July 2000. BBRA provides payments (in addition to PPS payments) to hospitals during the first three years of the PPS if their payments are less than they would have received prior to the PPS. This provision is intended to provide a temporary transition for hospitals to adjust to the new PPS when it is implemented by offering incentives to improve efficiency while protecting hospitals from large financial losses.

Provisions Affecting Medicare Parts A and B. BBRA delays the BBA's 15 percent payment reductions to home health agencies until one year after implementation of the PPS. It also requires the Secretary of HHS to report to Congress on the need for a 15 percent reduction, or for any reduction, within six months of implementing the PPS. This provision is designed to increase access to home health care services. The BBA established an "interim payment system" for home health care to temporarily replace the former system, which reimbursed home health agencies for the lesser of their reasonable costs or a limited amount per visit. BBA required the Secretary of HHS to implement a PPS for Medicare home health care beginning on or after October 1, 1999, and required that the new system be designed to reduce the initial aggregate cost of Medicare home health care by 15 percent. The BBA allowed a transition period to implement the new system of no longer than four years. The BBA also specified that if the new PPS was not ready for implementation on October 1, 1999, the existing interim payment system would be changed to reduce cost and per beneficiary limits by 15 percent.

The BBRA established a national average per resident payment amount, adjusted for differences in area wages, starting on or after October 1, 2000. Hospitals will receive the greater of the national average amount per resident or a blended amount of the hospital-specific amount and the national average amount, subject to a transition period. BBRA provides a five-year transition period for hospitals that had resident levels above the national average. Medicare pays hospitals for its share of direct graduate medical education costs in approved programs using a count of the hospital's number of full-time equivalent residents and a hospital-specific historic cost per resident, adjusted for inflation. The provision is intended to establish a more equitable structure for direct graduation medical education payments to teaching hospitals nationwide.

Rural and Other Critical Access Providers. The BBA established criteria for a small, rural, limited service hospital to be designated as a critical access hospital (CAH). These are geographically remote, rural, nonprofit or public hospitals that are certified by states as necessary providers. CAHs provide 24-hour emergency services, have up to 15 acute-care inpatient beds, and have hospital stays of less than 96 hours except under certain circumstances. The BBRA (1) permits certain urban hospitals to apply for rural designation; (2) updates and supplements federal criteria used to designate rural providers; (3) incorporates state designation of rural areas or providers; and (4) permits urban hospitals to be classified as sole community hospitals. Medicare's payments to an acute-care hospital vary depending on the geographic location of the hospital. The Medicare Geographic Classification Board may reclassify a hospital to determine its standardized payment amount, its wage index, or both. An urban or rural hospital may apply for redesignation if it can prove that its geographic assignment is inappropriate because it competes for patients and employees with hospitals located in other areas. The measure is intended to provide hospitals with greater flexibility so that they may participate in Medicare as CAHs or sole community hospitals. BBRA includes a number of provisions designed to strengthen and provide increased flexibility for CAHs. Specifically, it (1) applies the 96-hour limitation on length of stay on an average annual basis; (2) allows nonprofit hospitals to qualify for designation as CAHs; (3) allows hospitals that have closed within the past ten years or facilities that have downsized to convert to CAHs; (4) permits CAHs to elect either a cost-based hospital outpatient service payment plus a fee schedule for professional services or an all-inclusive rate; (5) eliminates coinsurance for clinical laboratory tests; and (6) clarifies CAHs' ability to participate in the swing-bed program.

BBRA extended the Medicare Dependent Hospital (MDH) Program through FY 2005. MDHs are small, rural hospitals that are not classified as sole community hospitals and that treat relatively high proportions of Medicare patients. (The BBA reinstated and extended the MDH Program to FY 2001.) BBRA permits sole community hospitals that were paid the existing federal rate to transition over time to Medicare payment based on their FY 1996 costs. A sole community hospital is paid based on certain factors and which factor yields the greatest Medicare reimbursement. The BBRA permits rural hospitals to increase their resident limits by 30 percent for both direct medical education and indirect medical education payments and allows non-rural facilities that operate separately accredited rural training programs to increase their resident limits. The BBA had limited the number of residents that hospitals could count for graduate medical education to the total recognized by the hospital on or before December 31, 1996.

Some rural hospitals must be able to use "swing beds" and be reimbursed accordingly because of the smaller number of beds and requirement for access to care. The BBRA eliminates the requirement that states review the need for swing beds through the certificate of need process. It also eliminates length-of-stay constraints. Medicare permits certain rural hospitals with fewer than 50 beds to use their inpatient facilities to furnish long-term care services. Rural hospitals with fewer than 100 beds can operate swing beds under certain circumstances. These provisions are intended to provide flexibility for hospitals with between 50 and 100 beds that want to participate more extensively in the Medicare swing-bed program.

Additional funding has been allocated to rural hospitals under BBRA to enable them to become PPS-ready. BBRA permits rural hospitals with fewer than 50 beds to apply for grants of up to $50,000 to meet the costs associated with implementing new PPSs, such as purchasing computer software and hardware and educating and training staff. The BBA replaced and modified the existing Essential Access Community Hospital (EACH) program with the Medicare Rural Flexibility Program. As part of the program, the Secretary of HHS is authorized to award grants to states for rural health care services. In addition, the BBA had established a telemedicine demonstration project to improve primary care for diabetics who live in medically underserved areas. BBRA directs the Secretary of HHS to award the authorized grants within three months of enactment and changes certain specifications of the project design.

Medicare Part C. BBRA slows the implementation M + C payment rate adjustments to more accurately reflect differences in per enrollee costs. In 2004, M + C rates will be risk adjusted based wholly on data from multiple settings. This provision is intended to give M + C plans additional time to transition to the new risk adjustment methodology to avoid dramatic changes in M + C payments that may destabilize the program and limit choices for seniors. For areas without M + C plans, the measure authorizes financial incentives to health care providers that enter counties that do not currently offer managed care plans. In some counties beneficiaries have access to only one Medicare option: the fee-for-service program. In addition, under certain circumstances BBRA allows a plan to re-enter a county if there is a legislative or regulatory change that increases M + C payments in the area within six months of the plan's notification of its intent to terminate its contract.

The BBRA (1) allows M + C beneficiaries an open enrollment period when they learn that their plan is ending its contract; (2) allows beneficiaries more time to enroll in M + C or Medigap plans when health plans withdraw from markets; (3) allows cost contracts with HMOs to be renewed through 2004; (4) requires the Secretary of HHS to continue to compute and publish adjusted annual per capita cost data; (5) sets aside funding annually (from graduate medical education funds already authorized) for payments to hospitals with nursing and allied health education programs when they provide inpatient care to patients enrolled in an M + C plan; (6) eases certain requirements that limit how potential providers design and market managed care products to offer to Medicare beneficiaries; (7) modifies and extends a number of demonstration projects; and (8) increases M + C payment rates in 2002.

Medicaid. The BBRA permanently extends special rules relating to DSH payments to safety-net hospitals. Previous law limited how much Medicaid DSH payments most hospitals could receive to 100 percent of their uncompensated care. Some public hospitals are now allowed up to 175 percent. This provision was enacted in 1997 to avoid destabilizing the delivery of care that safety-net public hospitals provide. Prior law capped the federal share of Medicaid DSH payments for each state at specified levels through 2002, increasing individual state allotments adjusted for inflation starting in FY 2003. BBRA bill increased allotments for several states and the District of Columbia in FYs 2000, 2001, and 2002. This provision was considered necessary to mitigate the cumulative impact of several BBA provisions that produced an unintended financial burden on DSH hospitals.

BBRA authorizes states to create a new Medicaid PPS for community health centers and mini-clinics that recognizes the cost of providing health coverage in rural and underserved areas and the high volume of uninsured patients treated in these health centers. Under the BBA, community health centers and mini-clinics could lose as much as $1.1 billion over a five-year period and more than 1.3 million uninsured community health center and mini-clinic patients could lose access to health care services. This BBRA provision was intended to maintain state flexibility and give states budgetary certainty by capping payments to community health centers and mini-clinics through an inflation index.

State Children's Health Insurance Program. BBRA contains provisions addressing the allotments to states under CHIP. It modifies the CHIP allotment formula by adding floors and ceilings to the system in order to provide greater stability to the financing structure. Of the total amount available for allotment under CHIP, 0.25 percent is allotted to commonwealths and territories to be divided among them based on specified percentages. Commonwealths and territories also received an additional $32 million in FY 1999. To permanently correct the underrepresentation of territory population reflected in the original formula established by the BBA, BBRA authorizes an additional $34.2 million for each of FYs 2000 and 2001, $25.2 million for each of FYs 2002–2004, $32.4 million for each of FYs 2005 and 2006, and $40 million for FY 2007 for commonwealths and territories.

Q 7:64   What is the Competitive Pricing Advisor Committee?

The Competitive Pricing Advisor Committee (CPAC) is an independent commission created by the BBA to design the demonstration to bring competitive bidding to M + C plans. The BBA mandated two competitive-bidding demonstration projects to test whether market principles could help Medicare to secure health services more efficiently. One project focused on durable medical equipment and services (except physician services). [BBA § 4318] The other centered on health plans, because CPAC was expected to call for competitive pricing. During nine public meetings held between May 1998 and October 1999, CPAC examined the experience of innovative purchasers of health insurance that could inform the demonstrations and heard testimony from a number of private and public sector health insurance purchasing experts. Two cities were chosen to host demonstration projects that would test the effectiveness of competition in the Medicare program: Maricopa County, Arizona, and the twin cities of Kansas City, Kansas, and Kansas City, Missouri. Both were opposed by local officials and congressional representatives and eventually were blocked by BBRA. [Pub L No 106-113 (Dec 3, 1999)]

At its last meeting, CPAC decided to continue producing its final report on the project, also mandated by Congress. The report covers six areas: lessons learned during the creation and initial implementation of the project, design considerations for future projects, the inclusion of Medicare fee-for-service, quality activities, rural projects, and benefit structure. Committee members discussed draft chapters on each topic and suggested that the section on lessons learned be adapted to reflect the fact that CPAC and the area advisory committees (AACs), which worked on the project at each site, completed their work as required by Congress, although the projects were never implemented. (For more information on CPAC, see http://www.hcta.gov/medicare/cpacrept.pdf.)

Although the 106th Congress stalled the implementation of the demonstration project designed by CPAC with the enactment of BBRA, some important design issues were raised by CPAC in evaluating previous and future Medicare demonstrations:

1. Should fee-for-service Medicare be included in the demonstration?
2. How aggressively should the government manage competition for Medicare beneficiaries?
3. Should there be a standard benefit package?
4. Where should the government contribution be set?
5. What form of risk adjustment is appropriate?
6. What kinds of comparative health plan information should be collected and disseminated to beneficiaries?

At its January 12, 2000, meeting, CPAC voted to produce the reports BBRA asked for and to work with the health policy leadership in Congress and the next administration to try to implement competitive-pricing demonstrations in the future despite its disillusionment with the political process.

Issues in Medicare and Medicaid

Q 7:65   What effects will health care costs have on Medicare and Medicaid spending?

Spending for all health care in the United States topped $1.2 trillion in 1999, up 5.6 percent from 1998, continuing a six-year trend of growth below 6 percent annually. Despite a one-time savings from the BBA, health care spending was projected to resume growing as a share of gross domestic product (GDP) in 2000 and is expected to reach 15.9 percent by 2010. The key factors behind this expected trend are strong household income growth, a slowdown in economic growth, continued advances in medical technology, and the inability of insurers to sustain the initial cost savings that resulted from the shift to managed care.[35]

Annual growth in Medicare spending remains low—only 0.1 percent in 1998 and 1 percent in 1999. This is well below the annual average of 9.2 percent recorded for 1993 to 1997. The two-year slowdown is attributed primarily to the effects of changing payment systems for home health care facilities and nursing homes, falling hospital case mix, slower growth in general health care costs, and continuing efforts by the federal government to detect and reduce fraud and abuse. Medicare spending represented 17.6 percent of every dollar spent on health care in 1999, falling from a peak of 19.3 percent of national health care expenditures in 1996 and 1997.[36]

The Medicaid share of total health care spending, without SCHIP funding, is projected to continue to rise, from 15.4 percent in 1999 to 16.8 percent by 2010.[37]

Private spending for health care grew by 6.2 percent and public spending by 4.9 percent from 1999 to 2000. The higher growth in private spending is expected to continue through 2000, in large part because of rapid growth in spending on prescription drugs, which are generally not covered by Medicare. Reductions in drug coverage, an increase in the number of prescriptions filled, a larger number of new, high-priced drugs in the marketplace, higher prices for existing drugs, and an increase in direct-to-consumer advertising expenditures all contribute to the higher spending growth rate for drugs. Drug spending is projected to increase by 12.6 percent per year on average from 2001 to 2010, reaching 16 percent of personal health spending by 2010, compared to 9.4 percent in 1999.[38]

Q 7:66　What is the Medicare, Medicaid, and SCHIP Benefits Improvement and Protection Act of 2000?

BIPA is a rider to a tax reform package that contained over $30 billion in Medicare and Medicaid provider funding restorations, including a total of about $11 billion for M + C plans over five years. The major provisions of BIPA are summarized in Table 7-1.

Q 7:67　What is the Medicare Payment Advisory Commission?

MedPAC is an independent federal body that advises Congress on issues affecting Medicare. It was established by the BBA, which merged the Prospective Payment Assessment Commission (PPAC) and the Physician Payment Review Commission (PPRC). The MedPAC has 17 members who have a wide range of expertise in the financing and delivery of health care services. MedPAC is supported by a full-time executive director and a staff of about 30 analysts. The analysts typically have backgrounds in economics, health policy, public health, or medicine. The primary outlets for MedPAC's recommendations are two reports required by statute to be issued in March and June of each year. MedPAC also advises Congress through other avenues, including comments on reports to Congress by the Secretary of HHS, testimony, formal comments on proposed regulations, briefings for congressional staff, and a series of short issue briefs. One of MedPAC's largest projects is a report on the implementation of comprehensive risk adjustment by CMS, which is required by BBRA.

The BBA gave HCFA (now CMS) authority to implement the risk adjustment payment system for M + C plans starting January 1, 2001, along with the authority to collect the data needed to create the system. HCFA began collecting hospital inpatient encounter data from M + C organizations in October 1998. Collection of physician encounter data began October 1, 2000, and submission of encounter data for hospital outpatient care began January 1, 2001. MedPAC is required by the BBA and BBRA to submit several reports to Congress on various aspects of the M + C program, including risk adjustment, payments for frail, elderly beneficiaries, and the prospective principal inpatient (PPI) diagnostic cost group system. BBRA set the phase-in schedule at 90 percent demographic method/10 percent risk adjustment for 2000 and 2001, 80/20 in 2002, and 70/30 in 2003. In

2004, rates will be determined based 100 percent on the risk adjustment methodology.

BBRA also requires MedPAC to complete several reports on various topics, including (1) special payments for skilled nursing facilities in Alaska and Hawaii; (2) Medicare payment policy for professional training of non-physician health care professionals within 18 months of December 1999; (3) the treatment of rural and cancer hospitals under the hospital outpatient PPS; and (4) appropriate quality improvement standards for all types of M + C plans.

Q 7:68 What will drive future reforms in Medicare and Medicaid?

Each year, Medicare beneficiaries account for over 1 million physician visits and 3 million claims and Medicare pays out almost $1 billion. Medicare serves 39 million beneficiaries and deals with 1 million providers. By many measures, Medicare is a remarkable success, processing an extraordinary volume of transactions with a high degree of accuracy at relatively low cost. Nevertheless, there are increasing concerns about the complexity of Medicare's operations and decision-making processes for both beneficiaries and providers and its failure to live up to contemporary standards of customer service and public communication.[39] In the executive summary of their published report, Bruce Vladek and Barbara Cooper noted the following concerns and suggestions for improvement voiced by Medicare beneficiaries, providers, and program administrators.[40]

1. Despite significant improvements (e.g., the Medicare handbook, the beneficiary hot line, and the Medicare Internet site), beneficiaries still need better customer service. Many Medicare beneficiaries cannot obtain assistance with their Medicare questions and problems. Each beneficiary should have access to an individual to assist with Medicare problems. There should be at least one Medicare representative in every Social Security office in the country.

2. Beneficiaries face unintended financial liabilities because they often do not know whether Medicare will pay for a service until after it has been received. Uncertainty and unplanned spending coiuld be reduced by requiring carriers to provide beneficiaries and providers advance guidance on coverage of certain procedures or services.

3. Beneficiaries are subjected to too much confusing paperwork, particularly if they have Medigap coverage. Paperwork could be reduced by requiring Medicare and Medigap health insurance carriers to transfer information and claims to one another electronically.

4. The accelerated fraud and abuse activities have created an atmosphere of distrust and fear among providers of Medicare services. Comity and provider confidence in Medicare could be increased by eliminating the application of the False Claims Act to bills submitted by providers.

5. Many providers cannot obtain assistance with their Medicare questions and problems. Each provider should be assigned an account executive, and the number of contractor and CMS staff interacting with providers should be increased.

6. The paperwork requirements for physicians, particularly surrounding documentation of evaluation and management (E&M) activities, are exceedingly onerous. E&M codes should be replaced with a simpler classification system, such as length of time of visit.

7. CMS's response to issues and problems is slowed considerably because of the multiple layers of bureaucracy in the DHHS and competing constituencies. Responsiveness and timeliness could be improved by making CMS an independent agency, along the lines of the Social Security Administration.

8. Medicare operations are severely underfunded, reducing efficiency, timeliness, and customer service. Customer service and efficiency could be improved by funding CMS operations from a trust fund appropriation, similar to that of the Social Security Administration and Medicare professional review organizations.

9. The Medicare process for determining whether a new item or service will be covered is slow, confusing, and extremely contentious. Availability of up-to-date, effective technologies could be ensured by delegating national coverage decisions to an independent advisory board.

10. Efficient organization, performance, and oversight of Medicare fiscal intermediaries and carriers (contractors) is hampered by legislative prohibitions against competition and

financial incentives for good performance. Contractor performance could be improved by modernizing legislative authorities, including the authority to compete for contracts and financially reward good performance.

When weighing future options for reforming Medicare and Medicaid, the U.S. Comptroller General suggested in a March 1999 presentation to Congress the following considerations for reform proposals:

1. *Affordability.* Reforms should address the current programs' incentives inhibiting effective cost containment.

2. *Equity.* Reforms should not impose a disproportionate burden on particular groups of beneficiaries or providers.

3. *Adequacy.* Reforms should account for the need to foster cost-effective and clinically meaningful innovations, furthering Medicare's tradition of technology development.

4. *Feasibility.* Reforms must provide for such administrative essentials as implementation and monitoring.

5. *Acceptance.* To make program costs more transparent to the public, reforms must provide for sufficiently educating the beneficiary and provider communities to the realities of trade-offs required when significant policy changes occur.

Most important, reforms need to address the sustainability of Medicare and Medicaid and ensure that they do not consume an unreasonable share of our productive resources and do not encroach on other public programs or private sector activities. An incremental approach to changes of the magnitude likely required will enhance both their feasibility and acceptance.

Q 7:69   What demonstration pilots were established under the BBA?

The BBA authorized several demonstration pilots, including the Medicare Military Retiree Subvention, a six-site Medicare managed care subvention demonstration between HCFA (CMS) and DOD. Under this demonstration, the DOD was to be paid a reduced percentage of the M + C reimbursement rate in return for providing Medicare-covered services to eligible military retirees who are also eligible for Medicare. Enrollment began in January 1998, with the first DOD managed care sites providing health care services in February 1998. The pilot was authorized for three years; start-up problems delayed its implementation by about one year. The pilot has been operating in Colorado Springs, Colorado; Dover, Delaware; Biloxi, Mississippi; Tacoma, Washington; San Antonio, Texas; and San Diego, California. In May 2000, the House of Representatiaves approved a DOD authorization bill (H.R. 4205) that included provisions extending prescription drug coverage to elderly military retirees and expanding this demonstration and making it permanent.

Other demonstrations authorized under the BBA include the following:

MSA Demonstration. The BBA includes an M + C option that is a combination MSA plan providing health insurance (with a deductible limited to $6,000) and an M + C MSA. MSA plans are limited to a demonstration pilot that is capped at 390,000 enrollees.

Medicare Competitive Pricing Demonstration. The BBA required the Secretary of HHS to establish a demonstration project under which payments to M + C organizations are determined in accordance with a competitive pricing methodology. According to HCFA's 1999 Active Projects Report, a demonstration design and sites have been selected for the project.

M + C Disenrollment Demonstration. The BBA authorized the Secretary of HHS to conduct a three-year demonstration using a third-party contractor to conduct the M + C plan enrollment and disenrollment functions. This demonstration must be conducted separately from the Medicare competitive pricing demonstration.

Social Health Maintenance Organizations. The BBA extended an existing demonstration project with regard to social HMOs through December 31, 2000. The Secretary of HHS was to submit a plan for integrating social HMOs and similar plans as an option under M + C plans.

Medicare Coordinated Care Project. The BBA authorized the Secretary of HHS to conduct demonstration projects to evaluate case management and other models of coordinated care that improve the quality of items and services provided to targeted individuals and reduce Medicare expenditures for such items and services. A targeted individual is an individual who has a chronic illness, as defined and identified by the Secretary of HHS, and who is enrolled in a fee-for-service program under Parts A and B of Medicare. CMS and its contractor for the project, Mathematica, have collected information on "best practices" in coordinated care.

Municipal Health Services Transition Project. The Secretary of HHS was allowed to extend demonstration projects for the orderly transition of municipal health services through December 31, 2000, but only with respect to individuals who received at least one service during the period beginning January 1, 1996, and ending on the date of enactment of the BBA.

Long-Term Care and Managed Care

Q 7:70   What is PACE, and how does it relate to Medicare and Medicaid?

PACE, Programs of All-Inclusive Care for the Elderly, provides an alternative to institutional care for persons who are age 55 and over and require a nursing facility level of care. The PACE team offers and manages all care services, including health, medical, and social services, and makes preventive, rehabilitative, curative, and support services available. PACE is provided in day health centers, homes, hospitals, and nursing homes. Its focus is to preserve independence, dignity, and quality of life.

PACE, created by the BBA, functions within Medicaid and Medicare and operates through contractual relationships regardless of the ultimate source of payment. PACE providers receive payment only through the PACE agreement and must make available all items and services covered under Titles XVIII and XIX of the Social Security Act without limiting amount, duration, or scope of services and without application of any deductibles, copayments, or other cost sharing. PACE therefore respresents a significant use of managed care. Individuals who enroll in PACE receive benefits only through PACE.

Children's Health Insurance Program

Q 7:71   What is the Children's Health Insurance Program?

CHIP, enacted as part of the BBA, is a program that gives $24 billion to the states over five years to provide health coverage for uninsured children. The money became available to the states on October 1, 1997, according to DHHS. CHIP gives the states flexibility to design insurance programs for children not covered by Medicaid. Many states, including Texas, have adopted legislation to provide such programs and to match the federal funding through a specified formula.

States have considerable flexibility on how to spend the money, including the ability to define eligibility. There is an income ceiling of 200 percent of the poverty level for states where the Medicaid eligibility ceiling is below 200 percent of the poverty level and an income ceiling of 50 percent above the current ceiling for states where the Medicaid eligibility ceiling is in excess of 200 percent of the poverty level. Options for state implementation of CHIP include the following:

- Expanded Medicaid coverage
- Enrollment of uninsured children in health plans by private health insurers
- Direct provision of health services to children (including immunizations, well-child care, and services provided by DSHs, using no more than 10 percent of the grant money for noncoverage purposes (e.g., administration, outreach, or services)
- Offering benefits equal to those provided in one of three benchmark benefit packages (see Q 7:72), those provided by a state-administered program, or those of the same actuarial value as one of the three benchmark benefit packages and including at least inpatient and outpatient hospital services, physicians' surgical and medical services, laboratory and x-ray services, and well-baby and well-child care (which include age-appropriate immunizations).

Q 7:72 What are the three benchmark benefit packages?

The three benchmark benefit packages under CHIP are

1. The standard Blue Cross/Blue Shield PPO service benefit plan offered under FEHBP;

2. The health coverage that is offered and generally available to state employees; and

3.   The health coverage offered by the HMO with the largest commercial enrollment in the state.

A benefit package whose aggregate actuarial value is at least equal to one of the benchmark benefit packages must meet the following requirements:

1.   The package must include coverage for inpatient and outpatient hospital services, physicians' surgical and medical services, laboratory and x-ray services, and well-baby and well-child care (including immunizations).

2.   If the benchmark benefit package selected by the state for the purpose of establishing the actuarial value of benchmark equivalent coverage includes any of the following services—prescription drugs, mental health services, vision services, or hearing services—the actuarial value of each of these categories of service in the benchmark equivalent coverage package must be at least 75 percent of the value of that category of service in the benchmark benefit package selected by the state.

3.   If the benchmark benefit package does not cover one of the categories of service listed in item (2), the equivalent plan may, but is not required to, provide coverage for that category of service.

The Secretary of HHS must ensure that these requirements are met prior to approving a state's plan.

Q 7:73   If a state chooses to expand coverage through its Medicaid program, must the benefit package meet all Medicaid requirements?

Yes. Medicaid rules apply to any expanded coverage provided under a state's Title XIX Medicaid program.

Q 7:74   Can CHIP funds (including the 10 percent for non-insurance-related items) be used to pay for health coverage for children who are illegal aliens?

No. The only federal funds available for undocumented immigrants cover only the cost of emergency services (services relating to a medical condition that would place the patient's health in serious jeopardy, or would result in serious impairment of bodily functions), regardless of age. These funds are provided through Medicaid. Emergency services are available to all undocumented immigrants if they would otherwise meet Medicaid eligibility requirements.

Q 7:75　What children are excluded from participation in CHIP?

Children deemed ineligible for participation in CHIP include children who are

1. Eligible for Medicaid;

2. Covered by individual health insurance;

3. Covered under a group health plan;

4. Inmates of a public institution or patients in an institution for mental diseases; or

5. Members of a family eligible for health benefits coverage under a state health benefit plan on the basis of a family member's employment with a public agency in the state.

Q 7:76　Are Native American and Alaska Native children eligible for CHIP?

Yes. Native American and Alaska Native children are eligible for CHIP on the same basis as other children. Children may be eligible for CHIP if they meet state eligibility standards based on the definition of a targeted low-income child.

The eligibility of Native American children for CHIP is not affected by the fact that they may also be eligible for or be recipients of health care services funded by the American Indian Health Service. CHIP specifically exempts programs operated or financed by the American Indian Health Service from the requirement to prevent duplication between CHIP and other federally operated or financed health programs.

CHIP requires each state to describe, in its CHIP plan, the procedures to be used to ensure the provision of child health assistance to targeted low-income children who are Native Americans or Alaska Natives.

Q 7:77   **If a child is enrolled in CHIP because no health insurance was available at the time of application but insurance becomes available later, is the state obligated to cancel coverage?**

No, the state is not obligated to cancel coverage if insurance becomes available to a child enrolled in CHIP. The CHIP definition of targeted low-income child specifies that children who are not covered under a group health plan or other health insurance coverage are eligible to participate in CHIP if they meet the income and state-specific standards. Therefore, the mere availability of health insurance does not necessarily preclude a child from participation in CHIP. There is an exception, however, for children who are eligible for a state health benefit plan on the basis of a family member's employment with a public agency. The availability of a state health benefit plan to a child does, in general, preclude the child's participation in CHIP if the state subsidizes dependent coverage for any of the plans.

CHIP requires states to describe in their CHIP plans how they will ensure that coverage under CHIP does not substitute for other coverage, including procedures for follow-up screening. States may want to conduct periodic redeterminations of a child's continued eligibility for CHIP utilizing the same methods and criteria as used in the initial determination, or may propose some alternate method of conducting follow-up screening, such as requiring families to notify the program when they become covered under another insurance plan. If a child is found not to meet the definition of targeted low-income child as a result of follow-up screening, the state is obligated to cancel coverage under CHIP.

Q 7:78   **Can a state give money to community health centers to cover children for certain services?**

Yes. A state can pay a community health center to obtain the minimum child health assistance benefits coverage for eligible children. In that instance, a community health center would, if qualified, furnish such coverage independently. Alternatively, a community health center could provide some of the health benefits and develop arrangements with other providers to furnish the rest of the coverage. A community health center could also provide some part of the minimum coverage under an arrangement or a contract with an entity responsible for furnishing the overall coverage. CHIP also permits payment for other child health assistance for low-income children, which could be provided through community health centers through contracts with the state. In addition, CHIP allows the state to request a waiver from the Secretary of HHS to permit the state to exceed the 10 percent limit on the use of funds for noncoverage purposes. This waiver applies to services meeting the coverage requirements of Section 2103 of the Social Security Act, as long as the services (1) do not cost more (on an average per child basis) than coverage provided under section 2103 and (2) are provided through a community-based health delivery system or through hospitals such as those that receive DSH payments.

Q 7:79   Has CHIP been effective in reducing the number of children without health insurance?

Yes. Census Bureau data for 1998 and 1999 show the percentage of Americans without health insurance declined from 16.3 percent in 1998 to 15.5 percent in 1999, the first drop in at least 12 years. The actual number of uninsured Americans declined from 44.3 million to 42.6 million. Two out of three of the newly insured are children. The rate of uninsured children dropped from 15.4 percent to 13.9 percent. The rate of uninsured near-poor children dropped from 27.2 percent to 19.7 percent, mainly as a result of CHIP. States that have aggressively expanded their CHIP and Medicaid programs have the lowest numbers of uninsured residents.[41]

There was only a 0.1 percent decrease in the number of persons covered under Medicaid. The government credited increased awareness of continued eligibility for Medicaid in the wake of welfare reform for the minimal decline. The number of Medicaid enrollees had been declining for the prior three years. The percentage of the population covered under Medicare remained constant at 13.2 percent.[42]

Among the states, New Mexico had the highest percentage of uninsured residents in 1999, 25.6 percent. Texas ranked next to last, with 23.3 percent; in 1998, it was 50th at 24.5 percent. Rhode Island had the smallest percentage of uninsured residents in 1999, 6.9 percent, followed by Minnesota at 8 percent. Among the Census Bureau's other findings for 1999 are these:[43]

1. More Hispanics (33.4 percent) were likely to be uninsured than any other of the major racial or ethnic groups. The percentage fell from 35.3 in 1998.

2. Adults age 18 to 24 remained the most likely to be uninsured (29 percent). The figure was 30 percent in 1998.

3. The percentage of uninsured foreign-born residents declined from 34.1 percent in 1998 to 33.4 percent in 1999. The percentage of uninsured U.S.-born residents fell from 14.4 percent in 1998 to 13.5 percent in 1999.

Q 7:80 What has been the experience with CHIP since its implementation in 1998?

As of July 1, 2000, all of the states, the District of Columbia, and five U.S. territories had implemented CHIP, covering over 2 million children. In addition, the number of children enrolled in Medicaid has increased because of state-wide outreach and eligibility simplification efforts. Of these approved plans, 15 states have created a separate child health program, 23 states have expanded Medicaid, and 18 states have developed a combination of a separate state program and a Medicaid expansion program. Many states have already amended their programs to expand eligibility beyond their original proposal. Prior to CHIP's creation, only four states covered children with family incomes up to at least 200 percent of the FPL ($35,300 for a family of four in 2001).

Q 7:81 What is "crowd out," and how does it affect employer-based insurance programs?

According to a study by the Kaiser Family Foundation,[44] because Medicaid enrollments tended to increase at the same time that employer coverage was declining, some observers have suggested that the expansion of Medicaid eligibility contributed to the decline in employer coverage. According to the "crowd out" hypothesis, the expansion of Medicaid eligibility to cover pregnant women and children with incomes above the poverty line may have caused some people with employer coverage to drop it. For example, low-income workers whose children became eligible for Medicaid as a result of the expansions may have dropped their private family coverage (for which a premium contribution is typically required) and substituted less expensive Medicaid coverage. Another possibility is that some

employers—especially employers with a low-income workforce—
decided to stop offering coverage in light of the Medicaid expansions.

Recent empirical studies have sought to determine how much of
the growth in Medicaid enrollments was due to a substitution of
Medicaid for private insurance. Most of this literature suggests that
the extent of crowd-out was small: less than 20 percent of the total
increase in Medicaid coverage during the period of the eligibility
expansions (1987–1992) was attributable to coverage of individuals
who were previously privately insured. These estimates suggest that
crowd out played only a small role in the overall decline in coverage,
since only a small proportion of newly eligible Medicaid enrollees
were previously insured and Medicaid enrollment growth due to the
expansions was small relative to the decline in employer coverage.
For example, if it is estimated that 3.5 million individuals gained
Medicaid coverage between 1987 and 1992 as a result of eligibility
expansions, the crowd-out estimates suggest that 700,000 of these
new enrollees (20 percent of 3.5 million) were previously insured.
Since approximately 9.9 million people lost employer coverage during this period, only about 7 percent (700,000 of the 9.9 million) of
the decline in employer coverage during this period may be explained by crowd out.

Other Government Programs

Q 7:82 What other government programs use managed care arrangements?

FEHBP, administered by OPM and the Military Health Services
System, administered by DOD, use managed care arrangements. The
Military Health Services System, comprising the Army, Navy, and
Air Force military treatment facilities, provides health care services
to 2.1 million active-duty military personnel. DOD also manages
CHAMPUS, which covers 6 million military family members and re-
tirees. In October 1995, DOD overhauled its programs to coordinate
CHAMPUS with the Military Health Services System under a new
program referred to as TriCare.

Federal Employees Health Benefits Plan. FEHBP is the health benefit payer for federal employees, including the President of the United

States and members of Congress. It has been suggested as a model for national health care reform. FEHBP offers four types of health benefit plans to federal employees and retirees. The plans are grouped into two basic categories: fee-for-service plans and prepaid plans. More than 300 prepaid plans participate in FEHBP; the majority are licensed HMOs. Federal qualification or licensure of the HMOs is not specified in the FEHBP statute or regulations.

OPM enters into contracts with indemnity plans, PPOs, HMOs, and POS plans to cover FEHBP eligibles. It has expressed an interest in proposals from prepaid plans that have a POS option. Including a POS option in a prepaid plan is considered a way to increase HMO enrollment. Since only a few states permit licensed HMOs to offer a POS option as part of the same plan, many HMOs offer a POS option as a stand-alone feature underwritten by the HMO. Alternatively, HMOs can use a wraparound plan through subcontracts with an indemnity or PPO subcontractor.

The Blue Cross and Blue Shield Association contracts with OPM on behalf of many Blue Cross and Blue Shield plans across the country to provide some of FEHBP's fee-for-service plans. These contracts are decreasing in number in view of cost-containment efforts to include managed care features in fee-for-service plans.

TriCare. TriCare is a comprehensive managed care program for the Military Health Services System. Military regional managers run TriCare, supported by private managed care plan contracts throughout the country. The program is implemented through managed care support contracts with civilian providers and is coordinated with military treatment facilities. As of September 1999, TriCare was operating in 15 regions in the United States, Europe, Latin America, and Canada.

TriCare has six enrollment categories: (1) active-duty members, who must be enrolled in TriCare Prime, the HMO option; (2) other TriCare Prime enrollees, who must be CHAMPUS eligible; (3) TriCare Standard enrollees, who are in the standard fee-for-service CHAMPUS and who do not select a managed care option; (4) Medicare-eligible beneficiaries, who, although not eligible for TriCare Prime, can participate in other TriCare programs; (5) participants in other TriCare managed care programs, when such affiliation arrangements are made; and (6) active-duty members who live more than 50 miles from a PCP, who must enroll in TriCare Prime Remote, which allows them to choose a local PCP (who is TriCare certified).

References

1. Matthew Broaddus, Shannon Blaney, and Annie Dude, *Expanding Family Coverage: States' Medicaid Eligibility Policies for Working Families in the Year 2000* (Washington, DC: Center on Budget and Policy Priorities, 2001).
2. *See* http://www.cms.gov/medicaid/dualelig/bbadedef.htm.
3. *See* Health Care Financing Administration, U.S. Dep't of Health and Human Services, "Link Between Medicaid and Temporary Assistance for Needy Families," Fact Sheet #1 (1996); Center for Budget and Policy Priorities, "An Analysis of the AFDC-Related Medicaid Provisions in the New Welfare Law" (unpublished memorandum Sept. 19, 1996); National Health Policy Forum, *Impact of the New Welfare Law on Medicaid,* Issue Brief No. 697 (Washington, DC: Feb. 7, 1997), as referenced in the PPRC Report at 416.
4. *See* Health Care Financing Administration, U.S. Dep't of Health and Human Services, "Link Between Medicaid and the Immigration Provisions of the Personal Responsibility and Work Opportunity Act of 1996," Fact Sheet #3 (1996), as referenced in the PPRC Report at 416.
5. *See* J. Iglehart, "The American Health Care System—Medicaid," *New Eng. J. Med.,* 340:403, 1999.
6. S. Zuckerman, A. Evans, and J. Holahan, "Questions for States as They Turn to Medicaid Managed Care" (Urban Institute, Issues and Options for States, No. A-11), available at www.urban.org/'content'/research/Newfederalism/aboutANF/about.ANF.htm.
7. N. McCall, *The Arizona Health Care Cost Containment System: Thirteen Years of Managed Care in Medicaid* (Menlo Park, CA: Henry J. Kaiser Family Foundation, July 1996).
8. O. Carasquillo, A. Carasquillo, and S. Shea, "Health Insurance Coverage of Immigrants Living in the United States: Dif-

ferences by Citizenship Status and Country of Origin, *Am. J. Pub. Health,* June 2000.

9. *See* Zuckerman et al., *supra* note 6.

10. *See* Health Care Financing Administration, U.S. Dep't of Health and Human Services, *Health Care Indicators: Key Trends in the Health Care Sector—Fourth Quarter 1999,* at http://www.hcfa.gov/stats/indicatr/default.htm.

11. *See Medicaid Managed Care: A Guide for States,* 3d ed., Jane Horvath and Neval Kaye, eds. (Portland, ME: National Academy for State Health Policy, 1997); M. Gold, M. Sparer, and K. Chu, "Medicaid Managed Care: Lessons from Five States," *Health Affairs,* 15(3):153–166, 1996; General Accounting Office, *Medicaid States Efforts to Educate and Enroll Beneficiaries in Managed Care,* GAO/HEHS96-184 (Washington, DC: GAO, Sept. 1996), as referenced in the PPRC Annual Report to Congress 1996, at 439.

12. *See BNA Medicare Report,* 10(30):842, July 23, 1999.

13. *See* Office of Inspector General, U.S. Dep't of Health and Human Services, *Medicare + Choice HMO Extra Benefits: Beneficiary Perspectives,* OEI-02-99-00030 (Mar. 6, 2000); *cf.* "Medicare and the American Health Care System Report to Congress" (Prospective Payment Assessment Commission June 1996) 133; L. Nelson et al., "Access to Care in Medicare Managed Care," *Health Affairs,* 16(2):148–56, Mar.–Apr. 1997.

14. Id.

15. *See* Report of the Employee Benefit Research Institute published at http://www.ebri.org.

16. EBRI Notes No. 2, which features "Medicare Beneficiaries with Dual Sources of Coverage," summarized at www. ebri.org/ebripubs.htm.

17. For more information about the Consumer Union's ratings of Medigap policies, see http://www.consumerreports.org. Information on the different forms of Medigap coverage and a comparison of policies can be found at http:// medicare.gov/mgcompare/home.asp. For more information, call 800-638-6833 for the "Guide to Health Insurance for People with Medicare" or your state insurance department.

18. *See* Health L. Rep. (BNA), Vol. 11, No. 10, Mar. 10, 2002, reporting on S. Crystal, "Out-of-Pocket Health Care Costs Among Older Americans," *J. Gerontology/Soc. Sci.*, Mar. 6, 2000.

19. Id.

20. Id.

21. For more information on this fee-for-service M + C option, see http://www.cms.gov/pubforms/transmit/memos/comm_date_dsc.htm.

22. For more information, see Health Care Financing Administration, Dep't of Health and Human Services, *Medicare Managed Care Contract Monthly Summary Report,* available at http://www.cms.gov/stats/mmcc.htm. In a subsequent publication by HCFA in November 2000, it was reported that beneficiary enrollment in the M + C program fell by 0.2 percent in October 2000, from 6,237,012 to 6,224,212.

23. "Managed Care: Low Reimbursement Rates, Overregulation Cause More Pullouts From M+C Program," *Health L. Rep. (BNA),* 9(27), July 6, 2000.

24. "Managed Care: HCFA Issues List of M+C Pullouts; More than 900,000 Enrollees Affected," *Health L. Rep. (BNA),* 11(30), July 28, 2000.

25. *See* www.medscape.com (visited Nov. 9, 2000).

26. A. Cassidy, *Medicare+Choice in 2000: Will Enrollees Spend More and Receive Less?* Commonwealth Fund Report, *cited in* Vol. 11, No. 33, Aug. 18, 2000, Bureau of National Affairs, Inc., Washington, D.C.

27. J. Kasten, M. Moon, and M. Segal, *What Do Medicare HMO Enrollees Spend Out-of-Pocket?* Commonwealth Fund Report, *cited in* Vol. 11, No. 33, Aug. 18, 2000, Bureau of National Affairs, Inc., Washington, D.C.

28. G. Dallek and D. Jones, *Early Implementation of Medicare+Choice,* Commonwealth Fund Report, *cited in* Vol. 11, No. 33, Aug. 18, 2000, Bureau of National Affairs, Inc., Washington, D.C.

29. *See* Health Care Financing Administration, U.S. Dep't of Health and Human Services, *HMO Withdrawals: Impact on Medicare Beneficiaries,* OEI-04-00-00390, available at http://www.hhs.gov/oig/oei.

30. *See* http://www.cms.gov/Medicare/OPL124.htm.

31. *See* National Committee on Vital and Health Statistics, *Core Data Elements: Report of the National Committee on Vital and Health Statistics* (Washington, D.C.: U.S. Dep't of Health and Human Services, Aug. 1996), as reported in the PPRC Report, at 170.

32. *See* Richard H. Friedman, Office of Information Systems and Data Analysis, Medicaid Bureau, Health Care Financing Administration, Personal Communication to the Physician Payment Review Commission, Nov. 21, 1996, as reported in the PPRC Report at 171.

33. HIPAA looks to Congress or the Secretary of HHS to develop measures to protect the confidentiality and security of medical information.

34. *See* National Committee for Quality Assurance, *A Road Map for Information Systems: Evolving Systems to Support Performance Measurement* (Washington, DC: National Committee on Quality Assurance, 1997), as reported in the PPRC Report at 174.

35. *See* www.hhs.gov.us (visited Apr. 2001).

36. Id.

37. Id.

38. Id.

39. Bruce C. Vladek and Barbara S. Cooper, *Making Medicare Work Better* (New York: Institute for Medical Practice, Mt. Sinai Medical School, Mar. 2001).

40. Id. at 6–8.

41. *See* http://www.census.gov/Press-Release/www/2000/cb00-160.html.

42. Id.

43. Id.

44. Kaiser Family Foundation, *Uninsured in America* (Menlo Park, CA: Kaiser Family Foundation, 1998).

Chapter 8

Legal and Regulatory Issues in Managed Care

In 2001, *Managed Care Answer Book* identified a number of important legal issues predicted to be of importance to those involved in managed care arrangements.[1] The issues that continue to attract the attention of regulators and courts include the following:

- Health plan regulation and litigation
- Fraud and abuse
- Health information privacy
- Advances in genetics that pose questions of biomedical ethics

Issues that received less attention from regulators and jurists over the past year include these:

- Health care antitrust issues
- Physician unionization
- Tax and tax-exemption issues

The American Medical Association's (AMA's) top two issues for 2001 were patients' bill of rights legislation and collective bargaining by individual physicians. Other issues on its agenda included increasing patient safety and reforming Medicare to reduce the burdens the program places on physicians.

At the top of the list of pending federal legislation are patients' rights, prescription drug benefits, and health insurance access in the wake of September 11, 2001. Legislation relating to bioterrorism is also pending in Congress. States have focused their attention not only on health information privacy but also on mandated benefits, prescription drug coverage, and managed care reforms such as "prompt payment."

Legal issues to watch are those related to bankruptcy, health plan liability (Employee Retirement Income Security Act of 1974), preemption, and privacy of health information. Health care bankruptcies involving physician groups and health systems began to rise in the late 1990s, according to the American Bankruptcy Institute. In the ERISA arena, the U.S. Supreme Court has agreed to hear a controversial case involving the application of ERISA preemption to state-mandated independent review of medical necessity determinations by health plans. The Department of Justice (DOJ) has submitted an amicus brief on behalf of the Bush Administration supporting the proposition that ERISA should not prevent state law independent review of medical necessity determinations. This is the second time this issue has been brought before the Supreme Court.

Dramatic health care cost increases and the growing number of uninsured Americans will most likely make it difficult for Congress to pass a patients' rights bill or impose new mandates on managed care plan coverage. The effort to pass a patients' bill of rights was stalled after the terrorist attacks of September 11, 2001, and Congress has not returned to its discussions of this legislation despite growing bipartisan support of the last version of the bill.

The pending implementation of the administrative simplification portions of the Health Insurance Portability and Accountability Act of 1996 (HIPAA) will have a dramatic impact on how health care information is accessed, transmitted, and protected. With implementation scheduled to begin in 2003, there is tremendous pressure on health care providers, insurers, and clearinghouses to become HIPAA compliant.

Laws and Regulations Affecting Managed Care

Q 8:1   What is the legal environment in which managed care systems operate?

Managed care operates in an evolving industry that is highly regulated by federal and state laws and regulations.

Antitrust

Antitrust Theory

Q 8:2   What is the basis of U.S. antitrust law?

The U.S. economic system depends on free enterprise and open competition. The antitrust laws are aimed at preventing activities that interfere with the normal operation of supply and demand in a free market, on such matters as price, volume of production, marketing territory, sources of supply, and channels of distribution. The main thrust of almost all the antitrust laws is to protect competition. The theory underpinning this protection is that competition naturally creates an impetus to reduce prices and to increase efficiency, quality, and innovation.

The first antitrust statutes were enacted to prevent a device known as the "business trust" from being used to concentrate economic power and to eliminate competition in entire industries. Since then, elaborate federal and state antitrust laws have been enacted to prevent such anticompetitive practices as price fixing, vertical restraints of trade, monopolization, price discrimination, exclusive dealing and tying arrangements, and anticompetitive mergers and acquisitions. Each of these practices is antithetical to free and open competition. Some rely for their success on agreement, collusion, or coercion. Some involve the necessary effect of lessened competition and increased economic concentration. Apart from the need to avoid the penalties imposed for violation, compliance with the U.S. antitrust laws is in the best interests of both employers and employees.

The four principal federal antitrust laws relating to managed care arrangements are the Sherman Act, the Clayton Act, the Robinson-Patman Act, and the Federal Trade Commission (FTC) Act.

Antitrust Issues in Managed Care

Q 8:3   Why are there antitrust issues associated with health care and managed care?

In the past, members of the health care industry attempted to defend against antitrust claims by claiming that they were protected by three special defenses particular to health care and related fields:

(1) the "learned profession" defense (i.e., that learned professions are not commerce), (2) the local character of health care, preventing it from having an effect on interstate commerce, and (3) the non-profit nature of many health care entities. Each of these defenses has been overruled by case law, except—to a limited extent—the not-for-profit defense, which has been overruled with respect to FTC jurisdiction (but not with respect to DOJ enforcement or private plaintiff actions) and with respect to certain purchases of supplies by nonprofit institutions.

Now, whenever there are contractual relationships between potential competitors, merger activities between competing providers, or dealings between a system that holds a sizable market share and its prospective purchasers or participants, there is increased risk for antitrust law violation. Any of these activities can affect competition, which is the subject of antitrust regulation. Violation of federal or state antitrust laws can result in a broad range of penalties, from civil monetary damages (trebled) and criminal penalties to injunctive relief, attorneys' fees, and consent decrees obtained by the DOJ, the FTC, state attorneys general, or even individual competitors adversely affected by the anticompetitive activity. With the increase in integration among health care providers through acquisition and merger in response to managed care, the antitrust risk also increases.

Q 8:4 What antitrust laws apply to health plans and managed care?

Health plans are subject to certain federal antitrust laws that attempt to ensure fair business practices and promote competition. These federal antitrust laws are in addition to state antitrust laws and include Sections 1 and 2 of the Sherman Act [15 USC §§ 1, 2], which prohibit monopolies and conspiracies; Section 7 of the Clayton Act [15 USC § 18], which governs mergers of commercial entities, such as health plans; and the Hart-Scott-Rodino (HSR) Act [15 USC § 18a], which requires that certain mergers be approved by the FTC and the Antitrust Division of the DOJ. Health plans are also subject to Section 5 of the FTC Act [15 USC § 45], which prohibits unfair or deceptive practices affecting commerce.

Other important antitrust laws include the Robinson-Patman Act [15 USC §§ 13, 13a], which prohibits commercial entities from offering different prices to buyers for the same goods. Although the

Robinson-Patman Act does not apply to the sales of services, some health plan activities may be subject to its regulation.

Q 8:5   How are antitrust laws enforced?

The FTC is a law enforcement agency charged by Congress with protecting the public against anticompetitive behavior and deceptive and unfair practices. The FTC's antitrust arm, the Bureau of Competition, is responsible for investigating and prosecuting "unfair methods of competition," which violate the FTC Act. The FTC shares responsibility with the DOJ for prosecuting violations of the Clayton Act. Private rights of action are also available to affected competitors, and state attorneys general can enforce federal as well as state antitrust laws.

When litigation is inevitable, many of the FTC's adjudicative matters are conducted in administrative proceedings before an FTC administrative law judge. Appeals from these FTC administrative proceedings go directly to the federal courts of appeal. The FTC has authority to seek preliminary injunctions in federal district court whenever it has reason to believe that a party is violating, or is about to violate, any provision of law enforced by the FTC. Such preliminary injunctions are intended to preserve the status quo, or to prevent further consumer harm even if administrative action is pending before the FTC. The FTC also has authority to seek a permanent injunction in federal district court.

In the mid-1970s, the FTC formed a division within the Bureau of Competition to investigate potential antitrust violations involving health care. The Health Care Services and Products Division consists of approximately 25 lawyers and investigators who work exclusively on health care antitrust matters.

The FTC and DOJ have provided guidance to health plans and other managed care organizations (MCO) through the publication of guidelines in 1981 (physician-controlled prepaid medical plans or independent practice associations (IPAs), 1992 (horizontal merger instructions), and 1993 ("safety zones" from antitrust scrutiny). The 1993 guidelines on safety zones were updated in 1994 to include several safety zones that applied specifically to physician network joint ventures, multiprovider networks, providers' collective provision of fee data to purchasers, and providers' collective provision of nonfee data to purchasers. These guidelines were revised again in 1996 to give some relief to providers seeking to form physician network joint ventures and multiprovider networks. A most important step taken by the DOJ was to provide advisory opinions to providers who want a business review of case-specific situations.[2]

In early 2002, the federal government implemented recommendations by a DOJ-FTC task force to reorganize the DOJ by eliminating the Antitrust Division's 16-attorney Health Care Task Force. The reorganization is part of an effort to modernize the Antitrust Division to accommodate new industries and economic trends. The health care fraud operations of the DOJ's Criminal Division will not be affected by this restructuring.

Q 8:6   What does the Sherman Act prohibit?

The Sherman Act, which was enacted in 1890, was the first modern U.S. antitrust law, and it remains today the most important. The key portions of the Sherman Act are Section 1, which prohibits joint actions by two or more companies to unduly or unreasonably restrain trade, and Section 2, which bars any act of monopolization or attempt to monopolize any market. This Act is the only antitrust statute that provides for criminal sanctions as well as civil penalties. The Sherman Act prohibits actions that constitute unreasonable restraints of trade. Section 1 of the Act states that "every contract, combination in the form of trust or otherwise, or conspiracy, in the restraint of trade or commerce among the several States, or with foreign nations, is hereby declared to be illegal." Section 2 of the Act prohibits monopolization or attempts to monopolize and states, "Every person who shall monopolize, or attempt to monopolize, or combine or conspire with any other person or persons, to monopolize any part of the trade or commerce among the several States, or with foreign nations, shall be deemed guilty of a felony."

The elements of restraint of trade under Section 1 of the Sherman Act concern (1) a concerted action by distinct entities (2) that has an unreasonable anticompetitive effect (3) on interstate commerce.

The elements of monopolization under the Sherman Act include (1) market power (defined as the power to control prices or exclude competition in a given market) and (2) the willful acquisition or maintenance of that power as distinguished from growth or development arising from a superior product, business acumen, or historic accident. Attempted monopolization under Section 2 of the Sherman Act includes intent to monopolize and actions in furtherance of that intent that have the probability of success. These activities are illegal, punishable as a felony with penalties of up to $10 million for a corporation, up to $350,000 for an individual, and/or up to three years of imprisonment.

Q 8:7   What does the Clayton Act prohibit?

The Clayton Act deals in greater specifics than does the Sherman Act, and seeks to prevent anticompetitive practices at the outset. It declares that various activities are illegal if their effects may be to "substantially lessen competition or tend to create a monopoly." Section 2 of the Clayton Act, commonly known as the Robinson-Patman Act, prohibits discrimination between similar customers in pricing or promotional practices. This section of the Clayton Act, which originally prohibited price discrimination in sales of commodities, was amended by the Robinson-Patman Act and affects sales of products by nonprofit organizations.

Section 3 of the Clayton Act prohibits the sale of a company's products on the condition that the customer not deal in competitive products when the effect is to substantially lessen competition or tend to create a monopoly. [15 USC § 14] This section covers exclusive dealing arrangements, tying sales, and requirement contracts involving the sale of commodities when the effect may be to substantially lessen competition.

Section 7 of the Clayton Act prohibits mergers, joint ventures, consolidations, or acquisitions of stock or assets that may have the effect of substantially lessening competition or tending to create a monopoly or otherwise unreasonably restraining trade. [15 USC § 18] In addition, Section 7a [15 USC § 18a], known as the HSR Act, requires that certain proposed mergers and acquisitions involving a level of stock or assets receive approval from the FTC and the DOJ before consummation. This premerger notification is subject to a formula. This section does not apply to individuals buying stock in a company for investment if the purchase does not substantially lessen competition. It is also permissible for a company to form a subsidiary if it does not lessen competition.

Section 8 of the Clayton Act prohibits interlocking directorates between competitors if the jurisdictional limits are met. Section 8 of the Clayton Act bars, with certain exceptions, an individual from serving on the boards of directors of competing corporations. Over the years enforcement has been sporadic at best. The 1990 Antitrust Amendment Act, however, made significant changes concerning interlocking directorates that may lead to more aggressive enforcement. It created a series of safe harbors that, if met, permit interlocking directorates and officers. The three *de minimis* safe harbor rules exempt corporations from the strictures of Section 8 of the Clayton Act if (1) the competitive sales of either corporation are less than $1 million (adjusted annually; $1,530,800 as of January 11, 1999), (2) the competitive sales of either corporation are less than 2 percent of the total gross revenues of that corporation, or (3) the competitive sales of each corporation are less than 4 percent of the corporation's gross revenues.

The *de minimis* exemptions were created because a ban on interlocking directorates serves no functional purpose when the corporations are not in competition with one another to a significant degree or if they compete in a line of business that is not economically significant in relation to their overall operations. The *de minimis* exceptions may work to increase government enforcement of Section 8 of the Clayton Act, because they will serve to pare down the number of competitively significant Section 8 violators to a manageable number. It should be emphasized that common directors and officers who fall within the new Act's safe harbor will continue to face exposure to criminal or civil liability under Section 1 of the Sherman Act for exchanges of sensitive information or coordination of decisions. Another significant change is the inclusion of officers under the new Section 8, which continues to leave all indirect interlocks, vertical interlocks, and interlocks between potential horizontal competitors unregulated. For example, competing corporations that have directors who sit together at a third, related corporation and who do not compete will still not be in violation.

Q 8:8   How does the Sherman Act differ from the Clayton Act?

Under the Sherman Act, an activity must have an actual adverse effect on competition before it is considered illegal. Under the Clayton Act, if the activity might have an effect on competition, it is illegal.

Q 8:9   What does the Federal Trade Commission Act cover?

The FTC Act, which is more accurately described as a trade regulation statute than as an antitrust law, established the FTC to supplement the enforcement activities of the Antitrust Division of the DOJ. The FTC Act is basically a catchall statute designed to encompass unfair methods of competition and deceptive practices not expressly covered by the other federal antitrust statutes.

Q 8:10   How does the FTC Act relate to other federal antitrust laws?

The FTC Act's broad proscription of unfair methods of competition was intended to ensure that antitrust enforcement would not be limited to specific activities prohibited under the Clayton Act. Consequently, the FTC Act is interpreted quite broadly, and violations of the Sherman and Clayton Acts are also violations of the FTC Act.

Q 8:11   What is the purpose of the Hart-Scott-Rodino Act?

The HSR Act provides for premerger notice and a waiting period for certain corporate mergers and acquisitions. The HSR Act was amended on December 21, 2000. The amendments, which became effective on February 1, 2001, modify the jurisdictional tests for determining whether filings under the HSR Act are needed in connection with planned or proposed transactions. A filing with the FTC and DOJ is required in advance of a merger when (1) any voting stock or assets of a company with at least $10 million in total assets or annual net sales are being acquired by an entity with total assets or annual net sales of at least $100 million, or (2) any voting stock or assets of an entity with annual net sales or total assets of at least $100 million are being acquired by an entity with total assets or annual net sales of at least $50 million. Notification is required only if the acquiring corporation will own $50 million of the voting securities or assets of the company being acquired. Following notice, the parties must wait 30 days from the date notification is received by the FTC and DOJ before they can close the deal. For cash offers, the waiting period is 15 days. The FTC or DOJ may request additional information prior to the expiration of the waiting period, which will extend it for 20 days and 10 days, respectively.

Some transactions are exempt from the HSR Act, such as (1) transfer of goods or realty in the ordinary course of business; (2) acquisition of nonvoting securities (e.g., bonds, mortgages, or deeds of trust); and (3) acquisition of voting securities when the acquiring party already owns 50 percent of the voting securities.

Q 8:12   What are the consequences of violating the HSR Act?

The FTC or DOJ may file a motion for a preliminary injunction against the consummation of the transaction if it certifies that the injunction is necessary to protect the public's interest. A violation of the HSR Act is punishable against any person, officer, director, or partner by a fine of up to $10,000 for each day of the violation. A federal court can require the party to substantially comply with the notification requirements or request for information.

Q 8:13   Does information disclosed to the FTC and the DOJ as part of the HSR Act become public information?

No. Information filed under the HSR Act may not be made public, except if relevant to a judicial or administrative proceeding. Congress has access to this information.

Q 8:14   What does the Robinson-Patman Act protect against?

The Robinson-Patman Act is intended to protect against illegal price discrimination for services and facilities. The price discrimination becomes illegal if it substantially harms competition, tends to create a monopoly, or injures or prevents competition with any person who either grants or receives the benefit of the discrimination, or with its customers. The Act permits different prices when the differences are based on manufacturing, sale, or delivery costs associated with the purchasing methods or quantities.

If the government demonstrates price discrimination, the alleged perpetrator has the burden of justifying its practice. For example, lowering one's price to meet that of a competitor is sufficient justification in the absence of other factors. Otherwise, the FTC can terminate the price discrimination.

Persons who engage in interstate commerce may not pay or accept commissions or brokerage fees in conjunction with the purchase or sale of goods except if the broker or agent actually performed the service. It is also illegal to pay anything of value to or for a customer unless the payment is available to other customers. A seller is prohibited from selectively providing services to buyers in conjunction with the sale of a commodity bought for resale. Any services the seller offers must be offered proportionally to all buyers.

It is illegal for anyone engaged in interstate commerce to knowingly induce or receive a discriminatory price for goods. It is also illegal to sell or contract to sell goods at lower or unreasonably low prices for the purposes of destroying competition or eliminating a competitor. Persons violating the Robinson-Patman Act are subject to a fine of up to $5,000 or imprisonment for up to one year.

Q 8:15   Do states regulate anticompetitive activity?

Yes, the majority of states have antitrust laws modeled after the federal antitrust laws, particularly the Sherman Act and the FTC Act. In fact, recent state investigations involving potential antitrust activity relating to market dominance have been targeting large hospital networks in the greater Boston area. Since the 1990s, hospitals in that market have either merged or affiliated with each other in large networks. This market dominance by a few hospital systems has resulted in complaints by consumers to state consumer protection agencies, triggering investigations related to tying arrangements.[3]

Q 8:16   What are the standards of review under federal antitrust law?

Ordinarily, business practices are illegal under antitrust law only if they have or may have an adverse effect on competition. The courts have held, however, that some arrangements and actions are so indefensible that they are conclusively presumed to be unreasonable restraints on trade under Section 1 of the Sherman Act and therefore conclusively presumed to be illegal. These actions are called per se offenses. These restraints are not permitted regardless of the business justification or procompetitive effect. No argument will even be entertained that such restraints were harmless or beneficial in any particular case. For this reason, per se offenses are particularly important to avoid. Moreover, federal enforcement policy encourages criminal prosecution for these per se offenses.

Conduct that is not labeled a per se offense is tested by a rule-of-reason standard. This analysis must determine if the purpose or effect of the activity or agreement actually harms competition or if the arrangement has redeeming economic benefits. One must show actual and unreasonable harm to competition under this standard. The existence of market power is often an essential ingredient in the analysis.

Q 8:17   What are the per se violations of antitrust laws?

The per se violations of antitrust laws include the following:

Horizontal Price Fixing. Perhaps the most notorious type of per se offense is price fixing, which is the antitrust violation most frequently prosecuted criminally. Horizontal price fixing typically involves agreements between competitors as to prices they will charge to buyers or pay to suppliers. A specific price need not be set. It is unlawful to agree on (1) maximum or minimum prices; (2) in some cases, on a common sales agent; (3) on terms or conditions of sale (such as credit terms or discounts); or (4) on an exchange of price information if there is a stabilizing effect on prices. The agreement itself can be inferred from any series of otherwise apparently innocent conduct, such as telephone calls or meetings followed by uniform price action.

Vertical Price Fixing (Resale Price Maintenance). In a competitive economy, prices should not be fixed either between competitors or between manufacturers and distributors. The latter arrangement is referred to as vertical price fixing. Although the courts have been substantially more relaxed recently with respect to nonprice vertical restrictions, any agreement between a manufacturer and a distributor or retailer that effectively fixes the price at which the distributor or retailer can resell the goods is per se unlawful. This includes efforts by a manufacturer to set maximum, as well as minimum, resale prices. Again, as in all per se offenses, the reasonableness of the resale price fixed, or any other justification for the price restraint imposed, is no defense to an antitrust charge.

Agreements Between Competitors. Any agreements or other arrangements between or among competitors having the purpose or effect of limiting competition between these competitors is per se unlawful. Included in this category are agreements between competitors to limit production, allocate customers or territories, boycott customers or suppliers, or establish common methods or plans of distribution. The anticompetitive purpose and effect of such horizontal agreements is conclusively presumed to be unlawful. Participants in the same market are expected to compete for the same customers on the basis of quality and price; any agreements, discussions, or "gentlemen's understandings" to limit that competition violate Section 1 of the Sherman Act.

Agreements Between Suppliers and Distributors (Group Boycotts and Tie-Ins). In much the same way that competitors cannot agree to boycott a reseller or customer for anticompetitive purposes, a manufacturer should not agree with its distributors or customers to refuse to deal with or terminate another distributor or customer. This area of the law is very delicate because a manufacturer may terminate a distributor lawfully, even following complaints by other distributors about predatory practices by the distributor being canceled. The facts in each case must be studied carefully to determine if the termination is lawful. An agreement representing a group boycott (which is per se unlawful) can be inferred from evidence of communications regarding the refusal or termination. Tying arrangements (the sale of one product on the condition that the buyer purchase another) are also in certain circumstances per se offenses.

Q 8:18   What are some general guidelines to avoid potential antitrust violations?

When dealing with competitors with respect to pricing, follow these guidelines:

1. Do not exchange past, present, or future price or cost information with competitors.

2. Do not make any agreements and do not enter into any discussions with competitors concerning the prices, terms, or conditions on which to purchase or sell. Agreements with respect to the inclusion of costs in prices are as dangerous as outright price fixing; penalties may include fines and imprisonment.

3. Do not attend any meeting where competitors will be present—including, for example, trade association meetings—or prices may be discussed either formally or informally; if pricing is discussed at any such meeting, leave at once.

4. Avoid any unnatural uniformity of action between competitors, such as raising prices simultaneously. Make every impor-

tant decision as to price that follows or may be followed by competitors only after internal deliberations, carefully recorded, that are not preceded or followed by discussions with competitors.

To avoid per se illegality in nonprice areas, follow these rules:

1. Do not make oral or written agreements or "gentlemen's agreements," or have any understandings with competitors, regarding geographic markets, sales territories or shares of any market, scope or methods of product distribution, or reciprocal purchases.
2. Do not exchange information with competitors (except for general statistical information).
3. Do not adopt or implement important decisions regarding any change in established practices that may be followed by other members of the same industry without carefully recording internal deliberations that are not discussed or shared with competitors.

In dealing with "customers" or downstream "users," the following guidelines are suggested to avoid "tying arrangements or group boycotts":

1. Do not adopt or announce a policy of automatic elimination of certain classes of persons or firms without justification.
2. Do not discuss or make any agreements with competitors regarding the selection of distributors.
3. Do not discuss allocation of products among various distributors with other distributors or competitors.
4. Do not give favored treatment to particular similarly situated distributors or customers with respect to price or service.

Q 8:19   What are the more common antitrust issues associated with managed care activities?

There are always antitrust issues associated with market dominance, control, or related impact by health care entities. Apart from the types of conduct that are per se illegal, such as price fixing, dividing markets, and boycotts, the most common focus of regulators evaluating managed care arrangements involving provider-sponsored organizations (PSOs) and health maintenance organizations

(HMOs) is market power. Market power is usually defined as the ability to control profits by controlling prices for a sustained period of time.

A secondary issue is that of inclusion and exclusion from provider panels. This is becoming more controversial as provider networks and payers become more selective. If decisions concerning inclusion or exclusion of providers are engaged in by economic competitors in a provider-controlled plan, there is an antitrust risk of group boycott, which is subject to the per se rule. If implemented by a non-provider-controlled plan, the agreement is a vertical nonprice restraint and is analyzed under the rule of reason.

Although more suits brought by plaintiff providers excluded from managed care plans are anticipated, such cases are difficult for plaintiffs to win. Selective and exclusive contracting are generally considered procompetitive because they force providers to compete with each other. Exclusive contracting (contracting with only one group of providers for a particular service) can, however, raise antitrust concerns under limited circumstances, particularly when competing and potentially competing providers are excluded from such a percentage of the market that they cannot survive. These exclusive arrangements are tested under the rule-of-reason analysis. The ultimate question is not whether the excluded providers are harmed, but rather whether the exclusive contract will adversely affect the terms and conditions on which the service in question is offered. The items to consider in this analysis include (1) whether the contract is truly exclusive; (2) the degree of the restriction or foreclosure to the market; (3) the contract's duration; (4) the plan's belief about the contract's effect on competition; (5) the prevalence of exclusive contracts in the market; (6) the exclusive contractor's market share; (7) the level of entry barriers; (8) the exclusive contract's effect on market performance; and (9) the efficiencies associated with the existence of the exclusion.

Q 8:20 What constitutes price fixing?

When there is not sufficient business integration or sharing of economic risk with new product development, any agreement between parties with respect to pricing may constitute price fixing under antitrust laws. [Arizona v Maricopa County Med Soc'y, 457 US 332 (1982); see also Boulware v Nevada, 960 F 2d 793 (9th Cir 1992) antitrust laws apply to hospitals the same as to other economic entities)] Many managed care provider organizations such as physician-hospital organizations (PHOs) and IPAs appear to be structurally integrated, but may not have sufficient operational integration to be deemed a common organization or risk-sharing joint venture for antitrust purposes. As a result of recent antitrust enforcement activity, there has been a change in the way partially integrated organizations such as PHOs and IPAs must negotiate prices with their members. In the past, these organizations were able to use a modified messenger model by obtaining an agreement as to a price floor and having advance approval to accept, collectively, contract rates on behalf of all providers in the network. Now, the conservative view is to use the pure messenger model, which requires each physician to opt in or out of the contract on a per agreement basis.

Q 8:21   How can division of markets give rise to antitrust liability?

When competitor organizations divide up a market, there is per se violation of the antitrust laws. Even if it can be shown that the market division is procompetitive, in order for the enterprise to proceed, such market division may still be deemed a legal restraint. [Polk Bros v Forest City Entertainment, Inc, 776 F2d 185 (7th Cir 1985)] For example, in small communities where there is a limited number of providers, the organization of two geographically distinct integrated delivery systems or other integrated entity involving hospitals and physicians can be perceived as having tacitly agreed to divide the local market. In that particular situation, it will likely be the payer that will complain.

Q 8:22   How does exclusive dealing create antitrust liability?

Although exclusive contracts have been upheld in limited circumstances, if they are intended to prevent competition from developing, they are likely to create antitrust liability.

Q 8:23   Does a covenant not to compete create antitrust liability?

Not necessarily. If a party agrees in a lawful contract not to compete because such an agreement is necessary to protect a legitimate business interest or property of the entity, that agreement will usually be upheld provided it is reasonable and limited in duration and scope. Federal and state antitrust enforcement agencies, however, have expressed increasing concern as to the potential anticompetitive effects of such agreements, which are commonly used in the syndication documents of integrated delivery entities to protect the integrity of the investment from participants competing with the integrated entity. With the alignment of providers and payers in managed care arrangements, such agreements will likely be tested in the courts or challenged by enforcement agencies.

Q 8:24   What is a most favored nation clause?

A most favored nation (MFN) clause is a clause often found in contracts between MCOs and providers in which the provider agrees to give the MCO its most favorable rate. Also called nondiscrimination clauses, these clauses are often negotiated as part of exclusive or other favorable managed care agreements between payers and providers.

Although these clauses do not constitute illegal price fixing because they do not affect what a physician charges, they have been recognized by some courts as rising to the level of an unreasonable restraint on trade if they result in a sufficient number of providers who would be unwilling or unable to participate in programs offering less reimbursement than the payer imposing the clause. The courts have evaluated these activities using a rule-of-reason analysis. In *United States v. Delta Dental of Rhode Island* [943 F Supp 172 (DRI 1996)], the court upheld a government challenge to an MFN clause as an anticompetitive agreement in violation of Section 1 of the Sherman Act and, in doing so, helped to clarify the circumstances under which an MFN clause will raise antitrust concerns. The key anticompetitive effects identified in this case include (1) increased costs of competitors' products, which restrict competition between a dominant buyer and its rivals or potential rivals, and (2) facilitating horizontal price coordination among suppliers.

Q 8:25   How has the federal government responded to the increased integration of providers in response to managed care?

The DOJ and the FTC have issued three sets of policy statements specifying safety zones from antitrust challenges. The first policy statement, issued in September 1993, provided, with respect to physician activities, that absent extraordinary circumstances, the agencies would not challenge (1) the collective provision by physicians of medical information to help purchasers of their services resolve issues about the mode, quality, or efficiency of medical treatment; (2) joint purchasing agreements between health care providers, as long as they meet conditions designed to ensure they do not become vehicles for collusive purchasing or for price fixing; or (3) physician network joint ventures composed of no more than 20 percent of the physicians in any specialty in a geographic market who have active hospital staff privileges and who share substantial financial risk.

In September 1994, the DOJ published "Statements of Enforcement Policy and Analytical Principles Relating to Healthcare and Antitrust," in which it recognized that some level of cooperation among independent competitors was not only procompetitive but also necessary. These policy statements address a number of situations ranging from hospital mergers and information-sharing arrangements to multiprovider networks. For purposes of analyzing multiprovider networks, the agency will look at such factors as degree of integration, joint pricing and joint marketing, market definition, competitive effects, exclusivity, exclusion of providers, and inefficiencies. Key to this analysis is the relevant geographic market definition used by the agency under the particular facts and circumstances.

In the 1996 "Statements of Antitrust Enforcement Policy in Health Care" (1996 Policy Statements), the DOJ and the FTC announced that they will apply the more flexible rule-of-reason legal standard in determining whether physician-run networks are anticompetitive. This will apply to fee-for-service arrangements as well arrangements involving risk sharing and is expected to accelerate the development activity of provider-sponsored networks.

On January 9, 1997, the Antitrust Health Care Advancement Act of 1997 (AHCAA) was proposed by House Judiciary Chair Henry Hyde to ease the scrutiny federal antitrust enforcers applied to health care provider networks by mandating a rule-of-reason analysis for provider networks in all respects, including for those that would have been per se illegal.[4] In two recent cases (one in Danbury, Connecticut; the other in St. Joseph, Missouri), the DOJ challenged two PHOs, both of which included a majority of the physicians in the town and had a common fee schedule without any risk sharing among physicians. [See United States v HealthCare Partners, Inc, Trade Reg Rep (CCH) ¶ 50,787 (D Conn 1995) (consent order);

United States v Health Choice, Inc, Trade Reg Rep. (CCH) ¶ 50,786 (WD Mo 1995) (consent order).] In both cases, the hospital, the IPA, and the PHO accepted consent orders in which they agreed to use a common fee schedule only if the provider panel represented less than 30 percent of the physicians for each specialty within the area and where there was true sharing of the risk among the physicians (e.g., capitated, risk contracts, or withholds). Otherwise, the DOJ and FTC mandated that a messenger model be used.

Finally, in 1999, the FTC and the DOJ issued new "Antitrust Guidelines for Collaborations among Competitors" (Competitor Collaboration Guidelines). These guidelines are intended to describe how the FTC and DOJ will analyze certain antitrust issues raised by collaborations among competitors. Competitor collaborations and the market circumstances in which they operate vary widely. Although no one set of guidelines can provide specific answers to every antitrust question that might arise from a competitor collaboration, these guidelines describe an analytical framework to assist businesses in assessing the likelihood of an antitrust challenge to a collaboration among competitors. A competitor collaboration comprises a set of one or more agreements, other than merger agreements, between or among competitors to engage in economic activity, and the economic activity resulting therefrom. Competitor collaborations involve one or more business activities, such as research and development (R&D), production, marketing, distribution, sales, or purchasing. Information-sharing and various trade association activities also may take place through competitor collaborations.[5]

Q 8:26 How is a competitor collaboration distinguished from a merger?

Mergers completely end competition between the merging parties in the relevant market or markets. By contrast, most competitor collaborations preserve some form of competition among the participants. This remaining competition may reduce competitive concerns, but also may raise questions about whether participants have agreed to anticompetitive restraints on the remaining competition. Mergers are designed to be permanent; competitor collaborations are more typically of limited duration. Thus, participants in a collaboration typically remain potential competitors, even if they are not actual competitors for certain purposes (e.g., R&D) during the collaboration. The potential for future competition among participants in a collaboration requires antitrust scrutiny different from that required for mergers.

In some cases, competitor collaborations have competitive effects identical to those that would arise if the participants merged in whole or in part. The FTC and DOJ treat a competitor collaboration as a horizontal merger in a relevant market and analyze the collaboration pursuant to the Horizontal Merger Guidelines if (1) the participants are competitors in that relevant market; (2) the formation of the collaboration involves an efficiency-enhancing integration of economic activity in the relevant market; (3) the integration eliminates all competition among the participants in the relevant market; and (4) the collaboration does not terminate within a sufficiently limited period by its own specific and express terms.[6] Effects of the collaboration on competition in other markets are analyzed as appropriate under these guidelines or other applicable precedent.

Q 8:27 What are the general principles used by the FTC and DOJ to evaluate agreements between competitors?

In reviewing agreements between competitors involving collaborations, the DOJ and FTC will evaluate according to the following principles:

1. *What are the potential procompetitive benefits?* The DOJ and FTC recognize that consumers may benefit from competitor collaborations in a variety of ways. For example, a competitor collaboration may enable participants to offer goods or services that are cheaper, more valuable to consumers, or brought to market faster than would be possible absent the collaboration. A collaboration may allow its participants to better use existing assets, or may provide incentives for them to make output-enhancing investments that would not occur absent the collaboration. The potential efficiencies from competitor collaborations may be achieved through a variety of contractual arrangements, including joint ventures, trade or professional associations, licensing arrangements, or strategic alliances. Efficiency gains from competitor collaborations often stem from combinations of different capabilities or resources. For example, one participant may have special

technical expertise that usefully complements another participant's manufacturing process, allowing the latter participant to lower its production cost or improve the quality of its product. In other instances, a collaboration may facilitate the attainment of scale or scope economies beyond the reach of any single participant. For example, two firms may be able to combine their research or marketing activities to lower their cost of bringing their products to market, or reduce the time needed to develop and begin commercial sales of new products. Consumers may benefit from these collaborations because the participants are able to lower prices, improve quality, or bring new products to market faster.

2. *What are the potential anticompetitive harms?* Competitor collaborations may harm competition and consumers by increasing the ability or incentive profitably to raise price above or to reduce output, quality, service, or innovation below what most likely would prevail in the absence of the relevant agreement. Such effects may arise through a variety of mechanisms. Among other things, agreements may limit independent decision making or combine the control of or financial interests in production, key assets, or decisions regarding price, output, or other competitively sensitive variables, or may otherwise reduce the participants' ability or incentive to compete independently. Competitor collaborations may also facilitate explicit or tacit collusion through facilitating practices such as the exchange or disclosure of competitively sensitive information or through increased market concentration. Such collusion may involve the relevant market in which the collaboration operates or another market in which the participants in the collaboration are actual or potential competitors.

3. *What is the overall collaboration, and what are the agreements?* A competitor collaboration comprises a set of one or more agreements, other than merger agreements, between or among competitors to engage in economic activity, and the economic activity resulting therefrom. In general, the DOJ and FTC assess the competitive effects of the overall collaboration and any individual agreement or set of agreements within the collaboration that may harm competition. Two or more agreements are assessed together if their procompetitive benefits or anticompetitive harms are so intertwined that they cannot

meaningfully be isolated and attributed to any individual agreement.

4. *What is the potential harm to competition?* The competitive effects of a relevant agreement may change over time, depending on changes in circumstances such as internal reorganization, adoption of new agreements as part of the collaboration, addition or departure of participants, new market conditions, or changes in market share. The DOJ and FTC assess the competitive effects of a relevant agreement as of the time of possible harm to competition, whether at formation of the collaboration or at a later time, as appropriate. An assessment after a collaboration has been formed, however, is sensitive to the reasonable expectations of participants whose significant sunk cost investments in reliance on the relevant agreement were made before it became anticompetitive.

Q 8:28   What analytical framework is used by the FTC and DOJ to make their determinations of potential antitrust violations?

The analytical framework that the FTC and DOJ use to evaluate the competitive effects of a competitor collaboration and the agreements of which it consists divides those agreements into (1) agreements that are so likely to be harmful to competition as to have no significant benefits (per se illegal) and (2) agreements that can be analyzed under a rule of reason. Under the rule of reason, the central question is whether the relevant agreement likely harms competition by increasing the ability or incentive profitably to raise price above or reduce output, quality, service, or innovation below what likely would prevail in the absence of the relevant agreement. As a result of the great variety of competitor collaborations, rule-of-reason analysis entails a flexible inquiry and varies in focus and detail, depending on the nature of the agreement and market circumstances. Rule-of-reason analysis focuses on only those factors, and undertakes only the degree of factual inquiry necessary to assess the overall competitive effect of the relevant agreement accurately.

Q 8:29   What are the competitor collaboration antitrust "safety zones"?

First, absent extraordinary circumstances, the FTC and DOJ do not challenge a competitor collaboration when the market shares of the collaboration and its participants collectively account for no more than 20 percent of each relevant market in which competition may be affected.[7]

Second, absent extraordinary circumstances, the FTC and DOJ do not challenge a competitor collaboration on the basis of effects on competition in an innovation market where three or more independently controlled research efforts in addition to those of the collaboration possess the required specialized assets or characteristics and the incentive to engage in R&D that is a close substitute for the R&D activity of the collaboration. In determining whether independently controlled R&D efforts are close substitutes, the agencies consider, among other things, the nature, scope, and magnitude of the R&D efforts; their access to financial support; their access to intellectual property, skilled personnel, or other specialized assets; their timing; and their ability, either acting alone or through others, to commercialize innovations successfully. This antitrust safety zone does not apply to agreements that are per se illegal, or that would be challenged without a detailed market analysis, or to competitor collaborations to which a merger analysis is applied.

Q 8:30   What has been the effect of the 1996 Policy Statements on managed care arrangements?

On August 28, 1996, the DOJ and FTC revised Statements 8 and 9 of the nine enforcement policies dealing with provider networks (physician and multiprovider) (see Q 8:25). These two policies create greater flexibility for the agencies' analysis of health care provider networks, both physician and multiprovider (e.g., PHO), in two ways.

First, the agencies will recognize new forms of integration that will justify the rule-of-reason standard of review by which provider networks engage in price negotiations (see Q 8:16 for a discussion of standards of review). This policy will allow networks that are not "economically" integrated to avoid per se treatment for engaging in pricing and related activities.

Second, the agencies have extended the list of risk-sharing arrangements that will qualify as being economically integrated. Specifically, the 1996 Policy Statements

1. Expand the definition of "shared financial risk" to include not only capitation and withholds but also per case payments and financial rewards based on utilization;

2. Retain the two safety zones for physician networks without change, but extend the reach of these safety zones through the expanded definition of shared financial risk;

3. More specifically set forth the factors that should be considered in determining whether a network is exclusive;

4. For networks that engage in risk and nonrisk contracting, allow joint pricing discussions to take place for both types of contracts if the efficiencies from the risk contracts extend to the nonrisk contracts;

5. Allow substantial clinical integration to be a substitute for substantial financial risk sharing in the agencies' analysis of such networks; and

6. Allow the messenger model to involve an agent that receives advance authority to accept a contract offer on behalf of the authorizing individual providers.

Q 8:31   What constitutes nonfinancial integration as described in the 1996 Policy Statements?

The most obvious form of nonfinancial integration is clinical integration. Clinical integration has been described in the 1996 Policy Statements as "an active and ongoing program to evaluate and modify practice patterns by the network's physician participants and create a high degree of interdependence and cooperation among the physicians to control costs and ensure quality." Under 1996 Policy Statements, such a program could include (1) mechanisms to manage utilization to control costs and ensure quality, (2) selection criteria based on efficiency objectives for network participants, and (3) investment of human and monetary resources in the infrastructure required to realize the network's efficiencies. The mechanisms include the following:

- Quality and utilization management programs

- Credentialing and performance evaluation of providers, including monitoring of practice patterns and use of practice guidelines

- Case management, preauthorization of services, and concurrent and retrospective review of inpatient stays
- Information system technology
- Outcome measures and reports
- Full-time medical director
- Practice standards and protocols used as part of provider appraisal

It is important to note that the 1996 Policy Statements will not insulate networks that intend to fix prices and engage in anticompetitive activity that uses the foregoing indicators of clinical integration as a ruse. The DOL and FTC will look to evidence indicating such anticompetitive intent through statements, history of anticompetitive behavior, absence of substantial use of the mechanisms to achieve the efficiencies, the presence of anticompetitive collateral agreements, the absence of mechanisms to prevent spillover collusion outside the network, and networks that use form over substance to achieve obvious anticompetitive objectives.

Q 8:32   What other types of risk-sharing arrangements will satisfy the 1996 Policy Statements?

In addition to the two recognized forms of risk sharing discussed in Qs 8:30 and 8:31 (economic integration and clinical integration), other risk-sharing arrangements that will satisfy the 1996 Policy Statements include (1) an arrangement by which networks engage in capitated contracting and (2) an arrangement in which networks establish substantial withholds to be distributed only if the network meets established goals. Three new standards are

1. Percentage of plan premiums or revenues;
2. Payments tied to performance targets or goals; and
3. Global or all-inclusive case rates.

Q 8:33   What is the significance of the 1996 Policy Statements for the messenger model?

Previous policy statements effectively precluded a "nonintegrated" network from using the modified messenger model. Under the 1996 Policy Statements, the messenger can now accept contract offers on behalf of network participants. The messenger may also help providers understand contract offers by giving objective information, including comparison of offered terms with other contracts agreed to by network participants; however, the messenger must function as an "honest broker," and may not express an opinion regarding the terms offered or decide which information should be conveyed.

Q 8:34 Is there always antitrust liability when potential competitors get together in response to managed care?

No. Whenever there are agreements between competitors that affect some aspect of competition in an industry, there is concern for potential violation of antitrust laws and regulations. The per se (see Q 8:17) rule as established for the most obvious anticompetitive activities. As discussed in Q 8:25, however, regulators have moved away from the per se rule in many health care ventures, such as integrated health care delivery systems, and are more likely to use a rule-of-reason analysis. Under this rule, the court examines such factors as the market share of each party and the purpose and competitive effects of the activity.

Antitrust Issues in Managed Care Organizations

Q 8:35 How does the degree of provider integration affect the antitrust analysis?

As discussed in chapter 6, antitrust analysis will differ depending on whether the entity involves a joint venture-type organization, such as an IPA or PHO, or involves a more integrated organization, such as a fully integrated medical group or an organized delivery system. Most managed care entities such as PHOs, IPAs, preferred provider organizations (PPOs), and management service organizations (MSOs) are partially rather than fully integrated. This means that the parties have combined only some of their business activities through the network. With regard to activities that are outside the network, they remain economic competitors. Even if the organization is a single legal entity such as a corporation or limited liability company, if it is only partially integrated and controlled by otherwise independent competing providers, regardless of its business form, it will be treated as a combination or agreement between the persons controlling it for purposes of antitrust analysis. The antitrust risk diminishes if the entity is not controlled by the competitors or if it achieves full economic as well as legal integration.

In evaluating the antitrust risk for partially integrated, provider-controlled arrangements, the following questions should be asked:

1. Does the process used by the network to establish and negotiate prices for its services with payers constitute a per se unlawful price-fixing agreement?

2. Is it likely that the network can exercise market power by raising the prices of its members' services above what they otherwise would be?

3. Do the network's decisions about which providers may participate result in an unlawful group boycott of providers excluded by the network?

4. Do the network's decisions about which providers may participate result in an exclusive dealing contract?

5. Does the network have any "collateral agreements" between participating providers that unreasonably restrain competition but are not really necessary for the network to achieve its "procompetitive benefits"?

Q 8:36 What are the common integration strategies involving hospitals, physicians, and payers?

As discussed in chapter 6, integration strategies are a market response to managed care. Activities inherent in such strategies include the formation of provider-controlled networks and mergers and/or acquisitions among providers or with payers. Integration among health care providers and payers can take three forms—horizontal, vertical, and conglomerate:

1. Horizontal integration involves the integration of similar businesses that may otherwise be direct economic competitors (e.g., the merger of physician practices or the affiliation and merger of two hospitals).

2. Vertical integration involves the integration of businesses that may be economically related but are not direct competitors

(e.g., the merger of a hospital with a medical group). Sometimes the transaction can involve both a horizontal and a vertical merger. For example, once the hospital has acquired a medical group (a vertical merger), it subsequently acquires another medical group (a horizontal merger).

3. Conglomerate integration is the integration of businesses that produce unrelated products or services. This form of merger should have little antitrust risk.

Q 8:37 What are the major factors in analyzing a horizontal merger?

If the merger is horizontal, two fundamental questions must be answered. First, will the merger result in a group that is sufficiently large that it will be able to exercise market power by itself? Second, will the merger result in a market that is so concentrated that any one competitor's decision creates an interdependent result so as to allow competitors to make competitive decisions and thus exercise market power as a group?

The DOJ and FTC have outlined, in their 1992 Horizontal Merger Guidelines [57 Fed Reg 41552 (Sept 10, 1992)], the following steps for undertaking this analysis:

1. Define the relevant product market, especially from the perspective of the managed care plans that purchase services from the merging groups.

2. Define the relevant geographic market.

3. Identify competitors in the relevant market.

4. Compute all competitors' market shares in each relevant market based on capacity, sales, and production.

5. Compute the postmerger market share of the merging parties.

6. Apply the Merger Guidelines concentration standards to determine how serious a problem, if any, the merger might raise.

7. Determine whether the postmerger market share of the merging parties is more than 35 percent, which is the general benchmark used to determine market power.

8. If the level of concentration is significantly above guidelines levels or the postmerger market share is above 35 percent, examine other factors.

9. Examine the level of entry barriers—that is, how difficult and likely would it be that new parties would enter the market if those already in the market attempted to exercise market power by raising prices.

10. When the only issue is the group's postmerger market share, examine how difficult it would be for competing groups in the market to increase their capacity and output quickly if the merged firm increased prices.

11. Examine other factors suggesting whether collusion would occur, and if so, whether it would be successful.

12. Examine the extent of efficiencies in the new, merged system.

13. Balance the procompetitive with the anticompetitive effects.

It is rare for physician practice acquisitions or mergers to create significant antitrust concerns, because most physician markets are not concentrated; however, this potential should be carefully observed as the market consolidates.

Q 8:38 What are the major factors in analyzing a vertical merger?

A merger is vertical if it is between organizations in the same chain of production or distribution. This can encompass mergers between physician practices and hospitals and between physician practices and third-party payers. The key questions to address in a vertical merger analysis are the same as those asked in a horizontal merger analysis (discussed in Q 8:37), questions relating to market power and market concentration rendering competitor individual behavior joint behavior.

The major concerns associated with a vertical merger are that (1) it may foreclose a substantial percentage of the market to competitors at either the purchaser or seller level sufficient to place it in market dominance at one of those levels; (2) it can raise barriers to entry, inhibiting new participants from entering the market because they will be foreclosed from customers or suppliers; and (3) it may reduce the number of competitors in the market to the extent that interdependent, oligopolistic business behavior could result.

Q 8:39   What are the implications of hospital-hospital joint ventures or mergers under current antitrust law?

Hospital mergers have increased recently in response to managed care activities. One implication is that with managed care, formerly defined "local markets" for antitrust purposes may now be part of regional markets for the delivery of health care services. [See Federal Trade Comm'n v Freeman Hosp, Trade Reg Rep (CCH) ¶ 23,936 (FTC 1995); United States v Mercy Health Servs. 1995-2 Trade Cas (CCH) ¶ 71,162 (ND Iowa 1995).] In *Santa Cruz Medical Clinic v. Dominican Santa Cruz Hospital* [1995-2 Trade Cas (CCH) ¶ 70,915 (ND Cal 1995)] the court rejected the plaintiff's motion for summary judgment on the merger issue because there was a genuine dispute as to whether the product market was limited only to general acute hospital services. Because hospital merger cases historically were evaluated against a product market consisting of "general acute hospital services," this case represents what may be a precursor to the inclusion of other entities, such as outpatient clinics, as competitors with an interest in hospital services.

Q 8:40   What are the implications of hospital-physician joint ventures or mergers under antitrust law?

The FTC and state attorneys general have begun to look at hospital acquisitions of physician practices from an antitrust perspective. The concern is that vertical integration in the health care industry, such as hospitals' acquisition of physicians, may foreclose access to physicians by competing hospitals or interfere with the ability of a competing managed care plan to obtain any foothold in the market. For example, in Missouri, a compromise and settlement was entered into with the attorney general in 1994 to resolve state antitrust concerns about the acquisition of physician practices and the hiring of those physicians by a hospital in Springfield, Missouri. The settlement specified nine specialty areas in which the hospital agreed to limit itself to under 40 percent of the physician specialists in the relevant geographic area. [68 Antitrust & Trade Reg Rep (BNA) 24 (Jan 12, 1995)]

In January 2002, the Massachusetts Attorney General sent investigative subpoenas to a number of hospitals asking for a wide range of information relating to competition in the greater Boston area. Health care antitrust enforcement remains a priority in other states, especially in California, Colorado, and Connecticut.

Q 8:41 What are the implications of physician practice acquisitions, joint ventures, and mergers under antitrust law?

Physician practice acquisitions and physician practice mergers have not yet become the target of antitrust enforcement, although that is likely to change now that the physician markets are becoming more concentrated. This is particularly the case with the increasing number of physician practice management companies (PPMCs) that use as their business strategy the development of "captive medical practices" through physician practice acquisition and management.

Forms of physician practice acquisitions that may raise antitrust issues include (1) mergers among physician practices, (2) practice acquisitions by hospitals, (3) practice acquisitions by third-party payers, and (4) practice acquisitions by PPMCs. The analysis for antitrust purposes will include a review of whether the transaction results in a single entity or whether the parties to the transaction remain separate after the transaction. (See Q 8:47 concerning fully versus partially integrated delivery systems.) If the physicians develop an MSO to function as their PPMC and negotiating agent, there is also a risk that the government would disregard the existence of the separate legal entity to raise the issue of horizontal price fixing among the affiliated physician groups.

Q 8:42 Can an integrated delivery system become so large it incurs antitrust risk?

Yes. Remember the Bell Telephone litigation that resulted in the creation of all the "Baby Bells"? Even if an organization is sufficiently integrated to overcome antitrust problems associated with price fixing or market divisions, its size creates the potential for group boycott. When a group excludes competitors to gain a monopoly in the market, there is potential violation of antitrust laws. When a group refuses to bargain in good faith and a payer is unable to obtain managed care contracts, there is a risk of group boycott.

Antitrust Issues in Provider Exclusion

Q 8:43   Do antitrust laws apply to the exclusion of health care providers from managed care plans or networks?

It depends. Provider membership decisions made by provider-controlled entities can be subject to antitrust scrutiny under theories of group boycott or concerted refusals to deal with potential participating providers. If the selection criteria used result in reduced competition, there may be antitrust implications. It is highly unlikely, however, that the inclusion or exclusion decisions of an IPA or PHO will have antitrust consequences unless the decisions are based on unfair and discriminatory criteria or the purpose of the decision is to punish a competitor.

Factors to be considered in analyzing antitrust risk in exclusionary practices include whether (1) the organization that engages in the exclusionary activities has significant market power or exclusive access to essential facilities or services; (2) the purpose is to disadvantage a competitor; (3) the boycott is used to enforce an agreement that is per se illegal; and (4) the activity can be justified by efficiency or procompetitive considerations. Providers that are excluded from managed care systems may challenge the action as an illegal restraint of trade and group boycott. To show an illegal group boycott, there must be more than one party, an anticompetitive event or the absence of a legitimate reason for the conduct, and a certain degree of market power by the actor. Although group boycotts in other industries are subject to a per se analysis, this is not always so in the context of managed care. In *U.S. Healthcare, Inc. v. Healthsource, Inc.* [986 F 2d 589 (1st Cir 1993)], the court stated that "per se condemnation is not visited on every arrangement that might, as a matter of language, be called a group boycott or concerted refusal to deal." In that case, the court of appeals upheld an exclusive contract that required primary care physicians to do business with only one HMO. A competing HMO claimed it had been unsuccessful in recruiting physicians in New Hampshire because of the restrictive covenant. The court used a rule-of-reason analysis to determine that competition was not lessened by the exclusivity provision.

Before the per se rule will be applied to an agreement to exclude providers, the entities involved in the exclusive arrangement must have sufficient market share, because exclusive dealing arrangements are not per se illegal. An unreasonable anticompetitive effect must be shown before an exclusive dealing arrangement will be deemed illegal. [See Jefferson Parish Hosp Dist v Hyde, 466 US 2 (1984); Tampa Elec Co v Nashville Coal Co, 365 US 320 (1961)] The market share threshold for application of a per se rule to an exclusive dealing arrangement has not yet been determined; however, there is some indication that the DOJ might look at an arrangement that involved more than 35 percent of the relevant market.

Exclusion of a defined group of providers may be deemed a group boycott in violation of antitrust rules if it is determined that there is not a legitimate business purpose for the exclusion. Several nonphysician groups such as podiatrists, psychologists, and chiropractors have successfully challenged exclusion from managed care arrangements using a group boycott theory under a rule-of-reason standard of review.[8]

Q 8:44   Can an individual provider's unilateral decision not to do business with another party constitute an illegal group boycott?

No. A group boycott, by definition, requires more than one party. Thus, if a single individual or entity makes a unilateral decision not to do business with someone, it is not illegal unless it rises to the level of a monopoly because of market position.

Q 8:45   How do antitrust laws relate to the peer review process?

When a peer review committee takes action against a peer provider, there are potential antitrust concerns because the adverse actions are often those of the affected practitioner's competitors. With the increase in competition among physicians under managed care, excluded or censured practitioners will often use antitrust as a basis for challenge of the adverse action. The reality, however, is that with the federal Health Care Quality Improvement Act of 1986 (HCQIA) as guidance for good-faith peer review, the majority of cases are either dismissed or found in favor of the peer review organization absent egregious facts. (The peer review process is discussed more extensively at Qs 8:81–8:92.)

Q 8:46 How can antitrust risk associated with provider exclusion be reduced?

When the selection decisions are made by a non-provider-controlled entity such as an insurer, HMO, or other managed care company, there is minimal antitrust liability. When the provider entity is making the selection decisions, the key to reducing the antitrust risk in all inclusion or exclusion decisions is to establish and follow clear, fair, and objective criteria for participation and removal. Individuals should not be precluded from participation for improper reasons such as sex, race, religion, or disability. To the extent a removal or exclusion decision is based on quality of care concerns, immunity for such credentialing or peer review is available to physicians under HCQIA. Economic credentialing factors are not covered by HCQIA.

Q 8:47 How can an integrated delivery system minimize its potential liability for provider selection and deselection decisions?

An integrated delivery system can minimize its liability exposure in the selection and deselection of providers by taking action in the following areas.

Sufficient Integration. To the extent the entity is sufficiently integrated, it is less likely to incur antitrust liability for its decisions related to provider selection or deselection. Criteria used to measure integration include whether the entity is a joint venture that (1) pools capital; (2) shares risk of loss; (3) employs utilization review protocols; (4) engages in joint marketing, claims administration, and collection; and (5) competes for business with similar entities.

Objective Membership Criteria. The use of objective membership criteria established by someone other than the competitors to whom the criteria will be applied should reduce the risk of antitrust liability relating to admission to and termination from the organization if the criteria are applied objectively and consistently.

Inclusion of Allied Health Professionals. Membership criteria should not arbitrarily exclude any class of practitioner.

Existing Business Plan. There should be a business plan addressing the specific levels of provider participation, based on geographic and specialty diversity. It may be preferable to use an objective third party to establish these levels.

Use of an Application and Quality Assurance Process. There should be a thorough and fair application process and a quality assurance process that adhere to the principles of substantive due process, such as limitation of direct competitors in the review or selection process and use of objectively determined criteria such as practice guidelines or parameters.

Limited Role of Competitors. Where competitors are insulated from making the business, selection, credentialing, and other decisions affecting other competitors, liability exposure should be limited.

Recent and Future Antitrust Issues

Q 8:48 What is being done to reduce the uncertainty of antitrust enforcement in the health care market?

Over the past several years, the DOJ and FTC have attempted to clarify their enforcement policies through the release of three sets of policy statements (see Qs 8:25–8:34). Although they do not plan to release any further enforcement statements in the near future, the agencies may do so as issues requiring clarification are brought to their attention.

The FTC and DOJ provide expedited business reviews and advisory opinions on any matter contained in the enforcement statements within 90 to 120 days of receiving all material necessary to respond. The process and guidelines for obtaining such reviews or opinions are contained in the FTC Web site (www.ftc.gov).

Q 8:49 What are the top issues of concern to the FTC and DOJ?

At a meeting of the American Bar Association in March 2001, representatives of the DOJ said health care enforcement priorities include reviewing new Internet business models, managed care mergers and contracts, and overinclusive physician groups.

Q 8:50 What recent antitrust activities affect physicians?

Many states have followed Texas's lead in obtaining state-legislated relief from the antitrust risk associated with groups of physicians negotiating with managed care companies. The Texas law provides physicians with an antitrust exemption and allows them to negotiate collectively with insurers on fees and other contract provisions. [Texas Insurance Code, Chap. 29, Art. 29.1–29.14]

Federal antitrust regulators continue to monitor the activities of doctors coming together to discuss contracts with health plans, particularly use of the messenger model by IPAs and PHOs. Regulators are concerned about abuses of the model, especially using it as a shield for collective bargaining. As of early 2002, the FTC is investigating several physician groups in Colorado, Texas, and California, all states where the FTC has moved to block what it saw as abuse of the messenger model in the past.

The medical community has long expressed concerns about whether current antitrust enforcement policy unduly restricts physicians' ability to compete effectively in the medical marketplace under managed care.[9] Physicians are concerned that market pressures to reduce costs will ultimately reduce access to quality care. They argue that they are effectively blocked under existing antitrust laws from organizing and collectively negotiating payment rates. The ability to organize would offset insurer market power, which is increasing in the wake of insurer consolidations. Collective bargaining by physicians is still one of the AMA's top issues.

Physicians also argue that, in comparison to insurers, they face additional requirements in setting up plans to reduce antitrust risk. These additional requirements include substantial risk sharing (or use of the messenger model-style price negotiation process) and limits on concentration of certain specialties (no more than 30 percent) for exclusive arrangements in a given market.

There is currently insufficient evidence to support the physicians' allegations of unequal enforcement policies. Little is known about physician-sponsored joint ventures; recent estimates suggest that about 15 to 20 percent of managed care entities are provider run.[10] Most of the evidence on "chilling" consists of anecdotal material from agency records that are not entirely clear. DOJ and FTC records suggest that they have been far less aggressive in health care-related activities than is generally perceived. Between 1981 and 1993, only 68 of 397 hospital mergers resulted in preliminary investigations; of these, only 15 were challenged.[11] Only two physician networks have been challenged under the per se rules, and only one of nine advisory opinions concerning physician-sponsored PPOs issued by the FTC between 1986 and 1994 indicated a risk of challenge to the proposed plan. Finally, none of the 11 business review letters concerning provider-sponsored networks issued by the DOJ between 1987 and 1994 indicated that the proposed ventures would be challenged.[12]

Q 8:51   What is the history of physician unions?

Physician unions have been in existence since the 1930s, and the number of unions representing physicians, as well as the number of physician members, is expected to grow. The AMA estimates that between 14,000 and 20,000 physicians are members of a union, which is far below the proportion for other health care workers.[13] Unions representing physicians include the Committee of Interns and Residents (founded in 1957), the Union of American Physicians and Dentists (founded in 1972), and the Federation of Physicians and Dentists (founded in 1981). Non-health care unions that have had physician members include the Office Professional Employees International Union; the Service Employees International Union; the American Federation of State, County, and Municipal Employees; and Local 56 of the United Food and Commercial Workers.

The AMA entered the field as a union organizer and representative when its 494-member house of delegates voted in favor of forming a "national labor organization" within the AMA to represent employee positions. On March 9, 2000, the AMA's collective bargaining arm, Physicians for Responsible Negotiation (PRN), won the right to represent the Wellness Plan's employed physicians in contract negotiations with management.

Q 8:52   Which physicians can be unionized?

Only employed physicians can be unionized. Self-employed physicians are prohibited from engaging in collective bargaining activities by federal antitrust laws. This prohibition was the reason for the Texas law discussed in Q 8:50 and for activity in Congress relating to physician collective bargaining.

In June 2000, the U.S. House of Representatives passed the Campbell-Conyers bill [HR 1304] by a vote of 276 to 136. This bill, known as the Quality Health Care Coalition Act, would provide a three-year waiver of antitrust law so that independent health care professionals could bargain collectively with health plans. It was sponsored by Rep. Tom Campbell (R-CA) and Rep. John Conyers (D-MI) and was adopted by a comfortable bipartisan majority. Both the DOJ and the FTC testified against the bill. To date, no further action has been taken on the measure.

Private sector opponents of the bill include insurers, nonphysician provider groups, and business groups such as the U.S. Chamber of Commerce and the National Association of Manufacturers. These groups claim the bill would allow physicians and other health care providers to collude, raising the cost of health care for everyone while enriching providers. The Congressional Budget Office (CBO) estimated the bill would increase total private health care costs by 1.6 percent by 2006 if it stayed in effect that long. A series of studies commissioned by the Health Insurance Association of America (HIAA) and the American Association of Health Plans (AAHP) have estimated the cost to be much higher. In a report issued by AAHP, it was predicted that U.S. health care costs would rise 8.6 percent if providers were allowed to bargain collectively.[14] Absent specific legislative exemption or state action, the exemptions available to union activity apply only when the union representation is with respect to an employment relationship. Otherwise, the use of a union to negotiate on behalf of a physician does not prevent the application of antitrust laws. In *AmeriHealth, Inc. and United Food & Commercial Workers Union, Local 56, AFL-CIO* [No. 4-RC-19260 (NLRB Aug 27, 1998)], a divided National Labor Relations Board ruled to allow New Jersey physicians to proceed to hearing, at which that unionization was allowed. It was determined that they were entitled to be recognized as an appropriate unit for bargaining purposes on the basis that the HMO-physician relationship created a de facto employment relationship. [329 NLRB No. 55, Oct. 18, 1999]

Q 8:53   What are the legal and ethical implications of physicians joining unions?

Physicians find themselves associated with hospitals or managed care plans as (1) full-time employees, (2) interns or residents completing medical training, (3) independent contractors of hospitals and facilities being reimbursed on a fee-for-service basis, (4) independent contractors through HMO and PPO contracts, and (5) independent contractors through joint venture contracts. Previously, physicians had limited choices in attempting to engage in "balanced" negotiations. For physicians seeking to organize into groups to negotiate collectively with health plans and hospital systems, antitrust laws imposed significant limitations on their ability to negotiate collectively on fees and other material terms of service. Others considered forming unions to qualify for a number of exemptions to antitrust laws with respect to collective bargaining concerning wages and other terms of employment. The dilemma for physicians considering union affiliation concerns the compromise of independent practice with employee status. Physicians must also consider whether they can accept the union's potential use of a "strike" activity to obtain a favorable contract and its conflict with their ethical duty of care to their patients.

Q 8:54 What antitrust developments are anticipated in health care in 2002?

FTC and DOJ health care enforcement priorities for 2002 include new Internet business models, managed care mergers and contracts, and overinclusive physician groups.

Based on recent high-profile cases, such as those involving Microsoft and Intel, some experts have predicted that future antitrust enforcement will be directed at single firm conduct and vertical restraints that affect competition. This emphasis may have antitrust implications for relationships between hospitals and physicians, with particular relevance to the practice of economic credentialing.

It is also expected that FTC enforcement measures will become tougher. Rather than just imposing "cease and desist" orders, the FTC will likely use more aggressive measures, such as immediate divestitures or similar actions. In a recent consent agreement, for example, an IPA-type organization not only had to "cease and desist" its conduct in colluding to fix prices and prevent managed care from entering the market but also had to terminate the membership of physicians who were part of the alleged conspiracy.[15]

Despite concerns raised by federal agencies relating to exclusive contractng arrangements involving MCOs and providers, the Texas Attorney General issued an opinion that said "exclusive dealing arrangements do not, as a matter of law, violate the [Texas Free Enterprise and Antitrust Act of 1983]." [See Tex Bus & Com Code Ann

§§ 15.01–15.52 (Vernon 1987 & Supp 2002)] The facts underlying this opinion involved a hospital that held an exclusive provider point of service (POS) agreement with a health plan to the exclusion of the local ambulatory surgery center.[16]

It can be expected that the merger activity involving large health plans will also come under increasing scrutiny by the FTC. In September 1999 the AMA filed a letter with the DOJ challenging the proposed merger of Aetna Health Plans with Prudential on the basis that the market power of Aetna created by the merger would limit choices of patients and employers, reduce competition, and further erode the ability of physicians to make medical decisions based on science and the medical needs of their patients. Although not in direct response to the AMA letter, the FTC ordered Aetna to divest its interest in NYLCare in certain markets because of market dominance. As of the date of this writing, Aetna has initiated the process of selling off its interest in NYLCare, an HMO that has substantial operations in Texas.

Q 8:55   What other issues are on the horizon for health care antitrust enforcement?

A number of lawsuits have been filed recently, including claims arising under federal and state antitrust laws. These claims have been targeted at plans leaving Medicare managed care markets following aggressive marketing, misuse of data, and possible conspiracy among drug companies to "inflate" or hold drug prices at a high level.

Conspiracy Among Health Plans to Withdraw from Medicare Managed Care. On March 6, 2000, a northern California woman sued five HMOs, alleging they engaged in fraud, antitrust violations, and a conspiracy by inducing elderly and disabled individuals to enroll in Medicare + Choice (M + C) when the plans intended to abandon the market. In *Green v. Aetna* [No. 412180 (Cal Super Ct filed Mar 6, 2000)], a class action lawsuit, the plaintiff alleges that Aetna U.S. Healthcare, Inc., CIGNA Corp., Lifeguard, Inc., Prudential Healthcare Group, Inc., and United HealthCare Corp. colluded to withdraw from the market in Santa Clara and San Mateo counties, redlined and boycotted certain areas so the MCOs that remained could charge more for service, and exerted greater pressure on the providers to accept lower fees. The lawsuit seeks injunctive relief; treble damages under the Cartwright Act, California Business and Professions Code Section 16720, for redlining and group boycott claims; compensatory and punitive damages on the fraud and negligent misrepresentation claims; and treble damages on the unfair business and unfair advertising practices claims under California Business and Professions Code Section 17200 et seq.

Misuse of Provider Data Creating Reduced Levels of Payment. A Maryland company that creates databases and sells them to insurance companies allegedly engaged in actions that resulted in the unlawful reduction of payments on medical claims, according to a complaint filed on May 16, 2000, in the U.S. District Court for the District of Maryland, Southern Division. [Knudsen v ADP-Integrated Med Solutions, No AW00CV1409 (D Md filed May 16, 2000)] In a lawsuit that seeks class status, Dr. Kirsten Knudsen and policyholder Carmel Loizon sued Automatic Data Processing-Integrated Medical Solutions (ADPIMS), of Bethesda, Maryland, alleging antitrust and Racketeer Influenced and Corrupt Organizations (RICO) Act breaches. The complaint states that National Biosystems, Inc., the predecessor to ADPIMS, created a database of charges for medical services and procedures based on charges submitted by health care providers across the United States to the federal Health Care Financing Administration (HCFA) for Medicare charges. "National, or ADPIMS, had purchased HCFA information since the 1980s which are among the lowest in the nation," according to the complaint. ADPIMS then used a methodology that had the effect of further lowering the calculation of coded charges from what could have been paid under Medicare. The data were then sold to the company's "insurer" clients. As a result, a substantial number of all claims for medical services submitted by ADPIMS's insured clients for processing through its computer database and program were deemed unnecessary and were not reimbursed, according to the complaint.

Prescription Drug Price Fixing. In December 2001, a federal judge sentenced TAP Pharmaceutical Products Inc. (PPI) to pay a $290 million criminal fine and serve five years of probation for admitting fraudulent pricing and marketing of a prostate cancer drug. [United States v TAP Pharmaceutical Prod Inc, No 01CR10354 (D Mass sentencing Dec 6, 2001)] In addition, the court found that TAP caused losses to Medicare, Medicaid, and other federal health care programs amounting to $145 million. These issues have also caught the attention of the Office of Inspector General (OIG) of the Department of

Health and Human Services as discussed in more detail in Qs 8:136–8:167. This followed an inquiry to the Attorney General regarding the investigation of collusion among drug companies to "fix" prices at artificially high levels.[17]

Bankruptcy in Health Care

Q 8:56   How do the bankruptcy laws apply to health care entities?

The Bankruptcy Code provides a mechanism for health care organizations to unwind over the objection of third parties while preserving the "going concern" value of their assets. A bankruptcy case may fall under either Chapter 7 or Chapter 11 of the Bankruptcy Code.

Under Chapter 7, a debtor starts a straight liquidation case, involving the termination of the debtor's business and the appointment of an independent trustee to take control of and liquidate the debtor's nonexempt assets and distribute the cash proceeds to creditors based on the priority of their claims. Alternatively, a debtor can file a petition for relief under Chapter 11, which allows the debtor to continue to possess and control its assets while "working out" its debts under a specific and supervised arrangement. Under either chapter, the debtor can be unwound and its assets sold free and clear of claims, interest, and liens. Only Chapter 11, however, allows reorganization so that an operation can go forward, unencumbered by past debt.

Q 8:57   How pervasive is insolvency among health care entities?

The rate of isolvency among health care entities varies from one state to another. The insolvency rate in a state depends, in part, on the penetration of risk-based managed care in the state and the degree to which health care organization revenue is tied to such arrangements.

According to a report prepared in the fall of 2001 by the California Department of Managed Health Care, of physicians who participate in risk-based managed care arrangements, about 25 percent of the groups reporting had assets worth less than 70 percent of the amount they owed others.[18] On a separate measure, 20 percent of groups had a negative net worth and barely any tangible assets. In the summer of 2001, the state reported that 56 percent of the more than 200 medical groups in the state failed at least one of the four measures of fiscal solvency in the first quarter. Groups were first required to report this information to the Department of Managed Health Care in March 2001. The public reporting of this information is being disputed between the California Medical Association and the California Department of Managed Health Care, a fact that underlines the significance of the situation.

Despite this report from California, health plans reported a decrease in plan failures from 2000 to 2001 and appear to be stabilizing in general. On the other hand, hospitals, particularly in rural areas, have experienced a significant increase in closures associated with insufficent funds to continue operations and constitutional prohibitions against insolvency.

Q 8:58 What are the warning signs of impending insolvency?

According to a report published by Cain Brothers Investment Bankers and Capital Advisors, there are 13 warning signs that forecast a potential risk of bankruptcy:

1. Increase in accounts receivable and/or accounts payable;
2. Decrease in operating margin;
3. Decrease in cash;
4. Decrease in market share;
5. Loss of key admitting physicians;
6. Inability to measure monthly financial and operating performance and report it in a timely manner to the members of the board;
7. Negative variations from approved budgets;
8. Inability of the organization to respond to regulatory actions or placing blame on regulatory actions for all problems;
9. Turnover of advisors (including especially legal or accounting advisors);
10. Rating agency debt downgrades and/or change of outlook to negative;

11. Violations of restrictive covenants contained in borrowing and credit enhancement agreements;

12. Evidence that there is not independence on financial issues (such as preferred loans to management);

13. Management recommendations to diversify to increase revenue when internal operations are not well controlled.

Trustees and management both need to be focused on proactively attending to these warning signs and taking action when necessary to avoid similar situations.[19]

Q 8:59 Under what circumstances can a debtor obtain financing to continue operations while reorganizing the company under Chapter 11 of the Bankruptcy Code?

An important Chapter 11 financing concept related to, but distinct from, the use of cash collateral is debtor-in-possession financing (DIP financing). DIP financing is often employed when the amount of available cash collateral may not be sufficient to permit the debtor to operate in Chapter 11 at a level of productivity or profitability necessary to the formulation of a reorganization plan. DIP financing is the provision of new loans to the debtor in Chapter 11 generally secured by a line of credit on all or substantially all of the debtor's pre–Chapter 11 and post–Chapter 11 assets. DIP financing is best employed when the debtor can be reorganized readily through the judicious rejection of burdensome contracts, through the sale of unnecessary assets, and through creditors' readily identifying incentives for cooperating with the debtor.

Q 8:60 Who is eligible to be a debtor under the Bankruptcy Code?

Section 109 of the Bankruptcy Code sets forth the entities eligible to seek bankruptcy relief. An individual, corporation, or partnership may seek reorganization protection under Chapter 11. A debtor need not demonstrate insolvency or an inability to pay debts as a condition for filing. [11 USC § 109(b)(2), (d)] There is a split in case law, however, as to whether HMOs or other insuring organizations are eligible entities because they may be deemed domestic insurance providers.

In evaluating HMO eligibility to be a debtor, the courts use one of three basic tests: (1) the independent classification test, which relies on Congress's failure to expressly exclude HMOs from bankruptcy; (2) the state classification test, which relies on the state's definition of an insurance company; and (3) the alternative relief test, which allows courts to look at available state procedures and congressional intent to determine whether bankruptcy relief is available.

Q 8:61   How does a bankruptcy case start?

A voluntary bankruptcy case under either Chapter 7 or Chapter 11 of the Bankruptcy Code is initiated with the filing of a petition with the bankruptcy court by the eligible debtor. [11 USC § 301] This filing automatically constitutes an "order for relief" under the chapter and results in an automatic "stay," which prevents creditor organizations from taking any action against the debtor organization. No allegation of insolvency is required; however, the petition must be filed in "good faith" and not in an effort to deter or harass creditors. The court will look to a state's corporate laws with respect to any authorities required to file the petition.

Under Chapter 11, a debtor is authorized to continue to operate its business for the benefit of creditors without receiving preapproval of each action by the bankruptcy court as long as the operations are "in the ordinary course of business." The debtor's management and board of directors remain in control of the debtor's business operations, subject to certain restrictions and the oversight of the creditors' committee or the U.S. trustee. A Chapter 11 debtor-in-possession can exercise all the powers of a trustee (see Q 8:64).

An involuntary bankruptcy petition may be filed if a debtor has fewer than 12 creditors, and one creditor with a claim of at least $10,000 that is not contingent as to liability and not subject to a bona fide dispute. [11 USC § 303(b)(3)(A)] If a debtor has more than 12 creditors holding claims, three of such creditors with claims aggregating at least $10,000 more than the value of any liens against the debtor's property must join in an involuntary petition. The debtor has 20 days after service of a summons to contest or accept the involuntary petition. Creditors may seek to liquidate a debtor by filing an involuntary petition under Chapter 7 or may seek to reorganize the debtor and preserve its "going concern" value by filing an involuntary petition under Chapter 11. Creditors of a tax-exempt, nonprofit organization, however, may not file an involuntary bankruptcy petition. [11 USC § 303(a)] In cases involving a health care facility, particularly if nonprofit, the primary purpose of a Chapter 11 filing is to allow the facility to be reorganized, either through a sale of all assets as an operating concern or to restructure its debt.

Between the time of petition and plan confirmation, the DIP will face numerous issues, such as (1) attempts by creditors to obtain relief from stay; (2) court permission to use cash collateral (the DIP cannot use cash unless ordered by the court to do so); (3) obtaining postpetition credit; and (4) efforts to force assumption or rejection of executory contracts. Before confirmation, the debtor must have a disclosure statement that is approved by the bankruptcy court and contains sufficient information concerning the plan that an informed creditor can make an informed judgment about the plan. [11 USC § 1125] Once the disclosure statement has been sent to all creditors and interest holders, the plan must be confirmed by the bankruptcy judge after a hearing. [11 USC §§ 1128, 1129] The plan of reorganization may not, as a general rule, allow the owners of a debtor to retain ownership interest in the debtor unless all other creditors of a higher priority (including unsecured creditors) are paid in full. If the plan is "fair and equitable," the bankruptcy court may confirm the plan over the objections of the dissenting classes through a process known as "cram down." [11 USC § 1129(b)] On confirmation, the DIP is fully discharged of all debts, claims, and interests arising prior to confirmation [11 USC § 1141(d)] and becomes reinvested with all property of the bankruptcy estate, and most important, such reinvestment is "free and clear" of all interest and claims. [11 USC § 1141(b), (c)] The plan must be implemented "postconfirmation." Usually, the bankruptcy court maintains jurisdiction to hear all matters concerning the plan.

Q 8:62   Who are the key players in a bankruptcy case and what are their roles?

The key players in a bankruptcy proceeding are (1) the debtor-in-possession; (2) the unsecured creditors through their official representative, the unsecured creditors committee; (3) the U.S. Trustee; (4) major secured creditors, lessors, and holders of key contracts (e.g., payers, provider groups); and (5) the bankruptcy judge.

Debtor-in-Possession. The entity that files for reorganization under Chapter 11 of the Bankruptcy Code is called a debtor-in-possession, or DIP, after filing because the entity (now a debtor) remains in control of its business during the bankruptcy proceeding unless a trustee is appointed or the case is dismissed or converted to a Chapter 7 liquidation proceeding. [11 USC § 1101(1)]

Unsecured Creditors Committee. An unsecured creditors committee (UCC) usually consists of 6 to 12 creditors (usually those having a large claim or a particular interest in the debtor) appointed by the U.S. Trustee at the first meeting of creditors. The UCC represents unsecured creditors as a whole; this means it must take positions adverse to any single creditor or group of creditors when it is in the best interest of the unsecured creditors, as a whole, to do so. The scope of the UCC's role and duties is set forth in Bankruptcy Code Section 1103 . Its primary role is oversight: the right to investigate and to be heard on all issues. [11 USC § 1103] The UCC plays an important role in (1) supporting the DIP against secured creditors, government agencies, and others who often try to "overcontrol" or shut down the DIP and (2) supporting the DIP in confirming the plan of reorganization. The UCC's interest is to protect the unsecured creditor's ability to receive a distribution or benefit from the reorganization process.

U.S. Trustee. The U.S. Trustee is responsible for general supervision of administration of all bankruptcy cases. [28 USC § 586(a)(3), (b)] Important powers include (1) ability to appoint a creditor committee, (2) right to be heard on all matters on all issues, and (3) power to issue its own rules and regulations regarding various reporting requirements concerning financial matters.[20]

Bankruptcy Judge. Before 1997, the bankruptcy judge (then known as the referee) had significant day-to-day control over all judicial and administrative aspects of a bankruptcy case. Today, most bankruptcy judges perform legal functions such as (1) establishing short discovery periods to cause settlements in lawsuits and (2) using pretrial conferences in adversary proceedings and contested matters to make their position clear in order to force settlement. Almost all trials before the bankruptcy judge are "judge" trials.

Q 8:63 What is the ultimate goal of a Chapter 11 case?

The ultimate goal of a Chapter 11 case is a confirmation and consummation of a plan of reorganization that effectuates the method of reorganization. A plan of reorganization is basically a contract between the debtor and its creditors that sets forth how each creditor is to be treated, a means for effectuating the plan, and how each claim or creditor will be treated. The plan divides all claims into different classes, based on the nature and priority of claims, and all creditors within a class must be treated the same. Only a debtor can file a plan of reorganization. [11 USC § 1121(b)] After the expiration of 120 days, however, any party in interest (including a competitor combining with one or more creditors) can file. [11 USC § 1121(c)] The debtor then loses complete control over its case and, ultimately, its facility.

The key benefit to reorganization of a health care facility is the broad discharge granted by a Chapter 11 plan confirmation order. [11 USC § 1141(c)] It even discharges claims that were not discovered until after confirmation unless the debtor engaged in some misconduct regarding the claim.[21]

Q 8:64   What are the critical stages in a bankruptcy case?

Bankruptcy requires careful planning and execution to achieve the desired outcome, particularly in Chapter 11 cases. The critical stages include (1) prebankruptcy planning, (2) initial stages of the bankruptcy proceedings, (3) continued facility operations, and (4) reorganization. The approaches to managing these issues will differ between debtor and creditor.

Suggestions for debtors include the following:

1. Prior to filing bankruptcy, meet with all existing significant lenders and attempt to strike a prefiling agreement on use of cash collateral or continue or obtain new financing.

2. Prior to filing, meet with critical payers and attempt to reach an understanding or agreement on postfiling payment for services so that postpetition cash flow can be maximized by reducing possible recoupment efforts.

3. Review the special conflict rules regarding professional persons and make sure there is bankruptcy counsel at the outset of the case that cannot be disqualified.

4. Identify the need for outside professionals and have them available for proceedings.

5. Prepare for postpetition litigation involving cash collateral, adequate protection, and relief from stay by accumulating information in preparation of the case.

6. Prior to filing, try to obtain a cash collateral stipulation from secured lenders for a two- to three-week period.

7. Immediately begin gathering financial data and other documents needed to continue operations by preparing key reports for the U.S. Trustee and include long-term projections of cash flow for use in future "adequate protection" arguments and for objections to relief from stay.

8. "Forum shop" to the extent possible.

9. If the goal is to reorganize through a sale, start hiring a marketing expert and start marketing as soon as possible.

10. Prepare due diligence materials.

11. Analyze future operating requirements and cash flow requirements to determine whether a loan will be needed in the future.

12. Adhere to the debtor's exclusivity period at all costs.

13. Use the time between the filing of a petition and the filing of a plan of reorganization to reach as many agreements with competitors as possible.

14. Become allied with the UCC.

15. Market nationally and include both for-profit and not-for-profit entities.

16. Use publicity and political action to increase pressure on state agencies to (a) reduce or subordinate their claims and (b) support the particular plan of the debtor.

17. Emphasize the policy goals of the state to cause it to reduce claims, particularly Medicaid claims.

18. Use broad notice and end dates of key procedural events to quantify and limit the amount and kind of claims so that as many creditors and parties as possible will be bound to the plan of reorganization.

19. Provide extensive notice of key events, particularly the plan of reorganization, to maximize the chances that the sale will be free and clear.

20. Be sure that the plan, the disclosure statement, and the con-
    firmation order contain key provisions concerning successor
    liability (property being sold free and clear of all liens, to the
    fullest extent of the discharge).

21. Use discharge of liability to bolster the value of the sale.

Suggestions for creditors include the following:

1. File proofs of claims and special requests for notice, despite
   notices to the contrary.

2. Serve on the UCC.

3. Obtain and review as much ongoing financial information
   related to the DIP as possible.

4. Maintain consultant contact with counsel for the UCC.

5. For secured creditors, require the debtor to provide adequate
   protection.

6. For payers and providers, force assumption or rejection of
   executory contracts at the earliest date possible.

7. Use any available remedy allowed despite automatic stay.

8. Use the period from filing to the commencement of the plan
   process to reach a deal with the DIP.

9. Create opportunities to obtain leverage in negotiating a good
   deal.

10. Do not oppose everything the debtor seeks unless it affects
    creditor interests directly.

11. Review the plan and disclosure statement and be involved
    in the confirmation process.

Q 8:65 What is the benefit of using bankruptcy to unwind an integrated delivery system?

The benefit of using bankruptcy to unwind an integrated delivery
system in its ability to allow the sale of all or substantially all of the
assets of the system, or the assets of the integrated subsidiary, free
and clear of any liens, interests, or claims of third parties (see chapter
10). This must be done under the direct supervision and with the
approval of the bankruptcy court.

The Bankruptcy Code also provides special treatment for contracts entered into prior to the filing of the petition when material

performance remains incomplete (executory contracts) for both parties and for unexpired nonresidential real property leases. Executory contracts include provider agreements with Medicare or Medicaid programs or other third-party payers, employment and independent contractor agreements, joint venture agreements, supply contracts, and leases of real or personal property. It is unlikely, however, that any contract with a specified doctor can be assumed and assigned over the objection of the contracting physician. [11 USC § 365(e)(2)(A)] Executory contracts can be treated in one of three ways: (1) the debtor can assume them, so they constitute ongoing, postpetition obligations of the company; (2) the debtor can assume them and then assign them to other parties; or (3) the debtor can reject them, in which case the debtor is no longer bound. [11 USC § 365(a)–(c), (f)]

Using what is called a "cramdown" provision of a plan of reorganization, the plan of reorganization can provide for the integrated delivery system debtor to consummate any corporate transaction, including the sale of assets to a third party, and merge into a new entity. Using a mechanism that divides creditors into classes, the plan is subject to creditor approval, which does not have to be unanimous. A plan is approved if at least half of the number and two thirds of the dollar amount of claims in each class vote in favor of the plan. [11 USC § 1126(c)] The effect of the positive vote is to "cram down" the plan on dissenters within a consenting class, who will all be bound to the terms of the plan as long as it does not discriminate between members of the dissenting class.

Q 8:66   How have the states handled failing HMOs?

HMOs are not immune from the economic stress in the managed care market. Unlike other health care entities such as hospitals or nursing homes, HMOs have separate obligations relating to insuring and covering the health care costs of members who subscribe. Most state insurance laws focus on solvency standards in the interest of consumer protection.

Under Massachusetts General Laws Chapter 143, insolvent HMOs will be removed from liquidation under federal bankruptcy laws. The statute grants protections to HMO members, hospitals, and providers. It provides a safety net for members by giving them a 30-day period in which they can switch health carriers without any restrictions on preexisting conditions. The first case to test this law involved Harvard Pilgrim Health Care. Under the law, the Massachusetts Attorney General obtained a court order placing Harvard Pilgrim Health Care into receivership after getting word that the company expected losses for fiscal 1999 to exceed original projections. [Ruthardt v Harvard Pilgrim Health Care, No SJ-2000-0003 (Mass order Jan 4, 2000)]

The California Department of Managed Health Care took over a failing nonprofit HMO following a state audit of the HMO's financial records. The state ordered corrective action, but in the absence of sufficient cash flow, the HMO was unable to continue to implement the corrective action, necessitating the state's intervention.[22]

Finally, some states have passed legislation to "bail out" failing HMOs. In New Jersey, the legislation uses a "Robin Hood" approach by requiring new plans in New Jersey to contribute to a fund intended to salvage two failed plans. In April 2000, the New Jersey governor signed legislation requiring HMOs that do business in New Jersey at any time during the next three years to contribute a total of $50 million to help repay the debts of two failed HMOs. The New Jersey Insolvent Health Maintenance Organization Assistance Fund Act of 2000 creates a $100 million fund to compensate physicians and hospitals for services they provided to members of the now-defunct HIP Health Plan of New Jersey and American Preferred Provider Plan before the state declared them insolvent in 1998. The state estimated the two plans owed providers a total of $150 million. To receive any reimbursement from the fund for unpaid claims, providers are required to forgive one third of the amount owed to them. The legislation calls for New Jersey's 16 commercial HMOs to pay a total of $50 million in equal installments over a three-year period into the fund. The industry contribution is augmented by $50 million from money the state receives under the national tobacco settlement.

Q 8:67 What effect has managed care had on the number of bankruptcy filings in health care?

The change in and amounts of reimbursement under Medicare, the delays in payment by health plans, and other factors leading to severe financial distress have led a number of health care organizations to seek protection of the bankruptcy courts as a means of avoiding further losses. Long-term care has been affected dramatically by these changes. In a recent press release published in *IHS Medicare/Medicaid Update,*[23] the Multicare Companies and a principal owner, Genesis Health Ventures, were reported to have filed for Chapter 11 bankruptcy protection citing drastic unanticipated cuts in Medicare reimbursements. Multicare Companies, based in Kennett Square, Pennsylvania, has obtained as much as $50 million in short-term working capital through Mellon Bank to continue to operate its 141 nursing home facilities nationwide. It reported that deep cuts in Medicare reimbursements, which far exceeded all government forecasts, coupled with chronic underfunding of Medicaid reimbursements, severely impacted its ability to service its current capital structure.

Skilled nursing facilities (long-term care) are not the only sector of the health care industry affected by changes in Medicare, Medicaid, and managed care. Hospitals are experiencing substantial cuts in revenues. The Balanced Budget Act of 1997 (BBA) alone accounted for $50 to $70 billion in Medicare cuts for 1998 through 2002. Most payment reductions are "end-loaded," which means that the major cuts take effect in 2001 and 2002.

HMOs and health plans are also facing major financial difficulties. The number of employees enrolled in HMOs has declined, profit margins have decreased, and government regulation has increased along with legal liability.

Q 8:68   What are the special issues involved in reorganizing health care entities?

Because of the extensive regulation of the health care industry, use of the bankruptcy process must be balanced against the special issues associated with licensed, Medicare-certified health care entities. Issues that are unique to health care entities include (1) recoupment, (2) executory contracts, and (3) conflicts with state or federal regulatory agencies.

Recoupment. There has been much litigation over the right of a private payer, including Medicare, to exercise the doctrine of recoupment to recover prefiling overpayments to facilities after the filing of a bankruptcy petition.[24]

Executory Contracts. An executory contract is a contract "pursuant to which the obligations of both parties are so far unperformed

that the failure of either party to complete performance would constitute material breach."[25] When in bankruptcy, a troubled health care
entity may reject or terminate a burdensome executory contract or
assume or assign favorable executory contracts despite termination
limitations or antiassignment clauses in the contract. [11 USC § 363]
On the other side of the coin, the ability of a holder of an executory
contract to force the DIP to assume or reject the contract provides
substantial leverage to lessors, payers, or providers. If a contract is
assumed, the DIP can and must pay all prefiling debt owed under
the contract and provide "adequate assurance of future performance." [11 USC § 365(b)(1)(C)] This topic is discussed in more
detail in Q 8:72.

Interplay Between Bankruptcy and State Regulatory Agencies. Various state agencies exercise control over a health care entity's day-
to-day operations and have control over the restructuring or sale of
the health care facility directly or indirectly through such powers as
licensing, certificates of need (CON), and Medicaid. The state will
often be a holder of large claims against the DIP because of amounts
owed for state income tax, sales tax, licensing fees, and Medicaid
and other state programs. These payment programs often pay for
the anticipated health care services on a prospective interim payment (PIP), which is paid in advance to a facility based on historical
usage. This means that the state wears several hats: (1) creditor for
pure state debts, (2) claims payer under Medicaid, (3) facility regulator and licensor overseeing consumer protection and quality health
care, (4) enforcer of CON laws, (5) economic developer maintaining
jobs in the community, (6) recipient of tax income from facilities,
and (7) political entity.

Q 8:69   What is the impact of bankruptcy on members of an integrated delivery system's board of directors?

The obligations of an integrated delivery system's board members
before, during, and after a bankruptcy proceeding are governed by
corporate law and the fiduciary duty of care and loyalty. Board members should be aware that their fiduciary duties shift from shareholders to creditors after a corporation files for bankruptcy, but they may
not be aware of director duties in the "zone of insolvency." In some
states, boards operating near insolvency owe allegiance to the corporate enterprise as a whole; this puts creditor and shareholder inter-

ests on an equal footing. In other states, fiduciary duty to the creditor comes first. In either case, directors can be sued for breach of duty if they do not act to pay back debts as soon as possible.

Essentially, the governance and other corporate activities should continue as before. Board members who act in good faith with respect to a plan of reorganization are generally subject to immunity from liability.

Q 8:70 Does bankruptcy shield a corporation and its officers, directors, and advisors from liability?

It is clear that bankruptcy protects a company from its creditors on insolvency, but not from its conduct in becoming insolvent. This was highlighted in the bankruptcy of the nonprofit, tax-exempt Allegheny Health, Education, and Research Foundation (AHERF), which resulted in a number of lawsuits by public and private organizations against AHERF executives and advisors on the basis of their conduct before, during, and after seeking bankruptcy court protection.

AHERF had grown from a single Pittsburgh hospital in 1986 to a statewide network in 1997 of 14 hospitals and 304 other sites employing 31,000 people. From July 1997 to May 1998, the system abruptly lost $330 million. In bankruptcy papers filed in July 1998, AHERF declared $1.3 billion in debt and 65,000 creditors. Following this "crash," in February 2000, claims were brought by the Pennsylvania Attorney General and Tenet Health Systems (Tenet) seeking nearly $80 million from former officials of the bankrupt AHERF who had allegedly transferred the money out of charitable trust accounts as the hospital system collapsed. [In re Allegheny Health, Educ, & Research Found, (No 98-25773 Bankr WD Pa filed Feb 23, 2000)] Tenet joined the complaint because it had purchased eight AHERF hospitals in a bankruptcy sale for $345 million in November 1998 and was required to maintain two tax-exempt foundations, the Philadelphia Health and Education Corp. and the Philadelphia Health and Research Corp., to protect the remaining charitable assets. The action alleged eight counts of violations of state charitable laws and fiduciary duties, negligence, and conspiracy. The complaint asked the bankruptcy court for judgments against the defendants, jointly and severally, on compensatory and punitive damages to be decided at trial, plus attorneys' fees.

In March 2000, the AG filed criminal charges against three former key executives of the bankrupt AHERF claiming it illegally spent $52.4 million in charitable endowments between February and July 1998 to postpone the health system's financial collapse. [Pennsylvania v Abdelhak, No CR-113-2000 (Pa CP filed Mar 15, 2000); Pennsylvania v McConnell, No CR-114-2000 (Pa CP filed Mar 15, 2000); Pennsylvania v Wynstra, No CR-118-00 (Pa CP filed Mar 20, 2000)]

To make matters more complex, four former employees of the bankrupt AHERF were allowed to proceed with their civil racketeering claims against 16 former AHERF trustees and top managers on the basis of alleged fraud by management and trustees. [Spitzer v Abdelhak, (No 98-CV-6475 ED Pa, memorandum and order Dec 15, 1999)] In that case, plaintiffs claimed the loss of patients and income and harm to their reputations they allegedly suffered as a result of the alleged fraud would have occurred even if AHERF and its Philadelphia-area operations had not filed for bankruptcy. The tentative settlement filed in January 2002, would restore $90 million to intended charitable recipients.

Q 8:71 Can individuals who have defrauded Medicare use bankruptcy to avoid liability and payment of civil monetary penalties?

Under current bankruptcy law, most individuals and entities that file for bankruptcy, including health care providers, are entitled to protections that put a hold on creditors' recovery efforts. This "loophole" in the Bankruptcy Code allows debtors, including those who have defrauded Medicare, to avoid recovery efforts by declaring bankruptcy.

Q 8:72 Can bankruptcy be used by the debtor to terminate executory contracts?

Yes. Executory contracts comprise the various contractual agreements to which the debtor is a party. The primary legal characteristic of an executory contract is that, at the time of the bankruptcy filing, there remain unperformed material obligations held by each party to the contract. Examples of executory contracts are real estate leases, equipment leases, intellectual property licenses, insurance policies, managed care contracts, and collective bargaining agreements with employees.

The Bankruptcy Code permits the debtor to reject an executory contract to the extent the debtor demonstrates that it is excessively burdensome to its ongoing operations. During the period before a court order authorizes such rejection, the debtor may be required to remain current on its financial obligations under the contract pending rejection by the court. For example, if the debtor seeks to reject a real estate lease in bankruptcy, it may be required to continue to pay rent under the terms of the lease until the court enters a rejection order.

The Bankruptcy Code contains special provisions for the protection of the rights of the nondebtor parties when the debtor is a lessor of real estate or a licensor of intellectual property. Even if the debtor elects to reject the real estate lease or intellectual property license, the nondebtor party to the contract may continue to enforce its rights for the remainder of the term of the contract and any contractually stipulated renewals. The debtor is simply relieved of any financial obligations it may have under the terms of the lease or contract.

Q 8:73   What is the effect of a bankruptcy on employment relations?

If the business is not a "going concern," but rather is winding up its affairs, the amounts owed to employees as back pay may not be given priority in a bankruptcy proceeding, even in view of the Worker Adjustment and Retraining Notification (WARN) Act. The WARN Act requires employers to inform their employees and holds the employers liable for back pay; however, in a Third Circuit case [In re United Healthcare Sys, Inc, Official Comm of Unsecured Creditors of United Healthcare Sys, Inc v United Healthcare Sys, Inc, No 98-6490 (3d Cir, Dec 29, 1999)], the court would not treat the 1,300 furloughed employees as being entitled to back pay and found that they were not entitled to first priority administrative claim status in the bankruptcy proceeding.

Q 8:74   Are Medicare fraud proceedings subject to the automatic stay in bankruptcy?

It depends. Medicare has the right to suspend payments to a health care provider if it has evidence of fraud being committed by the provider or that an overpayment exists. Providers often seek injunctive relief to compel Medicare to continue postpetition payments, arguing that suspension violates the automatic stay. [11 USC § 362(a)(1)] The government usually argues that the suspension is exempt from the automatic stay as an exercise of its regulatory powers.

The determination of whether the stay applies is based on a two-part test: (1) the public policy test and (2) the pecuniary interest test. Under the pecuniary interest test, the bankruptcy court must determine whether the government action relates primarily to the protection of the government unit's pecuniary interest in the debtor's property. Government proceedings intended to safeguard a pecuniary interest are subject to stay. Under the public policy test, the bankruptcy court has to determine whether the government unit is attempting to enforce its policy or regulatory power or to adjudicate private rights.

When a debtor is facing a fraud investigation, bankruptcy is often a consideration, in part to avoid the defense costs associated with pending litigation. The automatic stay of bankruptcy, however, is not likely to shelter a debtor from the costs of such litigation. In fact, False Claims Act cases brought by the U.S. government may continue through enforcement of judgment as an exercise of the government's policy powers.[26]

Q 8:75   What efforts has Congress made to change the laws relating to Medicare and health care insolvency?

Bankruptcy reform legislation approved by Congress includes three very important changes affecting the health care industry: the automatic appointment of a "patient ombudsman" to protect and defend the interests of patients; a process for disposition of patients' medical records by bankrupt providers; and an exception to the automatic stay to permit the federal government to exercise its right to exclude providers from participation in the Medicare program. As of February 2002, this bill, HR 333, was still in conference.

Corporate Practice of Medicine

Q 8:76   What is the corporate practice of medicine doctrine?

Under this doctrine, a corporation cannot practice medicine or employ or retain a physician as its agent to practice medicine. This doctrine, which exists in a number of states, prohibits a lay corporation or individual from employing a licensed physician, receiving his or her fees, or in any way influencing the delivery of medical services unless the individual is a physician or the corporation or entity is owned or controlled entirely by physicians. This doctrine is based on the principle that businesses, organizations, and entities that are not licensed by the state to practice medicine cannot engage in medical practice and exploit the special relationship between a physician and his or her patients.

In analyzing corporate practice problems, considerations include the degree of control by a lay entity over professional judgment; the potential for a lay entity to exploit the physician-patient relationship commercially; and the conflict of interest arising between physician and patient attributable to the influence of a nonphysician third party.

Corporate practice issues often arise in the context of employment, professional organizations, and fee splitting associated with physicians and medical practice. With respect to the third situation, in many states a licensed professional cannot divide and share a professional fee or profit with another professional or nonlicensed person. Some states expressly prohibit this activity; others treat fee splitting as assisting in the unauthorized practice of a licensed profession.

Q 8:77 What is the legal basis for the corporate practice of medicine doctrine?

Most corporate practice of medicine prohibitions are grounded in state licensing laws. The doctrine has also developed under common law based on public policy concerns. One of the earliest decisions in this area, *Painless Parker v. Board of Dental Examiners* [216 Cal 85, 14 P 2d 67 (1932)], involved a corporation formed to provide dental services through the employment of salaried dentists. In that case, the California Supreme Court held that the actions of the corporation violated the state's unlawful practice statutes and that Dr. Parker, the dentist, violated the state's aiding and abetting statute.

In recent years, the doctrine has been criticized as archaic in light of changes in the health care delivery system. Some states have narrowed the application of the doctrine, either through legislation or through court decisions. Even states that historically upheld the prohibition against the corporate practice of medicine, such as Texas and California, have seen this policy erode over time. The California Supreme Court denied review of an appellate court ruling that the state's corporate practice of medicine ban does not apply to University of California hospitals, even if the university operates facilities that may compete for paying patients with privately owned providers. [California Med Ass'n v Regents of the Univ of Cal, No S084269 (Cal June 21, 2000)] This landmark case overturns years of case law upholding the corporate practice prohibition in all circumstances in favor of allowing a state institution to engage in the practice of medicine without using the nonprofit health clinic exception. The statutory exception to the corporate practice of medicine has been used in Texas and California by organizing a nonprofit corporation to provide health care services.[27] This situation is discussed further in chapter 6.

Q 8:78   Do all states prohibit the corporate practice of medicine?

Not exactly. Although all states have some form of medical practice act setting standards and qualifications required for an individual to obtain a license to practice medicine, states vary in both their interpretation and their enforcement of activities that would constitute the corporate practice of medicine. Consequently, no clear rule defines the scope of the corporate practice of medicine, which must be addressed on a case-by-case as well as a state-by-state basis.

In some states, any person or entity can employ or contract with physicians. Other states allow only certain entities to employ or contract with physicians. Still others allow specific entities to contract with physicians only on an independent contractor basis. Finally, some states allow only licensed professional corporations, other physicians, or physician-owned entities to employ or contract for medical professional services.[28]

Q 8:79   How do corporate practice of medicine issues affect managed care and provider organizations?

In the context of managed care and integrated delivery systems, corporate practice of medicine laws may affect the ability of a risk-sharing organization to provide both professional and facility services, or to establish a single-provider risk-sharing organization. These state-imposed limitations on corporate practice may have an important effect on the form and structure as well as the manner of operation of PSOs.

In the IPA relationship with its physicians, unless the IPA is organized as a recognized "medical practice" entity, there may be corporate practice issues if the IPA attempts to hold the provider contract and assume direct obligations to provide the medical or professional services. PHOs that operate in a corporate practice jurisdiction cannot employ physicians or hold the managed care contract for the provision of medical or professional services. Often, the PHO serves as a contracting vehicle only, facilitating the contract with the managed care company or payer on behalf of the physicians and hospital. An MSO, unlike a provider organization, serves a business purpose and has some risk for fee splitting if the payment arrangement for management services is not structured properly. For example, payment on the basis of a percentage of gross revenues does not have the appearance of profit sharing between the physician or medical group and MSO that payment on the basis of a percentage of net revenues might have.

Q 8:80 Is the corporate practice of medicine doctrine an anachronism under current managed care structures?

Many take the position that the corporate practice of medicine doctrine is no longer necessary to protect consumers from those who would exploit the sacred trust between physician and patient. Because it limits the manner in which organizations can provide health care services, contracting and capitation arrangements are affected by the doctrine.

Others say that in view of the exceptions available in most states that maintain strict enforcement, and in view of the ability in most states to circumvent the corporate practice of medicine through "captive" practices, the doctrine is no longer effective. Most states that have strictly enforced corporate practice doctrines also have specific exceptions to allow physicians to provide services through a corporate structure. For example, IPAs can be organized as professional organizations permitted by statute to engage in medical practice by contracting with physicians. Other methods include the use of MSOs to manage the business and administrative activities not associated with clinical practice. (See chapter 6 for more detail on MSOs and "captive" practices.) Many state HMO acts contain an express corporate practice exception, which permits an HMO to employ or contract with physicians and other licensed professionals.

Credentialing and Peer Review

Q 8:81 What are credentialing and peer review?

Credentialing. Credentialing is a risk management function that involves the review of the clinical competence, training, and experience of practitioners who seek to provide care to patients in a hospital, clinic, medical group, or managed care setting. In the health care industry, it provides a means of quality control through the application of minimum standards to the particular practice situation. The primary purpose of credentialing is to ensure that the individual practitioner providing medical care is competent and qualified. Credentialing is an ongoing process that begins with the establishment of standards and criteria against which applicants can be reviewed. It is important to have a systematic way to evaluate practitioners.

Peer Review. Peer review is the review of a practitioner's clinical skills and professional conduct by a committee composed of the practitioner's peers. Entities that engage in a credentialing program perform regular and ongoing review of clinical practice activities using a peer review process based on quality and utilization criteria.

Credentialing and peer review in managed care are subject to a number of legal and accreditation considerations.

Q 8:82 What standards are used in the credentialing process?

Most standards used in the credentialing process come from the accreditation organizations involved with MCOs. As discussed in chapter 10, consumers are demanding higher standards of quality in health care, and purchasers are seeking to ensure that MCOs can provide quality care by requiring accreditation by a recognized organization. Major accrediting organizations that establish standards for credentialing include the following:

- National Committee on Quality Assurance (NCQA)[29]
- Joint Commission on Accreditation of Healthcare Organizations (JCAHO)[30]
- Commission (URAC)[31]
- Accreditation Association for Ambulatory Health Care (AAAHC)[32]
- AMA's "American Medical Accreditation Program" (available in New Jersey and the District of Columbia)

These organizations are discussed in more detail in chapter 10.

Q 8:83　Why is credentialing important in managed care?

Credentialing is done in managed care for several reasons:

- To comply with federal and state legal requirements
- To achieve organizational accreditation
- To reduce liability for unqualified practitioners
- For marketing purposes

Courts have long held hospitals liable when practitioners on their medical staffs are found negligent. [Johnson v Miseracordia Comm Hosp, 99 Wis 2d 708, 301 NW 2d 156 (1981)] This principle is now being applied in the context of managed care to hold HMOs, insurance companies, and even employers liable to enrollees or employees for selection of negligent providers. In *Harrell v. Total Health Care, Inc.* [781 SW 2d 58 (Mo 1989)], the court of appeals indicated that an HMO had a duty to protect its members from foreseeable risk of harm and would have imposed on the HMO a duty to conduct a reasonable investigation of the physician applicants. This duty is similar to that of hospitals to impose an independent duty to credential members of the medical staff. In *McClellan v. Health Maintenance Organization of Pennsylvania* [413 Pa 128, 604 A 2d 1053 (Pa Super Ct 1992), *appeal denied,* 616 A 2d 985], a Pennsylvania court held that the plaintiff had a cause of action against an IPA-model HMO for liability resulting from actions of a contract provider.

Thus, the managed care entity employer or insurer has a duty to evaluate the expertise of the and its provider selection and monitoring criteria. The theories under which an MCO may be held liable include (1) corporate negligence for negligent supervision and credentialing; (2) *respondeat superior*, which holds an employer responsible for the negligent acts of its employees; and (3) ostensible agency, which is based on the perception by an injured patient that an agency relationship exists between the parties, thereby justifying vicarious liability of one to the other for one party's negligence (see discussion of liability issues, beginning at Q 8:181). With the federal government and many states considering legislation to allow direct claims against health plans and MCOs for the legal liability consequences of their utilization review decisions, there is increased focus on credentialing as an important risk management tool.

Q 8:84 What is involved in the credentialing process?

Application. The credentialing process is initiated with a request for application. Some hospitals and provider networks use the request for application as a screening tool to ascertain the general eligibility and fitness of a prospective applicant. This "preapplication" process has been used successfully to avoid the cumbersome and expensive "due process" required under most state laws, under HCQIA, and as a condition of most accreditation organizations such as JCAHO and NCQA. The application should contain, at a minimum, the information listed in Figure 8-1. Figure 8-2 is a checklist of primary source documents for evaluating an applicant.

Information Verification. Verification of the information on the application is of central importance in managed care. The AMA, many state medical associations, and private organizations such as InterQual maintain a data bank for physician information and, for a fee, will make profile information on physicians and other licensed practitioners available. Much of this information is available on the Internet as well. NCQA allows verification from certain organizations as sufficient primary source information. Information that requires primary source verification includes (1) licensure; (2) controlled substance registration with the Drug Enforcement Administration (DEA); (3) board certification or eligibility; (4) training (routine if practicing medicine for fewer than ten years); (5) hospital affiliations; and (6) professional liability insurance and malpractice experience. Query of the National Practitioner Data Bank (NPDB) is required under NCQA and JCAHO accreditation standards. The NPDB was established as part of the HCQIA as a data repository for records of adverse actions or claims and settlements involving physicians. There is a mandatory obligation for hospitals to query the NPDB as well as to report when adverse actions have been taken.

Valid Selection Criteria. The MCO should have written provider selection criteria for evaluating each complete application. Those criteria will differ depending on the organization's structure, contracting strategy, and circumstances. The most important aspect of this part of the process is to be sure that the criteria are objective and are applied consistently to all applications. Only after review and approval of the application should the prospective participating provider be furnished with an agreement that describes in much greater detail the terms and conditions of participation in the provider panel.

Delineation of Privileges. NCQA standards require that the credentialing process extend beyond eligibility and fitness evaluation to include specific granting of privileges to participate as a provider in the health plan or network. Included in the review process is an on-site office visit and record review.

Due Process. If the applicant is not approved on the basis of any finding relating to clinical practice or quality, there is a right granted under most state laws to some form of due process before the applicant is rejected. This requirement may be deemed to apply even when the decision not to offer the applicant a contract to participate in the managed care network is based solely on such "nonclinical" reasons as sufficiency of providers in the applicant's specialty, or on purely administrative deficiencies such as lack of specialty board certification.

Figure 8-1. Application for Privileges

1. Personal and business information
   - Name
   - Corporate office name (if different from above)
   - Office and residence addresses and telephone numbers
   - Date of birth, birthplace, citizenship

- Social Security number
- Employer identification number

2. Professional information
   - DEA number and expiration date
   - State licenses and numbers
   - Medicare and Medicaid numbers
   - Education and training
   - References
   - Board certification status
   - Continuing medical education
   - Hospital affiliations, staff category, and privileges
   - Medical society or specialty society and association memberships
   - Malpractice insurance information
   - Managed care plan participation

3. Other office information
   - Patients per day and new patient acceptance
   - Office hours
   - Coverage arrangements
   - Foreign languages, public access accommodations (wheelchairs, etc.)
   - In-office ancillary services

4. Limitations on practice
   - License suspensions or limitations
   - Hospital privilege actions or limitations
   - Malpractice judgment, settlement, or pending claims
   - Other state or federal agency, health care organization, or plan proceedings
   - Other disciplinary actions

5. Health status information
   - Drug or alcohol abuse
   - Chronic or debilitating illnesses

6. Felony charges or convictions

Completeness review of application:

1. Are questions answered and is the application signed?
2. Are copies of requested information included?
3. Are there chronological gaps in professional and practice activities?
4. Are there frequent moves or short stays without justification?
5. Is there documentation of residency, fellowship, and/or formal training in the practice specialty?
6. Is the applicant board certified or eligible?
7. Have there been residency program changes within same-specialty training?
8. Is insurance coverage, limits, and carrier information included?
9. Is other relevant information included?

Figure 8-2. Credentials: Information Checklist

☐ Application (new hire)

☐ Cover letter to accompany application (new hire)

☐ Education (one time)

☐ Residency (one time)

☐ Hospital affiliations (current)

☐ State license (current)

☐ Release statement (current)

☐ Proof of insurance (current)

☐ Copy of licenses (current)

☐ Copy of DEA registration (current)

☐ AMA form

☐ Curriculum vitae (update)

☐ Continuing medical education

Q 8:85   On what basis are most provider credentialing recommendations made?

In MCOs, provider credentialing recommendations are based on several factors: (1) defined needs of the MCO and its contracted payers for different specialties or categories of participating providers; (2) documented clinical competence, training, and experience in the applicant's particular area of practice and geographic location; and (3) capability of the applicant to meet the utilization and quality review standards, as well as economic criteria, established by the MCO for continued participation. Many of the credentialing criteria used in managed care have been developed by such accrediting bodies as the American Accreditation Program, Inc. (AAPI), JCAHO, AAAHC, or NCQA.

NCQA credentialing standards require (1) maintaining written policies and procedures for the credentialing and recredentialing of physicians and dentists every two years according to policies and procedures adopted by the MCO's governing body and implemented through a credentials committee; (2) formal review and approval of the credentialing policies and procedures; (3) credentialing all physicians and other licensed independent practitioners identified in the MCO's marketing or membership literature; (4) designating a credentialing committee or other peer review body to make recommendations regarding credentialing decisions; (5) obtaining, at a minimum, the applicant's license, DEA certificate (drug prescription authority), a training assessment work history, professional liability history, evidence of good standing at a hospital, and evidence of adequate medical malpractice insurance coverage; (6) obtaining a statement by the applicant as to disciplinary activity, physical and mental status, license history, criminal record, lack of impairment, and the correctness and completeness of the application; (7) making inquiries to the NPDB and the applicable state licensing board and as to Medicare and Medicaid sanctions; (8) using an integrated appraisal process including member complaints, quality review results, utilization management records, and member satisfaction surveys; (9) visiting each primary care physician's office to review the site and the physician's recordkeeping; (10) maintaining a written description of delegated activities and the delegate's accountability; and (11) maintaining a mechanism for suspension, reduction, or termination of participation of providers.

Some states have statutes that describe what must be considered in making credentialing decisions. In addition to considerations of competence, character, and patient care concerns, institutional objectives may be considered. [See, e.g., NY Pub Health Law § 2801-b; Fla Stat § 395.011.] Other states include provisions that expressly prohibit an HMO from discriminating against certain types of providers such as chiropractors and psychologists.

Q 8:86 How have different MCOs approached physician credentialing?

Determining who is in and who is out of any managed care provider organization or integrated delivery system is not simple. In the immature managed care market, the tendency is to be overinclusive in order to avoid the political and potential legal issues associated with provider selection. In the more mature managed care markets, however, many provider organizations are making their selection decisions based on legitimate business criteria such as specialty needs, coverage of service area, and economic considerations. With the promulgation of specific credentialing standards by JCAHO and NCQA, the credentialing of physicians has become an important factor in the competitiveness and success of a provider network in contracting with payers.

Q 8:87 Are the laws and standards relating to provider credentialing in managed care consistent?

No. According to a recent study performed by URAC, the laws that govern the manner in which an MCO must investigate the credentials of its physicians vary substantially from state to state. The study also found that the credentialing activities of physician licensure boards differ within individual states as well.[33]

Q 8:88 What should a provider organization consider in developing its credentialing plan?

Based on the standards of the NCQA and JCAHO, it is suggested that a provider organization be selective in its credentialing of participating providers. Whether the provider organization is predominantly primary care in focus, multispecialty in composition, or entirely composed of subspecialists will significantly affect the credentialing program. In addition to routine checks of clinical competence and conduct, provider organizations should focus on the candidate's ability to participate effectively in a managed care arrangement. Exclusivity in provider relationships is another factor. Although exclusivity is desirable for a well-controlled program, its effect on existing referral relationships will need to be considered.

In developing a credentialing plan for selection and deselection of providers, a provider organization should evaluate the relevant antitrust issues, state case law, HCQIA implications, and applicability of state insurance laws (provider protection or "any willing provider" laws).

Q 8:89 What is delegated credentialing and how does it arise in managed care arrangements?

Delegated credentialing is the practice of delegating credentialing to another entity. Many MCOs (PPOs, HMOs, and exclusive provider organizations) and other health service purchasers (employers and third-party administrators) have established criteria based on the particular requirements of the health benefit plan. Plans can either perform their own credentialing at the plan administration level or delegate the credentialing process to the MCO. In organizations such as PHOs or IPAs, it is possible contractually to delegate the credentialing documentation and data gathering to the hospital medical staff office, on proper authorization, to avoid duplication of effort. If an MCO decides to delegate its credentialing responsibility, it should consider a contract that contains the following provisions:

- Retaining the right to approve new providers or sites and to terminate or suspend providers
- Requiring indemnification from the credentialing entity for losses attributable to negligent credentialing
- Ensuring that the credentialing entity carries adequate errors and omissions insurance coverage
- Requiring the MCO to be named as an additional insured

Q 8:90 When an MCO delegates its credentialing responsibilities to a hospital, what information from the NPDB can the hospital share with the MCO?

If the hospital has been given full responsibility for peer review and the MCO plays no role in the peer review process, information obtained from the NPDB query cannot be shared with the MCO. The hospital can share the cover sheet containing the list of names queried as long as the result of each query (match or no match) has been removed. If the practitioner in question has signed a waiver specifically allowing the release of the queried results, the hospital can disclose this NPDB information to the MCO. If the MCO plays a role in the peer review process, the hospital can share the queried information with the MCO provided that it is used for its intended purpose of peer review.

Q 8:91 What is a credentials verification organization?

A credentials verification organization (CVO) is an outside organization that contracts with an MCO, hospital, network, or other health care entity to perform the credentialing or recredentialing function, including primary source verification. If the CVO is accredited by NCQA, URAC, or other accrediting bodies, the health care entity can defer to the CVO the requirement of compliance with accreditation standards.

In selecting a CVO, health care entities should look for certification by a recognized accrediting organization, a proven track record of being able to handle the volume for which it contracts, and electronic data capability. Other issues to consider are whether the CVO provides regular work-in-progress reports and practitioner audit summaries. Does it have specific turnaround or performance standards? Does it have a quality management program to monitor operating performance on an ongoing basis? Can it service allied health credentialing?

Q 8:92 Should MCOs do their own credentialing?

Most MCOs are moving toward performing their own credentialing. Many, however, delegate credentialing responsibility to a medical group, IPA, or even a hospital. According to the AAPI, if a PPO relies on a hospital to do its credentialing, it will be downgraded in the AAPI accreditation report. NCQA standards require a written description of the delegated activities and the delegate's accountability for these activities.

Q 8:93 What is the Health Care Quality Improvement Act, and how does it apply to managed care arrangements?

HCQIA [42 USC § 11101 et seq] provides limited antitrust immunity to health care entities under defined circumstances for their peer review activities. It defines health care entities subject to limited immunity protection to include hospitals, medical group practices, and HMOs. [42 USC § 11151(4)(A)] In some ways an MCO meets the definition of health care entity. To enjoy immunity under HCQIA, the entity must provide full procedural due process as set forth in HCQIA as well as report the outcome of those actions, if adverse, to the NPDB. [42 USC §§ 11112, 11133(a)]

Q 8:94 What is the relevance of the HCQIA to selection and deselection of providers in an integrated delivery system?

Deselection is the process by which a health care entity denies a provider initial access, or terminates the membership or privileges of, or its contract with, a participating practitioner. The law accords certain minimal rights to practitioners who are either denied affiliation or removed from an existing relationship with an MCO. Some of these rights are a matter of common law, and others are imposed under state or federal law.

In organizing an integrated delivery system or MCO, the organizers should determine whether the benefits of HCQIA protection, including antitrust immunity and access to the NPDB, outweigh its drawbacks, which include mandatory reporting to the NPDB of adverse credentialing decisions based on clinical competence or conduct and compliance with the requirements of statutorily defined due process. Due process, at a minimum, means that the entity must offer the affected provider notice of the reasons for the adverse action and an opportunity to respond to or rebut them. A debate exists among attorneys and other interested parties as to whether an integrated delivery system should afford due process to providers who either are not selected or are deselected from participation and whether HCQIA even applies to entities such as integrated delivery systems.

Q 8:95 Does the denial of an application for participation trigger a reporting requirement to the NPDB?

If the basis of the denial is not associated with quality of care concerns, but is based on the applicant's failure to meet the criteria for participation, or on the existence of excess capacity for that medical specialty on the panel, it need not be reported. In fact, the definition of health care entity used in HCQIA does not extend to provider organizations such as PHOs or IPAs. The intent of the reporting requirement in HCQIA is to identify physicians with potential quality of care problems.

Q 8:96   Who must report to the NPDB, and what must be reported?

Medical malpractice insurers must report payments made on behalf of physicians, dentists, or other licensed health care providers. State licensing boards must report adverse licensing and disciplinary actions involving physicians or dentists. Professional societies must report professional review actions that adversely affect professional memberships and revisions to such actions for physicians and dentists. Professional societies must report professional review actions involving physicians and dentists, and may report actions involving other licensed health care practitioners. Although the original legislation did not extend reporting to other categories of licensed health care practitioners, amendments through the Omnibus Budget Reconciliation Act of 1990 (OBRA) [Pub L No 101-508] allow the collection of "any negative action or finding" by state licensing authorities as well as by peer review organizations and private accreditation entities. Proposed regulations implementing Section 1921 of the Social Security Act will extend the activities of the NPDB to all licensed health care practitioners and entities. Hospitals and other health care entities must report professional review actions concerning physicians and dentists, and may report actions involving other licensed health care entities.

In 1997, Medicare and Medicaid exclusion reports (MMERs) were added to the list of items reportable to the NPDB. This information identifies practitioners who have been sanctioned by the DHHS OIG and declared ineligible to participate in Medicare or Medicaid or in certain state health care plans under the Social Security Act.

Q 8:97   Can an improperly made or filed NPDB report invite liability?

Yes. Courts have recognized that the filing of an improper or inaccurate NPDB report can create liability exposure not insulated by the immunity provisions of OBRA. In *Brown v. Presbyterian Health Care Services* [101 F 3d 1324 (10th Cir 1996)], following a termination of a physician's privileges for violating the terms of previous sanctions, a competitor physician was found not protected by HCQIA's immunity when he used an adverse action code (incompetent/

malpractice/negligent) to describe the adverse action despite the physician's objection to the coding. The court determined that the use of this code when the adverse action was based on a failure to seek consultation was false and that the competitor knew it was false but used it anyway.

In *Odom v. Fairbanks Memorial Hospital* [999 p 2D 123 (Alaska Mar 17, 2000)], the plaintiff physician who alleged that his staff privileges and anesthesiology agreement were terminated on the basis of his plans to open an outpatient surgery center was successful in obtaining reversal of a lower court's dismissal of claims on the basis that there were sufficient facts found to sustain his allegations of antitrust violations, breach of contract, defamation, and emotional distress; however, the court held that claims based on the hospital's NPDB report were properly dismissed, citing 42 U.S.C. Section 11137(c), which immunizes a person making a report from liability unless he or she knows the falsity of the report.

Q 8:98   Are MCOs required to report to the NPDB?

Whether an MCO must report to the NPDB depends on whether the organization qualifies under the two eligibility criteria of HCQIA: (1) the organization provides a health care service and (2) the organization is engaged in professional review activities through a formal peer review process.[34] The DHHS regulations define a formal peer review process as "the conduct of professional review activities through formally adopted written procedures which provide for adequate notice and an opportunity for a hearing."[35] If a nonhospital provider does not meet the eligibility criteria, it cannot claim the HCQIA peer review immunity, and does not have to report to the NPDB.

A DHHSOIG report issued on June 11, 2001, exposed rampant underreporting by MCOs to the NPDB. The OIG found that 84 percent of all MCOs have not submitted adverse action reports in the last nine years. This report follows a 1995 OIG report that 75 percent of all hospitals in the United States did not report a single adverse action to the NPDB during the three years covered by the study.[36]

Q 8:99   Who can query the NPDB?

Organizations and entities that can request information from the NPDB include (1) hospitals; (2) state licensing boards; (3) other health care entities; (4) professional societies; (5) plaintiffs' attorneys; and (6) the individual physician, dentist, or other health care practitioner (regarding his or her own file). Query of the NPDB is mandatory for hospitals and voluntary for all other organizations or entities. The general interpretation used by the regulators in evaluating the application of limited immunity protections under HCQIA is that an organization may become qualified to query the NPDB provided it also reports actions to the NPDB. Organizations such as IPAs and PHOs, therefore, may be eligible to obtain numbers from the NPDB to allow them to query legally.

Q 8:100　What is the Health Care Integrity and Protection Data Bank?

The Health Care Integrity and Protection Data Book (HIPDB) was established under HIPAA [Pub L No 104-191] as part of the overall government crackdown on health care fraud and abuse; it requires reporting of certain final adverse actions against health care providers, suppliers, or practitioners by federal or state agencies and health plans, and health care entities affiliated or associated with health plans. The HIPDB is maintained by the same people who developed the NPDB, the Health Resource Service Administration (HRSA) Divisions of Quality Assurance. Final regulations for the HIPDB were published in the Federal Register on October 26, 1999 [64 Fed Reg 57740], with a correction to Section 61.15 pertaining to the accuracy of the HIPDB information published in the Federal Register on December 20, 1999. [64 Fed Reg 71041]

Of importance is the fact that the HIPDB is exempt from the HIPAA privacy rules, which have been published in the Federal Register. [65 Fed Reg 34986 (June 1, 2000)] The exemption is intended to apply to investigative materials compiled for law enforcement purposes.

Q 8:101　What entities are eligible to query or report to the HIPDB?

Entities eligible to report to or query the HIPDB must register with the HIPDB and include, but are not limited to, federal and state government agencies and health plans or programs, as follows:

1. A health plan or program is defined as an entity that provides health benefits, whether directly or through insurance, including the following—

- A policy of health insurance
- A contract of a service benefit organization
- A membership agreement with an HMO or other prepaid plan
- A plan established by an employer or a group of employers
- An insurance company

2. Information from the HIPDB will be available to the following or its authorized agents:

- Federal and state government agencies
- Health plans
- A health care practitioner, provider, or supplier requesting information concerning himself, herself, or itself
- A person or entity requesting statistical information (without identification of any individual or entity)

Hospitals cannot query the HIPDB. MCOs that delegate participating provider credentialing to medical groups, IPAs, and others can use information obtained from the HIPDB provided that the MCO has been designated as their authorized agent.

Q 8:102   What actions are reportable to the HIPDB?

Actions that must be reported to the HIPDB include the following:

- Civil judgments against health care providers, suppliers, or practitioners in federal and state courts relating to the delivery of a health care item or service (regardless of whether the civil judgment is the subject of an appeal)
- Federal and state criminal convictions against a health care provider, supplier, or practitioner relating to the delivery of a health care item or service (regardless of whether the conviction is the subject of an appeal)
- Actions by federal and state agencies responsible for licensing and certification of health care providers, suppliers, or practitioners
- Exclusion of a health care provider, supplier, or practitioner from participation in federal and state health care programs, including exclusions that were made in a matter in which there

are no findings or admissions of liability (regardless of whether the exclusion is the subject of a pending appeal)

- Other adjudicated actions by federal or state government or a health plan that include formal or official final actions taken against a health care practitioner, provider, or supplier, including the availability of a due process mechanism, and are based on acts or omissions that affect or could affect the payment, provision, or delivery of a health care item or service (adjudicated actions exclude clinical privileging actions; overpayment determinations by federal or state government programs, their contractors, or health plans; and claims denial determinations)]

Q 8:103 What procedures are common to both the NPDB and the HIPDB?

The published procedures for the NPDB and the HIPDB can be found in the *National Practitioner Data Bank Guidebook* and the *Healthcare Integrity and Protection Data Bank,* published by the DHHS (January 1999 and February 2000). [45 CFR § 61] Information about how the data banks function can be obtained by calling the data bank help line at 1-800-767-6732, or by visiting the data bank Web site at http://www.npdb-hipdb.com.

Common features of the NPDB and the HIPDB include the following:

Disputes. A practitioner who disagrees with a report may dispute it as to facts or process, or as to the eligibility of the reporting entity to make the report.

Self-Query. Self-queries are allowed, but there is a charge for self-queries, whereas a report is sent to the practitioner automatically without charge or request following its receipt.

Query Procedures. Regarding all other queries, there is a charge for electronic queries. Eligible entities must register with each data bank separately, because individual passwords are given at the time of registration. An entity representative may include one or more individuals who are authorized by staff title to report to or request information from the data banks. The entity representative may designate an authorized agent to query or report on the entity's behalf.

Immunity for Reporting. Individuals, entities, or their authorized agents will be immune from civil action filed by the subject of a report unless the report was submitted with actual knowledge of its falsity.

Confidentiality. All information reported to the data banks is considered confidential and is not disclosed except as specified in the data bank regulations. The NPDB confidentiality provisions have been interpreted as applying only to information given to the NPDB and not to documents and information relating to the peer review proceeding.[37] The House Commerce Committee's Oversight and Investigation Subcommittee has held hearings on whether the NPDB should be opened to patients. To date, no legislation has been introduced.

Q 8:104   Has the peer review immunity protection been successful?

For the most part, compliance with the provisions of HCQIA has insulated participants in good-faith peer review from antitrust liability; however, the process of ensuring that any challenge to the peer review process is subject to the immunity must be carefully structured to avoid falling outside HCQIA's purview. Usually, a peer review immunity defense is won through a motion for summary judgment made early in the case and based on a record of a fair hearing during the peer review process. These motions are usually won because the burden of proof is on the challenging physician to show that HCQIA procedures were not followed, or that the matter is not subject to HCQIA protection. If the peer review process is deficient in any way, the protections of HCQIA will not apply. This was the situation in *Brader v. Allegheny General Hospital* [64 F 3d 869 (3d Cir 1995)], in which the motion for summary judgment was premature in view of the deficiency in the peer review record. In *Brown v. Presbyterian Healthcare Services* [101 F 3d 1324 (10th Cir 1996), *cert denied*, US Apr 14, 1997; 117 S Ct 1461 (1997)], the Tenth Circuit upheld a $500,000 jury verdict (pre-trebled) for the plaintiff physician because of deficiencies in the peer review process.

Two recent state supreme court cases have further defined the scope of the immunity provided by HCQIA. In the first, the Nevada Supreme Court ruled that HCQIA does not grant peer reviewers immunity when a physician is dismissed for whistleblower activities. [Clark v Columbia/HCA Information Servs Inc, No 29995 (Nev June 21, 2001)] In the second, the Colorado Supreme Court ruled that a hospital review in that state followed proper HCQIA procedures, and thus the peer reviewers were immune from liability. [North Colo Med Ctr Inc v Nicholas, No 00SC418 (Colo June 25, 2001)]

To avoid liability when terminating a physician from a health plan, there should be valid reasons for the deselection based on published criteria that are applied consistently. By defining the criteria in advance, and providing the physicians with feedback during their reviews, liability associated with termination should be minimized.

Q 8:105 Are the credentialing materials used by an MCO discoverable?

The discoverability of confidential credentialing information has been the subject of many treatises and court decisions. The most common request is from plaintiffs' attorneys requesting information in malpractice suits and from physician plaintiffs in antitrust suits. In the absence of a statutory privilege protecting against the discovery of such information, a few courts have allowed discovery of peer review documents. [Kenney v Superior Court of Cal, 255 Cal App 2d 106 (Ct. App 1967)] Most courts, however, have tended to restrict discovery by the malpractice plaintiff, reasoning that the harm to the peer review process outweighs the advantages to the plaintiff, who has other means of obtaining the information. Courts have been more liberal in granting discovery requests by physician plaintiffs, reasoning that they have a due process right to the information pertaining to their own case and a greater need for information pertaining to general practices of the peer review committee; however, in *Memorial Hospital–The Woodlands v. McCrown* [927 SW 2d 1 (Tex 1996)], the scope of protection of confidential peer review information was extended to include initial applications for staff membership, requests for information related to an applicant's qualifications, and responses to such requests.

Judicial interpretation of peer review statutes varies by state. Protections run the gamut from absolute in Georgia, where a peer pre-view privilege is absolute, to almost nonexistent in Kentucky, where protections from discovery do not apply at all in medical malpractice cases. The Kentucky Supreme Court in *Sisters of Charity Health Systems Inc. v. Dones* [984 SW 2d 464 (Ky 1998)] cleared up confusion over Kentucky's statute by limiting the privilege to lawsuits against peer review entities.

In Illinois, a court held that incident reports submitted to peer review committees and the results of peer review investigations are not covered by the privilege. [Chicago Trust Co v Cook County Hosp, 698 NE 2d 641 (Ill App Ct 1998)] A Florida court reached the same conclusion, that the peer review investigation was privileged, but the resulting report was not. [Bayfront Med Ctr Inc v Florida, 741 So 2d 1226 (Fla Ct App 1999)] In Georgia, documents available from another source are not covered by the privilege, according to *Cobb County Kennestone Hospital Authority v. Martin.* [430 SE 2d 604 (Ga Ct App 1993)] In that case, original hospital data used to create a peer review report was found not to be covered by the privilege. California physicians in 1996 lost their privilege against state medical board subpoenas in *Arnett v. Dal Cielo.* [923 P 2d 1 (Cal 1996)] This brought California in line with other states, according to an amicus brief filed on behalf of the defendant and appellant. "State medical boards often do have access to peer review records," it said.

In *Babcock v. Bridgeport Hospital* [742 A 2d 322 (Conn 1999)], Connecticut's, highest court limited the peer review privilege to documents created by a peer-review committee expressly for the purpose of peer review. That decision allowed studies by an infection control committee to be discovered. In addition, the Illinois statute (and laws in other states) immunizes only the committee, not summary actions taken by individuals, according to *Berry v. Oak Park Hospital.* [628 NE 2d 1159 (Ill App Ct 1993)] In Virginia, a trial court ordered the discovery of hospital peer review records in a case involving a doctor's defamation claim against a television broadcast. As part of its defense, the television station sought the doctor's peer review records at four hospitals. The trial court ordered disclosure, finding the peer review protections in Virginia Code Section 8.01-581.17 did not apply in the context of a tort action unrelated to a medical malpractice action. [Levin v WJLA-TV, No L-175329 (Va Cir Ct Oct 22, 1999)] The Virginia Supreme Court took direct appeals in December 1999. [HCA Health Servs of Va Inc v Levin, No 992934,

(Va Dec 23, 1999); Inova Health Sys v Levin, No 992935 (Va Dec 23, 1999)]

Q 8:106   Does the immunity from discovery of peer review records apply in federal cases?

In cases that arise under federal law, there is no immunity from discovery. Federal courts do not have to recognize a state privilege. In antitrust, civil rights, and Emergency Medical Treatment and Active Labor Act (EMTALA) cases, federal courts have declined to apply state statutory protections against discovery. Federal courts will not recognize a state confidentiality privilege in a suit brought in federal court under federal law. The court in *Burrows v. Redbud Community Hospital District* [187 FRD 606 (ND Cal 1998)] ordered discovery of a doctor's peer review records in a case brought under EMTALA. The decision was affirmed on appeal and the U.S. Supreme Court declined to review.

In *Virmani v. Novant Health Inc.* [No 00-2423 (4th Cir Aug 1, 2001)], the Fourth Circuit granted a physician's motion to obtain peer review records relating to his allegation that racial and national origin bias played a role in a hospital's decision to terminate his staff privileges. This case suggests that extra caution is warranted when the subject of a peer review inquiry is a member of a protected class.

Peer review privilege does not apply when hospitals are sued by physicians for employment discrimination under the Americans with Disabilities Act (ADA). [Mattice v Memorial Hosp of S Bend, (No 3: 98-CV-303 RM (ND Ind Oct 15, 2001)]

Q 8:107   What has been the trend in upholding immunity in peer review proceedings?

Although peer review protections against discovery are eroding, civil liability immunity provided to peer review participants has been strengthened by recent cases. In *Sugarbaker v. SSM Health Care* [190 F 3d 905 (8th Cir 1999)], the court held that a hospital's peer review conduct was covered under the immunity granted by HCQIA. Summary judgment was granted to the health center in an antitrust complaint brought by a physician. In *Ironside v. Simi Valley Hospital* [188 F 3d 350 (6th Cir 1999)], the court applied both Tennessee and

HCQIA immunity to a California hospital that sent a factually correct though negative peer review letter to a Tennessee hospital.

Q 8:108 How does the ADA affect the credentialing process in managed care?

The ADA states that an employer with more than 15 employees cannot "discriminate" against a "qualified individual with a disability" on the basis of that disability with regard to job application procedures, hiring, advancement, training, compensation, discharge, or terms, conditions, and privileges of employment. [42 USC § 12112 et seq] A disability is defined as a physical or mental impairment that substantially limits one or more major life activities, a record of such an impairment, or being regarded as having such an impairment. To be protected under the ADA, the individual need not currently have a disability and, in fact, may never have actually had a disability.

Employers are required to make reasonable accommodation to the known disability of a qualified disabled person unless it would result in undue hardship. A qualified individual is one who has skills, experience, education, and other job-related capabilities for a position and who can, either with or without reasonable accommodation, perform the essential functions of the job in question. Essential functions are the fundamental duties intrinsic to the position. In analyzing ADA issues, the following questions are useful:

1. Is the applicant or employee qualified?
2. Is the applicant or employee disabled?
3. Can the applicant or employee perform the essential functions of the job with or without reasonable accommodation?

If the answers to these questions are all yes, and there is no direct threat to others from his or her employment, the person is protected by the ADA.

Under the ADA an MCO or integrated delivery system must not discriminate against qualified persons with disabilities through its credentialing program; yet the MCO or integrated delivery system must ensure patients of a high level of quality care. The requirements of the ADA appear to be, in some instances, in conflict with the duty to provide quality care. This conflict is most evident in cases of providers with alcohol or drug dependency. With respect to the ADA's application to credentialing, as long as the MCO or integrated delivery system can show that the adverse employment (contract) action is directly and necessarily related to quality of care issues, it may be able to reconcile its duty with the ADA requirements. By questioning specific job-related functions rather than general health status, the MCO or integrated delivery system should be able to achieve ADA compliance in its application process.

To avoid violating the ADA, the following should be considered:

1. Do not require a medical examination prior to accepting the application. The offer can be made conditioned on a satisfactory physical examination.

2. Do not ask questions as to health status, last physical examination, hospitalizations, use of alcohol or drugs, or any mental or physical limitations.

3. Do not withdraw an offer on the basis of the results of medical information unless the information is job related or the condition is a threat to the health or safety of the applicant or another individual.

In a case filed in federal district court in San Antonio, Texas, in 2000, a physician terminated from employment with a 5.01(a) organization (Texas Foundation) unsuccessfully raised claims under the ADA on behalf of his patients, alleging discrimination in care on the basis of their being enrolled in HMO plans.[38]

The U.S. Supreme Court declined to review the appeal of a physician who was terminated by her employer based on appearance of intoxication and her refusal to compelte a plan of treatment required by her employer. The physician claimed that the ADA protected her against the firing. The appeals court decision, left standing by the Supreme Court, held that even though the physician could establish that she was regarded as an alcoholic, her employer had a legitimate, nondiscriminatory reason for firing her. The court found that the employer presented enough evidence to show it was justified in discharging her on the ground that she posed "an immediate risk to patients." Under the ADA, an employer may defend an otherwise discriminatory condition placed on a disabled person's employment (e.g., a treatment plan and testing) if it can establish that the condition is consistent with business necessity, and that without it, the person's employment would constitute "a direct threat to the health or safety of other individuals in the workplace."[Bekker v Humana Health Plan, Inc, No 00-1294 (US Apr 16, 2001) (denying review)]

Q 8:109   Is due process required to be given to physicians who are terminated from a managed care provider network?

In deciding whether due process is appropriate for deselection, several factors should be considered:

1. Is the practitioner an employee or an independent contractor?

2. Is the adverse action being taken at the initial application phase or during the existing contract?

3. Is the termination occurring during the contract term or is it a nonrenewal or expiration of the contract at the end of its term?

Whether a physician is entitled to due process when a managed care contract is terminated or is not renewed is the subject of several significant court cases and recent legislation in a number of states. Many courts have determined that a physician who is terminated from a managed care provider network should be given some degree of due process; for example, the physician should be afforded an opportunity to know the basis of the termination and be given a chance to respond.[39]

In *Potvin v. Metropolitan Life Insurance Co.* [54 Cal App 4th 936, 63 Cal Rptr 2d 202 (Ct App 1997)], the court ruled that a physician was entitled to a "fair procedure" before the termination of his participation in the insurer's managed care networks. This right of fair procedure applied despite the insurer's reliance on a "no cause" termination. The court justified its decision on the basis that Dr. Potvin was entitled to due process based on the California courts' longstanding recognition of a common law right to fair procedure in protecting individuals from arbitrary exclusion or expulsion from private organizations that control important economic interests. A wealth of case law has developed in the hospital medical staff context. This duty to provide a fair procedure also comes into play when private organizations are "tinged with public stature or purpose" or attain a "quasi-public significance." Therefore, considerable judicial precedent supports a finding that this duty applies to managed care provider organizations but not to purely private associations, such as "clubs."

Q 8:110 Can an MCO remove a participating provider for any reason?

One of the major issues affecting providers who participate in managed care arrangements is the economic impact of being removed from a provider panel and losing the patients of that managed care plan. The deselection of physicians from these provider panels has been the subject of many lawsuits and has served as the impetus for enactment of many "any willing provider" and similar laws. Generally, claims by providers against MCOs for exclusion or expulsion are framed on antitrust or due process grounds. Claims of this type are strongly analogous to medical staff credentialing litigation and the courts are certain to rely on that body of law in addressing similar litigation against MCOs. Although there is presently very little appellate law on this issue, some cases warrant consideration.

In *Napoletano v. CIGNA* [680 A 2d 127 (Conn 1996)], the Connecticut Supreme Court considered companion suits, one brought by a group of physicians who had been removed from CIGNA's provider network and a second suit brought by CIGNA plan members complaining of the same action. The court concluded that these claims were not preempted by ERISA and could proceed to trial under Connecticut law. In finding no preemption by ERISA, the court focused on the U.S. Supreme Court's decision in *New York State Conference of Blue Cross & Blue Shield Plans v. Travelers Insurance Co.* [514 US 645 (1995)] In that decision the U.S. Supreme Court elaborated on the scope of ERISA preemption, and its language has provided support for courts seeking to narrow the preemptive scope of ERISA.

In *Harper v. Healthsource New Hampshire, Inc.* [674 A 2d 962 (NH 1996)], the New Hampshire Supreme Court held that a physician could maintain a claim for wrongful termination of provider status on the ground that the termination violated public policy. The application of the public policy doctrine to an exclusion case was a creative and somewhat unexpected approach.

California has recently seen three decisions relevant to this topic. In *Delta Dental Plan v. Banasky* [33 Cal Rptr 2d 381 (Ct App 1994)], the court held that due process requirements that historically applied to medical staffs and other professional associations also applied to expulsion from a managed care plan. In *Ambrosino v. Metropolitan Life Insurance Co.* [899 F Supp 438 (ND Cal 1995)], a federal judge determined that a plan's expulsion of a provider on charges of substance abuse violated the clinician's due process rights because the clinician was not afforded a fair hearing. Finally, in *Potvin v. Metropolitan Life Insurance Co.* [95 Cal Rptr 2d 496; S Ct Cal (filed May 8, 2000), docket 5061945, *affirmed*], Dr. Potvin was terminated from the MetLife provider panel without cause or due process. The trial court granted summary judgment in favor of MetLife's termination of Dr. Potvin from its provider panel, but Dr. Potvin won in the court of appeal, which largely relied on *Delta Dental* and *Ambrosino* in concluding that Dr. Potvin had a right to some sort of due process hearing before being expelled from the panel. The case was appealed to the California Supreme Court and in May 2000, the court ruled that managed care plans cannot arbitrarily terminate physicians from provider panels. The court said any such removals must be "both substantively rational and procedurally fair." In its 4–3 ruling, the court relied heavily on an amicus brief submitted by the California Medical Association and the AMA, adopting their argument that insurance companies, in making such arbitrary decisions, have tremendous power to destroy medical practices. "If participation in managed care arrangements is a practical necessity for physicians generally, and if only a handful of health care entities have a virtual monopoly on managed care, removing individual physicians from preferred provider networks controlled by these entities could significantly impair those physicians' practice of medicine," the ruling said. The court also found that there is a concern for the public interest because under managed care, patients often cannot choose their own doctors and are limited to physicians who are on a health plan's panel. When a plan arbitrarily terminates a physician, the patient is arbitrarily deprived of a relationship with that physician.

Q 8:111   Should termination be based on the credentialing plan or the provider contract?

One of the most common dilemmas for an MCO in assessing a termination decision is to determine whether it should be based on a practitioner's written contract or the integrated delivery system's credentialing plan. Ideally, there should be coordination between the written contract and the plan. Most MCOs, however, complete a contract before they process the credentialing information.

Usually, the plan will provide for discipline and termination based on specific criteria relating to qualifications, competency, and quality of care. Plans usually provide for a peer review process. The contract, on the other hand, will impose various requirements on the practitioner, including compliance with MCO criteria relating to quality of care; it will also address other requirements such as office hours, coverage, and staffing. Contracts generally include provisions for termination "with" or "without" cause, and the credentialing plan only addresses "for cause" terminations.

In reconciling the contract with the credentialing plan, the MCO should consider the following issues:

1. When is the credentialing plan to be used in cases involving termination?

2. Does termination without cause trigger obligations under the credentialing plan? Should it be subject to a different process?

3. Should all terminations for cause be implemented pursuant to the credentialing plan, or should there be a different process for terminations based on economic or business considerations?

4. Should there be a separate process for employed versus independent contract or practitioners?

Q 8:112 What is economic credentialing and how does it differ from the standard credentialing process of hospitals?

Economic credentialing is a process of determining or evaluating qualifications for membership or privileges that involves the use of economic criteria unrelated to quality of care or professional competency, such as cost and utilization rates. The argument in favor of this practice is that quality and outcomes justify the profiling of a physician's practice patterns and limiting privileges based on such data. Standard credentialing does not consider such economic criteria.

Q 8:113 What has been the impact of economic credentialing on physicians?

There have been few economic credentialing cases, and those that were upheld were linked to quality of care issues. In one case involving economic credentialing unrelated to quality of care [Rosenblum v Tallahassee Mem'l Reg'l Med Ctr, No 91-589 (Fla Cir Ct June 12, 1992)], a Florida court upheld the hospital's denial of privileges to a heart surgeon on the basis that he was under contract with a competing hospital to develop a heart surgery program. In another managed care case [Hassan v Independent Practice Assocs, 698 F Supp 679 (ED Mich 1988)], the district court upheld the termination of two allergists who had failed to practice in a cost-effective manner.

Q 8:114 What is exclusive credentialing?

Exclusive credentialing is credentialing in which hospitals require physicians to commit to admitting their patients to a particular hospital as a condition of medical staff membership. The AMA is concerned about the use by hospitals of admitting privileges as leverage in controlling admitting patterns because it threatens not only the physician-patient relationship but ultimately physician autonomy and livelihood. This practice has been reported to the DHHS as being fraudulent.[40] The AMA and several state medical groups charge that some hospitals require physicians to sign loyalty pledges in exchange for staff privileges. Such exclusive credentialing arrangements may also require physicians to pledge to send 90 percent or more of their patients to the hospital or lose their privileges, or to sever all ties with competing institutions even if those institutions could offer better patient care.

Q 8:115 How has the Internet affected credentialing?

Numerous Web sites containing credentialing information on health care providers—including licensure actions, federal program debarments, and board specialty society decisions—have sprung up. This publicly available information has empowered consumers to participate in the credentialing process. Patients can go to the Internet and personally "credential" the physicians on a health plan's provider list before they make an appointment. For this and other reasons, professional organizations such as the National Association of Medical Staff Services (NAMSS) and their state affiliates have begun to modify their credentialing standards and embrace the Internet-available Web sites as another source of information. Such Web sites include the following:

- Association of State Medical Board Executive Directors (www.docboard.org)
- American Board of Medical Specialties (www.abms.org)
- Federation of State Medical Boards (www.fsmb.org)
- American Medical Accreditation Program (www.ama-assn. org/amap)
- DHHS OIG (www.dhhs.gov/progog/oig)

As discussed in more detail in chapter 6, there is also an interest in centralizing the credentialing process and using an electronic platform for exchanging such information. In January 2000, Florida became the first state to implement a centralized electronic credentialing system designed to save physicians time and excess paperwork. Officials at the Florida Department of Health, which oversees the Internet-based CoreSTAT system through its Division of Medical Quality Assurance, said a number of states have expressed interest in establishing similar programs. CoreSTAT allows providers to gather "core" credentialing information 24 hours a day, seven days a week over the department's Web site (www.corestat.net).

Q 8:116　What is the likelihood that managed care plans will adopt a uniform credentialing form for providers?

The prospects for eliminating the cumbersome process of completing a separate application for and obtaining a separate credential from each managed care plan look good. In May 2000, the Dallas/Fort Worth Business Group on Health obtained approval from the major health plans, medical associations, and the state's Medicaid program of a common form to be used by the different health plans and hospitals to obtain background information on physicians before granting or renewing their privileges to see patients. The form seeks a wide range of information, including education, type of practice, licensure, and training, as well as office hours, languages spoken, facility affiliations, and malpractice claims history. This two-part, 24-page application can be found at the Web site of the Texas Medical Association (http://www.texmed.org).

Q 8:117   How does credentialing fit into a corporate compliance program?

In an era of corporate compliance, querying the data banks (NPDB and HIPDB) will be critical to a hospital's or health plan's compliance program. Credentialing goes to the heart of a compliance program because it utilizes a systematic process to review and assure quality and competence in patient care. The HIPDB also impose a higher level of accountability on health care organizations to ensure that the providers they credential are not perpetrators of health care fraud and abuse.

Q 8:118   What are the legal implications for a hospital, an IPA, or other MCO of retaining a physician who has been or is in the process of being excluded from Medicare?

Most hospitals and MCOs lack formal procedures for dealing with staff members who have been excluded from federal health care programs despite the significant institutional liability risk posed by those practitioners. Some 17,000 individuals and entities are barred from billing federal health programs under the BBA [42 USC §§ 1320a-7a(a)6, 1395y(e)(1)(B); 42 CFR § 1001.1901] About 3,000 practitioners and companies are hit with the government sanction every year for alleged billing fraud or other misconduct. Hospitals can be fined up to $10,000 for each item or service improperly billed, plus up to three times the amount billed, if hospital officials "knew, or should have known" of a potential claim by an excluded individual "under contract," according to regulations. In September 1999, the DHHS OIG issued a special advisory bulletin on the rule. The dilemma for hospitals is that federal exclusion does not explicitly require practitioners to be removed from a medical staff, but hospitals can be penalized for any improper billings by those physicians. According to final regulations published in the Federal Register [64 Fed Reg 39420, (July 22, 1999)], "A medical staff relationship, in the absence of any employment or contractual relationship or arrangement, in and of itself, remains outside the scope of these regulations. However, when claims are generated by physicians having privileges in the hospital for services they furnish, order, or prescribe, the hospital must be held accountable if the items or services are provided by excluded physicians."

Emergency Medical Treatment and Active Labor Act

Q 8:119   What is the effect of the Consolidated Omnibus Budget Reconciliation Act and the Emergency Medical Treatment and Active Labor Act on managed care arrangements?

EMTALA requires hospitals with Medicare provider agreements to provide an appropriate medical screening for emergency patients to determine if they have an emergency medical condition. Hospitals must take steps to stabilize such patients so that their condition does not materially deteriorate during transfer to another facility. In addition, EMTALA requires hospitals to report to the Centers for Medicare and Medicaid Services (CMMS), formerly the HCFA, or a state agency if it believes it has received an individual who has been transferred illegally from another facility. EMTALA, which was enacted as part of the Consolidated Omnibus Budget Reconciliation Act of 1985 (COBRA) [42 USC § 1395dd et seq (1992)], applies to hospitals with an emergency department that participate in Medicare. An MCO with hospital participants must ensure that the hospitals comply with COBRA, which requires the hospitals to treat alike all patients who present in an emergency room and request an examination or treatment. EMTALA requires hospitals to develop screening criteria that identify critical conditions and to apply those criteria uniformly. [See Summers v Baptist Med Ctr, 69 F 3d 902 (8th Cir 1995)]

Under these laws, a person with an emergency condition (including a pregnant woman having contractions) must be given treatment to stabilize the medical condition or be provided with an "appropriate transfer" to another medical facility. There is no liability if the patient has been stabilized. If the patient is not stabilized, however, the hospital may not transfer the patient unless the patient requests a transfer after being informed of the hospital's obligations or a physician certifies that the benefits of transfer outweigh the risks.

Q 8:120   When does EMTALA apply?

Courts have split on the issue of whether EMTALA duties apply only to emergency medical conditions identified as a result of the medical screening examination or to any emergency medical condition that is identified when a patient is in the hospital. The issue is significant because the second interpretation results in a broader application of EMTALA. For example, in *Lopez-Soto v. Hawayek* [175 F 3d 179 (1st Cir 1999)], the court found that EMTALA applied to care provided to an infant during both labor and delivery. On the other side, courts restrict application of EMTALA to emergency services and hold that EMTALA does not apply to patients admitted for treatment or care provided outside the emergency department. In *Baxter v. Holy Cross Hospital of Silver Spring* [155 F 3d 557 (4th Cir 1998), *cert denied*, No 98-1169 (US Mar 22, 1998)], the court determined that when a patient received stabilizing treatment for over two weeks, there was no liability under EMTALA. The U.S. Supreme Court's denial of certiorari in *Baxter* may be an indication that the stricter view will ultimately prevail.

The Sixth Circuit affirmed a district court ruling that a state hospital was entitled to 11th Amendment immunity against allegations that it violated EMTALA by allowing a patient to leave the hospital while his condition was worsening. [Drew v University of Tenn Reg'l Med Ctr Hosp, No 99-5070 (6th Cir May 1, 2000)] James H. Drew was brought to the University of Tennessee Regional Medical Center Hospital by ambulance after experiencing seizures from chronic alcohol abuse. He was admitted to the hospital and the next day was seen by the attending physician during rounds with a team that included medical students. The third morning, a medical student who was part of the team checked on the patient. The student then relayed to the attending physician that the patient refused to be examined and was upset about being in the hospital. The student stayed on the patient's floor until the physician arrived. When they went to the room, the patient was gone. His body was discovered in a nearby lake about a week later.

Q 8:121   Is there a private right of action against a health care provider for violating EMTALA?

There are no private causes of action by the patient or family against a physician under EMTALA, although a hospital may be sued for alleged violations. [See Baber v Hospital Corp of Am, 977 F 2d 872 (4th Cir 1992), King v Ahrens, 16 F 3d 265 (8th Cir 1994).] In addition, penalties for COBRA violations can be substantial. Civil monetary penalties may be assessed against the hospital and responsible physician in the form of fines of up to $50,000 for each violation. Hospitals that fail substantially to meet the requirements of CO-BRA are subject to termination of their Medicare provider status.

In *Malavee v. Hospital Doctor's Center Inc.* [No. 99-1833 (DPR Mar 10, 2000)], the court ruled that only patients, and not their relatives, were entitled to a cause of action under EMTALA. In pursuing an EMTALA claim, the court explained that it is up to the patient to show that the hospital failed to follow the screening policy or standard of care that it regularly follows for other patients presenting "substantially similar conditions."

Q 8:122 Do the EMTALA guidelines impose EMTALA risk on physician entities owned or controlled by hospitals?

In guidelines issued in May 1999, the EMTALA screening and stabilization requirements were expanded to cover off-campus hospital facilities that operate under the same hospital Medicare provider number. This means that clinics, such as urgent care or specialties centers owned and operated by hospitals may need to develop policies and procedures addressing EMTALA and be educated accordingly. The guidance provides:

> If a patient comes to a hospital-owned facility which is non-contiguous or off-campus and operates under the hospital's Medicare provider number, Section 1867 applies to that facility. The facility must therefore screen and stabilize the patient to the best of its ability or execute an appropriate transfer according to EMTALA guidelines if necessary.

[HCFA, State Operations Manual Transmittal No 2, "Responsibilities of Hospitals in Emergency Cases," Appendix V, Tag A406, Interpretive Guidelines § 489.24(a)(May 1999)]

Experts suggest that nonhospital providers that fall within the preceding definition should review their policies to ensure compliance with EMTALA because of the impact of the penalties associated with violations.

Q 8:123 What effect will the prospective payment system rule have on hospital emergency services in light of EMTALA?

The HCFA's April 1999 final rule setting a new Medicare outpatient prospective payment system (PPS) significantly changed the regulations that define "comes to the emergency department" under EMTALA. The rule changed "comes to the emergency department" to mean, with respect to an individual requesting examination or treatment, that the individual is on the hospital property.

The rule has created confusion as to where responsibility lies in areas over which the hospital has no control. Hospital property is defined in the final rule as "the entire main hospital campus as defined by the cross reference to the provider-based rules, which is § 413.65(b)," including the parking lot, sidewalk, and driveway, as well as any facility or organization that is located off the main hospital campus but has been determined under Section 416.35 to be a department of the hospital. [65 Fed Reg 18433 (Apr 7, 1999)] This means that under the definition adopted for "comes to the emergency department," the emergency department is larger than the hospital.

ERISA

Q 8:124   What is the Employee Retirement Income Security Act of 1974?

ERISA is a federal law that regulates welfare benefit plans of employers and employee organizations engaged in or affecting interstate commerce. For purposes of ERISA, an employee welfare benefit plan is any plan, fund, or program established or maintained by an employer, employee organization, or both for the purpose of providing participants or their beneficiaries, through the purchase of insurance or otherwise, any of the following:

- Medical, surgical, or hospital care or benefits
- Benefits in the event of accident, sickness, disability, death, or unemployment
- Vacation benefits
- Apprenticeships or other training programs
- Day-care centers
- Scholarship funds
- Prepaid legal services

- Any benefit (other than pensions at retirement or death and insurance to provide such pensions) described in Section 302(c) of the Labor Management Relations Act of 1947 (including severance benefits and financial assistance for employee housing)

[ERISA § 3(1); DOL Reg § 2510.3-1(a)(2)]

An ERISA plan is required to (1) have fiduciary responsibility on the part of the employer to the participants and beneficiaries; (2) have written terms that specifically allocate various administrative responsibilities; (3) have plan assets held in trust; (4) keep participants and beneficiaries informed about their benefits and rights under the plan; and (5) comply with reporting requirements.

In 1986 and 1993, Congress amended ERISA to require that most employers offer continued availability of group health coverage for 18 to 36 months to all former employees or beneficiaries who otherwise would lose coverage. Through ERISA, plan participants have certain rights, such as the right to file suit to recover benefits due them and protection against discrimination. Although an employer cannot terminate the employment of an individual to avoid paying medical expenses, it can terminate its own health benefit plan or modify its terms. This right was affirmed by the courts after a company rewrote its health benefit plan to place a $5,000 cap on AIDS benefits. [McGann v H&H Music Co, 946 F 2d 401 (5th Cir 1991)]

When ERISA was enacted in 1974, few knew that it would be a hot topic in legal seminars into the next century. In recent years, as MCOs have flourished, ERISA has come under fire from commentators, politicians, lawyers, and even a few judges. According to Department of Labor (DOL) estimates, ERISA applies to approximately 125 million U.S. citizens.[41]

Q 8:125 What was the original purpose of ERISA?

The original purpose of ERISA was to remedy problems relating to pension fraud and mismanagement, such as inadequate funding and poor investment of pension plans. It therefore contains extensive reporting requirements for pension plans. It also imposes some reporting requirements on health benefit plans, such as furnishing a summary plan description to all plan participants and filing an annual financial report with the DOL.

ERISA's goals are to establish uniform national standards, safe-guard employee benefits from loss or abuse, and encourage employers to offer employee benefits. To achieve these goals, ERISA imposes strict requirements on pension plan administrators not only for reporting and disclosure,[42] but also for participation and vesting,[43] funding,[44] and performance of fiduciary obligations.[45] ERISA does not mandate that employers offer benefit plans, but provides a structure for national uniformity of administration once such plans are offered.

Only a few of these requirements apply to health benefit plans, in part because Congress did not pursue the implications of regulating both pension and health benefit plans under a single statute. In addition, Congress could not have anticipated the dominance of the managed care model. As a result, ERISA provides almost no federal regulation of health plans.

Q 8:126   How does ERISA affect physician autonomy in managed care arrangements?

ERISA has three provisions that directly affect physician autonomy: (1) the preemption clause, (2) the limitation on remedies, and (3) fiduciary duty obligations.

ERISA Preemption. Traditionally, states have been responsible for regulating health care delivery, and litigation against health care providers has been resolved under state law.[46] Medical liability lawsuits are rarely heard in federal courts. ERISA alters the traditional approach by preempting state law, which means that state laws purporting to regulate health plans may not be enforced in any court. In assessing whether a particular state law is prohibited, courts look sequentially to each of the three parts of ERISA's preemption provision. First, courts must decide whether the state law "relates to" an employee benefit plan. Courts consider whether the challenged law burdens the administration of plan benefits or has only a remote impact on them. Courts generally hold that ERISA preempts state laws that bind employers or plan administrators to particular benefit choices or that preclude the uniform administration of an employee benefit plan. Laws with only a remote or incidental effect on plan administration, such as a surcharge on hospital services, may not "relate to" the employee benefit plan. A law is not preempted merely because it "relates to" a plan. Courts must also interpret two qualifying provisions: the savings clause and the deemer clause. ERISA's savings clause provides that laws regulating the business of insurance, even if they "relate to" a managed care plan, will not be preempted. This provision allows states to continue to enforce state laws governing the business of insurance by saving state regulation of health insurance, such as solvency requirements, from preemption. The deemer clause qualifies the savings clause. The deemer clause prevents states from deeming (or characterizing) an ERISA-covered plan as the business of insurance. States may not characterize a self-funded plan as an insurer to circumvent the effect of the "relates to" clause.

ERISA's Limited Remedies. Although much state litigation is preempted, ERISA provides some relief for injuries to health plan participants through its civil enforcement scheme. A plan participant or beneficiary may bring a civil action against an administrator who fails to comply with a request for information about the plan to recover claimed benefits, to enforce rights under the terms of the plan, or to clarify rights to future benefits.[47] A plan participant may also bring suit against a plan fiduciary who breaches any fiduciary duties and may seek to enjoin practices that violate ERISA or the terms of the plan. Even if a suit is successful, recovery under ERISA is generally limited to the amount of the benefits that should have been provided, as well as certain incidentals such as attorneys fees. This is a much more limited remedy than what is available under state law claims, through which the participant might be able to recover damages for any economic losses, noneconomic damages for pain and suffering, and punitive damages (especially in cases alleging bad-faith insurance denial).[48]

Fiduciary Duties. ERISA imposes a fiduciary duty on those who make discretionary decisions on behalf of the employee benefit plan. A fiduciary must discharge his or her discretionary functions "solely in the interest of the participants and beneficiaries" of the plan.[49] Courts have traditionally held that MCOs are subject to this fiduciary duty when making certain decisions, such as reviewing the appropriateness of a physician's treatment recommendations. In exercising this fiduciary duty, the MCO has an obvious problem when the clinical needs of one patient conflict with the MCO's economic interests. This has resulted in an increasing number of lawsuits by disappointed plan participants claiming breach of fiduciary duty and challenging the denial of physician-prescribed benefits on the basis of a potential conflict of interest. (See discussion of *Pegram v. Herdrich* in Q 8:181.)

Q 8:127   How does ERISA apply to managed care arrangements?

Because of the regulation of medical plans under ERISA, it is important that the MCO consider plan design and sponsorship in contracting for the provision of health care services. At present, ERISA does not mandate any particular benefit design or provide for any particular arrangement in the provision of benefits. Once an ERISA plan is in place, however, certain exclusive remedies are available to plan participants and providers claiming payments from a plan. Of particular relevance to managed care arrangements are the following issues.

Fiduciary Liability. Under ERISA, a plan fiduciary is personally liable to make up to the plan any losses resulting from the breach of the fiduciary's duty of care to participants and their beneficiaries. A person is an ERISA fiduciary to the extent that he or she exercises discretionary authority or control with regard to the management or disposition of the assets of an ERISA plan. If a managed care provider organization accepts payment on a capitated basis, this fiduciary liability could extend to individuals who make health care determinations, such as specialty care referrals or hospitalization. It is reasonable to conclude that an HMO, an entity acting as agent for and governing the operations of a PPO, a utilization review firm, or any other service provider engaged by a plan to assist its fiduciary in evaluating the performance of other fiduciaries would be considered a fiduciary with respect to a medical plan. Whether a participating provider in an ERISA plan is a fiduciary subject to liability depends not only on plan design but also on the activities of the provider under the plan. A fiduciary can be liable for another fiduciary's breach of fiduciary responsibility if the fiduciary (1) participates knowingly in, or knowingly undertakes to conceal, an act or omission of that other fiduciary, knowing such act or omission is a breach; (2) enables the other fiduciary to commit a breach by failing to comply with his or her specific fiduciary responsibilities; or (3) has knowledge of the breach by the other fiduciary and does not make reasonable efforts under the circumstances to remedy it.

Prohibited Transactions. ERISA prohibits certain transactions, absent a statutory exemption, between a plan and a party in interest as well as self-dealing by plan fiduciaries. A party in interest includes (1) any plan fiduciary (including any administrator, officer, trustee, or custodian), counsel, or employee of the ERISA plan; (2) any person providing services to the plan; (3) an employer that has any employees covered by the plan; (4) anyone having 50 percent or more control of an employer with employees covered by the plan; (5) a relative (spouse, ancestor, lineal descendant, or spouse of a lineal descendant) of anyone listed in (1) through (4) above; (6) any organization that is 50 percent or more owned by anyone in (1) through (4) above; and (7) any employee, officer, director, or 10 percent or more shareholder (or 10 percent or more partner or joint venturer) in (1), (3), or (6) above. [ERISA § 3(14), (15)]

Prohibited transactions between a plan and parties in interest include (1) a sale, exchange, or lease of any property; (2) a loan of money or other extension of credit; (3) the furnishing of goods, services, or facilities; (4) the transfer or use of plan assets by or for the benefit of a party in interest; and (5) the acquisition or holding of nonqualifying or excess qualifying employer securities or real property by the plan. [ERISA §§ 406–408] Acts deemed to be self-dealing by a fiduciary include (1) dealing with assets of the plan in his or her own interest or for his or her account; (2) receiving any considerations for his or her own personal account from any party dealing with the plan in any transaction involving the plan; or (3) acting on behalf of a party whose interests are adverse to the plan, or of its participants or beneficiaries, in any transaction involving the plan. [ERISA § 406(b)]

To the extent a provider could benefit if a service is not provided to the patient, depending on how the financial arrangements are structured, he or she could be placed in the impermissible position of dealing with the plan in a transaction in which he or she has a personal interest.

ERISA Preemption. With the exception of Hawaii's Prepaid Health Care Act (which was enacted before ERISA), ERISA preempts all state laws that relate to employee benefit plans. Courts have interpreted ERISA's preemption very broadly to preempt state laws relating to employer contributions to welfare benefit plans [see Stone & Webster Eng'g Corp v Ilsley, 690 F 2d 323 (2d Cir 1982), *aff'd without opinion sub nom* Acrudi v Stone & Webster Eng'g Corp, 103 S Ct 3564 (1983)], claims practices of insurance companies, and claims and administrative services provided to self-insured plans. [See Insurance Bd Under Social Ins Plan of Bethlehem Steel Corp v Muir, 819 F 2d 408 (3d Cir 1987)] Exceptions to preemption of state laws are based on whether the savings clause applies to preclude preemption. [ERISA § 415(2)(A)] The most significant exception applies to state laws that regulate the business of insurance. Although the courts have broadly applied ERISA preemption to protect a provider from punitive damages for bad-faith claims arising under state law, the courts have been reluctant to extend the scope of ERISA (and its protection against punitive damage awards) to medical malpractice claims. In fact, the most recent court decisions reflect an erosion of the preemption "shield."

Q 8:128   Why is the ERISA preemption clause so significant in managed care?

The ERISA preemption clause prevents state regulation of health plans subject to ERISA regulation. The scope of this preemption, however, remains ill-defined and has been interpreted by many experts as posing a barrier to state health care reform. States argue that ERISA waivers are critical to allowing innovative plans. Business and labor groups, however, believe that ERISA serves an important purpose because it allows multistate employers to offer identical benefit packages to all workers and saves them from the burden of state-by-state compliance. ERISA preemption has also served to shield employers and plans from state tort claims.

Many state programs have been challenged under the ERISA preemption clause. For example, in New Jersey and New York, hospital rate-setting legislation was challenged on the ground that ERISA's fiduciary standards prevent the use of plan assets to fund the care of nonplan members. In *United Wire, Metal & Machine Health & Welfare Fund v. Morristown Memorial Hospital* [995 F 2d 1179 (3d Cir 1993)], the Third Circuit upheld the state system on the grounds that states can indirectly impose costs on employer health plans as long as they do not require plans to structure or administer benefits in a particular way. In *New York State Conference of Blue Cross & Blue Shield Plans v. Travelers Insurance Co.* [115 S Ct 1671 (1995)], the U.S. Supreme Court concluded that the hospital rate-setting legislation was not preempted by ERISA, reversing the Second Circuit C decision in *Travelers Insurance Co. v. Cuomo.* [14 F 3d 708 (2d Cir

1994)] Although the Supreme Court did not give much guidance on interpreting preemption issues, it appeared to leave issues such as state provider tax, rate-setting, and Medicaid HMO enrollment schemes to the states.

The ERISA preemption clause has generally been held not to apply to state "any willing provider" laws because of the rights reserved to the states to regulate the business of insurance. Regardless of these state laws, however, an ERISA plan may not be treated as being in the business of insurance for purposes of provider deselection. Challenges to provider deselection brought by both beneficiaries and deselected providers under "any willing provider" laws against HMOs providing coverage under an ERISA plan have been unsuccessful. [See Hollis v Cigna HealthCare of Conn, Inc, 138 Conn 216, 680 A 2d 127 (1996)] In 2001 the issue of preemption was submitted to the U.S. Supreme Court in the form of two state court decisions. The first case concerns whether a state's independent review process is preempted by ERISA.[50] The second concerns whether ERISA preempts a state's "any willing provider" law.[51] The Court has not issued opinions on these cases as of this writing.

Q 8:129 What is the potential impact of lifting ERISA preemption?

A number of studies have attempted to analyze the cost of lifting ERISA preemption. In a study commissioned by the AAHP, the Barents Group gathered data on current liability insurance costs to physicians and hospitals and forecast that managed care premiums would increase 2.7 to 8.6 percent through the five-year period 1999 to 2003.[52] Two other studies, one by Muse and Associates for the consumer group Patient Access to Responsible Care Alliance and another by the nonpartisan CBO, predicted smaller premium increases.[53] Surveying expert opinion, the CBO estimated a 60 to 75 percent increase in health plans' liability costs, resulting in a 1.2 percent rise in premiums for employer-sponsored health insurance over a ten-year period. The Muse study suggested that eliminating ERISA preemption would result in an increase of no greater than 0.2 percent of average managed care premiums; it contended further that this extra cost might be offset by savings from a decline in medical injury costs in a legal environment in which fewer medically necessary services would be denied. Overall, these studies vary widely in the types of costs they build into their estimates and in other aspects of their methodologies. In a study performed by David M. Studdert, William M. Sage, Carole Roan Gresenz, and Deborah R. Hensler published in *Health Affairs,* the finding of the potential effect of lifting ERISA preemption was deemed "uncertain."[54]

Q 8:130   In which types of cases has ERISA preemption been deemed to apply?

It seems that the types of cases in which ERISA preemption has been held to apply involve laws that "relate to" ERISA, such as (1) laws that regulate the type of benefits or terms of ERISA plans; (2) laws that create reporting, disclosure, funding, or vesting requirements for ERISA plans; (3) laws that provide rules for the calculation of the amount of benefits to be paid under ERISA plans; and (4) laws and common law rules that provide remedies for misconduct growing out of the administration of ERISA plans.[55] If a state's laws regulate the business of insurance, such as "any willing provider" statutes, they are "saved" from preemption. These statutes spread risk among all insureds by including all providers, relating to cost and treatment, and being expressly limited to the insurance industry.[56]

Based on a finding that ERISA preempted issues relating to plan administration, the Third Circuit, in *Pryzbowksi v. U.S. HealthCare Inc.* [No 99-5920 (3d Cir Mar 27, 2001)], held in favor of ERISA preemption of a health plan participant's state law claim that she was injured because the plan negligently delayed approving care by out-of-network physicians. In so ruling, the appeals court rejected arguments that the participant's claims involved the quality of her care and not plan administration.

Q 8:131   In what types of cases has ERISA preemption been deemed not to apply?

A number of court decisions have eroded ERISA preemption, but ERISA preemption is now the subject of U.S. Supreme Court review, as discussed in Q 8:128.

Negligent Misrepresentation. ERISA did not preempt a state law negligent misrepresentation claim that physicians who failed to disclose an alleged conflict of interest in their contract with an HMO caused a patient to forgo consultation with a specialist that might have saved his life. [Shea v Esensten, 107 F 3d 625 (8th Cir 1997)]

Premature Discharge of a Patient. In *Bauman v. US Healthcare, Inc.* [193 F 3d 151 (3d Cir 1999)], the defendant's policy of discharging a newborn within 24 hours without adequately considering the medical appropriateness in a given case could be challenged in state court as substandard quality of care. This decision signaled that the courts may be giving clinical authority back to physicians. It is one thing to deny treatment when potential liability rests with the treating physician, but it is another to deny the claim when the organization might also be held responsible.

Delay in Treatment. In *Pappas v. Asbel* [724 A 2d 889 (Pa 1998)], the Pennsylvania Supreme Court held a quadriplegic's claim against an HMO over a treatment delay was not preempted by federal law, and remanded the case for further consideration.

Claims Arising Under the Americans with Disabilities Act. Although state antidiscrimination statutes, as part of the overall enforcement scheme contemplated by ADA, are exempt from ERISA preemption, the failure to state a cause of action under ADA will subject the state claims to ERISA preemption. In *Tompkins v. United Healthcare of New England Inc.* [No 99-1449 (1st Cir Feb 11, 2000)], the First Circuit dismissed the ADA claims on grounds that they failed to state a cause of action and ERISA preempted the state statutory and common law claims.

Class Action by Providers Seeking Payment. ERISA does not preempt a proposed class action against Aetna U.S. Healthcare Inc. brought on behalf of Louisiana physicians, hospitals, and medical providers alleging that Aetna willfully breached its contracts by failing to make payment for services rendered in a timely and reasonable manner, the U.S. District Court for the Eastern District of Louisiana ruled. [Lakeland Anesthesia, Inc v Aetna US Healthcare, Inc, No. 00-1061 (ED La June 14, 2000)] Lakeland Anesthesia, on behalf of similarly situated Louisiana physicians, hospitals, and medical providers, brought state law actions against Aetna, asserting breach of contract, violation of the Louisiana Insurance Code, and unjust enrichment. Lakeland Anesthesia alleged, among other things, that Aetna "adopted a routine practice of intentionally and/or negligently delaying payment of 'complete,' 'clean,' or otherwise valid claims beyond 30, 45 and even 90 days," and that Aetna "routinely classi-fied complete and clean claims as 'incomplete.'"

Q 8:132   How is ERISA used to manipulate the forum of a lawsuit?

Because ERISA is a federal law, removal to federal court from state court is always allowed on proper motion. The determination of whether ERISA applies is made by the federal court, with the state court often retaining jurisdiction over any state-based claims pend-ing the ERISA challenge. Cases involving the use of ERISA preemp-tion to manipulate the forum include the following:

1. *Giles v. NYLCare Health Plans, Inc.* [172 F 3d 332 (5th Cir 1999)] The *Giles* plaintiff originally asserted claims for negli-gence, vicarious liability, misrepresentation, breach of con-tract, and breach of warranty. After the case was removed based on the complete preemption doctrine, the plaintiff filed an amended complaint, admitting that the misrepresentation, breach of contract, and breach of warranty claims were com-pletely preempted. Because NYLCare did not argue that the negligence and vicarious liability claims were completely pre-empted, the decision on remand was focused entirely on whether the district court was right to remand the arguably not preempted state claims of negligence and vicarious liabil-ity after the three preempted claims were dropped. NYLCare argued that the federal district court should have retained ju-risdiction to prevent forum manipulation by the plaintiffs. The Fifth Circuit rejected the forum-shopping argument and, citing the traditional factors for discretionary remand, concluded that the balance of factors favored remand.

2. *Silva v. Kaiser.* [No 3-98-CV-0767-I (ND Tex May 26, 1999)] Following the Fifth Circuit's opinion in *Giles,* Federal District Court Judge Sam Lindsay of the Northern District of Texas recognized the continuing breadth and scope of ERISA pre-emption in issuing an order denying plaintiffs' motion to re-mand.

3. *Copling v. Container Store, Inc.* [174 F 3d 590, 596 (5th Cir 1999)] The court held that complete preemption applies re-gardless of how artfully a claim is disguised as a state court action. This case explains the two types of preemption: (a) complete and ordinary and (b) defensive.

4. *Smith v. Texas Children's Hospital.* [84 F 3d 152 (5th Cir 1996)] The court held that once a district court remands to state court for lack of jurisdiction, the district court's statements regarding preemption of state law claims by federal law would have no preclusive effect on the state court's consideration of any substantive preemption defense.

5. *Benoit v. W.W. Grainger, Inc.* [1998 WL 749444 (ED La No 98-1315, US Dist 1998)] Decided by the U.S. District Court for the Eastern District of Louisiana one month after Judge Gilmore questioned the vitality of *Corcoran v. United Health Care, Inc.* [965 F 2d 1321 (5th Cir 1992)] in her opinion in *Corporate Health Insurance, Inc. v. Texas Department of Insurance* [12 F Supp 2d 597 (SD Tex 1998)], this court rejected the argument that *Corcoran* is no longer good law in the Fifth Circuit:

   Benoit does not attempt to distinguish *Corcoran*. Rather, he claims that *Corcoran* has been undermined by more recent holdings of the Supreme Court and other circuits and is no longer "good law" in the Fifth Circuit. With this the Court cannot agree.

6. *Hull v. Fallon.* [188 F 3d 939, 942 (8th Cir 1999)] The plaintiff filed a medical malpractice action in state court alleging failure to diagnose and treat his heart disease, resulting in myocardial infarction. The plaintiff also filed a claim against the health plan, claiming vicarious liability for the physician's alleged negligence. The health plan removed the case to federal court and filed a companion motion to dismiss under ERISA. The court commented that, although the plaintiff characterized his claims in medical malpractice terminology, the essence of his claims was a denial of benefits, and they were therefore preempted by ERISA. Thus, the Eighth Circuit has joined the Seventh Circuit in finding preemption of vicarious liability claims against health plans.

Q 8:133   What are the future implications of ERISA in managed care arrangements?

For most health plans, ERISA will continue to apply to the claims brought by disaffected enrollees. As discussed in this chapter and elsewhere in this book, however, there have been some important trends in the determination of ERISA duties and in its preemption of state law claims. The forthcoming U.S. Supreme Court cases will be (see Q 8:128) important, since they will likely force some legislative action on the part of Congress.

Federal Employees Health Benefits Act

Q 8:134 What does the Federal Employees Health Benefits Act govern?

The Federal Employees Health Benefits Act (FEHBA) governs the employee benefit plans of federal employees (see chapter 7). FEHBA [5 USC § 8901] is administered by the Office of Personnel Management (OPM), which enters into contracts with indemnity plans, PPOs, HMOs, and POS plans to cover federal employees eligible to participate in the Federal Employees Health Benefits Program (FEHBP).

Q 8:135 What is the significance of the FEHBA preemption clause?

FEHBA preemption operates much like ERISA preemption. In 1998, the FEHBA preemption provision was amended to mirror the ERISA preemption clause:[57]

> The provisions of any contract under this chapter which relate to the nature or extent of coverage or benefits *shall supersede and preempt any State or local law which relates to health insurance or plans* to the extent that such law or regulation is inconsistent with such contractual provisions.

[5 USC § 8902(m)(1) emphasis added] It is clear that this amendment is intended to broaden the preemptive effect of FEHBA.[58] The express preemption provision of FEHBA prohibits certain claims by enrollees of FEHBA plans that attack the administration of the health plan. Many claims and allegations raised in managed care litigation may implicate the express preemption clause of FEHBA.

Health Care Fraud and Abuse

Overview

Q 8:136   What types of activities do health care fraud and abuse laws prohibit?

Various fraud and abuse laws will apply whenever health care transactions involve licensed health professionals or facilities as consumers or business partners, or involve the advertising, promotion, or purchase of goods and services that are provided by licensed health professionals or facilities, or that are required to be provided only pursuant to a physician's order, such as prescription drugs.

Health care fraud and abuse laws generally prohibit two types of activities: (1) fraud and false statements and (2) kickbacks and self-referral.

Fraud and False Statements. A number of federal criminal laws prohibit a wide range of fraudulent conduct, which can be defined roughly as any scheme designed to obtain money or something of value under false pretenses. Civil fraud remedies are also available when the federal government is the victim of fraud. Federal law prohibits making false statements to federal agencies, including statements made to obtain payment from the federal government or in connection with information provided to regulatory agencies, such as the Food and Drug Administration (FDA) or the CMS.

Kickbacks and Self-Referral. The federal antikickback statute makes it a crime, punishable by up to five years in prison, to provide anything of value, money or otherwise, directly or indirectly, with the intent to induce a referral of a patient or of a health care service. Significantly, liability attaches to both parties to the transaction: the entity or individual providing the prohibited remuneration and the entity or individual receiving it.[59] Federal law also prohibits physicians and other health care providers from referring beneficiaries in federal health care programs to clinics or other facilities in which the physician or health care provider has an interest.[60] These practices, kickbacks and self-referrals, are prohibited under federal law because they tend to corrupt the exercise of a medical professional's independent judgment.

Q 8:137   What activities of MCOs are subject to health care fraud and abuse laws?

With respect to MCOs, whenever an arrangement directs the flow of health care to any one provider or whenever any one party exercises undue influence over a patient's health care decisions, there is the potential for violation of health care fraud and abuse laws, which prohibit the following MCO activities:

Kickbacks for Referrals. In the context of Medicare and Medicaid, the health care fraud and abuse laws [18 USC § 1347] prohibit arrangements that encourage or influence referrals of patients. [42 USC §§ 1320a-7, 1320a-7a, 1320a-7b] In *United States v. Greber* [760 F 2d 68 (3d Cir 1985), *cert. denied,* 474 US 988 (1985)], the court adopted a very broad test that provided that even if "one purpose" of the arrangement was to induce referrals, the statute was violated.

Fee Splitting. Fee-splitting laws prohibit a licensed professional from splitting his or her professional fees with an unlicensed person or entity. Sometimes the prohibition is related to an impermissible intent, such as inducement of referral. In other cases, the fee-splitting prohibition is related to a ban on the corporate practice of medicine (see Qs 8:76–8:80).

Billing Fraud. In addition, the Fraud and Abuse Act defines two general categories of conduct as having the potential for violating its provisions: (1) filing false claims and (2) giving or receiving payment for referrals. Such violations can result in criminal penalties if performed willingly and knowingly and can result in civil monetary penalties and program exclusion, even in the absence of intent. [42 USC § 1320a-7b]

Self-Referral. Under legislation commonly referred to as the Stark laws, a physician or immediate family member cannot make patient referrals to an entity for furnishing Medicare- or Medicaid-reimbursed designated health services if the physician or a family member has an ownership or investment interest in, or a compensation arrangement with, the entity. [42 USC § 1395nn] An ownership or investment interest may involve equity, debt, or other means and includes an interest in an entity that holds an ownership or investment interest in an entity providing designated health services. Designated health services include the following:

- Clinical laboratory services
- Radiology or radiation therapy services
- Physical and occupational therapy services
- Durable medical equipment and supplies
- Parenteral and enteral nutrients, equipment, and supplies
- Prosthetics, orthotics, and prosthetic devices and supplies
- Outpatient prescription drugs
- Home health services
- Inpatient and outpatient hospital services

The Stark II regulations have been published in the Federal Register. [63 Fed Reg 1659–1728 (Jan 9, 1998)]

Q 8:138   What managed care activities are currently under increased government scrutiny?

The DHHS OIG has recently focused on failure of MCOs to authorize payment for emergency treatment and false statements concerning the MCOs' adjusted community rates (ACR). Of particular interest to the OIG is electronic health information.

Emergency Treatment Authorization and Patient Dumping. The DHHS OIG is developing guidance on reviewing organizations that fail to provide or authorize emergency treatment, including the failure of hospitals to do a medical screening examination regardless of whether the MCO provides authorization (see discussion of EMTALA, beginning at Q 8:119). The OIG anticipates imposing civil monetary penalties on hospitals and physicians who engage in "patient dumping" because of managed care incentives.

False Adjusted Community Rate Statements. Under the M + C program, participating managed care plans must submit ACR information to CMS. The ACR is the premium that the contract would charge its non-Medicare enrollees for Medicare-covered services, adjusted for the Medicare members' greater use of services. CMS will be evaluating whether any M + C organizations make false statements relating to their calculation of the ACR. (See chapter 7 for more information on M + C plans and ACR calculations.)

Denial of Services. In a presentation to the Hospital Council of Northern and Central California and Healthcare Financial Management Association on May 22, 1998, James Sheehan, chief of the civil division of the U.S. Attorney's Office for the Eastern District of Pennsylvania, told the audience that the focus of fraud investigation will shift from billing schemes to denial of care. He indicated that MCOs can avoid problems by using "clinically valid, objectively based guidelines." Compliance plans for MCOs are encouraged.

Gainsharing. The OIG issued a special advisory bulletin in July 1999 regarding gainsharing arrangements and civil monetary penalties for hospital payments to physicians to reduce or limit services to beneficiaries. Under Section 1128A(b)(1) of the Social Security Act, a hospital is prohibited from making a payment, directly or indirectly, to induce a physician to reduce or limit services to Medicare or Medicaid beneficiaries under the physician's direct care. Hospitals that make (and physicians that receive) such payments are liable for civil monetary penalties of up to $2,000 per patient covered by the payments. On August 24, 1999, the OIG released a letter clarifying this special advisory bulletin as applying only to fee-for-service systems and not to Medicare or Medicaid managed care plans.

Internet Health Fraud. Two federal laws protecting the privacy of individuals are particularly important to the electronic health industry. First, the FTC Act prohibits businesses engaged in interstate commerce from engaging in a broad range of unfair or deceptive trade practices. According to the FTC, collecting or disclosing personal information in violation of a Web site's written privacy policy may constitute an unfair or deceptive trade practice. The FTC announced that it has launched an investigation into the privacy practices of a number of health care Web sites, prompted in part by the California Healthcare Foundation study that found several well-known sites were violating their own posted privacy policies.[61] Second, and potentially more important to the electronic health industry, is HIPAA, under which new medical records privacy standards have been developed by DHHS.[62] Because Congress failed to meet its own deadline for enacting comprehensive medical records privacy legislation, HIPAA authorized and directed the Secretary of Health and Human Services to develop privacy regulations for certain electronic health care transactions. These regulations apply to health care providers, health care plans, and health care clearinghouses.

HIPAA also required DHHS to develop minimum standards for the security of electronic health information.[63]

Q 8:139 What types of activities involving a managed care entity could constitute fraud under the Fraud and Abuse Act?

Fraud under the Fraud and Abuse Act includes any intentional deception or misrepresentation that an individual knows to be false and that could result in an unauthorized benefit to himself or herself or some other person. Examples of such activities are billing for services not rendered, misrepresentation of services rendered, kickbacks, deliberate application for duplicate reimbursement, and false or misleading entries on cost reports.

Q 8:140 What types of activities involving a managed care entity could be deemed abusive under the Fraud and Abuse Act?

Abuse under the Fraud and Abuse Act includes any incident or practice that may directly or indirectly cause financial losses to government health programs or to beneficiaries or recipients (which is almost anything that the government agent considers unacceptable but does not rise to the level of actionable fraud). Examples of such activities are unnecessary services, breach of assignment agreement, "gang" visits (in which a physician charges for multiple patients during a single encounter), improper billing practices, routine waiver of coinsurance and deductibles, failure to maintain adequate records or accounting to substantiate costs, and excessive compensation to owners, administrators, or owner-related employees.

Q 8:141 How do Medicare and Medicaid reimbursement rules apply to managed care arrangements?

For MCOs, the most significant reimbursement issues arise under the related-organization principle and the restrictions: on reassignment of Medicare and Medicaid payments.

Related-Organization Principle. When a provider is paid on a cost basis, it is subject to a limitation on costs applicable to services, facilities, and supplies when they are furnished by organizations related by ownership or control. Costs for items furnished by a related party are limited to the cost to the related organization and cannot exceed the price of comparable items or services that could be purchased elsewhere. In the context of an integrated delivery system, if an MSO buys services from the hospital that formed it, the principle applies unless the MSO qualifies under the following exception to the principle: (1) the supplying organization is a bona fide separate organization; (2) a substantial part of the supplying organization's business activity of the type carried on with the provider is transacted with other organizations not related to the provider and the supplier by common ownership or control, and there is an open, competitive market for the type of services or supplies furnished; (3) institutions such as the provider typically obtain services, facilities, or supplies from outside sources rather than producing them internally; and (4) the charge to the provider is in line with the charge for similar items in the open market and no more than the charge made under comparable circumstances to others by the supplying organization.

Restrictions on Reassignment. Under Medicare Part B, payment for physician services and other medical and health services may be made either to the beneficiary or directly to the provider of services under an assignment agreement. Although a beneficiary can assign his or her rights to payment to the physician or supplier, these parties are prohibited from reassigning rights to receive payment to others absent certain exceptions, such as payment to an employer as a condition of employment or payment to an agent who provides billing and collection services. In the context of a managed care entity, the mechanism for billing Medicare or Medicaid must consider these prohibitions against reassignment.

For systems that are fully integrated, such as those that employ the providers, there is greater protection under the existing statutory exceptions and under applicable safe harbor regulations for violating any federal or state antireferral laws or regulations. To analyze the potential liability of any provider organization or its activities under federal antifraud and abuse laws and regulations, each structure has to be evaluated in the context of each activity in which it is engaged. For example, an IPA is far less at risk for fraud and abuse than an MSO because of its limited function as a provider organization that facilitates contracts.

Q 8:142   What is Operation Restore Trust?

Operation Restore Trust (ORT) is a DHHS program to combat fraud and abuse in Medicare and Medicaid. It began in 1995 in the five states that have more than one third of all Medicare and Medic-aid beneficiaries: California, Florida, New York, Texas, and Illinois. In May 1997, DHHS announced it had identified almost $188 million owed to the government as a result of ORT. The program has been expanded to 12 more states: Arizona, Colorado, Georgia, Louisiana, Massachusetts, Missouri, New Jersey, Ohio, Pennsylvania, Tennessee, Virginia, and Washington.

ORT has focused on Medicare and Medicaid fraud in home health agencies, nursing homes, and durable medical equipment sales. CMS is going after fraud and abuse in these areas by reviewing facilities with especially high Medicare reimbursement rates, by using statistical models to identify targets for investigations, by training members of local seniors' organizations to spot and report fraud, and by collaborating with state agencies (through the federal Fraud and Abuse Control Program) to survey providers' compliance with Medicare billing and quality requirements. ORT also has a telephone hot line so that the public can report suspected fraud and abuse directly to DHHS.

Over time, DHHS plans to expand ORT nationwide and across the various program areas of Medicare and Medicaid. Other DHHS projects to combat fraud and abuse include the following:

1. The Physicians at Teaching Hospitals initiative is investigating institutions for billing residents' services as if they had been performed by faculty.
2. The Medicare Integrity Program is allowing CMS to contract with fewer reviewers of provider behavior.
3. Greater efforts are being made to ensure that Medicare does not pay inappropriately when another insurer is the primary payer.
4. Information systems have been developed to identify questionable billing patterns, flag inappropriate payments before they are issued, and identify excluded providers and others who have engaged in improper billing.

Illegal Remuneration and Kickbacks

Q 8:143   What is the purpose of the federal antikickback statute?

The purpose of the federal antikickback statute, which has been on the books since 1972, is to protect patients and the federal health care programs from fraud and abuse by curtailing the corrupting influence of money on health care decisions. Straightforward but broad, the law states that anyone who knowingly and willfully receives or pays anything of value to influence the referral of federal health care program business, including Medicare and Medicaid, can be held accountable for a felony. Violations of the law are punishable by up to five years in prison, criminal fines of up to $25,000, administrative civil money penalties of up to $50,000, and exclusion from participation in federal health care programs.

The antikickback statute prohibits the knowing and willful solicitation, receipt, offer, or payment of any remuneration directly or indirectly, overtly or covertly, in cash or in kind, in return for (1) referring an individual to a person for the furnishing or arranging for the furnishing of any item or service for which payment may be made in whole or in part by Medicare or Medicaid, or (2) purchasing, leasing, ordering, or arranging for or recommending purchasing, leasing, or ordering any good, facility, service, or item for which payment may be made in whole or in part by Medicare or Medicaid. [42 USC § 1320a-7b]

Q 8:144   Are there any statutory exceptions to the prohibitions of the federal antikickback statute?

Yes. The following are not subject to the antikickback statute:

- Discounted goods or services (discounts or other price reductions are allowed if the reduction in price is properly disclosed and appropriately reflected in the costs claimed or charges made by the provider)
- Employer-employee relationship (payments by an employer to a bona fide employee who furnishes the covered items or services are allowed)
- Group purchasing arrangements (payments by a vendor of goods or services to an authorized purchasing agent for a group of providers are allowed provided there is adequate disclosure and a written agreement between the purchasing agent and the providers)
- Arrangements falling under safe harbors issued by the DHHS OIG

Q 8:145   What are the safe harbors?

There are 23 antikickback safe harbors in the Code of Federal Regulations (CFR), in 21 subparagraphs. These safe harbors set out exceptions to activities that might otherwise be deemed in violation of the federal antikickback statute.

Published Safe Harbors. As of November 1992, the DHHS OIG had published final safe harbors in the following areas: investment interests, space and equipment rental, personal services and management agreements, practice sales, referral services, warranties, discounts, employer-employee relationships, group purchasing organizations, waiver of beneficiary coinsurance and deductibles, and managed care arrangements.

In September 1993, DHHS proposed eight additional safe harbors. In 1999, these were published in final form:

1. *Investment in ambulatory surgery centers (ASCs) where physicians provide services directly to patients.* This safe harbor protects certain investment interests in four categories of free-standing Medicare-certified ASCs: surgeon-owned ASCs, single-specialty ASCs (e.g., all gastroenterologists), multispecialty ASCs (e.g., a mix of surgeons and gastroenterologists), and hospital and physician-owned ASCs. In general, to be protected, physician investors must be physicians for whom the ASC is an extension of their office practice pursuant to conditions set forth in the safe harbor. Hospital investors must not be in a position to make or influence referrals. Certain investors who are not existing or potential referral sources are permitted. The ASC safe harbor does not apply to other physician-owned clinical joint ventures, such as cardiac catheterization laboratories, end-stage renal dialysis facilities, and radiation oncology facilities.

2. *Group practices composed of active physician participants.* This safe harbor protects investments by physicians in their own group practices if the group practice meets the physician self-referral (Stark) law definition of a group practice. The safe harbor also protects investments in solo practices in which the practice is conducted through the solo practitioner's professional corporation or other separate legal entity. The safe harbor does not protect investments by group practices or

members of group practices in ancillary services' joint ventures, although such joint ventures may qualify for protection under other safe harbors.

3. *Specialty care referrals.* This safe harbor protects certain arrangements under which an individual or entity agrees to refer a patient to another individual or entity for specialty services, and in return, the party receiving the referral agrees to refer the patient back at a certain time or under certain circumstances. For example, a primary care physician and a specialist to whom the primary care physician has made a referral may agree that when the referred patient reaches a particular stage of recovery, the primary care physician should resume treatment of the patient. The safe harbor does not protect arrangements involving parties that split a global fee from a federal program. The safe harbor requires that referrals be clinically appropriate, rather than based on arbitrary dates or time frames.

4. *Cooperative hospital service organizations.* This safe harbor protects cooperative hospital service organizations (CHSOs) that qualify under Section 501(e) of the Internal Revenue Code (IRC). CHSOs are organizations formed by two or more tax-exempt hospitals, known as patron hospitals, to provide specifically enumerated services, such as purchasing, billing, and clinical services, solely for the benefit of patron hospitals. The safe harbor will protect payments from a patron hospital to a CHSO to support the CHSO's operational costs and payments from a CHSO to a patron hospital that are required by IRS rules.

5. *Physician recruitment.* This safe harbor protects recruitment payments made by entities to attract needed physicians and other health care professionals to rural and urban health professional shortage areas (HPSAs), as designated by the Health Resources and Services Administration. The safe harbor requires that at least 75 percent of the recruited practitioner's revenue be from patients who reside in HPSAs or medically underserved areas or are members of medically underserved populations, such as the homeless or migrant workers. The safe harbor limits the duration of payments to three years. The safe harbor does not prescribe the types of protected payments, such as income guarantees or moving expenses, leav-

ing that determination to negotiation by the parties. Because of the risk of disguised payments for referrals, the safe harbor does not protect payments made by hospitals to existing group practices to recruit physicians to join the group or payments made to retain existing practitioners. Such arrangements remain subject to case-by-case review under the antikickback statute.

6. *Rural hospital purchases of physician practices.* This safe harbor protects hospitals in HPSAs that buy and "hold" the practice of a retiring physician until a new physician can be recruited to replace the retiring one. To qualify for this safe harbor protection, the sale must be completed within three years and the hospital must engage in good-faith efforts to recruit a new practitioner.

7. *Investment in rural areas (joint ventures).* Often health care ventures in medically underserved areas have difficulty attracting needed capital, and often the best available sources of capital are local physicians. Many underserved area ventures cannot fit in the existing safe harbor for small entity joint ventures because that safe harbor limits physician ownership and the revenues that can be derived from referrals from physician investors. The underserved area joint venture safe harbor relaxes several of the conditions of the existing joint venture safe harbor. The new safe harbor permits a higher percentage of physician investors, up to 50 percent, and unlimited revenues from referral source investors. The new safe harbor protects joint ventures in underserved urban, as well as rural, areas. To qualify, a venture must be located in a medically underserved area, as defined by DHHS regulation and 75 percent of its patients must be medically underserved patients.

8. *Obstetric and malpractice insurance subsidies in underserved areas.* This safe harbor protects a hospital or other entity that pays all or part of the malpractice insurance premiums for practitioners engaging in obstetric practice in HPSAs. To qualify for protection, at least 75 percent of the subsidized practitioners' patients must be medically underserved patients. [42 CFR § 1001.952]

Managed Care Safe Harbors. In 1992, DHHS issued interim safe harbor regulations that indicated that typical managed care arrangements such as provider discounts and beneficiary incentives to use network providers were within the antikickback statute's scrutiny. The final rules, published and effective January 25, 1996, somewhat expand the scope of the safe harbors. These rules address protections for certain forms of enrollee incentives offered by health plans to encourage use of in-network providers, reductions offered to health plans by contract health care providers, and hospital in-patient coinsurance and deductibles. In January 1996, the DHHS OIG also published some revisions to the original safe harbors relating to Medicare and Medicaid managed care arrangements. [61 Fed Reg 2122 (Jan 26, 1996)] Most important was the risk-sharing arrangements exception contained in the HIPAA regulations and published in the Federal Register on November 19, 1999. When Congress enacted the exception to the antikickback statute for certain shared-risk arrangements, it directed DHHS to issue regulations through a negotiated rule-making process. The negotiating committee, composed of industry and government representatives, issued a joint committee statement in January 1998 that describes the agreement reached by the committee and served as a guideline for the government's rule making. This statement is available on the Internet at www.hhs. gov/progorg/oig/negrule/index.htm.

Q 8:146   What is the effect of these safe harbors?

These safe harbors immunize certain payment and business practices that are implicated by the federal antikickback statute from criminal and civil prosecution under the statute. To be protected by a safe harbor, an arrangement must fit squarely within the safe harbor, but failure to comply with a safe harbor provision does not mean that an arrangement is per se illegal. Compliance with safe harbors is voluntary, and arrangements that do not comply with a safe harbor must be analyzed on a case-by-case basis for compliance with the antikickback statute. Parties who are uncertain whether their arrangements qualify for safe harbor protection may request an advisory opinion. Instructions on how to request an advisory opinion are available on the Internet at www.hhs.gov/oig/advopn/index.htm.

Referral Restrictions

Q 8:147   What laws regulate physician referrals?

Some state laws prohibit a physician from having a financial relationship with any entity to which he or she refers a patient, or at a minimum, require the physician to disclose the relationship he or she has with the entity. These laws apply to all patients and all sources of payment.

Under the Ethics in Patient Referrals Act (also known as the Stark I and II laws), referrals by a physician to a clinical laboratory in which or with which the physician has a financial interest or relationship are expressly prohibited. When enacted in 1989, this Act did not apply to services provided directly by a physician (or under a physician's direct supervision) or to non-Medicare-covered services. Effective December 31, 1994, however, the prohibition was extended to cover not only clinical laboratory services but also physical therapy services; occupational therapy services; radiology or other diagnostic services; radiation therapy services; durable medical equipment; parenteral and enteral nutrients, equipment, and supplies; prosthetics, orthotics, and prosthetic devices; home health services; outpatient prescription drugs; and inpatient and outpatient hospital services. Future proposed amendments to the Stark laws will extend them beyond Medicare-covered services to include all services for which payment is made with federal funds. Penalties for violating the Stark laws include not only nonpayment for services subject to prohibited referrals and program exclusion but also civil monetary penalties of up to $15,000 per service, civil monetary penalties for each day that a required disclosure is not made, and civil monetary penalties of up to $100,000 for participation in any circumvention scheme.

Q 8:148 Are there any exceptions to the prohibitions in the Stark laws?

Yes. There are a number of general exceptions to the prohibitions in the Stark laws. Those most relevant to provider-sponsored entities are the exceptions for (1) referrals for physician services provided personally by (or under the personal supervision of) another physician in the same group practice as the referring physician [42 USC § 1395nn(b)(1)]; (2) referrals for in-office ancillary services [42 USC § 1395nn(b)(2)]; (3) compensation to a bona fide employee [42 USC § 1395nn(b)(2)]; (4) compensation pursuant to personal service arrangements [42 USC § 1395nn(b)(3)]; and (5) prepaid plan payments and referrals. [42 USC § 1395nn(b)(3)]

The most important exception is the medical group practice exception, under which a physician provides most of the services; the group provides, bills, and collects for the services; the expenses and income are allocated by the existing system; there is no compensation for volume or value of referrals; and 75 percent of the patient encounters are conducted by group members. This exception does not apply to the offering of durable medical equipment (other than infusion pumps) or parenteral or enteral nutrients, equipment, or supplies.

There are published exceptions for ownership in publicly traded securities and for ownership and investment in services provided by hospitals located in Puerto Rico, by rural providers, and when the physician is authorized to perform the services and the investment or ownership interest is in the hospital itself and not merely a subdivision of the hospital. Other exceptions exist for prepaid plans or other HMOs as defined by statute, rental of office space or equipment, hospital employment and service arrangements, physician recruitment, other service arrangements, and other isolated financial transactions.

The self-referral ban does not apply to bona fide employment relationships in which the employer is paying the employee for the provision of designated services. The test for a bona fide employment relationship requires a finding that (1) the employment is for identifiable services; (2) the remuneration is consistent with the fair market value of the services and is not based on the volume or value of referrals; (3) the remuneration is provided under a commercially reasonable agreement; and (4) such other requirements as the Secretary of Health and Human Services (HHS) may impose. [42 USC § 1395nn(e)(2)] Productivity bonuses are allowed, provided they are based on services performed personally by the physician. This requirement is more restrictive than the productivity bonus available under the group practice exception.

Q 8:149   What are the differences between the federal antikickback statute and the Stark laws?

The Stark laws do not include criminal sanctions, whereas the federal antikickback statute does. Evidence of corrupt intent is critical to a violation of the antikickback statute, but it does not apply to the Stark laws.

Antikickback Issues. Several arrangements that are fundamental components of an MCO, HMO, or integrated delivery system are within the scope of the antikickback law but do not fall within any current safe harbor: (1) incentives to encourage use of a provider panel; (2) incentives to encourage preventive care; (3) provider discounts; and (4) Part B coinsurance discounts under Medicare Select.

Self-Referral Issues. Provider integration is a natural end product of the evolution of the health care system as it moves toward increased cost effectiveness. Vertically integrated structures will own or control their ancillary services such as laboratory and radiology facilities. Such organizations may offer physicians a financial stake in the cost-effective practice of medicine through ownership interests. Although there is no motive in the structure to "over-refer" for profit, under the Stark laws any physician ownership in an entity (except those qualified under Section 1876 of the Social Security Act as cost risk contractors or as federally qualified HMOs) subjects the entire arrangement to regulatory scrutiny. With the sunset of employer mandates to offer federally qualified HMOs, there will be less incentive for HMOs to seek federal qualification unless they intend specifically to service Medicare and Medicaid programs. Even the contractual arrangements with physicians can create a problem under the Stark regulations.

Physician Incentives. In an effort to respond to fears surrounding increased use of managed care in government programs, DHHS issued regulations that place limitations on incentive arrangements that may influence a physician's care decisions. Final rules were published on March 27, 1996,[64] and apply to physicians providing medical care through HMOs, competitive medical plans, and health insuring organizations. Key provisions include the following:[65]

- Prohibitions against making specific payments for limiting or reducing medically necessary services
- Defining a medical group as having "substantial risk" if more than 25 percent of its potential payment is at risk for services it does not provide
- Providing for adequate stop-loss coverage for physicians at substantial risk
- For physicians at substantial risk, use of annual beneficiary surveys of enrollees and disenrollees on indicators of satisfaction, quality, and access to services

Q 8:150   Do managed care arrangements using integrated delivery systems and MCOs create any risk for violating laws that regulate physician referrals?

Yes. Laws at both the state and federal levels addressing physician self-referral define financial relationships to include ownership or investment arrangements and compensation arrangements. Therefore, these laws must be taken into consideration in structuring the various managed care provider organizations. Activities of HMOs, MCOs, and integrated delivery systems are subject to scrutiny under the antireferral laws (and the anti-kickback laws) regardless of the existence of a specific Medicare or Medicaid contract.

Implications of Fraud and Abuse for Managed Care

Q 8:151   How can MCOs, integrated delivery systems, and HMOs reduce their regulatory risk for violating the fraud, antikickback, and antireferral laws?

There is no simple answer to this question. Each arrangement must be analyzed based on its unique facts and circumstances. The DHHS OIG fraud alerts, administrative review letters, and other guidance can serve as excellent sources of information for unsuspecting providers. Activities that have been identified as problems include the following:

- Routine waiver of copayments or deductibles under Medicare Part B
- Joint venture arrangements that fail to fall within a safe harbor, and contain the following questionable features:
  - Choosing investors because they are in a position to refer
  - Giving physicians in a position to make more referrals greater investment opportunities or incentives
  - Requiring physicians who fail to meet quotas or who leave the practice to divest their interests
  - Tracking referrals and disseminating the information to investors
  - Investment interests that are "nontransferable"
  - Investments that are disproportionate to returns
  - Allowing physicians to "borrow" the amounts to be invested

- Hospitals or other providers engaging in arrangements that provide incentives for physicians to refer

- Hospitals engaging in gainsharing programs to provide incentives for physicians to engage in activities that "reduce" care and cut costs

- Aggressive marketing schemes by prescription drug companies that include valuable, nonmedical benefits in exchange for the physicians' selection of specific prescription drugs

- The provision of something of value to a source of referrals to a clinical laboratory

- Waiver of charges for managed care patients to retain referrals of fee-for-service patients

Q 8:152 Does Medicare regulate physician incentive arrangements under managed care?

Yes. On December 31, 1996, HCFA published final rules amending its earlier rules governing physician incentive plans operated by federally qualified HMOs and competitive medical plans. The objective of the rules was to prohibit the use of physician payments to limit or reduce necessary services to enrollees. In addition, the rules impose certain disclosure and stop-loss requirements on HMOs when payments put physicians at substantial financial risk for referral services. Plans with direct contracting and subcontracting arrangements that shift substantial risk must disclose the following information on an annual basis: (1) whether referral services are covered by the incentive plan; (2) the type of payment arrangement used (e.g., withhold or capitation); (3) the percentage of total income at risk for referrals; (4) the amount and type of stop-loss coverage; (5) the number of enrollees and whether enrollees were pooled to achieve the total; (6) for capitated physicians, the previous year's percentage of payment that was for primary care services, specialty referral services, hospital services, and other types of providers; and (7) a summary of enrollee survey results. Physician groups that do not transfer substantial risk to their own physicians are not required to disclose this information. Intermediaries such as IPAs are required to report their incentive arrangements, regardless of the risk transferred.[66]

Q 8:153 How does the BBA affect Medicare and Medicaid regulations against fraud and abuse?

The BBA supplements the antifraud, waste, and abuse provisions of HIPAA by adding the following provisions:

1. Those convicted of three health care–related crimes on or after the date of enactment are premanently excluded from participating in Medicare and Medicaid. Exclusion is mandatory.

2. DHHS can refuse to enter into Medicare agreements with a physician or supplier that has been convicted of a single felony if the Secretary determines it to be in the best interest of the program.

3. Explanation of benefits forms and itemized bills provided to Medicare beneficiaries must state that Medicare fraud, abuse, and waste are problems and must include a toll-free number for persons to report suspected fraud, abuse, and waste in Medicare.

4. An entity controlled by a family member of a sanctioned individual is excluded from participating in Medicare and Medicaid.

5. Individuals who knowingly contract with an excluded individual or entity are subject to civil monetary penalties. This provision creates a civil monetary penalty of $50,000 for each violation of the federal antikickback statute, including civil monetary penalties of up to $25,000 for health plans that fail to report adverse actions as required under the HIPAA Fraud and Abuse Program.

6. Suppliers of durable medical equipment, home health agencies, comprehensive outpatient rehabilitation facilities, and other rehabilitation facilities must provide surety bonds in amounts not less than $50,000. Durable medical equipment suppliers must also provide information as to persons with an ownership or control interest in the durable medical equipment supplier, or in any subcontractor in which the durable medical equipment supplier has a 5 percent or greater ownership interest.

7. Advisory opinions on whether a physician self-referral to designated health services (other than clinical laboratories) is

prohibited are binding on DHHS and the parties requesting the opinion.

The BBA is discussed in more detail in chapter 7.

Trends and Future Issues

Q 8:154   What are the top issues for regulators in the area of health care fraud and abuse?

The DHHS OIG has set the following as its target areas for investigation in 2002:

- Pharmaceutical industry
- Quality of care in nursing homes
- Hospital and physician billing
- Kickbacks
- Internet fraud
- Managed care
- HIPAA and medical privacy
- HCA-The Healthcare Company final settlement

Federal agencies, particularly DHHS, have been increasing their efforts to curb waste, fraud, and abuse in the health care industry. Stepped-up agency activity is reflected in OIG's recent investigations of large systems, such as Columbia/HCA, followed by a payment in 2000 of $745,000 in civil claims. Of note are the fraud and abuse provisions of HIPAA, the availability of advisory opinions for business arrangements, negotiated rule making for managed care exceptions to the federal antikickback statute, corporate compliance, and the Stark regulations.

Fraud and the Internet

Q 8:155   What types of Internet-based health activities are the focus of current federal fraud enforcement?

Federal fraud enforcement is focusing on the following types of Internet-based health activities: *Web Sites Offering Basic Business-to-Consumer Health Care Information.* For Internet health care (e-health) companies that simply provide information to consumers, without charging consumers or third-party payers for services, a key concern should be ensuring that the Web site's privacy practices are consistent with any stated privacy polices. The FTC has announced investigations into a number of health care Web sites that collected or distributed personal information in violation of the site's posted privacy policy.

Online Operations of Health Care Providers, Health Care Plans, and Health Care Clearinghouses. The HIPAA privacy regulations impose significant privacy safeguards on health care providers, plans, or clearinghouses that engage in certain electronic transactions, including health claims, health care payment and remittance advice, and referral certification or authorization. For example, if a physician practice submits claims electronically to a third-party insurance company, both the physician practice and the insurance company are required to comply with the HIPAA privacy regulations. Online pharmacies will also need to comply with these privacy regulations.

I-Health Companies Providing Goods or Services Reimbursed by Federal Health Programs. I-health companies that provide goods or services to beneficiaries of federal health care programs, including Medicare and Medicaid, or that contract with such companies, must be mindful of the full range of antifraud safeguards in federal law. For example, the DHHS OIG has stated that it is illegal for a hospital to provide a health care provider with telemedicine equipment with the intent of encouraging that provider to consult with specialists at the hospital where such consultations are reimbursed by a federal health care program. Similarly, the Stark self-referral laws also attach to situations in which health care goods or services are reimbursed by federal health care programs, whether online or off-line. This business model is being emphasized because at least one market analyst expects the business-to-business side of the i-health industry to reach $370 billion by 2004. Since the federal government pays for a substantial percentage of all health care goods and services consumed in the United States, it seems fair to assume that some of the business-to-business market will involve goods and services reimbursed by federal health care programs. I-health companies should also be aware of the prohibition on employing or contracting with individuals or entities that have been excluded from participation in federal health care programs for misconduct. In an era of tight labor markets and the "outsourcing" of many business operations, it is easy to overlook the need for careful screening of employees and potential business partners. For example, an online pharmacy cannot hire or contract with a pharmacist who has been excluded by the DHHS OIG if the pharmacy receives federal reimbursement for the drugs.

I-Health Companies Selling or Marketing Drugs or Medical Devices. I-health companies that sell or promote drugs or medical devices must be aware of the comprehensive federal regulatory framework that safeguards patient health and safety. The FDA and FTC regulate advertising of drugs and medical devices, whether online or off-line. Similarly, online pharmacies and other i-health companies engaged in the sale of prescription drugs must comply with the Food, Drug, and Cosmetic Act. More stringent safeguards are imposed on the manufacture, sale, and promotion of controlled substances, and more serious criminal and civil penalties attach for violations of the federal Controlled Substances Act. According to John Bentivoglio, Special Counsel for Health Care Fraud and Chief Privacy Officer, DOJ, the FDA's Office of Criminal Investigations has initiated 134 Internet-related investigations, including 88 open criminal investigations and 46 preliminary investigations. Of these 134 investigations, 54 involve sites selling prescription drugs and 80 are related to various types of health fraud or unapproved drug products.[67] In 2000, 36 arrests and 17 convictions have resulted from FDA investigations into the illegal sale of drugs or medical products over the Internet. Figures for 2001 are similar.

Q 8:156 What are the future legal and liability issues associated with electronic health commerce?

Legal and liability issues associated with electronic health commerce (e-health) will involve transactions between one business and another and transactions between business and consumers with respect to health content and the provision of health services. These issues are discussed in more detail in chapter 15.

Business-to-Business Transactions. These transactions involve the following:

- Insurance claims processing; payment of providers; physician directories
- Data warehousing services

- Supply procurement
- Provision of disease-specific content, often through co-branded Web sites
- Access service providers; Internet service providers

Business-to-Consumer Transactions. These transactions involve direct interaction with consumers and are the biggest targets of future regulation:

- "Ask the doctor" Web sites (virtual or real)
- Physician-patient interaction
- Mental health counseling
- Online pharmacies
- Sales of durable medical equipment to consumers
- General health information, including disease states, symptoms, and predictors; physician directories and credentialing information; medication information
- Clinical trials information and enrollment
- Personal medical records

Mixed Transactions. Mixed business-to-business and business-to-consumer transactions include the following:

- Telemedicine
- Devices (e.g., diabetes blood sugar testing using glucometers)
- Transmission of information and data warehousing
- Provider consultations and other forms of peer interaction

Q 8:157 What legal and liability issues are associated with Web site content?

Legal issues associated with Web site content include the following:

- Terms of use—disclaimers relating to medical advice or services; use of intellectual property; disclaimer of warranties
- Privacy policies—authorization for use of user information; disclosure

Liability issues associated with Web site content include the following:

- Potential liability for inaccurate or misleading information
- Notices of posting or other disclosure on Web sites
- Availability of liability insurance

Q 8:158 What should a company engaged in e-health do to avoid violating antifraud and other health care laws?

Any company engaged in e-health should conduct a comprehensive assessment of its business practices, focusing on several key areas, including privacy practices, compliance with fraud and abuse laws, and compliance with regulations governing the sale and promotion of drugs and medical devices. Questions to ask include the following:

1. Do you collect or disclose personal information? If so, are you a health care provider, plan, or clearinghouse as defined in the HIPAA privacy regulations? Have you taken steps to protect such data against cyberattacks?

2. Are you required to submit information to the federal government, such as information required by the FDA or another regulatory agency? If so, do you have systems in place to ensure the data is accurate?

3. Do you receive, directly or indirectly, reimbursement from the federal government for health care goods or services, or are you contracting with an individual or entity that does? If so, have you examined your operations to ensure you are in compliance with all federal health care fraud laws, including the antikickback and self-referral statutes? Have you instituted steps to screen employees and contractors to ensure your company has not hired an individual who has been excluded from participation in federal health care programs?

4. Are you dispensing or promoting drugs or medical devices over the Internet in a manner that would subject you to regulation by the FDA, FTC, or state regulatory agencies?

It is suggested that e-health businesses that will rely, in whole or in part, on reimbursement from federal health care programs develop compliance programs that contain, at a minimum, the components identified by the DHHS OIG in model compliance guides for various segments of the health care industry.

Compliance Programs

Q 8:159   What components of a compliance program have been identified by the DHHS OIG as model compliance guides?

The DHHS OIG has suggested that all corporate compliance programs have seven elements. These elements track the 1991 federal Sentencing Guidelines for Corporations. Courts are required to follow the guidelines in the sentencing of all organizations convicted of federal felonies and Class A misdemeanors. If an organization has an "effective" compliance program in place, the organization may have its culpability reduced. The seven elements of an effective compliance program are as follows:

1. *Compliance standards and procedures.* The organization should establish compliance standards and procedures to be followed by its employees and other agents that are reasonably capable of reducing the prospect of criminal conduct.

2. *Oversight responsibilities.* Specific individuals in high-level positions of the organization should be assigned overall responsibility to oversee compliance with such standards and procedures.

3. *Delegation and authority.* The organization should use due care not to delegate substantial discretionary authority to individuals who the organization knew, or should have known through the exercise of due diligence, had a propensity to engage in illegal activities.

4. *Employee training.* The organization should take steps to communicate its standards and procedures effectively to all employees and other agents, such as through required participation in training programs or by disseminating publications that explain what is required.

5. *Monitoring and auditing.* The organization should take reasonable steps to achieve compliance with its standards through monitoring and auditing systems reasonably designed to detect criminal conduct by its employees and other

agents, and by having in place and publicizing a reporting system for employees or other agents to make reports of suspected improper conduct without fear of retribution.

6. *Enforcement and discipline.* The standards must have been consistently enforced through appropriate disciplinary mechanisms, including, as appropriate, discipline of individuals responsible for the failure to detect an offense. Adequate discipline of individuals responsible for an offense is an important component of enforcement.

7. *Response and prevention.* After an offense is detected, the organization should take all reasonable steps to respond appropriately to the offense and to prevent further similar offenses, including modifications to its program to prevent and detect violations of law.

The DHHS OIG model compliance guidelines specific to key categories of providers are available at www.os.dhhs.gov/oig/modcomp and include the following:

- Home health agencies [63 Fed Reg 42410 (Aug 7, 1998)]
- Third-party medical billing [63 Fed Reg 70138 (Dec 18, 1998)]
- Clinical laboratories [62 Fed Reg 9435 (Mar 3, 1997), as amended at 63 Fed Reg 45076 (Aug 24, 1998)]
- Durable medical equipment companies [64 Fed Reg 4435 (Jan 28, 1999)]
- M + C plans (see Q 8:165)
- Hospices
- Nursing homes [63 Fed Reg 70137 (Dec 18, 1998)]
- Individual and small medical group practices [65 Fed Reg 59434 (Oct 5, 2000)]

Q 8:160 What has contributed to the importance of compliance programs in health care?

Health care providers and suppliers have come under increased scrutiny by the government, commercial payers, and consumers in an effort to eliminate fraud, waste, and abuse in the health care industry. In 1995, the government began waging war on Medicare fraud and abuse through ORT. In 1996, with the passage of HIPAA, the government received a new weapon to combat health care fraud through HIPAA's antifraud provisions, which gave the government the authority to levy increased fines and damages and introduced four new health care crimes: health care fraud, embezzlement, false statements, and obstruction. The government's antifraud initiative was further strengthened by the passage of the BBA, which added more antifraud provisions, the authority to impose civil fines of up to $50,000 for violations of the federal antikickback statute, and a "three strikes" provision to impose mandatory lifetime exclusion from Medicare and Medicaid programs after the third conviction for a health-related offense.

Q 8:161   On what areas is the OIG focusing regarding compliance?

The OIG is focusing on a number of areas:

- Evaluation and management services
- Audits of physicians at teaching hospitals
- New laboratory codes in chemistry and hematology (with special attention on panels and profiles)
- Procedures performed in conjunction with visits
- Physicians with excessive nursing home visits
- Physician certification of durable medical equipment
- Diagnosis code validation
- Hospital ownership of physician practices
- Multiple hospital discharge billing for a single stay
- Critical care billing
- Physician billing for services rendered by a physician assistant
- Anesthesia services personally performed
- Improper billing for psychiatric services

Q 8:162   Why is corporate compliance important to a health care organization?

A corporate compliance program reduces the likelihood of wrongdoing, aids in the early detection of problems, and establishes a structure for internal reporting and investigation. In addition, a compliance program will go a long way toward helping when the government conducts an investigation. A compliance program indicates a lack of corporate intent to perform unlawful acts; thus, in cases where the government uncovers fraud, it shows that reasonable, good-faith efforts have been made by management to prevent and detect misconduct in the entity. Generally, the OIG will look to the compliance program as a factor when determining the level of sanctions, penalties, and/or exclusions to be imposed on the provider.

A compliance program also makes good business sense. It sends a clear message to employees and the public that an organization is committed to ensuring that its work is being done in an ethical and legal manner. A compliance program serves to protect both the integrity of the individuals in leadership positions of the organization and the organization itself.

Because of the criminal nature of health care fraud, the government does not have to prove that breaking the law was intended in order to indict and convict. It is enough that the crime occurred. More important, however, is the fact that corporate compliance is required. Organizations that do not have or have ineffective compliance programs face many risks:

1. *Probation and court-imposed compliance program.* If a company has no compliance program and is convicted of a crime, it faces not only a higher fine but also a court-imposed compliance program, which may be far more rigorous and may include judicial oversight.

2. *Government-designed corporate integrity program.* In the context of Medicare and/or Medicaid fraud and abuse, the DHHS OIG has stated that not only will a compliance plan be a "necessary component of all settlements," but any existing plan will be a "relevant factor" in negotiating settlements. A company without a compliance plan can expect more severe punishment than one with a compliance plan.

3. *Medicare and Medicaid program exclusion.* A danger of conviction for Medicare and/or Medicaid fraud is exclusion from the programs altogether. If an organization is convicted of criminal fraud, exclusion is mandatory. The existence of a corporate compliance program may change the mandatory exclusion to a permissive exclusion.

4. *Asset forfeiture.* The federal government and many states have the authority to seize assets before any adjudication of wrongdoing.

5. *Management liability.* Individuals have always been subject to fines and prison for their involvement in a crime. This liability can extend to corporate officers and managers.

6. *Shareholder lawsuits.* Another risk to management and the board of directors that is often overlooked is civil litigation by disgruntled shareholders against officers and directors.

7. *Legal counsel liability.* As seen in the cases against the attorneys advising a hospital in Kansas City, there is a risk to the legal advisors to an organization that is engaging in health care fraud.[68]

8. *Qui tam lawsuits.* The Fraud and Abuse Act has both criminal and civil penalties that can be initiated through private individuals on behalf of the government. These suits involve "whistleblowers," who can be competitors, employees, or even patients of a health care provider.

Q 8:163   What is a corporate integrity agreement?

A corporate integrity agreement is an agreement that the DHHS OIG imposes on health care providers or entities that settle civil fraud cases. In return for agreeing to operate under a corporate integrity agreement, the OIG agrees not to exclude the health care provider or entity from participation in Medicare, Medicaid, and other federal health care programs. The typical corporate integrity agreement lasts for five years and requires a provider or entity to put compliance measures in place to ensure the integrity of federal health care program claims submitted by the provider or entity. Such measures include requirements to do the following:

• Hire a compliance officer and appoint a compliance committee

• Develop written standards and policies

• Implement a comprehensive employee training program

• Audit billings to federal health care programs

• Establish a confidential disclosure program

• Restrict employment of ineligible persons

• Submit a variety of reports to the OIG

The corporate integrity agreement annual report checklist and answers to frequently asked questions are available on the OIG Web site at http://www.hhs.gov/oig/new.html.

Q 8:164　What is the responsibility of a compliance committee and of a compliance officer?

A compliance committee is established at the direction of the organization's governing body. It provides oversight and leadership to the compliance activity and ensures reporting and accountability to the governing body. The committee serves as an advisory body for employees who request reviews or those who make complaints. Finally, the committee is intimately involved in fashioning corrective actions when departures from compliance policies are observed or reported.

A compliance officer appointed by the organization's governing body works with the compliance committee and is responsible for educating the committee and monitoring its work.

Q 8:165　How important are compliance programs for M + C organizations?

In 1999 the federal government began to focus considerable attention on MCOs in its expansion of fraud and abuse enforcement.[69] In its fiscal 1999 work plan, DHHS included 15 managed care-related initiatives, and HCFA's February 1999 Comprehensive Plan for Program Integrity included managed care as one of five priority areas with respect to program integrity. In the M + C regulations issued in June 1998, a provision was included requiring M + C organizations to have a compliance plan. [42 CFR § 422.501(b)(3)(vi)]

In addition to the seven basic elements of a compliance plan (see Q 8:159), the DHHS OIG recommends that an M + C organization compliance officer be given "full authority to stop the submission of data that he or she believes is problematic until such time as the issue in question has been resolved." In addition, the OIG recommends that M + C organizations establish an intranet compliance Web site for employees to serve as "a centralized source [of] statutory, regulatory and other program guidance." M + C organizations are required to consult HIPDB before hiring or contracting with a provider.

Q 8:166　What are the important fraud risk areas unique to MCOs?

Each MCO must identify its own risk areas. The DHHS OIG, however, has identified seven areas that are of particular concern to the OIG based on its own audits, investigations, and evaluations:

Marketing Materials and Personnel. The OIG is concerned that marketing materials be complete and accurate, and that they do not mislead, confuse, or misrepresent any aspect of the plan. This concern arises as a result of a recent General Accounting Office (GAO) study that reviewed marketing materials used by 16 MCOs and found that all 16 organizations had distributed inaccurate and incomplete information. Of particular concern to the OIG is the importance of stressing in these materials to potential enrollees (1) the concept of a "lock-in," which requires beneficiaries to select providers from an authorized network, and (2) that beneficiaries may be terminated from enrollment because CMS refuses to renew the M + C organization's contract, or because the M + C organization elects not to participate in the program in that geographic area or renew its M + C contract.

Selective Marketing and Enrollment. The OIG is concerned about marketing schemes designed to select healthier (and therefore less costly) enrollees. The first scheme, known as "cherry-picking," involves discriminatory marketing and enrollment practices to attract healthier and less costly Medicare eligibles. The second scheme, called "gerrymandering," involves eliminating high dollar risk areas from the organization's service area. Any discrimination among enrollees based on perceived degree of risk for costly or prolonged treatment is illegal (with the exception of end-stage renal disease).

Disenrollment. The OIG has discovered a pattern of disenrollment by managed care enrollees who were on the verge of receiving expensive inpatient services. Although the reasons for such disenrollment are unknown, the OIG is sensitive that enrollees not be encouraged to disenroll except as permitted by law.

Underutilization and Quality of Care. Underutilization, or "stinting," is defined by the OIG as the inappropriate withholding or delay of medically necessary services. This practice can take many forms, including (1) failure to employ or contract with sufficient numbers of providers or supplies, (2) failure to ensure that providers and services are obtainable from a particular geographic area, (3) the imposition of unreasonable and burdensome utilization review procedures, (4) the categorical denial of claims, and (5) failure or delay in approving referrals to specialists. Delays in scheduling appointments or obtaining telephone access can also be considered stinting. Therefore, M + C organizations must develop policies and procedures that ensure that their enrollees receive appropriate access to medically necessary care. The types of policies that the OIG focuses on include the following:

- Policies prohibiting gag rules (rules that interfere with the ability of health care professionals to communicate openly with beneficiaries concerning the beneficiaries' health status, treatment options, and the risks, benefits, and consequences of treatment and nontreatment)
- Policies that ensure that any incentives offered to physicians or physician groups to control utilization comply with the rules regulating physician incentive plans, which prohibit incentives aimed at limiting medically necessary care, and under some circumstances, require the use of satisfaction surveys and adequate and appropriate stop-loss insurance
- Policies to ensure that enrollees receive medical care from health care professionals who are properly qualified and licensed and who have clinical privileges in good standing

Data Collection and Submission. The OIG recommends that M + C organizations implement policies and procedures to ensure that "all required submissions to [CMS are] accurate, timely and complete." Of particular concern to the OIG is the submission of data that influence the amount of payment received by an M + C organization from CMS. This includes enrollment data, encounter data, and information needed to determine adjusted ACR$ for the plan.

Antikickback Statute and Other Inducements. The OIG recognizes that the federal antikickback statute is broad and may be applied to certain managed care arrangements. In recognition of the inapplicability of such incentives in managed care risk arrangements, the OIG has implemented a safe harbor to immunize many of the financial arrangements between MCOs paid on a capitated basis and providers and suppliers, as well as the downstream subcontractors of such providers and suppliers. [42 CFR § 1001.952]

1. There will be no protection for "swapping" (the practice of offering M + C organizations heavy discounts for services covered by a capitation rate in exchange for fee-for-service business).
2. The safe harbor will protect only risk-based managed care plans that do not claim any payments from federally funded health care programs other than the capitated fee.

3. The safe harbor will apply only to remuneration for health care items and services.

In a reversal of its position outlined in the original proposed regulations, the OIG now states that the beneficiary inducement law (section 1842 of the Social Security Act) is not implicated by a plan's offering incentives to a beneficiary to induce enrollment in the plan.

Antidumping. M + C organizations must not interfere with federal antidumping laws, which require hospitals to provide emergency screening and stabilization to a patient who comes into an emergency facility, regardless of the patient's insurance status and without obtaining prior authorization from the insurer (see EMTALA discussion beginning at Q 8:119). This includes avoiding the practice of "dual staffing," whereby an MCO stations its own staff in the emergency facility for screening and treatment of enrollees.

Q 8:167   What is a gainsharing arrangement, and how does it affect managed care arrangements?

Although there is no fixed definition of a gainsharing arrangement, the term typically refers to an arrangement in which a hospital gives physicians a percentage share of any reduction in the hospital's costs for patient care attributable in part to the physicians' efforts. In most arrangements, for the physician to receive any payment, the clinical care must not have been adversely affected. In addition, many plans require a determination by an independent consultant that the payment represents fair market value for the collective physician efforts. Medicare Part B and Medicaid payments to physicians are generally unaffected by a gainsharing arrangement.

Gainsharing arrangements seek to align physician incentives with those of hospitals by offering physicians a share of the hospital's variable cost savings attributable to Medicare and Medicaid reimbursement. Since the institution of the Medicare Part A diagnosis-related group (DRG) system of hospital reimbursement and with the growth of managed care, hospitals have experienced significant financial pressures to reduce costs. Because physicians are paid separately under Medicare Part B and Medicaid, physicians do not have the same incentive to reduce hospital costs. Gainsharing arrangements are designed to bridge this gap by offering physicians a portion of the hospital's cost savings in exchange for identifying and implementing cost-saving strategies.

The DHHS OIG recognizes that hospitals have a legitimate interest in enlisting physicians in their efforts to eliminate unnecessary costs. Savings that do not affect the quality of patient care may be generated in many ways, including substituting lower cost but equally effective medical supplies, items, or devices; reengineering hospital surgical and medical procedures; reducing utilization of medically unnecessary ancillary services; and reducing unnecessary lengths of stay. Achieving these savings may require substantial effort on the part of the participating physicians. Obviously, a reduction in health care costs that does not adversely affect the quality of the health care provided to patients is in the best interest of the nation's health care system. Nonetheless, the plain language of Section 1128A(b)(1) of the Social Security Act prohibits tying physicians' compensation to reductions or limitations in items or services provided to patients under the physicians' clinical care. In a private review letter published by the OIG on January 18, 2001, however, the OIG reviewed a gainsharing arrangement involving a hospital and its cardiac surgeons that appeared to fall within the proscriptions of gainsharing. The OIG said it would decline enforcement because of the protections in place to prevent reductions in the level of care. [See OIG Adv Op 01-1 (Jan 18, 2001)]

HIPAA

Q 8:168   What is the Health Insurance Portability and Accountability Act of 1996?

HIPAA [Pub L No 104-191] is a federal health care reform law. Enacted on August 21, 1996, it was the first major reform of the health care system since ERISA and Medicare. HIPAA contains five titles:

Title I.   Guarantee of health insurance access, portability, and renewal (see chapter 5)

Title II.   Prevention of health care fraud and abuse, promoting administrative simplification

Title III. Authorization of medical savings accounts and health insurance tax deductions for self-employed individuals (see chapter 3)

Title IV. Enforcement of group health plan provisions

Title V. Revenue offset provisions

Fraud and Abuse Enforcement

Q 8:169 What are the key fraud and abuse provisions of HIPAA?

The most widely discussed aspects of HIPAA were those that allowed people to carry their health coverage from one employer to another. The Act also represents a major expansion of the government's efforts to fight health care fraud and abuse. The following statements summarize HIPAA's key fraud and abuse provisions:

1. HIPAA creates the criminal offense of health care fraud. This crime entails defrauding any health care benefit program, public or private. Violators may receive fines or prison terms of ten years, up to 20 years if the fraud resulted in serious injury, and life imprisonment if the fraud resulted in a patient's death. HIPAA also creates criminal sanctions for theft and embezzlement from a health care program and for making false statements relating to health care benefits.

2. HIPAA increases maximum civil monetary penalties by 500 percent (plus three times the amount of the claim) for fraud against federal health care programs. It also changes the standard of intent for fraudulent claims by authorizing civil monetary penalties against those who should have known that a claim was inappropriate.

3. HIPAA creates and funds the federal Fraud and Abuse Control Program, which coordinates the enforcement efforts of the DHHS OIG and the DOJ.

4. HIPAA enables a beneficiary to receive a portion of the proceeds the government collects when the beneficiary reports fraud or abuse.

5. HIPAA applies the Medicare and Medicaid antikickback statute to all federal health care programs.

6. HIPAA creates an exemption to the antikickback statute for organizations and individuals that join in risk-sharing arrangements.

7. HIPAA requires DHHS to issue advisory opinions relating to the antikickback statute and to inducements to limit services to beneficiaries.

8. HIPAA excludes those who have been convicted of health care fraud from future participation in federal health care programs.

9. HIPAA shifts the responsibility for conducting medical necessity and fraud reviews from carriers to federal contractors that are likely to be more strict.

Q 8:170 When might health care fraud and abuse laws affect e-health?

Although the health care fraud and abuse laws were written to apply to traditional providers of health care (i.e., to licensed health professionals and facilities, such as physicians, pharmacies and hospitals), these laws have the potential to affect e-health entities in both business-to-business and business-to-consumer transactions when the transactions involve licensed health professionals or facilities as consumers or business partners, or involve the advertising, promotion, or purchase of goods and services that are provided by licensed health professionals or facilities, or that are required to be provided only pursuant to a physician's order, such as prescription drugs.

Q 8:171 Under what circumstances do health care fraud and abuse laws apply to e-health transactions and activities?

The federal health care fraud and abuse laws apply only when goods or services are reimbursed directly or indirectly by federal health care programs, such as Medicare and Medicaid. Because of the severity of the sanctions for violations of these laws (including program exclusion or debarment, recoupment of reimbursement, and civil and criminal fines and imprisonment), as a jurisdictional matter, it must be determined whether

1. Any party to the transaction (the Internet company, the consumer, or the business affiliate or partner) is a licensed provider that participates in federal health care programs; or

2. Any goods or services provided by and through the Web site are reimbursed in whole or in part by federal health care programs. Outpatient prescription drugs are covered by Medicaid and, with more limitations, by Medicare. Laboratory tests and x-rays are covered by both. Professional medical services and hospital services delivered through an electronic medium currently have limited coverage under telemedicine provisions.

If either of the foregoing conditions is met, the entire chain of financial interactions must be reviewed for compliance, because most federal health care fraud and abuse laws affect both direct and indirect actions.

An activity may be lawful in one state and unlawful in another. Laws vary significantly from state to state in both the scope of activities covered by fraud and abuse laws and the persons subject to jurisdiction. For example, some state antikickback laws apply only to Medicaid services; others apply to all payers. Some state self-referral laws apply only to equity interests; others apply to any financial relationship between a health care provider and a third party. Some self-referral laws apply only to physicians; others apply to all facilities and professionals. Designing or modifying an Internet product to comply with all state fraud and abuse laws may present administrative and operational challenges for an Internet company and its business clients and consumers.

Q 8:172 Why do the fraud and abuse provisions of HIPAA concern the managed care industry?

Beneficiary Incentives for Reporting Health Fraud. The Secretary of HHS is authorized to provide financial rewards to patients for reporting activities that could be the basis for civil penalties, exclusion, or prosecution under any number of laws. Specifically, the Secretary can pay a beneficiary for a tip that leads to a recovery of at least $100 for the government. In addition, HIPAA requires the issuance to beneficiaries of explanation of benefit forms even when no copayment is required, thus expanding the chances that a patient may discern improprieties. In 1998, there were 439 defendants and 326 convictions.

Greater Government Subpoena Power. HIPAA grants increased subpoena authority to the U.S. Attorney General in investigation of health care offenses. As a result of this statutory change, federal prosecutors have the power to force a provider to deliver to them all their records, including those in electronic form. In other words, a particularly vindictive investigator could require a physician to turn over all patient charts as well as computers pending investigation. The risk here is not hypothetical. In March 1997 the FBI raided Columbia/HCA's facilities and hauled out computers and truckloads of files.

Expanded Scope of the Antikickback Statute. HIPAA expands the scope of the federal antikickback statute to cover all federal health care programs except FEHBP. The antikickback statute forbids the offering or solicitation of any kind of remuneration in exchange for referrals. Previously, many providers could place their transactions outside the scope of this law by excluding Medicare or Medicaid patients. The expansion of the law's applicability could create risk for certain existing arrangements. If providers have structured their deals on the Medicare-Medicaid exclusion principle, they may need to revisit those transactions.

Increased Civil Money Penalties. HIPAA expands the financial penalties the government can impose on wrongdoers in the health care industry and the number of activities to which such penalties may be applied. The civil monetary penalty law now allows the government to collect $10,000 (instead of $2,000) per false claim, plus treble damages rather than double damages. When one considers how many times a physician might bill a specific procedure in a particular year and that each procedure could represent a false claim, the potential fines are staggering.

In addition, HIPAA lowers the government's burden of proof in these cases. To exact civil monetary penalties, the government need only demonstrate that the provider should have known that the claim submitted was false or that the provider acted "in deliberate ignorance of the truth or falsity of the information" or acted "in reckless disregard of the truth or falsity of the information." No proof of specific intent to defraud is required. Thus, a reckless pattern of upcoding or unnecessary care could result in civil fines of bankrupting proportions.

Perhaps more disturbing to the managed care industry, civil monetary penalties are authorized when the government can demonstrate a pattern of up-coding or providing unnecessary care as a result of deliberate ignorance, reckless disregard of the truth, or lack of due diligence as to the accuracy of a claim. Civil monetary penalties are also authorized for offering remuneration to Medicare or Medicaid beneficiaries if the offeror knows or should know that doing so will influence the patient to order or receive items or services from a particular provider or supplier. Remuneration is defined to include the waiver of coinsurance and deductible amounts and the transfer of items or services for free or for other than fair market value. Although the legislative history indicates that the provision of items of nominal value is not intended to be covered by this section of the law, providers need to be careful not to offer substantive "freebies" in an effort to lure patients into their offices. At this juncture, there is no specific information available as to what items the enforcement authorities are likely to consider items of nominal value. The Federal Register [65 81; 2440 Apr 26, 2000] uses refreshments and medical literature as examples.

Greater Chance for Exclusions. Provider exclusions from participation in federal and state health care programs are likely to become more frequent as a result of HIPAA. Individuals or entities that are found to have submitted, or caused to be submitted, claims for excessive charges or to have furnished unnecessary items or services must be excluded from these programs for at least one year. Further, any felony conviction relating to health care fraud likewise will result in program exclusion, regardless of whether the offense was Medicare or Medicaid related.

New Federal Health Care Fraud Offense. HIPAA creates a new federal felony offense—health care fraud—punishable by up to ten years in prison and/or fines. Health care fraud is defined as "knowingly and willfully" executing or attempting to execute a scheme (1) to defraud any health care benefit program or (2) to obtain, by means of false or fraudulent pretenses, money or property from any health care benefit program. [18 USC § 1347] This criminal provision applies to any public or private health care benefit program, not just to those that are federally sponsored.

Reduction of Risk for Certain Risk-Sharing Arrangements. One of the redeeming features of HIPAA is that it recognizes that providers need additional protection from the antikickback statute in the managed care setting. Before enactment of HIPAA, there was some concern that the antikickback statute could technically prohibit many of the financial arrangements necessary to make managed care plans viable; however, HIPAA protects many arrangements under which providers accept financial risk. Under a DHHS negotiated rule-making process, the Negotiated Rulemaking Committee on the Shared Risk Exception unanimously endorsed a statement setting forth two new safe harbors on January 22, 1998.

Advisory Opinions. In HIPAA, Congress directed the Secretary of HHS, in consultation with the U.S. Attorney General, to provide advisory opinions on request with respect to whether a specific arrangement is prohibited by the antikickback statute or falls under an exception. The DHHS OIG issued an interim final rule regarding the process for seeking an advisory opinion in which it specified that an advisory opinion may be relied on only by the requestors and it may not apply if the facts of the arrangement are materially different from those given to the OIG in the request. Further, to request an opinion, the arrangement must already exist or the requestors must be about to engage in the arrangement. [63 Fed Reg 1645–58 (Jan 9, 1998)]

Security and Privacy Provisions

Q 8:173   What do the administrative simplification provisions of HIPAA address?

The administrative simplification provisions of HIPAA (Title II) address consumer protection and the simplification of the administration of health care transactions. Included are transaction standards, standard code sets, unique health identifiers, security standards, electronic signature standards, information communicated between plans, and privacy and confidentiality standards.

Before enactment of these provisions, health information security and confidentiality were subject to regulation under state law, with the limited exception of federally assisted substance abuse treatment facilities [Public Health Service Act § 543, 42 USC § 290dd-2; 42 CFR p 2], records in some federally assisted programs (e.g., Medicaid state agencies) covered by specific statutes, and data held directly by the federal government and its contractors covered by the Privacy Act of 1974. [5 USC § 552a]

Q 8:174   What are the important security and privacy provisions in Title II of HIPAA?

There are four important security and privacy provisions in Title II of HIPAA:

1. Health care providers do not have to participate in electronic data transactions, but if they do, they must comply with the data transactions requirements of HIPAA.

2. Health plans must be able to accept health care data in electronic format without delaying the data's processing.

3. Those subject to the HIPAA security standards must protect the health care data they maintain or transmit electronically from improper access, alteration, or loss.

4. Those subject to the HIPAA privacy standards must not disclose individually identifiable health information.

Q 8:175   Have regulations been issued on the HIPAA security and privacy provisions?

Yes. On August 12, 1998; the DHHS published proposed regulations to implement certain of the administrative simplification provisions of HIPAA. The goal was to develop and implement national standards and procedures for the electronic storage and transmission of health care information. The proposed regulations set forth a framework of standard minimum protocols and procedures for ensuring the safety, security, integrity, and privacy of electronically stored and transmitted health care information. The final rules took effect on April 14, 2001.

The proposed regulations would affect any health information that is created or received by a health care provider, health plan, public health authority, employer, life insurer, school or university, or health care clearinghouse. The breadth of the definitions of these entities means that nearly every record relating to health care (other than one's personal memorialization of health care delivered to oneself or one's family) is covered by these regulations:

1. *Health plan* means "any individual or group health plan that provides, or pays the costs of medical care" and includes any government-sponsored health insurance or health care programs, such as Medicare and Medicaid, CHAMPUS, the Indian

Health Service, and the like; any Medicare supplement program; any HMO or similar state-regulated entity such as a
PPO, a medical foundation, or a competitive medical plan; any
licensed insurance company subject to state oversight; and
any employee welfare benefit program or group health plan
sponsored by employers.

2. *Health care clearinghouse* (if engaged in certain electronic transmission activities) means any entity that processes health care
information into standard data elements for electronic or other
transmission, such as a billing service, management information system, or community health information system.

3. *Health care provider* (if engaged in certain electronic transmission activities) means any person or entity that furnishes or
bills and is paid for health care services in the ordinary course
of business.

Only providers who maintain or transmit health information electronically (as opposed to on paper records and claims) would be
subject to the proposed regulations.

In addition, entities that may be hired by any of the above (business partners) will be subject to the same requirements as imposed
on the covered entities.

Despite the caveats and limitations in the proposed regulations,
just about every person or entity engaged in the electronic creation,
transmission, or storage of health information for other individuals
would be subject to the HIPAA standards for data elements (when
promulgated), security, and electronic transmission.

Q 8:176 What are the HIPAA regulations' security standards?

DHHS used extensive research into current marketplace security
standards to develop the security standards in the proposed regulations. The security standards would not require the use of specific
technologies or particular hardware or software, but instead would
require health plans, health care clearinghouses, and health care
providers who electronically store and transmit health information
to comply with certain minimum threshold protocols and procedures
in four broad categories. These categories relate to different aspects
of ensuring the integrity, confidentiality, and availability of electronically stored and transmitted health information. The categories are

(1) administrative procedures; (2) physical safeguards; (3) technical protections relating to data storage; and (4) technical protections relating to access to and transmission of data. The comments to the proposed regulations indicate that DHHS would require every element of compliance with each of the four categories to be documented, monitored, reviewed, and regularly updated, as follows:

1. *Administrative procedures to guard data integrity, confidentiality, and availability.* The proposed regulations would mandate in detail 12 distinct areas in which policies and procedures must be implemented and documented by every regulated entity: certification of data systems to evaluate compliance with security standards (DHHS apparently expects certification by third-party entities); "chain of trust" agreements between the regulated entity and each other entity with whom health information is exchanged; a contingency plan to ensure continuity and preservation of data in the event of an emergency; formal data processing protocols; formal protocols for controlling access to data; internal audit procedures; security features for initial clearance, ongoing supervision and training, and overall monitoring of activity by personnel with access to health information; "security configuration management," meaning procedures to coordinate overall security, including documentation, hardware and software systems review, and virus checking; protocols for reporting and responding to breaches of security; establishment of a security management structure that features continuous risk assessment and thorough sanction policies and procedures; specific procedures (such as changing locks and passwords) in the event of personnel terminations; and training programs for all security management.

2. *Physical safeguards to guard data integrity, confidentiality, and availability.* These requirements relate to the literal physical protection of data systems and data from intrusion and environmental hazards. Regulated entities would be required to assign security responsibility to a responsible person or entity; develop controls on access to and the physical manipulation of hardware components such as disks, keyboards, and monitors; develop disaster and intrusion response and recovery plans; implement personnel identification verification procedures for physical access to data sites; maintain mainte-

nance records; enforce security clearance hierarchies on a "need-to-know" basis; and implement detailed protocols regarding activities and security at the workstation level.

3. *Technical security services to guard data integrity, confidentiality, and availability.* These requirements relate to software controls and protocols within and surrounding particular data systems to, among other things, regulate access to particular privilege classes, including provision for emergency access during crises; ensure internal systems audits and controls; provide for data authentication (to prove stored data are neither altered nor inappropriately accessed or processed); and ensure user or communicator authentication and access control (using such methods as automatic log-off, user identification, and other access controls such as biometric identification, passwords, a callback function, or token-based systems).

4. *Additional technical security mechanisms relating to the transmission of data.* These requirements relate to software controls and protocols incident to electronic storage and transmission of health information to ensure that data cannot easily be accessed or intercepted or interpreted by unauthorized third parties. Proposed implementation features include integrity controls (internal verification that data being transmitted or stored are valid); message authentication (ensuring that the messages sent and received are the same); and either access control to transmissions (such as dedicated lines secure from tampering) or encryption. If an entity chooses to attempt to control transmissions, rather than everything, DHHS would also require alarms to signal abnormal communication conditions; automatic recording of audit trail information; and a means of entity authentication.

Q 8:177   What are the HIPAA regulations' privacy and confidentiality standards?

The privacy and confidentiality standards of the HIPAA regulations were published November 3, 1999, in the absence of legislation. These rules were finalized on April 14, 2001, and will become effective for most covered entities in 2003. Of all the HIPAA regulations, these have posed the greatest challenge for regulators and have generated the most comments. The goals of these standards are to ensure that individually identifiable information is used only for the purposes for which it was acquired, unless otherwise authorized; patient-care decisions are based on complete, accurate information; access to individually identifiable health information is based on professional need to know; and everyone is accountable for handling confidential information properly.

The following principles are enumerated in the regulations:

1. Patients have the right to examine and copy their records (with limited exceptions).
2. Policies governing the use and disclosure of confidential information should be in place.
3. Confidentiality requirements should apply to patient records, regardless of format.
4. All information should be accorded the same high level of protection.
5. Federal standards should preempt state laws.
6. Personal identifiers should be removed as soon as feasible, while maintaining the usefulness of the data.
7. Formal oversight should govern research use.
8. Privacy protections should follow the data.
9. Health care organizations should implement security safeguards.

More information regarding HIPAA standards and published guidance is available at www.hhs.gov/ocr/hipaa/.

Q 8:178   What are the sanctions for noncompliance with these standards?

Congress provided for civil and criminal penalties for covered entities that misuse personal health information.

Civil Penalties. Health plans, providers, and clearinghouses that violate these standards will be subject to civil liability. Civil monetary penalties are $100 per violation, up to $25,000 per person per year for each requirement or prohibition violated.

Federal Criminal Penalties. Under HIPAA, Congress also established criminal penalties for knowingly violating patient privacy.

Criminal penalties are up to $50,000 and one year in prison for obtaining or disclosing protected health information; up to $100,000 and up to five years in prison for obtaining protected health information under "false pretenses"; and up to $250,000 and up to ten years in prison for obtaining or disclosing protected health information with the intent to sell, transfer, or use it for commercial advantage, personal gain, or malicious harm.

Q 8:179   What guidance has been given by DHHS on HIPAA compliance?

On July 6, 2001, after the HIPAA privacy regulations were finalized, the Office of Civil Rights (OCR, the enforcement agency of HIPAA privacy) issued published guidance. The guidance, which is available at http://www.hhs.gov/ocr/hipaa, sets forth DHHS's official interpretation of the regulations.

OCR noted that DHHS intends to propose modifications to the regulations to

1. Expand the rights of parents to access their children's medical records;
2. Permit pharmacists to fill phoned-in prescriptions before obtaining the patient's written consent;
3. Permit providers receiving a first-time patient referral to schedule appointments, surgery, and other procedures before obtaining written consent;
4. Ensure that oral communications required for health care treatment remain clearly permissible; and
5. Clarify that certain common practices, such as the use of sign-in sheets, x-ray lightboards, and bedside patient charts fall outside the "minimum necessary" standard.

The OCR intends to publish more guidance to answer frequently asked questions.

Other Privacy Issues

Q 8:180   What significant cases have addressed protection of privacy interests?

Cossette v. Minnesota Power & Light [188 F 3d 964 8th Cir 1999)] held that individuals who agree to voluntary medical examinations at an employer's request have a claim under ADA when the employer fails to keep confidential all information obtained through the medical examination.

In *In re Medtronics, Inc.* [No 98-3804, 1999 WL 529245, (8th Cir July 26, 1999)], the Eighth Circuit overturned the trial court's order for Medtronics to turn over medical device reports (reports of adverse events involving its medical devices) on the basis that the names of all pacemaker recipients were being sought. The decision is important because it upheld the federal protections of privacy with respect to physician-patient privilege.

Biddle v. Warren General Hospital [715 NE 2d 512 (Ohio 1999)] allowed a tort action for breach of confidentiality when a hospital transmitted patient information to its attorneys as part of its effort to recover payment for outstanding bills. The court held that there could be a cause of action against third parties for intentionally inducing a medical provider to disclose confidential medical information.

Humana Medical Plan, Inc. v. Fischman [Nos 98-3651, 99-0311, 1999 WL 1243873 (Fla Dist Ct App Dec 22, 1999)] held that as a matter of law, Humana could not require the defendant physician to release the medical records of patients who had not given consent, despite provisions in the provider contract to the contrary.

United States ex rel. Chandler v. Cook County [No 00-4110 (7th Cir Jan 22, 2002)], the Seventh Circuit held that a discovery order requiring Cook County, Illinois, to hand over certain drug treatment records was incompatible with federal privacy regulations. At issue were the privacy rules governing confidentiality of alcohol and drug abuse patient records, rather the federal medical privacy rule.

Liability Issues

Major Areas of Liability in Managed Care

Q 8:181   What are the major areas of liability exposure in managed care?

The major area of liability exposure in managed care are as follows:

Tort Liability. Tort liability exposure for an MCO can arise through its various relationships with providers, other insurers, plan administrators, utilization review agents, and even employers. An MCO's liability can also occur as a consequence of its own acts or omissions that result in injury or harm to persons or property. An MCO may be liable for malpractice and professional liability under an independent corporate liability theory for failure to supervise and monitor its program and providers, or it can be directly liable for the utilization review process itself. An MCO can also be vicariously liable for the activities of providers who are either employed or under contract with the MCO. Finally, an MCO may be liable for intentional or negligent infliction of emotional distress, unfair business practices, or wrongful interference in the doctor-patient relationship. Tort liability exposure has been identified in the following areas:

1. *Intentional interference with the doctor-patient relationship.* In *deMeurers v. Health Net* [No 239338 (Cal Super Ct Riverside Cty, Dec 13, 1995)], an arbitration panel found that HMO officials had forced a physician to reverse his treatment decision.[70]

2. *Breach of fiduciary duty.* In *Wickline v. California* [192 Cal App 3d 1630, 239 Cal Rptr 810 (Ct App 1986)], the court noted a physician's fiduciary duty to the patient to give priority to the patient's needs over the concerns of all others, including the physician. In the later case of *Ching v. Gaines* [No 137878 (Cal Super Ct Ventura Cty, Nov 15, 1995)], a judge overruled the HMO's pretrial attempts to eliminate a cause of action based on breach of fiduciary duty relating to financial incentives not to refer patients to specialists.

3. *Negligence per se.* Another potential cause of action could be raised by using violation of criminal statutes in a civil action to show negligence per se. For example, California Penal Code Section 206 states: "Every person who, with the intent to cause cruel or extreme pain and suffering for the purpose of revenge, extortion, persuasion or for any other sadistic purpose, inflicts great bodily injury upon the person of another, is guilty of torture." This has not yet been presented as a cause of action under managed care.

4. *Negligence and vicarious liability relating to treatment.* In *Dukes v. U.S. Health Care Systems of Pennsylvania* [57 F 3d 350 (3d Cir 1995), *cert denied*, 115 S Ct 564 (1995)], the widow of a plan subscriber was successful in maintaining a cause of

action despite the defendant's efforts to seek ERISA preemption on the basis that the HMO arranged for the actual medical treatment for plan participants. A plaintiff's efforts to hold an HMO liable under a theory of vicarious liability for its selected physicians' activities was also upheld in *Chaghervand v. Care-First*. [909 F Supp 304 (D Md 1995)]

5. *Negligent selection and credentialing of physician providers.* See *Dukes* in item (4).

6. *Restrictions on access and choice of provider. Rodriguez v. Pacificare of Texas, Inc.* [980 F 2d 1014 (5th Cir 1993), *cert denied*, 113 S Ct 2456 (1993)], an employee went outside his HMO to consult an orthopedic surgeon who placed him in therapy. When the HMO refused to cover the unapproved expenses, Rodriguez filed suit in Texas state court against the HMO and primary care physician for failing to provide prompt and adequate medical care and coverage.

7. *Negligent utilization review decisions.* In *Corcoran v. United Healthcare, Inc.* [956 F 2d 1321 (5th Cir 1992), *cert denied*, 506 US 1033 (1992)], the court determined that despite the adverse outcome of the utilization review decision regarding benefits, the role of utilization review affects the benefits available under a benefit plan and, therefore, is subject to ERISA preemption.

8. *Negligent design of financial incentives or cost-containment programs.* An HMO has a fiduciary duty under ERISA to disclose physician financial incentives discouraging patient referrals to specialists. [See Shea v Esensten, 107 F 3d 625 (8th Cir 1997), *cert denied*, 522 US 914 (1997)]

Contract Liability. ERISA imposes a fiduciary duty on plan administrators and even employers. Liability arising out of a breach of this duty has been found when employers mislead employees regarding future employment benefits [Varity Corp v Howe, 516 US 489, (1996)]; when financial incentives are offered to contracted physicians (see *Shea*, item (8) in list above); and with respect to fraudulent inducement to forgo benefits and breach of contract. [Smith v Texas Children's Hosp, 84 F 3d 152 (5th Cir 1996)] Insurance professionals may also become liable for professional negligence outside of ERISA. [See Coyne & Delany v Selman, 98 F 3d 1457 (4th Cir 1996)]

Breach of Contract or Warranty. Breach of contract claims are also part of the claim of bad faith. These claims arise from an implied covenant of good faith and fair dealing found in the insurance contract. Many states view bad-faith claims as a tort, and courts have held that insurance companies owe their insureds a duty of good faith and fair dealing in evaluating claims.[71] Bad-faith claims may be asserted in connection with insurance-type functions, such as claims handling and utilization review, and the design and administration of an MCO's system. This theory has logical extension to direct contract arrangements. The elements of a bad-faith claim include the absence of a reasonable basis for denying benefits and the insurer's knowledge or reckless disregard of the lack of a reasonable basis for denying the claim. Factors viewed by the courts as having significance in determining bad faith include the following:

- An insurer's failure to contact the patient's attending physician to discuss the patient's condition before denying coverage
- Failure to obtain the patient's progress notes and follow procedures for claims review before determining the services were not medically necessary
- Failure to inform a member of his or her right to appeal an adverse decision and settle disputes through arbitration

Breach of Fiduciary Duty. The same conduct that supports a bad-faith claim may also support a breach of fiduciary duty claim by a plaintiff against a physician or an MCO. A physician may owe a fiduciary duty to his or her patient.[72] The law is less clear as to whether an MCO owes a fiduciary duty to plan members.[73] The determining factor is whether the MCO is deemed an insurer or a provider. ERISA imposes a fiduciary duty on a plan administrator to implement the plan properly; however, most states do not recognize the existence of a fiduciary relationship between an insurer and a policyholder. In *Pegram v. Herdrich* [530 US 211, 120 SCt 2143, 2158 (2000), *rev'g* 154 F3d 362 (7th Cir 1998)], the U.S. Supreme Court overturned the lower court's finding that there could be a triable issue of fact relating to the issue of fiduciary duty arising under ERISA. The Justices' unanimous ruling said patients cannot use a federal law to sue HMOs for giving doctors a financial incentive to cut treatment costs. Such lawsuits could mean the end of HMOs, which are based on financial incentives, the Court said. "The fact is that for over 27 years the Congress of the United States has promoted the formation of

HMO practices," Justice David H. Souter wrote for the Court. "The federal judiciary would be acting contrary to the congressional policy . . . if it were to entertain [a claim] portending wholesale attacks on existing HMOs solely because of their structure." [Id at Section III B]

In *Pegram v. Herdrich*, what started out as a routine medical malpractice case turned into a claim based on violation of state unfair trade practice and consumer fraud law because of a compensation system that was alleged to have rewarded physicians financially if they kept medical costs down. When a federal district court ruled that Herdrich's claim was preempted by ERISA, she recast it as a breach of fiduciary duty claim under ERISA, and in 1998, the Seventh Circuit held 2–1 that Herdrich was entitled to a trial on the question of whether the existence of physician financial incentives violated ERISA, a federal law that regulates employer-sponsored benefit plans. Herdrich won a state law medical malpractice claim against Pegram and other defendants and was awarded $35,000 in damages. A major issue in this case is the elevation of a physician's duty of care when participating in capitated managed care arrangements from what has been historically "ordinary" care to a much higher standard of care predicated on a fiduciary duty to the patient.

Misrepresentation. An MCO may have liability based on misrepresentation or false advertising if it either misrepresents or fraudulently omits in oral or written communications to subscribers the standard or quality of medical services, or promises benefits that it cannot or does not deliver. A plaintiff may allege that an MCO has made misrepresentations or omissions regarding (1) covered benefits; (2) provider qualifications; (3) quality of care provided; (4) financial incentives; or (5) administrative processes involved in determining coverage and appeal rights.

Tortious Interference with Contract. Plaintiffs may also claim that an MCO interfered with the physician-patient contract by implementing cost containment that discourages medically necessary care or that prohibits physician disclosure of information about the MCO (gag clauses). Claims may also be raised that MCO cost containment interferes with employees' rights to benefits from employers.

Disease and Demand Management. MCO liability in connection with disease and demand management may arise from (1) improper nurse triage; (2) negligently designed treatment of patients with a specific disease such as diabetes, cancer, or stroke; and (3) the conduct of aggressive large-case management. Telemedicine and other techniques are as yet untested in the courts, but potential liabilities are associated with the application of this system. Disease and demand management are discussed in more detail in chapter 9.

RICO. Claims against health plans and MCOs may be raised under RICO. RICO allows for private claims to be brought as class actions if there is intent to defraud. A 1999 U.S. Supreme Court decision paved the way for a Nevada class of individuals to sue Humana, Inc., under RICO for health insurance fraud on the basis that they overpaid millions of dollars in medical copayments during the 1980s.[74] The class action alleged that Humana negotiated secret discounts that were never passed on to the subscribers, and that these actions were not immune from antitrust liability under the McCarran-Ferguson Act.[75] More recently, on May 25, 2000, the California Medical Association (CMA) filed a federal lawsuit against the three largest for-profit national health plans in California for imposing unfair contract terms, unnecessarily denying and delaying payments for procedures patients need, and reimbursing physicians at rates that are insufficient to cover costs.[76] More specifically, CMA claimed that Blue Cross of California, PacifiCare Health Systems Inc., and Foundation Health Systems Inc. forced physicians to suffer under patently unfair contract terms that set reimbursement rates at unconscionably low levels that were not adequate to cover medical services. The health plans also delay and decrease payments, and unfairly deny claims, CMA claimed. The health plans' unlawful, coercive, and extortionary conduct has forced physicians to leave their practices and terminate their CMA memberships, the complaint alleged.

Q 8:182 How have MCOs been affected by these theories of liability?

Since 1997, MCOs and their plans have been increasingly threatened by claims from patients asserting liability on the part of the plan for medical malpractice. Such claims may be based on a theory that the MCO itself was directly negligent in some respect, or that it is vicariously liable for negligent acts of the involved health care providers. Many of these cases have involved "coverage litigation," which involves utilization decisions relating to denial of care.

Q 8:183   What are the general categories of claims brought against entities involved in managed care?

From a litigation perspective, managed care claims generally fall into three categories: medical claims, systems claims, and corporate claims. The ability to categorize claims into one or more of these categories will depend on how the claim is phrased in the complaint as well as the subject matter of the claim.

Medical Claims. The medical claim case tends to involve claims of pure medical malpractice and relates to the conduct of the health care provider at issue. The medical case involves issues of duty, breach, proximate cause, and damages. This portion of the managed care claim will involve traditional allegations such as failure to diagnose, failure to treat, informed consent claims, and other simple medical negligence and gross negligence claims.

Systems Claims. The systems claims case typically challenges the policies, procedures, and internal operations relating to how health care is delivered within the MCO. Examples of systems subject to challenge include the following:

- Physician compensation mechanisms
- Hospital-based physician teams
- Utilization review (including disease and demand management)
- Resources management
- Quality assurance
- Quality improvement
- Use of nonphysician personnel
- Risk management activity
- Claims review activity
- Telephone triage or advice systems
- Out-of-plan transfer programs
- Recordkeeping issues
- Experimental treatment issues

Claims relating to systems concern the administration of the health plan. For this reason, many of the systems allegations are preempted by ERISA, FEHBA, and other federal preemption provisions. Therefore, attacks on systems are commonly cloaked in the following causes of action:

- Negligence—inappropriate system arrangement
- Negligence—systems failure
- Deceptive Trade Practices Act
- Fraud
- State insurance code violations
- Breach of fiduciary duty
- Tortious interference
- Texas Commercial Bribery Statute
- Breach of contract
- Corporate practice of medicine

Allegations in pleadings that make up direct attacks on the system include the following:

- Failure to provide adequate policies to facilitate the ordering of the proper diagnostic tests for the patient
- Failure to provide adequately trained or skilled health care providers to diagnose and treat the patient's medical condition properly
- Failure to provide adequately trained or skilled health care and medical providers to care for the patient
- Failure to have adequate policies with respect to the medical treatment, medical testing, and referral of patients with medical symptoms and conditions like the patient's
- Failure to have adequate quality assurance medical systems in place
- Failure to have measures in place to see that the patient was sent to the nearest emergency room
- Failure to provide adequate referral services, which would have made an appropriate specialist available to the patient
- Financially discouraging doctors and health care providers from providing necessary medical services, including but not limited to medical testing, outside referrals, emergency room treatment, and early necessary hospitalization

- Inappropriately penalizing treating physicians for ordering testing or specialist referrals necessary for the proper diagnosis and provision of necessary medical services
- Failure to provide proper incentives to provide quality health care
- Failed to establish and enforce an effective quality control program
- Having incentives for doctors and managers to meet budgets, but not to provide quality health care
- Failure to maintain continuity of care
- Failure to establish a medical care system with continuity of medical treatments and plans for members
- Penalizing treating physicians for ordering medically necessary medical testing for the proper diagnosis and provision of necessary medical services
- Failure to develop and maintain an organization data system to provide necessary patient data to all health care providers
- Instituting policies and procedures to reduce the number of hospital days incurred by members without regard to the negative impact on members' health

Corporate Claims. Corporate claims cases involve control and agency issues among the various managed care entities and individuals. Efforts to establish vicarious liability or direct negligence theories of liability focus on the following subjects:

- Contractual arrangements
- Business plans
- Financial relationships
- Organizational structure
- Profit or nonprofit status of the organization

Q 8:184   What are the legal theories most often used in managed care litigation?

The following theories are often pled in managed care litigation in an attempt to tie in remote managed care entities with very little or no involvement in the direct delivery of health care to managed care members:

1. Joint enterprise and "de facto" partnership—

   a. The defendants are and were involved in a joint enterprise. They acted and continue to act as a tight-knit partnership and enjoyed a symbiotic relationship, depending on each other and sharing the profits of the health plan.

   b. The financial compensation arrangements show the existence of a partnership that emphasized cost savings instead of appropriate treatment.

2. Single business enterprise—

   a. The defendants integrate their resources to achieve a common business purpose, and they are not operated as separate business entities.

   b. The defendants' operations satisfy the elements of a single business enterprise because they are not operated as separate entities and they integrate their resources for a common business purpose.

3. Respondeat superior and alter ego—

   a. The individuals involved in the health care and treatment were the agents, employees, or representatives of all defendants, acting within their scope of authority granted by the defendants.

   b. The corporate defendants are responsible for the conduct, acts, and omissions on the part of the health care providers under the doctrine of *respondeat superior* and alter ego.

4. Ostensible agency and agency by estoppel—

   a. The health care providers appeared to the plaintiffs and their families to be the apparent ostensible agents of the health plan, either actual or constructive.

   b. Because of the actions and representations of the health plan, it appeared to the plaintiff that the physicians were employed by the HMO defendant.

5. Other corporate attacks—

   a. The defendants, through violations of the commercial bribery and antikickback statute, engaged in fraudulent concealment and tortious interference with the physician-patient relationship, which resulted in actual damages to the plaintiff.

b. The defendants' emphasis on cost reduction and saving prevented members from receiving proper care and treatment.

c. The defendants are guilty of fraud in that such corporations have been conceived and operated to deceive the public by failing to disclose their financial arrangements.

d. The misrepresentations and nondisclosures by defendants in their advertising and marketing materials constitute unfair, deceptive, untrue, and misleading advertising.

e. The defendants have engaged in fraudulent and unfair business acts and practices in violation of state law.

f. The defendants failed to disclose material facts relating to the actual operation and financial arrangements and thus are guilty of fraudulent concealment.

g. The health care providers and the managed care entities combined and conspired with each other to avoid or delay appropriate medical care.

h. The defendants breached the provisions of their agreements, written and oral, with the plaintiff to provide and authorize timely and appropriate medical care.

Q 8:185   How does a managed care entity become legally liable?

As an organization, the managed care entity has a duty of care and may have direct or indirect liability for its action or inaction. Most lawsuits brought against an HMO for negligence relate to either the exercise of judgment by the HMO in medical decisions or the selection and retention of participating providers. An MCO making a coverage determination subjects itself to ERISA preemption. This relates most often to decisions affecting utilization and medical necessity.

Actions of managed care entities that are most likely to create liability exposure include the following:

1. *Selection and retention of providers.* Because an MCO directs its enrollees or subscribers to use particular providers, it has a duty to exercise care in selecting and monitoring those who serve as its participating providers. This independent duty of

care has been established over the years for hospitals and has direct applicability to MCOs. In *Harrell v. Total Health Care, Inc.* [1989 WL 153066 (Mo Ct App Apr 25, 1989), *aff'd*, 781 SW 2d 58 (Mo 1989)], the concept of corporate responsibility for provider selection was imposed on an HMO following a patient injury. In *McClellan v. Health Maintenance Organization of Pennsylvania* [604 A 2d 1053 (Pa Super Ct 1992)], the court held that an IPA-model HMO had a nondelegable duty to select and retain only competent primary care physicians. The court noted that to establish liability against the HMO, the plaintiff would have to show (a) the HMO had undertaken to render services to the subscriber that the HMO should recognize as necessary for the subscriber's protection; (b) the HMO failed to use reasonable care in selecting, retaining, or evaluating the primary care physician; and (c) the risk of harm to the subscriber was increased as a result of the HMO's failure to use reasonable care.

2. *Selection of utilization review organizations and denial of care.* When an MCO contracts with a utilization review organization (URO) for utilization review services, it exposes itself to liability for negligent selection of its URO. In the first of many cases based on utilization review decisions, *Wickline v. California* [192 Cal App 3d 1630, 239 Cal Rptr 810 (Ct App 1986)], the court noted, "Third party payers of health care services can be held legally accountable when medically inappropriate decisions result from defects in the design or implementation of cost containment mechanisms as, for example, when appeals made on a patient's behalf for medical or hospital care are arbitrarily ignored or unreasonably disregarded or overruled." As with provider selection, an MCO should focus on the following three criteria in selecting and monitoring UROs: determine whether the utilization review entity or personnel are properly licensed (if required by state law) and comply with the American Board of Quality Assurance and Utilization Review or other certification groups; make sure the policies and procedures are clear and are followed consistently; and review the qualifications of the utilization review personnel (e.g., nurse reviewers should be appropriately licensed and trained, with specified experience). The procedures used in utilization review should ensure that the proper personnel review the cases; physician reviewers practice in the area of

medicine relevant to the cases they review; there is discussion with the attending physician before issuing a denial; the basis of denials and the protocols followed are documented; patients and physicians have the right to appeal denials and a procedure exists for doing so; medical criteria are based on local practice standards (unless dealing with a specialty hospital); and denials are communicated to the patient, who is informed about his or her rights.

3. *Financial Incentives.* An approach increasingly seen in lawsuits is to target the MCO's use of financial incentives to control costs and influence access to care. In Florida, Humana Health Insurance Co. of Florida had to pay nearly $80 million to the father of a nine-year-old girl with cerebral palsy for improperly terminating her from a special treatment program for catastrophically ill patients. After a 14-day trial, the jury deliberated two days before awarding Mark Chipps more than $1 million in compensatory damages for unpaid medical bills and intentional infliction of emotional distress and $78.5 million in punitive damages for the care of his daughter, Caitlyn. Charges brought in the lawsuit included breach of an insurance contract, fraud in the inducement, bad-faith action, intentional infliction of emotional distress, and promissory estoppel. Caitlyn was among 100 to 150 catastrophically ill children systematically denied benefits in a medical case management program offered by Humana as part of its preferred provider network coverage. [Chipps v Humana Health Ins Co of Fla, No CL 96-000423 AE (Fla Cir Ct award Jan 4, 2000)] The federal government and 21 states have statutes or regulations that prohibit financial incentives to limit medically needed care.[77] In fact, ERISA and the Medicare and Medicaid programs require disclosure of financial incentives (see chapter 7) The Texas Attorney General sued six HMOs on the basis that they violated Texas law by giving physicians a financial incentive to limit patient care.[78] In the lawsuit, originally filed in December 1998, Texas had accused Aetna of offering financial incentives to doctors to compel them to limit care and penalizing doctors who declined. In reaching a settlement with Aetna Health Plans of Texas, the Texas Attorney General stated in a press release that the settlement would gives more decision-making authority to doctors and would eliminates financial incentives to limit patients' medical care.[79] As part of

the agreement, Aetna will establish a consumer ombudsman office for Texas health plan members and will disclose how it makes coverage decisions by posting guidelines and policies at the Aetna U.S. Healthcare Web site and by telling patients who request such information by phone or in writing.[80]

Q 8:186   Can a health plan be sued for assigning too many patients to a provider's panel?

An HMO can be sued for institutional negligence for allegedly assigning more Medicaid patients to a physician than the physician is capable of serving, the Illinois Supreme Court held on May 18, 2000. In *Jones v. Chicago HMO Ltd.* [301 Ill App 3d 103 (May 18, 2000)], the court held that the doctrine of institutional negligence may be applied to HMOs. The court affirmed the Illinois Appellate Court's ruling that the HMO had a duty to refrain from assigning an excessive number of patients to a physician and that the HMO negligently adopted procedures requiring patients to call for an appointment before obtaining medical care.

Q 8:187   Can an MCO incur liability for using telephone triage?

Yes. Many managed care systems have incorporated telephone triage systems and other complex arrangements to review and approve medically necessary health care. These complex arrangements often give rise to claims specifically derived from the arrangements of these complex systems. The issue is usually the use of telephone triage as a way to screen calls for medical care. In states that adhere to strict corporate practice of medicine prohibitions, the use of non-physicians in telephone triage may also be an issue in a claim against the MCO.

Many MCOs have implemented a telephone triage system affording members 24-hour access to a nurse and medical information. These telephone triage systems appear in many different forms, from simple "nurse advice lines" to more complex arrangements. Commonly pleaded claims relating to the organization and operation of telephone triage and medical advice nursing centers include the following:

- Professional negligence
- Gatekeeping

- Corporate practice of medicine
- Negligent operation and arrangements
- Negligent protocol formulation or implementation
- Interference with the physician-patient relationship

Telephone triage and the use of nursing and nonphysician health care providers may give rise to alleged causes of action relating to the traditional prohibition of the corporate practice of medicine. Additionally, plaintiffs may assert this claim in cases involving partnership, alter ego, and agency theories. In this context, plaintiffs often assert claims of negligence per se, relying on definitions of the practice of medicine in the Medical Practice Act.

Defenses to these novel claims usually include reference to the fact that these licensing statutes simply do not afford private causes of action to plaintiffs in civil litigation. Furthermore, the factual bases for these theories are usually premised on federally preempted subject matters, including ERISA, FEHBA, and the federal HMO Act. The application of these defenses should be explored early in any case involving allegations relating to the corporate practice of medicine.

Q 8:188   How can a managed care entity be at risk for medical malpractice claims?

Hospitals and other health care providers have been liable under conventional theories of liability such as vicarious liability, *respondeat superior,* and corporate negligence. Managed care entities are now being directly sued for medical malpractice. These suits may include allegations that the MCO itself was actively negligent in discharging its duties in a way that harmed an enrollee.

Direct Negligence. Claims of direct negligence asserted against an MCO typically fall into one of two categories:

1. *Action or failure to act that directly affects the care provided to the claimant.* The more a plan "manages" the care available to its members, the greater the risk that it may be found directly liable for malpractice. The most common methods by which plans manage member care include the following:
   - Limiting access to specialists through gatekeepers and requiring primary care physicians to handle many medical

situations that would previously have resulted in a referral to a specialist

- Restricting lengths of stay in in-patient settings and lowering the level of intensity in those settings
- Establishing medical policies that dictate the availability or nonavailability of certain types of treatments for various injuries and illnesses
- Requiring plan physicians to limit drug prescriptions to plan formularies

2. *Failure to credential health care providers properly.* An MCO may also incur direct liability for negligent provider selection and retention. *McClellan v. Health Maintenance Organization of Pennsylvania* [604 A 2d 1053 (Pa Super Ct 1992)], the HMO was sued on a theory of both apparent agency and negligent credentialing. In addition to finding support for a theory of apparent agency, the court found sufficient allegations to state a cause of action for negligent credentialing on the basis that the HMO had a duty of care to "select and retain only competent physicians [and] formulate, adopt and enforce adequate rules and policies to ensure quality care for [its subscribers]."

Vicarious Liability. MCOs can incur similar liability exposure through the negligent acts of their employees or medical staff or through the negligence of those perceived by enrollees or members as having a relationship (agency or otherwise) on an ostensible basis:

1. *Respondeat superior (employer) liability.* In a bona fide employment relationship, an employer is liable for the negligent acts of its employee under the theory of *respondeat superior.* In *Shleier v. Kaiser Foundation Health Plan* [876 F 2d 174 (DC Cir 1989)], the court returned a $825,000 verdict against an HMO for wrongful death arising from an employed physician's negligent failure to diagnose and treat a patient's coronary disease. In states with a strong corporate practice prohibition, the courts have rejected liability under this theory on the basis that physicians had to be independent contractors because they could not be employees.

2. *Ostensible or apparent agency liability.* An MCO may have vicarious liability exposure for its nonemployed participating

providers under a theory of ostensible or apparent agency if the patient reasonably views the entity rather than the individual provider as the source of care, and the entity engages in conduct that leads the patient to reasonably believe that the source of the care is the entity, or the provider is an employee of the entity. *Boyd v. Albert Einstein Medical Center* [547 A 2d 1229 (Pa Super Ct 1988)], a plaintiff sued the HMO for negligent failure to diagnose breast cancer, alleging that the HMO should be liable under apparent agency for the negligence of its nonemployed participating physicians. The court considered the following factors as sufficient to justify the patient's perception of an agency relationship: the payment of fees to the HMO and not the physician; HMO control over the list of physicians from whom the patient could choose; the requirement of referral by the primary care physician to a specialist; and other representations that would cause the patient to perceive the HMO as the provider of care. In *Raglin v. HMO Illinois, Inc.* [595 NE 2d 153 (Ill App Ct 1992)], however, the court did not deem the HMO's quality assurance program to have sufficient control over the medical groups or physicians with which it contracted for medical services.

Q 8:189 What sources of information can be accessed or discovered in litigation to establish sufficient evidence of control to impose vicarious liability on an MCO?

The following sources of information can be used in a lawsuit to find evidence of MCO control:

- HMO contract with members
- HMO contract with providers
- Member handbook
- Advertising brochures
- Physician lists
- Claims forms
- Financial records
- Depositions of HMO employees

Q 8:190   What are the more recent legal threats to physicians who practice under managed care arrangements?

Physicians operating under managed care arrangements are encountering novel theories of liability beyond claims for medical malpractice. These theories, such as breach of fiduciary duty, are often based on the results of economic credentialing [see Wickline v California 192 Cal App 3d 1630, 239 Cal Rptr 810 (Ct App 1986)], directed patient care, gatekeeping, and the use of economic incentives to ration or withhold care. Causes of action being brought against groups that participate in managed care arrangements include (1) medical malpractice, (2) intentional or negligent interference with a contractual relationship, (3) intentional or negligent infliction of emotional distress, (4) wrongful interference with the doctor-patient relationship, (5) intentional or negligent misrepresentation, and (6) breach of fiduciary duty.

Physicians have become more aggressive in challenging some of the actions and policies of MCOs. These MCO actions may range from economic or punitive fiscal policies to deselection of physicians from the plan. Physicians are responding by bringing legal actions against MCOs under theories of slander, breach of contract, failure to afford due process, and retaliation.

Q 8:191   What are the liability issues associated with denial of benefits and withholding of care?

There has been significant attention given over the past several years to "coverage litigation," which involves utilization decisions relating to denial of care. These decisions have come under scrutiny by state regulators and have been the subject of legislative reform. Advocates for patients who have been denied health care benefits describe the optimal outcome as one in which the patient can obtain the desired treatment without personal financial responsibility. If ERISA does not preempt the case, factors to consider are (1) the specificity of the plan documents or insurance policy, (2) the grievance and dispute resolution system, and (3) the disclosures to and expectations of patients.

Some plaintiffs have attempted to use the prohibitions against reducing care under the M + C antifraud and abuse rules as a means of establishing culpability in cases alleging denial of benefits or withholding of care.

Q 8:192 What are some of the risk management strategies that can be used to reduce liability exposure in managed care?

Strategies to reduce liability exposure in managed care include the following:

- Obtaining appropriate insurance to cover malpractice risk
- Having an effective and well-qualified medical policy team that can carefully consider policies on access to specialists, length of stays, and level of intensity of in-patient care, and so forth
- Meaningful and appropriate credentialing of the plan's panel of providers, which should include periodic recredentialing to ensure that providers continue to qualify and a program to deal with impaired providers (This duty may be contractually delegated to IPAs or large medical groups with requirements that the groups defend or indemnify the plan if litigation arises.)
- Possibly including a requirement in plan documents for binding arbitration or mediation of any malpractice disputes
- An external review process for controversial or high-risk claims
- Employing a good risk manager who can work with plan providers to lower risk and improve quality of care
- Involving knowledgeable counsel in policy decisions and high-risk individual situations to ensure that the plan is in compliance with the many state and federal laws that dictate management of certain medical problems (e.g., length-of-stay legislation

Q 8:193 What effect does ERISA have on tort claims?

As discussed in Q 8:124, as a general rule, ERISA will govern employee benefits issues if the plaintiff receives employee benefits from a private employer. Therefore, any lawsuit will be heard in federal court. State law will govern if the plaintiff fits within certain exceptions such as those for school districts, church employees, or one who directly contracts for health care benefits with an HMO.

The purpose of the federal statute, as stated in ERISA Section 2 [29 USC § 1001(b)], is to protect participants in employee benefit plans and their beneficiaries by requiring the disclosure and reporting to participants and beneficiaries of financial and other information with respect those plans; by establishing standards of conduct, responsibility, and obligation for fiduciaries of employee benefit plans; and by providing for appropriate remedies, sanctions, and ready access to the federal courts. Accordingly, ERISA preempts any state laws related to an employee benefit plan. The courts have broadly interpreted the phrase *related to an employee benefit plan.* This means that a state tort claim filed against an HMO for negligence or breach of contract for wrongful denial of benefits will generally be preempted by ERISA. If, however, the basis of the claim is related to the corporate or administrative aspects of the plan, including quality of care, ERISA preemption may not apply to bar the state law claim.

The courts are not in agreement on whether ERISA preemption applies to malpractice claims. Pure malpractice actions are more likely to escape ERISA preemption under theories such as vicarious liability of the MCO or HMO for the acts of its agents or employees. It seems that the cases concerning ERISA preemption make a distinction between utilization review and benefit determination (which are preempted) and cases involving clinical decision making during treatment. For example, in *Dukes v. U.S. Healthcare, Inc.* [57 F 3d 350 (3d Cir 1995), *cert denied,* 116 S Ct 564, (1995)], the plaintiff brought action in state court alleging medical malpractice against several defendants, including the physicians and the ERISA-covered HMO. When the HMO sought removal to federal court under ERISA, the plaintiffs sought to remand the case to state court on the ground that ERISA did not preempt their state claims. The case was ultimately remanded by the appellate court to remain in state court, with the court finding that the claim about the quality of a benefit received is not a claim under ERISA Section 502(a)(1)(B) to "recover benefits due . . . under the terms of [the] plan."

Until *New York State Conference of Blue Cross & Blue Shield Plans v. Travelers Insurance Co.* [514 US 645 (1995)], ERISA preemption was given broad interpretation to encompass claims based on state laws that were even remotely related to an ERISA plan. As a result of the rapidly changing role of the HMO in providing or arranging for medical care, however, the scope of ERISA preemption has been narrowed dramatically. The trend today indicates claims for medical malpractice and negligent selection and retention of physicians will increasingly be found to fall outside of ERISA preemption.

In January 2002, *Rush Prudential HMO Inc. v. Moran* [No 00-1021 (US argued Jan 16, 2002)] was argued before the U.S. Supreme Court to determine if the process of submitting a claim for independent medical review for determination of "medical necessity" is pre-empted by ERISA or subject to state law court review. Over 40 states currently have laws giving plaintiffs the right to submit their claims for independent review of denials in coverage.

Q 8:194   Does Medicare law preempt negligence claims against Medicare plans?

In *Wartenberg v. Aetna U.S. Healthcare, Inc.* [2 F Supp 273, 279 (EDNY Apr 13, 1998)], the court held that wrongful death and negligence allegations arising under state law are not preempted by the Medicare Act when the claims are not based on a claim for payment of benefits or to reimburse payments. The court the case back to the state court on the basis that the claims arose from the administrative acts of the Medicare benefit administrator and did not arise under the Medicare Act. Citing *Ardary v. Aetna Health Plans of Southern California* [98 F 3d 496 (9th Cir 1996)], the court held that the complaints were not based on the benefits ascribed to the Medicare Act, but on a state common law ground involving negligence. The court went on to note that unlike ERISA, which contains express language regarding preemption of state law, the Medicare Act does not contain a preemption provision.

Q 8:195   Under what circumstances does Medicare preempt state law claims?

Managed care claims may also be subject to federal preemption under the Medicare Act (see chapter 7). Whether a claim "arises under" the Medicare Act and therefore completely preempts state law is determined by either one of two tests enunciated by the U.S. Supreme Court. First, a claim "arises under" the Medicare Act if "both the standing and the substantive basis for the presentation" of the claim is the Act. [See Heckler v Ringer, 466 US 602, 615 (1984); Zamora-Quezada v HealthTexas Med Group, 1998 WL 892608, at *3 (WD Tex Nov 30, 1998)] Second, a claim "arises under" the Medicare Act if it is "inextricably intertwined" with a claim for medical benefits. [See Heckler, 466 US at 624] Administrative review is not necessary when a claim is wholly collateral to a claim for benefits and a colorable showing has been made that the claimant's injury cannot be remedied by the retroactive payment of benefits. [See id at 617]

Although the Medicare Act does not contain an explicit preemption provision comparable to ERISA Section 514 [29 USC § 1144], the Medicare Act has been accorded preemptive effect in the field of coverage disputes because of the need to maintain uniform administration of Medicare coverage rules and to effectuate Congress's intention that DHHS preside over the adjudication of these disputes subject to limited federal court review. Cases in which the Medicare Act has been used to find preemption include the following:

1. *Bodimetric Health Service v. Aetna Life & Casaulty Co.* [903 F 2d 480, 483 (7th Cir 1990)] In this case, the Seventh Circuit held that Medicare's administrative system bars a health care provider from seeking Medicare reimbursement outside that system: "If litigants who have been denied benefits could routinely obtain judicial review of these decisions by recharacterizing their claims under state and federal causes of action, the Medicare Act's goal of limited judicial review for a substantial number of claims would be severely undermined."

2. *Levy v. Pacificare of California.* [1999 WL 1241072 (Cal Ct App 4th Dist)] In *Levy,* the plaintiff brought an action against his HMO alleging that he was wrongfully denied access to a second medical opinion concerning a cancer diagnosis and was then denied coverage for corrective surgery. In holding that the plaintiff's complaint was inextricably intertwined with his claim for benefits under the Medicare Act, the appeals court noted his state law causes of action would necessarily require the court to review the merits of the Medicare claims decisions. Thus, the appeals court held that the plaintiff's claims were subject to the Medicare Act's exclusive review provision.

Two cases decided in California (one in state court, the other in federal court) held that plaintiffs' claims against their health plans were not preempted by the Medicare Act:

1. *Albright v. Kaiser Permanente Medical Group.* [1999 WL 605828 (ND Cal Aug 3, 1999)] On August 3, 1999, the U.S. District Court for the Northern District of California remanded a case filed by a Medicare beneficiary against her health plan.

The plaintiff filed an action in state court alleging unfair business practices, violation of the covenant of good faith and fair dealing, and fraud. The defendants removed the case to federal court, claiming complete preemption under the federal Medicare Act, and they filed a motion to dismiss on the basis of failure to exhaust administrative remedies. After the plaintiff amended her complaint, alleging that she had exhausted her administrative remedies, the defendants filed a second motion to dismiss. The district court reviewed the absence of authority for complete preemption under the Medicare Act and remanded the case to state court.

2. *McCall v. Pacificare of California, Inc.* [87 Cal Rptr 2d 784 (Ct App 1999] The California Court of Appeal, 4th District, Division 3, reversed a demurrer granted without leave to amend on the patient's claims for negligence, intentional and negligent infliction of emotional distress, unfair business practices, and fraud. The patient suffered from progressive lung disease, and he sued his HMO for allegedly refusing to refer him to a specialist for a lung transplant in an effort to save money. The California Court of Appeal held that the action was not one for reimbursement of benefits so as to arise under the Medicare Act and therefore it was error to grant the demurrer without leave to amend.

Q 8:196   Is the current system of resolving medical liability claims appropriate for managed care?

Experts suggest that the current medical liability system does not adequately prevent medical injuries or compensate injured patients. As managed care expands, the medical liability system's performance will become increasingly important to maintain quality of care and not impede efforts to provide appropriate, cost-effective care. This has been reflected in the numerous proposals by state and federal governments to reform the medical liability system. These issues were discussed in depth in the Annual Report to Congress of the Prospective Payment Review Commission in 1991, which listed reduction of medical injury as the number one goal. A second goal was to give fair compensation to patients who experience a medical injury. It was noted that the existing liability system promotes the practice of defensive medicine and may impede efforts to improve the cost effectiveness of care.

Q 8:197   Are there other legal barriers to MCO liability?

Yes. In states that strictly adhere to the prohibition against the corporate practice of medicine, there is a legal barrier to holding an MCO directly liable or accountable for patient care outcomes on the basis that the MCO does not engage in the practice of medicine. As a matter of law, then, the MCO could not be held liable for malpractice. This doctrine, which exists in a number of states, prohibits a lay corporation or individuals from employing a licensed physician, receiving his or her fees, or in any way influencing the delivery of medical services unless the individual is a physician or the corporation or entity is owned or controlled entirely by physicians. This doctrine is based on the principle that businesses, organizations, and entities that are not licensed by the state to practice medicine cannot engage in medical practice and exploit the special relationship between a physician and his or her patient.

Other Areas of Liability in Managed Care

Q 8:198   What are the liability implications of clinical practice guidelines or practice parameters?

Many managed care entities advocate the use of practice parameters or clinical guidelines, which are discussed in greater detail in chapter 9. Guidelines are advocated as having a positive effect not only on cost containment but also on liability. Opinions differ as to the use of guidelines in the liability arena. Some hold that clinical guidelines or practice parameters reduce malpractice litigation because, if followed, they standardize care and treatment protocols. Others, however, argue that these guidelines or parameters give plaintiffs' attorneys a potential weapon to use in malpractice cases. A Harvard study found that plaintiffs are introducing guidelines more often than defense attorneys.[81] In the absence of current case law, the role of practice parameters from a liability standpoint is still unknown.

Q 8:199   What are the liability issues associated with sharing information and data systems?

As discussed in much greater detail in chapter 15, information systems are an important component of any integrated delivery system or MCO. These systems rely on clinical data to evaluate the quality and cost effectiveness of the providers they select. If an individual practitioner loses privileges at a hospital, the MCO has an interest in obtaining that information. Unlike hospitals, however, MCOs have no direct access to such information and must rely on others to provide it. This need to obtain clinical data raises several legal issues, including a patient's right to privacy and the continued availability of the peer review privilege and immunity protections.

With the passage HIPAA, DHHS imposed far-reaching regulations on health care organizations, including requirements relating to (1) health insurance transferability and (2) expanded fraud and abuse prohibitions. Included were the administrative simplification provisions [HIPAA §§ 261–264, 42 USC § 1320d-2 et seq], which call for national standards to facilitate the electronic exchange of health information to make financial and administrative health care transactions more efficient. Because of the concern about electronic transmission of health care information leading to widespread dissemination of private and sensitive information, HIPAA also called for the promulgation of national privacy standards. [HIPAA § 264] These standards were issued on November 3, 1999 [64 Fed Reg 59918] and can be found at http://aspe.hhs.gov/adminisimp.

Patient Privacy. With provider records undergoing multiple levels of review by outside reviewers under managed care, ensuring the continued privacy and confidentiality of this information becomes a paramount concern. An MCO must be aware of its liability exposure for the unauthorized public release of patient-identifying information. Since the states have varying regulations relating to confidential medical records, physician-patient privilege, and AIDS-related or chemical dependency-related information, the MCO must be attentive to the various means of obtaining and communicating this information. The rules for security and privacy of "protected health information" (individually identifiable health information transmitted or maintained in electronic form), the use of the information (transaction standards), the privacy of the information (privacy standards), and the protection of that information (security standards) are all pending republication in the Federal Register.

Peer Review Privilege and Immunity. Some states' statutes define the privilege available to protect the proceedings of peer review committees as broad enough to cover MCO peer review activities. The importance of this privilege is the protection from legal discovery it gives to the information and proceedings of peer review committees that are responsible for evaluating provider competence and performance. To the extent a state statute also grants immunity to peer review participants and to persons who furnish information to peer review committees, the exchange of such information as part of the peer review process should be subject to the same immunity that exists for hospital peer review of its medical staff.

Q 8:200 What issues are raised in disability claims arising under managed care?

The ADA applies in the context of public accommodations and employment. It has been used as a basis for claims against health plans and MCOs by both patients and their providers. Title I of the ADA states that an employer with more than 15 employees cannot "discriminate" against a "qualified individual with a disability" on the basis of that disability with regard to job application procedures, hiring, advancement, training, compensation, discharge, or terms, conditions, and privileges of employment. [42 USC § 12112 et seq] A disability is defined as a physical or mental impairment that substantially limits one or more major life activities, a record of such an impairment, or being regarded as having such an impairment. To be protected under the ADA, an individual need not currently have a disability and, in fact, may never have actually had a disability.

Employers are required to make reasonable accommodation to the known disability of a qualified disabled person unless it would result in undue hardship. A qualified individual is one who has the skills, experience, education, and other job-related capabilities for a position and who can, either with or without reasonable accommodation, perform the essential functions of the job in question. Essential functions are the fundamental duties intrinsic to the position.

The trend in recent case law is moving from generalized review of the application of the ADA to more individualized analyses by the courts. For example, in *Sutton v. United Air Lines, Inc.* [527 US 471, (1999)], the U.S. Supreme Court found plaintiffs seeking jobs as commercial pilots were not covered by the ADA because they were not disabled as defined under the ADA. They relied on corrective lenses and had been denied employment on the basis of a minimum uncorrected vision requirement of 20/100.

In a more significant case, the Court held in *Olmstead v. L.C.* [527 US 581, (1999)] that unnecessary institutionalization of a disabled person was "discrimination per se" under the ADA. This case involved a state's unjustified delay in moving plaintiff patients from an institutionalized setting to community-based programs for which they qualified.

In an important case in which an ERISA plan's distinction between physical and mental disabilities for purposes of qualifying for long-term disability was at issue, the Tenth Circuit found in *Kimber v. Thiokol Corp.* [196 F 3d 1092 (10th Cir 1999)] that the ADA does not guarantee equal disability benefits with respect to physical and mental disabilities.

At issue in a case of first impression filed in federal district court in San Antonio, Texas were the theories of managed care contrasted against theories relating to the ADA. The case, *Zamora-Quezada v. HealthTexas Medical Group of San Antonio* [WD Tex Nov 30, 1998], was filed in the U.S. District Court for the Western District of Texas, San Antonio Division, under several theories of liability, including wrongful termination as to Dr. Zamora and a novel theory by Drs. Zamora and Guerrero and certain patients involving the ADA. The core issue in the case was whether the managed care plans and contracted physicians discriminated against individuals with disabilities to get them to "disenroll" so that they could save the costs of treating "costly" medical conditions. The case was settled for an undisclosed amount after it was sent to the jury.

Liability Reform and Managed Care

Q 8:201   What role do punitive damages play in litigation generally and in managed care litigation?

The role of punitive damages is somewhat unsettled in the courts and legislatures.[82] As of 1996, 43 states allowed punitive damages; 14 of these states imposed some kind of cap, typically a multiple of the dollar amount of the compensatory damages awarded in a case.[83] In addition, several bills have been introduced in Congress to curb punitive damages.[84]

What is clear is that punitive damages are quite common in certain types of litigation. A study by the DOJ found that in 1991–1992, one third of awards in libel and slander cases, one fifth of fraud awards, and one quarter of awards involving employment suits included a punitive damages component.[85] A study of civil jury verdicts by RAND found awards of punitive damages in 24 percent of all verdicts against insurers.[86] The relationship between punitive damages and the insurance cases in which bad faith has been alleged appears to be even stronger, although not all states recognize this type of claim.[87] In contrast, the awarding of punitive damages has been relatively rare in medical malpractice litigation. Studies have indicated that punitive damages are awarded in less than 1.5 percent of verdicts in malpractice cases.[88]

With the changes in the managed care industry, such as consolidation of health plans and use of financial incentives to reduce health care costs, as well as the legislative and judicial trends relating to liability reform, health care insurers have been thrust into the liability spotlight, introducing into health care litigation an entity that readily fits the profile of the classic defendant in cases involving punitive damages. As managed care businesses get larger, it is likely that juries will believe that punitive damages are necessary to get management to pay attention.

Q 8:202 What is the potential impact of punitive damages on managed care?

Opening up managed care plans to litigation and punitive damages is one way to force change in how health care decisions are made; however, litigation also disrupts the economics of managed care for the insurer. If managed care plans are saddled with the costs of litigation and payment of damages, especially punitive damages, then their management strategies may no longer be economically rational. In this way, a substantial increase in costly litigation could considerably reduce or modify the scope of managed care. It is likely that awards of punitive damages will affect the behavior of insurers.[89]

A litigation crisis managed care will be costly, and many will be affected. Use of the tort litigation system to effect reforms in the insurance and managed care industries is the least effective means of achieving managed care reform. In an intriguing article published in the *New England Journal of Medicine*,[90] Dr. Troyen Brennan of the Harvard School of Public Health and Mr. David Studdert of RAND analyzed the effect of punitive damages arising under managed care. Brennan and Studdert note that two outcomes are certain: millions of dollars will go toward attorneys' fees, and such costs will need to be paid, at least in part, out of health insurance premiums. These considerations should be weighed as legislatures consider bills that would promote litigation in lieu of other forms of dispute resolution or a more sophisticated approach—namely, carefully crafted regulatory oversight that is responsive to the need to reconcile the protection of patients and quality assurance, on the one hand, with the cost containment that consumers demand from managed care, on the other.

Q 8:203   What has been the impetus behind managed care liability reform?

A major impetus behind managed care liability reform is growing dissatisfaction with certain forms of managed care that limit access to care, choice of provider, and disclosure about the plan; restrict coverage; and establish incentives for health care providers to ration health care services.

The federal government has been trying to enact a patients' bill of rights as part of its efforts to address access and choice, disclosure, grievance procedures, and quality of care. During the last several years, many state legislatures have increased efforts to pass managed care liability acts in an attempt to create state law causes of action against health plans. Texas was the first state to pass a managed care liability act holding managed care entities to a duty of "ordinary care." [Texas Managed Care Liability Act, Tex Civ Prac & Rem Code Ann ch 88] More recently, California and Georgia have passed managed care liability statutes. Managed care liability bills were introduced in the vast majority of state legislatures over the past five years, with efforts continuing on the state level to enact liability bills in the wake of the federal stalemate.

Q 8:204   What effect has the Texas managed care liability act had on other states?

In 1997, efforts to pass managed care liability bills met with success in only one state: Texas. By 1998, managed care liability bills were considered in 28 states, but none of the measures survived. In 1999, measures to expand health plan liability were introduced in 38 states, with two states passing liability bills and legislation dying in 25 states. In 2000, important state reform efforts since the Texas bill was enacted include the following:

1. *California.* The California Managed Health Care Insurance Accountability Act of 1999 [Chapter 536 Cal Stat of 1999], signed into law by Governor Gray Davis in September 1999, became effective January 1, 2001. This Act accompanied the creation of an independent physician review system. The Act provides for liability after the enrollee has exhausted the independent review procedures, with certain exceptions. One exception relates to cases in which the alleged substantial harm has already occurred; in those cases enrollees are exempt from the independent review requirements. The bill defines substantial harm as death, loss or significant impairment of limb or bodily function, significant disfigurement, severe and chronic physical pain, or significant financial loss. Like the Texas Managed Care Liability Act, the California Act removes the ability of managed care entities to shift responsibility for liability to health care providers by contractual or other indemnity.

2. *Georgia.* During the 1999 legislative session, Georgia passed its own version of an HMO liability act. HB 732, which amended Chapter 1 of Title 51 of the Georgia Code, created a cause of action and other remedies against MCOs. The substantive text of the Act can be found at Georgia Code Annotated Sections 51-1-48 and 51-1-49. The Act also provides for an external review procedure. [Ga Code Ann § 33-20A-5] The external review procedure, which is very similar to the Texas procedure, requires exhaustion of the grievance procedure or an allegation that harm has already occurred prior to filing suit.

3. *New York.* [AB 1400 (1999–2000)] In 1999, AB 1400, was introduced in the New York Assembly. AB 1400 would have held health care organizations, defined as HMOs and insurers, liable for any personal injury, death, or damages caused by a delay, failure, or refusal to approve, provide, arrange for, or pay for in a timely manner any health care service to a person when the plan was contractually obligated to do so. The bill

passed in the Assembly, its chamber of origin, in 1999, but died in the New York Senate on January 5, 2000.

Q 8:205   What lessons can be drawn from the Texas initiative to hold HMOs legally accountable?

As other state legislatures and the federal government look to the Texas legislation and propose similar legislation to hold HMOs accountable for their actions or inactions, some important lessons can be learned from the Texas experiment in legislating managed care liability:

1. *Define key terms affecting the scope of the legislation.* Terms such as *managed care entity* and *medical treatment decisions* should be precisely defined. Without great specificity, MCOs are unfairly exposed to litigation and are not given sufficient opportunity to comply with the legislation.

2. *Apply any tort reform protections equitably to MCOs.* Although some may disagree, MCOs are an integral part of the health care delivery system. The next generation of health care litigation now emerging will involve both MCOs and health care providers as defendants. If a state has enacted tort reform protections for health care providers in health care liability litigation, MCOs should be given the benefit of those protections.

3. *Make any independent review process mandatory.* To be an effective method for resolving disputes without resort to litigation, any internal or independent review process should be mandatory, with an exception only for instances in which the enrollee can show imminent harm to health or safety. Similarly, failure of an enrollee to exhaust the internal or independent review process should result in dismissal of the case. By strengthening the independent review process, legislatures will encourage MCOs and enrollees to resolve disputes earlier and without the expense and burden of litigation.

4. *Consider repealing the corporate practice of medicine prohibition.* The corporate practice of medicine prohibition, which is recognized in some form in a majority of states, is unfair to MCOs in light of the enactment of managed care liability laws. If MCOs are now to be held accountable for the actions of the health care providers with whom they contract to deliver care, MCOs should be given the legal authority and right to control

the providers' actions—through repeal of any corporate practice of medicine prohibition. If such control by MCOs is not desired or is deemed contrary to public policy, the statutory causes of action should be drafted to hold MCOs accountable only for their actions, not for the actions of health care providers.

Q 8:206   What consumer protection initiatives have been enacted with respect to managed care?

A number of initiatives relating to the impact of managed care on consumers and provider groups have been introduced over the past year. Consumers are concerned about limits on freedom of choice, particularly for out-of-network and emergency care; providers have taken issue with provider network rules, gag clauses, and the absence of due process provisions; and there are increasing concerns about the privacy of health information.

In response to these concerns, regulators and legislators in almost every state and in the federal government have considered new consumer protection laws and regulations. Their goal is to increase scrutiny of managed care plans in the areas of consumer and provider protection. Most of these initiatives involve (1) "any willing provider," freedom of choice, and direct access laws; (2) coverage for emergency services; (3) consumer grievance and appeal procedures; (4) length of stay; (5) gag clauses and due process measures; and (6) physician financial incentives.

According to the National Conference of State Legislatures, more than 1500 bills were introduced in state legislatures between 1995 and 1999 to regulate managed care. HMO liability laws, however, have failed in 30 states.[91] Several of these initiatives were comprehensive consumer protection reforms. Most of these reforms addressed access and quality issues, coverage of experimental treatments, and grievance procedures and appeals. Going into 2000, reform of the managed care industry remained the hottest topic of debate in most state legislatures. Many of these bills focused on external review, mental health parity, drug formularies, and HMO liability. Although external review laws were enacted in more than half of the 20 states where they were being considered, few of the states enacted legislation allowing health plans to be sued.

"Any Willing Provider" Laws. These laws require health plans to admit to their networks and provider panels any qualified provider willing to comply with the terms and conditions of the provider agreement and who otherwise meets the credentialing criteria of the plan. State legislative activity in this area has decreased. One reason for the slowdown is the success of several challenges raised by insurers and employers that the laws are preempted by ERISA.

Freedom of Choice Laws. Freedom of choice laws focus on the interests of consumers to access covered health care services from any qualified provider they choose, regardless of whether the provider is in the health plan's provider network. These laws usually allow enrollees to seek care from out-of-network providers without reduction in benefits as long as the provider agrees to accept the insurer's level of payment for the services. Most of these laws apply to pharmacies, certain specialists, and other defined providers. Few apply to all types of managed care plans. Legislative efforts in this area have been unsuccessful in view of alternative measures aimed at enhancing the quality of care through direct access to specialists and mandating minimum stays for new mothers and mastectomy patients.

Direct Access Laws. Direct access laws limit the ability of managed care plans to direct the flow of patients toward specific providers. They ensure access to certain providers such as obstetrician-gynecologists, dermatologists, ophthalmologists, and psychiatrists without requiring a referral from a primary care physician. Even in the absence of specific legislation, many MCOs have responded to consumer pressure for direct access by developing new products that permit patient self-referral to certain categories of specialists such as orthopedic surgeons, obstetrician-gynecologists, and mental health providers. This topic is discussed in more detail in chapters 3, 4, and 5.

Emergency Services Coverage. EMTALA (see Q 8:119) requires that all patients who present to a hospital emergency room be evaluated and triaged. Many states have passed laws mandating that managed care plans cover emergency services received by patients even when the ultimate diagnosis shows there was no emergency. These statutes generally apply a "prudent layperson" standard to the situation in which emergency services are sought by the patient.

Consumer Grievance and Appeal Procedures. Although most HMO licensing statutes require some form of enrollee grievance procedure, many consumer advocacy groups have deemed them inadequate and nonresponsive. Many states have adopted rules relating to "timely responses" to medical necessity determinations that are appealed.

Coverage Mandates. Many states have adopted mandatory benefit and coverage laws in response to consumer groups and specific situations that have been held up as contrary to public policy. The most notable of these situations are "drive-through" deliveries, that is, the 24-hour maternity stays allowed by many health plans. Federal law (Newborn and Mothers Health Protection Act of 1996, PL 104-204) and most state laws enacted in response to this situation mandate at least 48-hour hospital stays for mothers and their newborn babies following normal delivery.

Gag Clauses. Gag clauses are contractual provisions that may restrict physicians from fully informing patients about treatment options or about which options are covered by a plan; they may also prohibit referrals to providers for services that are not covered. Other contract clauses may prohibit the physician from criticizing the health plan, disclosing financial incentives, or discussing how authorizations relating to care are made by the plan. Many states and the federal government have enacted laws and issued policy statements restricting or banning gag clauses.

Provider Due Process. Another area that has been addressed by many states through legislation and rule making is disclosure of the criteria and process used to select and deselect (remove) providers from managed care networks.

Financial Incentives. CMS (formerly HCFA) issued final rules on physician incentive payment plans. Under such arrangements, physicians or physician groups may receive economic incentives based on utilization criteria. CMS rules require disclosure and stop-loss insurance on Medicare and Medicaid HMOs when payment methods place the physicians at substantial financial risk for referral services.

Other Litigation Devices—Class Actions

Q 8:207   What is a class action lawsuit?

To be certified as a class action suit, the action must be associated with a significant number of claimants and have a certain commonality, typicality, and adequacy of representation. In the context of potential litigation against an MCO, the requirement of numbers should be easy to attain, with the consideration that the number must be such that joinder of all members, individually, would be impracticable. The second requirement, commonality, requires that questions of law or fact be common to the class. Typicality is intended to measure the extent to which the representative party or parties can truly speak for the other members of the class. Typicality tends to merge with commonality. Finally, the representative party must be able to convince the court that he or she or they "will fairly and adequately protect the interests of the class." This requires that the representatives be part of the class and possess the same interest and suffer the same injury as the other class members.[92]

Some cases have been brought as class actions against certain activities of managed care companies. The most common challenge has been to the risk-shifting aspects of managed care, which have led some patients to express concerns about quality of care through class action lawsuits.[93] Although these cases have not directly resulted in a finding of liability against the MCO, the fact that the court certified the class resulted in settlements in some cases, and changes in insurance industry practices in others. State regulators have initiated investigations into some of these practices as a result of the litigation efforts.

Q 8:208 What types of cases are most appropriate for class action litigation?

Class actions are most appropriate in cases involving civil rights and discrimination arising under federal civil rights statutes, the ADA, or the Age Discrimination in Employment Act (ADEA). In the context of managed care, suits involving "discount cases" in which claims are based on breach of fiduciary duty under ERISA, fraud, or violation of a state disclosure statute may be appropriate for class action because the individual's ability to recover may be significantly limited in comparison to a class potential for recovery. Another issue lending itself to class action is that of quality of care (not involving personal injury claims). Finally, claims related to access to care and services may be appropriate for class action. In *Grijalva v. Shalala* [946 F Supp 747 (D Ariz 1996)], a group of Medicare beneficiaries whose HMOs had denied them service filed a class action lawsuit in federal court alleging that the federal government had failed to adequately monitor and sanction HMOs serving Medicare patients. The court certified their class as meeting the requirements to assert the claims using the class action format.

Q 8:209   Why are class action lawsuits being used so extensively in cases involving managed care?

The main force behind the rise in class action lawsuits targeting managed care is a group of plaintiffs' class action lawyers who call themselves the "REPAIR team" and who include former tobacco, asbestos, and gun control litigators. These attorneys have decided to go after the managed care industry, as they have other industries, on the basis that MCOs violated federal employee benefits and racketeering laws by creating undisclosed incentives for physicians to skimp on medical care to which the MCOs' enrollees were entitled. Humana, Aetna, Foundation, Kaiser, and PacifiCare are among the companies that have been sued in state and federal courts by lawyers who earlier were involved in class actions against the tobacco companies. The theory of the class actions being brought by these attorneys is that the MCOs are deceiving their enrollees by representing that they provide coverage based solely on medical considerations and physicians' independent judgment, when in fact their decisions are driven by cost considerations. The complaints attempt to state claims under two federal laws: ERISA and RICO:

1. Under ERISA, the class actions allege that the MCOs violated their fiduciary duty to enrollees both by implementing a system of financial incentives to contain costs and by failing to disclose those incentives to enrollees.

2. Under RICO, the suits claim that the MCOs engaged in racketeering by inducing enrollees to sign up for their health plans based on false representations concerning the scope and nature of coverage under the plans.

Q 8:210   On what theories of liability are class actions against managed care entities based?

Class action managed care lawsuits have been based on creative theories of liability ranging from breach of fiduciary duty claims under ERISA to novel state consumer protection statute theories based on alleged false and deceptive advertising. Among the currently litigated managed care class action causes of action and claims are the following:

- Breach of contract
- Unfair or deceptive trade practices
- Breach of fiduciary duty
- ERISA violations: breach of fiduciary duty
- Fraud and misrepresentation
- RICO violations
- False and misleading advertising
- Tortious interference with the physician-patient relationship
- Tortious interference with a business relationship
- Violations of state insurance statutes pertaining to timing of reimbursement payments
- Bad faith or breach of the duty of good faith and fair dealing
- Violations of state insurance statutes pertaining to disclosure of physician financial incentives
- Lanham Act violations: false advertising
- Civil conspiracy
- Vicarious liability, including de facto partnership, single business enterprise, *respondeat superior*
- Direct corporate negligence (control theory)
- Apparent agency
- Ostensible agency
- Agency by estoppel

Regulation of Insurance

Q 8:211   What activities are regulated by states as the business of insurance?

To the extent the activities are not subject to preemption under ERISA for self-insured health benefit plans, states regulate a number of activities that directly and indirectly relate to the business of insurance. These activities include utilization review, third-party claims administration, HMOs, and prepaid contract arrangements, as well as the larger assumption of risk for a range of services, the spreading of risk over groups of potential patients, and the sharing of risk with groups and networks of providers. As traditional indemnity and HMO plans are replaced with "nontraditional" forms of health care coverage, and as the distinction lessens between entities that finance health care and those that deliver health care, insurance regulators are increasing their focus on and scrutiny of these organizations and their activities in the interest of consumer protection.

Q 8:212 What is a risk-bearing entity, and why is risk bearing important in managed care?

The National Association of Insurance Commissioners (NAIC) defines a risk-bearing entity as "one or more persons that contract with individuals, employers or other groups to arrange for or provide health care benefits on a basis that involves the assumption of risk by the risk-bearing entity."[94] It is the bearing of insurance or actuarial risk that triggers regulatory scrutiny.

Risk assumption falls into three categories that are important in any regulatory analysis:

1. *Insurance risk.* Insurance risk typically involves the assumption and spreading of risk of loss in return for compensation and is, accordingly, regulated risk. In managed care contracting, certain controllable portions of the financial risks that together constitute the total insurance-type risk are shifted to the providers that presumably can control certain aspects of the risk.

2. *Pricing, or financial, risk.* Distinguished from insurance risk, provider financial risk is more accurately described as pricing, compensation, or business risk. Provider financial risk does not necessarily involve assumption of insurance-type risk, even though it does involve transfer of a portion of an "insurer's" own financial risk to a provider.

3. *Operational risk.* Insurers, providers, and managed care entities alike bear numerous operational risks that can affect the extent of financial risk as well as the scope of insurance risk. The financial or operational risks that providers bear may, in and of themselves, give rise to regulatory issues. For example,

both the amount of financial and/or operational risk and the manner in which either is transferred to a provider may influence regulatory interpretation. Potential questions include whether insurance-type risk has been transferred to or assumed by the provider; whether the entity placing the provider at risk is permitted to abate its own risk in this particular manner; and how management of the various types of risks by any of the risk-bearing parties may affect the underlying "contract" with the "insured" person.

Q 8:213   What analysis do regulators use to determine whether the (improper) business of insurance is being conducted by an individual or entity not licensed as an insurer or an HMO?

The analysis usually tracks the following course:

1. The insured possesses an insurable interest in his or her health.

2. The insured faces substantial risk of loss through the occurrence of disease or accident and the expenses associated with treatment.

3. The overall risk of loss is assumed by the "insurer" under the terms of the contract; that is, the insurer promises to pay an ascertainable sum or perform some act of value in the event of loss.

4. Both insured and insurer lack substantial control over the risk of loss.

5. Risk is spread or distributed among a large group of insureds who have similar risks of loss.

6. The insurer accepts some form of pecuniary consideration or "premium" that is usually distinct from payment for covered services in the event of loss.

[See generally *Couch on Insurance,* 3d ed, ch 1 (West Group 1997).]

As discussed in chapters 6 and 13, the statutory definitions of regulated insurance-type risk, whether borne by an insurer or an HMO, focus on (1) indemnification, reimbursement, or coverage for loss through direct payment for or delivery of health care expenses; (2) assumption and spreading of the risk for which the insurer will be called on to provide indemnification or expense reimbursement or for which the HMO will have to provide coverage by delivering health services; and (3) acceptance of an advance premium regardless of the form of such payment.

Q 8:214   What are the specific issues associated with the regulation of HMOs?

All states regulate HMOs. Most states have patterned their laws after the Model HMO Act developed by NAIC. Because HMOs have a service delivery function that does not exist for traditional insurers, they are subject to regulations that relate to their structure, quality of service delivery, and financial solvency. Most state HMO regulations include provisions relating to reserve, capital, and deposit requirements. They also require that HMOs maintain a quality assurance program and an appeal and grievance procedure that is approved by the appropriate state agency. Most states divide responsibility for the regulation of HMOs between the department of insurance and the department of health.

HMOs must provide consumers with protection against plan insolvency, either through hold-harmless clauses in their provider agreements or a requirement of continued coverage for some time period following insolvency. Other consumer protection provisions address minimum levels of health services and benefits, information to be furnished to enrollees, and prohibitions against misleading or abusive marketing practices.

Because of the problems that occurred with HMO insolvency in the mid- to late 1980s, both federal and state regulators increased standards relating to solvency and administration of HMO plans. Amendments were added to the federal HMO Act [Pub L No 93-222] to strengthen the solvency standards that federally qualified HMOs must meet and to eliminate grants and loans to HMOs. States modified their HMO regulations by becoming more involved in the review of fiscal solvency, consumer protection, quality assurance, utilization management, and the structure of delivery networks.

Q 8:215   What specific issues are associated with the regulation of PPOs?

Health care organizations that do not bear financial risk may be subject to regulation either directly, under state PPO laws, or indirectly, under laws relating to the regulation of insurance companies. Many states have enacted PPO laws based on NAIC's Preferred Provider Arrangement Model Act.

Although less comprehensive than the NAIC Model HMO Act, the NAIC Preferred Provider Arrangement Model Act contains requirements relating to disclosure, access, and provider contracts to ensure that PPO members are informed of differences in benefit levels and that providers are not unfairly discriminated against in opportunities to participate or remain participants in a PPO plan.

Tax and Tax-Exemption Issues

Q 8:216   What federal tax exemptions are most often used in managed care?

A health plan that meets the federal tax code's definition of a "charitable" or "social welfare" organization may be exempt from federal income taxes unless a significant portion of its activities is devoted to the business of commercial insurance. Exemptions exist for the following types of organizations:

1. *Charitable organizations.* A Code Section 501(c)(3) exemption is available to health care corporations, funds, or foundations organized and operated exclusively for religious, charitable, scientific, or educational purposes.

2. *Social welfare organizations.* Health care organizations may be exempt under Code Section 501(c)(4) if they are not organized for profit and they are operated for the promotion of social welfare. The organization's net earnings must be devoted exclusively to charitable, educational, or recreational purposes.

3. *Exclusion of commercial-type insurance and HMOs.* Code Section 501(m) was enacted in 1986 as part of the Tax Reform Act of 1986 for the purpose of causing Blue Cross and Blue Shield organizations to become taxable as insurance companies because a substantial part of their activities consisted of providing commercial-type insurance.

Q 8:217   What tax issues arise most often in managed care arrangements?

There are two areas in which the IRS expresses concern about the development of managed care arrangements. The first is in the choice of entity as a nonprofit or for-profit corporation. Some entities, such as PHOs or IPAs, are organized as nonprofit taxable corporations. Other entities, such as medical foundations, are structured as nonprofit, tax-exempt corporations to take advantage of the benefits of tax-exempt status. MSOs must be structured as for-profit entities because of their business purpose, and to offer their investors opportunities to receive profit distributions from the cash flow.

The second area of concern is in the pension or profit sharing plan rules under Code Section 414(m) (called affiliated service group rules) applied to qualified retirement plans. [IRC § 414(m)(2)(ii), as amended] Qualification of a plan allows the employer contributions to it to be tax-deductible and allows deferral of an employee's obligation to pay income tax on plan contributions. For an IPA, which may be composed of one or more legal entities and individuals, these rules may treat all involved as a single entity for purposes of testing the qualification of the various retirement plans.

Q 8:218   To what extent may a tax-exempt organization participate in election or political activities?

Tax-exempt organizations are absolutely prohibited from participating in any political campaign activity. The determination of a violation is made by the IRS based on the facts and circumstances. Violations may be found even if the activity was inadvertent. The penalty for violating the political campaign activity prohibition is loss of exemption for the organization. The types of activities at issue include participation in or intervention in (including publishing of statements or their distribution) any political campaign on behalf of or in opposition to any candidate for public office. Prohibited support may be financial or nonfinancial. Code Section 501(c)(3) organizations may not establish or support a political action committee (PAC) nor allow their facilities, personnel, or other financial resources to be used for the benefit of a PAC.

A Code Section 501(c)(3) organization may carry on educational activities advocating particular viewpoints and positions provided that the activities satisfy the IRS's "methodology test," which is outlined in Revenue Procedure 86-43. [1986-2 CB 729] This test applies to the determination that none of the following are true: (1) the presentation of the position is unsupported by the facts; (2) the facts supporting the position are distorted; (3) the presentation uses inflammatory and disparaging terms and expresses conclusions reflecting strong feelings; and (4) the approach being used is not aimed at developing an understanding on the part of the audience because it does not consider background or training in the subject matter. As a result, it is necessary to look not just at the activity itself but at the intended consequences of the activity.

The following activities by a charitable organization are generally considered to be a violation of the prohibition:

- Publishing or distributing written statements, or making oral statements, on behalf of or in opposition to any candidate for any federal, state, or local office
- Distribution of partisan campaign literature
- Provision of financial or in-kind support (use of volunteers, paid staff, equipment, mailing lists, etc.) to a candidate for any federal, state, or local office
- Establishment or support (financial or in-kind) of a PAC

The following activities of a charitable organization may be considered to be a violation of the prohibition:

- Inviting a particular candidate to make an appearance at an organization event
- Sponsoring candidate forums or distributing voter guides that may evidence a bias in favor of one particular candidate
- Allowing a PAC to use the organization's name in the PAC's distributed materials
- Using issue advocacy in fund-raising materials to affect voter preference

The following activities of a charitable organization should not result in violation of the prohibition:

- Unbiased voter education
- Nonpartisan public debates
- Nonpartisan get-out-the-vote drives

Q 8:219   What are the advantages and disadvantages of using a tax-exempt, nonprofit entity in managed care?

The major advantages of tax-exempt status are (1) exemption from paying federal income taxes for income associated with the entity's exempt purposes; (2) exemption from state property or income taxes; (3) deductibility to donors of charitable contributions made to the entity; and (4) availability of tax-exempt financing.

The major disadvantage of tax-exempt status is the restrictive conditions required to obtain and maintain that status.

Q 8:220   What is required to qualify for tax-exempt status?

To qualify for tax-exempt status under Code Section 501(c)(3), an organization must establish that it is organized and operated exclusively for religious, charitable, scientific, testing for public safety, literary, or educational purposes. The provision of medical care has been determined by the courts and the IRS to qualify as a charitable purpose. In Revenue Ruling 69-545 [1969-2 CB 117], the IRS established the following criteria to determine whether the charitable community benefit of an exempt hospital was being met: (1) the operation of an active emergency room; (2) control by a board of trustees composed of independent civic leaders; (3) maintenance of an open medical staff with privileges available to all qualified physicians; (4) a policy of leasing available space in the hospital's medical office building to physicians on its active medical staff; and (5) the use of surplus funds from operations to improve the quality of patient care, expand facilities, and advance the hospital's medical training, education, and research programs.

Q 8:221   What types of activities create problems for tax-exempt organizations?

The types of activities that create problems for tax-exempt organizations include compensation arrangements and joint venture arrangements. The IRS has granted favorable tax-exemption determinations in some circumstances for certain types of MCOs such as HMOs and integrated delivery systems.

Compensation Arrangements. The effect of the various compensation arrangements between a tax-exempt organization and nonexempt entities or persons, such as physicians or medical groups, depends on the nature of the arrangement and its purpose. Salaries may be paid by an exempt organization to a nonexempt entity or person if they are reasonable. The determination of reasonable compensation is a facts-and-circumstances test based on whether (1) the compensation is a result of arm's-length negotiations; (2) the party receiving the compensation has any control or influence over the exempt organization or compensation process; (3) the compensation is reasonable in terms of the responsibilities and activities required; (4) the salary would qualify as an expense deduction under Code Section 162(a); (5) the payments serve a real and discernible business purpose of the exempt organization independent of any purpose to operate for the direct or indirect benefit of the employee; (6) the compensation depends principally on the incoming revenue of the exempt organization or on the accomplishment of the objective of the contract; and (7) there is a ceiling or reasonable maximum to avoid the possibility of a windfall benefit. [Treas Reg § 1.162-7(b)(3) (1958)]

Income Guarantees. Income guarantees, which are used extensively in physician recruitment activities, have been suspect under both IRS guidelines and, more recently, Medicare fraud and abuse regulations. The IRS position is that it does not intend to create a negative presumption that such arrangements constitute per se inurement or private benefit. [GCM 39674 (June 17, 1987)] It is clear, however, that income guarantees must have reasonable terms, such as specified duration of support and an obligation to repay in cash or services. [IRS 1992 Examination Guidelines for Hospitals § 333.3(7)(a)]

Incentive Compensation Arrangements. Incentive compensation arrangements may be permitted if the arrangement qualifies as a profit sharing plan under Code Section 401(a). This arrangement allows exempt organizations to pay a percentage of profits as additional compensation as long as the payment is pursuant to a qualified plan. The IRS has determined by private letter ruling that a hospital incentive compensation plan would further the exempt purpose of the organization. [Ltr Ruls 8807081, 9112006]

Rental Abatement. Rental abatement in hospital-owned office buildings was at one time a common physician recruitment device. Under the IRS Examination Guidelines for Hospitals, these arrangements must meet a test of reasonable rental rates. In view of the position taken in evaluating potential violations of the Medicare fraud and abuse provisions, these arrangements will be suspect.

Management and Support Services. Support staff and practice management services are two other popular recruiting and retention methods. The test is whether the charge for such staffing and services is reasonable. If services are provided at below-market cost or at no charge, the exempt organization will have to demonstrate that the benefit is necessary to induce physicians to practice in an underserved area and that the overall compensation is reasonable.

Loans and Cash Assistance. Loans by an exempt organization to an insider at below-market rates or without adequate security will be suspect. A reasonable rate of interest has been defined under the Exemption Guidelines for Hospitals as prime plus 2 percent. [IRS 1992 Examination Guidelines for Hospitals § 333.3(10)] Cash assistance, such as a one-time recruitment bonus, may be permissible if it is based on the value associated with recruiting a particular physician service competence and not on the anticipated services to be rendered. [GCM 39498 (Apr 24, 1986)]

Equipment Purchase. The purchase of expensive equipment by an exempt organization for a nonexempt entity's use could jeopardize the exempt organization's tax exemption unless it can demonstrate that the public benefit with only incidental private benefit. To minimize private benefit, the arrangement should include elements such as retained ownership with a right to use or limited transfer with reversionary interest.

Hospital-Physician Joint Ventures. In General Counsel Memorandum 39005 [June 28, 1983], the IRS set out a three-part test regarding joint ventures involving exempt organizations. First, does the joint venture serve a charitable purpose? Second, does the joint venture allow the exempt organization to act exclusively in furtherance of its exempt purposes without conflict under applicable state law? Third, does the arrangement result in anything more than an incidental private benefit to the other nonexempt participants? These factors will not insulate an exempt organization that is deemed to be engaging in a joint venture relating to sharing of its net revenue stream.

In General Counsel Memorandum 39862 [Dec 2, 1991], the IRS reversed three private letter rulings relating to this form of joint venture, finding it a form of private inurement on the basis that (1) it causes the exempt organization's net earnings to inure to the benefit of private individuals; (2) the private inurement is not merely incidental to the public benefits achieved through the operation of the joint venture; and (3) these transactions may violate Medicare and Medicaid fraud and abuse laws that prohibit the offer, solicitation, payment, or receipt of any remuneration in return for or to induce the referral of a service that may be paid for under Medicare or Medicaid.[95] This ruling is significant because it represents the first time one federal agency, the IRS, has sought to identify and regulate an area subject to regulation by another federal agency, the DHHS OIG. Moreover, the favorable determination letters issued by the IRS for the Friendly Hills and Facey Medical Foundation integrated models on acquisition of physician practices are in conflict with the OIG's stated position on the inclusion of goodwill and other intangible assets in a health care transaction.[96]

Q 8:222   Is the IRS considering relaxing any of its standards of review with respect to exempt organizations in view of changing health care delivery systems?

Beginning with the exemptions issued to the Friendly Hills and Facey systems, the IRS has been moving toward recognizing the integration of health care providers within a single system. Since the fall of 1994, the IRS has applied a 20 percent safe harbor when analyzing the role of insiders on boards of exempt health care organizations only in the context of initial applications for exemption. More recently, the IRS has shown movement away from the strict application of the 20 percent safe harbor and has indicated that a health care organization seeking an initial determination of exempt status may have up to 49 percent insiders on the board of directors and still qualify for exemption if it has a strong conflict-of-interest policy in place.

In the first significant guidance in almost a decade, the IRS issued a technical advice memorandum in 1998 [98 TNT 243-2 (Doc 98-37129)] regarding HMOs' continued qualification for exemption as a charitable organization or as a social welfare organization. The key factors identified by the IRS in supporting a Code Section 501(c)(3) determination included the following:

- Community benefit or public purpose
  - Community representation on the governing body (only 20 percent physician insiders)

—An open patient care policy accepting Medicare and Medicaid patients as well as providing charity care procedures

—Existence of projects and programs that improve health care in the community, including expansion of health care resources, creation of new providers, improving modalities, and reducing the costs of health care

—Open medical staff policies at affiliated hospitals

- No private inurement issues

—Paying fair market value for all assets [Rev Rul 59-60, 1959-1 CB 237]

—Using professional and independent appraisals

—Arm's-length negotiations

- Fee schedule and physician compensation issues

—Determined by an independent community board

—Pay comparable to what physicians are paid in the community (taking into account the transfer of capital assets)

- Unrelated business income issues

—Management services provided by a tax-exempt organization may constitute an unrelated trade or business [Rev Rul 72-369, 1972-2 CB 245; Ltr Rul 9232003]

—Management services provided to a rural for-profit hospital and improving the quality of care in the community do not constitute unrelated business [Ltr Rul 9204033]

Q 8:223   What are the tax-exemption issues associated with physician recruitment?

One of the challenges facing tax-exempt health care organizations is competition with for-profit systems that are not encumbered by inurement concerns. On April 21, 1997, the IRS released its physician recruitment ruling in final form. [Rev Rul 97-21, 1997-1 CB 121] This ruling gives hospitals greater flexibility in documenting recruiting arrangements following the controversial closing agreement involving Hermann Hospital.

Permitted exemptions under the ruling include (1) signing bonus; (2) payment of malpractice insurance premiums for a limited period; (3) subsidized office rent for a limited period; (4) home loan guaranty; (5) reimbursement of moving expenses as defined in the regulations; (6) reimbursement of malpractice tail insurance for a physician's prior practice; (7) private practice net income guaranty for a limited period at an amount within the range of national or regional salary surveys for physicians in the same specialty, after reasonable practice expenses; and (8) financial assistance in the form of a loan for practice start-up expenses that is "properly documented" and provided on "reasonable terms." These exemptions supplement incentives that were approved previously, such as practice management services, life insurance premiums, providing scholarships to interns and residents during medical training, and paying the educational expenses of a medical student in exchange for subsequent practice in the community.[97]

Of significant deviation from the Hermann guidelines are the "cross-town" and retention recruitment incentives. These incentives may be allowable provided there is sufficient justification documented in all other areas but may still pose problems under Stark and antikickback laws.

References

1. *See* S.T. Dacso and C.C. Dacso, *Managed Care Answer Book 2001 Supplement* (New York: Aspen Publishers Inc., 2000), ch. 8.

2. Information regarding advisory opinions is contained in *Topic and Yearly Indices of Health Care Advisory Opinions by Commission and by Staff* and can be obtained from the FTC Public Reference Section. The index and advisory opinions issued since October 1993 can be found at http://www.ftc.gov.

3. "Government Regulators Still on Health Care Antitrust Beat Despite DOJ Task Force Demise," (BNA) Health L. Rep., 11(4), Jan. 24, 2002.

4. H.R. 2925, 104th Cong. (1996), was initially introduced on February 1, 1996. Although approved by the House Judiciary Committee on June 27, 1996, it did not survive a full vote of Congress and was reintroduced on January 9, 1997, as H.R. 415, 105th Cong. (1997).

5. *See* http://www.ftc.gov.

6. In general, the FTC and DOJ use ten years as a term indicating sufficient permanence to justify treatment of a competitor collaboration as analogous to a merger. The length of this term may vary, however, depending on industry-specific circumstances, such as technology life cycles.

7. For purposes of the safety zone, the FTC and DOJ consider the combined market shares of the participants and the collaboration. For example, with a collaboration between two competitors when each participant individually holds a 6 percent market share in the relevant market and the collaboration separately holds a 3 percent market share in the relevant market, the combined market share in the relevant market for purposes of the safety zone would be 15 percent. This collaboration, therefore, would fall within the safety zone. If, however, the collaboration involved three competitors, each with a 6 percent market share in the relevant market, the combined market share in the relevant market for purposes of the safety zone would be 21 percent, and the collaboration would fall outside the safety zone. Including market shares of the participants takes into account possible spillover effects on competition within the relevant market among the participants and their collaboration.

8. For a more detailed discussion, see the Competitive Impact Statement filed with the complaint and proposed final judgment in *United States v. Women's Hospital Foundation,* No. 96-389-B-M2 (M.D. La. filed Apr. 23, 1996).

9. J.R. Biereg, "Antitrust and Physician Involvement in Managed Care: Reform Is Needed!" (paper presented to the Physician Payment Review Commission, Jan. 11, 1995); E.B. Hirschfeld, "The Case for Antitrust Reform for Physician Groups" (Chicago: American Medical Association, June 8, 1994); J.S. Todd, "Physicians as Professionals, Not Pawns," *Health Affairs,* 12(3):145–47, 1993; *see also* "Government Regulators Still on Health Care Antitrust Beat Despite DOJ Task Force Demise," *supra* note 3.

10. Based on unpublished data of the American Managed Care Review Association, 1995, and "Provider-Owned Managed Care Networks Take Off," *Managed Care Wk.,* Oct. 31, 1994, at 1, 2.

11. As reported in the Annual Report to Congress of the Prospective Payment Review Commission (PPRC Report), *Medicare and*

Medicaid Guide Part 2, at 295 (CCH 1995), nd published in the report of the General Accounting Office, Federal and State Antitrust Actions Concerning the Health Care Industry (Washington, D.C.: GAO Aug. 1994).

12. *See* M.J. Horoschak, Bureau of Competition, Federal Trade Commission, advisory opinion letter to Paul W. McVay, President, ACMG Inc., July 1994; report of oral testimony of Mark J. Horoschak before the Prospective Payment Review Commission, Oct. 28, 1994.

13. Remarks by Ed Hirshfeld at his presentation on "Physicians, Unions, and Antitrust" before the National Health Lawyers Association Annual Seminar on Antitrust in Health Care, Feb. 19, 1998.

14. "Health Provider Bargaining Bill Passes House by 2-1 Margin," *Health L. Rep.* (BNA), 9(27), July 6, 2000.

15. *See* North Lake Tahoe Medical Group, Inc., FTC File No. 981-0261 (proposed consent order), 64 Fed. Reg. 14730 (Mar. 26, 1999).

16. Tex. Att'y Gen. Op. No. JC-0447 (Dec. 27, 2001).

17. "Prescription Drugs: Price-Fixing in Drug Industry Alleged; Congressman Asks Reno to Investigate," Health L. Rep. (BNA), 11(25), June 23, 2000.

18. C. Orstein. "25% of Doctors Groups Face Insolvency," *L.A. Times,* Aug. 22, 2001.

19. Cain Brothers Investment Bankers and Capital Advisors, "Lessons from a Health Care Bankruptcy: South Fulton Hospital," *Strategies in Corporate Finance,* Summer 2001.

20. *See* 11 U.S.C. § 586(a)(3)(A)–(H); G.M. Treister, J.R. Trost, L.S. Forman, K.N. Klee, and R.B. Levin, *Fundamentals of Bankruptcy Law* 91 (3d ed., 1993).

21. *See* In re Emmer Bro. Co., 52 B.R. 385, 395 (D. Minn. 1985).

22. *See* "State Managed Care Regulator Seizes Nonprofit Plan, Cites $59 Million in Debts," Health L. Rep. (BNA), 10(33), Aug. 16, 2001.

23. *See IHS Medicare/Medicaid Update,* Vol. 00-23, June 26, 2000, at mmu@ihshealth.com.

24. *See* Magera, "The Bankruptcy Code, Medicare Regulators and the Medicare Provider Relationship in Bankruptcy: When May the Government Recover Medicare Overpayments from Bankrupt Health Care Providers," *54 U.P. Health L. Rev.* 1085 (1993).

25. Weintraub and Resnick, *Bankruptcy Law Manual* (Boston: Warren, Gorham & Lamont, 1998).

26. *See* In re Commonwealth Co., 913 F.2d 518 (8th Cir. 1990); In re Selma Apparel Corp., 132 B.R. 968 (S.D. Ala. 1991) (both holding that suits for violation of the False Claims Act were not subject to automatic stay).

27. In Michigan, the doctrine was expressly limited. Virginia and Iowa have adopted a case-by-case analysis of whether the corporation controls professional practice (Virginia opposing counsel, Att'y Gen., Dec. 7, 1992; Iowa opposing counsel, Att'y Gen., July 12, 1991). In Kansas and Oklahoma, where the doctrine is rarely enforced, hospitals have been granted an express exclusion.

28. For a comprehensive 50-state survey of corporate practice statutes, see the seminar presentation materials of Dana Rister Gache, "Corporate Practice of Medicine 50 State Survey," NHLA Health Law Update and Annual Meeting, June 5–7, 1996.

29. *See* http://www.ncqa.org.

30. *See* http://www.jcaho.org.

31. *See* http://www.urac.org.

32. *See* http://www.aaahc.org.

33. For more information on the URAC survey, *see* www.urac.org.

34. *National Practitioner Data Bank Guidebook: A Reference for Individuals and Entities Reporting to and Querying the Data Bank,* (Washington, D.C.: U.S. Dep't of Health and Human Services Aug. 1992).

35. 45 CFR § 60.2 (formal peer review process).

36. *See* http://www.hin.com/sw/hospital_HSmanagement.html (Aug. 25, 2001).

37. In *LeMasters v. Christ Hospital*, 791 F. Supp. 188 (S.D. Ohio 1991), although the information reported to the NPDB was considered confidential, the peer review files were discoverable.

38. *Zamora-Quezada v. HealthTexas Medical Group of San Antonio* was filed May 16, 1997, in the U.S. District Court for the Western District of Texas, San Antonio Division, under several theories of liability, including wrongful termination as to Dr. Zamora and a novel theory by Drs. Zamora and Guerrero and certain patients involving the ADA. The case was settled for an undisclosed amount after it was sent to the jury.

39. *E.g.*, Harper v. Healthsource N.H., Inc., 674 A.2d 962 (N.H. 1996); Potvin v. Metropolitan Life Ins. Co., 54 Cal. App. 4th 936, 63 Cal. Rptr. 2d 202 (Ct. App. 1997).

40. *See* "Staff Privileges: AMA Calls 'Exclusive Credentialing' by Hospitals a Fraud Violation," Health L. Rep. (BNA), 9(10), Mar. 9, 2000.

41. Hearings Before the Senate Comm. on Labor and Human Resources. 105th Cong., 2d Sess. (1998) (testimony of Meredith Miller, Deputy Assistant Secretary, Pension and Welfare Benefits Administration).

42. 29 USC §§ 1021–1031 (1999).

43. 29 USC §§ 1051–1061 (1999).

44. 29 USC §§1101–1114 (1999).

45. *Id.*

46. K.A. Jordan, "Travelers Insurance: New Support for the Argument to Restrain ERISA Preemption," Yale J. on Reg., 13:255–336, 1996.

47. 29 USC §§ 1132 (1999).

48. McEvoy v. Group Health Coop. of Eau Claire, 570 N.W.2d 397 (Wis. 1997).

49. 29 USC § 1104(a)(1) (1999).

50. In *Rush Prudential HMO Inc. v. Moran*, No. 00–1021 (U.S. filed Mar. 26, 2001), the Court will decide whether a state law requiring independent review of medical necessity decisions made by an

HMO conflicts with ERISA. In November 2001, the DOJ provided its brief to the Court, saying that ERISA should not bar external review of claims.

51. In *Kentucky Association of Health Plans Inc. v. Miller,* No. 00-1471 (U.S. filed June 25, 2001), the Court asked the Bush Administration to weigh in on the ability of the states to regulate managed care networks, by inviting the Solicitor General to file a legal brief on whether state "any willing provider" laws are superseded by ERISA.

52. Barents Group LLC, Health Economics Practice, "Impacts of Four Legislative Provisions on Managed Care Consumers: 1999–2003" (prepared for the American Association of Health Plans, Apr. 22, 1998).

53. S. Nystrom et al., "The Health Premium Impact of H.R. 1415/S. 644, The Patient Access to Responsible Care Act (PARCA)" (Washington, D.C.: Muse and Associates, June 29, 1998); Congressional Budget Office, H.R. 3605/S. 1890: Patients' Bill of Rights Act of 1998 (Washington, D.C.: CBO, July 16, 1998).

54. D.M. Studdert, W.M. Sage, C.R. Gresenz, and D.R. Hensler, "Expanded Managed Care Liability: What Impact on Employer Coverage?" *Health Affairs,* 18(6):7–27, 1999.

55. Martori Bros. Distribs. v. James-Massengale, 781 F.2d 1349 (9th Cir. 1986), *amended,* 791 F.2d 799 (1986).

56. *See* Stuart Circle Hosp. Corp. v. Aetna Health Management, 995 F.2d 500 (4th Cir. 1993), *cert. denied,* 510 U.S. 1003 (1993); Texas Pharm. v. Prudential Ins. Co. of Am., 105 F.3d 500, 1035, 1040-42 (5th Cir. 1997; *cert. denied,* 522 U.S. 820 (1997)).

57. On October 20, 1998, President Clinton signed into law a new FEHBA preemption provision. Until then, FEHBA's preemption provision read: "The provisions of any contract under this chapter which relate to the nature or extent of coverage or benefits (including payments with respect to benefits) shall supersede and preempt any State or local law, or any regulation issued thereunder, which relates to health insurance or plans to the extent that such law or regulation is inconsistent with such contractual provisions."

58. The legislative history of the new FEHBA preemption provision shows that Congress meant to broaden FEHBA's preemptive scope: "[T]his bill broadens the preemption provisions in current

law to strengthen the ability of national plans to offer uniform benefits and rates to enrollees regardless of where they live. This change will strengthen the case for trying FEHB program claims disputes in Federal courts rather than State courts. It will also prevent carriers' cost-cutting initiatives from being frustrated by State laws." H.R. Rep. No. 105-374, at 9 (1998).

59. 42 USC § 1320a-7b(b). Various statutory and regulatory safe harbors have been established for beneficial arrangements that might otherwise violate the statute. *See* 42 USC § 1320a-7b(b)(3) (statutory safe harbors); 42 CFR § 1001.952 (regulatory safe harbors).

60. 42 USC § 1395nn (codifying Stark I and Stark II statutes).

61. "FTC Reviews Privacy Issues at Health Web Sites," W. St. J., Feb. 18, 2000, at B6.

62. *See* U.S. Dep't of Health and Human Services, Notice of Proposed Rule Making for Standards for Individually Identifiable Health Information, 64 Fed. Reg. 59917–60065 (Oct. 23,1999). Also available at www.hhs.gov/hottopics/healthinfo/index.htm.

63. *See* U.S. Dep't of Health and Human Services, Notice of Proposed Rule Making for Security and Electronic Signature Standards, 63 Fed. Reg. 43263–69 (Aug. 12, 1998).

64. 61 Fed. Reg. 13430–13450 (Mar. 27, 1996).

65. 42 CFR §§ 417.479, 417.500, 434.44, 434.67, 434.70. These rules require any HMO or other covered managed care plan that has an incentive arrangement with physicians to disclose these arrangements to DHHS and make such disclosures to every Medicare beneficiary or Medicaid recipient.

66. *See* 61 Fed. Reg. 13430 (Mar. 27, 1996); Health Care Financing Administration, Dep't of Health and Human Services, Office of Managed Care Operational Policy Letter No. 96.045, Dec. 3, 1996, as referenced in the PPRC Report, 242, *supra,* at note 11.

67. Presentation by John T. Bentivoglio at the Symposium on Health Care Internet and e-Commerce, Legal, Regulatory and Ethical Issues, Washington, D.C., Mar. 27, 2000.

68. *See* United States v. Anderson, 85 F.Supp. 2d 1084, 1103 (D.Kan. 1999).

69. *See* "Enforcement: Top DOJ Official Says No Easing of Crackdown on Health Care Fraud," *HFRA*, 3:385, May 5, 1999, "Managed Care: Federal Officials Detail Types of Fraudulent Activities under Investigation Involving MCOs," *HFRA*, 3:148, Feb. 24, 1999.

70. This case was a *Time* magazine cover story, "The Soul of an HMO," by Erik Larson, Jan. 22, 1996, at 44–52.

71. In *Viking v. Enterprise Financial Group, Inc.*, 148 F.3d 1206 (10th Cir. 1998), the court found that under Oklahoma law, an insured may bring a cause of action in tort for bad faith if the insurer breaches its duty to deal fairly and act in good faith with its insureds.

72. *See* McCarroll v. Reed, 679 P.2d 851 (Okla. Ct. App. 1983) (holding that a physician was liable for bad-faith breach of duty entitling the patient to punitive damages).

73. *See* Silver v. Slusher, 770 P.2d 878 (Okla. 1988) (holding that Oklahoma does not recognize the existence of a fiduciary relationship between insurer and insured).

74. *See* Humana v. Forsyth, 114 F.3d 1467, *aff'd*, No. 97-303 (U.S. Jan. 21, 1999).

75. 15 USC § 20.

76. *See* California Med. Ass'n v. Blue Cross of Cal. Inc., No. C 00-1894 (N.D. Cal. filed May 25, 2000). The plans named in the lawsuit include California Blue Cross, Foundation Health Systems, Inc., and PacifiCare, which are the major HMOs operating in California. For more information, see the CMA Web site at http://www.cmanet.org/upload/RICOsuit.pdf.

77. *See* D. Pimley, "States Tell Health Plans that Incentives May Not Limit Medically Necessary Care," Health L. Rep. (BNA), 7(40):1581, 1998.

78. *See* Texas v. Humana Health Plan of Tex., Inc., No. 98-13973 (Tex. Dist. Ct. 261st Jud. Dist. Dec. 16, 1998); Texas v. Aetna U.S. Healthcare, Inc., No. 98-13972 (Tex. Dist. Ct. 250th Jud. Dist. Dec. 16, 1998); Texas v. PacifiCare of Tex., Inc., No. 98-13971 (Tex. Dist. Ct. 201st Jud. Dist. Dec. 16, 1998).

79. The Assurance of Voluntary Compliance (AVC) can be found on the Texas Department of Insurance Web site at http://www.oag.state.tx.us/notice/avc_fin1.pdf.

80. The consumer information can be found on the Aetna Web site at www.aetnaushc.com. Also named in the suit were Humana Health Plan of Texas, NYLCare Health Plans of the Gulf Coast, NYLCare Health Plans of the Southwest, and PacifiCare of Texas.

81. *See* "Getting the Goods on Guidelines," *Hosps. & Health Networks,* Oct. 20, 1994, at 72.

82. *See* BMW of N. Am., Inc. v. Gore, 517 US 559 (1996), TXO Prod. Corp. v. Alliance Resources Corp., 509 U.S. 443 (1993).

83. T. Eisenberg and M.T. Wells, "Punitive Awards after BMW, a New Capping System, and the Reported Opinion Bias," *Wis. L. Rev.,* 1:387–425, 1998.

84. H.R. 956, 104th Cong. § 201(b) (1995); H.R. 955, 104th Cong. § 8(a) (1995); S. 1554, 105th Cong. (1997).

85. C.J. DeFrances et al., "Special Report: Civil Justice Survey of State Courts, 1992: Contract Cases in Large Counties," NCJ-15346 (Washington, D.C.: Dep't of Justice (July 1995).

86. E. Moller, N.M. Pace, and S.J. Carroll, "Punitive Damages in Financial Injury Jury Verdicts," MR-888-ICJ, (Santa Monica, CA: RAND, 1997).

87. J.C. Kelso and K.C. Kelso, "Jury Verdicts in Insurance Bad Faith Cases" (Sacramento, CA: McGeorge School of Law, University of the Pacific, Aug. 5, 1999); *see* http://www.mcgeorge.edu/ilp_verdicts_bad_faith_cases.htm.

88. M.L. Rustad, "Unraveling Punitive Damages: Current Data and Further Inquiry," *Wis. L. Rev.,* 1:15–69, 1998.

89. M. Galanter, "Shadow Play: The Fabled Menace of Punitive Damages," *Wis. L. Rev.,* 1:1–14, 1998.

90. T. Brennan and D.M. Studdert, "The Problems with Punitive Damages in Lawsuits against Managed Care Organizations," *N. Eng. J. Med.,* 342:4, Jan. 27, 2000.

91. P. Butler, "Key Characteristics of State Managed Care Organization Liability Laws: Current Status and Experience" (Menlo Park, CA: Kaiser Foundation, 2001).

92. The ability to form a class for purposes of bringing legal action arises under Federal Rule of Civil Procedure 23, which autho-

rizes class actions in the federal courts and outlines procedures for their maintenance, conduct, notice, judgment, dismissal, and compromise. Rule 23 is intended to give rights to groups of people who individually would be without effective strength to bring their opponents to court.

93. *See* Anderson v. Humana, Inc., 24 F.3d 889 (7th Cir. 1994) (rejecting a statutory claim alleging that the class was misled into selecting an HMO by fraudulent information); Teti v. U.S. Healthcare, Inc., No. 88-9808, 1989 U.S. Dist. LEXIS 14041 (E.D. Pa. Dec. 28, 1989) (unpublished opinion dismissing fraudulent disclosure claim); Weiss v. CIGNA Healthcare, Inc., 972 F. Supp. 748 (S.D.N.Y. 1997) (class action alleging that important medical decisions concerning patients' treatment were not made by the patients' primary care physicians, but by the MCO "bureaucrats" who are primarily motivated by cost reduction); Drolet v. Healthsource, Inc., 968 F. Supp. 757 (D.N.H. 1997) (alleging health plan's nondisclosure policies affected beneficiaries' ability to make informed medical decisions); Lynch v. Intergroup Healthcare Corp., No. CV 94-15694 (Ariz. Super. Ct. filed June 27, 1995) (class action alleging that HMO "intentionally failed to disclose a system of financial incentives given to contracting physician groups to encourage them to reduce the medical services" provided to HMO enrollees).

94. NAIC, The Regulation of Risk-Bearing Entities, at 1 n.3.

95. The private letter rulings affected by GCM 39862 are Ltr. Ruls. 8820093 (Feb. 26, 1988), 8942099 (July 28, 1989), and an unpublished 1984 letter ruling. The antikickback statutes referred to are found at 42 USC § 1320a-7b(b) (West Supp. 1991).

96. *See* IRS Determination Letters: Friendly Hills Healthcare Foundation, Jan. 29, 1993, and Facey Medical Foundation, Mar. 31, 1993, on exemption of integrated health care delivery systems; *see also* Dec. 22, 1992, letter from D. McCarty Thornton, Associate General Counsel of DHHS, DIG to the IRS Office of the Associate Chief Counsel.

97. *See* GCM 39498 (Apr. 24, 1986); GCM 39674 (June 17, 1987); Ann. 92-83, 1992-22 IRB 59, § 333.3(3)(a), (7)(c); GCM 39670 (June 17, 1987); Miss Georgia Scholarship Fund, Inc. v. Commissioner, 72 T.C. 267 (1979); Rev. Rul. 73-313, 1973-2 CB 174; Ltr. Rul. 8629045 (Apr. 22, 1986).

Chapter 9

Medical Care Management*

Utilization management lies at the core of managed care and is the major reason that managed care is so unpopular with patients and physicians alike. The imposition of controls by a third party can take many forms, ranging from the most strict lock-in gatekeeper model to a loosely managed discount of fees negotiated with a preferred provider organization (PPO). Medicare is on another plane, since it does not thoroughly manage care by imposing fee schedules via resource-based relative value scales (RBRVS) and shifting utilization controls to the provider using diagnosis-related groups (DRGs). Management control methodologies have in common control of provider utilization and conservation of economic resources. Demand management, a term borrowed from other industries, focuses on controls imposed prior to the utilization of resources.

Managed care plans use many strategies to reduce health care spending. Among these strategies are case management, demand management, and utilization review. Utilization review employs measures designed to manage the use of services and spending.

*The disease management section of this chapter was written by Kara McArthur, M.A., Academic Coordinator, Department of Medicine, Baylor College of Medicine. The case management section was contributed through the courtesy of Fred Spong, M.D., Milliman & Robertson, as adapted from *The Risk Contracting and Capitation Answer Book: Strategies for Managed Care* (Gaithersburg, MD: Aspen Publishers, Inc., 1999), 115–131.

A key feature of the health benefits and insurance industry, including indemnity plans, utilization review works to control costs, to monitor patient use, and to avoid services deemed unnecessary or inappropriate. Case management is a founding principle of managed care that uses clinically based criteria to manage care and control cost. Demand management is the control of services prior to utilization by education or prescriptive pathways.

Utilization management varies among plans in response to market forces such as price competition, payer pressure to control premium growth, and acceptability of managed care techniques to covered beneficiaries. Included in any modern utilization management strategy are clinical practice guidelines intended to improve patient outcomes and increase the value of health expenditures by facilitating informed decision making. Of great interest is the accelerating trend to reduce controls imposed by health plans and even to reduce the gatekeeper role.

Overview

Q 9:1 What is utilization review?

Utilization review (UR) is a cost-control mechanism used by some insurers and employers to evaluate health care on the basis of appropriateness, necessity, and quality. Predicated on external evaluations designed to enforce cost-control efforts, UR usually works hand in hand with a quality assurance strategy. It is the process by which health care services are examined to ensure that they are both necessary and cost efficient. In UR, the health care services provided to a specific patient are compared to an established norm of services provided to comparable patients.

Arguments in UR focus on definitions of appropriateness, necessity, and quality. These disputes form the basis of so-called patient protection legislation because they are at the heart of the practice of medicine. Many plans, rather than engage in these battles, have decreased the intensity of their URs and their procedures for preauthorization. Preauthorization is authorization from a plan prior to embarking on a therapy or medical procedure.

Q 9:2   What is the goal of utilization review?

The goal of UR is to control the quantity of health care services delivered and ultimately the cost of health care by eliminating "unnecessary" and "inappropriate" treatment.[1] In UR, it is important to discover

1. Whether care, including duration and frequency of service, is medically necessary and appropriate;
2. Whether lower-cost forms of care are available and efficacious; and
3. Whether patients improve as a result of treatment.

Utilization Management

Q 9:3   What is utilization management?

Utilization management (UM) is the entire process—including preadmission certification, concurrent review, and retrospective review—used to evaluate health care on the basis of appropriateness, necessity, and quality. It incorporates UR into a case management context. UR is a central element of UM, which extends to treatment and discharge planning as well as case management. Physician profiling and adoption of clinical practice guidelines are also part of modern UM programs and are used to help payers, health plans, and hospitals make decisions about managed care contracting. An effective UM program enables the provider to manage the allocation of resources for the benefit of the patient and the provider. Ideally, the patient receives health care services that are medically necessary and delivered in the most appropriate setting, and the provider delivers quality care with maximum reimbursement potential.

Methods used in many UM programs also include provider selection, provider education, economic incentives for both provider and patient, and claim review. The core parts of UM have come under attack as managed care has changed from the lock-in model of the 1980s and 1990s to the loosely managed but more expensive model of the twenty-first century.

Q 9:4   What was the impetus for utilization management in health care?

The historical impetus for UM in health care was the need to contain national health care expenditures, which began escalating in the mid-1960s. As the public and private sectors began to focus on cost containment, UM became a means of "managing cost." Integrating control over financing and delivery of care in order to manage care was the impetus for the development of health maintenance organizations (HMOs), which use an integrated means of managing care and costs through both programmatic systems and financial incentives. Capitation, limits on "out-of-network" care, gatekeepers, prospective and retrospective review of care, precertification, and second opinions are some of the methods used to manage care and reduce the inappropriate utilization of resources.

Q 9:5   What concerns are there about utilization management?

Arnold Milstein has voiced the following concerns about UM.[2]

1. Utilization levels have already been significantly reduced.
2. There is little evidence on the safety of UM programs or on their acceptability to patients.
3. As UM expands beyond UR, it is more difficult to scrutinize from the perspective of patient safety.

4. The point at which UM begins to affect quality is difficult to measure.

5. There are few safeguards.

Although these are real concerns, the culture of limited resources has permeated medical education for the past 15 years. As a consequence, physicians are very aware of costs and outcomes.

Q 9:6 What safeguards have been instituted for utilization management programs?

Efforts to safeguard consumers in the application of UM techniques include the following:

Accreditation. UM has been the focus of a number of accreditation organizations, including the Utilization Review Accreditation Commission (URAC), whose standards for utilization review organizations (UROs) focus on consumer safety issues.

Benefit Plan Labeling. Methods of informing purchasers and consumers of health plans as to the UM methods used by the health plan, hospital, and medical group have been developed. When effective, labeling occurs at the point of plan enrollment and provider selection.

Clinical Ombudspersons. Patient advocates are common in hospitals, and ombudspersons are common in many long-term care facilities. These individuals help patients obtain independent assessments of the appropriateness of treatment recommended by their physicians or health plans and evaluate options based on personal values. The objectivity of these persons must be able to withstand scrutiny to counteract the suspicion of bias.

Evidence-Based Utilization Management. Many government and private organizations have propounded evidence-based standards of practice. The American College of Physicians has accepted a grading scheme for evidence-based medicine that assesses a recommendation or standard from A to C depending on the quality of the underlying data. The Agency for Healthcare Research and Quality (AHRQ), the successor organization to the Agency for Health Care Policy Research and Quality (AHCPR), has assessed standards and publishes its assessment on their Web page, www.ahrq.gov.

Q 9:7   What are some of the methods benefit plans use to manage utilization?

Methods commonly used by managed care organizations (MCOs) and employers to manage utilization include managing provider referrals, monitoring provider practice patterns, case management for high-dollar cases, demand management, and service and coverage authorization. For a more detailed discussion of case management, see Qs 9:25–9:44.

Referral Management. Traditional HMOs prohibit enrollees from accessing specialty services without a referral from their primary care physician. Exceptions exist for certain services based on plan design, such as self-referral to a gynecologist for a "well woman" examination. Although PPOs do not absolutely restrict provider access, they shift costs to enrollees who receive medical treatment outside the network. Recent data[3] indicate that restrictions placed on specialty access by managed care plans were useless in that specialty medical care use is the same whether or not a gatekeeper model is used. Thus, it is reasonable to conclude that the gatekeeper model, the core of the closed-network HMO, did little to conserve cost and much to anger consumers. Of course, many patients prefer that their primary care physician coordinate their care. Acceptance of this model has been an unintended benefit of managed care.

Monitoring Provider Practice Patterns. Many professional medical organizations, medical staffs of managed care plans, and the AHRQ have developed guidelines for the medical management of specific health care conditions. Although many managed care plans use these guidelines to educate providers about more efficient or cost-effective approaches to the delivery of care, the guidelines are also used in peer review and to monitor physician performance.

Case Management for High-Dollar Cases. Another UM technique is case management for long-term or chronic illnesses. The scope and design of case management programs vary by plan, but there are two basic models. High-intensity programs focus on managing service use across all health care settings, with case managers spending significant amounts of time with the patient. Low-intensity programs focus on inpatient hospitalization and prior authorization for services. Fundamental to both types of program are patient selection, development of a care plan for patient services, and monitoring of care over time.

Demand Management. Programs are developing to help physicians and patients manage their expectations regarding health care services. Patients historically accessed medical services without regard to necessity or cost. Physicians acted on the basis of economic incentives, access to technology, and patient demands. Demand management programs use decision support tools such as practice guidelines and balanced financial incentives to counter over- or underutilization.

Service and Coverage Authorization. Most health plans use one of three general methods to authorize services:

1. Precertification, the most popular method, is a way to control the setting, the services, and the anticipated case monitoring for patient care. Preadmission notification allows the plan to anticipate a claim.
2. Concurrent review allows the plan to monitor and limit the length of stay following admission. Plan staff monitor patients during their hospitalization.
3. Retrospective review is based on the submitted claim and assesses accuracy of charges and patterns of care provided by the institution.

Q 9:8 How does management of medical processes affect utilization?

Medical management is critical for success in a competitive environment. In medical management, physicians agree both to define and to implement treatment plans with the goal of standardizing routine, uncomplicated care. Variation in medical care is common and often confounds management. Yet that variation is enormously costly at best and unsafe at worst. Physicians must learn not to equate medical management with a "cookie cutter" approach to care. Medical management does not seek to diminish the patient-physician relationship. Medical management will work best when there is alignment of incentives between the plan, the managers, the hospitals, the patients, and the physicians.

Q 9:9 What is evidence-based medicine?

Evidence-based medicine is a response to efforts to balance clinical judgment (based on experience) and medical evidence (results based on research) in reaching a medical decision. In the *Health Policy Newsletter*, Dr. David B. Nash[4] reports on an approach taken by D.L. Sackett and colleagues to manage the use of evidence in clinical practice.

The steps outlined by D.L. Sackett[5] for practicing evidence-based medicine are the following:

1. Converting information needs into answerable questions;
2. Tracking down with maximum efficiency the best evidence from all sources with which to answer the questions;
3. Appraising the evidence for its validity and usefulness in a critical fashion;
4. Applying the results of this appraisal in everyday practice; and
5. Evaluating performance and feeding back the information to those involved in the process.

Q 9:10 How does evidence-based medicine link outcomes to utilization management?

Associating differences in the delivery of care with differences in outcome may help to identify which services are worth providing, which services have been misused, and which services require more evidence about their effectiveness. The ability to measure and incorporate outcomes into protocols based on "best evidence" provides additional tools for managing care. The key to the success of managing care is the convergence of information technology and evidence-based decision making.

Evidence-based medicine is far from a panacea to ending the variation in medical care, although it is a strong contributor to the movement to place a scientific foundation under the practice of medicine. For many clinical situations there is no firm scientific evidence to guide therapeutic decisions. In these cases, the physician relies on probabilities, ancillary knowledge, and even some intuition.

Q 9:11 What are the advantages and disadvantages of concurrent review of hospitalizations as a utilization management technique?

Concurrent review is the preferred method when review is performed because it allows the maximum opportunity for intervention and negotiation. Unfortunately, many avoidable medical admissions are unscheduled and occur from emergency rooms. For surgical admissions, rigorous criteria are lacking.

Concurrent review suffers from three major flaws:

1. The system reacts to what might have happened because it is based on assignment of length of stay from retrospective data.
2. Physician participation is often inadequate.
3. The efficacy of concurrent review is based on the certainty of punishment—withholding payment—and thus it produces an adversarial rather than cooperative environment.

Q 9:12 What are "continuum of care" services?

Continuum of care services are services that provide an appropriate intensity and location for medical care based on the intensity of the patient's illness. From the most intense to the least intense, these services generally include the following:

- Intensive care unit
- Step-down unit
- Hospital bed
- Long-term acute-care facility
- Sub-acute-care facility
- Skilled nursing facility
- Rehabilitation facility
- Custodial care
- Home health care
- Adult day care
- Hospice care

Support services included in the continuum of care include the following:

- Durable medical equipment
- Infusion services
- Personal care and homemaker assistance
- Telephone support

- Transportation
- Wellness program

Q 9:13   What tools are available to manage the delivery of continuum of care services?

The tools available to manage delivery of continuum of care services include the following:

- Clinical guidelines
- Critical pathways
- Delivery system infrastructure elements
- Case management
- Disease management

The Institute of Medicine has defined clinical guidelines as "a systematically developed statement to assist practitioner and patient decisions about appropriate health care for specific clinical circumstances." Other names for the same thing are practice parameters, practice protocols, and practice algorithms.

Q 9:14   How does provider selection serve utilization management objectives?

One UM method many HMOs and PPOs have used is selection of physicians with efficient utilization practices. Exclusion of inefficient physicians can reduce health care costs; however, there are some legal risks to provider exclusion in states that have "any willing provider" statutes (see chapters 5 and 12 for more information on these regulations). Another barrier to using provider selection procedures is the absence of meaningful data about physician utilization practices and performance. Obtaining such data or developing such databases can be time consuming and expensive and raises real questions about ensuring patient confidentiality under the Health Insurance Portability and Accountability Act of 1996 (HIPAA). As networks become more open, physician profiling is falling into disuse as a UM tool.

Q 9:15   What is the role of provider education in utilization management?

Historically, physicians had little or no training in costs associated with specific medical procedures. In one pioneering study conducted in 1981, community physicians estimated only 14 percent of medical costs correctly, and physicians in one teaching hospital estimated only 50 percent of costs correctly.[6] Medical education, including continuing medical education, has now incorporated evidence and cost into medical decision making.

Q 9:16   How are economic incentives used in utilization management?

The use of economic incentives to reduce provider utilization is controversial and much less commonly employed as a cost reduction method. The Centers for Medicare and Medicaid Services (CMS) has been very concerned about provider incentives and uses them as major review items in site visits for accrediting Medicare managed care plans. (The implications of using of physician incentives are discussed in chapters 8 and 13.)

Q 9:17   What is the role of the patient in utilization management?

Patient-directed incentives and education are important elements of any UM program. A Rand Corporation study in the early 1980s showed that patient cost sharing can dramatically reduce utilization.[7]

An unintended consequence of managed care has been to make the consumer of medical care suspicious of the quality of the care and the motives of the providers. This has spurred a movement for self-education, which has been fueled by the easy access to information provided by the Internet. Internet information, however, is unscreened and often placed by individuals with motives more questionable than those of physicians. Thus, physicians are often asked to interpret Internet data for patients.

Q 9:18   What are the major obstacles to an effective utilization management program?

There are at least five fundamental barriers to optimal UM: (1) lack of effective execution; (2) absence of a standard based on scientific data; (3) claims data limitations (inaccuracies and inconsistencies); (4) limitations of the medical record; and (5) professional autonomy and disdain for external controls.

Q 9:19   What types of utilization review are there?

Typically, there are five types of UR: prospective, concurrent, retrospective, second opinion, and case management.

Prospective review is performed to determine medical necessity before the initiation of treatment. It usually entails some form of preadmission certification or other process involving notification by the provider to the UR entity of the patient's diagnosis and proposed treatment. Following this notification, the UR entity authorizes a treatment or a length of stay for the patient. If the proposed treatment is not deemed medically necessary, the payer will not pay for that treatment.

Concurrent review is performed during treatment to ensure that the care continues to be appropriate and necessary. If it does not, the payer may refuse to authorize or pay for additional care.

Retrospective review is performed after treatment has been completed and is used primarily to evaluate the care provided. If the review indicates that the medical care was not necessary, the payer may deny the claim retroactively.

Second opinion review usually concerns either surgical or complex medical procedures and is intended to eliminate unnecessary treatment. Second opinion review can be either mandatory (benefits are reduced or eliminated if the second opinion is not obtained) or voluntary (no impact on the level of benefit, but a second opinion is paid for).

Case management is performed by a clinical case manager who reviews a case to determine whether an alternative plan of care could provide the necessary medical services more effectively. Case management is generally used in cases of catastrophic illness or injury. (This topic is discussed in more starting with Q 9:25.)

Some companies provide the following additional UR services:

- Preadmission testing
- Presurgical procedure review
- Outpatient and ambulatory facility surgical review
- Home health care review
- Birthing center, hospice, nursing home, and hospital bill audit

- Mental health (including substance abuse) review
- Dentistry review
- Chiropractic review
- Podiatry review
- Private-duty nursing review
- Managed case management (focusing on specific illness and injury episodes)
- Managed second medical opinion (identifying cases that benefit from second medical opinions and waiving second opinion requirements for others)
- Prospective fee negotiation (which occurs during UR)

Q 9:20 How do payers use these types of utilization review?

Most insurance companies and MCOs rely on prospective and concurrent review because they enable the payer to ascertain whether proposed treatment is deemed medically appropriate before the care is provided and resources are expended. Prospective review has had a far greater effect on cost containment and quality than retrospective review. Arnold Milstein identified five important areas for innovation in prospective UR.[8]

1. Expansion of review and case management programs, including development of medical necessity criteria and price control databases for hospital outpatient services, for ambulatory care facilities and settings (including ambulatory surgery), for physician office care, for long-term care, for home-based services, and for allied health practitioners;

2. Targeted case management programs with complete ancillary services at negotiated reimbursement for a variety of health care services, including durable medical equipment, home health services and infusion therapy, psychiatric residential treatment, physical and occupational therapy, rehabilitation services, and prescription drugs;

3. Quality assurance as a stand-alone product line offered by vendors, and by hospitals and physicians, including (a) defining quality of care in operational terms and then managing it; (b) redefining hospital and physician data collection and analysis mechanisms; (c) identifying underutilization and

overutilization of services; (d) incorporating indices for intensity of services and severity of illness; and (e) developing inpatient and ambulatory care outcome measures.

4. Integration of claims data and UR information, which would lead to expanded analytical and reporting capability and capacity, and hence to (a) reports that indicate savings by different types of UR procedures and by case management; (b) targeting high-incidence illnesses by diagnoses and procedure; (c) in-depth provider profiling; (d) online modification of fee schedules; and (e) far more sophisticated price and fee negotiation; and

5. Program specialization and specification, including, for example, (a) increased use of clinical expertise in case management; (b) UR conducted by medical and nursing specialists trained in treating a patient's particular illness; (c) use of review resources designed to focus on particular problem areas; (d) identification of tertiary-level DRGs by specific institutions; and (e) identification of centers of excellence based on superior surgical or treatment results.

Q 9:21 How effective is utilization review?

The effectiveness of UR is a subject of debate. UR decreases the use of services, particularly in hospital settings. Effective UR identifies underutilization as well as overutilization, and thus is distinguished from rationing.

In one case study, a major HMO reported numerous coding and billing errors by physicians, errors of data entry by payers, and duplicate submission of bills by patients. These problems were identified using the following computer data screens:[9]

- Volume and intensity of service
- Practice patterns, including the following:
  - Upcoding of office visits
  - Frequency of consultations
  - Frequency of x-rays and ultrasounds
  - Frequency of laboratory tests
  - Frequency of injections
  - Frequency of referrals

- — Frequency of visits by diagnosis
- — Misuse of procedure and service codes
- — Misuse of new-patient codes
- — Misuse of anesthesia times
- — Misuse of hospital discharge codes
- — Misuse of phlebotomy codes
- — Misuse of breast cyst excision codes
- — Misuse of medical service codes by mental health professionals
- — Misuse of office visit codes for physical therapy
- Quality issues, such as the following:
  - — Readmission within 31 days
  - — Cesarean section rate
  - — Failed outpatient rate
- Contract compliance, including the following:
  - — Noncompliance issues
  - — Failure to obtain preauthorization
  - — Admission to noncontracted facility
  - — Billing for archaic procedures
  - — Billing for assistant surgeons in absence of medical need
  - — Billing for cosmetic and experimental procedures
  - — Unnecessary hospitalization
  - — Data entry by payers
- Identification of billing errors such as the following:
  - — Hospital and office visits during follow-up period
  - — Surgery charges without hospitalization
  - — Anesthesia charges without surgery
  - — Fragmentation
  - — Surgery package fee
  - — Maternity package fee
  - — Exploratory laparotomy
  - — Extended anesthesia times

Q 9:22   What should be considered in evaluating a utilization review program?

The means by which UR is performed is important to the employer, the purchaser of health care services, the payer, as are the financial integrity and legitimacy of the UR company and the experience of those performing the UR. In evaluating a UR program, the following should be considered as part of an overall risk and fiscal management review:[10]

Organizational Competence and Fiscal Responsibility. Just as many networks use a credentialing process to evaluate the qualifications and competence of providers, the purchasers of health care services should apply similar criteria to their selection of UR services. These criteria should include the experience and credentials of the professional reviewing staff; the levels of liability insurance covering provider networks and UR companies; the financial integrity of the company, particularly its ability to indemnify the employer, purchaser, or payer; the role of the employer, purchaser, or payer in deciding coverage issues for specific medical services (e.g., experimental or high-risk procedures) about which the patient may need to be informed in order for the payer and provider to avoid liability; and the nature of the review process and those responsible for carrying it out.

Standards and Procedures Used in Administering the Program. Risk management occurs through the administration and operation of the UR program, including the familiarity of the physician reviewer with the specialty area in which the patient is involved; consultation with the attending physician by the physician reviewer prior to issuing a denial; discussion of the case with the attending physician; familiarity of the physician reviewer with the case documentation; and, in some cases, examination of the patient by the physician reviewer prior to issuing a denial. Emergency admissions should be exempted from preauthorization review. Time frames for review by nurses and physicians should be specified, and denials should be subject to an appeal process by either the patient or the physician (in addition to any second opinion rights of the UR program). Medical criteria used in UR should be based on local practice standards and subjected to review and approval by the employer, purchaser, or payer being implemented.

Data Collection and Management Capability. Another critical feature of an effective UR program is its ability to accumulate and analyze data quickly and accurately. A data management system should have an adequate computer system, experienced staff, and compatibility between the UR computer system and the provider network system. The computer system should meet the needs of the provider and of the purchaser, employer, or payer. The data gathered must be appropriate (e.g., cost per period, volume of services by category or medical specialty, or cost per provider), and the system should be capable of generating appropriate reports and data within a brief turnaround time. (The management of information is discussed in chapter 15.)

Q 9:23 Is utilization review generally included in a managed care organization's services?

The answer depends on the type of managed care organization (MCO) or type of health plan. A health maintenance organization (HMO) cannot unbundle UR from its plan. PPOs, however, are not subject to the same legal restrictions. Many insurers and large employers try to require providers to use their UR programs as a condition of the contract. Because most PPOs and providers have their own UR programs, this requirement can lead to duplication and inconsistency. Whose UR program is used and who oversees the UR are significant issues between the payer and the provider that go to the heart of a UR program's integrity and data capture capability. Reconciling UR programs is more than merely a question of reducing duplication. Duplicating UR increases costs and can send mixed and even conflicting messages to providers. From the perspective of a health plan, it is difficult to delegate UR to more than one entity while maintaining the integrity of a cohesive UR program.

Case Management

Q 9:24 What is case management?

Case management is a process intended to improve the quality of medical care by improving the management of health care delivery outcomes. It encompasses a range of strategies that culminate in the design and implementation of comprehensive plans of action. Case management entails a determination of the level and extent of medical care needed and includes identification of appropriate treatment modalities and settings.

The Case Management Society of America (CMSA), founded in 1990, is an international, not-for-profit professional society with more than 7,000 members. CMSA describes case management as "a collaborative process which assesses, plans, implements, coordinates, monitors and evaluates options and services to meet an individual's health needs through communication and available resources to promote quality, cost-effective outcomes." Ideally, case management ensures continuity, timeliness, and appropriateness of care to produce planned clinical and resource management outcomes. The process involves a myriad of health care resources and professionals to achieve these outcomes. Physicians, nurses, social workers, discharge planners, hospitals, home health agencies, skilled nursing facilities, and extended care facilities are among the providers mobilized to meet patient and family needs.

Q 9:25 How is case management used to manage care and cost?

Comprehensive case management is more than the coordination of health care providers and services; it is an ongoing process of patient, family, and provider education. The case manager helps all stakeholders (i.e., patients, families, providers, community agencies, and payers) to understand available care and treatment options, participate in health care decision making, navigate the delivery system, and adhere to the plan of care.

Q 9:26 What are the key components of traditional case management?

Traditional case management involves a number of interrelated processes derived from nursing practice. The processes are often performed simultaneously.

Assessment. Relying on information from the patient, family, and providers, the case manager develops a preliminary assessment and treatment plan. The plan includes measurable objectives such as projected length of stay, recovery in terms of ability to perform activities of daily living, and anticipated need for postdischarge care (e.g., transfer to a sub-acute-care facility, home health care, outpatient treatment).

Planning. The case manager must develop a consensus on the treatment plan among all stakeholders. It is especially important that the patient and family participate in the planning and concur with treatment goals; in the absence of such support, adherence to the prescribed treatment and satisfaction with care are compromised.

Implementation. Before starting the treatment plan, the case manager must conduct a benefits review and obtain necessary authorizations. The treatment plan begins when all parties are informed and concur about the actions needed to produce the desired clinical and resource management outcomes.

Coordination. This process ensures timely access to needed services. Coordination also prevents duplication or provision of unnecessary services and enhances continuity of care.

Monitoring. The treatment plan must be monitored to ensure adherence and may be altered or fine-tuned in response to the patient's needs.

Evaluation. Case managers determine the extent to which clinical and resource management objectives are achieved as well as patient, family, provider, and payer satisfaction with the course of treatment and planned follow-up.

Communication. Case management requires clear and frequent communication with patients and families, providers, and payers. Along with conducting in-person and telephone meetings, case managers must maintain detailed written records and document authorization for treatment, changes to the treatment plan, follow-up, and evaluation.

Cost-Benefit Analysis. Because one desirable outcome of case management is optimal, cost-effective resource utilization, case managers must continually assess the costs and benefits of all planned treatment. Conversant with available community health care resources, they are often instrumental in guiding providers and directing patients to the most appropriate treatment setting.

Q 9:27 How is case management practiced?

Historically, case management was performed episodically, in response to catastrophic illness or in anticipation of prolonged hospitalization or highly intensive, costly services. This form of inpatient
case management bears a strong resemblance to clinical crisis intervention, a patient-focused, payer-driven process involving provider
organizations and furnished by consultant firms. It is short term,
intense, and performed separately from UM.

In contrast, outpatient case management seeks to prevent the episodes of care monitored by hospital-based case managers. Identifying individuals at risk (e.g., patients suffering from chronic diseases or frequent users of hospital-based urgent or emergency
services), case managers seek to educate patients about their illnesses to prevent the acute exacerbations of illness that result in
hospitalization. Case managers also focus on changing patterns of
outpatient utilization, by redirecting patients from the acute setting
to lower levels of care. For example, patients diagnosed with chronic
conditions such as asthma, hypertension, low back pain, or diabetes
may be referred to patient education and/or peer support groups
mediated by allied health professionals in place of frequent office or
clinic visits.

Outpatient case management has also been applied to managing
community-based health and social services for chronically impaired
older adults. By bridging the chasm between the formal medical care
delivery system and informal helping networks, several states have
developed fully integrated models of managed care for older adults.
These model programs provide incentives for the delivery of appropriate acute and long-term care in the least restrictive setting. Case
managers coordinate and facilitate service delivery for frail older
adults requiring complex, multidisciplinary care in a continuum of
settings ranging from acute, day hospital and skilled nursing care to
home care and respite for caregivers.

Q 9:28 Who tends to get involved in case management decisions?

There are many participants in case management decision
making.

Physician. The treating physician is critical to case management to ensure continuity of care. If a physician does not have privileges at a participating hospital, this can affect the patient's care and case management. Thus, hospital staff membership is generally a prerequisite for joining a payer's panel. The MCO with which the physician has contracted generally will have executed a contract with the hospital separately. In an integrated delivery system, the hospital and the physicians are one entity, and no such separate negotiation need be entered into. From the point of view of the case manager, integration clearly simplifies negotiations. For mental health issues, the hospital team is at times more important than the attending physician. A well-functioning hospital team discusses the patient's progress on a regular basis, and decisions are made about treatment and care with the physician's input and recommendation.

The referral relationships among physicians are also an important factor. When the case manager facilitates the transfer of care from one provider to another, the ability of the providers to communicate and establish some rapport is important to patient care and case management.

A new type of program, stimulated by managed care, has helped to facilitate integrated delivery. Groups of physicians, usually internists, who define themselves variously as "intensivists," "hospitalists," or "criticalists," confine their practice to the hospital and manage a patient during his or her hospital stay. Much as primary care physicians do, these internists coordinate specialty referrals and procedures to minimize the length of stay, complications, and expense. For primary care physicians, the rise of this new specialty has the benefit of keeping them in their most efficient environment, the office. For the patient, care coordination by a single physician, the paradigm of managed care, can be carried into the hospital. For the MCO, the hospital stay can be reduced beyond the limit circumscribed by an outpatient physician's hospital rounding schedule. The notion of the hospitalist seems to be best accepted among the highly capitated plans under which the physician derives great economic benefit from minimizing hospital expense. The hospital can be a beneficiary when it is paid on a case-rate, DRG, or other risk basis. Some progressive hospitals are sponsoring the development of hospitalist practices for this reason.

Family. The patient's family can exert a tremendous influence on case management. Sometimes the family resents the intrusion of the case manager into the physician-patient relationship. Other times, the family welcomes the presence of an external facilitator. The skilled case manager is able to understand the family's perspective and balance it with the needs of the patient, the payer, and the physician. Often the family's travel time influences the location of the care facility ultimately selected. A family's ability to provide care for the patient at home can greatly influence the timing of the patient's discharge.

Discharge Planner. Many case managers view a facility's discharge planners as more influential than its physicians. Often, discharge planners understand the role of case managers. Some facilities have case management departments made up of social workers, nurses, and counselors, who help in planning and anticipating discharges and setting goals for the patient and family. These workers are sometimes differentiated as internal and external case managers. The more the key participants are in agreement and supportive of discharge planning, the greater the patient's chance for recovery and success. With chemical dependency cases, implicit in discharge planning is the aftercare plan and the patient's compliance with it as part of the reintegration of the patient into the workplace.

Q 9:29 Are case managers certified, licensed, or regulated?

One of the goals of the CMSA is to implement uniform standards for case management practice. Currently the practice of case management requires neither licensure nor mandatory certification. Voluntary certification is available from the Commission for Case Management Certification (CCMC), an independent credentialing body established in 1995.

The CCMC defines case management as a specialized area of practice, rather than a profession. The intent of CCMC credentialing is to establish a national certification process attesting to an individual's mastery of fundamental case management principles and practice. The designation of certified case manager (CCM) was designed to serve as an adjunct to other professional credentials in the health and human services profession.

The renewable, five-year CCM credential is awarded to practitioners who satisfy specific educational and employment requirements and pass the CCM examination. Applicants for certification renewal must verify that they continue to maintain the license or certificate they held at the time the credential was issued and must demonstrate ongoing professional development by completing an approved program of continuing education or reexamination.

Efforts to license and stipulate training of case managers have been endorsed by a number of other professional organizations, including the American Nurses Association, the Association of Rehabilitation Nurses, and the National Association of Professionals in the Private Sector. Although the optimal education, training, and experience of case managers are debated within professional societies, all concur that to perform effectively, case managers must possess superb interpersonal, communication, and teaching skills.

UROs and firms that offer case management services are subject to regulation in at least 28 states. Minimally, most states require UROs to notify the provider or enrollee about UR decisions; use written, clinical review procedures that are periodically reviewed and updated; disseminate a written description of the appeal process to providers; allow ample time for providers to submit necessary clinical information for review; and prohibit reimbursement tied to the number or frequency of claims denials. Since 1991, UROs conforming to national standards established by the URAC have been granted voluntary accreditation. The stated purposes of the URAC standards are:

1. To encourage consistency in the procedures for interaction between UROs and providers, payers, and consumers of health care;

2. To establish UR processes that cause minimal disruption to the health care delivery system;

3. To establish standards for the procedures to certify health care services and to process appeals of the determinations;

4. To provide the basis for an efficient process for accrediting UROs; and

5. To provide an accreditation mechanism that can be applied efficiently in states that choose to regulate URO activities.

Hospital-Based Case Management

Q 9:30 What is hospital-based case management?

Hospital-based case management is intended to improve quality of care by providing planned outcomes, which include a goal of length of stay and anticipated need for postdischarge care.

Q 9:31 What are the basic mechanisms of hospital-based case management?

The basic mechanisms of hospital-based case management are preadmission screening, admission review, continued stay review, and discharge planning.

Preadmission Screening. Hospital-based case management begins with preadmission screening to determine the medical necessity of the admission and the appropriate level of care. During preadmission screening, the patient and family are the foci of teaching to prepare for the planned activities of the admission (e.g., diagnostic testing, surgical or medical intervention); identify posthospitalization needs; plan discharge options; initiate the community resource referral process; and when necessary, perform financial screening.

Admission Review. Generally conducted within 24 hours of admission, this chart review entails a comparison of clinical guidelines with the documented admission data to establish the medical necessity for treatment in an acute-care setting. Admission review targets nonelective entry to the hospital—that is, direct admissions from the physician's office and patients admitted through the hospital emergency department.

Continued Stay Review. At various points during the hospital stay, focused chart review is used to confirm or question the need for continuing care in the acute-care setting. It may also be used to modify or amend the discharge plan.

Discharge Planning. Discharge planning occurs during preadmission screening for all elective admissions. The discharge plan must retain considerable flexibility to respond to changing needs and circumstances of the patient and family. Along with continued stay review, ongoing communication with multiple caregivers is required to determine the need for changes in the goal length of stay and/or the discharge plan.

Q 9:32   What are the roles of physicians and nurses in hospital-based case management?

Essentially a collaborative process, case management involves the patient and family, case manager, physician, nurses, and allied health professionals. In many instances, case management may also be subject to institutional review from a provider or payer UM group.

The physician is responsible for diagnosis and treatment as well as development and direction of the care plan. Physicians engaged in case management must regularly confer with the nurses who implement and document the plan, the case manager tracking the plan, and the patient and family.

Effective case management requires considerable support from nursing personnel. They must be thoroughly conversant with the case management guidelines in their specialties (e.g., medicine, surgery, obstetrics, rehabilitation). Individual nursing departments often must be realigned to support overall UM goals. For example, preoperative testing and screening provide the opportunity for nurses to preassess discharge planning needs and discuss the goal length of stay with the patient and his or her family. Case management guidelines and criteria must be incorporated into the nursing care plan. The nursing care plan should document the goal length of stay and any potential obstacles (e.g., medical, family, social, or financial impediments to discharge) to achieving the goal length of stay. Nurses facilitate timely communication between all stakeholders. They notify case managers when family members are available for conferences, participate in multidisciplinary rounds, and alert attending physicians when the results of laboratory or other diagnostic tests arrive. Further, nurses promote timely changes in the care plan by apprising the physician of patient progress throughout the day, such as improving dietary tolerance.

Q 9:33   How does hospital-based case management differ from MCO case management?

Hospital-based case management addresses resource utilization during and after inpatient admission. It is characterized by short-term, intense case management relationships aimed at optimizing individual patient outcomes. Patient and family education centers on management of the illness or condition that precipitated hospitalization. The effectiveness of hospital-based case management is measured in terms of clinical outcomes, such as goal length of stay. Financial outcomes are assessed by determining cost savings per patient.

MCO case management not only incorporates hospital-based case management techniques but also considers outpatient care. Its emphasis is on preventing hospitalization and illness. The case manager seeks to educate members about illness avoidance by promoting primary prevention and wellness programs.

Targeting members considered to be at risk for hospitalization or greater than average utilization (e.g., older adults, members with multiple medical problems and/or chronic illnesses), MCO case managers maintain long-term relationships with members. In general, they are less frequently called on to perform the crisis intervention services associated with management of catastrophic illness than their hospital-based counterparts. The efficacy of MCO case management is measured using population-based outcomes such as hospital days per month, utilization of emergency or urgent care services, and overall cost savings per population.

Managed Care Organization Case Management

Q 9:34 What are the goals of MCO case management?

Along with coordinating care and ensuring timely treatment in the most appropriate setting, MCO case management aims to enhance quality service delivery by preventing morbidity associated with chronic diseases. It has assumed an increasingly prominent role in MCO UM programs in response to the swelling numbers of older adults enrolling in Medicare-risk and other MCO programs.

Although the majority of MCOs provide only limited skilled nursing or extended care facility benefits, many MCO case managers make use of a continuum of long-term care resources to shift frail elderly, and chronically or terminally ill members from higher-cost hospital settings to nursing homes and home care programs. These innovative case managers follow members over time and across treatment settings.

The education goals of MCO case management differ significantly from the patient teaching conducted by hospital-based case managers. Proactive MCO case management encourages assessment and teaching of medical self-care skills and adherence to prescribed treatment regimens. Case managers also instruct MCO members about how best to negotiate the delivery system (e.g., how to seek urgent care, obtain a referral to a specialist, resolve claims disputes).

Case managers play a pivotal role in monitoring and improving MCO member satisfaction. Many case managers help members select a personal physician, orient them to the MCO service delivery system, and provide referral to MCO and community-based health programs and support groups. Able to identify, document, and intervene to resolve recurring delivery system problems, case managers serve to increase reported levels of member and provider satisfaction.

Optimal clinical outcomes and resource utilization, as opposed to cost containment, should be the overriding goals or stated purposes of case management, especially MCO case management. Designating cost containment as the primary goal of the MCO case manager serves only to exacerbate tension resulting from the case manager's competing roles of advocacy and gatekeeping. Ultimately, the financial outcomes of MCO case management should be assessed as population savings, using lifetime expense profiling, as opposed to the individual cost savings attributable to catastrophic care or hospital-based case management.

Q 9:35 When should MCO case management begin?

When instituted as a primary prevention program, MCO case management must identify the need for active intervention on member enrollment, prior to service utilization. Early identification, via new-member surveys, health status questionnaires, and other member self-report mechanisms, enables the case manager to triage members to office or clinic visits with physicians, mid-level practitioners, or nurses. The case manager may also refer members to MCO-sponsored and community-based health education, wellness, chronic disease, and disease management programs.

Q 9:36 At what point does the case manager get involved in a case?

This varies from program to program, depending on the type of organization involved. Some case managers get involved on a referral basis from the UR team, unless the case management program is part of a broader UM program. Others get involved immediately on hospitalization.

Q 9:37 What are the key requirements for a successful MCO case management program?

Effective CMO case management programs share the following characteristics:

Management Commitment. Without an earnest management commitment, the case manager will have neither the responsibility nor the authority to effect change.

Physician Commitment. The presence of strong physician support for case management is essential. Physician involvement in the design of the case management program, in-service education delineating the goals and mechanics of the program, and incentives for participation are among the strategies used by MCOs to generate physician support for case management.

Designated Case Managers. Although case management is a collaborative process conducted by a team of providers working in concert with patients and families, it requires a central locus of control. The designated case manager performs this function, serving simultaneously as a clearinghouse for information, source of information and referral, patient advocate and educator, and coordinator of care.

Accountability. Every individual involved in case management should have a clear understanding of his or her role and responsibilities in the process. Despite considerable overlap of functions (e.g., multiple members of the case management team may communicate with the patient and family), written statements of accountability should, for example, identify the team member responsible for obtaining a skilled nursing home placement.

Ongoing Team Member Education. All persons involved in case management require regular updates about service utilization patterns and resource availability as well as feedback about the overall effectiveness of the case management program.

Data Collection and Analysis. The case management process presents multiple opportunities to identify and address patient care and delivery system problems. To fulfill this promise, case managers must systematically document and communicate quality issues related to coordination, timeliness, and appropriateness of care.

Q 9:38   To perform effectively, what types of resources must be available to the MCO case manager?

Along with support from administrators and providers, the case manager must be equipped with a complete understanding of the MCO delivery system, benefits, and covered services. Similarly, case managers should have full knowledge of and referral relationships with local community health and social service agencies, and other providers.

From an organizational standpoint, the practice of case management requires management information and communication systems. The case manager and providers must have reliable, timely data to permit advances in the plan of care. Delayed reports of laboratory or other diagnostic tests may result in unnecessary hospital admission or prolonged hospital lengths of stay. For example, a member with chest pain admitted to a short-stay or observation unit may linger unnecessarily if the laboratory data confirming noncardiac chest pain is not reported and conveyed quickly.

Lapses in communication not only have the potential to delay access to care but also may compromise adherence to treatment and satisfaction with care. If, unable to obtain provider consent, payer authorization, or cooperation from agencies external to the MCO, the case manager fails to "deliver" even one element of the agreed-upon plan of care (e.g., referral to a physician specialist, reliable home health care, institutional placement), the case management process disappoints all stakeholders.

Though not requisite to the effective practice of case management, the availability of immediate electronic information transfer streamlines the process. Hand-held computer notepads enable the case manager to generate requests for referrals, coding, and billing at the patient's bedside.

Q 9:39 Which subpopulations of MCO enrollees benefit from case management?

The following MCO members benefit from case management: members with multiple, active chronic diseases; members taking multiple medications; members who have had multiple hospitalizations; members who are age 75 or older; members who have had multiple emergency department visits; and members with significant impairment in the activities of daily living.

Q 9:40 Where should the responsibility for case management rest in MCOs?

There is a compelling argument favoring assumption of responsibility for case management by the component of the delivery system that bears substantial financial risk. Some MCOs place hospitals at risk and many require medical groups or independent practice associations (IPAs) to assume a share of the financial risk associated with providing care for the enrolled population. Others place an integrated delivery system at risk for financial performance. Proponents of assignment of responsibility to the entity or group at greatest financial risk contend that case management is best performed by those with the financial imperative and incentive to do it.

Other industry observers believe that the health plan or medical administration of the MCO should assume responsibility for supervision of the case management function. Advocates of health plan or administrative oversight view case management as a key component of quality improvement, rather than simply a cost-containment program. They contend that the objective results of case management— that is, planned, predictable clinical and financial outcomes—constitute administrative accountability. Further, case management outcomes, when reported as performance measures of quality, significantly enhance MCO marketability among employer and consumer groups.

Measuring Case Management Performance

Q 9:41 How are the outcomes of case management measured?

Traditionally, case management has been measured, and its effectiveness assessed, in terms of dollars saved per patient. Case management consistently and unequivocally demonstrates the ability to control the costs associated with health care delivery. To date, the most dramatic savings have been realized as the result of hospital-based case management. These savings are immediate and easily documented. The cost savings resulting from anticipatory, preventive case management are still largely estimates of lifetime expense profiles—that is, long-term, projected savings per population.

Case management can and should be appraised by its capacity to improve quality by reducing variance from established norms (i.e., critical paths or clinical practice guidelines). It should act to optimize resource management and utilization and measurably contribute to consumer and provider satisfaction with health care service delivery.

Case management programs must continue to demonstrate and communicate success in improving health care delivery quality using clinical, financial, and patient satisfaction outcome measures. In the presence of quantifiable objectives and results, case management programs will earn the support of all managed care stakeholders (i.e., employers, providers, payers, and consumers).

Q 9:42   How should a case manager or case management program be evaluated?

The following are key factors in the evaluation of case management programs:

Geographic Scope of Coverage. Although it is desirable to use a case management firm or program that has regional or national coverage, health care is a local matter. Case managers must be familiar with community resources; physician, hospital, and practitioner practice patterns; and the cost of services and providers in their area.

Independent Versus Integrated Programs. It is preferable for the case management program to be part of a UM program in order to obtain the benefits of a comprehensive program; however, this may result in compromising the most qualified provider for the overall convenience of a comprehensive program.

Program Ownership. Whether the case management program is owned by an individual, an independent UR firm, a carrier, or the group at risk may affect results and cost containment. If the group at risk is providing the case management, there may be a perception that costs will affect the determination of medical necessity and be given greater attention than the quality of care. A case management program that is not at monetary risk can better balance the goals of quality and cost.

Case Managers' Qualifications. The qualifications of individuals who call themselves case managers range from nurse reviewers with an understanding of claims and benefits to nonclinical individuals with relevant clinical knowledge and claims experience. The individuals doing the case management should have expertise compatible with the case being managed. For example, specialists in chemical dependency and psychiatry should not manage high-risk pregnancies and premature infant cases.

In addition to the breadth and depth of qualifications of the case managers themselves, management style and personnel satisfaction should be taken into consideration. A high turnover rate in case management staff may signal internal organizational problems.

Availability of Physician Consultants. A case management program should have physician consultants from a broad range of specialties. This is a very important quality indicator and an important consideration in gaining cooperation from physicians interacting with a case management program.

Telephone Versus On-Site Services. Not all companies provide on-site management; the cost can be prohibitive. Telephone services are usually sufficient unless there are unusual circumstances involving the patient, the patient's family, or the care team. The disadvantage of telephone case management is that the case manager is not able to assess a problem fully. All the information is secondhand at best. On-site case management that includes all significant persons in the case can be far more comprehensive.

Identification of Cases. The ability to identify cases in a timely and efficient manner is important to case management. This is often accomplished through UR of diagnosis, length of stay, and/or frequency of admissions. Cases may also be identified by reaching certain dollar thresholds or from employer referrals.

Quality Improvement Capability. There should be a means to measure outcomes and improvement in the care being managed. The program should have written standards and should include techniques to measure quality.

Ability to Measure Outcomes. Outcomes measures are complex. If the desired result is cost savings, the savings should be measurable. Measures should be credible and based on stated expectations. Cost is measured relatively easily and thus is often used as a yardstick for outcome measurement, but it is a crude measure and can obscure more important issues. To managed care payers with very slim profit margins, cost becomes paramount; thus, the case manager has the difficult job of balancing other measures of outcome, such as readmission rates and patients' quality of life, with the more objective measure of cost. Satisfaction surveys are often used, although they are subjective.

Ability to Report Case Management Activities and Results. Case managers should routinely report on the status of their activities at hospital patient care conferences, managed care administrative meetings, and education symposia.

Medical Management

Q 9:43   What is medical management?

Medical management is the oversight of all aspects of the continuum of care by a physician. Prior to the advent of managed care, medical management was performed by the individual physician in coordination with other health care professionals, such as nurses and social workers. It often took the form of discharge planning, the effort to provide continuity between the hospital and the outpatient setting; and this effort was restricted to the illness episode. In a managed care setting, the goal of medical management is to prevent an illness episode and, when one occurs, to provide care that is as efficient and effective as possible.

Q 9:44   What is integrated medical management?

Integrated medical management is medical management that emphasizes a number of features critical to success in a managed care environment:

- Cost effectiveness
- Patient satisfaction

- Health status outcomes that are satisfactory for both the individual and the population
- Preventive care
- Management of information
- Blurring of the boundaries between payer and provider (the provider becomes an MCO)

As integrated medical management develops, providers become more independent, able to manage their own medical care protocols and their own risk. The provider, therefore, assumes more responsibility for the continuum of care and thus must learn how to manage that care and the resources associated with it. This requires more standardization and the use of pathways or "care maps."

Q 9:45 What are examples of medical necessity and appropriate care?

The medical director is asked to judge the appropriateness of a procedure or a test based on "medical necessity." This can be a simple task, as when an MRI is ordered as a first test for migraine headaches or a thallium treadmill is ordered prior to obtaining an electrocardiogram, but often, the issue of "medical necessity" is confused with issues of coverage. The medical director should never be asked to adjudicate issues of coverage, only of appropriateness of treatment.

Q 9:46 What is the role of the medical director in medical management?

The medical director is generally the physician in charge of medical care delivered on behalf of the MCO, and hence is in charge of medical management. There is a distinction between being in charge and the actual delivery of medical care. In many HMOs, the medical director does not see patients at all but is responsible for overall quality and assuring members of that quality. In recognition of the role of the medical director, some HMOs have begun calling the most senior physician in the organization "chief medical officer." The medical director brings a perspective to the MCO that is clearly different from that of the MCO management but, ideally, synergistic with it.

Legal and Regulatory Issues

Q 9:47   Is utilization review subject to state or federal regulation?

Yes. Most states regulate UR professionals and organizations. Although these laws and regulations differ from state to state, they generally cover issues such as telephone access, employee qualifications, time requirements for review, appeals, confidentiality, and criteria development.

At the federal level, the UR activities of multiemployer pension programs and employee welfare and benefit plans, including employer-sponsored medical insurance policies, are regulated under the Employee Retirement Income Security Act of 1974 (ERISA), which preempts state law (see chapter 8). [29 USCA §§ 1001–1461] ERISA preemption poses a barrier to most plaintiffs who attempt to file a common-law negligence claim under state law against an insurer or employer based on a UR denial. Although the passage of ERISA preceded the use of most current cost-containment strategies, health care reform may result in a reevaluation of this barrier for claims arising from improper UR decisions. Further, as more insurers incorporate UR into their standard employee health insurance packages, thereby firmly establishing UR in the business of insurance, plaintiffs may be able to overcome ERISA preemption more easily by claiming to be subject to a state action or law. (These issues are discussed in more detail in chapter 8.) Patient protection legislation under consideration at the Federal level may preempt ERISA but this has not been settled at the time of this writing.

Q 9:48   At what point does utilization management become the practice of medicine?

The use of various UM techniques has been the subject of much discussion as it relates to the degree to which these activities constitute the practice of medicine. The managed care industry maintains that UM decisions based on medical necessity are payment and coverage decisions, and not medical decisions. Until July 1997, this was the position accepted by the courts and state attorneys general. In *Murphy v. Board of Medical Examiners* [949 P2d 530 (Ariz Ct App 1997)], however, the court determined that a decision to deny pre-certification for gallbladder surgery was a "medical" decision and that the state Board of Medical Examiners had jurisdiction over the state-licensed physician who made that decision on behalf of his health insurer employer. In subsequent cases around the country, the courts have increasingly focused on the activities of physicians associated with UM determinations in reaching decisions regarding the physicians' authority to engage in these activities without being licensed in the state in which the determination is being made. Although this is a subject of debate in the courts, many states have adopted legislation imposing license requirements and jurisdiction based on the exercise of medical judgment by physicians involved in UM decisions (see chapter 8).

These court cases reflect an increase in scrutiny over the role of the insurer in medical necessity determinations. In addition to the corporate practice issues discussed in chapter 8, there are liability and regulatory considerations. Many MCOs rely on their medical directors to oversee clinical issues. This has created some concern on the part of states that have strict corporate practice of medicine statutes and medical practice acts.

Q 9:49   Does a medical director have to be licensed in the state where the MCO does business?

Some states have attempted to regulate UR by requiring that medical directors be licensed in the states to which their responsibilities extend. Recent legislation in Texas concerning UR activities did not impose the requirement of licensure in the state of Texas but did require that UR activities be overseen by a licensed physician.[11]

It is obvious from the language of managed care contracts that the medical director plays an important part in the review of medical necessity determinations and grievances regarding denial of services. Although most MCOs take the position that they do not engage in medical practice and that UM decisions relate to coverage and not to treatment, recent case law and legislation suggest otherwise. The real issue is whether the treating physician can realistically pursue a course of treatment once coverage has been denied based on UR criteria. These issues are discussed in more detail in chapter 8.

Q 9:50   What other mechanisms exist to establish standards for utilization review?

The leading organization involved in accrediting UROs is URAC. URAC was established by the American Managed Care and Review

Association (AMCRA, now part of the American Association of Health Plans (AAHP)), a trade association of UR firms, PPOs, and HMOs, which seeks to standardize organizational UR procedures in order to avoid the necessity of government regulation of UR activities at the state or federal level. The URAC accreditation process is intended to offer an alternative to state regulation and to provide a national set of standards for UR.

URAC's goal is to improve the quality and efficiency of interaction between the UR industry and the providers, payers, and purchasers of health care. Its standards are process oriented and not intended to evaluate the adequacy of the UR criteria and protocols. URAC sets standards for (1) applicability to providers; (2) responsibility for obtaining certification; (3) information on which UR is conducted; (4) procedures for review determinations; (5) appeals of determinations not to certify; (6) confidentiality; (7) staff and program requirements; and (8) accessibility and on-site review procedures.

Q 9:51   What legal risks does utilization review impose on payers and utilization review organizations?

Because of the role of the third-party payer or URO in medical treatment decisions, UR places these nonmedical organizations in a position of substituting their judgment for that of medical professionals. If the third party becomes involved to the extent that it changes the course of medical treatment, the third party may incur liability exposure for any injury the patient suffers as a result of this change. Until recently, courts had rejected the idea that third-party payers, UROs, or other MCOs could affect the course of treatment through decisions to refuse coverage or payment for a patient's medical care; however, there is an increasing trend toward holding third-party payers, UROs, and related organizations legally accountable under several theories of liability.

MCOs that hold contracts with UROs may be held liable for the acts of the URO under the doctrine of ostensible agency (see chapters 8 and 13). The determination of ostensible agency is a subjective test based on the perception of the subscriber or patient. Absent specific clarification of the independent contract relationship, the MCO may be held liable for the URO's actions.

Just as other health care entities such as hospitals have an independent corporate duty to a patient to select and monitor their professional medical staff carefully, the MCO has an independent duty to evaluate and monitor the performance of its URO.

Q 9:52 Can a health care provider (hospital or physician) or third-party payer, including the employer, be held liable for substandard care attributable to improper utilization review activities in managed care?

Yes. Providers and third-party payers are liable for inappropriate UR or UM if there is injury to the patient attributable to the UR activities. As discussed in chapter 8, many states and the federal government have passed or are considering HMO liability legislation designed to hold MCOs legally accountable for their UR decisions. There is growing concern that employers, too, may have some liability exposure when an employee's freedom of choice in provider selection and level of health care services is limited by the employer's health benefit plan. Employers can protect themselves from most managed care liability claims by taking the following steps:

1. Do some form of due diligence on the managed care vendor, including its provider selection criteria, to ensure that there is a means of monitoring quality of care prior to contracting (consider using a request for proposal). This will reduce potential independent corporate or ostensible agency liability.

2. Ensure that the provisions in the contracts address risk financing and risk assumption by those servicing and administering the health plan.

3. Maintain appropriate liability insurance coverage and require those administering or servicing the health plan to maintain appropriate insurance coverage.

4. Look into the ERISA safeguards of effective communications, plan documents, and contracts with vendors.

Q 9:53 Under what theories can action related to utilization review and utilization management be brought against a provider, purchaser, employer, or payer?

There are a number of theories under which providers, purchasers, employers, and payers can incur liability exposure for managed care activities such as UR and UM. The following theories of liability are discussed further in chapter 8.

Negligence of Insurer. To maintain a common-law negligence claim against an insurer, a plaintiff must establish not only that the UR at issue falls within the practice of insurance but also that the state law on which the action is based actually regulates insurance.

Ostensible Agency Liability. A theory used in the absence of an employment relationship is to hold an MCO or other perceived controlling party legally responsible under an ostensible agency theory, based on the employee's or patient's perception of an employment or other controlled relationship.

Corporate Negligence. If the courts identify an independent duty of care on the part of a party to prevent foreseeable harm to a patient or employee, there may be liability exposure under a theory of corporate liability.

ERISA Considerations. If the health plan is employer sponsored and subject to ERISA regulation, there can be some protection because of the preemption by ERISA of state common-law actions in tort or contract.

UR Liability. Liability for injuries associated with UR determinations has been the basis of recent litigation involving managed care, UR, and medical management.

Q 9:54   How have courts ruled on utilization review liability?

The two cases that raised the consciousness of many UROs and MCOs regarding their own liability exposure are *Wickline v. State of California* [239 Cal Rptr 813 (Ct App 1986), *cert dismissed, remanded,* 741 P2d 613 (Cal 1987)] and *Wilson v. Blue Cross of Southern California* [271 Cal Rptr 876 (Ct App 1990)].

In *Wickline,* the patient underwent major vascular surgery to replace a section of the artery that supplied blood to her right leg. Prior to surgery, the physician had obtained authorization from Medi-Cal (California's Medicaid program) for the surgical procedure and 10 days of hospitalization. Following surgery, there were complications, and the vascular surgeon determined that an eight-day extension of the hospital stay was medically necessary. The Medi-Cal nurse reviewer referred the case to a Medi-Cal consulting physician, who authorized only four additional days. Although the three physicians involved in the patient's care could have attempted to obtain a further extension of the patient's hospital stay, none did so, and the patient was discharged at the expiration of the extension. Nine days later, she was readmitted as an emergency patient and her leg had to be amputated to save her life.

In her lawsuit, Mrs. Wickline claimed that the state of California negligently discontinued her Medi-Cal eligibility, causing her to be discharged prematurely while she was in need of continuing hospital care. The court focused on whether a third-party payer of health care services could be held legally responsible when medically inappropriate decisions resulted from defects in design or implementation of the cost-containment mechanism of UR. Although the court concluded that such liability was possible, it reversed a jury verdict in favor of the plaintiff and absolved Medi-Cal from liability. The court held it was the responsibility of the treating physician to request an extension and added, "A physician who complies without protest with the limitations imposed by a third party payer, when his medical judgment dictates otherwise, cannot avoid his ultimate responsibility for the patient's care." [239 Cal Rptr at 819] The court also added that

> [t]he patient who requires treatment and who is harmed when care that should have been provided is not provided should recover for the injuries suffered from all those responsible for the deprivation of such care, including, when appropriate, health care payers. Third-party payers of health care services can be held legally accountable when medically inappropriate decisions result from defects in the design or implementation of cost-containment mechanisms, as, for example, when appeals are made on a patient's behalf for medical or hospital care and arbitrarily ignored or unreasonably disregarded or overridden.

In the *Wilson* case, the court extended the application of the *Wickline* decision to the private sector. In this case, the plaintiff suffered from major depression, drug dependency, and anorexia. He was admitted to the hospital, where his physician concluded that he needed three to four weeks of inpatient care. Ten days into his treatment, his insurance company determined that it would not pay for further hospitalization. Wilson was discharged because he could not pay for the continued treatment, and 20 days after discharge he committed suicide. In its lawsuit against California Blue Cross, the family relied on the theory raised in *Wickline*. In reversing the dismissal of the case in the lower court, the appellate court found that the *Wilson* case could be distinguished from *Wickline* and, consequently, *Wickline* was not controlling. For example, the court in *Wilson* made a strong statement that the physician is not responsible when a third-party payer refuses to pay for medically necessary treatment. Because the physician's medical decision was appropriate, the potential liability lay with the party that had the fiscal key to the hospital door. The fiduciary duty was thus shifted from the physician to the third-party payer.

A landmark settlement in California against HealthNet, an HMO, provided a family $89.3 million for the HMO's refusal to pay for a costly, experimental procedure to treat the breast cancer that ultimately killed the insured. This case represents the largest judgment to date in cases involving denial of medical benefits. [Fox v HealthNet, No 21692 (Cal Super Ct Riverside County filed June 19, 1992, settled Apr 6, 1994)] These liability issues are discussed further in chapter 8.

Q 9:55   What have utilization review organizations learned from *Wickline*, *Wilson*, *Fox*, and other court cases?

UROs have learned these lessons from those court cases:

1. Conduct a thorough and complete investigation before denying a claim. [Hughes v Blue Cross of N Cal, 245 Cal Rptr 273 (Ct App 1988)]

2. Advise patients of their appeal rights when denying a claim. [Davis v Blue Cross of N Cal, 600 P2d 267 (Cal 1987)]

3. Communicate the reason for the denial in a manner that can be understood. [Kent v Central Benefits Mut Ins Co, No 88 AP-758 (Ohio Ct App Feb. 9, 1989)]

4. Give the patients the correct information; do not mislead or misinform. [Aetna Life Ins Co v Lavoie, 470 So 2d 1061 (Ala 1984)]

5. Make sure there is adequate and appropriate communication with physicians. [Hughes v Blue Cross of N Cal, 245 Cal Rptr 273 (Ct App 1988)]

6. Avoid using inappropriate or defamatory language concerning the provider's conduct in the determination of a claim. [Slaughter v Friedman, 185 Cal Rptr 244 (Cal 1982)]

Clinical Practice Guidelines

Q 9:56   What is behind the development of clinical practice guidelines?

The major incentive behind the development of clinical practice guidelines is the desire to ensure quality while controlling costs and to address the unexplained variations in health care delivery patterns across the country. To place a value on health care services in a managed care system, there must be some notion of what is necessary and appropriate with respect to treatment and prevention of medical conditions. Clinical practice guidelines and their applications are intended to bring some consistency to the evaluation of the appropriateness of health care services and to allow determination of what is effective in the patient care setting. At the core of clinical practice guidelines is the concept that clinical services should be judged based on scientific and objective rather than administrative and subjective standards. This concept underlies the various quality assurance and accreditation standards used in managed care.

Another major reason for clinical practice guidelines is to change physician behavior. Ample data have been accumulated emphasizing the differences in practice patterns among physicians. Utilization rates have been studied for coronary surgery, prostate surgery, cesarean section, and routine prescribing. These studies generally show a wide variation in procedures and costs for the same or similar conditions, which results from factors such as availability of technology, reimbursement schemes, community standards, peer expectation, concentration of specialists, managed care controls, and patient expectations.

Q 9:57   Are clinical practice guidelines the same as utilization review protocols?

No. UR protocols used by hospitals and MCOs and clinical practice guidelines developed by professional societies should not be confused. They are entirely different from each other. UR protocols are usually economically based, whereas clinical practice guidelines are medically based.

Q 9:58 What has experience shown regarding the implementation of practice guidelines?

Many studies have shown that dissemination of guideline information alone is not sufficient to integrate the guidelines into medical decision making. Considerations for implementing guidelines include the following:

1. Is the guideline broad enough to be generally applicable yet narrow enough to provide real guidance?
2. Is the guideline applicable to "real world" practice?
3. Does the guideline address an important clinical problem that needs standardization?
4. Is there actually a "best strategy" for the clinical situation under study?
5. Is the guideline intended to be prescriptive or to serve as a suggestion?
6. Can implementing the guideline be expected to improve clinical care?
7. Has the production of the guideline involved enough clinical expertise to make it acceptable to practicing clinicians?

At the local level, many health plans, hospitals, and other organized health care delivery systems are adopting nationally developed guidelines for their own use; however, the effort required to produce these guidelines is enormous and taxes the good will of physicians who are not paid to perform that kind of work. Most health plans that use practice guidelines rely on their own medical staffs for internal development of many of the guidelines they use.

Q 9:59 How is guideline information disseminated?

Guideline developers and others use a number of means to put guidelines in the hands of physicians and other health care decision makers. Guidelines are often disseminated through independent means by the agency that created them and through the specialty societies. The extent of dissemination depends on the issuing organization and the perceived importance of the guideline. Managed care plans disseminate guidelines among their own providers and consumers. Specialty societies publish guidelines in their professional journals or otherwise distribute them to their membership.

Organizations such as the American Medical Association (AMA), the National Library of Medicine (NLM), Emergency Care Research Institute (ECRI), and American Association of Health Plans (AAHP) have collected guidelines and assisted in their mass dissemination. For example, since 1989, the AMA's Practice Parameters Partnership and Forum has annually issued a directory of practice parameters developed by government and specialty groups that lists guidelines by subject, sponsor, and title. The NLM has developed an online database with full text of guidelines, consensus conference reports, and technology assessments of the AHRQ, the National Institutes of Health, and the U.S. Preventive Services Task Force. ECRI has developed a database of information for more than 24,000 practice guidelines, technology assessments, standards of care, and state and federal laws. The AAHP has compiled practice guidelines developed in or modified by HMOs, which must use the AAHP's guidelines to be included in its listing.

Q 9:60   From what sources can clinical guidelines be obtained?

Clinical guidelines can be obtained from these sources:

- Agency for Health Care Policy and Research (www.ahcpr.gov)
- National Guideline Clearinghouse (www.guideline.gov)
- American Medical Association Directory of Practice Parameters
- Specialty societies (American Heart Association, American Gastroenterological Association)
- Integrated delivery systems (Intermountain Healthcare)
- Consulting firms (Milliman and Robertson, Deloitte & Touche Consulting Group "Best Practices")

Q 9:61   How can physicians be encouraged to comply with guidelines?

Physicians may balk at using practice guidelines because of the stigma of "cookbook medicine." Several factors aid physician acceptance and use of guidelines:

- Education on the content and use of guidelines to decrease unnecessary hospital admissions
- Information on costs associated with different modalities of care
- Development of a physician-friendly information and reporting system
- Use of those who can influence decisions by teaching as change agents

For guidelines to be successful, however, there has to be an efficient and complete infrastructure supporting the clinical practice. This may include some of the following elements:

- Rapid treatment unit
- Outpatient surgical center
- Case or care manager
- Availability of services 24 hours per day, 7 days per week
- Home health care
- Outpatient intravenous therapy and pharmacy
- Availability of facilities in the full continuum of care

Q 9:62 What have been the most controversial issues associated with the development and use of practice guidelines?

The most common challenge to efforts to standardize care is the establishment of formal and rigid "cookbook" medicine. Concerns include the justifiability of the scientific principles underlying the standards, fear that the development of guidelines is a disguised cost-control technique, and a belief that national standards are inappropriate because medical practice is local. Finally, there are sometimes conflicts between different published guidelines for the same condition.

Fear of litigation has stymied guideline preparation for many years. Clinicians are always concerned about laying themselves open to liability at the plaintiff bar. This problem can be mitigated by "using practice guidelines and clinical pathways to improve the quality and consistency of patient care [and not using them to] reduce the costs of care, manage utilization, [or] deny access to health care services."[12]

Q 9:63 How has the AHRQ responded to concerns about guidelines?

The AHRQ turned to the Institute of Medicine (IOM), a part of the National Academy of Sciences, to assist in the development of practice guidelines. The IOM established the Committee to Advise the Agency, which immediately developed a statement of the attributes of good practice guidelines. These attributes included projected health outcomes, projected costs, relationship between the evidence and the guidelines, preference for empirical evidence over expert judgment, thorough literature review, methods used to evaluate the scientific literature, strength of the evidence, use of expert judgment, strength of expert consensus, independent review, and pretesting. These criteria support the guiding principle that a good guideline is both scientifically supported and reproducible. Another important principle developed by the IOM committee is that guidelines must be periodically reviewed, for medicine is not static. Finally, documentation of a guideline is critical to both its development and its use.

Other public agencies besides AHRQ are involved in developing guidelines. For example, the Food and Drug Administration, National Institutes of Health, Centers for Disease Control and Prevention, Health Care Financing Administration, U.S. Preventive Services Task Force, and Congressional Office of Technology Assessment have been involved in such activities.

Q 9:64 What goes into the selection of topics for development of a set of guidelines and how are they developed?

In selecting topics for guideline development, the AHRQ considers several criteria, such as (1) the potential for reducing clinically significant and unexplained variations in practice or outcomes; (2) the number of persons affected by the condition; (3) the adequacy of scientific evidence; (4) the amenability of the condition to prevention; (5) the needs of Medicare and Medicaid beneficiaries; and (6) the cost of the condition to all payers, including patients.

An expert panel of consumer representatives, nonphysician practitioners, and physicians from relevant disciplines develop guideline recommendations and content. The guidelines are subject to peer review for scientific validity and pilot testing before issuance by the AHRQ.

Guidelines incorporate evidence on health outcomes into sets of recommendations concerning appropriate management strategies for patients with specific conditions. When evidence is insufficient, the panel of experts provides an opinion in some cases. AHRQ-sponsored guidelines have been validated by the relevant medical specialty societies, which support them as being well-researched, credible interpretations of the evidence.

Q 9:65   What are the advantages of clinical practice guidelines?

Clinical practice guidelines help to facilitate informed medical decision making. Their intent is to help patients get the care they need and prevent their exposure to unnecessary services by identifying when services are beneficial and when they are not. Clinical practice guidelines can also support cost-containment efforts by providing information on the benefits, risks, and costs of a service to allow patients and physicians to make decisions in an environment of limited resources. Cost containment is not their sole objective.

Use of practice guidelines in medical decision making may allow patients to have input into their own care. Increased patient involvement in medical decision making is attractive to some health plans because of the potential for increased patient satisfaction and perception of quality. Cost savings may also be achieved through more informed decision making by patients and their physicians.

Purchasers of health care services view practice guidelines as a positive step in improving the quality of care and placing a value on their health care expenditures. Practice guidelines can be used to define appropriate care, and criteria or standards derived from practice guidelines may be a measure of quality. The Health Plan Employer Data and Information Set uses standards and criteria derived from practice guidelines to measure health plan performance. This is discussed in more detail in chapter 10.

As health care systems continue to evolve, it is anticipated that clinical practice guidelines will be used in the credentialing and selective contracting process. Provider profiling is being used on an increasing basis by MCOs, integrated delivery systems (IDSs), and even hospitals, based on provider conformity with practice guidelines.

One of the intended beneficiaries of practice guidelines at the federal level is Medicare. Medicare peer review organizations are changing their focus from identifying and penalizing instances of poor quality of care to evaluating practice patterns and facilitating quality improvement. At the state and local levels, practice guidelines have appeared in legislation related to health care reform and are being used as a "standard of care" in medical malpractice suits in a few states.[13]

Q 9:66   What are the potential legal liabilities associated with using clinical practice guidelines?

There are two areas of potential legal liability. They are associated with the responsibility of the parties that develop and disseminate the guidelines and with the parties whose practices seek to conform to the guidelines.

Liability in Development and Implementation. There is concern that those responsible for the development of the guidelines will incur product or warranty liability risk based on the potential status given to practice guidelines by the public and medical practitioners. There is also concern as to the significance and weight practice guidelines will be given as evidence in a court of law. The AHRQ has attempted to address this issue in its guidebook. Another area of potential product liability risk to guideline developers is the translation of guidelines into derivative products such as medical review criteria, performance measures, and standards of quality.

Malpractice Issues. There is a risk that MCOs that select and apply guidelines may be held legally responsible for the outcomes of care. Unlike peer review organizations, which have had a statutory exemption since 1988, MCOs have been subject to malpractice actions related to their control over medical decision making. Recent legislation links malpractice protection to guideline use, but no published court cases explicitly use guideline adherence as a basis for protection from malpractice liability. These issues are addressed further in chapter 8.

Q 9:67 What steps should be taken to maximize the effectiveness of practice guidelines?

According to John C. West, Director of the Sisters of Charity Health Care Systems in Cincinnati, Ohio, several steps should be taken to ensure maximum effectiveness of practice guidelines,[14] including the following:

1. Each guideline should delineate its intended purpose.
2. The types of guidelines should be differentiated in a descriptive manner.
3. Physicians should be given incentives to use practice guidelines.
4. Practice guidelines should be based on a consensus of opinion in the specialty being scrutinized.
5. Controversial practices should not be developed into guidelines.
6. Guidelines should be disseminated and practitioners should be educated about them before they are used for any measurable outcome.

Disease Management

Q 9:68 What is disease management?

Disease management is a coordinated population-based approach to maximizing the effectiveness and efficiency of patient care in a specific disease. It identifies persons who are at risk for or have a particular illness; manages their care with preventive and therapeutic tools, including protocols and guidelines, and manages their compliance with education and support; and then measures the outcomes.

Q 9:69 What has been the impetus behind disease management?

Disease management in the United States is a response to the fact that a relatively small number of patients with chronic diseases generate most health care costs. It supposes that many of the costly and debilitating complications of chronic illness can be avoided if caregivers follow established clinical practice guidelines and if patients are more informed about their diseases. The underlying concepts of disease management are not new, and in fact, have long been acknowledged as the cornerstones of primary care; what is new, however, is disease management's targeted, systematic, reproducible approach.

Q 9:70　What has been the impact of disease management on the health care market?

Disease management is big business in the United States, with hundreds of disease management programs in effect and hundreds more planned. "For-profit companies are scrambling to get their hands into the $500 million chronic disease pot."[15]

Q 9:71　What are the risks associated with disease management?

There are several risks associated with disease management:

- Diminished physician autonomy
- Increased use of intermediaries in the doctorpatient relationship
- Use as a carve-out program contributes to the fragmentation of U.S. health care
- Possibility of adverse selection (i.e., the program may attract sicker patients to the plan, and thereby change the distribution of risk)
- High failure rate

If a provider group or payer expends energy, good faith, and money on establishing a program that does not deliver results, that failure will likely hurt the organization's ability to implement new programs in the future.

Q 9:72　Why should an MCO implement a disease management program?

A good disease management program proposes to achieve lower costs while maintaining or improving quality of care, improving patient satisfaction, and leveraging the efforts of physicians. Cost savings are achieved through avoiding complications, hospitalizations, emergency room utilization, and other consequences of poorly controlled disease. For conditions such as congestive heart failure, these savings can be immediate and dramatic. For other conditions, like hypertension, years of investment are required before savings are apparent.

Patient satisfaction can be increased in both tangible and intangible ways. Tangible benefits to the patient are related to quality of care and outcomes. Intangible benefits to the patient include the sense of caring and security that comes from having medical professionals personally assigned to and on call for the patients.

Finally, disease management leverages physicians' ability to provide care by giving them access to a highly coordinated and specialized group of allied professionals and by using information technology to educate and monitor patients on an ongoing basis, employing protocols to screen data and flag problems for physician attention. Thus, a sophisticated disease management program can relieve physicians of the responsibility for most of the time-consuming elements of primary care (patient education, patient questions, follow-up, case management) while enhancing its quality.

Q 9:73 How does disease management differ from case management?

Case management is performed on an individual basis, assessing an individual patient's needs and determining the appropriate care for his or her case. In contrast, disease management is population based; once patients are identified, efforts are made to follow standard, "best practices" care as much as possible, and savings are measured for the group as a whole rather than on a case-by-case basis. Disease management does, however, rely on case management principles, and disease management programs frequently employ de facto or actual case managers.

Q 9:74 Where does disease management fit into a utilization management program?

Disease management is a UM tool and can be included in a UM strategy along with other standard instruments, such as quality assurance and UR. Disease management programs manage utilization by implementing treatment guidelines that help standardize routine, relatively uncomplicated care and by enlisting the patient as an ally in reducing inappropriate utilization. Disease management follows quality management principles.

Disease management differs from UR in two important ways. It is not a normative method of external control over caregivers and it expects patients to be active participants in their care because they are ultimately responsible for their own health.

Q 9:75   How does disease management differ from other commonly used outcome management techniques?

Disease management is designed to be more of the "real world" and less "ivory tower." Thus, it is a practical approach rather than a theoretical one. Clinical trials generally use a very narrow segment of a population meeting strict entry criteria. Although, ideally, this population is representative of the behavior of the disease or the intervention in clinical practice, this is often not the case in actual practice. R.S. Epstein and L.M. Sherwood write that "the basic premise behind disease management is that here is a more optimal way to manage patients, which results in lowered costs and improved health outcomes."[16] This premise is based on three assumptions:

1. Medical practice varies. (If not, why impose "best practices" or optimal care?)
2. This variation is related to different outcomes. (If not, why bother to intervene?)
3. It is possible to develop and implement a system of care that improves outcomes.

Q 9:76   What conditions are amenable to disease management?

Conditions amenable to disease management include the following:

- Diabetes mellitus (both type I and type II)
- Hypertension
- Asthma (adult and childhood asthma have different disease management challenges)
- Emphysema
- Congestive heart failure

- Hyperlipidemia
- Rheumatoid arthritis
- Endometriosis

Q 9:77 What are the minimum requirements for establishing a disease management program?

The most important prerequisite for establishing a disease management program is to have providers who will support it. Passive resistance by physicians who do not see the benefit or rationale for disease management can kill a program before it begins. This physician "buy-in" goes beyond simply adopting clinical algorithms. Physician flexibility is also required because the process of disease management involves change. An essential feature of good disease management is constant adaptation of practices and the program itself in response to data and experience.

The second most important requirement is good data. Launching a successful disease management program requires solid baseline utilization data (to identify candidate diseases and to monitor the effectiveness of interventions) and patient profiles (not only to recruit patients but also to help the program reach them at the optimal point in the progression of their disease). It is important to stress that quality data cannot be bought. A vendor may be able to sell an organization a powerful disease management package, but if the organization cannot access trustworthy information about its patient population, the program will never succeed.

Every program must include a method for monitoring its performance. (Some advice for designing outcomes studies for disease management is provided in chapter 10.) One of the most common mistakes in this regard is made at the prerequisite stage: some programs never clearly state what they are trying to achieve. Because results cannot be analyzed without a clear hypothesis, clinical and financial goals for patient and provider satisfaction should be determined and their measurement should be clearly articulated at the outset.

A minimal level of integration between the hospital, MCO, and physician group is also helpful. At the least, it is necessary to be able to track participating patients' use of services. Of course, close cooperation between the primary care physician, payer, and tertiary and quaternary care providers contributes greatly to the strength of any disease management program.

Q 9:78 What are the elements of a successful disease management program?

A successful disease management program must contain several important features. First, the program must be clinically based. That is, it must not rely solely on traditional case management techniques. Second, the types of diseases to be included must be identified in advance to be sure that the program and its clinicians can support the management on a clinical basis. Other important program features include the following:

- Reliance on primary care
- Adherence to accepted clinical guidelines (e.g., National Institutes of Health consensus statements)
- Use of nonphysician case managers to coordinate patient care and provide emotional and clinical support
- Close monitoring of disease
- Extensive patient education
- High expectations for patients to participate in their own care
- Measurement of outcomes

Many programs that call themselves disease management programs do not actually attempt to manage disease. Instead they focus on a single area, like patient compliance, and attempt to use it to reduce overall costs and improve outcomes for a population. Most such programs are actually providing pharmaceutical management, demand management, or patient education.

Q 9:79 How does one select which disease or diseases to manage?

A good return on investment in disease management requires both an economy of scale and the opportunity for cost savings. The best candidates for disease management are both highly prevalent in the patient population and costly to the payer. A Medicare HMO, therefore, would be wise to target congestive heart failure, but a self-insured corporation might want to purchase a disease management program for back pain, which is a major cause of employee absentee-ism and disability.

The next criterion is the opportunity to improve the quality of care. Quality is difficult to define and measure in health care (see chapter 10), but for the purpose of disease management, a good proxy for quality is the extent to which plan providers are conform-ing to accepted "best practices."

For a number of diseases there is a strong consensus on treatment in the literature, yet low adherence to that consensus among provid-ers. Asthma and diabetes are good examples. Despite the fact that the medical community's understanding of asthma underwent a par-adigm shift in the early 1990s, many physicians continue to treat it under the old model, with much less effective results.

Opportunity for improvement with disease management also ex-ists when there is high variability in how a disease is treated. Lipid measurement rates for type II diabetes in Medicare patients range from 8 to 70 percent, depending on the region of the country, and the sex, ethnicity, and educational level of patients has been shown to affect how aggressively hypertension and heart disease are treated.

To realize savings before their participants change plans, payers should choose diseases for which results can be seen in the short term. With the turnover rate for managed care plans averaging 20 percent or more per year, payer-sponsored disease management pro-grams are likely to plan in terms of months rather than years (e.g., high-risk pregnancy).

Although it makes sense for both providers and payers to begin their disease management by targeting a disease that others have successfully managed, providers should also consider their own ex-perience and expertise. Other considerations when choosing a target disease include complexity of management, prevalence and number of co-morbid conditions, and amenability to integration of care.

Q 9:80 What are the advantages of purchasing a disease management program?

Contracting for a packaged program from a vendor is the fastest way to launch a disease management initiative. In addition to quick implementation, contracting offers a lower initial investment. Because much of the cost of disease management comes at the beginning of the program, these savings can reduce overall costs substantially.

The most attractive advantage to purchasing a disease management program is guaranteed savings. Many vendors will assume the risk for reducing the total costs (including the cost of the program itself) for a disease. In addition, some vendors will assume risk for the cost of co-morbid conditions.

Outsourcing disease management can also provide leverage for smaller practices that do not have the patient volume to support an in-house program. An experienced vendor with a successful track record can offer a tested program and proven success, but buyers should not accept that record without carefully reviewing the supporting data. Potential problems with the methods that vendors use to demonstrate effectiveness include:

1. Generalizing from a highly controlled environment to the population at large;

2. Using samples that are too small to be statistically significant; and

3. Reporting results from samples with selection bias, no randomization, and no controls.

A good disease management study will

1. Develop a baseline of clinical events, hospitalizations, and procedures described as rates per thousand in the membership under and over age 65;

2. Determine the baseline economic burden of disease on a per-member per-month (PMPM) basis for those under and over age 65;

3. Ascertain the effect of the program in reducing the rates per thousand from baseline, adjusted for age and membership differences; and

4. Measure the economic effect PMPM of the intervention, adjusted for age and membership differences.

Q 9:81 What are the advantages of developing a disease management program in-house?

The major advantage to an organization developing its own disease management program is ownership. Ownership should translate into less resistance from participating providers because the program is not imposed from outside. In fact, involving the physicians who will be implementing the program in its development is likely to increase provider satisfaction and compliance with the program. Other advantages include the following:

- Greater control
- Ability to tailor the initiative more closely to the organization's expertise, experience, and situation
- Having all savings accrue to the organization
- Possibility of becoming a vendor and selling the program to others

Q 9:82 What are the steps to developing an in-house disease management program?

The first step is to perform a health needs assessment that specifically identifies physician practice patterns and patient compliance issues.

The next step is to develop protocols from established guidelines. This point in the process offers an excellent opportunity to educate the organization's physicians about disease management and to get their "buy-in." Physicians, administrators, and other members of the team should then articulate short-term (one-year) and long-term (three-year) goals for the project. Of course, some diseases will require more time to realize savings (e.g., hypertension and diabetes).

It is now axiomatic in managed care that incentives need to be aligned among all of the partners in a risk-contracting situation. Ensuring that the incentives are aligned remains an essential step in the planning process because it can make working for one's own goals equal to working for the good of the whole.

Information technology options should be considered to streamline disease management, improve communication and education, and collect and analyze data. The gold standard for such systems would gather data from patients in a user-friendly manner, alert physicians to abnormal lab tests and prompt them with treatment protocols, and feed data back into the system for rapid evaluation. The most successful solutions in the literature have been fairly simple Web-based applications.

Q 9:83 What are the steps to implementing an in-house disease management program?

Implementation begins with creating supporting materials (e.g., mailing lists, patient education tools) and training workers in the program's protocols and systems. All members of the team must be well informed about the program, although specific training should be tailored to the job role. For example, physicians may want to work through the patient education materials themselves to see what their patients will be learning, and data-entry personnel will want more hands-on computer time.

The next steps will vary with the specific program, but should always include the following:

- Identification of patients
- Assessment and stratification of patients
- Program launch (i.e., patient education, monitoring, triage, and acute intervention)
- Outcome analysis
- Adjustment of the program to reflect the results of the outcome analysis

Q 9:84 What are physicians' concerns about disease management?

Physicians are right to be skeptical of catchwords and trends that promise to solve the problems of health care, and disease management is certainly a hot topic right now. There are other concerns as well that are specific to disease management and the way it changes how physicians practice medicine.

Reduced Autonomy. Disease management can be viewed as reducing physician autonomy. Protocols and guidelines are attempts to introduce some consistency into a highly variable world, and they have the potential to degenerate into "cookbook" medicine. The challenge of disease management is to develop protocols and standards that are sensitive to the needs of exceptional patients.

Population-Based Rather Than Patient-Based Approach. A similar challenge to disease management comes from the fact that it is population based, in contrast to the practice of medicine, which has always centered on the individual doctor-patient relationship. Fortunately, disease management is not one of the many forces that are assailing that previously inviolable sphere: although disease management programs address the needs of a population, physicians in the program can continue to treat patients as individuals, rather than as representatives of a group.

Team Rather Than Group Approach. Finally, disease management requires a team approach, and physicians have traditionally had sole responsibility for their patients' care. To participate in disease management programs, physicians have to work as part of a team. The experience of disease management so far, however, is that it has supported, rather than undermined, physicians' ability to provide high-quality care. Of course, it is also important to remember that the team approach has its limitations: physicians will always be ultimately responsible, both legally and morally, for their patients' care.

Demand Management

Q 9:85   What is demand management?

Demand management is the "use of decisions and self-management support systems to enable and encourage its consumers to make appropriate use of medical care."[17] It is a rational and information-based program that developed as a UM tool to help physicians and patients manage their expectations regarding health care services. Not to be confused with "demand reduction," these programs focus on appropriate use of medical care and not reduced use of medical care.

Patients have historically accessed medical services without regard to necessity or cost. Physicians acted on the basis of economic incentives, access to technology, and patient demands. Demand management programs use decision support tools such as practice guidelines and balanced financial incentives to counter overutilization or underutilization.

Q 9:86 How do demand management programs reconcile demand versus need for clinical services?

Health policy makers often focus on the need to manage the supply of medical resources rather than on why there is a demand for such services. Medical need is the "medically modifiable morbidity burden of a defined population," such as heart attacks, trauma, cancers, and other forms of illness that can be modified through prevention. Medical demand, on the other hand, is the patient's request for medical services, which may not necessarily be related to medical need.

To reconcile these two issues, James Fries has recommended the following approaches:[18]

1. Develop programs that focus on preventing or postponing illness and that promote health.
2. Support programs that promote patient self-management, backed by appropriate resources to help consumers decide what action to take when a symptom arises.
3. Use telephone triage.
4. Use clinical guidelines to support medical care.
5. Focus on chronic disease management using the tools of "disease management."

This approach is supported by an article by Dr. David Levy in which he suggests that the optimal way to manage care is to focus on the individual patient.[19] By returning the patient to the center of the health care delivery system and applying the tools of practice guidelines, disease management, and case (or care) management, it is possible to manage large populations of individual patients.

References

1. C.E. Schlessler, "Liability Implications of Utilization Review as a Cost Containment Mechanism," *J. Contemp. Health L. & Pol'y*, 8:379–406, Spring 1992.

2. Arnold Milstein, "Managing Utilization Management: A Purchaser's View," *Health Aff.*, 16(3):87–90, May–June 1997.

3. T.G. Ferris, Y. Chang, D. Blumenthal, and S.D. Pearson, "Leaving Gatekeeping Behind—Effects of Opening Access to Specialists for Adults in a Health Maintenance Organization," *New Eng. J. Med.*, 345:1312–1317, 2001.

4. David B. Nash, "Higher Quality at Lower Cost: Is Evidence-Based Medicine the Answer?" *Health Pol'y Newsl.*, Jan. 1999.

5. D.L. Sackett, *Evidence-Based Medicine: How to Practice and Teach EBM* (New York: Churchill Livingstone 1997).

6. J. Eisenberg and S. Williams, "Cost Containment and Changing Physicians' Practice Behavior: Can the Fox Learn to Guard the Chicken Coop?" *JAMA*, 246:2195–2201, 1981.

7. J. Newhouse et al., "Some Interim Results from a Controlled Trial of Cost Sharing in Health Insurance," *New Eng. J. Med.*, 305:1501–1507, 1981.

8. A. Milstein et al., "In Pursuit of Value: American Utilization Management at the Fifteen Year Mark," in Peter Boland (ed.), *Making Managed Healthcare Work: A Practical Guide to Strategies and Solutions* (Gaithersburg, MD: Aspen Publishers, Inc. 1993), 371–388.

9. This list is adapted from Nigel Roberts and Ed Zalta, "CAPP Care: Utilization Review of Ambulatory Services," in Peter Boland (ed.), *Making Managed Healthcare Work: A Practical Guide to Strategies and Solutions*, (Gaithersburg, MD: Aspen Publishers, Inc. 1993), 389.

10. URAC Standards, URAC, 127 25th St. NW, Suite 620, Washington, DC 20037.

11. HB 1090 77th Legislature, 2001, Sec.1(4), Art. 5.76-3 Insurance Code. *See also* Ind. Code Ann. § 27-8-6-8(b)(1); Minn. Stat. Ann. § 62Q.12 (West 1996), both requiring that appeals or denials of care be made only by professionals licensed to provide the services in question.

12. M. Crane, "When Doctors Are Caught Between Dueling Guidelines," *Med. Econ.*, 71:15, Aug. 8, 1994.

13. In Maine, for example, the use of guidelines is limited to certain specialties and can be raised as an affirmative defense

to a claim of malpractice. Guidelines may not be used by a plaintiff to establish liability.

14. John C. West, "The Legal Implications of Medical Practice Guidelines," *Health & Hosp. Law,* 27(4):97–103, Apr. 1994.

15. T. Bodenheimer, "Disease Management: Promises and Pitfalls," *New Eng. J. Med.,* 340:1202–1205, 1999.

16. R.S. Epstein and L.M. Sherwood, "From Outcomes Research to Disease Management: A Guide for the Perplexed," *Ann. Internal Med.,* 124:832–837, 1996.

17. D.M. Vickery and W.D. Lynch, "Demand Management: Enabling Patients to Use Medical Care Appropriately," *J. Occupational & Envtl. Med.,* 37:5, May 1995.

18. James F. Fries, "Beyond Health Promotion: Reducing the Need and Demand for Medical Care," *Health Aff.,* 17(2):70–84, Mar.–Apr. 1998.

19. David Levy, "Patient Centered Care as the New Paradigm of Health Care Management," *Managing Employee Health Benefits,* 6(3):1–9, Spring 1998.

Chapter 10

Trends in Quality Management and Consumer Rights

The discussion of quality in health care has changed dramatically in the past few years. Whereas quality in health care had previously been assessed as compliance with guidelines and regulations, the debate now focuses on patients' rights, outcomes, and a cost-benefit analysis. Largely as a result of the work of John E. Wennberg, M.D., M.P.H., at Dartmouth College and Donald Berwick, M.D., M.P.P., of the Institute for Healthcare Improvement in Boston, health care quality became an objective science. Once, quality health care could have been defined merely as something that quality doctors provided, but the application of scientific principles requires the production of data and now there is external oversight and review.

The original Consumer Bill of Rights and Responsibilities proposed as part of the Balanced Budget Act of 1997 (BBA) had three goals: (1) to strengthen consumer confidence by assuring consumers that the health care system is fair and responsive to their needs and to provide consumers with credible and effective mechanisms to address their concerns, thus encouraging them to take an active role in improving and maintaining their health; (2) to reaffirm the importance of a strong relationship between patients and their health care professionals; and (3) to reaffirm the critical role consumers play in safeguarding their own health by establishing both rights and responsibilities for all participants in improving health status.[1]

The biggest challenge in the health care industry and under managed care is to maintain and improve quality while reducing or containing costs. At the heart of the national health care debate is whether quality can be maintained in the presence of financial incentives to limit utilization.

Because there is no single measure of quality, this chapter examines quality from the perspective of managed care's major constituencies: physicians, patients, and purchasers. The chapter focuses on the concept of value, which includes quality and price. It also describes some of the methods used to achieve and measure quality in health care, including voluntary accreditation, credentialing, and peer review. Compliance plans as a tool for achieving organizational quality improvement are discussed.

Overview

Q 10:1   What is quality health care?

Definitions of quality in health care are wide ranging. The Agency for Health Care Research and Quality offers a short but accurate definition:

"Quality health care means doing the right thing, at the right time, in the right way, for the right person, and having the best possible results."[2] This suggests that (1) quality performance occurs on a continuum, ranging from acceptable to unacceptable, (2) the focus is on services, (3) quality may be evaluated from the perspective of the ultimate user, (4) evidence from research must be the basis for identifying services that improve health outcomes, and (5) these criteria have yet to be developed in the absence of scientific evidence.

Q 10:2   What are the major challenges to quality in US healthcare?

Several types of quality problems in health care have been documented through peer-reviewed research. They include:

Avoidable errors. Too many Americans are injured during the course of their treatment, and some die prematurely as a result. For example, a study of injuries to patients treated in hospitals in New York State found that 3.7 percent experienced adverse events, of which 13.6 percent led to death and 2.6 percent to permanent disability, and that about one-fourth of these adverse events were due to negligence.[3] A national study found that from 1983 to 1993, deaths due to medication errors rose more than twofold, with 7,391 deaths attributed to medication errors in 1993 alone.[4]

Underutilization of Services. Millions of people do not receive necessary care and suffer needless complications that add to health care costs and reduce productivity. For example, a study of Medicare patients with myocardial infarction found that only 21 percent of eligible patients received beta blockers and that the mortality rate among recipients was 43 percent less than that among nonrecipients.[5] An estimated 18,000 people die each year from heart attacks because they did not receive effective interventions.[6]

Overuse of Services. Millions of Americans receive health care services that are unnecessary, increase costs, and often endanger their health. For example, an analysis of hysterectomies performed under seven health plans estimated that one in six was inappropriate.[7]

Variation in Services. There is a continuing pattern of wide variation in health care practice, including regional variations and small-area variations. This is a clear indication that the practice of health care has not caught up with the science of health care to ensure evidence-based practice in the United States.

The word *appropriate* is a slippery slope. It has been a shibboleth for managed care and has been used as an excuse to deny payment for expensive or nonstandard care. In this context, *appropriate* means that there is evidence that the type of care proffered is likely to affect the disease or condition under consideration in a favorable way. Sometimes, doing nothing is more appropriate than intervening when intervening cannot be shown to affect the outcome of a clinical condition beneficially.

Q 10:3 What has driven the emphasis on quality in managed care?

Early managed care's focus on managing costs has driven the emphasis on quality. Although there is little evidence that the overall health of the population was adversely affected by control of health care costs, certain spectacular incidents focused the public's attention on mere cost containment. *Fox v. HealthNet* [No. 219692 (Cal Super Ct Riverside County Dec 28, 1993)] centered on the failure of a health maintenance organization (HMO) to pay for autologous bone marrow transplantation for a patient with advanced breast cancer. The result of this denial was an enormous judgment against the HMO. Although the procedure has subsequently not proved to be highly efficacious for breast cancer, the case is instructive in decision making based on cost.

The current debate is about measurable quality. Several successful initiatives have shown that it is possible to measure quality. Nonetheless, medication errors abound. Although controversial, the Institute of Medicine of the National Academy of Science has reported a significant number of deaths and complications from medication errors in hospitals.[8]

Q 10:4 How is quality measured?

Researchers have found that methodologies for measuring quality have their limitations. They find that automated medical records, not claims data, are the most reliable data source for measuring quality.

The definition of quality and its measure are the focus of several accreditation organizations, such as the Joint Commission on Accreditation of Healthcare Organizations (JCAHO) and the National Committee for Quality Assurance (NCQA). JCAHO has identified nine components of quality in health care: accessibility of care, appropriateness of care, continuity of care, effectiveness of care, efficacy of care, efficiency of care, patient perspective issues, safety of the care environment, and timeliness of care.[9]

Q 10:5   How important is quality to the consumer?

In choosing a health plan, people say quality of care is their top priority over cost and choice. They tend to rely on recommendations from their physicians, family members, and friends rather than on information produced by independent organizations. In fact, when choosing a doctor, patients are more concerned about how well the doctor communicates and how caring the doctor is than about whether the doctor is board certified or highly regarded by the managed care plan. Nonetheless, the AHRQ has cited a number of examples of purchasers of health care using quality metrics:

1. GTE provides its employees and their families with financial incentives to enroll in "exceptional quality" plans (those with high ratings on quality measures and satisfaction surveys). Employees receive report cards on plans so that they can choose a plan based on cost and quality. Initial analysis of this approach showed that employees who considered making a health plan change were most sensitive to cost; however, they also relied significantly on specific quality information, with 30 percent considering GTE's designation of "exceptional quality" and 45 percent considering the quality scores based on the Health Plan Employer Data and Information Set (HEDIS) and participant satisfaction measures.[10]

2. General Motors blends several measures of health care quality into one amalgamated quality measure and draws from direct indicators of quality from HEDIS, employee satisfaction measures, accreditation status, and impressions gained from site visits. It also works with its plans to develop quality improvement strategies and facilitate the sharing of best practices.[11]

3. Digital Equipment Corporation emphasizes value (which it defines as the sum of quality of care and consumer satisfaction, divided by costs) in its health care purchasing decisions. Using information from its performance reporting requirements, it identifies the best plan in each region as the benchmark plan and bases its contribution to the cost of health coverage on the premium charged by that plan.[12]

4. The Pacific Business Group on Health requires HMOs to set aside 2 percent of premiums and allows plans to keep that money only if they attain the performance standards set in customer service, quality, data collection, and other areas.[13]

5. Seven leading business and employer organizations recently announced a new initiative, the Employer Quality Partnership (EQP), to "accelerate the growing emphasis on quality in private health plans." EQP has released informational guides and launched a Web site as part of its effort to educate the public about the role of employers as health care purchasers.[14]

6. The United Auto Workers requires quality accreditation for all health plans offered to its members, and it is working on a strategy to provide information, including NCQA accreditation status and some quality assessment based on HEDIS measures.[15]

Q 10:6 What is the key component of quality accountability to the consumer?

The key component of a health plan's accountability to the consumer is its demonstrated ability to meet or exceed community-based performance and quality standards. These standards are based, in substantial part, on a perception of value to the purchasers and health care consumers. Satisfaction surveys provide an important vehicle for reporting on health plans and establish a sense of accountability to the consumer. As discussed in Qs 10:19–10:21, however, these surveys must be able to appropriately measure quality and establish consumer perceptions of value. When correctly interpreted and acted on, consumer satisfaction surveys can provide critical information for improving the quality of health care services and their delivery.

EQP suggests making quality metrics part of an employer's negotiation with a health plan. For an example of quality metrics, see the table at http://www.eqp.org/sampleper.html.

Q 10:7 Is there a relationship between quality and cost?

Yes. Although there is no direct relationship between quality and cost, the difficulty in measuring quality makes many purchasers of health care services focus on cost. Paying more for health care, how-

Figure 10-1.   Theoretical Relationships: Quality and Outcome

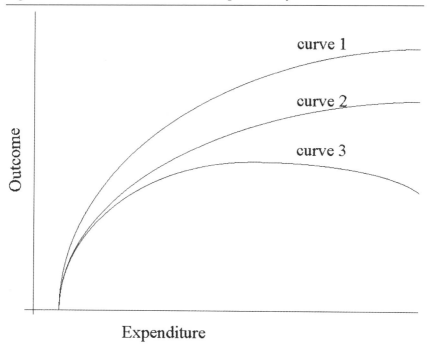

ever, does not ensure higher quality. In fact, providing unnecessary care can even diminish the quality of the care.

There are three theoretical relationships between cost and outcome, as shown in Figure 10-1. In curve 1, as expenditure increases, outcomes continue to improve. In curve 2, there is a point at which outcomes cease to improve no matter how much more is spent. In curve 3, there is a point at which increasing expenditures actually produces a poorer outcome. Cases can be adduced for each curve, but there is no agreement as to which curve, if any, is accurate. It is clear, however, that an equilibrium point exists at which decreasing expenditures adversely affects outcome, and this is demonstrated in each curve.

Q 10:8   What are some of the issues in the cost-quality balance?

Robert Brook and others pose eight salient questions related to the cost-quality balance:[16]

1. As the transformation to a fully managed care system progresses in the United States, how can the nation be certain that a focus remains on quality of care?

2. As physicians shift from patient-based to population-based medicine, how do they balance the needs of the individual with the demands of managing the population?

3. One of the casualties of a highly managed care system is likely to be physician contact time. As that time is reduced, how does the physician maintain knowledge of the patients' social, psychological, and even economic milieu? Similarly, how does the physician ensure that he or she has communicated risks and benefits, has advised about complications, and has been receptive to patients' needs for information when time is constrained?

4. As cuts are made in health care, will they be rational and related to patient needs or "across the board" and draconian?

5. How will information be disseminated to the public to allow public assessments of health plans and some degree of control over the medical marketplace?

6. Will needs assessments result in just the "right" number of physicians to fill the demand, or will a surplus of physicians be needed to allow timely access?

7. Will data be disseminated to the public in a valid and understandable form to allow consumers to make rational choices?

8. Will high-quality and technologically sophisticated care be accessible to all, regardless of income or social status?

The critical issues Brook addresses focus on communication and resource allocation. Communication between providers remains stymied by the presence of multiple, noninterchangeable information systems and proprietary software. This communication block is the cause of many quality mishaps but a solution is not in sight.

Q 10:9 Are there any emerging standards in cost-effectiveness analysis?

Yes. The U.S. Public Health Service has convened an expert panel called the Panel on Cost-Effectiveness in Health and Medicine. One of the major problems in cost-effectiveness analysis is comparability. That is, can one analysis performed in a unique geographic, social, and economic environment be comparable to another? Further, how can a cost-effectiveness analysis become prescriptive without standardization? The panel defines cost-effectiveness analysis as follows:

> Cost-effectiveness analysis is a method for evaluating the outcomes and costs of interventions designed to improve health. The results are usually summarized in cost-effectiveness ratios that demonstrate the cost of achieving a unit of health effect (e.g., the cost per year of life gained) for diverse types of patients and for variations of the intervention. In a cost-effectiveness ratio, changes in health due to an intervention, compared to a specific alternative, are captured in the denominator; and changes in resource use, compared with the same alternative and valued in monetary terms, are captured in the numerator.

The panel proposes the inclusion within cost-effectiveness analysis of a "reference case" using quality-adjusted life years (QALYs) as the standard measure. The panel also emphasizes that this type of reference case analysis is useful for population-based decision making and will not give guidance for decision making at the bedside.[17]

Q 10:10 Is there regional variation in quality of care?

Yes. Evidence is accumulating to suggest that there is substantial regional variation in the rate of use of many surgical procedures that cannot be explained by variations in the patterns of disease. Best studied have been hysterectomy, prostate surgery, and coronary surgery versus angioplasty. A 1997 study highlights the complexity of regional comparisons.[18] The study compared rates of coronary surgery in similar populations in New York and Ontario, Canada, and found substantial regional variation suggesting overuse of some procedures in the United States and underuse of others in Canada. These variations emphasize the difficulty in assessing the "right" rate for any intervention. The authors imply that a thorough analysis needs to take into account not only the number of procedures performed but also the outcomes of the procedures and their impact on quality of life.

Similar analyses have been performed among constituent hospitals of the same HMO, and variations in the use of procedures have been documented.

Q 10:11   What is a quality report card?

The notion that a report card can be issued for a health care plan or provider is new. Only recently, with the rise of commercial health plans and their competition, has the notion of a publicly available accounting been seen as a marketing tool. The presumption had been that health plans paid providers who, in turn, did the most and the best they could. This approach was driving health care costs to the stratosphere.

In the early 1990s, several pioneering health plans—United HealthCare, Group Health Cooperative of Puget Sound, Kaiser, United States Healthcare Corporation, and Ethix Corporation—set out to publish report cards on their activities. Many others have followed suit. Researchers from the University of Oregon found, however, that consumers disregard quality information that they do not understand, and often find report cards incomprehensible because of their inability to understand the context. Consumers are unsure what the many quality indicators are intended to tell them. Therefore, if informed consumer choice is to work, more information must be provided and the consumer must be educated regarding the significance of this quality of care information.[19]

Q 10:12   What are the key components of a report card?

Paul Kenkel has described the following components of one report card:[20]

1. *Access.* How timely is the provision of personal health services? How easy are the services to obtain?

2. *Appropriateness.* Was the care provided necessary? Was necessary care provided?

3. *Efficiency.* Was care provided in the most efficient manner? Were there unnecessary delays in the provision of care?

4. *Outcome.* Was the expected outcome achieved? Was the outcome achieved without complications?

5. *Health plan member satisfaction.* How satisfied were members with the health plan's services? Did the services provided have the desired effect on the member's functioning and quality of life?

Q 10:13 What is the difference between process studies and outcome measures?

Process data are accumulated by examining the steps involved in delivering a service to a plan enrollee, whether it be acute care or preventive care. Traditionally, process studies have been useful in identifying and eliminating areas of ambiguity, duplication, and inefficiency. Outcome measures, on the other hand, examine whether the desired effect was achieved. Both are important, but they measure different things. When examining report cards, it is important to know whether they represent process studies or outcome measures.

It is also important to know how the data for the report card were gathered. Claims data can be very crude. The best data are generated when studied prospectively with real-time observation. Paradoxically, as plans become more capitated, their data collection can become less accurate because the providers are less motivated to account for every step of the care process when they are no longer paid on a fee-for-service basis.

Q 10:14 What is risk-adjusted outcome rating?

Outcome indicators show whether a health care goal has been achieved: To ascertain the significance of any outcome indicator (e.g., mortality after coronary artery surgery), it is critical to adjust the finding for the expected frequency of the outcome. This comparison makes outcome measuring very difficult. The mortality rate after coronary artery surgery, for example, can be expected to be substantially different for 55-year-old female nonsmokers than for 75-year-old male smokers. If the outcome indicator is not adjusted for the population, it is not a fair representation of the health plan's quality of care. This is called risk-adjusted outcome rating.

Q 10:15 How does a quality management plan assure quality and performance in managed care?

A quality management plan serves to identify the techniques that measure treatment outcomes and to assure the continuous quality improvement mandated by payers, regulatory agencies, and employer groups. These parties look for documented assurances of quality as well as cost effectiveness. A quality management plan should begin with a statement of purpose explaining why the plan was developed, possibly a mission statement, and a statement of responsibility. Its goals should include but should not be limited to

1. Identifying "quality" standards of care;
2. Maintaining a system of quality assessment information to be utilized in contracting with and credentialing health care providers;
3. Implementing utilization guidelines based on quality outcomes;
4. Improving medical record documentation; and
5. Establishing, implementing, and monitoring corrective action plans for deficiencies.

Because health care is a service industry, many experts see quality improvement as service improvement. Consequently, for the service to improve, the results of any quality review studies and requirements should go to those providing the services. Some companies use consumer research as a tool to improve the quality of health care services.

Measuring Quality

Q 10:16   How does one measure the quality of service in health care?

Measuring the quality of service in health care is much less complicated than measuring the quality of health care. Quality of service usually relates to how the system performs in meeting the patient's nonclinical needs and expectations, including appointment waiting times, telephone response times, claims handling, courtesy, and overall responsiveness. Essentially, these factors relate to patient satisfaction.

Q 10:17   How do clinical and production efficiency fit into quality assessment techniques?

Clinical efficiency concerns the manner in which a practitioner manages the patient's clinical problems. Production efficiency is how an organization as a whole produces the goods and services out of which the care is provided. Clinical efficiency is under the control of the physician; production efficiency is directed and controlled by the managed care organization (MCO).

Q 10:18 How can quality be improved?

Approaches to quality improvement take many forms. Mark R. Chassin identifies four approaches to consider:[21]

Regulation. Regulation as a method of quality improvement is least favored because of its inability to accommodate variations in patient characteristics that affect physician decision making. Regulations offer limited flexibility, a cumbersome revision process, and little ability to encourage innovation. To the extent regulations could facilitate regionalization of specialized health care services (e.g., cardiac surgery, neonatal intensive care), there could be some benefit to patient care and improved quality.

Competition. Competition is a powerful motivating force that could affect quality if harnessed to a quality improvement strategy.

Continuous Quality Improvement. This strategy for improving quality of care uses industrial quality management techniques and applies them to health care. It is based on understanding how mistakes occur and then focusing on the practices that contributed to the mistakes as a means of emphasizing the process rather than the people. It is a dynamic strategy that emphasizes reducing variations in processes of care.

Financial Incentives. Economics have a powerful effect on human behavior. Most discussions related to payment and quality concern the potential for adverse effects. There is also a concern that payment methods affect quality of care. Fee-for-service payments encourage overuse, whereas capitation tends to result in underuse of health care services.

Q 10:19 What is a patient satisfaction survey?

A patient satisfaction survey can take many forms. At its simplest, a physician or caregiver asks: "Did I meet your needs? Are your questions answered?" More complicated questionnaires ask the patient about access, availability, continuity, financial aspects of care, interpersonal aspects of care, technical aspects of care, and general satisfaction.

A sample survey that the AHRQ suggests as a guide to making health care decisions is provided in Table 10-1. A more complete version can be downloaded from the AHRQ Web site (see below).

Table 10-1.   Quick Checks for Quality

Look for a plan that

- Has been rated highly by its members on the things that are important to you.
- Does a good job of helping people stay well and get better
- Is accredited, if that is important to you
- Has the doctors and hospitals you want or need
- Provides the benefits you need
- Provides services where and when you need them
- Meets your budget

Look for a doctor who

- Is rated to give quality care
- Has the training and background that meet your needs
- Takes steps to prevent illness (e.g., talks to you about quitting smoking)
- Has privileges at the hospital of your choice
- Is part of your health plan, unless you can afford to pay extra
- Encourages you to ask questions
- Listens to you
- Explains things clearly
- Treats you with respect

When choosing a treatment, make sure you understand

- What your diagnosis is
- Whether treatment is really needed at this time
- What your treatment options are
- Whether the treatment options are based on the latest scientific evidence
- The benefits and risks of each treatment
- The cost of each treatment

Look for a hospital that

- Is accredited by the JCAHO
- Is rated highly by state or consumer or other groups
- Is one where your doctor has privileges if that is important to you
- Is covered by your health plan
- Has experience with your condition
- Has had success with your condition
- Checks and works to improve its own quality of care

Look for long-term care that

- Has been found by state agencies, accreditors, or others to provide quality care
- Has the services you need
- Has staff that meet your needs
- Meets your budget

Source: AHRQ, http://ahrq.gov/consumer/quick.htm.

Q 10:20 Are patient satisfaction surveys an appropriate way to measure quality?

They can be. Patient and enrollee satisfaction surveys have been the most significant contributors to report cards on health plans and provider organizations that participate in managed care and play a major role in measuring performance and establishing accountability. Although the satisfaction survey is a good tool, certain pitfalls must be recognized and avoided to make the best use of it.

The first pitfall is in the design and content of the survey. Surveys that seek "marketing" information will not be useful for quality improvement. Instead, the survey should focus on "patient-defined" quality characteristics. The second pitfall involves the sampling strategy used in the survey process. The most common sampling technique is to use random sampling. Depending on the scope of the health plan's programs, a simple random sampling may not extend to the full range of programs and services to be included in the measure. The third pitfall to avoid is bias in the results of the survey. Telephone and face-to-face surveys are subject to interviewer bias, as are on-site surveys. Professional interviewers and consumer research companies may produce more reliable results. Finally, there is a pitfall associated with the use of the data and the data's availability to the end-user. The more simple the presentation of the results, the more meaningful they will be in achieving their desired effect of improving quality. Experts suggest that the survey process itself should be the subject of continuous quality improvement principles to be sure that the survey remains a meaningful tool as used by the surveyor.[22]

Q 10:21 What are the steps in developing a patient questionnaire?

Goldfield and others identify six steps useful in the development of a patient questionnaire:[23]

1. Perform an internal review to examine current patient questionnaires. Ask such questions as the following:

    • What does the institution need to measure?

    • Do existing questionnaires meet the need?

- What services do the best questionnaires measure?
- Are the questions reliable and valid?
- What was (or will be) done with the information?
- Who received (or will receive) the results?
- Was there (or will there be) any change based on the results?
- What was (or is anticipated to be) the impact of the change?

2. Convene a focus group of administrative personnel, health professionals, and outside customers (e.g., patients and employer group representatives). The group's role is to decide how the results of current questionnaires can best be incorporated into the quality improvement process and whether the current use of this information is optimal. Is there a need for other customer information?

3. Designate a portion of the focus group as a task force to confirm implementation of the recommendations. The task force should include individuals outside the organization, as well as internal staff members.

4. If the organization does not have someone in charge of consumer surveys, consider hiring such an individual as part of the quality management program. In a small institution, this person need not be full time.

5. Develop questionnaires in coordination with the medical staff.

6. Become familiar with patient-derived ratings before attempting to obtain patient reports, particularly when the reports are intended to produce information about physician practice.

Q 10:22   How can reproducible quality metrics be developed for American health care?

McGlynn and Brook, in a trenchant analysis of quality initiatives, take a dark view of the past and a hopeful view of the future. Their article,[24] which should be read in its entirety, identifies several opportunities for standardization of quality measures:

- Create quality champions. Fundamentally, we need a "war on poor quality" that has the same level of public commitment as the war on cancer or the campaign to put a man on the moon. We believe that the subsequent funding of needed research in response to this declaration of war will lead to the development of specific strategies that should be followed. Both the private and public sectors will have to demand a complete overhaul of medical practice, and implementing such change will necessitate leadership from clinicians and a vigilant constituency. . . .

- Develop a functional information system. . . . [H]ealthcare professionals and organizations need to embrace computer technologies that can be used to receive and transmit information. The private sector should lead the way by making investment in such systems an allowable expense in calculating health insurance premiums. The government should undertake an evaluation of tax incentives that might further spur the adoption of computer technologies in office-based medical practice. No serious advances in quality of care can be made without a functioning, computer-based information system of care. . . .

- Routinely monitor and report on performance. . . . [A]n independent group should routinely compile information into a national report on whether average levels of and variation in quality are increasing or decreasing. There have been scattered attempts to do this, including an effort mandated by Congress, but the amount of funding allocated to these efforts has been grossly inadequate. . . .

- Ensure adequate funding for quality measurement. To make all of this work, sustained investments must be made in the tools that are used to set standards, promulgate current and scientifically valid measures for monitoring, provide consistent information to physicians on best practices, make information easily accessible to decision makers, and so on. This is not a trivial enterprise. . . .

Accreditation

Q 10:23   What is accreditation?

Accreditation is a process used by an independent organization to evaluate an MCO's internal system from a qualitative perspective using standards developed by the reviewing organization. Accreditation serves as an external assessment of the structure and effects of health plans' internal quality assurance programs. The evaluating organizations survey compliance with standards using document review, on-site observations and interviews, review of medical records, and assessment of member service systems. Their role is not to endorse quality or to rank the organizations they review, but rather to give MCOs a way to measure their own performance and predict future performance.

It is unclear whether accreditation affects consumer choice; however, it is clearly favored by employers as a tool for measuring and evaluating the various managed care plans. An increasing number of companies are using accreditation as a way to assure employees that they are getting quality health care from their plan. In fact, several companies, including Xerox and PepsiCo, mandate accreditation for their MCOs.

Several states require accreditation or other external assessment of licensed HMOs or regulated MCOs as part of state-mandated QA requirements. Florida's Administrative Code requires accreditation by an approved accrediting organization within two years of an HMO's receipt of a certificate of authority. [Fla Admin Code Ann §§ 59A-12.0071, 59A-12.0072] Pennsylvania's Health and Safety Code requires external QA assessment by an expert in HMO review approved by the Pennsylvania Department of Health within one year of an MCO's receipt of its certificate and every three years thereafter. [28 Pa Code § 9.93 (1994)] Kansas requires MCOs to obtain on-site quality of care assessment by an independent quality review organization acceptable to the Kansas Insurance Commissioner at least once every three years. [Kan Stat Ann § 40.3211 (1993)]

Q 10:24   What organizations are involved in health plan and health care organization accreditation?

Several organizations play an important role in accreditation of various types of health care provider entities and health benefit plans in the private sector, including the NCQA, the American Accreditation Program, Inc. (AAPI), the Utilization Review Accreditation Commission (URAC), the Accreditation Association for Ambulatory Health Care (AAAHC), and the JCAHO. Others that focus on quality as part of an accreditation process include the National League of Nursing's Community Health Accreditation Program (CHAP), the Commission on the Accreditation of Rehabilitation Facilities (CARF), and the Medical Quality Commission (MQC).

National Committee for Quality Assurance

Q 10:25   What are the characteristics, standards, and experiences of NCQA?

Established in 1990 under the auspices of the Group Health Association of America (GHAA) and the American Managed Care and Review Association (AMCRA), NCQA evolved as an accrediting organization for MCOs through a grant from the Robert Wood Johnson Foundation and matching moneys from MCOs. NCQA uses HEDIS as its core set of performance measures. The HEDIS measures were developed in response to an employer's needs: to understand the value of the health care dollar in purchasing and to hold a health plan accountable for its performance.

NCQA review focuses on clinical and administrative mechanisms for QA and the communication process for problem identification, analysis, solution, and follow-up. It focuses on quality and not on an organization's legal structure or financial integrity. NCQA review is performed by a qualified team of physicians and administrators with experience in HMO quality management.

NCQA standards are used to evaluate an MCO in the areas of quality management and improvement, utilization management, credentialing, member rights and responsibilities, preventive health services, and medical records and to rate the organizations on a compliance scale ranging from full compliance to noncompliance. An organization that provides health services may apply for NCQA accreditation if it provides or arranges to provide comprehensive health services (1) through a defined benefits package, including preventive care; (2) to enrolled members through an organized delivery system; (3) in ambulatory and inpatient care settings; (4) within the United States and its territories; (5) in compliance with federal, state, and local laws and regulations; and (6) quality monitoring and improvement processes. The organization must also have been in operation for at least 18 months.

NCQA has been endorsed by the Managed Health Care Association (MHCA), a group of large employers dedicated to advancing managed care, as the most experienced of the accrediting organizations with the most comprehensive process for reviewing managed care plans.

Q 10:26   What are the NCQA accreditation categories?

On July 1, 1999, NCQA changed its accreditation designations to make them easier to understand and more intuitively meaningful for consumers and employers. It also added a new status, excellent, to recognize commitment to clinical excellence, customer service, and continuous quality improvement. In October 1999, NCQA awarded excellent status to 40 managed care plans that generally achieved scores in the top 25 percent on a slate of key performance measures such as mammography and immunization rates, beta blocker treatment after heart attacks, and overall consumer satisfaction.

NCQA's primary accreditation status levels are as follows:

1. *Excellent.* Excellent is NCQA's highest accreditation status. Full accreditation is granted for a period of three years. Plans earning this accreditation level are also recognized for having achieved HEDIS results that are in the highest range of national or regional performance.

2. *Commendable.* This three-year full accreditation level is awarded to plans that demonstrate levels of service and clinical quality that meet or exceed NCQA's rigorous requirements for consumer protection and quality improvement.

3. *Accredited.* This one-year accreditation level is granted to plans that have well-established quality improvement programs and meet most NCQA standards. NCQA provides the plans with a specific list of recommendations and reviews the plans again after a year to determine if they have progressed enough to move up to full accreditation.

4. *Provisional accreditation.* This designation is granted for one year to plans that have adequate quality improvement programs and meet some NCQA standards. These plans need to

demonstrate progress before they can qualify for higher levels of accreditation.

5. *Denial.* This designation is given to plans that do not qualify for any of the foregoing categories.

6. *Under review.* This designation denotes that a plan's initial accreditation determination is under review at the request of the plan.

Q 10:27 What does NCQA examine?

NCQA examines quality improvement, utilization management, credentialing, member rights and responsibilities, preventive health services, and medical records.

Quality Improvement. NCQA measures quality improvement through review of program structure, accountability and coordination with management, content of the program, and delegation. NCQA asks: Does the plan fully examine the quality of care given to its members? How well does it coordinate all parts of its delivery system? What steps does it take to make sure members have access to care in a reasonable amount of time? What improvements in care and service can the plan demonstrate?

Utilization Management. NCQA looks for a documented utilization management program that includes, as appropriate, delegated functions. NCQA asks: Does the plan use a reasonable and consistent process when deciding what health services are appropriate for patients' needs? When the plan denies payment for services, does it respond to member and physician appeals? How consistently do the medical records kept by the plan's physicians meet NCQA standards for quality care? For instance, do the records show that physicians follow up on patients' abnormal test findings?

Credentialing. NCQA looks for written policies and procedures for credentialing of physicians and other clinical practitioners, as approved by a governing body. Delegation of the credentialing activities involves the additional safeguards of verification of primary source information (e.g., licensing, work history, malpractice insurance, and claims history) and a process for periodic verification of a practitioner's credentials similar to that used in the initial review, but also including member complaint information, quality review, utilization management, and member satisfaction surveys. NCQA asks: Does the plan meet specific NCQA requirements for investigating the training and experience of all physicians in its network? Does the plan look for any history of malpractice or fraud? Does it keep track of all physicians' performance and use that information for their periodic evaluations?

Member Rights and Responsibilities. NCQA seeks documentation and information related to member rights and grievance procedures through existence of written policies, satisfaction reports, and access by members to information and confidentiality of patient information. NCQA asks the following questions: How clearly does the plan inform members about how to access health services, how to choose a physician or change physicians, and how to make a complaint? How responsive is the plan to members' satisfaction ratings and complaints?

Preventive Health Services. NCQA emphasizes an MCO's use of practice guidelines for preventive health services for the full spectrum of the enrolled population. NCQA asks: Does the plan encourage members to have preventive tests and immunizations? Does the plan make sure that its physicians are encouraging and delivering preventive services?

Medical Records. NCQA looks at the standards used for medical record completion, maintenance, and review to determine whether the records are current, detailed, and organized and allow for effective patient care and quality review. New standards include provisions for health plans to provide external review to enrollees for all denials of covered services based on a determination that the treatment or procedure is not medically necessary.

Q 10:28 How does NCQA accredit?

NCQA accreditation review consists of three phases.

Preassessment Survey. Following receipt of a completed application, NCQA schedules the on-site survey and obtains additional information for the first phase of the document review. This information relates to the organization's size, scope, structure, and operations.

On-Site Survey. This phase involves a two- to four-day on-site visit by the review team (usually an administrative reviewer and two or more physician reviewers). Using a predetermined schedule, the team reviews documents on-site and interviews key clinical and administrative personnel, the medical director, and other officers and directors of the MCO.

Post-Survey Activities. Based on the information obtained before and during the on-site visit, the review team prepares a preliminary report addressing each on-site survey. Following review of the draft by the review oversight committee, the draft is furnished to the MCO for comments. Accreditation is determined by the review oversight committee as full accreditation, accreditation with recommendations, provisional accreditation, denial or revocation of accreditation status, or deferral of accreditation review.

Q 10:29 What type of organizations does NCQA accredit?

NCQA reviews organizations that deliver managed health care services—including traditional staff and group-model HMOs, network and independent practice association (IPA)–model HMOs, mixed models, and open-ended HMOs—or point-of-service products. Other network-based systems may also qualify for accreditation.

Q 10:30 What are the NCQA criteria for in a medical report card?

The NCQA criiteria for a medical report card are uniform across health plans and include the following:

- Presence of guidelines for doctors about the need to provide immunizations and screening tests to plan members
- Effective communications that make doctors in the plan aware of the guidelines
- Effective communications that make plan members aware of what they can do to reduce illness, disease, and accidents
- Percentage of children under the age of two who have received recommended immunizations to prevent childhood diseases
- Percentage of children who, by the age of 13, have received recommended immunizations for continued protection against childhood diseases

- Percentage of Medicare members over the age of 65 who received an influenza vaccination to prevent the flu (only for health plans serving Medicare beneficiaries)
- Percentage of women ages 52 to 69 who received a mammogram within the past two years to detect breast cancer early
- Percentage of adult women who received a Pap smear within the past three years to detect cervical cancer early
- Percentage of pregnant women who received their first prenatal care visit during the first three months of pregnancy
- Percentage of new mothers who received a checkup within eight weeks after delivery
- A well-defined program for improving the quality of clinical care and service provided to plan members
- Individuals in the health plan responsible for overseeing quality improvement programs
- Actual improvements that the plan has made in care and service.[25]

Utilization Review Accreditation Commission

Q 10:31   What does URAC do?

URAC accredits organizations that use or offer utilization review (UR) services. URAC allows variation in its standards because of federal and state laws and regulations; however, where the URAC standard is higher than the state or federal standard, the URAC standard prevails. URAC standards apply to prospective, concurrent, and retrospective UR for inpatient and outpatient services.

URAC reviewers look at the background and qualifications of staff, the accessibility of the organization, and the procedures applied to certification decisions and appeals. URAC accreditation is for two years. As of October 1999, there were over 300 URAC-accredited MCOs.

URAC has been successful in 18 states in obtaining "deemed" status, which allows URAC accreditation to serve as a surrogate process for state licensing or certification requirements without the necessity of separate state review. In September 1995, URAC began to test new noncapitated network standards to accredit PPOs, physician-hospital organizations, physician organizations, and integrated delivery systems. Today it offers nine different accreditation programs for MCOs. Components of a URAC review include the following:

Confidentiality. UR organizations must have written procedures for ensuring confidentiality of patient-specific information. Data shared between the UR organization and its client are considered private and are governed by contract.

Responsibility for Certification. If a UR organization is responsible for certifying a health service, the UR organization must allow any licensed facility, provider, or patient representative, including family member, the right to assist in fulfilling the certification requirement.

Staff and Program Qualifications. UR organizations are required to have properly qualified, trained, and supervised staff members who use written clinical criteria and procedures. Use of health professionals in review who are not clinical peers must be limited to first-level clinical review, with second-level review done by clinical peers. The clinical peers must be practicing providers with board certification by either the American Board of Medical Specialties or the Advisory Board of Osteopathic Specialists.

Accessibility and On-Site Review Procedures. UR standards require access to review staff by phone at least from 9 a.m. to 4 p.m. each day, with written procedures for after-hours calls. There are specific requirements for UR personnel identification.

UR Information. UR organizations are to collect only information that is necessary to certify an admission, procedure, treatment, length of stay, or frequency or duration of service. Copies of partial or complete medical records may be obtained retrospectively. The cost of copies to be used other than for appeal or legal purposes should be reimbursed to the provider furnishing them.

Procedures for Review Determination. There must be written procedures to ensure that reviews are conducted in a timely fashion, that decisions are made in a timely fashion, and that notification of decisions is timely.

Appeals of Determinations Not to Certify. Procedures must exist for appeals of decisions not to certify admissions, medical procedures, services, or extension of stays. The appeal right belongs to the patient and attending physician or provider.

Q 10:32   Where are the URAC standards published?

The URAC standards are summarized on URAC's Web site, http://www.urac.org/programs/accreditationstandards.htm.

Joint Committee on Accreditation of Healthcare Organizations

Q 10:33   What is the role of JCAHO?

JCAHO accredits health care networks. It offers two options for networks meeting survey eligibility criteria: accreditation or third-party evaluation. Third-party evaluations are based on the same standards as accreditations but are tailored to the requester's needs. JCAHO focuses on organizational processes, including policies, mission, and other systems-related issues. JCAHO accredits HMOs, integrated delivery systems, PPOs, provider-sponsored organizations, specialty networks, and managed behavioral health care organizations. JCAHO standard implementation may be phased in for such areas as improving organization performance and management of information.

Q 10:34   What is a health care network, and what are the JCAHO standards for health care networks?

JCAHO defines a health care network as "an entity that provides, or provides for, integrated health care services to a defined population of individuals. A network offers comprehensive or specialty services and is characterized by a centralized structure that coordinates and integrates services provided by component organizations and practitioners participating in the network."[26]

The JCAHO standards for health care networks are as follows:

Rights, Responsibilities, and Ethics. In evaluating these standards, JCAHO looks for a written code of ethics related to the integrity of clinical decision making, regardless of financial incentives. Access to information and member involvement through mechanisms to ensure informed consent and patient participation in the clinical decision-making process, grievance procedures, systems to protect confidential information, and disclosure of the foregoing are components of these standards.

Continuum of Care. JCAHO requires that all health care services be provided by JCAHO-accredited organizations or through an organization that uses similar standards. JCAHO emphasizes integration of health care services but provides for oversight of components that are not accredited or eligible for accreditation.

Education and Communication. This standard requires the MCO to take a systematic approach to communicating with and educating members.

Health Promotion and Disease Prevention. JCAHO focuses on the maintenance of health, prevention of acute diseases and injuries, avoidance or delay of morbidity and disability, and health care resource use associated with chronic and degenerative diseases.

Leadership. JCAHO looks to the governing body, senior management, and leaders of the practitioners to provide the mission and plans for the MCO.

Management of Human Resources. JCAHO requires the MCO to establish staffing levels and procedures to determine the qualifications and competency of employed practitioners and/or licensed independent contracting practitioners, and to assess and improve competency on an ongoing basis.

Management of Information. Management information systems must be planned and designed to meet the MCO's information requirements.

Improving Network Performance. The organization must have a planned and systematic approach to designing, measuring, assessing, and improving its performance that is interrelated with the standards described above.

The chapters in JCAHO's standards manual on the accreditation of health care networks cover the following areas of performance: quality improvement; member rights and responsibilities; utilization management; credentialing of practitioners; medical records; preventive health services; ethical standards; withdrawal of care or end-of-life treatment policy; oversight of contracts with providers; satisfaction of consumers, providers, and purchasers; safety of the care delivery environment, including infection control; emergency preparedness planning; network planning based on the needs of members and the perspectives of practitioners and community leaders; compliance with laws and regulations; and ownership disclosure.

Q 10:35   What are JCAHO's categories of accreditation?

The JCAHO accreditation for networks can result in one of seven decisions:

Accreditation with Commendation. This is the highest accreditation decision awarded to a network. It is awarded when the network has demonstrated exemplary performance in all areas of measurement.

Accreditation Without Type I Recommendations. This accreditation is awarded when a network has demonstrated acceptable compliance with JCAHO standards in all performance areas.

Accreditation with Type I Recommendations. This accreditation decision results from a network receiving at least one recommendation addressing insufficient or unsatisfactory standards compliance in a specific performance area. Resolution of type I recommendations must occur within a stipulated time frame.

Provisional Accreditation. This accreditation decision results when a network has demonstrated satisfactory compliance with the selected standards applied during its first survey, and a second survey, or full survey, is conducted approximately six months later to allow the network to establish a track record of performance.

Conditional Accreditation. This accreditation decision results when a network is not in substantial compliance with JCAHO standards, but is believed capable of achieving acceptable standards within a stipulated time frame.

Preliminary Nonaccreditation. This accreditation decision is assigned to a network found to be in significant noncompliance with JCAHO standards or when its accreditation is initially withdrawn by JCAHO for other reasons (e.g., falsification of documents) before the final decision is made.

Not Accredited. This accreditation decision results when a network is in significant noncompliance with JCAHO standards, when the accreditation is withdrawn, or when the network voluntarily withdraws from the accreditation process.

Accreditation Association for Ambulatory Health Care

Q 10:36 What dos the AAAHC do?

The AAAHC primarily accredits ambulatory surgery centers, although it has accredited several HMOs, using two groups of standards: core standards for all organizations and adjunct standards that are applied as appropriate. Core standards apply to and include rights of patients, governance structure, administration, quality of care provided, quality management and improvement (which includes peer review and risk management), clinical records, professional improvement, and facilities and environment.

Quality from the Physician's Perspective

Q 10:37 How does a physician evaluate quality in managed care?

Physicians must consider many factors when evaluating a health plan or network for participation. One is the latitude that the plan allows the physician in planning courses of therapy, obtaining diagnostic information and ancillary services, and referring within established patterns. Another is the number and extent of barriers the plan places between the patient and recommended therapy. An example of this is the accessibility of the utilization and preadmission certification coordinators. Time spent waiting for authorization is time lost from patient care. Physicians call this the hassle factor.

The form of the network also influences the physician's measures of quality. In a completely integrated system, where incentives are completely aligned among the providers, measures of quality relate primarily to outcome and adherence to clinical pathways. In less-integrated systems, where there is still conflict between payers and providers, measures of quality will differ.

The physician wants the purchaser of health care to consider quality carefully because the physician will be judged on the quality standard. If quality is equated with price, there will be an inevitable diminution of service provided to the patient. If quality is defined as an objective measure of outcome, the physician will have to ask how that is determined and what systems are in place to track it.

Nothing intrinsic to managed care prevents the quality of medical care from being as satisfactory to the patient and payer as it is to the physician. The critical feature for both payer and physician is the alignment of goals and incentives to improve quality continually. For physicians, who to a great extent determine the expenditure of resources, the latitude with which they are allowed to deal with their patients becomes a measure of quality.

Decisions Regarding Allocations of Physician Time. The commodity that is most vaunted by the MCO is the contact between the physician and the patient. A physician judging an HMO will therefore be concerned about the allocation of his or her time and the amount of that time allowed for face-to-face contact with the patient. It is not uncommon for MCOs scheduling patients for a physician to determine the time allowed with the patient without considering the patients' needs.

Allocation of physician time is a crucial issue. When incentives are aligned among payers, hospitals, and physicians, the allocation of physician time becomes less a control issue than a quality issue. There is a theoretical relationship between cost of medical care and quality that implies that only so much can be shaved from the price of medical care. This has not been shown to be empirically true, largely because of a lack of accurate and reproducible measures of medical quality. Nonetheless, when evaluating an MCO, the purchaser should ascertain that the physicians' and payers' incentives are aligned or are approaching alignment.

Required Panel Sizes. Panel size is important both in staff-model HMOs and the less-structured IPA model. Where physicians are capitated for primary care, income is determined by panel size. Thus, the physician's motivation is to accept the largest possible panel. In a staff-model HMO, or one in which the physician receives a straight salary, the motivation is to minimize panel size to allow the greatest amount of discretionary time per patient. Compression of the time required to perform a task adequately produces stress and anxiety in both the patient and the physician. Physicians feel this is inimical to the therapeutic relationship.

Physicians' Problems in Managed Care Practice. Much ink has been expended on discussions of the "hassle factor" in the practice of medicine. Although this complaint has taken on the aspect of whining, its importance to the quality of an MCO cannot be overstated. One reason physicians seek managed care opportunities is to be relieved of the administrative and paperwork burden of practice. Thus, if the MCO substitutes one hassle for another, the net result is zero for the physician. Managed care concerns in a competitive market must focus on operating and profit margins. Some MCOs have therefore instituted tight administrative controls on their doctors, requiring external approval for virtually all activities that may affect the capitated dollar. This compromise of autonomy and discretion is displeasing to a person whose training has focused on individual responsibility and accountability. QA focuses on neither. A physician evaluating the quality of a managed care contract will therefore carefully examine the degree of external control imposed by management. Overemphasis on external controls implies that the administration of the MCO does not trust its physicians to practice in the best interest of the patient and feels they must be reined in. Similarly, a poorly designed and poorly implemented set of quality guidelines does not inspire in the contracting physician the sense that the MCO is committed to high-quality, cost-effective care.

Quality of the Staff. Because of the broad variety of products offered, a physician evaluating a managed care product will be interested in the number and quality of his or her clinical colleagues as well as the facilities in which he or she is to care for the contracted patient. Just as physicians are not truly fungible, hospitals, ambulatory surgery centers, and imaging centers are not either. Therefore, a physician embarking on a managed care contract will carefully evaluate where the patients are to be hospitalized as well as the clinical colleagues with whom he or she will exchange referrals. Consider the situation, in the crudest sense, of a primary care physician who is capitated for specialty care. He or she may have a financial incentive not to refer patients. If all the primary care physicians are and each specialty care physician is separately contracted, however, the physician does have a financial incentive to refer. Perverse incentives can be built into any MCO, and prudent physicians will carefully judge the quality of their colleagues.

Incentive Structure. Consider an MCO that capitates a cardiologist caring for a patient with coronary artery disease. Consider further that the managed care provider has the cardiologist share risk with the cardiovascular surgeon so that the cardiologist receives less payment for his or her services if the patient requires surgery. It takes a committed physician to refer questionable cases for a surgical opinion. Although this form of contract may well reduce the amount of cardiovascular surgery performed, the incentive to do so is not necessarily congruent with the best medicine for the patient. Such incentives can interfere with good medical judgment and result in increased liability for the physician. Physicians evaluating a managed care program will want to see that the incentive structure is fair and rewards the cost-conscious, good practice of medicine.

Physicians' Financial Interests. An adversarial relationship between the physician and the payer is bound to be reflected in the clinical care given to the patient. It can manifest itself in subtle ways—as delays in appointments for certain providers, for example—and more overtly, as outright hostility toward the payer in the examination room. Either of these, or any of a host of problems that the physician may have with the payer, can be devastating for the therapeutic relationship as well as damaging to the managed care provider at reenrollment time. Disenrollment is a symptom of the failure of the triangular relationship between physician, patient, and payer. Although disenrollment does not solely depend on that triangle, it is the only part of overall patient satisfaction under the control of the individual physician. In assessing the MCO, a physician will want to know the depth of the staff assigned to provider relations. Further, the physician is likely to want easy access to that person and to be assured that provider issues will be handled carefully and thoughtfully. The techniques employed by the managed care provider for dispute resolution are likely to be scrutinized as well. Physicians are not schooled in adversarial politics and are likely to think highly of an organization that negotiates rather than mandates. Physicians want provider relations staff to be more like associates in the medical process than adjudicators of a complaint department.

Organization's Medical Director. The importance of the medical director cannot be overemphasized. This person has the difficult task of mediating between the MCO and the physicians providing the clinical service. In an open-model product, the medical director must see that the interests of the patient, the company, and the provider are satisfied. Physician providers will view the medical director as their advocate. Open communication between the medical director and the providers is a requirement for patient satisfaction.

Q 10:38 How does a medical director's role affect quality and utilization management?

Quality and utilization management have many components and are critically important to a care delivery system for both the patient and the physician. The medical director uses the following issues in assessing quality and utilization:

- Cost effectiveness
- Appropriate utilization in the appropriate setting
- Service
- Patient or member satisfaction
- Outcomes for the individual
- Outcomes for a population of members under the care of the group
- Safety
- Limited variation

Q 10:39 What are the key components of a quality and utilization management program subject to medical director oversight?

The fundamental principle for a good quality and utilization management program is accountability, which includes the preparation and dissemination of a written description of the program that is reviewed annually and updated as necessary. During this updating, it is important that the quality work plan consider projects for the future, track and account for past projects, and provide a global evaluation of the quality and utilization management program. This should be fully documented in the quality committee meeting minutes.

Another important feature of a quality and utilization management program is coordination, which requires documentation of support from the leadership of the group or the MCO in the form of board or executive council minutes and a charge to the quality committee. Leadership must also review and comment on a periodic report of quality in the organization and provide top-level oversight of the quality and utilization management program. It is also important that quality and utilization management activities do not occur in a vacuum but rather permeate the entire organization.

Q 10:40   Does physician compensation affect quality of care?

Maybe. There is a saying in the retail industry: You get what you pay for. No one wants to admit that this could apply in the health care service setting, although many fear that it does. Federal regulators have attempted to protect Medicare recipients from incentive arrangements that increase compensation in return for "rationing" health care services; however, the reality is that economic pressures will affect availability.

The debate should focus on cost and quality rather than on compensation alone. The cost-quality conundrum has been addressed in numerous articles on managed care. David M. Eddy has identified several characteristics of managed care that affect the cost-quality conundrum:[27]

1. The MCO is responsible for the health of a defined population (e.g., all people who have paid).
2. For this defined population, the MCO is responsible for the entire spectrum of care, ranging from primary prevention to screening, diagnosis, treatment, rehabilitation, and support care.
3. Since the MCO's responsibility extends beyond providing care when the patient seeks it, the MCO must initiate contact with the patient.
4. MCOs impose clinical management systems on physicians.
5. The MCO can engage in centralized decision making.
6. The point of intersection between quality and cost is usually at the level of the medical director, who must improve quality while reducing cost.

Q 10:41   Do ethics ever play a role when making trade-offs between cost and quality in health care?

They should not. Ethical principles focus on concepts of fairness, equality, and optimality. According to David M. Eddy,[28] fairness means that if people contribute equally to a pool of resources from which the costs of treatment will be paid, they should expect to be treated equally in terms of the treatments they will receive." Equality means that if identical patients seek treatment for the same health problem, they should receive the same treatment. Optimality means that treatments should be chosen with the best health outcomes in mind, within the resources available and subject to applicable constraints. All medical practice should be subject to the principle of fairness. An ethical dilemma can arise when a person or entity with its own motives, such as a physician, an insurance company, or an MCO, has control over the patient's treatment and, ultimately, outcome.

Q 10:42 Is it possible to link quality and outcomes to physician compensation?

Probably not. Linking physician compensation arrangements to quality of care would provide a clear cause-and-effect relationship, but creating such a link is difficult. Part of the difficulty stems from the problem of defining quality. In the context of compensation arrangements, Eugene Ogrod notes that quality can take many forms:[29]

1. *Technical quality* looks at the intellectual or mechanical skill required to obtain certain results from medical or surgical intervention.
2. *Outcomes quality* looks at the ultimate impact on the patient.
3. *Process quality* looks at the steps in a treatment approach using a short-term approach.
4. *Service quality* looks at patient satisfaction measures such as convenience, politeness, attentiveness, and educational information.
5. *Physician standards* refer to minimum levels of training or skill such as that used in the credentialing process.

If quality is to be linked to compensation, which of the foregoing definitions of quality should be used? Is any one definition more important than another? Can any one of these types of quality be measured accurately?

Q 10:43 How do physicians get paid?

How physicians get paid varies according to the relationship the physician has with the health plan, the type of product involved, how the physician practices (e.g., IPA, group practice, or solo practice), along with many other factors. Most payments for health care services are made on a fee-for-service, capitated, salaried, or global capitation basis. Many of the regulations affecting managed care focus on physician compensation and incentives.

Fee-for-service arrangements may include full or discounted charges. The codes for services that define physician work under a fee-for-service system delineate the episodes of care. Some MCOs have implemented resource-based relative value scale (RBRVS) approaches to elevate fee-for-service reimbursement to a higher level because RBRVS approaches define care in terms of total physician work effort rather than in terms of incremental services.

Capitation is a budget-based system of payment. A certain amount of money is set aside, and the physicians work within that budget. Health care demand will vary, based on factors such as the age and sex of the patient population, and these factors must be considered when structuring capitation-based payments. Unfortunately, this adjustment often does not account for variability in frequency or severity of a patient's illness.

Salary arrangements are the least likely to provide strong incentives for physicians, and most studies show that production decreases when physicians are placed on a straight salary. Most salary systems include production and performance standards, hours to be worked, and availability to patients. Often these are linked in some way to patient satisfaction.

Global capitation has been shown to be one of the most successful compensation models because it puts the physician organization (IPA or medical group practice) at risk for the delivery of services to patients across a broad geographic area.

Quality form the Patient's Perspective

Q 10:44   Why is it difficult for consumers to measure quality in managed care services?

As inscrutable as quality is to a physician, it is more so to the patient. Under fee-for-service systems, patients had a virtually infinite menu of choices regarding medical care. Particularly in urban areas, available medical care may have ranged from low-cost community clinics to high-priced penthouse specialists. Managed care, regardless of its protestations, must limit choice. Without some limitations on choice, it is not managed at all. In the fee-for-service days, the patient was the physician's only customer, and thus the physician's entire efforts could be directed at satisfying that customer. This was accomplished first and foremost by providing high-quality care. Amenities were secondary and served to differentiate the high-quality (and high-cost) providers. Hospitals followed suit, competing to supply the largest and most diverse amenities. These maneuvers were reflected in market share, and thus the health care providers—physicians and institutions alike—pursued them. Patients equated external appearances with quality. For example, some of the finest hospitals in the country are the public teaching hospitals, yet if given a choice, many patients would steer clear of these institutions, not because of quality but because of the lack of amenities.

The AHRQ is a good source for patients who need a scoresheet to evaluate physicians and networks (http://ahrq.gov/consumer/index.html#plans).

Q 10:45 Are there any substitutes for board certification as an indicator of minimum competence?

Not any longer. The American Medical Association (AMA) had developed a program for accrediting physicians independent of their board certification. This was in recognition of the large number of practicing physicians who, for a variety of reasons, are not board certified and are thus vulnerable to exclusion from managed care contracting. The program, called the American Medical Accreditation Program (AMAP), provided a mechanism for uniform credentials verification, including primary source verification. Additional factors included in the following:

- Graduation from an accredited medical school
- Active license to practice medicine
- Unrestricted DEA certificate to prescribe narcotics
- Absence of disciplinary actions

Other standards were assigned a point value and contributed to the overall AMAP:

- Completion of an approved residency program
- Certification or recertification by an American Board of Medical Specialties member
- Minimal or no malpractice litigation experience
- No record of adverse experience with the National Practitioner Data Bank (NPDB)
- Membership in a medical association that subscribes to the AMA's principles of medical ethics
- Completion of continuing medical education courses
- Participation in clinical continuous improvement processes
- Office site review

Although these measures were sound philosophically, they were deemed by the AMA to be fiscally "not viable," and the AMAP was discontinued in 2000.

Q 10:46   What credentials should physicians have?

The first credentialing process for a physician occurs at the entrance to medical school. Most entering students have a bachelor's degree (although many schools do not require one). After graduation, almost all physicians enter a residency. This residency may train them for careers as generalists in family medicine, general pediatrics, or general internal medicine. After training, they take comprehensive board examinations, which cover all material from medical school through their specialty training.

A board examination is not a license to practice medicine. Licensure is granted by the state after fulfillment of that state's individual requirement. All states require some form of standardized licensure examination that covers all medical school subjects. States also perform a thorough credential check and personal interview. Some states have further requirements such as a jurisprudence examination. State licensure can be conferred without specialty boards, and this distinction must always be kept in mind. A licensed physician is not necessarily board certified.

Q 10:47   How are specialists trained and certified?

Physicians may specialize in areas not covered by the primary boards, for example, orthopedics, ophthalmology, or radiology. If a physician has completed a residency and passed the boards in a primary care discipline, he or she may further subspecialize in disciplines such as cardiology or geriatrics. Family medicine has no subspecialties; however, those with family practice boards are able to obtain certificates of added competence in areas such as geriatrics. The primary disciplines now require recertification after ten years. Voluntary recertification is available for physicians trained before introduction of the compulsory recertification requirement.

The board examinations generally accepted are endorsed by the American Board of Medical Specialties. Because of the cachet of board certification, many proprietary organizations are offering "board" examinations at the end of a required didactic course of study. These examinations are not endorsed by the American Board of Medical Specialties and thus are not regulated.

The issue of board certification has become more important as MCOs look for "gold standards" to credential their physicians. Using board certification in this way is problematic: because many senior physicians trained at a time when board certification was less important, they either did not sit for the examination or failed it once and never retook it. They may have been practicing successfully for many years but lack this critical credential. In addition, some physicians taking the board examination later in their careers may be hampered by the large amount of basic science on the examination. And physicians who took and passed the board examination in most primary disciplines (excluding family medicine, which has required recertification for years) before 1990 are not required to get recertified.

Q 10:48   Is there a difference in the outcome of a severe illness when the patient is cared for by a specialist versus by a generalist?

Yes. Many MCOs and health care plans require that all clinical care be either provided or overseen by a generalist. Evidence is accumulating that this may be, as many physicians have suspected, short-sighted. In fact, some MCOs have recognized that specialists may be more appropriate primary care providers than generalists. Jollis and colleagues performed a thorough analysis to answer the question of outcome in acute myocardial infarction when the patient was cared for by a primary care physician versus by a cardiologist.

Cardiologists had a higher rate of using invasive and sophisticated procedures and their patients did significantly better. Cardiologist-treated patients had a 12 percent decrease in likelihood of death in the first year following the event than did patients cared for by primary care physicians. The patients were well matched for severity of illness.[30] These data agree with previous studies that showed that the knowledge of sophisticated cardiologic procedures differed among family physicians, internists, and cardiologists.

The managed care implications of these findings are substantial:

1. MCOs must evaluate the appropriateness of the physician who is primarily in charge of the patient. In many chronic and stable conditions, particularly those with multiple organ involvement such as diabetes or cerebrovascular disease, an internist may be the logical choice with judicious consultation. This approach is no different from "old-fashioned" care.

2. When a patient managed by a primary care physician has an acute change in condition, timely "hand-off" to the specialist may be in order.

3. MCOs have to acknowledge the conflict in turning management of a patient over to a physician with full knowledge that the physician is likely to engage in more costly and resource-intensive interventions.

Q 10:49   How important are physicians' hospital affiliations?

Hospital affiliation is important. Another way patients can ascertain quality is through the physician's hospital affiliation. At the time of application to medical staff membership, accredited hospitals are required to determine their physicians' credentials. This process includes verifying primary data such as medical school graduation and board status and querying the NPDB. This database contains medical staff, licensure, and malpractice information on all medical practitioners in the country. It is not accessible to the general public, but is accessible to health care institutions. Failure to have any hospital affiliations may mean only that a physician does not care to do inpatient medicine.

Q 10:50   Is a physician's general reputation in the community a significant measure of quality?

No. A number of measures of medical practitioner quality have nothing to do with the physician's abilities. The most common of these, of course, is word of mouth. Although patient satisfaction is a reasonable measure of office efficiency or even the physician's personality, it is not objective or reproducible. Other such measures include AMA or county medical society membership. AMA membership requires only a medical degree and payment of dues; county medical society membership is rarely denied. Even less reliable measures of quality are listings in any number of "best doctor" books. Reputations required to gain selection by supermarket magazines as "best doctors" often have little to do with the practice of medicine.

Quality from the Purchaser's Perspective

Q 10:51 How do managed care plans monitor health care provider practices for quality?

Managed care plans use a variety of methods, including consumer surveys and outcomes studies, to monitor care and influence physician practice behavior. According to a survey of managed care plans conducted by Mathematica Policy Research (MPR) and the Medical College of Virginia (MCV) in 1994 on behalf of the Physician Payment Review Commission (PPRC), a number of methods are used in the private sector to affect health care delivery. Common methods used to monitor or influence care in managed care plans include UR, recredentialing of providers, written quality assurance plans, outcomes studies for particular conditions, targeted quality improvement initiatives, consumer surveys, profiles of practice patterns, and formal written practice guidelines. Of these methods, UR is the most widely used; practice guidelines and profiles of practice patterns are used least often. For a more detailed discussion of practice guidelines and UR, see chapter 9.

Q 10:52 What are the common features of most quality assurance programs in MCOs?

The common features of most QA programs in MCOs are as follows:

Monitoring Physician Practice. Most MCOs use a variety of means to monitor and influence physician practice behavior. HMOs use such techniques far more than PPOs, except for UR, which is done in almost all plans.

Oversight and Integrity. Many MCOs use the NCQA standards for governance of QA programs, provider credentialing, and member rights as internal standards. It appears that most MCOs, regardless of type, had similar features related to oversight of QA. These oversight features include individual accountability of a designated executive in the organization, existence of an oversight committee for quality management, and specified accountability and responsibilities of that oversight committee.[31]

Credentialing. Another feature of a QA program is the extent of its credentialing process and criteria such as licensure, board certification, and clinical training and current competence. Most MCOs have a credentialing process that involves at least an individual executive but may also include a separate internal or external committee process.

Member Rights and Grievance Procedures. Grievance procedures and other member rights provide important guarantees of consumer protection. Most HMOs include such rights and procedures, but PPOs have fewer safeguards. The methods used by MCOs to protect member rights and allow for a grievance process include specific policies and procedures addressing member rights and a formal system for addressing grievances.

Health Plan Employer Data and Information Set

Q 10:53   What is the Health Plan Employer Data and Information Set?

HEDIS is a set of standardized performance measures designed to ensure that purchasers and consumers have the information they need to compare the performance of managed health care plans reliably. It is sponsored, supported, and maintained by NCQA and includes multiple indicators of quality of care that are rate-based, population-specific measures of care. HEDIS measures are frequently evaluated and revised. The latest version, HEDIS 3.0, is designed for both commercial and public sector health plans. In 1999, NCQA reported that approximately 400 MCOs used its standards.

Q 10:54   How effective is the HEDIS performance report in evaluating health plan performance?

It is one effective measure. HEDIS 3.0, issued in early 1997 by NCQA, is recognized as the state of the art in health plan performance measures. The HEDIS measures address effectiveness of care (quality), access, member satisfaction, plan stability, service use, costs of care, outreach or member information services, and plan characteristics.[32] The major obstacle to comparing health plans, however, is ensuring that the data sets are of similar quality based on completeness and accuracy. To the extent health plans "self-report" without independent audit, their performance reports may be of limited value. Few health plans are able to generate the data needed to evaluate their performance using all the measures.

NCQA has tied accreditation to scores on HEDIS, putting pressure on health plans to participate in HEDIS. In its Accreditation 99 program, effective July 1999, HEDIS performance accounts for 25 percent of NCQA accreditation scores. These standards tie performance on clinical, satisfaction, and access measures to accreditation and include new consumer protections and performance measures.[33]

Consumer Protections. These provisions of HEDIS recognize the relative powerlessness of managed care patients to direct their own care:

1. Plans are prohibited from using financial incentives to encourage managers to limit or deny care.
2. Plans are required to have a process for approving exceptions to restricted drug formularies.
3. Patient rights include evaluation of whether plans unduly limit access to emergency department care.
4. Plans are required to coordinate medical and behavioral health care.

Performance Measures. These measures assess a plan's performance based on a broad range of quality indicators, such as immunization rates, education of smokers, prenatal care, and eye examinations for diabetics. They count for 25 percent of the accreditation score, are compared against national and regional averages and national benchmarks (or best performers), and must be audited according to the standards of NCQA's HEDIS compliance audit program.

Q 10:55 What are the attributes that characterize HEDIS 3.0 and that NCQA feels should characterize future versions of HEDIS?

Relevance. To be considered for inclusion in HEDIS 3.0, measures had to be relevant to purchasers and/or consumers to the extent that they addressed issues that were known to affect health outcomes significantly, to the extent that those issues were controllable (or at least could be influenced significantly) by the health plan, and to the extent that there was evidence that purchasers and consumers would use that information in selecting a health plan.

Scientific Soundness. Measures had to be scientifically sound for the development committee to have confidence that the information produced through measurement would lead to better decisions. The committee sought measures that were reproducible (produced the same results when repeated in the same populations and setting), valid (made sense logically and related to other measures looking at the same aspect of care), and accurate (measured what is actually happening). Measures also had to have sufficient statistical power to detect differences of the magnitude expected between health plans and had to include a strategy to adjust results for other factors (such as characteristics of the health plan population) that might lead to measured differences in health plan results.

Feasibility. The committee was interested in producing a measurement set that was useful in 1996. Although it was unwilling to be tightly bound by the limitations of current information systems—an explicit objective of the committee was to use HEDIS measures to stimulate improvements in information systems—it was also clear that potential HEDIS measures that were easy to produce would be of most value in the short run. To be feasible, a measure needed to be precisely defined in order to collect data in the same way; it had to be possible to produce the measure at a reasonable cost; and the collection of data for the measurement could not threaten the confidentiality of any patient information.[34]

Benchmarking

Q 10:56   What is benchmarking?

Benchmarking is a process by which each institution seeks to develop a means of measuring quality improvement and performance. Benchmarking involves the sharing of performance information to identify the clinical and operational practices that lead to the best outcomes. Health care organizations are often familiar with benchmarking as they work toward total quality improvement through a continuous quality improvement process.

Q 10:57   What are the types of benchmarking?

There are two types of benchmarking: internal benchmarking and external benchmarking. Internal benchmarking identifies internal functions to serve as pilot sites in new program development. External benchmarking compares a plan's performance against its toughest competitor.[35]

Q 10:58   What are the benefits of benchmarking?

Benchmarking offers a positive alternative to the more onerous performance measures used by MCOs such as economic credentialing or "report carding," which have more negative connotations. Those performance measures focus on the impact of money on the quality of care with the presumption that there is a correlation. The focus of benchmarking is on independent measures of cost and quality, with a specific drive toward excellence.

Benchmarking creates value in health care by focusing the organization and individuals on key performance gaps; bringing in ideas from external organizations and identifying opportunities; rallying the organization around the findings to create a consensus to move forward; and implementing ideas into operations to yield better-quality products and services.

The needs for improvement are defined by the customer. In health care, the customer may be the patient, the physician, or the payer.

Q 10:59   How can benchmarking be used to assess the need for physicians?

There has been extensive discussion of the national need for physicians since pioneering work in the early 1990s suggested a dramatic oversupply of physicians nationwide. Most planning for physician distribution is based on an estimation of needs or a projection of current demand. Goodman and others reviewed these methodologies and made a compelling argument for the use of benchmarking to assess the need for physicians.[36]

A needs-based model looks at the prevalence of illnesses and health conditions in a population and estimates the need for physicians based on these findings. A demand-based model looks at the requirements for physician services in certain environments and makes projections based on these demands. Goodman's approach of benchmarking identifies regions or health plans that are currently operating and compares them with other operating regions or systems. The goal is to examine the density of physicians in relation to clinical outcome.

Benchmarking is useful as a standardization tool using working situations in the real world. By this measure, there is an oversupply of both generalists and specialists nationwide.

Q 10:60   What are the legal and ethical issues associated with benchmarking?

Benchmarking is a new process that has not yet been fully evaluated under current legal principles. The major areas of legal concern are the confidentiality and proprietary protection of the shared information, antitrust issues that may be involved in the sharing of information among competitors, and the contractual commitments associated with a participation agreement by a health care entity in a benchmarking study.

Clinical Practice Guidelines

Q 10:61   What has been the experience with clinical guidelines as quality enhancement tools in clinical practice?

A well-studied example of the use of guidelines in clinical practice is the case of unstable angina. The standard of care has been to admit to a hospital all patients suspected of having unstable coronary disease because of the high risk of myocardial infarction (heart attack) and the possibility of life-threatening cardiac rhythm disturbance. This has, of course, led to the admission of a number of people who had cardiac symptoms from causes other than unstable angina, and some of these people have been subjected to cardiac catheterization and other extensive testing. This practice has always been consistent with good, conservative clinical practice; however, because of the expense and stress to patients and families associated with admitting all cases of unstable angina, the practice has come under intensive review. The Agency for Health Care Policy and Research (AHCPR), now the AHRQ, issued new and controversial guidelines for the management of unstable angina that include outpatient management for patients considered to be a "low risk."[37]

A study of the clinical applicability of these guidelines for unstable angina and their potential impact on hospital admissions found that the guidelines might have some unintended consequences in actual practice.[38] The guidelines were intended to reduce unnecessary hospitalizations by identifying a low-risk group that could safely be discharged to home. The empiric study found that patients who meet the guidelines' criteria for low risk are a very small proportion of the patients seen in an emergency department (only 6 percent). The small size of this group among emergency patients suggests that little reduction in hospitalization and, thus, cost can be expected from the guidelines. When the study's authors examined the guidelines' criteria and recommendations for high-risk patients, they found that strict application of the guidelines would place more patients in intensive care than would current practice. Therefore, the guidelines' actual impact on cost may be to increase the most expensive admissions while doing little to reduce overall cost, because there are so few patients that meet the low-risk criteria.

The study has limitations, but it does emphasize that clinical guidelines, even those generated by an expert panel after a thorough and competent review of the literature, require empiric validation and may be very population-specific.

Credentialing and Peer Review as Quality Management

Q 10:62   How can an integrated delivery system minimize its legal risk in provider selection and exclusion?

An integrated delivery system can choose a number of ways to minimize its liability exposure in the selection and deselection of providers.

Sufficient Integration. To the extent the entity is sufficiently integrated, it is less likely to incur antitrust liability for its decisions related to provider selection or deselection. Criteria used to measure integration include whether the entity is a joint venture that (1) pools capital, (2) shares risk of loss, (3) employs UR protocols, (4) engages in joint marketing, claims administration, and collection, and (5) competes for business with similar entities.

Objective Membership Criteria. The use of objective criteria established by someone other than the competitors to whom the criteria will be applied should reduce the risk of antitrust liability related to admission to and termination from the organization if the criteria are applied objectively and consistently.

Inclusion of Allied Health Professionals. Membership criteria should not arbitrarily exclude any class of practitioner.

Existing Business Plan. There should be a business plan addressing the specific levels of provider participation, based on geographic and specialty diversity. It may be preferable to use an objective third party to establish these levels.

Use of an Application and Quality Assurance Process. There should be a thorough and fair application process and QA process that adheres to the principles of "substantive" due process such as limitation of direct competitors in the review or selection process, and use of objectively determined criteria such as practice guidelines or parameters.

Limit Role of Competitors. Where competitors are insulated from making the business, selection, credentialing, and other decisions affecting other competitors, liability exposure should be limited.

Q 10:63 What is delegated credentialing, and how does it arise in managed care arrangements?

Many MCOs, such as PPOs, HMOs, and exclusive provider organizations, and other health service purchasers (employers and third-party administrators) have established criteria based on the particular requirements of the health benefit plan. They can either perform their own credentialing at the plan administration level or delegate the credentialing process to the MCO provider. In organizations such as physician-hospital organizations PHOs or IPAs, it is possible contractually to delegate the credentialing documentation and data gathering to the hospital medical staff office, upon proper authorization, to avoid duplication of effort. If an MCO decides to delegate its credentialing responsibility, it should consider a contract under which

1. It retains the right to approve new providers or sites and to terminate or suspend providers;
2. Indemnification from the credentialing entity is required for losses attributable to negligent credentialing;
3. The credentialing entity must carry adequate errors and omissions insurance coverage; and
4. The MCO must be named as an additional insured.

Q 10:64 Should MCOs do their own credentialing?

Yes. Most MCOs are moving toward performing their own credentialing. Many, however, delegate credentialing responsibility to a medical group or IPA, or even to a hospital. NCQA standards require a written description of the delegated activities and the delegatee's accountability for these activities.

Q 10:65 What is the Health Care Quality Improvement Act, and how does it relate to quality of care in managed care arrangements?

The Health Care Quality Improvement Act (HCQIA) provides limited antitrust immunity to health care entities under defined circumstances for their peer review activities. HCQIA defines health care entities subject to limited immunity protection to include hospitals, medical group practices, and HMOs. [42 USC § 11151(4)(A)]

Q 10:66 What is the relevance of HCQIA to selection and deselection of providers in an integrated delivery system?

In organizing an integrated delivery system or MCO, the organizers should determine whether the benefits of HCQIA protection, including antitrust immunity and access to the NPDB, outweigh its drawbacks, which include mandatory reporting to the NPDB of adverse credentialing decisions based on clinical competence or conduct and compliance with the requirements of the statutorily defined due process. Due process, at a minimum, means that the entity must offer the affected provider notice of the reasons for the adverse action and an opportunity to respond or rebut those reasons. There is a debate among attorneys and other interested parties as to whether an integrated delivery system should afford due process to providers that are either not selected or that are deselected from participation in the system and whether HCQIA even applies to entities such as integrated delivery systems.

Q 10:67   What is the National Practitioner Data Bank?

The NPDB is a federally overseen database that maintains records on physicians, dentists, and other health care practitioners. It is maintained by the Department of Health and Human Services (DHHS). It receives information from licensing authorities, insurance companies, and health care entities that perform peer review.

Q 10:68   What has been the experience with the reports received by the NPDB?

By December 31, 2000, the end of its 124th month of operation, the NPDB contained reports on 264,065 reportable actions, malpractice payments, and Medicare and/or Medicaid exclusions involving 164,320 individual practitioners. Of the 164,320 practitioners reported to the NPDB, 69.7 percent were physicians (including M.D. and D.O. residents and interns), 14.1 percent were dentists (including dental residents), 6.2 percent were nurses and nursing-related practitioners, and 10 percent were other health care practitioners.

About two thirds (65.4 percent) of physicians on whom reports had been made had only one report in the NPDB, 85 percent had two or fewer reports, 97.4 percent had five or fewer, and 99.6 percent had ten or fewer. Notably, few physicians had both medical malpractice payment reports and reportable action reports in the NPDB. Only 6.2 percent had at least one report of both types in the NPDB.

Approximately 53 percent of all reports received during 2000 concerned malpractice payments, although cumulatively reports concerning malpractice payments constituted 72.7 percent of all reports. The lower percentage of malpractice payment reports for 2000 reflects a large number of Medicare and/or Medicaid exclusion reports received during 2000 in conjunction with the opening of the Health Care Integrity and Protection Data Bank (HIPDB). These reports were also placed in the NPDB. During 2000, physicians were responsible for 80.3 percent of all malpractice payment reports; dentists were responsible for 12.2 percent; and all other health care practitioners were responsible for the remaining 7.5 percent. These figures are similar to the percentages from previous years.[39]

Q 10:69   What type of information is maintained by the NPDB?

If a medical malpractice lawsuit results in the payment of money on behalf of the practitioner, a report must be made to the NPDB. This is true even if the lawsuit is settled and no admission of guilt is made. Licensing boards are required to report actions on a practitioner's license. Health care entities are required to report actions on the credentials or privileging of practitioners to the appropriate licensing board. The board then notifies the NPDB. Even if a practitioner surrenders his or her license or voluntarily restricts activities in a health care entity, timely report must be made.

Q 10:70   Who must report to the NPDB?

A health care provider must report to the State Board of Medical Examiners any "professional review action" that adversely affects the clinical privileges of a physician for a period longer than 30 days. [42 USC § 11133] A health care provider must report any voluntary surrender of clinical privileges by a physician while the physician is under investigation for incompetence or improper professional conduct, or if the physician agrees to surrender privileges in order to avoid undergoing an investigation. Failure to report results in loss of the qualified immunity available under HCQIA.

Entities that routinely report to the NPDB include those that make medical malpractice payments on behalf of health care practitioners (extends to nonphysician practitioners), state licensing boards, health care entities that take adverse action as a result of professional review, and professional societies that take adverse action as a result of professional review.

Q 10:71   What are the consequences of not reporting to the NPDB?

In addition to the loss of qualified immunity under HCQIA for taking the adverse action, an organization required to report that fails to report may be liable for civil monetary damages or lose its

Medicare certification altogether. As a result of the Balanced Budget Act of 1997, civil monetary penalties may be assessed against a person or entity that fails to report medical malpractice payments, or improperly discloses, uses, or permits access to information reported to the NPDB. [42 USC § 1003.102(b)(5),(6)]

Q 10:72 Who can request NPDB information?

The following can request NPDB information:

1. Hospitals can request NPDB information on practitioners on their staffs.

2. Practitioners can request their own NPDB profile.

3. Licensing entities can request information.

4. Health care entities processing applications for employment from practitioners or evaluating applications for privileges can request information.

5. In medical malpractice suits, plaintiffs or plaintiffs' attorneys can request NPDB information if a hospital is also to be named in the suit and the hospital did not request NPDB information in credentialing the practitioner.

6. As part of a peer review process, health care entities may request NPDB profiles.

7. State medical and dental boards may query at any time.

8. Others can request statistical data from the NPDB, but the information divulged will not be identified as to individual practitioners.

Q 10:73 Can a practitioner dispute an NPDB report?

A practitioner who disagrees with an NPDB report can dispute either the factual accuracy of the information or whether the report was submitted in accordance with proper reporting requirements. This process is not an avenue to protest or challenge the reporting entity's underlying action, which could have been challenged earlier. If the practitioner believes that the report is inaccurate, he or she must first attempt to resolve the disagreement directly with the reporting entity. If the practitioner notifies the NPDB of the dispute, historical queries and future queries will be notified of the dispute. The reporting entity may correct the report, void the report, or decline to change the report. As to the third outcome, the practitioner may request the Secretary of DHHS to review the dispute. The review will be limited to factual information. The Secretary will not initiate review until after 30 days from the date the practitioner initiated discussions with the reporting entity.

Courts have recognized that filing an improper or inaccurate report can invite liability; however, there is immunity under HCQIA for any report made to the NPDB if the report is made without knowledge of the falsity or inaccuracy. [42 USC § 11137(c)]

Q 10:74 Does the denial of an application for participation in managed care trigger a reporting requirement to the NPDB?

If the basis of the denial is not associated with quality of care concerns, but is based on the applicant's failure to meet the criteria or on the existence of excess capacity for that medical specialty in the panel, the denial need not be reported. In fact, the definition of health care entity used in HCQIA for regulation under HCQIA does not extend to provider organizations such as physician-hospital organizations or IPAs. The intent of the reporting requirement in HCQIA is to identify physicians with potential quality of care problems. [42 USC § 11101 et seq]

Q 10:75 What is the Health Care Integrity and Protection Data Bank?

The HIPDB was created under the Health Insurance Portability and Accountability Act of 1996 (HIPAA) to require the reporting of certain final adverse actions against health care providers, suppliers, or practitioners by federal and state agencies, health plans, and health care entities affiliated or associated with health plans. The HIPDB is being developed by the same people who developed the NPDB, and its procedures track those for the NPDB.

Licensing and Certification

Q 10:76 What role do licensing and certification play in assuring quality?

Licensing is the mandatory government process of being granted a right to practice as an individual or operate as an institution. Practicing or operating without a license is technically illegal.

The historical bases of licensing came from Europe during the Middle Ages when an apprenticeship was required before one could be considered a skilled craftsman who was eligible to enter a guild. In Germany, this process was formalized for medical practice. In the United States, the use of licensing in medicine reappeared in the 1870s and 1880s, although with minimal requirements. State power to license evolved as a result of the Tenth Amendment to the U.S. Constitution, which grants states the power to regulate matters affecting the health and safety of their citizens.[40] Eventually, licensing laws were strengthened to require both a diploma from a reputable school and state examination.

Facility licensing is a more recent phenomenon. Most facility licensure laws in the United States were enacted after passage of the Hill-Burton Act of 1946. [Pub L No 79-725, 60 Stat 958 (1946), codified at 42 USC §§ 291-291n] This law, which primarily related to funding of construction of health care facilities, represented the first time the federal government addressed the regulation and improvement of hospital facilities.

Q 10:77 What are the distinctions between licensing, certification, and accreditation?

Although these three terms are often used together to describe the multilevel process of approval of health care providers and facilities, they are very different.

In the United States, licensure operates on a state-by-state basis. Licensed practitioners generally include physicians (M.D. and D.O.), optometrists, nurses and nurse practitioners, and other categories of practitioners. The scope of licensure as a means of regulating the health care industry is constantly expanding with the entry of complementary or alternative care practitioners. Licensed health care facilities generally include hospitals, ambulatory surgery centers, nursing homes, free-standing clinics and emergency centers, pharmacies, and sometimes diagnostic facilities.

Certification is the process for professionals and organizations to meet the qualifications for participation under certain government funding programs, such as Medicare and Medicaid. Although certification is voluntary, Medicare and/or Medicaid certification is critical to the economic survival of most health care practitioners and facilities because Medicare and Medicaid represent a significant proportion of the payment resources for health care services.

Accreditation is a private, voluntary approval process through which a health care organization is evaluated and can receive a designation of quality and compliance with certain accreditation standards (see Qs 10:23–10:37).

The functions of licensure, certification, and accreditation are often intertwined such that receipt of approval from one organization is deemed to represent satisfaction of the requirements of another. For example, accreditation by a recognized national accrediting organization will be "deemed" to satisfy federal conditions of participation or compliance with Medicare and/or Medicaid certification. Similarly, some states recognize Medicare and/or Medicaid certification or accreditation as sufficient to satisfy life and safety requirements for licensure. In fact, many state departments of health are delegated the responsibility for certification inspections along with responsibility for licensing a health care facility.

State and Federal Requirements

Q 10:78 What efforts have been undertaken by the federal and state governments to assure quality of health care?

State Initiatives. Most states have established regulations protecting consumers enrolled in health plans by requiring that the plans have internal QA programs. These requirements vary among the states, but they are all intended to assure plan quality and integrity. Based on a survey of state health and insurance departments conducted by the Intergovernmental Health Policy Project (IHPP) on behalf of the PPRC, most states focus on internal QA programs for HMOs. Some states regulate other types of MCOs as well. The methods of monitoring compliance vary among the states, ranging from review of written reports only, to monitoring of grievances, to onsite inspections. Fewer than one third of the states review a plan's accreditation status.

Federal Initiatives. Medicare instituted quality initiatives in 1993 when it revised its peer review organization (PRO) program. Under contract with Medicare, PROs reviewed medical records for quality and appropriateness of care. PROs have been using practice guidelines developed by the AHRQ.

In response to the national debate on assuring health care quality for consumers while managing costs, federal law enforcement agencies have increased their efforts to police delivery of health care within government programs. HIPAA expanded the types of crimes constituting "health care fraud." The Balanced Budget Act of 1997 set forth new antifraud provisions, including penalty provisions for exclusion from Medicare and Medicaid after three convictions for specific crimes. The courts have witnessed an explosion in health care lawsuits under federal fraud statutes. An important part of the national debate is how quality of care relates to fraud. Federal and state prosecutors are targeting denials of care or alleged quality problems in delivered care in their definition of fraud.

Even the Department of Labor (DOL), which oversees ERISA (Employee Retirement Income Security Act of 1974) plans, has issued an information letter in which it assessed the concept of quality in the context of the fiduciary obligations of a health plan. The DOL listed the following as factors a fiduciary should consider in assessing the quality of services: (1) the scope of choices and qualifications of medical providers and specialists available to participants; (2) ease of access to medical providers; (3) ease of access to information concerning the operations of the health care provider; (4) extent to which internal procedures provide for timely consideration and resolution of patient questions and complaints; (5) extent to which internal procedures provide for confidentiality of patient records; (6) enrollee satisfaction statistics; and (7) rating and accreditation of health care service providers by independent organizations.

Q 10:79 What is a compliance program?

Formerly the province of large industries, the term *corporate compliance* is gaining currency in health care circles, particularly those dealing with the direct delivery of health care, including organizations that employ or contract with physicians. In general, a compliance program can be defined as a comprehensive strategy to ensure that an organization consistently complies with the laws relating to its business activities.

Q 10:80 What are the elements of an effective compliance program?

An effective compliance program includes the following elements:

1. Written compliance standards are established and widely disseminated throughout the organization.

2. Top-down oversight is demonstrated. Ideally, top-down oversight is shown through decision making at the level of the governing body.

3. Those with discretionary authority are scrutinized.

4. Employees throughout the organization participate in educational programs about corporate compliance, and this is documented.

5. The organization's commitment to a compliance program is communicated and the steps involved in the program are extensive and documented.

6. Compliance is dynamic. There must be explicit programs in place to monitor compliance, audit compliance, and record the steps that have been taken in response to information uncovered.

7. Standards are investigated and enforced throughout the organization. When departures from the standards are discovered, they are corrected and measures are introduced to prevent recurrence.

8. Compliance should be demonstrated to be a criterion for promotion.

9. A hotline should be established and announced to create a rapid and anonymous route for reporting violations.

10. Measures are implemented to guard against retaliation directed toward an employee who exposes compliance violations.

11. Policies regarding record creation and retention are developed and adhered to.

Q 10:81 What are the benefits of a corporate compliance program to the organization?

An intact and vibrant corporate compliance program provides the following advantages to an organization that might be faced with an audit:

1. It demonstrates an organization's commitment to quality and excellence.
2. It sends a strong message and enhances employee awareness of conduct that is unacceptable.
3. It identifies problem areas early and promotes intervention.
4. It reduces the organization's exposure to civil and criminal liability.

Q 10:82 What is the responsibility of a compliance committee?

A compliance committee is established at the direction of the organization's governing body. It provides oversight and leadership to the compliance activity and ensures reporting and accountability to the governing body. The committee serves as an advisory body for employees who request reviews or those who make complaints. Finally, the committee is intimately involved in fashioning corrective actions when departures from compliance policies are observed or reported. A compliance officer appointed by the organization's governing body works with the compliance committee and is responsible for educating the committee and monitoring its work.

References

1. *See* http://www.hcqualitycommission.gov/final/ (last accessed Jan. 16, 2000).
2. *See* http://ahrq.org/consumer/qntascii/qntqlook.htm.
3. T.A. Brennan, L.L. Leape, N.M. Laird, et al., "Incidence of Adverse Events and Negligence in Hospitalized Patients," *New Eng. J. Med.,* 324(6):370–376, 1991.
4. D.P. Phillips, N. Christenfeld, and L.M. Glynn, "Increase in U.S. Medication-Error Deaths Between 1983 and 1993," *Lancet,* Feb. 28, 1998.

5. S. Soumerai, T. McLaughlin, E. Hertzmark, et al., "Adverse Outcomes of Underuse of Beta Blockers in Elderly Survivors of Acute Myocardial Infarction," *JAMA*, 277:115–121, 1997.

6. M.R. Chassin, "Assessing Strategies for Quality Improvement," *Health Affairs*, 16(3):151–161, May–June 1997.

7. S.J. Bernstein, E.A. McGlynn, A.L. Siu, et al., "The Appropriateness of Hysterectomy: A Comparison of Care in Seven Health Plans," *JAMA*, 269:2398–2402, 1993.

8. Institute of Medicine, *Crossing the Quality Chasm: A New Health System for the 21st Century* (Washington, D.C.: National Academy Press, 2001).

9. N. Goldfield, M. Pine, and J. Pine, *Measuring and Managing Health Care Quality* (Gaithersburg, MD: Aspen Publishers 1996) 4–6.

10. S. Sheffler, "What Do We Know About the Information That People Need or Use? Lessons from Employed Populations?" Presentation before the Henry J. Kaiser Family Foundation/ Agency for Health Care Policy and Research Conference— *Value and Choice: Providing Consumers with Information on the Quality of Health Care* (Arlington, VA, Oct. 29–30, 1996).

11. J. Meyer, L. Rybowski, R. Eichler, *Theory and Reality of Value-based Purchasing: Lessons from Pioneers.* AHCPR Publication No. 98-0004 (Nov. 1997).

12. Id.

13. T. Bodenheimer and K. Sullivan, "How Large Employers Are Shaping the Health Care Marketplace," *New Eng. J. Med.*, 338(14):1003–1007, 1998.

14. *See* http://www.eqp.org/.

15. AFL-CIO, *Union Guide to Quality Managed Care* (1997).

16. R.H. Brook, C.J. Kamberg, and E.A. McGlynn, "Health System Reform and Quality," *JAMA*, 276:476–480, 1996.

17. L.B. Russell, M.R. Gold, and J.E. Siegel, "The Role of Cost Effectiveness Analysis in Health and Medicine," *JAMA*, 276:1172–1177, 1996.

18. J.V. Tu, C.D. Naylor, D. Kumar, et al., "Coronary Artery Bypass Graft Surgery in Ontario and New York State: Which Is Right?" *Annals Internal Med.*, 126:13–19, 1997.

19. J.H. Hibbard and J.J. Jewett, "Will Quality Report Cards Help Consumers?" *Health Affairs,* 16(3):218–228, May–June 1997.

20. P.J. Kenkel, *Report Cards: What Every Health Provider Needs to Know about HEDIS and Other Performance Measures* (Gaithersburg, MD: Aspen Publishers 1995) 8.

21. M.R. Chassin, "Assessing Strategies for Quality Improvement," *Health Affairs,* 16(3):151–161, May–June 1997.

22. J.H. Seibert, "Patient Satisfaction and Quality Improvement: Strategies and Pitfalls," *Managing Employee Health Benefits,* 6(4):46–50, Summer 1998.

23. N. Goldfield, supra note 9, at 4–6.

24. E.A. McGlynn and R.H. Brook, "Keeping Quality on the Policy Agenda," *Health Affairs,* 20(3):82–90, May–June 2001.

25. *See* http://www.ncqa.org.

26. *See* http://www.jcaho.org.

27. D.M. Eddy, "Balancing Cost and Quality in Fee-for-Service Versus Managed Care," *Health Affairs* 16(3):162–173, May–June 1997.

28. Id.

29. E.S. Ogrod, "Compensation and Quality: A Physician's View," *Health Affairs,* 16(3):82–86, May–June 1997.

30. J. Jollis, E.R. DeLong, E.D. Peterson, et al., "Outcome of Acute Myocardial Infarction According to the Specialty of the Admitting Physician," *N. Engl. J. Med.,* 335:1880–1887, 1996.

31. Physician Payment Review Commission, Annual Report to Congress, Part 2, *The Medicare and Medicaid Guide* (New York: Commerce Clearing House 1994) 341.

32. HEDIS 3.0 consists of 74 measures and specifications for descriptive information. Another 30 items make up a testing set that will be considered for future versions of HEDIS. Some of these measures apply to all plan enrollees and others are specific to Medicaid, Medicare, or commercial enrollees.

33. This information is available on the NCQA Web site, www.ncqa.org.

34. Id.

35. P. Kongstvedt, *The Managed Health Care Handbook* (Gaithersburg, MD: Aspen Publishers 1996) 413.

36. D.C. Goodman, E.S. Fisher, and T.A. Bubolz, "Benchmarking the U.S. Physician Workforce," *JAMA*, 276:1811–1817, 1996.

37. E. Braunwald, D. Mark, R. Jones, et al., "Unstable Angina: Diagnosis and Managment," *Clinical Practice Guideline Number 10*, AHCPR, 1994.

38. D.R. Katz, J.L. Griffith, and J.R. Beshansky, "The Use of Empiric Clinical Data in the Evaluation of Practice Guidelines for Unstable Angina," *JAMA*, 276:1568–1573, 1996.

39. National Practitioner Data Bank 2000 Annual Report, www.npdb-hipdb.com.

40. For a more detailed discussion of the Tenth Amendment and its relationship to state regulation of health care, see Holzer, "The Physician's License: An Achilles Heel?," *J. Legal Med.*, 12:201–209, 1991.

Chapter 11

Managed Care Contracting and Negotiation Strategies

One of the most important aspects of any managed care arrangement is the written agreement. As a legal document, the contract controls the rights and responsibilities of the parties and can serve to protect or punish a party that does not comply with its terms.

As discussed in chapters 3 and 4, managed care products are becoming more numerous and more complex. As discussed in chapter 7, under the Balanced Budget Act of 1997 (BBA), Medicare + Choice (M + C) with its provider-sponsored organization (PSO) regulations offers managed care organizations (MCOs) more options when participating in M + C. The BBA also changes the types of MCOs allowed to assume the role of payer and dramatically affects the relationships MCOs will have with participating providers. These new products, new relationships, and new regulations take the contracting process to new levels of complexity. In addition, provider risk sharing, the predominant means of cost containment in managed care, is coming under increasing legal scrutiny as state legislators and the courts focus on cases involving economic failure. With the continuing evolution of plans and increasing legal scrutiny, negotiating managed care contracts will require knowledge of legal issues as well as business and political issues.

This chapter focuses on the negotiation of the managed care contract. Managed care contracts generally require extensive negotiations because of the many parties and interests involved. The negotiation process is key to the ultimate success of any managed care arrangement because the contracts affect payer-provider relationships and ultimately customer satisfaction. The process of negotiation described in this chapter is based on the principles developed by the Program on Negotiation and the Harvard Negotiation Project, which have been published in several texts, including the best-selling books *Getting to Yes: Negotiating Agreements Without Giving In*[1] and *Getting Past No: Negotiating Your Way From Confrontation to Cooperation.*[2] These principles appear to be generally applicable to managed care contract negotiation.

Some state legislatures have attempted to assist providers in the negotiation process by enacting legislation that allows providers to come together in collective bargaining units. These physician "unions" are discussed in more detail in chapter 8.

Fundamentals of Contracts

Q 11:1 What is a contract?

A contract is a legally enforceable agreement that involves at least one promise that has legal consequences. Not every agreement is a contract. A contract is formed when there is a promise of performance in exchange for value, or when two or more persons promise to do something on which each relies, or one person makes a promise in exchange for another's performance of some act or forbearance from acting. Contracts can be oral, written, or implied based on the understanding of the parties. They set forth the stated obligations of the parties and describe or define the consideration (something of value) that cements the obligation. Only competent parties can enter into enforceable contracts. If a contract involves an incompetent person (by either age or disability), there may not have been proper capacity for the parties to have a meeting of the minds to enter into a mutually obligating agreement.

Q 11:2 What is the purpose of a contract?

The primary purpose of a contract is to provide one or more of the parties with a legal remedy if another party does not perform his or her obligations. Another purpose of a contract is to specify, limit, and define the agreements that are legally enforceable. Contracts require parties to be specific in their understandings and expectations.

Q 11:3 What does it take to create a contract?

The test of what becomes a contract is the subject of many cases in law school texts. It is not uncommon, however, to look at the facts and circumstances of a relationship or agreement to evaluate whether there is a legally enforceable agreement. Contracts often arise when there is some form of offer by one party for which there is an acceptance by the other party. The existence of some form of consideration, or a consideration substitute such as reliance, makes the obligations of the parties mutual and enforceable. It is the consideration or exchange of value that creates the mutual obligations for which performance is legally enforceable.

Q 11:4   What happens if a party fails to perform as agreed in the contract?

Many things can happen when there is no performance. The party affected by the nonperformance can try to sue for damages or equitable relief in the form of seeking specific performance of the agreement. Specific performance describes the obligation imposed on a party to perform under an enforceable contract. Before one can claim that a person is in breach of a contract, however, it is necessary to determine whether the contract requires the event that was not performed. If performance of the event is neither specified in the contract nor easily inferred from the contract language, it may not be enforceable under the contract. Although certain oral agreements are legally enforceable as a contract, most written contracts include language that provides that the agreement represents the final agreement of the parties and cannot be modified by prior oral or written representations. (See chapter 8 for discussions related to contract liability in managed care.)

Sometimes performance of an agreement is excused either because the consideration used was illegal and therefore the contract is void, or there were events outside the control of the nonperforming party that make performance impossible. Courts tend to want to save a contract from being invalidated and will sometimes re-form the agreement to reflect the intent of the parties and allow them to accomplish the agreed purposes under the circumstances. Consequently, rescission of a contract (which involves returning the parties to their precontract status) is an extraordinary remedy to a breach, as is specific performance. Specific performance is an equitable remedy that will be imposed only if there is no adequate remedy at law, such as monetary damages, to make the affected party whole. In the context of a health care provider agreement, specific performance may not be available as a legal remedy to nonperformance needed, (5) the extent to which the agreement should delegate administrative duties, (6) the time needed to complete the transaction, and (7) the managed care maturity of the market.

A party entering into managed care contract negotiations should know as much as possible about the other party, amd that party's (1) senior management team, (2) financial strength or profitability, (3) corporate philosophy or business approach, (4) membership base, (5) payment methods and timeliness, (6) allocation of the premium dollar, (7) membership growth, (8) other contracting parties, (9) approach to care management, and (10) provider relationships.

This information may be obtained from colleagues, from the MCO itself, from employers, from patients, from state and federal regulatory authorities, and from private research organizations and consultants.

Q 11:9 What constitutes the managed care contracting "playing field"?

The managed care contracting playing field comprises subscribers, payers, intermediaries, and providers (see Figure 11-1 in Q 11:13).

Subscribers may be individuals, groups, or health insurance purchasing alliances (HIPAs), which broker or provide direct access to licensed health insurers for employees of (usually) small employers. If a HIPA provides direct access, it may collect premiums, but it does not usually assume insurance risk. [See, e.g., Cal Ins Code § 10730 et seq (1995); Colo Rev Stat § 6-18-101 et seq (1995); Tex Ins Code art 26.01 et seq (1995)]

Payers may be licensed indemnity plans (such as Blue Cross), HMOs and other prepayment plans, unlicensed health and welfare plans such as ERISA (Employee Retirement Income Security Act of 1974) plans or multiple employer welfare arrangements (MEWAs)), or governmental health benefit programs (CHAMPUS, Federal Employees Health Benefits Program (FEHBP), Medicare, or Medicaid). Some intermediaries perform an insurance function; others perform network functions.

Intermediaries are defined as entities that interface with payers and/or providers and that perform functions on behalf of one or the other or both. Intermediaries may include third-party administrators (TPAs), management services organizations (MSOs), physician-hospital organizations (PHOs), or independent practice associations (IPAs).

Providers are defined under the contract based on category of provider and scope of services under the contract. Providers may include physicians, hospitals, ambulatory surgery centers, home health agencies, and skilled nursing facilities.

Each type of managed care arrangement has different contracting considerations based on its unique characteristics. Depending on the type of contract, there will be different issues and negotiating strategies (see Q 11:13).

Q 11:10   What other factors will affect managed care contracting issues and negotiating strategies?

Numerous other factors will affect managed care contracting issues and negotiating strategies:

The Changing Health Care Marketplace. Some of the most important factors relate to changes in the health care marketplace, such as (1) diversification of managed care products, (2) consolidation of plans and providers, (3) medical practice integration, and (4) employer expectations of MCOs.

The Role of Managed Care Organizations. Other factors relate to defining the types of MCOs that might be involved. MCOs are characterized as organizations that combine financing with delivery of health care services through provider arrangements in which providers have been selected pursuant to certain selection criteria. MCOs monitor provider performance and rely on programs and systems to gather, monitor, and measure data on health services utilization, referral patterns, and other quality and performance measures. Most MCOs use incentives or impose requirements on their members to encourage use of preferred providers associated with the benefit plan, and use incentives and impose requirements on their providers to encourage appropriate utilization of resources. As discussed in chapter 3, the common types of MCOs include the following:

- Licensed insurers
- HMOs

- PPOs
- Integrated delivery systems (IDSs)
- Self-insured employer plans or employer coalitions (ERISA plans)

Products and Services. Numerous products and services are provided through MCOs, ranging from closed-panel plans, such as HMO and exclusive provider organization (EPO) plans, to POS plans and open-access PPO plans. These products and services are discussed in more detail in chapter 3.

Contracting Entities. MCOs must structure their contractual arrangements with providers to meet their service delivery obligations. Usually, an MCO will have separate types of form contracts for primary care physicians (PCPs), specialty care providers, multispecialty groups, IDSs, and ancillary care providers. This becomes important when designing risk contracts, because service and payment are usually separated into institutional services and medical-professional services. The ability of an organization to be contractually obligated for institutional services or medical-professional services, or both, will be subject to state law unless state law is preempted by ERISA. These arrangements are discussed in more detail in chapters 2 and 5.

Q 11:11   What issues should the parties consider before negotiating a managed care contract?

Before engaging in any managed care contract negotiations, the parties should consider the following issues:

General Issues

1. What are the parties' respective competitive positions?
2. What are the status and stage of managed care in the relevant market?
3. Where do the existing patients come from?
4. What are the relative health care costs?
5. What is the "bottom line" or best alternative to a negotiated agreement?
6. Has there been a careful analysis of the managed care plan?

MCO Issues

1. Has there been a proper review of the MCO's legal structure and authority to contract?
2. Can the MCO produce a reasonable volume of patients that will make the financial risk of the contract worth taking?
3. What is the financial position of the MCO and its ownership structure?
4. Does the MCO maintain professional liability insurance? Have there been any claims against it?
5. What percentage of the MCO's enrollees are over age 65?
6. What has been the MCO's utilization experience for hospital and physician services?
7. With what providers and employers does the MCO currently hold contracts?
8. What is the MCO marketing strategy?
9. For HMOs, what has been the record on distribution of withheld funds or payment of incentives?

Provider Issues

1. Is the health care provider ready to engage in managed care contracts?
2. Can the provider furnish the required services?
3. Will the provider be required to expand existing services or facilities in order to meet the contract requirements?
4. Will the provider be able to accept patients under the existing plan, and will it be able to accept new patients in the future?
5. Is the provider able to assume the financial risk under managed care?
6. Are the provider's prices competitive?
7. Does the provider have systems in place to manage care under contract (provider network, information management, and so on)?
8. Does the provider know its costs?
9. Does the provider understand the managed care market in which it is competing for contracts?

10. Is the provider prepared, politically, for the impact of managed care contracting on its other business relationships? For example, have physicians contracted with the plan? Are they affiliated with the appropriate hospitals? Are they committed to managed care?

Q 11:12   What information about a managed care plan must be gathered to perform careful analysis of the plan?

Information about a managed care plan is available from a number of sources, including the plan itself, regulatory agencies, consultants, and the plan's existing providers. Information that should be obtained and reviewed before contracting with a plan includes the following:

- Organizational structure, ownership, and affiliated organizations
- Status of applicable licenses and certifications
- Length of time the plan has been in business
- Management structure and personnel
- Number and types of current and expected enrollees
- Market share, strategy, and business plan
- Financial solvency status and performance
- Geographic service areas covered and enrollee distribution
- Other participating providers
- Criteria for selection and review of providers
- Current claims, litigation, or administrative actions
- Quality and scope of documentation
- Timeliness of payment
- Business reputation with employers, enrollees, and providers
- Attitude toward negotiations with providers
- Policies and procedures related to claims, utilization and quality management, and grievance procedures

- Certification under the National Committee for Quality Assurance (NCQA) or a comparable accreditation organization

Types of Managed Care Contracts

Q 11:13   What are the different types of managed care contracts?

As shown in Figure 11-1, the different types of managed care contracts are the following:

- Coverage (or subscription) agreements (type 1 contracts; see Q 11:14)
- Payer-provider agreements (type 2 contracts; see Q 11:15)

Figure 11-1   The Contracting Playing Field

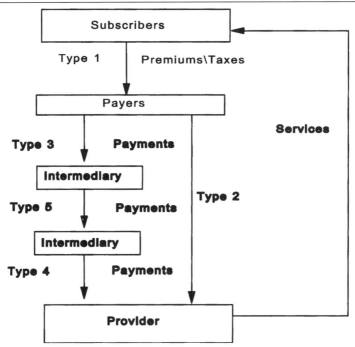

- Payer-intermediary agreements (type 3 contract; see Q 11:16)
- Intermediary-provider agreements (type 4 contract; see Q 11:17), and
- Network intermediary-provider (or network-sharing) agreements (type 5 contract; see Q 11:18)

Type 1 Contracts: Coverage

Q 11:14   What issues are considered in negotiating a type 1 (coverage) contract?

The relationship defined under a coverage (or subscription) contract is that between the ultimate purchaser or subscriber and the payer. The ultimate purchaser or subscriber is usually the employer, the ERISA plan administrator, or the government purchaser. The payer may be an insurer, HMO, or some other MCO. The tension in this relationship arises because the purchaser wants a broad base of providers in the panel for access, but the payer, which wants to offer the purchaser a broad panel of providers, must do so at a competitive price. The providers will participate in anticipation of increased volume or directed referrals, despite the discount on charges.

The following issues are considered in negotiating a type 1 contract:

Scope of Services. A comprehensive plan requires a full spectrum of health care services, including primary, specialty, ancillary, and hospital care. Most MCOs will build from a primary care base and expand to include the specialty services based on primary care referral patterns. Essential specialty areas include allergy, cardiology, neurology, gastroenterology, general surgery, orthopedics, dermatology, ENT (ears, nose, and throat), ophthalmology, cardiovascular surgery, obstetrics and gynecology, urology, pulmonology, nephrology, hematology and oncology, neurosurgery, plastic surgery, infectious disease, rheumatology, and endocrinology. A key question is whether the services required by the payer include services that the provider is unwilling or unable to provide.

Incentives. There should be some expectation that members or enrollees will use participating providers. Does the coverage agreement set forth incentives to use the provider? Will the payer grant exclusivity? (See appendix 11-A for language that can be used in exclusive contracts.)

Network Adequacy. The scope of services and the ability to ensure direction of members or enrollees to certain providers will depend, to a great degree, on the composition, structure, and size of the provider network. The test for network adequacy, after review of specialty requirements, will be based on a member-to-physician ratio to ensure that the network includes an adequate number of providers.

Type 2 Contracts: Payer-Provider

Q 11:15   What major issues arise in negotiating a type 2 (payer-provider) contract?

When most people think of managed care contracts, they think of payer-provider agreements. Numerous issues arise in negotiating these contracts. Some issues involve nonfinancial terms, and others involve reimbursement and other financial considerations.

Nonfinancial Considerations

Provider Obligations:

1. What services is the provider obligated to provide?
2. Does the contract or any referenced policy or procedure of the payer require the provider to obtain licenses or certifications it does not already have?
3. Is the provider asked to provide clinical services it does not have, so it will be required to subcontract its services? If so, does the payer limit the provider's ability to subcontract the services it cannot provide?
4. Are the provider's obligations suspended in the event of an unforeseen tragedy or catastrophe?
5. What happens if the provider approaches maximum capacity?
6. Is the provider required to recruit certain providers to its business or medical staff?

Payer Obligations:

1. With how many other competing providers will the payer contract?
2. Will the payer share its encounter data and utilization reports with the provider?

Eligibility and Medical Necessity Determinations:

1. How does the contract or any referenced policy or procedure of the payer alter the provider's traditional means of verifying patient eligibility for benefits?
2. Does the payer or the provider bear the risk for an erroneous representation of eligibility?
3. How does the contract or any referenced policy or procedure of the payer alter the provider's traditional means of obtaining pretreatment approval?
4. Are precertification and eligibility verification requirements waived for emergencies?
5. By whom and under what process is medical necessity determined?
6. Is the utilization review/quality assurance plan consistent with accepted medical criteria?
7. Can the payer retroactively deny payment for an admission or procedure it had preapproved?
8. What are the procedures for an appeal of denied services?
9. Is the utilization review/quality assurance program in compliance with state and federal guidelines?

Insurance and Liability:

1. Does the contract or any referenced policy or procedure of the payer require the provider to carry insurance it does not already have?
2. Does the contract or any referenced policy or procedure of the payer require the provider to indemnify the payer?
3. Does the contract or any referenced policy or procedure of the payer allow payer access to confidential peer review files, hearings, and committees?
4. If arbitration is required under the contract, to what types of disputes does it apply?
5. What insurance coverages does the payer maintain?

Term and Termination:

1. What term is the contract?
2. Can the contract be terminated without cause?

3. What, if any, are the for-cause grounds for termination?

4. What procedures are to be followed to terminate the contract?

5. What effect does termination have on a beneficiary under continuous treatment at the time of termination?

6. Are there tag-along or take-along affiliates of the provider whose contracts will follow the term and termination of the provider's contract?

7. How is the contract amended?

8. What documents are incorporated by reference, and how can they be amended?

9. How and how often are the payment rates adjusted?

Other Terms:

1. Are the payer's representatives exempt from provider policies regarding visitors and guests?

2. Does the contract or any referenced policy or procedure of the payer allow the payer access to private business records of the provider?

3. Does the contract give the payer authority to use the provider's name in marketing programs?

4. Does the contract or any referenced policy or procedure of the payer require the facility to admit certain providers to its medical staff?

5. Is the provider asked to modify its credentialing process in any manner?

6. Is the provider precluded from having closed department or exclusive contract arrangements?

7. Does the contract or any referenced policy or procedure of the payer alter the traditional means by which payers review and copy medical records?

8. Can the payer unilaterally modify policies and procedures or even the terms of the contract? If so, how is the provider notified of any changes, and can the provider escape these changes?

9. Is the provider's ability to sell the business limited?

10. Do federal or state laws dictate any terms of the contract? (See appendix 11-B for a Medicare contracting checklist.)

Financial Considerations

Payment Methodologies:

1. *Discounts* are usually stated as a percentage of the provider's charges. Sometimes the percentage discount will increase along a siding scale as volume increases.

2. *Per diems,* which first became popular with hospitals in the 1940s and 1950s, are currently used by many payers even in sophisticated markets. Providers run a tremendous risk of the intensity of service required being disproportionately low in relation to the price charged. Providers also run the risk that their price offer assumes a utilization rate higher than the payer intends. Stop-loss provisions and specialty service carve-outs can protect against the first risk, but not the second.

3. *Per case* payment is made for a specified illness. The Medicare diagnosis-related group (DRG) payment system is a per case method.

4. *Capitation* refers to a monthly fixed payment by the payer to the provider, usually computed per member, in return for the provider assuming responsibility for all or a specific list of covered benefits. The method of structuring a capitated payment is discussed in more detail in Q 11:22.

Type 3 Contracts: Payer-Intermediary

Q 11:16   What major issues arise in negotiating a type 3 (payer-intermediary) contract?

Type 3 contracts involve payers (i.e., insurers, HMOs, and ERISA plans) that contract with organizations such as TPAs, MSOs, PHOs, and other MCOs to access their contracted providers or to obtain specific support services.

Insurance Functions

1. What services are to be provided?
   - Processing and adjudicating, in accordance with the terms of the applicable benefit plan, all claims submitted by or on behalf of beneficiaries, including an explanation of benefit form reflecting the disposition of each claim

- Providing 800 number access for members or providers who wish to call directly for claims status
- Providing beneficiaries with an explanation of benefits form reflecting the disposition of each claim
- Medical review support, analysis, and expertise, including, but not limited to, the conduct of any investigation deemed necessary by insurers for the proper determination of claims under the benefit plans
- Preparation and mailing of IRS Form 1099 to providers
- Maintenance of an up-to-date eligibility list (sometimes using an 800 access number for members or providers who wish to call directly to check eligibility)
- Administration of the stop-loss program, including the filing of any claims with stop-loss insurers and the tracking and filing of claims with stop-loss insurers
- Actuarial services
- Benefit design and plan drafting
- Case management
- Underwriting services
- Quality assurance
- Mail and communications services including, but not limited to, printing and dissemination of all beneficiary identification cards, participating provider lists, manuals, and other administrative documents necessary for the proper operation of the benefit plans
- Management information services
- Regulatory and legal services
- Accounting and other financial services
- Purchasing and vendor contracting
- Record maintenance
- Personnel management, employee training, and related services
- Customer relations, including conducting grievance proceedings

- Collection of amounts owed to insurers by third parties, including, but not limited to, coordination of benefit and subrogation obligations
- Provider network development, including provider contracting, directories, selection, credentialing, and termination

2. Who has final discretionary authority over payment of claims and interpretation of the benefit plan?
3. Who is responsible for taxes, fees, and assessments for premium taxes, insolvency or guarantee funds, and claims paid?
4. Who is ultimately responsible for the payment of claims to providers?
5. If claims payment is a requested service, how does the intermediary access the funds of the payer?
6. Is the intermediary given incentives under the payment provisions? If so, does the intermediary assume insurance risk?

Network Functions

1. *Guarantees.* Provider-sponsored intermediaries accepting financial risk from payers and not passing all of that risk to the providers may be required to show their financial wherewithal to bear losses resulting from deficits in risk pools. For provided-sponsored intermediaries unable to demonstrate financial strength at levels commensurate with their risk, payers have started asking for guarantees from the intermediaries' parents. For many physician-hospital organizations (PHOs), this means the hospital.
2. *"Wholesale" HMOs.* Also called "shadow" and "provider" HMOs, these state-licensed HMOs do not issue their own subscriber agreements, but instead act as risk-bearing provider networks for other HMOs. Because these intermediaries are regulated as HMOs, there should be little concern over the nature of the relationship between the payer and intermediary other than to ensure that there is appropriate delegation and accountability.
3. *Medicare contracting.* Medicare expects to monitor the performance of intermediary organizations by requiring Medicare-certified HMOs to include in their HMO-intermediary contracts a clause requiring the intermediaries to give the Health

Care Financing Administration (HCFA) access to their books and records and to include in their intermediary-provider contracts all the same clauses that HMOs must include when they contract directly with providers. Appendix 11-B provides examples of federal contract requirements.

Type 4 Contracts: Intermediary-Provider

Q 11:17   What special issues are considered in negotiating a type 4 (intermediary-provider) contract?

Type 4 contracts are those between an intermediary organization, such as a PHO or IPA, and the individually contracted providers, such as hospitals or physicians.

Business Considerations

1. How many payers does the intermediary represent?
2. How exclusive is the intermediary's provider panel?
3. Can the provider refer patients outside the intermediary's provider panel? If not, how adequate is the intermediary's provider panel?
4. How does the intermediary alter the claim submission or claim payment process?

Other Considerations

- Agency authority
- Membership fees
- Exclusive bargaining agency
- Panel-by-panel termination

Type 5 Contracts: Network Intermediary-Provider

Q 11:18   What is a network intermediary, and what issues arise in negotiating a type 5 (network intermediary-provider) contract?

A network intermediary is an intermediary that holds contracts with providers as a PPO network. These intermediaries "rent" or charge for access to their provider networks.

Issues that arise in negotiating a type 5 contract include the following:

1. *Delegated credentialing.* If the payer delegates any credentialing (and recredentialing, recertification, or reappointment) activities to contractors, there should be oversight of the contracted activity for the payer to be accredited by the NCQA.

2. *Access fees.* Provider-sponsored intermediaries should become self-supporting pursuant to legitimate business plans. For example, significant fraud and abuse and Stark II issues (see chapter 8) arise if a hospital subsidizes a PHO, even one that is controlled in part by the hospital. For a tax-exempt hospital, private benefit and inurement issues will also arise. These issues arise because the tax and reimbursement officials at the federal level are of the opinion that PHOs are significantly controlled by (and at the very least operated on behalf of) physicians. There are only two customers from whom a PHO could conceivably earn revenue: the providers and the payers. Neither will pay willingly.

3. *Delegated Administration.* Many provider organizations and networks seek to be delegated certain administrative functions from the insurer or MCO. These functions include information management and reporting, claims payment, utilization review, and other functions that can be legally delegated by the licensed or regulated entity to the network. Sometimes the network will need appropriate licenses and certifications to perform these delegated functions.

Q 11:19   What can be done to avoid the "silent PPO" situation that can arise in a type 5 contract, that is, in a network-sharing arrangement?

One of the most problematic issues in developing network-sharing arrangements is the potential misuse by intermediaries or payers of the network as a silent PPO. Intermediaries usually want the broadest authority to engage any type of payer on behalf of a provider. Although such flexibility will certainly enhance the probability of the intermediary's success, such authority can worry providers. For example, some intermediaries contract with workers' compensation insurers, and the application of the provider's discount in this context is both unnecessary and inadvisable if those payments are established by law and a freedom of choice statute precludes any steering of patients. In addition, through the use of network-sharing agreements an intermediary can sell a provider's discount to another intermediary, *ad infinitum,* in a manner that would offer no assurance of patient volume for the discount provided. This situation establishes tension between providers and intermediaries, which is no greater than that in provider-sponsored intermediaries.

Texas has imposed regulations [Tex State Ins Code, Article 3.70-3C, § 7A] on the use of the silent PPO; however, the best way to protect against the silent PPO situation is to ensure that when signing PPO contracts, providers agree to the following:

1. Discounts will be extended only to enrollees of the PPO who have cards identifying them as such.

2. All PPO members eligible for discounts will be subject to steerage mechanisms.

3. The types of entities that can be added to the network will be identified in advance, and providers will receive timely notice when payers or employers are added.

4. All members added to the PPO will be subject to the same steerage mechanisms.

5. Any discounts applicable to a PPO enrollee will be disclosed at the time coverage is verified.

6. The sale or other unauthorized use of contract rate information will be specifically prohibited.

Things to look for in evaluating a PPO include the following:

- Provider directories
- Payer lists
- Member identification cards
- Employee-to-member ratio
- Credentialing
- Utilization management/quality assurance programs
- Fee schedules and financial incentives

Evaluating the Financial Risk in Managed Care Contracts

Q 11:20   How should the payment provisions of a managed care contract be analyzed?

There are many forms of reimbursement under managed care contracts. The most common payment arrangements for physicians (in order of increasing risk) are discounted fees, capped fee schedules, capped fee schedules with withholds, primary care capitation, and full capitation. For hospitals, the common payment methods are discounted charges, per diems, per stay or per case payments, and capitation arrangements. Detailed information for analyzing payment methods follow:

Nonrisk Payments

Discounted Fees. A discount on fees or charges is one of the most straightforward methods of payment to providers. This discount can be structured as a straight percentage discount, or for hospitals, as a sliding-scale discount whereby the percentage of discount increases with the volume of patient encounters. In analyzing a proposed discount arrangement, one should estimate the increased enrollee volume under the contract, predict the types and volume of services required by the enrollee, identify the variable costs of each service covered by the discount arrangement, determine the contribution to fixed costs required from reimbursement for the services covered by the discount, and predict any potential increase in variable and fixed costs over the period of the negotiated discount. Other questions to ask include these:

1. Are hospital-based physician professional fees included in the facility's negotiated rates?
2. How are additions to and deletions from the provider's service menu reflected in the negotiated payment rates?
3. How promptly will the payer pay a completed claim?
4. What remedies exist for tardy payments?
5. Under what circumstances can a payment be justifiably delayed?
6. Does the contract or any referenced policy or procedure of the payer alter the provider's traditional means of collecting patient deposits?

7. Does the contract or any referenced policy or procedure of the payer alter the provider's traditional means of collecting deductibles, coinsurance, copayments, and other cost-sharing payments?

8. Does the contract or any referenced policy or procedure of the payer alter the provider's traditional means of billing for noncovered services? At what rate?

9. Does the contract or any referenced policy or procedure of the payer alter the provider's traditional means of bringing a direct cause of action against the patient for nonpayment by either the payer or the patient?

10. Does the contract or any referenced policy or procedure of the payer alter the provider's traditional means of printing invoices and claim forms?

11. Has the payer promised not to pay the provider any less than any other provider?

12. Will the provider offer "most favored nation" (MFN) prices?[3]

13. Does the contract or any referenced policy or procedure of the payer alter the provider's traditional means of billing other payers in coordination of benefits cases?

14. Are there deadlines for the submission of the provider's claims? Do these deadlines affect billing for a long course of treatment?

15. Will the hospital be paid for providing statutorily mandated emergency medical screening and treatment?

Per Diems. The per diem charge method is often used for inpatient charges and is based on a single charge for each day the enrollee is hospitalized, regardless of the actual charges or costs incurred. This arrangement places the hospital at some risk for controlling internal costs and allows the plan to provide incentives to physicians who control admissions and lengths of stay. For high-intensity cases, it may be appropriate to negotiate a stop-loss threshold above which reimbursement will be paid under some discounted fee-for-service or other arrangement. Per diems can be negotiated as a fixed day rate for all inpatient services or can exclude expensive services such as intensive care or obstetrics. Alternatively, there can be multiple sets of per diem charges based on type of service or a combination of per diem and flat case rates depending on the type of inpatient services. Finally, there can be sliding-scale per diem rates similar to sliding-scale discounts based on total volume. Under this scenario, the payer negotiates an interim per diem that it agrees to pay for each bed-day in the hospital. Depending on the total number of bed-days in the year, the payer will pay either a lump-sum settlement at the end of the year or withhold an amount from the final payment for the year to adjust for an additional reduction in the per diem from an increase in total bed-days.

Capped Fee Schedules. A more common approach used by PPOs and HMOs is to cap fees using a maximum allowable fee, or fee cap, for each procedure. Physicians are paid charges up to the maximum amount. The advantage of capped fee schedules compared to discounted charges is that capped fee schedules limit the impact of fee increases and are more equitable for physicians with different fee schedules. The disadvantage is that reimbursement is based on the number of services performed, so there is no incentive to control utilization of services. A variation of the capped fee approach, which creates the incentive to control utilization, is to withhold a percentage of the payment to the physicians (usually 15 to 20 percent) and to pay out these withheld funds if certain performance goals are met. This arrangement has the advantages of a capped fee schedule with an incentive to control utilization. There is still a risk, however, that the physician will view the withhold as a discount and increase utilization to increase compensation levels.

Risk Payments: Capitation. Under a capitation arrangement, the provider receives from the payer a flat payment per enrollee per month (also called per member per month, or PMPM). In return for the monthly payment, the provider agrees to provide all or certain specified covered medical services to the payer's enrollees. These arrangements are volume driven, and utilization is at the provider's risk. Under primary care capitation, the PCP is capitated for a fixed list of services and receives the same payment regardless of the number of covered services performed. Usually, there is a withhold with primary care capitation. Under some circumstances (and depending on applicable state HMO laws), a physician may be fully capitated for both medical (primary and referral) and hospital services. For hospitals, the key to success in capitation arrangements is to have a relationship with a physician group or independent practice association (IPA) in order to address admissions and lengths of stay. To evaluate a capitation arrangement, there must be assumptions as to enrollee mix (age, sex, and so on), admission rates, case mix, and average length of stay. Under capitation arrangements, contracts must clearly specify which inpatient and outpatient services are covered by the capitation payment and which services are outside the capitation payment. Stop-loss insurance is an important consideration. Large providers should consider obtaining reinsurance similar to that used for liability insurance policies. Important questions to ask include the following:

1. What services is the provider obligated to provide under the capitated fee?

2. Is the provider bound by the payer's interpretation of the policy (particularly with respect to high-cost, new, and experimental techniques)?

3. Is the provider bound by the payer's amendments to the policy?

4. Can the provider provide all the services allocated to it under the capitation rate?

5. Does the payer limit the provider's ability to subcontract services it cannot provide?

6. Who between the provider and payer is responsible for out-of-area coverage of members assigned to the provider?

7. To whom are covered services due?

8. When is a person deemed to be eligible (for payment purposes)? How are member eligibility disputes handled?

9. To what extent is the payer allowed to enroll or disenroll members retroactively?

10. What fee schedule was used to build the payment rate? What utilization predictions were used to build the payment rate? Are they based on historical data of the same population? What information exists regarding the health, age, and sex of the expected membership population? Will the payer share its information, including actuarial assumptions, with the provider? Can the provider renegotiate the capitation rates if the risk status of the enrollee population changes, such as if the payer begins to sell its product to the Medicare and Medicaid population?

11. What information will the payer give the provider during the contract year?

Figure 11-2   Continuum of Reimbursement Methodologies

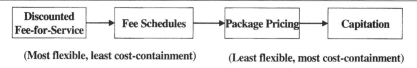

| Discounted Fee-for-Service | → | Fee Schedules | → | Package Pricing | → | Capitation |

(Most flexible, least cost-containment)   (Least flexible, most cost-containment)

12. When and how will the provider be paid? Will the capitation rates reflect adjustments for age, sex, plan benefits, and co-payment levels?

13. Who between the payer and provider is entitled to bill other health payers in coordination of benefits cases? In subrogation cases? If it is the payer, is it "chase and pay" or "pay and chase"?

14. What protection is available to the provider for unexpected utilization?

15. What protection is available to the provider for an unexpectedly small membership population?

16. Is there contract language made nonnegotiable by legislation or regulation?

17. Will the provider offer MFN prices?

18. Does the notice requirement for termination vary with the size of the membership population?

19. How are the risk pools constructed? (See Qs 11:56, 11:57.)

20. How much of the premium or capitation payment is allocated to plan administrative costs?

Figure 11-2 shows the continuum of reimbursement methodologies from most flexible to least flexible.

Q 11:21   What types of risk are inherent in managed care contracts?

There are five types of risk inherent in managed care contracts:

1. *Underwriting risk* is the risk identified by the insurer based on identification of the target population and the likely utilization of resources so that an appropriate premium charge can

be assessed. Actuaries establish the utilization risk associated with a particular population.

2. *Marketing risk* is the risk that enough individuals may not be sold on the program or plan to make it operationally and financially feasible. Low enrollment does not work in capitated arrangements.

3. *Financial risk* is the risk of financial collapse for lack of revenue, excess costs, or both.

4. *Operational risk* is the risk taken by the service provider to deliver the quantity and quality of services required to meet the perceived needs as well as the defined needs of the patient and payer population. This risk is set out in the payer-provider contract.

5. *Regulatory risk* is the risk associated with the MCO's meeting the requirements of the various regulatory agencies, such as state insurance regulators, HCFA, the National Institutes of Health (NIH), and the Department of Labor (DOL).

Which party bears the risks depends on the type of insurance product and the payment method. The allocation of these risks is shown in Table 11-1.

Table 11-1   **Allocation of Risk by Managed Care Entity Based on Type of Payment Plan**[4]

Payment Plan	Underwriting Risk	Marketing Risk	Financial Risk	Operational Risk	Regulatory Risk
Fee-for-service	Insurer	Insurer, provider	Insurer	Insurer	Insurer, provider
Fee-for-service with deductible and coinsurance	Insurer	Insurer, provider	Insurer	Insurer, provider	Insurer, provider
PPO with discounted fees	Insurer, provider	Insurer	Insurer, provider	Provider, insurer, patient	Insurer, provider
Capitation	Provider	Insurer	Provider	Provider, patient	Insurer, provider
POS plan	Insurer	Insurer, provider	Insurer, patient	Insurer, provider, patient	Insurer, provider

Q 11:22   How is a capitated payment structured?

To evaluate a capitated payment, it is important to understand how it is structured. First, the covered health care services are defined (e.g., inpatient hospitalization, mental health care, pediatrics). Second, the expected utilization of each of the covered services is predicted (usually expressed as the number of visits, patient days, prescriptions, or procedures during one year for 1,000 people). Third, the desired reimbursement rate for each of the covered services is decided (per day, per procedure, per visit) based on (1) premium-driven reimbursement rates, (2) provider cost-driven reimbursement rates, or (3) market-driven reimbursement rates using data from California Relative Value Studies, McGraw-Hill, Medicare (Resource-Based Relative Value Scale), or private databases. Fourth, the product of the second and third steps (the expected cost of health services) is reduced by the amount the insured is expected to pay in the form of copayments. Finally, the effect of age and sex on the expected utilization and expected cost of health services and the effect of contract administration, reinsurance, and profits (often 30 percent of total premiums) are predicted. The resulting amount is the capitation rate. Table 11-2 shows how capitation rates are constructed based on this methodology.

Q 11:23   What is a percentage-of-premium arrangement?

A percentage-of-premium arrangement is an arrangement under which the provider goes "at risk" with the payer and agrees to accept a percentage of the payer's monthly premiums in return for providing all covered medical services to the enrollees during that month. This method has the same level of risk as capitation, except that the provider must depend on the accuracy of the payer's actuarial

Table 11-2   Construction of Capitation Rates*

Covered Service	Utilization	Unit Cost	Annual Cost	PMPM Cost
Hospitalization (days)	0.450	$850.00	$382.50	$31.88
Primary care (visits)	3.680	$35.00	$128.80	$10.73
Drugs (prescriptions)	6.440	$40.00	$257.60	$21.47

*Not shown are the effects of copayments and age-sex conversion rates. Also not shown are insurer add-ons for administrative costs, reinsurance, and profits.

Table 11-3   Percentage-of-Premium Calculation

HMO Premiums		$127.60 PMPM
Percentage retained by HMO or MCO:	16%	$ 20.42
Percentage allocated to providers:	84%	$107.18
Option 1: HMO increases premium		$135.00
Result to provider at 84%		$113.40
Option 2: HMO decreases premium		$122.00
Result to provider at 84%		$102.48

assumptions in establishing the premium rate, which may be artificially lowered in order to be competitive with other rates in the market. For this arrangement to work, the provider must know that it will serve a clearly defined segment of a plan's enrollment. Solo community providers are likely candidates for this arrangement because they have reasonable assurance of exclusive utilization by the enrollees in the community. This type of arrangement may be subject to regulation under state insurance laws. The major difference between a percentage-of-premium arrangement and a capitation payment is that under the former, translating the percentage into a capitated PMPM amount reveals that the PMPM amount varies as the insurer bids for subscribers. The provider will enter into a percentage-of-premium arrangement with the assumption that the insurer will sell its policies at a certain PMPM amount, but market conditions may void that assumption. An example of a percentage-of-premium arrangement is shown in Table 11-3.

Q 11:24   How is the percentage of premium determined?

A percentage of premium payment rate is determined according to the estimated portion of the total premium dollar to be paid to the provider and the amount to be retained by the payer.

Q 11:25   What are risk pools?

Risk pools are a method of risk sharing often used in conjunction with one of the other reimbursement methods. This method usually involves withholding a certain percentage of the provider's reimbursement payments in a fund into which the payer may also deposit a portion of its premium dollars. In some cases, payments may be made from the fund over the course of the year to cover shortfalls when other sources of payment are insufficient. The fund can also be used to make up for shortfalls in contractually agreed-upon provider reimbursement rates. Any surplus remaining at the end of the year will usually be divided among the participating providers. If the fund has an insufficient balance to make up any shortfall or pay claims made against it during the year, the provider forfeits its withheld amounts and may even be liable to the payer for a share of the deficit. Other risk pool arrangements are used to create incentives for providers if certain utilization or claims targets are met and to penalize individual providers who do not meet their targets.

Q 11:26 From the payer's perspective, what are some of the more common contract provisions that affect its ability to control cost and shift risk?

Payers use escrows, risk pools, and payment withholds to control cost and shift risk. These devices should be evaluated by providers as to their purpose, how they will be applied, and when and under what conditions payments will be made to the providers.

Payers want to control increases in cost under contracts with providers. Providers should determine whether there is to be any reduction in the amount or rate of payments to the provider. If so, how and when will it be implemented? Will it be the subject of future negotiation?

Payers want to be sure that they have been given the opportunity to contract at the lowest possible cost or rate. To do so, they use clauses limiting the amount of the payment to the provider to the lowest it has contracted to receive from other payers for the same services. Alternatively, a provider may propose or demand a similar clause that extends to it the benefit of any higher reimbursement rate paid by the payer to another participating provider. As discussed in chapter 8, these clauses have come under some antitrust scrutiny.

Because most managed care contracts (and HMOs, by law) prohibit the provider from collecting any additional payment from enrollees, providers should not overlook these sources of payment. Payers will deduct from their payments to providers amounts allocable to deductibles and copayments, placing the burden on the provider to collect for these amounts. Coordination of benefits may result in delayed payments to providers and may be delegated to the providers or retained by the payers as a means of avoiding duplicate payments.

Payers will tend to hold on to a payment until they are absolutely sure of their responsibility for making the payment. Providers expect that one of the benefits of managed care contracting will be timely payment. To avoid any disputes related to payment obligations, payment provisions in the contract should include claims procedures that are clearly defined and consistent with applicable state law, including specific terms for timely payment and incentives for prompt payment (such as late payment charges).

Q 11:27 What common managed care contracting strategies can providers use to reduce their financial risk?

A number of provisions contained in managed care contracts can have an immediate and direct financial impact on the provider and thus must be recognized and addressed in the contract negotiation process. In addition to the items outlined in Q 11:28, common contracting strategies that reduce financial risk include the following:

Carve-Outs. If a provider can anticipate a higher cost or unusual circumstances involving certain services that would not be adequately covered in the standard contract reimbursement structure, the provider may want to carve out those high-cost or high-intensity services and negotiate a different reimbursement arrangement for them.

Stop-Loss Provisions. Whenever there is a risk of unanticipated volume or intensity of services that would pose a serious financial risk to the provider, a stop-loss provision should be included to set a threshold on which the reimbursement methodology will shift from per diem, capitated, or per case to standard or discounted charges. Under some circumstances, it may be appropriate to acquire reinsurance to protect a provider organization that is heavily invested in managed care in order to consolidate the financial risk exposure in a common insurance product.

Annual Adjustment in Rates and Compensation. Most providers should negotiate the right to review and periodically adjust the payment structure on a regular (but at most annual) basis to allow them to modulate the contract based on volume or patient mix.

Right to Bill for Noncovered Services. Under most managed care contracts, payers are required to reimburse for covered services only and the provider is obligated to accept the reimbursement as payment in full. In the event services not covered by the plan are provided, the provider should have the right to seek payment directly from the enrollee. Such provisions usually require some form of disclosure and consent from the patient or enrollee.

Copayments. Some contracts compute copayments on the basis of undiscounted charges. This arrangement would result in a lower payment being made to the provider and may represent a hidden loss of revenue. Any such provisions should be specified in the contract. The contract should also specify which party is responsible for collecting the copayments.

Emergency Services. Although most contracts include special provisions deferring preauthorization in circumstances involving emergency services, many contracts specify a time frame following the provision of those services in which the payer or UR organization is to be notified of the services. Disputes most often arise from the requirement of patient referral to participating providers, which may conflict with medical judgment and federal and state patient anti-dumping laws. (See chapter 8 for more information on these legal considerations.) Other problems arise with emergency room and covering physicians, who may not be participating providers and who expect to be compensated at usual and customary rates. One way to avoid financial exposure is for the hospital to give patients presenting in the emergency department a financial disclosure and consent form, which puts the patient on notice of his or her personal financial responsibility for the emergency services in the event the payer declines to pay.

Reconciliation of Payments. Some provision in the contract should address the reconciliation of accounts at year-end or at specified times during the contract term to reflect over- or underpayments. When the contract contains withhold provisions, an area of controversy between payer and provider is the timing of reconciliation of the withheld funds. This depends on the nature of the contract and the level of risk assumed by the provider. Providers should attempt to obtain reconciliation on at least a quarterly basis.

Obligations Following Termination of Contract. Most managed care contracts require providers to continue to provide services to enrollees who are either in the hospital or in need of ongoing care immediately following termination of the contract. Thus, the contract should specify the payment for such services until the patients can be safely transferred to another participating provider (see Q 11:44).

Periodic Interim Payments. If an enrollee is expected to be an inpatient over a long period of time (usually over one month) because of a particular illness, the provider may want to negotiate the ability to receive interim and periodic payments to minimize financial risk.

No Retroactive Denial. If a provider has received prior authorization for treatment of the patient and has relied on the authorization, a payer should not be able to deny payment retroactively without good cause.

Hold-Harmless Clauses. Except for copayments, deductibles, and payments for noncovered services, enrollees under most managed care contracts are to be held harmless of any liability for claims related to covered services, even if the payer becomes insolvent. This release is required under many state HMO laws.

Grievances and Appeal Rights. The contract should provide for a fair appeal process that the provider can pursue in the event that a claim is denied. The appeal process should be clearly delineated in the agreement, or incorporated by reference if it is part of the policies and procedures of the plan. Some states regulate the procedural parameters of claims submission and timing of payment or denials. Contract terms should track applicable state law.

Q 11:28 How do stop-loss, reinsurance, and other risk reduction methods help provide management of financial risk?

As risk transfer reimbursement methodologies become more popular and common, providers must understand how to establish appropriate financial protections. Risk protection strategies include (1) predicting the extent of financial risk (based on risk-taking reimbursement structure), (2) identifying and monitoring potential exposure, and (3) reducing risk through stop-loss, reinsurance, and other risk reduction methods.

The terms *stop-loss* and *reinsurance* are often used interchangeably, but they represent different methods of risk management. Stop-loss establishes the maximum direct exposure to the provider's risk pool. "Stop-loss" reinsurance is used to cover the excess exposure to the risk pool under circumstances of a catastrophic claim to a provider. Also available to provider organizations is an aggregate reinsurance policy to cover cumulative medical claims risk. This insurance is often used to protect hospital incentive funds and professional services risk pools. Some HMOs will withhold amounts to fund this policy. Some provider groups with extensive risk contracts in place will self-fund a reinsurance policy.

Other forms of risk protection involve low-enrollment guarantees from HMOs (usually set at 200 for an individual PCP, and 2,000 for a moderately sized physician group), fee-for-service guarantees, and disease-specific protection.

Low-enrollment guarantees allow the risk to be reduced during a start-up enrollment period and phased in as enrollment hits the established thresholds. Fee-for-service guarantees act as a form of aggregate reinsurance to protect the physician's income under a contract. Fee-for-service claims are submitted as encounters, which are valued using a fee-for-service equivalency calculation based on a prenegotiated relative value schedule, such as RBRVS. The total calculated value of the services is compared to the amount of total capitation payments paid to the physician over the same period for the same population. If the capitation payments represent less than some preagreed percentage (e.g., 60 to 80 percent) of the fee-for-service equivalency, the HMO will pay the physician additional reimbursement to meet the guarantee. Of course, some contracts stipulate a maximum of capitated revenue as a percentage of billed charges; this prevents the physician from benefiting from the upside potential of capitation. Finally, disease-specific protection is intended to protect the physician's reimbursement from catastrophic expenditures associated with specific diseases such as cancer, AIDS, or conditions requiring organ transplantation. This protection is particularly important if the PCP is responsible for the specialty services and referrals.

Provider Contracts

General Contract Terms

Q 11:29 What are the general contents of a managed care provider contract?

Most payer-provider agreements follow a general format and include the following provisions:

Title. The title can be used to describe the type of contract and the parties involved (e.g., Primary Care Physician Agreement, IPA Group Agreement, Hospital Agreement).

Caption. The caption is an introductory paragraph, or preamble, which provides either an effective date or a contract date. It also describes the parties to the contract.

Recitals. Recitals usually take the form of "whereas" clauses, stating the underlying purpose of the contract and the goals of the parties. Such clauses often become relevant in contract interpretation to resolve inconsistencies. Although these clauses generally are not part of the enforceable provisions of the contract, they can be made so by incorporating them by reference into the body of the agreement.

Definitions. The definitions section usually precedes the substantive provisions related to duties and responsibilities and is important to clarify and define key contract terms in order to reduce ambiguity in interpretation and enforceability. The federal government and most states have imposed definitions on specific terms that should be reflected in the contract.

Parties' Covenants. The rights and responsibilities of each party (provider, payer, and plan) are generally contained in separate provisions in the body of the contract. These provisions include specific conditions that must be met by each party to maintain the contract, the specific covenants and agreements of the parties, the manner in which these covenants are to be discharged, what happens in the event a party does not discharge a covenant, and a process for terminating the contract and resolving any disputes related to the contract.

Provider Obligations. The services to be furnished by the provider should be set out in the body of the contract or in an exhibit or attachment. The contract needs to define what is meant by a covered enrollee to whom the provider is obligated to provide services and explain how the provider will identify covered enrollees. Other provider responsibilities include referral and acceptance of enrollees and availability and coverage requirements in on-call situations. Hospital providers will want to address issues such as emergency care, preadmission authorization, and hospital-based physician services.

Payment Terms. The terms and conditions of payment, including copayments, deductibles, coordination of benefits, claims submission requirements, and timing of payments for services, should be specified either in the body of the agreement or in an attachment or exhibit. The manner of payment can vary from a risk-based capitation to a fee-for-service arrangement. Payment terms should include detailed procedures for claims submission, review, and processing; disputes; and timing of payment. Most provider contracts include hold-harmless clauses that preclude the provider from seeking payment for covered services from the enrollee regardless of the circumstances, including health plan insolvency. Most plans also include no-balance-billing clauses to prevent a provider from balance billing an enrollee for any payment owed by the plan, regardless of the reason for nonpayment. The provider may bill for copayments, coinsurance, or services not covered under the schedule of benefits.

Nondiscrimination. Most managed care contracts include provisions that require providers to furnish services to enrollees in the same manner that they would furnish services to other patients. Many contracts include a clause prohibiting discrimination on the basis of age, sex, race, religion, national origin, or disability. Nondiscrimination is mandated for federal contracts.

Acceptance of Enrollees. Most provider contracts include a clause that ensures that the provider will accept enrollees regardless of health status. Many provider contracts with PCPs provide for a minimum number of enrollees or members that the physician must accept into his or her panel.

Quality Assurance and Utilization Review. There should be specific information related to the quality assurance and utilization review programs to be used by the plan or payer that the provider is responsible for following. These provisions often raise questions related to access to data and patient information, including medical records.

Proprietary Information Protection. Many contracts include provisions that limit the ability of either party to use the other's name without express authorization. These proprietary rights extend to service marks or trademarks and to information specifically identified as confidential and proprietary that is not to be disclosed or used for any competitive purpose following contract termination.

Relationship of the Parties. For risk management reasons, most provider contracts contain a provision stating that the managed health care plan and the provider are independent contractors and that the agreement does not create any partnership, joint venture, or other shared business arrangement. For the same reasons, a clause that provides that it is the physician's and not the plan's responsibility to recommend any procedure or course of treatment is also often included in provider contracts.

Representations and Warranties. Managed care contracts should contain certain representations and warranties as to the legal integrity of the organization under various federal and state laws with respect to licensure, certification, and financial solvency.

Term and Termination. Some contracts leave the term of the agreement open-ended, with termination on notice with or without cause. Others provide for a specific term with renewal terms. Many contracts provide for termination without cause on 90 days' notice; however, the obligations of the providers to continue treatment of patients may survive the contract termination date for a specified period. In such situations, the plan's payment obligations should continue for the same period, either subject to plan coverage and payment terms or outside the contract under the provider's standard fees. Most contracts provide for termination with cause on loss of licensure, certification, or accreditation; financial instability of either party that would impair its ability to meet its obligations; cancellation of insurance; changes in the law or the reimbursement system that would significantly affect the contract; failure to make timely payments; sale of assets, merger, or change of control; or assignment of the contract. It is not uncommon to include an opportunity to cure if notice of termination is given for cause.

Insurance and Indemnification. Most contracts include insurance requirements related to coverages and limits for each party. Many contain reciprocal indemnification provisions. These should be carefully reviewed, because indemnification agreements are usually outside standard liability insurance coverage and may result in the organization's assets being placed at risk to protect the interests of the party seeking indemnification. If assets are insufficient or there is no evidence of contract indemnity insurance coverage, such clauses should be avoided.

Miscellaneous. Most contracts include a number of miscellaneous provisions, referred to as legal boilerplate, which are intended to address many of the general contract law issues such as *force majeure* (inability to perform because of an act of God), assignment, enforceability, amendments, notices, waiver, severability, binding effect, and governing laws.

Close and Testimonium. At the end of the contract, there will be a closing statement with signature lines. Often there will be specific reference to the authority under which the party is executing the contract.

Attachments and Incorporated Documents. It is not uncommon for contracts to contain exhibits and incorporate other documents by reference, although they are not contained in or attached to the actual contract. It may be preferable to use exhibits or attachments to reflect contract provisions that are commonly negotiated and re-negotiated, such as pricing and payment, so that these can be revised by attachment or addendum without affecting the body of the agreement.

Q 11:30   What is the primary purpose of the provider contract from the perspective of the MCO?

The primary purpose of the provider contract from the perspective of the MCO is to describe the relationship between the parties. The document must clearly describe the agreements reached by the parties through negotiations. The clarity and format of the contract add a lot to its effectiveness. Most contracts are organized according to a format that breaks down the sections by (1) purpose, (2) definitions, and (3) rights and responsibilities.

Some agreements between providers and MCOs concern multiple products. To the extent that there are different services and different methods of compensation associated with each product, these agreements should be placed in separate attachments to a master agreement. Each product should have its own attachment. Any unique characteristics of the product should be included in the attachment.

Identifying the Parties

Q 11:31   Why is identification of the parties important in managed care contracting?

A contract represents an agreement between parties to do certain things. If the performing party is not identified properly in the contract, its nonperformance of its contract obligations may not be legally enforceable. For example, a contract may identify a hospital by location, but if it has not described the entity based on its legal structure or ownership or imposed obligations on directors or shareholders to discharge the contract requirements imposed on the hospital, there may be difficulty or confusion in ascertaining the proper party for a lawsuit. Similarly, in dealing with a physician group, it is important to understand how the group is organized and how it will secure compliance with the terms of the agreement by each physician member.

It may also be important to include in the identification of each party the reason the agreement is made with that particular party rather than with someone else. For example, if the plan is contracting with a particular physician group because of geographic coverage or expertise in certain specialties, including this information in the recitals may be useful in subsequent renegotiation or termination. This practice is also good antitrust risk management, because it documents the reasonable basis for possible exclusion of other qualified providers.

Because of the legal duties and obligations imposed on parties to a contract, the parties should be identified accurately and thoroughly. This may be more complicated than anticipated if some parties are difficult to define.

Defining Services to Be Provided

Q 11:32 Why is it important to define the scope of covered provider services?

It is important for a health care provider such as a physician or hospital to define the services it is required to provide under the contract because a payer's objective is to require the provider to provide all covered services to enrollees, but the provider may need to limit its obligation to the services it customarily provides. A clear statement of what is included in covered services to be provided to enrollees is essential. Nothing in the contract should require a provider to furnish services it does not otherwise offer its patients.

If a payer offers different benefit plans to various enrollee groups, the contract should require the payer to furnish the provider with summaries or copies of each coverage document. A contract that stipulates that the services to be provided are those usual and customary for that provider leaves the provider at risk for having contractually committed to providing services that it may not be capable of providing or that would impose extraordinary financial risk based on the reimbursement structure. For example, if a physician group is contracting to provide services to plan enrollees, unless items such as immunization, laboratory, and x-ray services have been separately identified for special reimbursement, the physicians are economically and legally responsible for providing those services under the contract. If the provider is a hospital, the contract should specify the type of room accommodations.

Q 11:33   How should a provider address limitations in the scope of services it will provide?

If the provider is concerned that it may not have adequate staffing or facilities to provide additional services where enrollment is scheduled to increase, it can limit its obligation to provide covered services to the extent its facilities, staff, and resources allow and avoid becoming financially and legally responsible for arranging for services to be provided to enrollees at other facilities or by other providers. The provider should also review its ability to provide certain types of services and to provide services over certain geographic areas as may be required under the contract.

Q 11:34   What happens if the provider is no longer able to continue providing a covered service required under the contract?

To allow the provider some flexibility in the event it can no longer provide a covered service required under the contract, the contract should contain a notice provision that allows the provider to change its services for legal or business reasons. It will be up to the payer to determine the significance of the provider's discontinuing any covered service. The payer's ability to continue the contract may depend on its need for the specific service and the general availability of the service in the community.

Q 11:35   When hospital-based physician services (emergency room, radiology, and pathology) are included as covered services, who is responsible for paying the physicians providing these services?

A hospital provider may require that its hospital-based physicians participate in its managed care contracts either through the hospital's participation agreement or through separate contracts directly with the payer. Existing exclusive contracts with hospital-based physicians must be reviewed to avoid possible conflicts under payer contracts. Suggested approaches to working with hospital-based physicians are outlined in appendix 11-C.

Utilization Review and Quality Assurance

Q 11:36   How does medical necessity affect the provision of covered services?

For a covered service to be paid for under a managed care contract, it must be medically necessary. This requirement imposes a limitation on the provision of services and can be a subject of dispute and controversy between payer, provider, and patient. Contracts should define medical necessity as specifically as possible, and disputes related to determining medical necessity should be subject to appeal.

Q 11:37   Who decides what is medically necessary?

Most payers attempt to maintain control and responsibility over determinations of medical necessity. To avoid liability for an improper determination, it is important to document the payer representative responsible for the decision and the basis for that determination. To meet the standards established in *Wickline v. California* [192 Cal App 3d 1630, 228 Cal Rptr 661 (Cal App 2d Dist 1986)], the provider should exhaust all available review and appeal rights in the plan. Other situations that may create problems for coverage determinations include emergency services, preexisting conditions, and experimental procedures.

Q 11:38   Why do managed care contracts include provisions relating to utilization review?

Utilization review is a key component of any managed care arrangement. Most managed care contracts include language related to the plan's utilization review program and the provider's obligations to comply with the terms of such programs. The programs usually include preauthorization review, concurrent review, and retrospective review to ensure that enrollees have received medically necessary care and appropriate services. Although utilization review is under the payer's direction and control, the provider has an interest in ensuring that the contract provisions reflect a balanced process that does not unduly favor one party over the other.

Q 11:39   What are the important contract provisions relating to a utilization review program?

Many managed care contracts require the provider to comply with the payer's utilization review program but give no program description or detail. Because the type of program can have a significant impact on the level of reimbursement to the provider, these provisions should be carefully reviewed in advance of contract implementation.

Preauthorization Requirements. The contract should clearly address how the provider is to verify enrollee eligibility as well as financial responsibility for treatment provided to individuals later determined ineligible. Preauthorization requirements should be clear and practical. Changes in procedures for verifying eligibility should require advance notice to the provider. Common methods of verification include identification cards, enrollee lists furnished by payers to providers, telephone verification of eligibility, and any combination of these.

Emergency Services. Emergency services do not require preauthorization; however, many plans require notice of treatment within a specified period after care is rendered. The contract should include explicit directions for emergency care consistent with the anti-dumping provision of the Social Security Act [42 USC § 1395dd], which prohibits ascertainment of a patient's financial status prior to providing emergency care. Hospitals participating in Medicare must provide a screening examination to anyone seeking assistance through the emergency department and stabilize any individual with an emergency medical condition. Similar requirements are imposed under many state laws.

Concurrent Review. The contract should address and summarize how a payer will conduct concurrent review to determine the medical necessity of continued stay in the hospital. The contract's summary of the payer's concurrent review program should include information related to the type of admission or service subject to review, the frequency of the review, the time frames for providing this information, the procedures for accessing patient records, the time frames within which review decisions must be made, and whom the payer will notify with its review decision.

Retrospective Review. Retrospective review should be carefully defined in the contract, which should include specific provisions relating to appeal procedures, fairness, and limited payer discretion. When there are already strict preauthorization and concurrent review requirements, the provider may want to limit retrospective review to emergency care and other specific services.

Appeal Rights. Adverse utilization review decisions should be subject to appeal to an impartial reviewing body using appropriate standards of review. At a minimum, the appeal should be decided by a physician with training and experience in the specialty or service at issue. Appeal rights and procedures should be explained in the contract.

Q 11:40   Why are contract provisions relating to quality assurance important?

Quality of care and adherence to standards of care are important issues in contracting because the economic viability of a managed care plan depends on the delivery of quality, cost-effective care. In addition, recent court decisions have held managed care plans independently liable for the negligence of their participating providers. Finally, many employers look for a plan's accreditation by organizations such as the Joint Commission on Accreditation of Healthcare Organizations (JCAHO) and the NCQA as an indicator of quality. These accreditation organizations and standards are discussed in more detail in chapter 10. Contracts with providers should therefore address credentialing and peer review, contract participation standards, furnishing information to the plan, and whether corrective actions will be taken.

Term and Termination

Q 11:41   Should the initial contract term exceed one year?

It depends. In determining whether a contract should run for a short or long term, a provider should determine the economic viability of the initial contract arrangement to it as well as the long-term potential for payer viability. If the payer is viable and has a good track record, a longer term may be appropriate. If the parties are unsure of the efficacy of the relationship, however, a one-year trial is appropriate to allow the relationship to develop.

Q 11:42 How should contract renewal be structured?

Renewal provisions can take different forms. Many provider contracts provide for automatic renewal unless a party takes affirmative action to terminate the contract. Others provide for a preexpiration period of good-faith negotiation regarding contract renewal. It is not unusual for payers to request as much as six months' advance notice on either renewal or renegotiation in view of marketing considerations. One of the arguments in favor of renegotiated renewal is that it allows for renegotiated payment rates. If the contract is automatically renewed, it renews under all existing terms unless notice of nonrenewal or termination is given or automatic escalators are built into the payment provisions.

Q 11:43 Why are contracts terminated?

Contracts are usually terminated for cause or without cause. Termination for cause can be for specified causes such as becoming disqualified as a party to the contract (e.g., loss of license or accreditation status) or for reasons related to breach or nonperformance under the contract. Some contracts allow a time period within which to cure the underlying basis for the contract's termination. These specifications should be carefully evaluated, particularly under circumstances involving possible insolvency, because the bankruptcy laws lock in all potential creditors and prevent them from unilaterally terminating a contract on the filing of the petition in bankruptcy. Providers need to be able to terminate before any bankruptcy filing, which can be accomplished only through careful and ongoing review of the payer's financial position and use of solvency surveillance indicators.

Termination without cause is an important provision that should be included in almost all contracts. Although payers favor limiting termination without cause to contract expiration, providers should have the ability to terminate without cause with reasonable advance notice as a risk management device. Sometimes a valid contract will become illegal because of changes in the law or in regulations. Under such circumstances, there should be some provision that would attempt to save the contract rather than invalidate it in its entirety until the parties can reach agreement, in good faith and within a reasonable time frame, on a contract that complies with the law.

Q 11:44   What other considerations relating to contract termination should be addressed in the contract?

Many contracts require a provider to continue to provide services to an enrollee who is under a provider's care at the time of contract termination for a specified period of time and until the enrollee can be safely transferred to the care of another participating provider. Under these continuing obligation provisions, the areas to be negotiated are whether the provider will be subject to the payment provisions and the patient hold-harmless provisions of the contract following termination or expiration and whether the provider will be paid at usual and customary rates.

Insurance Coverage and Indemnification

Q 11:45   Why is insurance coverage required in a managed care contract?

Managed care arrangements carry significant risk of liability and financial loss. A managed care contract should limit risk by requiring liability insurance for professional liability claims and reinsurance (if appropriate) for financial risk under capitated and other risk-sharing arrangements. Each party should be required to carry its own errors and omissions insurance coverage and to show evidence of insurance coverage in specified limits. If one of the parties fails to carry appropriate insurance, it places the other party at increased risk of being a "deep pocket" for potential liability claimants.

Q 11:46   What is the difference between occurrence and claims-made insurance coverage?

Occurrence policies cover the insured for acts or omissions that form the basis for a claim of damages that arises during the policy period, regardless of whether the policy is in force at the time the claim is made. These policies are not readily available in the market and have been replaced by claims-made policies, which provide coverage for claims made during the time the policy is in force. That is, if a claim is brought against a provider that was and still is insured by the carrier at the time the claim is made, it will be covered. If, however, the claim is brought after the policy has either expired or been renewed under a different carrier, it will not be covered. To avoid the gaps in coverage related to claims-made policies, many insurance carriers offer either tail insurance coverage, which is purchased at the termination of the policy, or nose or prior-acts coverage going into the new policy. Managed care contracts should include these types of policies and coverages to avoid gaps in coverage and potential increased exposure of one party for the liability of the other.

Q 11:47 Should managed care contracts include provisions for mutual indemnification?

Only if there is contractual liability insurance coverage should one party accept the responsibility of indemnification of the other party. Indemnification clauses are used in managed care contracts to assign, through the contract, legal responsibility for assuming the defense and the cost of the defense and damages associated with claims brought against a nontortfeasor for the acts or omissions of a tortfeasor. If the payer is at fault for a claim but the provider is also sued because of the contractual relationship, an indemnification clause would allow the provider to demand that the payer indemnify and hold it harmless. Caution should be used in including any provision for indemnification, even if it is reciprocal, since it might impose direct and uninsured liability on and financially expose a party as an unintended consequence because contract indemnity is not covered by most standard policies of insurance. If a party does not have such insurance coverage, it is placing its assets at risk with every claim. Most MCOs are thinly capitalized; thus, there is increased exposure to the provider, which might be inadvertently placing its own assets at risk with each contract.

Claims Processing and Payment

Q 11:48 What issues should the contract address with regard to obtaining payment?

Many payers specify a time frame within which a claim must be filed in order to be acceptable for reimbursement to the provider.

These time frames, if required by the payer, should be reasonable and allow for extensions for good-cause delays. Another area of controversy concerns the accuracy and completeness of the claim form. Providers perceive that payers will refuse a claim if there is even a minor deviation from required format. There should be a clear understanding as to the billing form to be used and the time frame within which a claim must be rejected if it is not complete. Claims should be deemed clean claims after a specified period to trigger the running of the time frame for payment of the claim. If a claim is not paid within a specified period of time, the provider should have the option of seeking either its full, undiscounted charge as reimbursement or a penalty that accrues against the payer for each day the claim is unpaid beyond the specified time frame. There should also be provisions that would allow the provider to look to the enrollee for financial responsibility for copayments, deductibles, coinsurance, and noncovered services the enrollee has consented to receive.

Q 11:49 Should there be a provision for interim payments or payments pending utilization review?

Yes. Providers have financial risk for expensive cases during the pendency of claims submission and review. They also have significant exposure if a particular payer's enrollees make up a substantial part of the provider's patient base. Some contracts include provisions for interim payments when there is financial risk to the provider. Others restrict the payer's ability to delay payments beyond the specified time frame if the claim has been preauthorized. Payers have the ability to protect their economic interests by providing for periodic adjustments to future payments to offset any excess or deficiency in payments to providers.

Q 11:50 How should the contract coordinate benefits and subrogate claims?

Whenever there are multiple payers, there should be a mechanism for allocating responsibility among them for payment of any claim. Subrogation of claims involves the assignment of payment of liability claims to the payer to offset the amounts paid by the payer under the insurance policy for coverage of claims for injuries resulting from the act or omission of a third party. Many providers prefer that the payer make full payment and then be responsible for handling coordination of benefits and subrogation rights. On the other hand, payers may require that the provider handle coordination of benefits and subrogation of claims.

Records Retention, Access, and Disclosure

Q 11:51   How should the contract address ownership of and access to patient records?

Most managed care contracts provide for some form of access to medical record information by the health plan. The health plan requires certain information to satisfy reporting requirements under federal and state law; however, the health plan's right to confidential medical information is not absolute. As a general rule, the provider is responsible for custody and control of the patient's physical records and has a legal duty under state and federal law to maintain the records' confidentiality. Payers do not have an automatic right of access to medical records and should be required to provide some form of patient consent. (Federal law imposes a higher standard for access to drug and alcohol abuse records.) Although many payers attempt to incorporate a general, blanket release of medical records into their enrollment or application forms, these may have limited validity under state and federal law. In fact, some state laws extend statutory protections to patient medical information and make it a violation of medical practice acts to release confidential medical information without proper patient authorization.

Q 11:52   How can the contract protect a party's confidential and proprietary information and materials that are disclosed to the other as part of the relationship?

Contracts should first specifically identify which shared information and materials are to be considered proprietary to which party. The contract should provide for both confidentiality and nondisclosure, with appropriate legal sanctions (both injunctive relief and damages) if the proprietary information is wrongfully disclosed.

Q 11:53   How should the contract address confidential quality management and utilization review materials and records?

Most contracts require providers to cooperate with the plan's utilization review and quality management program; however, the potential access by the payer to a provider's confidential peer or quality review information may jeopardize the protection generally available under most state laws. To avoid losing legal protection, the provider may need to develop alternative means of providing quality and utilization information to the payer, such as summaries and reports, rather than provide the primary sources of information. Significant challenges related to protecting confidential information will arise as systems for communication of primary patient data become more sophisticated.

Q 11:54 What are the retention requirements for health information?

The retention requirements for health information vary by state and are subject to various regulatory and accreditation considerations. The Code of Federal Regulations includes record retention requirements for hospitals [42 CFR § 482.24(b)(1)], for home health agencies [42 CFR § 482.48(a)], for state and long-term care facilities [42 CFR § 483.75(l)(2)], and for specialized providers and suppliers [42 CFR § 485.60]. These federal record retention requirements are imposed on these health care providers as a condition of participation in certain federally funded health care programs. The Code of Federal Regulations does not specify a record retention period for hospices, ambulatory surgical services, HMOs, competitive medical plans (CMPs), or health care prepayment plans (HCPPs).

Accreditation organizations such as the JCAHO and the National Commission on Correctional Health Care for Health Services in Jails and Prisons impose record retention requirements, but the NCQA and the Commission on Accreditation of Rehabilitation Facilities do not prescribe specific retention requirements.

The American Health Information Management Association recommends that patient health information be retained for the following time periods:[5]

Patient health records (adult)	10 years
Patient health records (minors)	Age of majority plus statute of limitations period
Diagnostic images (x-ray film)	5 years

Disease index	10 years
Fetal heart monitor records	10 years after the infant reaches the age of majority
Master patient index	Permanently
Operative index	10 years
Physician index	10 years
Register of births	Permanently
Register of deaths	Permanently
Register of surgical procedures	Permanently

Risk Contracting with Prepaid Health Plans

Q 11:55 What types of risk-sharing arrangements are encountered by providers in a managed care contracting situation?

Under a risk-sharing arrangement, an MCO will contract with a provider or provider organization to provide a defined set of medical services at a negotiated capitation rate. Capitation rates can be negotiated as a flat amount PMPM; as a table of PMPM rates adjusted for age, sex, and benefit option; or as a percentage of the purchaser's premium payment.

Virtually any arrangement of prepaid health care is possible as long as the parties agree to the risks. Prepaid health care, of which capitation is the paradigm, is merely a mechanism to allow the broader sharing of risk coupled with strong controls on utilization. Thus, a broad spectrum of arrangements that promote the sharing of risk is possible under the rubric of capitation. Risk-sharing arrangements include full capitation, physician services capitation, subcapitation, and use of third-party intermediaries.

Full capitation, sometimes known as full risk, requires a managed care entity to assume responsibility for all the medical needs of the enrollees in or subscribers to a health plan. These needs will usually include hospitalization, durable medical equipment, and ancillary services such as x-ray, laboratory, and pharmacy services. Many of these services and supplies may be subcontracted to another organization on a discounted fee-for-service basis or on a subcapitated basis with the risk shared among providers.

Under physician services capitation, a managed care entity is responsible only for the physician services provided to the contracting entity. Although there may be "value-added" services provided, the managed care entity will not be responsible for providing any hospital, drug, or ancillary service. Under this arrangement, the physician group may elect to capitate only its PCPs and pay its specialists on a discounted fee-for-service basis. Some "primary care only" groups will subcapitate specialist services to other groups prepared to accept that risk.

Subcapitation exists when the initial risk-taking entity contracts with another for services or supplies on a risk basis by assuming a portion of the risk. This arrangement may take the form of the provision of specialized services or even primary care services for a certain area. In one of the more common subcapitation arrangements, the primary care group or the HMO itself subcontracts with specialists or subspecialists on a risk basis for services such as cardiology and oncology. Regional and nationwide networks have been constructed to accept this form of risk. In other forms of subcapitation, MCOs accept risk for some covered services such as home health, pharmacy, or laboratory services. Because the PMPM payment is typically small in subcapitation, successful contracts will require a large volume or population of members. If the enrolled population is too small, specialists who would normally be subcapitated should be paid on a discounted fee-for-service basis.

As a business organization, a management services organization (MSO) can manage contracts on behalf of its contracted physicians or physician groups. Some MSOs include physician investors who hold an equity interest in the MSO. If the contract pays the provider a capitation rate or a discounted fee with a withhold, the MSO may impose additional performance criteria on the manner of distribution of additional payments. The scope of activity of an MSO varies depending on state laws relating to the corporate practice of medicine. In some states, the MSO can participate in the risk-sharing arrangement. The MSO serves as an intermediary between the physician and the contracting entity and in some states may actually hold the contract in its name. In this situation, although the physicians may be part owners of the MSO, they generally participate in the actual patient care risk via capitation or a withhold pool.

Risk is even further diluted when a third-party intermediary distributes it. In this situation, the risk may be partly held by all or only a few of the parties involved in providing patient care. The intermediary may share in the risk or take a fee for managing the prepaid plan. The intermediary can be an MSO.

Q 11:56   What are the various risk-sharing models?

In risk-based relationships with provider networks, the financial and organizational models for managing and distributing funds include (1) the PCP capitation and shared-risk pool, (2) the provider organization capitation and shared-risk pool, and (3) full-risk capitation. A general example of a risk pool arrangement is shown in Figure 11-3.

Primary Care Physician Capitation with Shared-Risk Pool. Under this arrangement, only the PCPs are paid a capitation rate, whereas other providers are paid at a discounted fee-for-service rate as determined by the MCO. Often, the MCO retains a percentage of the capi-

Figure 11-3   Shared-Risk Funds

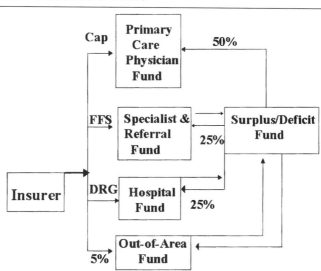

Figure 11-4   **Primary Care Physician Capitation**

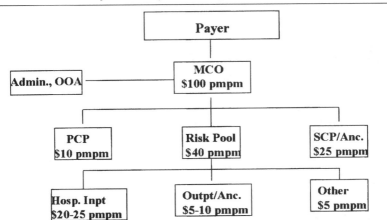

tation payment as a withhold to be used in the event network costs exceed the budget. Figure 11-4 shows an example of how this arrangement can be structured.

Provider Organization Capitation and Shared-Risk Pool. Under this arrangement, a provider group is capitated for professional services and a risk pool is established for hospital and other services. Hospitals are typically paid on a fee-for-service basis or on a negotiated per diem or case rate basis. The MCO holds the hospital budget pool and deducts hospital payments from that pool. Surplus funds remaining are shared by the health plan and physicians. This approach is shown in Figure 11-5.

Full-Risk Capitation. Under a full-risk or global capitation model, the provider organization is given a negotiated capitation rate to manage both hospitals and professional services. The provider organization also administers the capitation payment and may handle many of the administrative services as part of its responsibilities. This approach is shown in Figure 11-6.

Q 11:57   What are the basic elements of constructing a risk pool?

The structure of risk pools among providers under various managed care arrangements requires careful consideration of several elements, including the parties to be affected, the monies to be pooled,

Figure 11-5   Provider Organization Partial-Risk Capitation

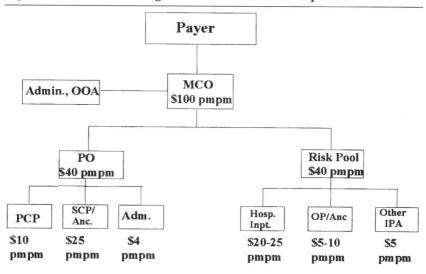

Figure 11-6   Provider Organization Full-Risk Capitation

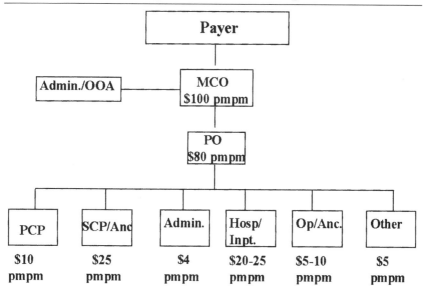

the period of time for risk pool settlements, and the level of participation. The analysis should be conducted as follows:

1. Who stands to benefit from or to be burdened by utilization variances?
   - PCPs
   - Specialists
   - Institutions
   - Provider network (PHO, PPO, MSO)
   - Insurers
   - Employers

2. What monies will be pooled?
   - Primary care
   - Specialist care
   - Institutional care
   - Prescriptions
   - Out-of-area care
   - Emergency care in area, but out of network
   - Coordination of benefits and third-party insurance recoveries
   - Reinsurance and stop-loss recoveries from third parties
   - Self-funded reinsurance, stop-loss, and withhold or risk stabilization pools

3. When will the computations be made?
   - Periodic computations with annual reconciliation
   - Moderating effect of withhold pools
   - Continually adjusting interim payments
   - Carryovers
   - Incurred but not reported estimates

4. Where (at what level) will participation in the pools be?
   - Individual or group
   - Own or combination of own and other services
   - Offsets of one pool against another

- Method of allocation among providers
  - Referrals
  - Per capita
  - Assigned enrollees
  - Visits or other utilization measure
  - Billed charges
  - Patient satisfaction
  - Severity adjusted
5. Why have risk pools?
   - Reward or punishment
   - Limitations
   - Performance variables
     - Inpatient days (1,000)
     - Prescriptions
     - Average length of stay
     - Patient satisfaction
     - Adherence to formulary
     - Referral budget (dollars or frequency)
     - Quality (morbidity rates, mortality rates, chart review)
6. How should risk pools be designed?
   - Internal variables (the structure)
     - Service responsibility
     - Charges against budget
     - Credits against budget
     - Timing of measurement
     - Incurred but not reported calculations
     - Surplus or deficit sharing
       Among pools
       Among providers of same class
       Among providers of different classes
       Percentages
       Allocation methodologies
       Performance measures

- External variables
  - — Enrollee population size
  - — Influence over utilization
  - — Cost of out-of-plan and out-of-network services
  - — Physician group internal compensation methodologies

Q 11:58   What legal issues commonly arise in managed care risk contracting?

Contracts between MCOs and providers are subject to complex government regulations. Some are imposed under federal law, and others are imposed under state law. These issues are discussed in more detail in chapter 8. They include the following:

Insurance Law. The ability of a provider to enter into a risk contract depends on state insurance law. Under many state insurance or corporation laws, entities that contract on a risk or global fee basis may be subject to state regulation. The focus of the regulators is on (1) whether the arrangement constitutes the business of insurance, (2) whether there is a licensed entity in the risk chain, (3) whether full or partial risk is being transferred, (4) the extent to which the provider is responsible for the cost of services beyond its scope of practice, and (5) evidence of the entity's solvency and accountability.

Government Programs. To the extent the arrangement involves federal contracts under Medicaid or Medicare, there are issues associated with managed care contracting. Medicare prepaid plans offered through HMOs and other MCOs have their own set of requirements that differ from state law requirements. The BBA created the opportunity for PSOs to contract with Medicare on a risk basis.

Antitrust. The Federal Trade Commission (FTC) and the Department of Justice (DOJ) have issued enforcement guidelines relating to MCOs and the shared risk aspect of the contracting process. Under the most recent enforcement statements on provider networks, there is an opportunity to use risk-sharing arrangements as a means of integrating provider organizations.

Corporate Practice of Medicine. Another legal issue that may arise in the contracting arrangement is whether the fee or compensation arrangement violates any corporate practice of medicine or medical practice acts. There are fee-splitting prohibitions under many state laws.

Underutilization. Many states have adopted rules that prohibit MCOs from offering financial incentives that would induce providers to limit services that are medically necessary. In *Shea v. Esenten* [1997 WL 78350 (8th Cir) (Feb 26, 1997)], the court held that administrators of health plans have a fiduciary duty to disclose to their enrollees that the plan offers financial incentives for participating health care providers to limit services. Similar protections are being developed as part of the Medicare fraud and abuse provisions to protect against rationing medically necessary health care services.

Physician Incentive Plans. Civil monetary penalties of up to $25,000 per occurrence may be imposed when certain MCOs substantially fail to provide medically necessary items and services to a covered individual and the failure adversely affected or had a substantial likelihood of adversely affecting the individual. [42 USC § 1395mm(I)(6)] No payment may be made to a provider as an inducement to reduce or limit medically necessary services provided to an enrollee. In January 1997, final incentive plan regulations became effective to curb the potential financial loss to physicians who are at substantial financial risk for populations that include Medicare or Medicaid eligibles. Under these incentive plan rules, if a plan places a physician or physician group at "substantial risk" for the cost of referrals, the plan must provide stop-loss protection and conduct periodic surveys of enrollees to determine the degree of access to care and quality of services. If a physician or physician group participates in a physician incentive plan, the information regarding the nature of the incentive program must be disclosed to HCFA.[6]

Bad-Faith or Financial Incentive Tort Liability. Some have found liability when application of a health plan's utilization review criteria resulted in injury or harm to a person. These cases (discussed at length in chapter 8) have resulted in new legislation regulating health plan conduct. Texas enacted Senate Bill 386, which holds HMOs and health plans liable for malpractice when their utilization review decisions are the primary cause of an adverse event involving a covered patient. [Title 4, Civil Practices and Remedies Code, chapter 88]

Q 11:59 What other items should be considered in risk contracting?

In addition to the issues discussed in Qs 11:55–11:58, practical considerations to any risk-based contract include the following:

Practicing Medicine versus Coverage Determinations. In analyzing the potential liability of each contracting party for the other's activities, it is important to focus on indemnification and hold-harmless clauses in the contracts. Because of the inequities in the economic relationship of the parties, and because most physician liability carriers do not extend the coverage of the physician's policy to a third party without express contractual liability endorsement, it is best that physicians not expressly indemnify the MCO for liability. Instead, the parties should ensure that each maintains appropriate malpractice insurance coverage for its respective acts or omissions.

Agency Relationships. There is a risk that the enrollee will perceive that there is more than a mere contractual relationship between the payer and provider. This perceived agency relationship can expose the payer to vicarious liability as a principal, with the provider as its "ostensible" agent. Not all vicarious liability claims that arise under such circumstances will be preempted by ERISA. (See chapter 8 for further discussion.)

Setting a High Standard of Care in Plan Documents. When plans describe the level of care and competence of their provider networks as being of "highest quality" with "good results," there is the risk that a standard of care will be imposed that exceeds what is "ordinary, customary, and acceptable."

Financial Incentives. As discussed in chapters 7 and 8, there is a regulatory risk when financial incentives adversely affect the patient. In the context of potential liability exposure, however, self-serving statements regarding the purpose of the financial incentive may help overcome such claims.

Other Considerations. What services are required under the capitation fee? How are new and experimental procedures handled under the policy? What are the preexisting-condition policies? Are there any contractual limitations to subcontracting for services not provided by the provider? How are out-of-area cases handled? What is the mechanism for accounting (in the capitation payment) for enrollment and disenrollment of members? How are member eligibility disputes handled? How was the capitation rate established? How was the premium rate established? What information will the payer give the provider? How is coordination of benefits handled? How should the provider protect itself from shrinking membership levels? How are the risk pools constructed?

Q 11:60   What are some of the precautions to take when considering a risk-sharing arrangement?

Questions to ask as part of a due diligence analysis of an entity that proposes to take risk for a population include the following:

1. Can the entity that is assuming the risk for medical care fulfill the contracted obligation? Although insurance laws in most jurisdictions ensure the entity's financial solvency as well as its ability to follow through with its financial obligations, this does not ensure that the entity will be able to deliver the services it is obligated to deliver.

2. Are controls in place to allow effective utilization review? Utilization review (see chapter 9) is a complex series of procedures designed to provide the most efficient care for patients. Utilization review is not denial of care, nor should it introduce needless hassles for patients and providers. Utilization review should be performed in a spirit of cooperation rather than confrontation. The purchaser of capitated care for employees should inquire diligently as to whether the utilization review function exists to facilitate or to deny care.

3. Does the entity control its own capitation, or is it subcontracted to a risk-managing company? The managed care industry has spawned a number of subsidiary functions serving it, among them the "capitation manager." In large MCOs, this function is often performed in-house; in others, it is subcontracted to an independent firm. The considerations are complex. On one hand, this function serves to provide the most cost-effective care. On the other hand, it determines profit margin. Some MCOs insist that this function be performed outside the confines of the organization purely for the purpose of maintaining objectivity. Other MCOs feel comfortable managing capitation themselves. Regardless, it is important to ensure that the capitation management and

information system is capable of producing and reporting data that can be used by the purchaser to manage the health care buying dollar intelligently.

4. Does the medical care entity understand the concept of appropriate as contrasted to minimal medical care? Few measures of value have been developed to allow the purchaser of managed care to make intelligent decisions regarding its provision. As discussed in greater detail in chapter 10, many efforts are under way to measure quality. Table 11-4 lists some value-added programs that MCOs have used to augment their normal role of providing medical care. Since *HMO* means health maintenance organization, it should come as no surprise that a number of value-added services are focused on prevention. Although little data exist on the efficacy

Table 11-4   Examples of Value-Added Services

Medical Services

- After-hours scheduled visits
- 24-hour physician availability
- Home visits
- Medical question "hot line"
- Multiple provider locations
- Medical school or educational institution affiliation
- Preventive medicine services
- Health maintenance services
- Travel medicine services
- Choice of primary care provider

Education

- Health fairs
- Health question telephone line
- Medical information packets
- Illness-specific information packets

Additional Services

- Home health services
- Rehabilitation and physical therapy services
- Range of out-of-area coverage

of prevention, no one would argue against the importance of immunizations, cancer screening, and nutrition education.

5. Does the managed care entity afford access, and can the entity define access in terms of what it means to the individual patient? Measures of access may be as mundane as the number of primary care doctors within a certain radius of each subscriber or as specific as average waiting time for a new-patient appointment or a specialist visit. It is important to remember that MCOs save money by managing care. As purchasers shift from traditional indemnity to managed care, discretion regarding access is progressively lost. Therefore, the managed care purchaser should not expect the same access to specialists or to the physician of one's choice as was provided under traditional indemnity coverage. It is, however, reasonable to expect standardization in provider competence and the credentialing process (see chapter 10). The purchaser of managed care must not be misled by large lists of physicians when few of them have open practices.

6. Where does the entity exert control of utilization? Prepaid health care requires control of utilization. Restriction of medical care services under capitation is a reality. Capitated systems do not purport to replicate fee-for-service systems, and the purchaser of managed care should expect change as the shift is made. This shift may, however, be accompanied by increased access to primary care and preventive services as well as better management of illness episodes. In other words, the overall quality of the health care received by a subscriber may improve. Nonetheless, if the patient or physician believes that this is accomplished by increasing the hassle required to get health care, the perceived benefit will be negated. As discussed in chapter 9, control of health care utilization can be achieved through many methods, including the following:

   - *Restriction of benefits.* The contents of the plan must be disclosed in detail. Managed care plans manage care by providing a defined set of benefits. That these benefits do not cause undue hardship to the patient is important in evaluating the plan.

   - *Restriction of capacity.* Many plans restrict access to specialists by requiring referral from a PCP, or by requiring a greater financial contribution from the patient to access an out-of-network specialist (e.g., POS plans). Inability of a patient to access an appropriate specialist in a timely way can adversely affect patient care.

- *Negative incentives for referral.* As the economic noose tightens on physicians, they are increasingly aware of being observed at every turn. PCPs can be, and have been, excluded from contracts on the basis of their utilization. This so-called economic credentialing is pervasive, and it is important for the managed care purchaser to know what form of economic credentialing is used. Rarely is it so blatant that the physician is economically punished directly for specialist referral. The coercion is generally more subtle and takes the form of financial incentives to the primary care "gatekeeper" through withholds and bonuses. These incentive schemes are not, by definition, nefarious; they may merely be cost effective. But that border must be recognized.

7. Who are the doctors? MCOs have different standards for credentialing their providers (see chapter 10). General practitioners, family physicians, general internists, and general pediatricians are all placed under the heading of "primary care physician," but a glance at the functional definitions given in Table 11-5 shows that these physicians are not alike. Another important issue is to what extent the MCO uses mid-level nonphysician practitioners such as nurse practitioners,

Table 11-5　Characteristics of Primary Care Physicians

Category	Primary Degree	Years of Training After Doctorate	Primary Certification
General practitioner	M.D. or D.O.	1*	None
General internist	M.D. or D.O.	3	American Board of Internal Medicine
Family physician	M.D. or D.O.	3	American Board of Family Practice
General pediatrician	M.D. or D.O.	3	American Board of Pediatrics

* Several states require no postdoctoral training for licensure. Thus, a substantial number of physicians licensed to practice medicine have had no postdoctoral training.

physicians assistants, nurse midwives, and nurse anesthetists.

8. Who operates the ancillary services such as laboratories and radiology facilities? Ancillary services, facilities, and supplies are a major expense for MCOs. Therefore, they carefully balance price and quality in making contracts. The same analysis used in investigating an MCO should be used in examining its ancillary services contracts.

9. Are value-added services, such as patient education, smoking cessation programs, weight-loss programs, health fairs, and immunizations, offered? (See Table 11-4.)

10. Is the entity associated with a medical education institution? The role of the teaching hospital in managed care is under debate. Teaching hospitals, residency programs, and medical student education have heretofore been funded by a complex web of interactions, including direct and indirect medical education payments by Medicare to teaching hospitals, "cost shifting" from third parties, research funding, and state payments. Each of these payers is saying, "no more," and medical education is scrabbling for funding. Yet the academic medical centers provide an environment where new knowledge is generated and amplified and the next generation of physicians is trained. As such, the academic medical centers provide unique resources in difficult-to-manage cases and suffer greatly from adverse selection when they are included in MCOs and provider panels. Should a managed care purchaser actively look for an organization affiliated with a teaching institution, or should it recoil in terror? The data to answer this question are being collected, and most of the reports are anecdotal. Certain cross-subsidization must continue if the non-revenue-generating activities of the academic medical center are to survive, but who will pay and how are questions of national policy that have yet to be answered.

Q 11:61 How are the compensation provisions of capitation and risk-sharing agreements structured?

The principal forms of provider risk sharing (capitation, withholds, and stop-loss arrangements) occur in provider agreements.

As health care costs continue to rise, health insurers, HMOs, and self-funded employers are looking to providers of health care as a source of risk sharing (and risk shifting). The methods of sharing risk vary among the types of providers as well as within provider groups.

Capitation. Capitation payment uses a set dollar amount PMPM paid by an MCO to a provider (or provider organization) to cover a specified set of services, without regard to the actual volume of services provided to any one patient. Capitation may cover the provider's own services, referral services, or all medical services and/or administrative costs. If the patient costs exceed the capitated amount, the provider absorbs the loss. If costs are below capitation, the provider keeps the additional money.

Withhold Pools. Withhold pools are funded through the deduction by the MCO of a percentage or a set dollar amount from each provider's (or provider organization's) payment (salary, fees, or capitation). The amount withheld is set aside in pools to pay for specialty referral services, inpatient hospital services, or unanticipated health care costs. The provider is at risk because the withhold pool funds may not be available if the cost of the health care services exceeds the amount in the fund. If costs exceed the budget, part or all of the withhold may be forfeited. If costs do not exceed the budget, part or all of the withhold may be returned to the provider. Withhold pools are used with either fee-for-service or capitation arrangements.

Global Fee Arrangements. Global fee arrangements have developed as a mechanism for shifting the risk of care to providers for certain categories of patients. For example, in obstetrics, the physician is paid an amount for antepartum through postpartum care, is financially responsible for rendering all obstetric services associated with the pregnancy, and receives no additional payment even if the actual costs exceed the global fee payment.

Per Diems for Hospitals. A per diem system pays hospitals a prospectively determined rate for each day of inpatient care provided. With per diems, as with DRGs, hospitals benefit if the actual cost of an inpatient stay is less than the per diem amount multiplied by the patient's length of stay in the hospital. Conversely, the hospital takes a loss if the actual costs exceed the cumulative per diem payment.

Per Case Rates for Hospitals. Per case reimbursement rates are much like DRGs in that the hospital is paid a prospectively determined amount based on the patient's diagnosis or based on the type of service to be rendered (e.g., obstetrics, cardiology, general surgery). The risk analysis is the same as it is for per diem arrangements.

Global Capitation. With the integration of health care providers into a single delivery system, payers are developing ways to shift the risk for a broad array of health care services to such organizations by paying the provider network a global capitation payment each month for each patient who elects to receive services from the network's panel of providers. The payment rate includes all health services rendered through providers under contract with the network, including physician and hospital services. The network is financially responsible for the compensation of all providers from the single global payment and is at risk if the total compensation to the providers is greater than the aggregate global capitation payment.

Bundled Fee Arrangement. Another way to pay physicians, hospitals, and other types of providers is through a single fee payment. Under a bundled fee arrangement, different classes of providers agree to be compensated for the individual services that each provider renders during an episode of treatment through a single fee negotiated between the payer and providers. This represents the fee-for-service approach to a global contracting arrangement. For example, a hospital-based anesthesiologist may agree to join with the hospital in negotiating with payers for a bundled fee payment for specific types of surgeries. Usually, the hospital will receive the bundled payment and will be financially responsible for paying other providers for services rendered.

Assuming a Corridor of Risk (Stop-Loss Coverage). Some networks assume a specified corridor of risk, which involves the purchase of stop-loss coverage from a licensed reinsurance company. Under this approach, an actuarial analysis of the anticipated risk to be assumed from the patient population of a particular payer is performed. The network agrees to a global capitation payment equal to 100 percent of the actuarially expected risk. To cover the risk above the specified level, the network arranges for the purchase of stop-loss coverage at an attachment point that approaches the global capitation payment as closely as possible on an actuarial basis. This results in the network assuming the corridor of risk between 100 percent of the actuarially expected risk and the attachment point for stop-loss coverage. The risk in this type of arrangement is the degree to which the stop-loss insurer starts to look like a traditional health insurer subject to state regulation as such. As the attachment point for excess loss coverage approaches 100 percent, there is increased risk of the reinsurer looking like an insurance company. Experts suggest that an attachment point for aggregate and/or specific stop-loss coverage that exceeds 125 percent of the actuarially expected risk is usually acceptable by most state regulators.

Q 11:62   How do the different payment methodologies align hospital and physician incentives?

One of the goals of risk contracting is to align provider incentives though a shared risk and reward system. The effectiveness of capitation is that it rewards providers for effective and efficient utilization. Table 11-6 shows the effects of different payment methodologies on hospital and physician utilization of certain services.

Q 11:63   What are the mandated provisions in a managed care contract?

A number of provisions in a managed care contract exist because of statutory, regulatory, or accreditation requirements. Such requirements include requirements of the following:

National Committee for Quality Assurance. NCQA is a major accrediting organization of MCOs, and the NCQA standards address (1) participation in quality assurance activities, (2) access to care, (3) delegation of certain functions and activities, (4) medical records

Table 11-6   Effects of Payment Methodologies on Utilization

	Discounted Fee for Services	Per Diem (Hospital Only)	Per Case (Hospital Only)	Capitation (Includes MD)
Admissions				
Hospital	Encourage	Encourage	Encourage	Discourage
Doctor	Encourage	Encourage	Encourage	Discourage
Length of Stay				
Hospital	Encourage	Encourage	Discourage	Discourage
Doctor	Encourage	Encourage	Encourage	Discourage
Ancillaries				
Hospital	Encourage	Discourage	Discourage	Discourage
Doctor	Encourage	Encourage	Encourage	Discourage

confidentiality and maintenance standards, and (5) preventive health services.

State Departments of Insurance. Standards applicable to PPOs extend to (1) applicants to insured PPO networks, (2) fairness standards, (3) no provider risk, (4) undercare restrictions, (5) freedom of choice by insureds, (6) continuity of treatment on termination, (7) emergency care standards, (8) provider diversity, (9) complaint resolution, (10) no retaliation, (11) due process on termination of providers, (12) economic profiling, (13) quality assurance using physician reviewers, (14) utilization review overseen by licensed physicians, (15) no indemnity required in PPO contracts, (16) standards on patient charges, and (17) standards on intermediary contracts. Standards applicable to HMOs include (1) financial hold-harmless requirements, (2) continuity of treatment on termination, (3) no retaliation for complaints and grievances, (4) restrictions on undercare, (5) no indemnity of an HMO for its own acts, (6) application process, (7) termination standards, (8) economic profiling disclosure, (9) capitation payments, and (10) emergency care requirements and coverage

State Departments of Health. Most state departments of health play a role in the oversight of managed care plans that are regulated by state laws. Most of these requirements track the standards of NCQA and relate to access to information, continuity of care on termination, contract requirements, and other quality and clinical standards.

State Boards of Medical Examiners. Sometimes there are provisions in contracts required by state medical practice acts that are intended to ensure that an unlicensed entity is not engaged in the corporate practice of medicine.

Medicare. Medicare imposes a significant number of contract requirements on HMOs as a condition of participation in a risk plan and on providers who provide services to Medicare eligibles. Of particular interest are financial hold-harmless provisions, cooperation with utilization review and quality assurance standards, anti-gag rule and disclosure provisions, medical records standards, and continuity of care on termination. There is an effort under way to obtain "deemed" status under Medicare for compliance if the health plan and contract are accredited by an approved accrediting organization such as NCQA or JCAHO.

Payer-Intermediary Arrangements

Q 11:64   What are the special issues related to insurance functions of a payer-intermediary arrangement?

These arrangements typically involve TPAs or administrative-services-only or contract management companies that perform management as well as other services for either the payer or the provider. The types of services vary, but can include the following:

- Marketing
  - Commercial (employer groups, government employees, individuals)
  - Medicaid
  - Medicare
- Enrollment
  - Membership files
  - Disenrollment
  - Maintenance of current eligibility lists
- Network operations and administration
  - Contracting and provider network development
  - Credentialing
  - Provider services
  - Administration of stop-loss program
  - Benefit design and plan drafting
  - Regulatory and legal services
  - Purchasing and vendor contracting
  - Record maintenance
  - Personnel management, employee training, and related services
- Member services
  - Toll-free telephone access, inquiries
  - Education (e.g., how to access services)
  - Explanation of benefits
  - Customer relations, including grievance proceedings and patient advocacy

- Claims administration
  - In versus out of network
  - Incurred but not reported (IBNR) claims
  - Processing and adjudicating claims
- Information management
  - Aggregate data for all departments on revenue, costs, utilization, and quality
  - External reports for regulators and reviewers
  - Management information services
  - Mail and communications services
- Finance
  - General ledger, accounts receivable and payable, budgeting, and payroll
  - Premium and capitation calculations
  - Preparation and mailing of IRS Form 1099 to providers
  - Actuarial services
  - Underwriting services
  - Accounting and other financial services
  - Collection of copayments, coordination of benefits, and subrogation payments
- Health services
  - Case management
  - Utilization management
- Quality management, including medical review support, analysis, and expertise

Direct Contracting

Q 11:65 What are the important issues to consider in direct contracting between a subscriber and a provider?

Practical operational as well as legal issues must be considered in any direct-contracting analysis. From a marketing and operational perspective, focus should be on the product: what it will take to sell the product and whether a particular purchaser is qualified to be a direct-contracting partner. The purchaser of the product has legitimate concerns about the quality of the product, the network associated with it, its financial solvency, and its track record. Important factors for a purchaser to consider in contracting with a provider organization include (1) the quality of the provider network's facilities and physicians, (2) its quality management program, (3) the availability of providers to enrollees in the network, (4) the flexibility of the network to accommodate multiple managed care arrangements (PPO, HMO, or POS) in a single delivery system or network, (5) the affordability of the services to the employer and employees based on cost per employee, and (6) the organizational and fiscal stability of the network and its participating providers.

Q 11:66 What are the precontracting considerations for direct contracting from the subscriber's or purchaser's perspective?

Medicare and Medicaid have specific rules associated with risk contracting for Medicare and Medicaid beneficiaries. In the private sector, however, self-funded employers have two options when purchasing a health benefit product on a direct-contract basis. They can buy health care services (with or without the administrative support) as a packaged product directly from provider organizations, or they can be part of a pooled purchasing arrangement. Many self-funded employers have become actively involved in the design and purchase of health care services. Because of the application of ERISA, the employer's choice of product and manner of participation will determine whether it must follow state and/or federal law.

Q 11:67 How does ERISA affect direct-contracting arrangements?

The unique feature of ERISA law for direct-contracting purposes is its preemption of state law. The ERISA preemption provisions are structured as three separate clauses: the preemption clause, the "savings" clause, and the "deemer" clause. If a state law relates to an employee benefit plan subject to ERISA, it is preempted. [29 USC § 144(a)] The savings clause provides an exception to preemption for state laws that regulate insurance, banking, or securities. The deemer clause, however, prohibits states from enlarging the scope of their regulatory authority by simply deeming self-insured ERISA plans to be insurance companies for purposes of state regulation. This analysis has been used to determine the scope of ERISA preemption and is subject to varying interpretation by the courts. Because of the federal preemption of state claims, ERISA has been used as a shield in negligence and related tort claims involving various managed care entities and arrangements that seek the limited liability protection of ERISA. State regulations such as "any willing provider" laws may not be preempted by ERISA.[7]

Q 11:68 What are the precontracting considerations for a provider organization that wants to engage in direct contracting?

The ability of a provider organization to engage in direct contracting with an employer or with a government program is subject to a number of statutory and regulatory considerations ranging from the state's regulation of the business of insurance and insurance products to antitrust and liability issues.

Q 11:69 What should be considered in the analysis of any direct-contracting arrangement under state law?

The first question to ask is whether the provider organization that accepts prepayments or engages in risk sharing is, by definition, an HMO health plan under the state's HMO law or is otherwise engaged in the business of insurance under the state's insurance law. Depending on state law, this concern may arise not only for direct contracts with employer benefit plans but also for contracts with licensed insurers or HMOs. Therefore, integrated provider groups, provider networks, and IDSs should carefully evaluate all their health care delivery arrangements, but especially those outside the context of contracts with licensed insurers or HMOs.

In addition to business of insurance and HMO licensure regulations, provider organizations must be aware of other state regulations. A provider organization may, for example, conduct operations—such as utilization review, claims payment, or other network administrative services—that are subject to separate state licensure and/or taxation. A provider organization may also be engaging in certain selective provider contracting, credentialing, or subcontracting activities that could subject it to "any willing provider" or freedom of choice laws.

Q 11:70   How do risk bearing and risk sharing by the provider organization affect direct-contracting arrangements?

Licensed insurers, licensed HMOs, provider-sponsored PPOs, and provider-sponsored integrated systems have, for years, offered provider networks directly to employee benefit plans as well as indirectly through other entities (TPAs, PPOs, and various types of brokers) that are contracted with employee benefit plans. Because of the financial arrangements used by some, these contract arrangements have been challenged by regulators as being the business of insurance or by competitors as not being subject to the insurance antitrust exemption of the McCarran-Ferguson Act. [15 USC § 20] Courts have produced several examples of what is not the business of insurance. These examples recognize that an employee benefit plan's direct contract with a network of providers does not necessarily indicate that the plan has entered into an insurance contract. Accordingly, these courts have concluded that such contracts do not cause the plan to lose the protection from state laws that is provided by the ERISA preemption clause. Examples of activities that were found not to be the business of insurance include the following:

- Use of a fee-for-service psychiatric program utilizing a provider network established by Blue Cross/Blue Shield, in which the employer plan retained all claims payment risk [Varol v Blue Cross & Blue Shield, 708 F Supp 826 (ED Mich 1989)]

- Use of a utilization review committee of providers to review the reasonableness of charges and medical necessity [Union Labor Life Ins Co v Pierno, 458 US 119 (1982)]

- Negotiated fee contracts with pharmacies participating in a network [Group Life & Health Ins Co v Royal Drug Co, 440 US 220 (1979)]

- Claims processing and administration and similar administrative services [NGS Am Inc v Barnes, 805 F Supp 462 (WD Tex 1992), *aff'd*, 998 F 2d 296 (5th Cir 1993); Self-Insurance Inst v Gallagher, ND Fla 1989, *aff'd*, 909 F 2d 1491 (11th Cir 1990); Insurance Bd of Bethlehem Steel Corp v Muir, 819 F 2d 408 (3d Cir 1987); Moore v Provident Life & Accident Ins Co, 786 F 2d 419 (4th Cir 1985), *cert denied*, 476 US 1170 (1986)]

- Utilization review and management services, even when the utilization review managers made decisions to withhold care that led to patient morbidity and mortality [Tolten v American Biodyne Inc, 48 F 3d 937 (6th Cir 1995); Kuhl v Lincoln National Health Plan, 999 F 2d 298 (8th Cir 1993), *cert denied*, 114 S Ct 694 (1994); Corcoran v United Healthcare Inc, 965 F 2d 1321 (5th Cir 1992)]

The sharing of a portion of the financial risks that are associated with the insurance risk or overall "risk of loss" does not necessarily constitute sharing of the insurance risk. A key factor in distinguishing a financial risk from an insurance risk is likely to be whether the provider assumes the risk associated only with the out-of-pocket cost of its own services and perhaps other costs over which the provider has some control, or whether the provider instead assumes or spreads the risk of costs associated with other, unaffiliated providers or services. In managed care contracting, there are insurance risks (which involve the assumption and spreading of risk in return for compensation), pricing or financial risks (a business risk to the provider), and operational risks. The financial and operational risks concern regulators because of the potential consequences to the "insured" person. Many observers have suggested that direct capitation compensation for a provider's own services (i.e., for services under the provider's direct control) is the clearest delineation of a pricing or financial risk. In fact, some state insurance laws and HMO acts specifically exclude contracts for individual professional services. On the other hand, just as many have insisted that capitation is actually the clearest example of insurance risk. Examples of financial risk-sharing compensation that are usually viewed as constituting less than insurance risk include hospital per diems, diagnosis-based rates, and case rates; physician or hospital withholds; direct provider capitation; and global or bundled fees and package prices for physician services, or for physician and hospital or other provider services, related to a specific episode or type of care.

Arguably, certain direct payment arrangements might be acceptable under many states' laws if the arrangement was simply a package rate or global fee mechanism for a relatively limited range of health care services, or if the arrangement did not constitute or appear to constitute the underwriting, indemnification, or reimbursement of the insurance risk of the costs of the health care services provided. This is not the position taken by the National Association of Insurance Commissioners (NAIC) and is not the interpretation of many states. Withholds, capitation, the range of bonus and penalty mechanisms, and a variety of cost-corridor arrangements have been targeted as constituting something more than simple price or business risk. There are risks associated with contracting that must be taken into consideration in the direct-contracting situation as well.

Operational Risk. For all parties involved in managed care contracting, especially within a provider organization, the operational risk is perhaps the most important factor in financial solvency. Operational risk for insurers and HMOs is assessed and monitored by regulators. Successful managed care providers do the same internally through various management information systems. Operational risk can be considered to include both revenue risks and the risks associated with more specific operating factors, such as administrative, medical, and patient costs.

Revenue Risk. Revenue risk refers to the predictability and variability of all sources of revenue from operations. Factors affecting revenue risk include the number of enrollees or covered lives, enrollment growth, disenrollment rate, competition, revenue mix (fee for service, capitation, and so on), stability of revenue sources and mix, and maximization of revenue (coordination of benefits, subrogation, and so on). Overall revenue risk is affected by the relative stability or variability of both revenue sources and revenue mix.

Risk-Bearing Issues. The question of state regulatory oversight is not so clearly established for the various types of provider entities that may enter direct contracts, particularly for provider organizations that are not themselves licensed health care providers, may not directly provide health care services, or may provide only a portion of the total contracted services (see chapter 6). Increasing regulatory vigilance, resulting from state insurance reform efforts, makes it imperative that provider organizations structure their reimbursement arrangements to avoid the business of insurance as established by state law. These concerns—and specific legal advice focused on operational and contractual details—are particularly critical if the provider organization enters into contracts directly with self-insured employers or other direct arrangements that do not involve an HMO or insurer, which as a licensed, regulated entity may impart some degree of regulatory protection to the integrated organization.

If an ERISA plan is involved, the state insurance department's view will be that an employer can retain risk. When that self-funded employer transfers the risk downstream, however, the party accepting risk becomes subject to state insurance laws.

State HMO Regulatory Analysis. Historically, insurance and HMO regulators in most states have taken the position that any capitated payments to providers of medical or hospital services are the hallmark of a prepaid health care plan and therefore that such arrangements are, by definition, subject to regulation under the state's HMO act. Most state HMO acts generally require an HMO certificate of authority for a network of physicians and/or facilities to furnish the full range of basic health care services on a prepaid basis.

Typically, a state's HMO act also specifies that an HMO includes any entity or person that either arranges for or provides a health care plan to enrollees on a prepaid basis. For example, the Texas HMO act defines a prepaid health care plan as

> any plan whereby any person undertakes to provide, arrange for, or reimburse any part of the cost of any health care services; provided, however, a part of such plan consists of arranging for or the provision of health care services, as distinguished from indemnification against the cost of such service, on a prepaid basis through insurance or otherwise.

[Tex Ins Code art 20A.02(h)]

Thus, the statute is applied to both the entity that offers the prepaid arrangements and the entities that provide services under the arrangements.

In the final analysis, "the line between insurance and non-insurance may be more fluid and unstable than many dare imagine."[8] For managed care contracting, the critical regulatory questions quickly become these:

1. Who can accept how much financial risk?
2. For which services?
   - Services they provide directly
   - Services they can arrange to provide directly
   - Services they are licensed to provide
   - Services they are not licensed to provide
3. How can the accepted risk be transferred?
   - Through subcapitation

- Through global contracts
- Between or among similarly licensed providers
- Between or among providers of various types
- Between or among unlicensed, provider-controlled entities

4. With whom can the risk be shared?

5. Who then is the insurer?

Q 11:71   What other legal issues arise in direct-contracting arrangements?

The liability analysis for any direct-contracting arrangement requires the prior consideration of many legal issues. The first level of any analysis is whether the arrangement is subject to ERISA. If so, then ERISA preempts the application of state laws and actions that relate to the employee benefit plan. The scope of that preemption, however, is not unlimited, based on the U.S. Supreme Court decision in *New York State Conference of Blue Cross & Blue Shield Plans v. Travelers Insurance Co.* [115 S Ct 1671 (1995)] *Travelers* represented the first time the Court finally addressed the scope of the "relates to" provision of ERISA preemption. The Court held that under the facts of the case, the state laws would have only an indirect economic impact on ERISA plans and therefore did not have the requisite "connection with" ERISA plans to trigger preemption.[9]

Regardless of the application of ERISA preemption to the employee benefit plan, the laws governing the conduct of the parties or entities involved in a direct-contracting arrangement must be considered in any risk analysis. In that analysis, antitrust, corporate structure, medical practice law, antireferral and antikickback law, liability, and taxation issues may arise out of the provider organization's internal structure as well as its contractual relationship with the purchaser.

Risk Contracting in the Public Sector

Q 11:72   Which major public sector programs are engaging in contracts with private sector MCOs and providers?

Contracting in the public sector on a risk basis occurs for Medicare, Medicaid, and CHAMPUS/TriCare. Contracting opportunities also exist under FEHBP. CHAMPUS covers military dependents, retirees, and some other military-connected personnel through contracts with the Department of Defense (DOD), which manages the Military Health Services System. In February 1995, the DOD proposed regulations to overhaul CHAMPUS to allow its coordination with the Military Health Services System under a new program called TriCare. CHAMPUS has a long history of selective contracting for services. Medicare risk contracting is relatively new, although becoming more widespread.

FEHBP, authorized by the Federal Employee Health Benefits Act [5 USC § 8901], is administered by the Office of Personnel Management (OPM), which contracts with indemnity health insurance plans, PPOs, and HMOs to cover FEHBP eligibles.

Q 11:73   What are the special considerations in public sector risk contracting?

Before passage of the BBA, most eligible MCOs that contract with HCFA under Medicare had to be either federally qualified or licensed HMOs. These MCOs were required to ensure that no more than 50 percent of their enrollment consisted of Medicare and Medicaid beneficiaries. This restriction was intended to serve as a QA mechanism to assure beneficiaries of coverage and benefits comparable to those received by other MCO enrollees. The BBA eliminated the 50-50 requirement for Medicare HMOs. HMOs are paid 95 percent of the adjusted average per capita cost (AAPCC) for each class of Medicare + Choice (M + C) enrollee.

The federal Medicaid program requires a state to allow any individual eligible for Medicaid benefits to obtain care from any qualified provider, including an MCO. State Medicaid programs can offer Medicaid recipients the option of enrolling in an MCO or can mandate enrollment in an MCO. The BBA eliminated the 75-25 rule related to Medicaid/non-Medicaid enrollment (see Q 11:76).

FEHBP specifies four types of health benefit plans that may be offered to federal employees and retirees. These plans are grouped into two general categories: fee-for-service and prepaid plans. Prepaid plans and HMOs refer to the three types of comprehensive medical plans described in the FEHBP statute. FEHBP does not give federal qualification the same status as Medicare and Medicaid do, nor does the FEHBP statute specifically require that the plan be offered through a licensed HMO. The OPM will consider proposals from prepaid plans that offer a POS option as a means of increasing enrollment in HMOs. Finally, there are fee-for-service plans that contract with OPM for FEHBP.

Medicaid Risk Contracts

Q 11:74   What are the common provisions in a Medicaid risk contract?

The Medicaid risk contract between an HMO and the state is used when the HMO assumes full risk for services provided to enrolled Medicaid beneficiaries. These contracts are discussed in more detail in chapter 7. A Medicaid managed care checklist is provided in Table 11-7. Contract provisions generally include the following:

Definitions. The definition section includes such terms as capitation payment, catastrophic coverage, categories of assistance, eligible person, emergency services, enrollee, primary care contractor, PCP, state plan, subcontract, and utilization control agent.

Eligibility, Enrollment, and Duration of Coverage. These provisions describe eligibility, the responsibility for and limits on enrollment of beneficiaries, termination of enrollment, and the enrollee's relationship with the primary care contractor.

Scope of Services. This section describes all the services required in the state plan (and any additional services), the exclusions and limitations of coverage, inpatient care parameters, health maintenance and promotion, emergency services, access, services to newborns, dual practice arrangements (fee for service), program changes, and HMO liability.

Obligations of Contracting Party. The obligations of the HMO should be set out with specificity. They include compliance with program standards, identifying enrollees, reporting, assessing quality, recordkeeping, and marketing. Agency obligations include eligibility verification and education of enrollees. Mutual obligations include compliance with federal and state laws and regulations, coverage of catastrophic claims, and reenrollment. Finally, reimbursement rates and provisions for additions and deletions are addressed.

Table 11-7   Medicaid Managed Care Checklist

- ❏ Services to be provided
- ❏ Expanded services
- ❏ Noncovered services
- ❏ Exempt services
- ❏ Eligible and ineligible recipients
- ❏ Availability and accessibility of services
- ❏ Minimum standards
- ❏ Staffing requirements
- ❏ Staff licensure
- ❏ Specialty coverage
- ❏ Physician choice
- ❏ Case management and continuity of care
- ❏ Emergency services (in and out of plan)
- ❏ Marketing
- ❏ Enrollment and disenrollment
- ❏ Enrollment levels and period
- ❏ Grievance procedures
- ❏ Quality assurance
- ❏ Medical records
- ❏ Medical audit
- ❏ Payment requests
- ❏ Newborn payment
- ❏ Rate adjustments
- ❏ Copayments
- ❏ Insolvency protection
- ❏ Reporting requirements
- ❏ Legal action notification
- ❏ Fidelity bonds
- ❏ Workers' compensation insurance
- ❏ Termination procedures
- ❏ Liquidated damages
- ❏ Gratuities
- ❏ Attorneys' fees
- ❏ Venue (for litigation)
- ❏ Assignment
- ❏ Dispute resolution

Source: Adapted from the AAHA Practice Guide Series 1993, Vol. 2, *Hospital-Affiliated Integrated Delivery Systems: Formation, Operation, and Contracts Handbook* 282. The Managed Care and Integrated Delivery Systems Committee of the American Academy of Hospital Attorneys, American Hospital Association, One North Franklin, Chicago, IL 60606.

Marketing and Service Area. These provisions address the requirement of listing approved primary care contractors and defining HMO marketing within specified market areas.

Term and Termination. All contracts include some provision related to term and termination. Most are annually renewable. Termination is triggered on withdrawal of federal financial participation, unavailability of state funds, loss of HMO license, or sanctions. Mutual termination provisions are available if a party refuses to renegotiate capitation rates on change of benefits or after failure to cure.

Subcontract Relations. These provisions address the right to use subcontractors and set forth their qualifications and contract requirements. Prior agency approval is required for all subcontracts.

Grievance Procedure. The grievance procedure requires prior written approval by the agency. All complaints must be in writing, and staff should be available to assist enrollees with the process.

Confidentiality. Confidentiality provisions are required.

Contract Sanctions. The agency may impose specified sanctions on an HMO that fails to comply with specified requirements. Notice and opportunity to cure rights exist for the HMO.

General Provisions. These provisions include such additional boilerplate provisions as disclosure by the HMO of other activities, prohibition against hiring state employees, agency waivers, and renegotiation on Department of Health and Human Services disapproval.

Q 11:75 What are the important Medicaid risk contracting issues?

Medicaid managed care capitation rates are developed based on the projected Medicaid fee-for-service cost per capita in a particular geographic region. Rates vary by eligibility category, age, and sex. Setting a rate for the AFDC (Aid to Families with Dependent Children) population is relatively straightforward because there is a lot of data on this population's utilization; however, developing rates for the elderly, blind, and disabled populations is much more complicated because of known utilization rates and less data on managing the care of that population. In structuring a Medicaid risk contract, the following factors are important:

1. The rate of turnover in the eligible and enrolled population makes continuity of care and case management difficult.

2. Accurate demographic data on the eligible population are difficult to access because there are many unidentified and underidentified members of the population.

3. New eligibles with preexisting conditions can be very expensive to the program.

4. Copayment often is not available, and there are few financial incentives for beneficiaries to use health services and providers appropriately.

5. Medicaid reimbursement is generally very poor compared to Medicare or commercial rates of payment.

To reduce financial risk and survive under a Medicaid managed care contract, the provider should:

1. Know who is in the enrolled population;

2. Become familiar with the risks and negotiate accordingly;

3. Identify the services covered by the capitation rate;

4. Develop a system that is oriented to the unique needs of the Medicaid population; and

5. Educate the population on "demand management" and use of less costly services.

Q 11:76   What has been the effect of the BBA on Medicaid managed care contracting?

Medicaid had been moving steadily toward managed care before passage of the BBA. The BBA expanded the options available to states under the federal Medicaid statute to make managed care more attractive and easier to attain than before. In the past, states that wanted to require Medicaid beneficiaries to enroll in MCOs had to obtain a waiver from the Secretary of Health and Human Services (HHS). Under the BBA, they can do so without seeking a waiver. The BBA also eliminated the requirement that at least 25 percent of the MCO enrollment had to be non-Medicaid enrollment. States may therefore contract with exclusively Medicaid HMOs. Finally, the BBA allows states that want to limit Medicaid beneficiaries living in urban areas to a choice between two MCOs to do so without seeking a waiver from the Secretary of HHS. States can restrict beneficiaries in rural areas to a single MCO.

Q 11:77   What standards does the federal government impose on states contracting with Medicaid MCOs?

Because of the level of federal funding given to states under the Medicaid program, the federal government imposes procedural standards on states contracting with Medicaid MCOs, including the following:

Conflict-of-Interest Safeguards. The BBA prohibits a state from entering into risk contracts with MCOs unless it has in effect conflict-of-interest safeguards with respect to officers and employees with responsibilities relating to such contracts. These safeguards are found in the Federal Procurement Policy Act. [42 USC 423] The BBA also imposes conflict-of-interest safeguards on state (and local) employees with Medicaid responsibilities other than those relating to MCO contracting. These safeguards apply to each state or local officer, employee, or independent contractor who is "responsible for selecting, awarding or otherwise obtaining items and services under the [Medicaid program]." This rule is intended to extend the safeguards to private entities such as enrollment brokers, external quality review organizations, actuaries, fiscal intermediaries, and claims processing organizations. [See 42 USC § 423] The BBA extended the federal criminal penalties applicable to individuals who violate these safeguards to independent contractors.

Enrollment and Enrollment Brokers. Many states have used enrollment brokers to educate and enroll Medicaid beneficiaries, giving the beneficiaries the right to choose their benefit plan. Enrollment brokers were allowed to enroll beneficiaries in MCOs on a "default" basis, without giving the beneficiaries a choice. The BBA bars federal matching funds for the cost of an enrollment broker unless (1) the enrollment broker is independent of any MCO or primary care case manage (PCCM) or health care provider participating in the state's program; (2) the broker does not have an owner, employee, consultant, or contractor with any "direct or indirect" financial interest in any such MCO or PCCM or health care provider; and (3) the broker does not have any owners, employees, consultants, or contractors who have been subject to sanctions under Medicaid or Medicare.

Under the BBA, states cannot assign default enrollees to MCOs that fail to comply with their Medicaid contract or with regulatory standards. The enrollment process must consider enrolling default beneficiaries so as to maintain existing relationships between patients and providers, and with providers that have traditionally served the Medicaid beneficiaries (e.g., significant traditional providers).

Payment Rates. To allow flexibility in achieving federal savings under the BBA, several federal minimum payment standards for various types of providers, including hospitals, nursing homes, federally qualified health centers (FQHCs), pediatricians, and obstetricians, were phased out. Federal minimum payments to MCOs were not affected; however, payment to MCOs must be made based on an "actuarially" sound basis, and capitation payments cannot exceed HCFA's upper limit for risk contracts, which requires that the payment not exceed the cost of providing the services on a fee-for-service basis. [See 42 CFR § 447.361] Disproportionate share hospital (DSH) payments can no longer be incorporated into the capitation rates paid to MCOs, but must be paid directly to DSHs.

Organizational Qualifications for Medicaid MCOs. Under the BBA, a state can contract on a risk basis with "any public or private organization," including an HMO, an "eligible organization" with a Medicare risk contract, a "Medicare + Choice organization" with a Medicare contract, or a PSO that meets state-determined HMO accessibility and solvency standards. A federally qualified HMO is deemed to meet the solvency and accessibility standards. These new federal standards apply to contracts entered into or renewed on or after October 1, 1997. The new federal solvency standards under the BBA apply to contracts entered into or renewed on or after October 1, 1998.

Federal Approval of State MCO Contracts. Under the BBA, risk contracts between state Medicaid agencies and MCOs in excess of $1 million are subject to prior approval by DHHS. This restriction likely applies to virtually all Medicaid MCO contracts.

Federal Standards for State Contracts with MCOs. The BBA substantially expands the minimum Medicaid MCO contract standards. As of October 1, 1997, the following standards became effective:

1. *Organizational qualifications.* The contracting MCO must be either an HMO, an eligible corporation with a contract with Medicare, an M + C organization, a PSO, or a public or private organization that makes services "accessible" to Medicaid beneficiaries and has adequate solvency.

2. *Actuarially sound payments.* Capitation payments must be made on an actuarially sound basis.

3. *Audits.* DHHS and the state or their designees have the right to audit and inspect the books and records of the entity and of any subcontractor relating to their ability to bear financial risk, the services performed under the contract, or the determinations of amounts paid.

4. *Nondiscrimination.* The MCO cannot discriminate among Medicaid beneficiaries on the basis of their health status or requirements for health care services in enrollment, reenrollment, or disenrollment.

5. *Disenrollment.* The MCO must allow a Medicaid beneficiary to disenroll for cause at any time and without cause during the first 90 days following enrollment and at least once every 12 months thereafter.

6. *Emergency care.* The MCO or state must reimburse hospitals and other providers not affiliated with the MCO for care provided to Medicaid enrollees when such care was immediately required because of unforeseen illness, injury, or other medical condition.

7. *Disclosure.* The MCO must provide full and complete information as to the identity of each person with an ownership or control interest in the MCO or in any subcontractor in which the MCO has a 5 percent or greater ownership interest. The MCO must also disclose certain related-party transactions.

8. *FQHCs and rural health centers (RHCs).* If an MCO has entered into a subcontract with an FQHC or RHC to provide services, the MCO must pay the subcontractor at least the "level and amount of payment" that the MCO would pay for such services if the provider were not an FQHC or RHC.

9. *Financial incentive arrangements for physicians.* The financial incentive arrangements that the MCO uses for its physicians must meet the same requirements as those for Medi-

care risk contractors under Section 1876 of the Balanced Budget Act.

10. *Encounter data.* The MCO must maintain sufficient patient encounter data to identify the physician who delivers services to Medicaid beneficiaries.

11. *Section 1932 requirements.*[10] The contract must specify the benefits that the MCO is responsible for providing. At a minimum, these benefits include the following:
   • Specification of benefits
   • Emergency services
   • "Gag rule" prohibitions
   • Protection against balance billing
   • External independent quality review
   • Timely payments to providers

12. Other minimum contracting requirements include the following:
   • Information to enrollees
   • Grievance procedures
   • Adequate capacity and services
   • No enrollee liability for payment
   • HIPAA standards for maternity care and mental health care (see chapters 5 and 11)
   • Quality standards
   • No affiliations with debarred individuals or organizations[11]
   • Marketing restrictions
   • Physician identifiers

Medicare + Choice Risk Contracts

Q 11:78   What are the CMS requirements of a Medicare + Choice risk provider contract under the BBA?

For an MCO to qualify for contracting with HCFA, it must demonstrate evidence of a health services delivery system. CMS guidance on HMO-provider contracts (still applicable with modification for

M + C plans) is reflected in appendix 11-B. For the CMS to meet HCFA's requirement of having a qualified health services delivery system, the MCO's application to the CMS must contain evidence of the following:

1. The provider agrees to serve the health plan members for a specific period of time, typically one year.

2. The provider agrees to provide specific services to all members and to provide a statement that plan members include commercial and Medicare enrollees (when applicable).

3. Payment for services are stated, along with incentive arrangements, if any.

4. The provider agrees not to bill health plan members. To be considered protection for members in the event of HMO or payer insolvency, however, the agreement must contain standard NAIC hold-harmless language. This is important if the HMO is using provider hold-harmless contract requirements for the covered expenses in its insolvency calculation.

5. The agreement is signed by both the HMO and the provider.

Regulatory Issues

Q 11:79   What are the significant regulatory issues associated with Medicare or Medicaid risk contracting?

Both Medicare and Medicaid laws governing prepaid health plans or organizations restrict the amount of risk they can place on a physician for services he or she does not provide. These rules define what is substantial financial risk based on specified risk thresholds when there is risk for services not provided directly by the physician or physician group (such as those provided by specialists through referrals).

Antikickback Laws. Managed care and direct-contract activities that could be subject to the broad language of the fraud and abuse prohibitions include situations in which (1) a provider offers a discount or other favorable pricing arrangement to a managed care plan in the hope of increasing or maintaining a particular volume of business, (2) a provider invests in a managed care company, or (3) a managed care plan offers enrollees additional benefits or reduced out-of-pocket expenses (such as waiver of coinsurance) to induce them to use the preferred providers.

Safe Harbors. In 1996, DHHS published safe harbor rules on typical managed care arrangements such as provider discounts and beneficiary incentives. These rules address protections for certain forms of enrollee incentives offered by health plans to encourage use of in-network providers, reductions offered to health plans by contract health care providers, and hospital inpatient coinsurance and deductibles.

The safe harbors also address certain negotiated price reduction agreements between health plans and health care providers under contract with the plans. The application of the safe harbors is subject to the following standards:

1. For risk-bearing plans that contract with Medicare or Medicaid or that operate under federal authority, providers cannot seek additional payment from Medicare or Medicaid unless the respective program says otherwise. This includes any attempts at cost shifting.

2. For Medicare or Medicaid plans paid on a cost or similar basis, the agreement between the plan and the contracted provider must span at least one year and must specify in advance the covered services and payment methodology. Reporting to HCFA and the state is required, and the plan cannot claim payment for any item or service not approved by HCFA or the state, or otherwise shift the burden of waived charges to HCFA or the state.

3. Plans that do not have a Medicare or Medicaid contract, are not operating under a federal pilot program, and do not capitate providers must comply with the following standards:

    • The plan's agreement with providers must span at least one year.

    • The agreement must specify in advance the services and items covered, the party responsible for filing claims with Medicare or Medicaid, and the provider fee schedule.

    • The fee schedule must remain in effect throughout the agreement, unless Medicare or Medicaid makes a payment update.

- The party submitting claims to Medicare or Medicaid cannot submit claims above the agreed-upon fee schedule amount.

- The plan and the provider must report fee schedule amounts on any Medicare or Medicaid cost report and comply with any request to furnish the terms of the plan-provider agreement and amounts paid under it.

- The party that is not responsible for filing claims cannot seek any money from Medicare or Medicaid for services furnished under the agreement or otherwise shift such costs to Medicare or Medicaid.

4. Plans that do not have a Medicare or Medicaid contract and are not operating under a federal demonstration waiver but capitate providers must comply with the following standards:

- The plan's agreement with providers must span at least one year.

- The agreement must specify in advance the services and items covered, the capitation rate, and applicable enrollee copayments.

- The capitation amount in the agreement must remain in effect during the entire agreement.

- The plan and the provider must comply with any request by HCFA or a state Medicaid program to see the terms of the agreement and amounts paid under it.

- The contracted provider cannot seek payment from Medicare, Medicaid, or its enrollees for any charges other than copayments.

- The plan cannot pay the provider more than the capitation rate in the agreement.

OIG-HCFA Rules for Medicare and Medicaid HMOs, CMPs, and Other Prepaid Plans. Under Medicare-Medicaid conditions of participation, sanctions apply specifically to managed care entities that participate in Medicare or Medicaid through either HMO or CMP contracts. HCFA can terminate an HMO or CMP from the program or levy intermediate sanctions against a plan if it (1) substantially fails to provide necessary care; (2) requires Medicare enrollees to pay excessive premiums; (3) improperly expels or refuses to reenroll an individual; (4) discriminates against potential enrollees with potentially high utilization needs; (5) misrepresents or falsifies information it furnishes to HCFA, an individual, or any entity; (6) fails to pay claims promptly; or (7) violates any enrollment standard. Additionally, M + C organizations are subject to intermediate sanctions for employing or contracting with an individual or entity excluded from Medicare or for violating the physician incentive payment regulations. Intermediate sanctions may involve (1) freezing the plan's Medicare enrollment during the sanction period, (2) suspending Medicare payments during the sanction period, or (3) suspending the plan's marketing to Medicare enrollees. Sanctions generally take place 15 days from the date of notification to the plan, unless earlier implementation is warranted by the conduct. HCFA may also exclude plans from the program, refuse to renew a plan's Medicare contract, or notify the OIG, which may impose civil monetary penalties.

Civil monetary penalties of up to $25,000 for each determination can be levied against Medicare and Medicaid HMOs, CMPs, and prepaid plans that engage in prohibited behavior such as (1) substantially failing to provide necessary services; (2) imposing excessive premiums; (3) illegally expelling or refusing to enroll a Medicare enrollee for reasons other than health status or need for services; (4) misrepresenting or falsifying information; (5) failing to pay claims promptly; (6) employing or contracting with or through a person or entity excluded from Medicare; or (7) failing to comply with the Medicare and Medicaid HMO physician payment incentive requirements. [42 CFR §§ 1003.100–1003.106] In the case of misrepresenting or providing falsified information to DHHS or a Medicaid state agency or discrimination against specific Medicare or Medicaid recipients based on health status, penalties may reach $100,000 per determination.

Medicare Secondary-Payer Issues. Under rules applicable to group health and other plans for which Medicare is a secondary payer, group health plans must offer employed individuals and their spouses who are age 65 or older the same benefits as those under age 65 receive. [42 USC § 1395y(b)] This requirement does not apply to group health plans of employers with fewer than 20 workers or to seniors who work at such small employers and are enrolled in multiemployer or multiple-employer group health plans.

The same requirement applies to Medicare-eligible end-stage renal disease (ESRD) coverage during the 12-month period starting when the person becomes eligible for Medicare Part A benefits, or if earlier, the first month in which the individual would have been entitled to Medicare benefits. There are exceptions for certain members of religious orders and special rules for aggregation of employees and employers.

Medicare will not pay for items or services to the extent they have been or can reasonably be expected to be covered by a group health plan, large group health plan, workers' compensation insurance plan, automobile or liability insurance policy, or other type of plan. When Medicare makes payment otherwise covered under another plan, it must be reimbursed when it is a secondary payer. If reimbursement is not made within 60 days, DHHS can charge interest. There are civil monetary penalties, assessments, and exclusions associated with violation of these rules.

Q 11:80   What effect do the regulations on physician incentive plans have on government contracts?

Physician incentive plans (PIPs) are subject to extensive regulation under various federal laws relating to health plans. [See, e.g., USC § 1395mm(1); 42 CFR § 17.479] Inducements relating to specific individuals are prohibited. Placing physicians at substantial financial risk triggers certain affirmative duties of the HMO, including the following:

- Conducting enrollee surveys for all current Medicare or Medicaid enrollees in the plan as well as those who have disenrolled in the previous 12 months for any reason except loss of eligibility or relocation
- Providing adequate stop-loss protection to physicians according to the size of the patient panel
- Disclosing to Medicare enrollees on request the following information:
  — Whether the plan uses an incentive arrangement that affects the use of referral services, and if so, the type of arrangement
  — Whether stop-loss is provided
  — Results of any survey required as a result of the incentive arrangement

A physician is at "substantial financial risk" when the incentive arrangement places the physician or group at risk based on the costs of referrals and the physician's patient panel contains fewer than 25,000 enrollees (or more than 25,000 through "pooling"), and (1) withholds exceed 25 percent of payment; (2) bonuses are greater than 33 percent of potential payments; (3) withholds plus bonuses equal more than 25 percent of potential payments; (4) the difference in maximum and minimum potential capitation payment is more than 25 percent of the maximum; (5) the physician's contract does not clearly explain minimum possible capitation payments; or (6) the physician is potentially liable for amounts exceeding 25 percent of potential payments, regardless of payment methodology.

Fundamentals of Negotiation

Q 11:81   What is negotiation?

Negotiation has been described as a give-and-take process whereby parties seek to reach agreement on issues. The negotiation process generally involves (1) a give-and-take between two or more parties, (2) a level of friction or discomfort between the parties resulting from their constraints and motivations, (3) an important issue that the parties wish to resolve, and (4) conflict between the positions of the parties.[12] In negotiating managed care agreements, parties often reach the bargaining table with positions that differ in strength. The payer has the ability to control the dollars and the patients but cannot provide the medical services. The provider has the ability to service the health plan, but not without reasonable compensation. These contracting issues are discussed in much greater detail in chapter 14.

Q 11:82   What are the common negotiating styles?

There are many approaches to the negotiation process. The most common styles are either confrontational or collegial.

Confrontational negotiators favor an aggressive approach and tend to focus on the real or perceived differences between the parties at the bargaining table. These negotiators may be particularly aggressive when the party they represent is perceived by all sides to be the dominant party. Unfortunately, confrontational negotiators overlook the importance of the parties' ongoing relationship, which may be sacrificed in the negotiating process, leading to distrust and continued positional bargaining. A number of managed care plans have used confrontational approaches to their detriment. For example, Maxicare Health Plan's confrontational approach cost it critical provider support when it later encountered financial difficulties.

Collegial negotiators attempt to build consensus among parties through the give-and-take of negotiations. This style is based on the idea that the outcome of the negotiations marks the beginning of the relationship between the managed care plan and its providers. This does not mean that collegial negotiators are weak or too quick to make concessions; it does mean that the dominant party refrains from unilaterally imposing its position on the other party.

Q 11:83   What is principled negotiation?

Principled negotiation, a method developed and taught by the Harvard Negotiation Project, is based on the merits of the issues rather than on the positions of the parties. [See www.pon.harvard.edu] Key to this method are the following principles:

1. Separate the people from the problem.
2. Focus on the interests of the parties, not their positions.
3. Generate a variety of possible solutions before agreeing on any particular solution.
4. Agree to use an objective standard for selecting the appropriate solution.

Q 11:84   What are the advantages of using principled negotiation techniques?

The major benefit of principled negotiation is that it eliminates the need for parties to engage in either confrontational or collegial styles of negotiation. It places the parties in a position to seek a mutually beneficial agreement rather than one that favors one party over the other. It also fosters the relationship of the parties over any one party's position.

In the context of managed care, for example, if the HMO agrees that the hospital is entitled to a fair level of return or contribution to margin, and the HMO is entitled to reimbursement rates that are no less favorable than those offered to other payers, with the definition of objective standards for each of these elements, it will be easier to reach a fair and workable agreement.

Q 11:85   What are the disadvantages of positional bargaining?

Positional bargaining can pose a number of problems. Arguing over positions is highly inefficient and can produce unwise agreements. Because of the emphasis on the different positions of the parties rather than their respective interests, there is a greater risk that the agreement ultimately reached will have sacrificed the relationship of the parties and be of far less value to each party than if they had used principled negotiation. The more parties involved in the negotiating process, the more problems positional bargaining will create.

Negotiation Strategies in Managed Care Contracting

Q 11:86   How should the parties prepare for negotiations?

Before beginning negotiations, the "deal points" should be identified. Core issues such as defining covered services, financial arrangements, parties' obligations under quality assurance and utilization review plans, and termination rights will be the most aggressively negotiated by the parties. The objectives of the providers will likely include (1) increasing or maintaining patient volume, (2) developing managed care experience, (3) creating or protecting revenue, (4) establishing relationships with payers, and (5) aligning with other providers.

Part of preparing for negotiations in managed care contracting is understanding each party's goals. A physician may want to attract patients covered by managed care plans in order to build his or her practice. A hospital may want to obtain an agreement for competitive purposes. The MCO may want to obtain the participation of a specific hospital because employer groups have demanded its inclusion as a condition of offering the health benefit plan.

To ensure that there is a common understanding of a party's goal, they should be reviewed with all involved in the internal decision-making process. The following questions should be considered:

1. What does the party hope to accomplish in negotiations? Preparation is crucial to the success of any negotiation. A complete list of the items the party hopes to gain from the negotiations should be prepared. The importance of each item on the list should be weighed against the anticipated give-and-take of the negotiation process.

2. What are the party's strengths and weaknesses, and how will they affect negotiations? It is important to recognize one's weaknesses because they will be quickly identified and used by the other side. Knowing the party's weaknesses can help the negotiator defuse them early in the negotiation process.

3. What is the corporate culture of the organization, and how will it affect its relationship with the other party? Is the organization seen as trustworthy or as overly aggressive? How the organization is perceived by outsiders is important information for the negotiator. It will influence how the negotiations are conducted, how the other party reacts to proposals, and whether the negotiator is perceived as credible.

4. How is decision making handled? Has the party identified its best alternative to a negotiated agreement (BATNA)? The BATNA should be established well in advance of any negotiations so that it does not have to be determined during the heat of negotiations.

These questions should also be asked to analyze the other party's goals. Most important in this analysis is ascertaining the other party's strengths and weaknesses and, if possible, its BATNA.

Q 11:87   What steps should providers take to prepare for negotiations?

Providers need to assess the capabilities and value of the MCOs operating in their geographic market. In addition to understanding the MCO's background, providers must be willing to examine their own place in the market and attempt to identify what the MCO will be looking for. Key components to a provider's self-assessment include identifying its credentialing deficiencies and examining the strengths and weaknesses of its network and participating providers.

After completing their self-assessment, providers should obtain relevant documentation from the MCO to assist their discussions and negotiations. Such documentation includes (1) utilization management and quality assurance policies and procedures, (2) historical utilization and cost data of the enrollee population, (3) historical utilization and cost data for the particular provider or provider group, (4) the MCO's stop-loss policy, (5) the scope of covered services, and (6) administrative procedures.

When comparing MCOs, the provider should consider the following questions:

1. Where do its patients come from?

2. How much revenue does the MCO represent to the practice?

3. How fast is the MCO's market share growing or declining?

4. Which MCOs have the most favorable reimbursement arrangements? Why?

5. Which MCOs work most cooperatively with providers?

Q 11:88 What is the primary concern of the MCO as it prepares for negotiation?

MCOs are interested in remaining competitive and satisfying their customers. Since the retail purchaser (e.g., individual employee) and the wholesale purchaser (e.g., employer) will want to know who is in the network and how much access to the network will cost, the MCO must be prepared to address their concerns regarding access and cost. Its primary concern will therefore be the composition and structure of the network.

Q 11:89 Is there a benefit to using requests for proposals in managed care contracting?

Yes. Often, managed care plans submit requests for proposals (RFP) to which various provider organizations respond. Sometimes they conduct preliminary discussions with the respondents before choosing a prospective contracting party. These preliminary discussions are usually for clarification of responses and general issues. After a proposal has been accepted, there are still details to be negotiated beyond the contents of the proposal received in response to the RFP. Nonetheless, the RFP process can expedite much of the contracting process for a managed care plan.

Q 11:90 Who should handle the negotiations in managed care contracting?

Selecting the members of the negotiating team is an important prenegotiation step. Negotiations should be conducted by individuals familiar with the negotiation process. The negotiating team for the provider should include several key parties, in addition to representatives of the provider organization. These key individuals include (1) legal counsel, (2) an accountant or other experienced financial advisor to provide actuarial support, and (3) consultants with expertise in managed care contract negotiations and strategies. Use of outside consultants or lawyers is common. Managed care plans usually include their provider relations personnel on the negotiating team because of their understanding of the local community. Often, at least one financial staff member is included because of the effect reimbursement levels have on premium rates. Depending on the importance of the contract to the plan, the plan's chief executive or chief operating officer may be part of the negotiating team.

Q 11:91 How should the negotiating team prepare for negotiations?

The negotiating team should review any proposal that has been received prior to the start of the negotiations, identify acceptable trade-offs, and understand the alternatives available to the other party. If the discussions will concern renegotiation of a contract, the team should review all aspects of the existing agreement to identify problems caused by the current arrangement and areas for change, including changes that may be requested by the other party.

Each negotiating team should familiarize itself with the other party's negotiating team. This can help in a number of ways, such as in determining the style of negotiation that the other team may use, predicting how the other team will approach the negotiation process, and identifying common interests and background to foster more congenial communications.

Q 11:92   Is the location of the negotiations important?

The site of the negotiations is not usually a decisive factor in the outcome. Sometimes there are preliminary exchanges of information and documents before the parties engage in any face-to-face negotiation.

Q 11:93   How should the negotiations be conducted?

Every aspect of the negotiation process can affect the outcome, even the site selected for the negotiations. Therefore, the negotiations should be conducted according to a carefully prepared format and procedure. At the outset, an agenda must be defined that will allow each party to state its position, make counteroffers, and critique the other party's proposal. There is no standard format used in the negotiation process, except to be sure that all parties clearly understand the rules of the game. It is also important at the outset to determine the limits of the other negotiating team authority to make an agreement on behalf of its organization. This avoids unnecessary delays.

Each negotiating team should designate a member to take notes on the discussion. These notes should reflect dates and locations of all the negotiating sessions, names and titles of all participants and observers, salient terms of all proposals that are made by either party (including who made the proposal), key points made during discussions of proposals (including who made the points), agreements made by the parties (including conditions and contingencies related to the agreements), and areas of disagreement between the parties. The notes are important for two reasons. First, they provide a document from which the parties can draft a memorandum of agreement that accurately reflects the agreements reached during negotiations. Second, they may be useful in showing intent if there is a subsequent dispute over the terms of the contract.

Negotiations should begin with a concise statement summarizing each party's position. It helps to have a written proposal for distribution at the initial negotiating session. This can frame the issues for negotiation and set the tone for the balance of the negotiations. The parties one should then identify areas of agreement and disagreement from which the contract will ultimately be negotiated. Agreement on the items to be negotiated can be an important first step toward building a relationship and invoking the use of principled negotiation (see Q 11:86). After bargaining on the issues that are difficult to resolve, the parties should prepare a memorandum of agreement, which each party initials and from which the definitive contract is developed.

Q 11:94 What is the fundamental objective in negotiating managed care agreements?

In negotiating managed care agreements, the single common objective is to provide health care services to a particular population. Although the parties may differ on the details of how this should be done, their objective is the same.

Q 11:95 What issues are most likely to be the subject of dispute between the payer and the provider in negotiating a managed care agreement?

A number of issues are often the subject of dispute between the parties to a provider agreement. Foremost among them is compensation for the health care services that everyone agrees are the goal of the contract. Payers will want to spend as little as possible, while providers will want to maximize reimbursement. Scope of covered services, timing of payments, exclusivity provisions, and patient volume are also issues ripe for conflict.

Q 11:96 From the perspective of the managed care plan, what are the major issues to consider in negotiations with providers?

The managed care plan usually has four main objectives in negotiations with providers: establishing an acceptable provider panel, setting reasonable levels of reimbursement, laying the foundation for a long-term relationship, and obtaining favorable contractual terms.

Acceptable Provider Panel. What constitutes an acceptable provider panel will depend on the type of managed care product; but whether the product is an HMO or a PPO plan, the important factors include availability of services and provider coverage, accessibility of the providers who offer the services required under the plan, availability of specialty coverage, and perception of quality.

Reasonable Reimbursement. What is considered reasonable reimbursement will vary according to the perspective of the party. From the plan's perspective, reasonable reimbursement is as low as possible and predictable.

Long-Term Relationship. Changing provider panels can be very disruptive to the enrollees and problematic for the plan. Plans prefer to maintain their provider relationships if at all possible. This can motivate them to consider renegotiating reimbursement rates.

Favorable Contractual Terms. Plans will usually propose terms that require providers to (1) abide by and cooperate with the utilization management and quality assurance protocols; (2) look solely to the plan for payment of claims, even in the event of plan insolvency (enrollee hold-harmless clauses); (3) submit claims in a specified format and within a fixed time frame; (4) continue to provide covered services for a specified period following contract termination; (5) refrain from soliciting enrollees to change coverage after contract termination; and (6) submit to binding arbitration all disputes involving the patients served by the providers under the plan.

Q 11:97 What tactics are commonly used by managed care plans to obtain provider concessions?

Negotiating styles of most managed care plans range from confrontational to amicable. Obviously, the durability of the relationship will depend on the tactics used in achieving an agreement, with an amicable or neutral approach having a higher probability of success than an aggressive, confrontational one. Tactics used by managed care plans to obtain favorable agreements include using competing proposals from other providers; threatening to move patients to other providers; playing one provider group against another; making last-chance offers; and using provider data such as cost and/or charge information.

The managed care plan may indicate either explicitly or implicitly that competing proposals on the table offer more advantages to the plan. Plans may threaten to move their covered lives to other providers if the parties fail to reach agreement. Providers should anticipate this threat and assess its implications before entering negotiations.

Some managed care plans play hospitals and physicians against each other in an effort to force compromises on various contract provisions. This tactic can be avoided if the hospitals and physicians are aligned and is one of the reasons for the development of IDS arrangements, as discussed in chapter 4. Managed care plans sometimes tell providers that there will be no later opportunity for them to participate. This ploy can sometimes backfire, and participating at the outset does not guarantee ongoing participation.

Some managed care plans prepare detailed analyses of provider cost and/or charge information for their markets. It is important that the providers have access to cost and utilization information as part of their response as well as their marketing effort.

Q 11:98 From the perspective of the provider, what are the major issues to consider in negotiations with managed care plans?

From the provider's perspective, the major issues to consider in negotiations with managed care plans are market share, competition among managed care plans, satisfaction of provider needs, favorable reimbursement, a foundation for future relationships, and favorable contractual terms.

Most providers participate in managed care plans either as a means of protecting their patient base or as a means of expanding their patient base.

Some providers believe they should participate in as many managed care plans as possible to prevent any single plan from becoming market dominant. Hospitals tend to contract with plans that have contracts with their medical staff. Other providers, such as hospitals, may participate in managed care plans because their physicians, as participating providers, must use participating hospitals. Their motives are to satisfy the needs of their physicians and to avoid losing physicians to competitor facilities. Physicians tend to contract with plans that include members of their patient population.

Optimal rates of reimbursement and predictability of payment are important factors in motivating provider participation in managed care. These issues pose the greatest degree of conflict and need for negotiation.

Most providers favor long-term relationships with managed care plans provided they can renegotiate reimbursement rates on an annual basis.

Important contractual terms for provider agreements include compliance with plan utilization and quality management programs, payment on disputed claims (clean claims) and timing of payment (prompt payment), assurances of protection of proprietary information and name use, minimal involvement of provider personnel in implementing plan procedures, elimination of retroactive denial of preauthorized services, and provider protection for plan insolvency.

Q 11:99   What are some common provider negotiation tactics?

Provider strategy in managed care contract negotiations may include joint physician-hospital negotiations through such provider organizations as PHOs, analyzing alternatives available to the managed care plan, threatening not to participate (although this can pose antitrust risk under certain circumstances, as discussed in chapter 8), and analyzing the managed care plan.

Q 11:100   What areas of conflict and confusion commonly arise in the negotiation process?

Areas of confilct and confusion that commonly arise in the negotiation process include party identification, definitions used in different benefit plans, determining the scope of services to be provided under each plan, evaluating and protecting against unreasonable financial risk, dealing with standard contract language and forms, complying with administrative requirements in the contract, and dealing with exclusivity provisions. Using a checklist can help to ensure that potential areas of conflict are identified as they are discussed. Items to include in the checklist are as follows:

- Develop provider objectives
- Develop provider deal points
- Identify payer and payer plans involved
- Identify provider and provider services involved
- Evaluate payer risk solvency, reputation, and enrollee population
- Secure and review payer financial documents

- Compare contract as offered against list of deal points
- Identify all payer administrative requirements and review written policies and procedures
- Review antitrust and practical impact of exclusivity clauses[13]

Q 11:101 What is driving the movement to unionize physicians?

Physicians are seeking collective representation as a last recourse in the negotiation and contracting process. With an increasing number of physicians being employed by some form of provider organization, and with the uncertainty in the market, physicians see participation in unions or recognized collective bargaining units as a means of economic survival. With the consolidation in the HMO market, many physicians are being put in a "take it or leave it" position with few alternatives and no negotiating options. IPAs have proved ineffective in the negotiation process. Participation in unions or recognized collective bargaining units represents an important option to the medical profession because it is the only way physicians can bargain collectively without violating antitrust laws.

References

1. Roger Fisher and William Ury, *Getting to Yes: Negotiating Agreements Without Giving In* (New York: Penguin, 1991).

2. William Ury, *Getting Past No: Negotiating Your Way From Confrontation to Cooperation* (New York: Bantam 1993).

3. Following is a list of what, from a provider's perspective, would be in a well written MFN clause: (1) MFN pricing should apply only to identical lines of insurance. The enrollment level of a payer who seeks benefit of MFN pricing must equal or exceed the enrollment level of the payer whose prices are allegedly better. (2) The contract term of a payer who seeks benefit of MFN pricing must equal or exceed the contract term of the payer whose prices are allegedly better. (3) A payer seeking the benefit of MFN pricing must be exclusive to the provider if the payer whose prices are allegedly better has given an exclusive contract. (4) In the case of a nonexclusive contract the number of competing network

providers (e.g., beds, specialists, primary care physicians) must be equal to or less than the payer whose rates are allegedly better. (5) Level of risk assumed under a contract with a payer seeking MFN pricing must be equal to or less than the payer whose rates are allegedly better.

4. Adapted from C.P. McLaughlin, "Managed Care and Its Relationship to Public Health: Barriers and Opportunities," in *Managed Care & Public Health,* Paul K. Harlverson, Arnold D. Kulazny, and Curtis P. McLaughlin, eds. (New York: Aspen Publishers 1998) 56.

5. *See* http//www.ahima.org.

6. Guidance on disclosure requirements to HCFA may be found on the Internet at http://www.aahp.org.

7. Despite *Stuart Circle Hospital Corp. v. Aetna Life Insurance Co.,* 995 F.2d 500 (1993), which the U.S. Supreme Court declined to hear, there is a likelihood that networks that include both insured and self-insured employers would be deemed to have voluntarily submitted to state law. *See also* Fort Halifax Packing Co. v. Coyne, 482 U.S. 1, 14 (1987).

8. Dennenberg, "The Legal Definition of Insurance," *J. Ins.,* 30: 319, 335, 1963, *quoted in* 63 Opposing Counsel of Md. Att'y Gen. No. 422, at 5 (1978).

9. The *Travelers* case involved several commercial insurers, their HMOs, and trade associations challenging New York's hospital surcharges on the ground that they were preempted by ERISA. This case narrowed the scope of the ERISA preemption by excluding from its scope state laws that have an indirect economic influence on an employee benefit plan.

10. Section 1932 of the Social Security Act permits states to require beneficiaries to enroll in managed care without a waiver from the Secretary of DHHS on the state's filing of an amendment to its Medicaid plan. The amendment, like the plan, must receive DHHS approval for the state to receive its matching funds. Under a Section 1932 waiver, the state does not have to demonstrate that its managed care initiative is either cost effective or budget neutral.

11. Debarred individuals are those who have been sanctioned (suspended, excluded, or otherwise prohibited) from participating in Medicare or Medicaid.

12. Donald B. Sparks, *The Dynamics of Effective Negotiation* (Houston: Gulf Publishing 1982) 3–5.

13. American Academy of Hospital Attorneys of the American Hospital Association, AAHA Practice Guide Series 1993, Vol. 1, *Managed Care Handbook.* Reprinted with permission.

Appendix 11-A

Suggested Language: Exclusive Contracts

Many providers bargain for exclusive contracts that will exclude their competitors from access to a particular payer. Others seek to bar exclusive arrangements through patient protection, due process, essential community provider, mandated point of service, any willing provider, and freedom of choice legislation. The following are examples of exclusive-contract drafting.

Example #1: Exclusive Provider. Nothing contained in the Agreement shall prevent Hospital from participating in or contracting with any insurer, preferred provider organization, health maintenance organization, or otherwise entering into contracts regarding health care delivery with any other entity. During the term of this Agreement, however, Payer shall not contract with any hospital provider of health care services that is physically located within the following geographic area:

Example #2: Differential Payments. At any time Payer does not have an agreement in force with _____ Hospital during the term of the Agreement, then Payer shall be entitled to pay Hospital and Hospital shall accept as reimbursement the rates set forth in Attachment B in lieu of the rates set forth in Attachment A.

Example #3: Differential Payments. During each month on or after the Effective Date of the Agreement that the number of licensed beds within [geographic area] exceeds _____ [##] in acute-care hospitals which are then participating hospitals under contract with Payer, Payer shall pay Hospital in lieu of the rates set forth in Attachment A the rates set forth in Attachment B.

Example #4: Right of First Refusal. Payer shall not offer a Payer Agreement to any acute-care hospital or provider sponsored physician-hospital organization located in counties of _____ without first offering the Payer Agreement to Provider and selected Participating Providers of Provider's Network. Provider shall have five (5) working days to notify Payer in writing of Provider's acceptance of the Payer Agreement and if Payer does not hear from Provider during that time, Payer may offer the Payer Agreement to any other organization or provider(s). This right of first refusal does not apply to the following clinical services, which shall not be offered to Payers through Provider: _____.

Example #5: Right of First Refusal. As part of the consideration for Hospital's commitment for the development of the HMO in the Service Area, HMO hereby grants Hospital the right of first negotiation respecting HMO's further or additional expansion in the area, subject to the following terms and conditions. As long as this Agreement is in effect HMO shall not approach any other hospital for the provision of hospital services to Beneficiaries within the area without first offering Hospital the opportunity to develop or exploit such expansion through a subcontract. If Hospital declines to participate in such expansion or Hospital and HMO, after engaging in good-faith negotiations for a period of ninety (90) days, fail to agree on the terms and conditions of the expansion, then HMO shall be free to offer direct contracts to any hospital in the expanded area.

Appendix 11-B

Medicare Requirements for Provider Agreements

DHHS, CMS, Office of Managed Care, provided guidance on HMO-provider contracts in the form of Attachment II (Important Notice) to HMO-CMP Medicare coordinators as part of its memorandum on "Improvements to Application Materials." This document was provided for information only in developing contracts between MCOs and providers of health care services.

Mandatory

- The provider must agree to serve the health plan members for a specified period of time, usually one year
- The provider must agree to provide specific services to all members, including a statement that plan members include commercial and Medicare enrollees (when applicable)
- The provider must agree not to bill health plan members
- Providers must agree to review of services provided to plan members by utilization management and quality assurance committees/staff
- Payments for services must be stated, and incentive arrangements must be described, if any
- The agreement must be signed and dated by both the HMO and provider

Legal

- Contract definitions must be consistent with Medicare definitions
- Identification of specific covered basic and/or supplemental health care services, including maximum benefits
- Provisions for insolvency protection, including a member hold-harmless clause stating financial liability in case of insolvency
- Describe contract termination process (minimum 60 days' notice except where patients are in danger) and continuity of care
- Include agreement to maintain adequate liability and malpractice coverage

- Include clause making the provider contract nonassignable without HMO consent
- Include member nondiscrimination clause

Enrollment

- HMO is to identify who is eligible to enroll in the Medicare product and maintain data system and mechanism for provider access
- State agreement to service the Medicare members
- Describe provider's responsibility for membership reporting

Payment

- Clearly describe payment arrangements, including physician incentive payment
- Obligate provider to collect copayments and deductibles
- Describe provider's coordination of benefits and subrogation responsibilities, if any
- Describe health plan's payment and administrative responsibilities
- Describe provider responsibilities for Medicare payment procedures, if any

Services

- Comply with the Medicare HMO peer review program
- Disclose advance directives to Medicare patients
- Comply with state patient confidentiality laws
- Disclose patient information to HCFA
- Explain Medicare appeals and grievance process
- Provide a detailed description of the health plan benefits
- Participate in the HMO's quality assurance activities, credentialing processes, utilization management program, and member grievance system
- Physician must have admitting privileges in at least one contracting hospital
- Physician must notify HMO of changes in licensure or admitting privileges

- Describe times of service
- Allow health plan approval and oversight of subcontractor agreements
- Identify administrative services, if any, to be performed by HMO

Intermediary Organization Contracts

Contract must require the intermediary to put in its contract with providers all of the clauses mentioned above

- HMO retains all statutory responsibilities
- HMO is to be third-party beneficiary of intermediary/provider contract
- HMO has veto power over intermediary credentialing decisions
- HMO must maintain copies of the intermediary's contracts or have ready access to them
- If intermediary pays claims, the HMO must monitor timeliness and appropriateness of payment and services, and HCFA should have access to books and records of intermediary

Membership

- Members referred to out-of-network providers cannot incur financial liability except for copays and deductibles
- Providers that see Medicare enrollees shall be paid more than they would have received under regular Medicare reimbursement

Appendix 11-C

Provisions Related to Hospital-Based Physicians

How can a hospital engage the cooperation of separately billing hospital-based physicians with the hospital's managed care contracting strategy? Many hospitals perceive that their strategy can be sabotaged if a separately billing hospital-based physician refuses to contract with HMOs and PPOs or demands unreasonable contract terms. One suggestion is to select a cooperative hospital-based physician at the outset. Consider the following excerpt from a hospital's request for proposals:

> Dear Doctor:
>
> St. Elsewhere Hospital is in the process of negotiating its single source anesthesia contract. Please indicate your group's willingness to:
>
> * * *
>
> Participate in good-faith negotiations regarding HMO/PPO contracts in which the hospital participates.

Also consider obtaining the hospital-based physician's covenant to cooperate.

Examples of hospital-based physician contract clauses:

Example #1: Weak. Physician agrees to work closely with Hospital to negotiate for managed care contracts and to participate, to the extent practicable, in the same managed care contracts as Hospital.

Example #2: Demanding. From time to time Hospital may enter into arrangements with third-party payers or their agents (such as HMOs, PPOs, employers, labor unions, and government payers) in which participation by Hospital is, in the estimation of Hospital, dependent upon Physician also entering into an arrangement with the payer or payer's designee that might alter Physician's usual separate billing procedures by requiring Physician to accept assignment, accept discounted fees, accept capitated risk payments, bill Hospital rather than the payer, or accept some other unique arrangement. In this event, Hospital will notify Physician of the payer's proposal. Physician shall have thirty (30) days to reach an agreement with the other party. If this deadline is not met, Hospital may retain the services of another to meet the needs of the payer, irrespective of any exclusive contractor provision of this Agreement or other understanding between the parties or any current or future Hospital or Medical Staff bylaw, rule, or regulation to the contrary.

Example #3: More Demanding. From time to time Hospital may enter into arrangements with third-party payers or their agents (such as HMOs, PPOs, employers, labor unions, and government payers) in which participation by Hospital is, in the estimation of Hospital, dependent upon Physician also entering into an arrangement with the payer or payer's designee that might alter Physician's usual separate billing procedures by requiring Physician to accept assignment, accept discounted fees, accept capitated risk payments, bill Hospital rather than the payer, or accept some other unique arrangement. In this event, Hospital will notify Physician of the payer's proposal. Physician shall have thirty (30) days to reach an agreement with the other party and shall reduce its charges by [insert one of following choices]. If this deadline is not met, Hospital may retain the services of another to meet the needs of the payer, irrespective of any provision of this Agreement or other understanding between the parties or any current or future Hospital or Medical Staff bylaw, rule, or regulation to the contrary.

[Choice 1] the same percentage reduction made by Hospital for that payer.

[Choice 2] the same percentage reduction made by the [IPA/ PHO] for that payer.

[Choice 3] no less than ____ percent (but need not be more than ____ percent) of Physician's current charges.

[Choice 4] the same percentage reduction made by the surgeons and attending physicians of Hospital's Medical Staff for that payer.

Finally, consider amending the medical staff bylaws to require participation in managed care contracts:

> The Board of Trustees may deny Medical Staff membership, departmental affiliation, or clinical privileges to an applicant

for reappointment if the applicant has not entered into managed care agreements consistent with Hospital's mission and objectives.

This opens the entire economic credentialing debate. California law precludes this type of economic credentialing:

> A hospital which contracts with an insurer, nonprofit hospital service plan, or health care service plan shall not determine or condition medical staff membership or clinical privileges upon the basis of a physician and surgeon's or podiatrist's participation or nonparticipation in a contract with that insurer, hospital service plan, or health care service plan.[1]

Texas approaches the issue differently. Current regulations affecting insured PPOs state:

> No insurer may contract with a hospital or institutional provider which, as a condition of staff membership or privileges, requires a practitioner to enter into a preferred provider contract.[2]

---

[1] Cal Health & Safety Code § 1322 (1996).
[2] Tex Dept Insurance, 28 Tex Admin Code § 3.3703(2) (1996).

Chapter 12

Alternative Dispute Resolution

Although alternative dispute resolution (ADR) such as arbitration and mediation has existed for over 20 years, it has only recently been embraced by the legal profession as a way to avoid the costs, delays, and acrimony of litigation. As the use of ADR to represent managed care disputes increases, it has become increasingly important to include ADR provisions in managed care contracts. A well-written agreement representing the results of a negotiation process can make the resolution of disputes easier and less costly. Unfortunately, as more lawyers begin to enter the ADR arena, there is concern that ADR is becoming more like than unlike litigation.

Previous editions of this book focused on ADR as the optimal means of conflict resolution in health care disputes, particularly those involving managed care. This edition adopts a more critical view of ADR and discusses its deficiencies as well as its advantages. This popular process has been abused in cases involving the use of mandatory arbitration to resolve consumer complaints against managed care plans.

Overview

Q 12:1   What is alternative dispute resolution?

ADR is a process that uses various techniques to resolve issues in conflict. It is employed most often in conflict management and involves such methods as arbitration, mediation, mini-trials, summary jury trials, and moderated settlement conferences. The goal of ADR is the speedy and cost-effective settlement of disputes. ADR procedures are structured to achieve this goal by relaxing the formal procedural and evidentiary rules of the courtroom. ADR refers to a variety of procedures for the resolution of disputes; each ADR procedure is an alternative to court adjudication.

Q 12:2   How prevalent is the use of ADR in business?

In an article by Elizabeth Kent published online in *Findlaw Library* by the Hawaii State Bar Association,[1] it was reported that a survey of ADR use among 1,000 of the largest U.S. corporations found the following:

1. Mediation was viewed as a cost-saving measure by 90 percent.
2. Mediation was used in the prior three years by 88 percent.
3. Arbitration was used in the prior three years by 79 percent.
4. Most litigate first and then move to ADR, or litigate only in appropriate cases and use ADR for all others.
5. Use of mediation and arbitration was widespread in commercial and employment disputes.
6. Mediation was considered a more satisfactory process than litigation by 81 percent.
7. Mediation was viewed as successful in preserving good relationships by 59 percent.

Q 12:3   Why is ADR favored by the judiciary?

In the article cited in Q 12:2, Kent reported that the judiciary favors ADR for a number of reasons, including the following:

1. ADR may save litigation costs.
2. Resolution may be speedier.
3. Business relationships may be preserved.
4. Creative resolutions are possible.
5. People often prefer making their own decisions.
6. There may be less of an emotional toll on the parties.
7. If more cases are resolved by ADR, judges have more time to work on cases that require judicial attention.
8. Privacy and confidentiality may be preserved (court is open to the public).

Q 12:4   What are the different forms or methods of dispute resolution?

Dispute resolution can be nonbinding or binding.

Nonbinding Processes. Nonbinding methods along the dispute resolution continuum include conflict avoidance, negotiation, conciliation, mediation, use of an ombudsperson, and evaluative methods (moderated settlement conference, summary jury trial, minitrial, early neutral evaluation, and nonbinding arbitration):

1. *Conflict avoidance.* Avoidance, which is the earliest and the easiest response to conflict, involves simply walking away from a dispute rather than challenging it.
2. *Negotiation.* Most legal disputes are settled by negotiation. Resolution requires that the parties be able to communicate and want to compromise.
3. *Conciliation.* Conciliation is like mediation. It involves a third party in a less formal process than mediation.
4. *Mediation.* Mediation is facilitated negotiation that involves a third party who has no authoritative decision-making authority, but who assists the parties in voluntarily reaching a mutually acceptable resolution of the issues in dispute.
5. *Ombudsperson.* An ombudsperson is a special type of grievance-handling official who investigates complaints and makes recommendations that directly relate to the merits of the dispute.

6. *Evaluative methods.* The following methods are often used to give the parties a sense of the value of their case and can provide a starting place for negotiations:

   a. *Moderated settlement conference.* A moderated settlement conference involves presentation of the case by counsel representing the parties to an impartial panel of experienced attorneys, with each side taking no longer than 30 minutes. The hearing involves questions from the panel, and counsel for the parties can make closing statements. The entire process is confidential. The conference gives the parties an opportunity to evaluate the strengths and weaknesses of their case. Although the parties do not participate directly in the conference, they may be present during the proceeding.

   b. *Summary jury trial.* A summary jury trial is conducted by a court in the same manner as a jury trial, except that the voir dire (jury selection process) and presentation of evidence are greatly limited, the rules of evidence are relaxed, and the jury verdict is advisory in nature. This approach allows the parties the opportunity to experience a formal court hearing and evaluate the jury's reaction to the case. Jurors selected for this panel are generally not aware of the advisory nature of their opinion until after they have reached a verdict.

   c. *Mini-trial.* The mini-trial is a private, consensual proceeding in which counsel for each party makes an abbreviated presentation of his or her best case before a representative of each party with full authority to settle the matter.

   d. *Early neutral evaluation.* Some jurisdictions and courts require early neutral evaluation. Under early neutral evaluation, parties to litigation are required to make presentations to a neutral evaluator. The evaluator is engaged to provide both parties with an assessment of the strengths and weaknesses of their respective positions and to facilitate resolution of the dispute. This device is used early in a litigation process, before substantial discovery and often at the request of the court. The parties may meet with a neutral party to discuss both sides of the case in confidence. The process serves a case management objective as well as a settlement objective by allowing the neutral party to give an evaluation of the case.

e. *Nonbinding arbitration.* Nonbinding arbitration allows the parties to present their facts and positions to a neutral party or panel who will render a nonbinding determination or opinion.

Binding Processes. Binding processes include administrative proceedings, arbitration, and formal adjudication:

1. *Administrative proceedings.* Administrative proceedings involve a third party or panel with subject matter expertise and the authority to make a binding decision.

2. *Arbitration.* Arbitration has a long history in labor disputes. Typically, a private person or a group of private persons is chosen by the parties or selected under specified procedures to resolve a dispute. It is less formal than a judicial proceeding but follows a specified procedure in an adversarial setting. In arbitration, a dispute is submitted to an arbitrator for a decision.

3. *Formal adjudication.* Litigation is the most common form of dispute resolution handled in the court system, with formalized rules and appealable decisions by a judge or jury. Courts in some jurisdictions, however, may have case management conferences, at which staff counsel or other court officers may take active roles in promoting settlement discussions.

Q 12:5   What are the advantages of ADR over litigation?

Conflict resolution mechanisms, including ADR, have a number of advantages over litigation. First, the resolution process can be as simple and flexible as the parties desire, so the parties can tailor the resolution mechanism to the specific dispute. Second, ADR allows a more efficient and prompt resolution than a long, contentious litigation process. Third, ADR tends to be less adversarial and allows the parties to preserve their relationship at the conclusion of the process.

Another advantage is that ADR does not result in a published opinion or court record. This allows a more open and protected process. Finally, ADR is much less expensive than litigation. Fees are generally set in advance, and expenses associated with the process are generally shared by the parties.

Q 12:6 How does a party access ADR services?

Parties desiring ADR can either "self-administer" a dispute resolution process or access ADR services through a number of resources, such as the American Arbitration Association and the Judicial Arbitration and Mediation Services. The American Health Lawyers Association offers dispute resolution services for parties involved in health care disputes.

Arbitration

Q 12:7 What is the difference between binding and nonbinding arbitration?

Binding arbitration involves having a neutral person (or a panel of neutral persons) decide a dispute after hearing each party's presentation of evidence and argument. The parties agree in advance that the decision (award) of the neutral agent will be final. Generally, there are no appeals from an arbitrator's award, although parties may seek judicial relief from binding arbitration if the arbitrator exceeds the authority conferred under the parties' agreement to arbitrate, or if the arbitrator denies a party a fair hearing or demonstrates bias or prejudice. Parties may sometimes seek judicial relief if there is an obvious mistake, such as a calculation error, that appears on the face of an award.

Parties may decide in advance whether arbitration will be binding (the parties must accept the award), or nonbinding (the arbitrator's award is advisory only). If the award is nonbinding, the parties may decide to accept the nonbinding opinion, use it as the basis for further settlement negotiations, or reject it and proceed to litigation. Those seeking nonbinding arbitration may wish to consider whether they might find nonbinding arbitration useful; they lose the value of finality but gain more flexibility.

Q 12:8 Can arbitration be mandated?

Yes. Arbitration can be mandated by court-ordered rules that require certain disputes to be submitted to arbitration, or can be mandatory under the terms of an agreement entered into by the parties in advance of any dispute. For example, the rules of the U.S. National Association of Securities Dealers require members to submit all disputes between them to binding arbitration.

Arbitration is more often voluntary than mandatory. Voluntary arbitration refers to the arbitration of a dispute submitted to an arbitrator by agreement of the parties. Typically, parties to a dispute submit their dispute to arbitration in order to minimize the expense, delay, or publicity that they perceive will accompany litigation. Parties enter into an agreement to arbitrate or into a submission agreement. The agreement to arbitrate may be entered into in advance of any dispute, and may, for example, be included in a dispute resolution clause of a contract. Alternatively, parties may agree to arbitrate a dispute at the time it arises, or at any time before a final judgment is entered in a court proceeding.

Q 12:9 Should commercial agreements include an arbitration clause?

Yes. There are several good reasons for including arbitration clauses in commercial agreements. Arbitration can be a prompt, and therefore inexpensive, way of resolving business disputes. Arbitration can also ensure that the dispute is decided by a person who is familiar with the commercial context in which the dispute arose. Consider a contract that relates to a particularly complicated matter—would it be preferable to have a dispute arising under that agreement decided by a member of the judiciary, who may be elected or appointed, and whose experience may be in government, criminal prosecution, or criminal defense, or by a businessperson or professional who is familiar with the nature of the industry?

Arbitration may also reduce the risk of punitive or exemplary damages. If the arbitration agreement authorizes the award of compensatory damages only, it is unlikely that any party to that agreement will be assessed punitive damages. Because the plaintiff will be required to arbitrate his or her claim, a punitive damage lawsuit will not usually be instituted until after the arbitration is concluded. If the plaintiff prevails in arbitration and receives compensatory damages, that party (and more important, his or her lawyer) will have little incentive to pursue litigation in which he or she will recover only if he or she establishes a punitive damage case. Conversely, if the plaintiff loses in arbitration, and receives no compensatory damages, the plaintiff will be barred from pursuing a punitive damage action in most jurisdictions.

Q 12:10   What are the disadvantages of arbitration?

Arbitration may not make sense under certain circumstances. For example, if extensive discovery of information will be required, that will undermine the use of arbitration. In addition, there may be a benefit to forcing litigation when the economic positions of the parties are unequal. A court may be a better forum when a dispute involves questions of law and there is a substantial body of precedents in favor of a party's position.

Q 12:11   How does arbitration compare with litigation?

Arbitration differs from litigation in a number of ways and has features in common with litigation:

1. Arbitration avoids all technical pleading requirements. The initial arbitration filing may be as simple as a letter addressed to the arbitration tribunal that briefly explains the dispute in layperson's terms, refers to the arbitration contract, and asks for arbitration to be started. Motion practice associated with pleadings (motions for more particular statements and motions to dismiss for failure to state a claim) simply does not exist in arbitration.

2. Arbitration filing fees can be more or less expensive than court filing fees, depending on the arbitration rules that are invoked. The American Arbitration Association has many different arbitration rules, each of which applies to a different type of dispute. Some of the arbitration rules require a nominal filing fee ($25 or $50), and other arbitration rules require payment of a filing fee that is based on a percentage of the amount in dispute (such fees can amount to thousands of dollars). Before drafting an arbitration clause, the arbitration rules should be reviewed to be certain that the rules referenced in the arbitration clause do not call for disproportionate filing fees. Of course, arbitration may be completely private (outside the auspices of an arbitration organization

such as the American Arbitration Association), in which case there need not be any filing fees.

3. When a dispute goes to court, the litigants need not be concerned with paying the judge's salary. In contrast, arbitrators must usually be paid. In some cases, arbitrators will serve at no charge (some commercial arbitration rules provide for arbitrators to volunteer a limited amount of time for smaller commercial disputes). Some arbitrators charge as little as $350 per day; others charge as much as $3,500 per day. Typically, payment of the arbitrator's fee is shared equally by the parties, unless the arbitration agreement provides otherwise.

4. In both litigation and arbitration, the parties can agree that the prevailing party must be awarded attorneys' fees. In the absence of such an agreement, neither courts nor arbitrators will award attorneys' fees, unless the governing law provides for an award of attorneys' fees.

5. In litigation, there is no charge for the use of the courtroom. In arbitration, the parties may need to rent a conference room at a neutral location, such as a hotel. This cost can usually be avoided by using attorneys' conference rooms, or even unused courtrooms.

6. Most jurisdictions permit extensive pretrial discovery. In contrast, few arbitration rules provide for discovery. Many states, however, have arbitration statutes that can be invoked to permit discovery in arbitration. In addition, parties can draft arbitration agreements so as to define the extent of pretrial discovery that will be permitted. Generally, discovery is freely available in arbitration as long as the discovery is not abusive. Most arbitrators will allow key witnesses to be deposed in advance of the arbitration hearing and will require opposing parties to make copies of documents available to their adversaries. Parties can confer on arbitrators the same powers as courts to issue orders compelling discovery and protective orders.

7. Arbitration offers a big advantage in scheduling a hearing on the dispute. Courts schedule matters without regard to the schedule of the litigants. Some judges have been known to schedule trials involving out-of-state parties shortly before holidays in order to attempt to stimulate settlement interest.

In contrast, arbitration hearings are always scheduled with a view to the convenience of the participants. Courts have substantial backlogs. Cases may take as long as one or two years to come to trial, and appeals may extend the dispute even longer. In contrast, most arbitration hearings take place and are concluded within six months after arbitration is invoked.

8. Arbitration can be conducted in private, and arbitration records can be kept private. Litigation is open to the public, and documents, unless sealed by the court, become public documents.

9. In court, preliminary matters may be handled by several different judges, or by a magistrate. In arbitration, it would be most unusual for anyone other than the arbitrator or arbitrators who will ultimately decide the case to hear any pretrial matters. Court cases are decided either by a jury of laypersons or by a single judge (in most jurisdictions), or as in Vermont, by a presiding judge and one or two lay judges (assistant judges). Arbitration usually involves a single arbitrator, and the arbitration agreement can set forth minimum qualifications for the arbitrator. If the parties prefer, they may choose to use several arbitrators. One common arrangement is for each party to the dispute to select an arbitrator and for those two arbitrators to select a third arbitrator. When more than one arbitrator is to be used, the parties should clarify whether they intend that all the arbitrators be neutral, or whether each party is entitled to select an arbitrator as that party's representative, with one or more "deadlock-breaking" arbitrators as true neutrals.

10. Some judges and some arbitrators get actively involved in settlement negotiations. Some arbitrators are particularly adept at mediation and are able to stimulate settlement before cases are heard. The same may be said of some judges. In arbitration agreements, the parties may determine the extent to which the arbitrator will attempt to mediate the dispute.

11. Courts typically use formal rules of evidence. Although the modern trend in the law of evidence is to allow most evidence to be introduced, a substantial body of law requires certain formalities in the presentation of evidence. In most

cases, witnesses will be required to come to the hearing in order to identify documents so that they may be introduced, hearsay statements will not be introduced, and lawyers will be constrained in the conduct of their examinations to comport with the rigorous requirements imposed by all rules of evidence. A different situation is presented in arbitration. Usually affidavits are accepted (unless the parties agree otherwise), and it is rare for an arbitrator to exclude anything from evidence. Questioning is informal, and most arbitrators will tolerate a few objections from opposing counsel. Most arbitrators are sophisticated enough to understand that a question is leading, or that a question calls for hearsay evidence, and they are apt to permit such questions, allowing them to affect the weight that the arbitrator will give to the testimony.

12. In most cases tried in court, some form of posthearing briefs are required. In jury trials, jury instruction briefs are likely to be required and will often involve the same sort of legal research needed to prepare a memorandum of law. In cases tried by a judge (trials by court), posttrial briefs are frequently requested by the court. In arbitration, the parties can agree (either in the arbitration agreement, or at the time of the hearing) on whether they want to file posthearing briefs. It is extremely rare for an arbitrator to request briefs, or to refuse to accept briefs, contrary to the wishes of the parties.

13. In jury trials, the decision is apt to take the form of a general verdict that simply indicates the party who prevailed and the amount owed. Courts may use special interrogatories to the jury that may give more detail on the decision, but this detail will be far short of a complete explanation as to the result.

14. In cases by a judge, most courts must provide, on request, written findings of fact and conclusions of law that explain, in detail, the rationale for the court's decision. Rarely will a court issue an oral decision from the bench at the conclusion of the hearing. In arbitration, the parties may dictate the form of the decision. Parties may specify that the arbitrator provide a written decision explaining his or her rationale, or they may agree that the arbitrator provide no explanation at all. Generally, if the parties truly want the arbitration pro-

ceeding to be final, they will prefer to have an arbitrator issue an award without any accompanying rationale. If the parties agree, the arbitrator will "rule from the bench."

15. In most jurisdictions, every party has the opportunity to appeal as a matter of right. The judgment of the court does not become final until the appeal is concluded. On appeal, the appellate court uses an appellate review standard under which facts found by the trial court will not be disturbed unless there is no evidence introduced in the trial court on the point in question. The appellate court will, however, review the law as applied by the trial court, and will not hesitate to set aside the trial court's decision if it finds that the trial court was wrong in applying the law. There is no automatic appeal from an arbitration award. Most arbitration proceedings purport to be "final and binding," with the result that courts are reluctant to review arbitration awards, even if a party alleges that the arbitrator found facts unsupported by evidence or misapplied the law. Most arbitration statutes permit an extremely limited review of arbitration awards and authorize courts to set them aside if

   a. Corruption or fraud is evident in the procurement of the arbitration award;

   b. Evident partiality is demonstrated by the arbitrator;

   c. The arbitrator exceeds his or her powers; or

   d. The arbitrator conducts the hearing in a grossly prejudicial manner.

   By and large, it is extremely difficult to set aside an arbitration award in court. Similarly, it is very difficult for a party to avoid his or her agreement to arbitrate. Most arbitration statutes require that courts compel arbitration of any matter that is even arguably within the scope of an arbitration clause.

16. In court, parties may obtain provisional remedies, including property attachment, temporary injunctions, and wage garnishment. The same remedies are generally not available in arbitration, unless the parties provide for provisional remedies in their agreement to arbitrate. If the parties fail to provide for provisional remedies in their agreement to arbitrate,

it still may be possible for a plaintiff to bring a lawsuit to obtain a provisional remedy while arbitration proceeds.

Q 12:12   Are there any statutes that govern arbitration?

Yes. The Federal Arbitration Act [9 USC § 1 et seq] governs arbitration agreements made in interstate commerce. Generally, it provides that such agreements are enforceable and that federal courts must compel parties to participate in arbitration on motion made by any party. Under the Federal Arbitration Act a party may waive arbitration by failing to move for an order compelling arbitration within a reasonable period of time. Parties may attempt to avoid arbitration under the Federal Arbitration Act by claiming that they were defrauded into entering into the arbitration agreement, or by claiming that the arbitration agreement is contrary to law. There is a substantial body of federal case law on both points, and federal courts are increasingly finding that arbitration does not offend statutes that provide federal court remedies. For example, the U.S. Supreme Court has ruled that the "exclusive remedy" provisions of the 1933 Securities Act are not offended by arbitration. It has also ruled that claims arising under the Racketeer Influenced and Corrupt Organizations Act (RICO) may be arbitrated.

The Federal Arbitration Act further provides that an agreement to arbitrate is subject to all the same defenses that may be raised to any contract. The federal courts have, over the years, construed this provision narrowly so as to favor arbitration. In *Broughton v. CIGNA Healthplans of California* [No S072583 (Cal Dec 2, 1999)], the court held that the Federal Arbitration Act did not compel private arbitration of public injunctions. In that case, a mandatory arbitration provision in the CIGNA MediCal contract was challenged in a medical malpractice action. The court allowed the mandatory arbitration to proceed on the malpractice claim, but left the injunctive action with the courts.

The Administrative Dispute Resolution Act of 1996 (ADRA) [5 USC §§ 571-583] made substantial changes in the arbitration provisions found in the ADRA of 1990. Specifically, the ADRA of 1996 authorizes the voluntary use of binding arbitration, without the 1990 Act's qualifying proviso that allowed heads of agencies to vacate an arbitrator's award. Before an agency can exercise this new power, it must issue guidance, in consultation with the Attorney General, on the appropriate use of binding arbitration. [See 5 USC § 575(c)]

The federal courts almost uniformly require that a party establish fraud in the making of an arbitration clause (not merely fraud in the making of the contract in which the clause is included) to allow the party to escape from the obligation to arbitrate a dispute. Federal courts have occasionally invalidated arbitration agreements when they have been found unconscionable or oppressive (e.g., when arbitration is required to be held in a distant locale at great cost to a litigant who cannot afford to pursue his or her claim in that locale).

Many states have their own arbitration statutes, and in a majority of the jurisdictions in the United States, these statutes are modeled after the Uniform Arbitration Act. In most states, enactment requires that courts compel arbitration on the motion of any party, much like the Federal Arbitration Act. It is important to review a state's law to ensure that the ultimate arbitration agreement will be enforceable. For example, under Vermont law, an arbitration agreement is unenforceable if there is not a prominently displayed "acknowledgment of arbitration" to ensure that both parties fully understood that the agreement contained an arbitration clause.[2] This requirement underscores the importance of knowing which state's law will apply to an arbitration agreement, including a choice of law clause in the contract, and thoroughly understanding the requirements of the law that is chosen to govern the dispute.

Q 12:13 Are arbitration clauses enforceable in international agreements?

Yes. Several international protocols govern arbitration agreements, and those who prepare an arbitration clause for inclusion in an international agreement must determine whether there is a treaty or convention that would pertain to the enforcement of the arbitration clause. Experienced counsel should be prepared to assist clients in any of the following proceedings, and should understand these proceedings well enough to draft the arbitration agreement with the client's objectives in mind:

- Actions to compel arbitration
- Actions to resist arbitration
- Actions to set aside arbitration awards

- Actions to modify arbitration awards
- Actions to enforce arbitration decisions

Q 12:14   What should be considered in drafting an arbitration clause in a contract?

No standard arbitration clause will fit all contracts; however, the following should be considered in drafting any arbitration clause: (1) keep it simple; (2) address how expenses will be handled; (3) establish in advance the number, qualifications, and manner of selection of arbitrators; (4) determine the extent to which discovery will be allowed during the proceeding; (5) establish scheduling guidelines; (6) address scope of privacy and confidentiality of the proceeding; (7) define the role of the arbitrators in the proceeding; (8) determine the scope of evidentiary rules to be used; (9) determine the use of briefing documents; (10) determine the ultimate format of the arbitrator's decision; (11) delineate the ability of a party to appeal the award or decision; (12) determine in advance the choice of law for the proceeding; and (13) determine the availability of mediation as part of the proceeding.

Q 12:15   How is the number of arbitrators involved in an arbitration proceeding determined?

The determination of the number of arbitrators involved in an arbitration proceeding is up to the parties, or can be addressed in the written contract. As part of the "disaster planning" that should be part of any written agreement, an attorney can determine the number of arbitrators during contract drafting and negotiation. There is no rule of thumb for making this determination, except that it may need to be related to the complexity of the dispute and the "worst case scenario." In arbitration, it is not uncommon to have more than one arbitrator; often a panel of three is chosen. The process of selection of the panel can be as random as having each party approve from a list one arbitrator and then having the two selected approve the third.

Q 12:16   What is the major difference between arbitration and mediation?

Arbitration uses an adversarial approach. Mediation stresses a collaborative, partnership approach.

Q 12:17   Why do attorneys prefer arbitration to mediation?

Most attorneys prefer arbitration to mediation because arbitration uses an adversarial approach that closely tracks the approach of the judicial system, whereby a third party hears evidence and testimony and then renders a decision. That decision can be binding or non-binding.

Mediation, on the other hand, requires special skills in the art of compromise and negotiation because it attempts to militate against the "win-lose" approach in favor of a negotiated resolution. The mediation forum is less antagonistic than arbitration, and because it is consensual, the parties are able to withdraw at any point in the process. Some attorneys are concerned about the need to "put all their cards on the table" as part of information gathering during mediation. This concern can be addressed before the commencement of mediation by an agreement that only the mediator will be given the information and that the mediator will not disclose it without the party's consent. Some states allow the process to remain confidential and preclude later "discovery" and use at trial of potentially damaging evidence.

Mediation

Q 12:18   What is mediation?

Mediation is a process for resolving disputes with the aid of a neutral agent. The neutral agent assists parties, privately and collectively, in identifying the issues in dispute and in developing proposals to resolve the disputes. Unlike an arbitrator, a mediator is not empowered to decide any disputes; accordingly, the mediator may meet privately and hold confidential and separate discussions with the parties to a dispute.

Q 12:19   What is the primary purpose of mediation?

The primary purpose of mediation is to reduce the hostility routinely associated with litigation. Mediation therefore stresses a collaborative, partnership approach, whereas adjudication and arbitration both use an adversarial approach. Mediation is not designed or intended to decide which party was right and which party was wrong, but rather to (1) give the parties an opportunity to vent and diffuse feelings; (2) clear up misunderstandings; (3) determine their underlying interests; (4) find areas of agreement; and (5) incorporate these results into solutions agreed to by the parties.

Q 12:20   Is mediation appropriate for all kinds of disputes?

No. There are some situations for which mediation will not achieve the desired result. For example, mediation will not work when a client wants to "send a message," that is, achieve a public victory that will serve to deter future disputes. Not all clients are able to handle the mediation process. Before engaging in mediation, an attorney should gauge the client's frame of mind and explore his or her motives for the case from both plaintiff and defense perspectives. The client should be counseled as to the strengths and weaknesses of the case and understand the "best alternative to a negotiated agreement" (BATNA) and the "worst alternative to a negotiated agreement" (WATNA).

There are three basic approaches to mediation:[3]

1. *Directive mediation.* After hearing input from both sides, the mediator suggests a resolution and then tries to sell both parties on the solution.

2. *Facilitative mediation.* The mediator focuses on the interests of both parties and works to open the lines of communication between them while suggesting various solutions based on the information obtained during the mediation. The mediator encourages the parties to become part of the negotiation process and "buy into" the solution.

3. *Transformative mediation.* The mediator works with both parties to develop empathy for the other side and to empower both parties to work toward a mutual agreement. This approach is valuable when the goal is to maintain a working relationship at the conclusion of the mediation.

Q 12:21   What is the role of a mediator?

According to the American Arbitration Association, the role of a mediator is to clarify and interpret each side's position, persuade and inform the parties of the pros and cons of each side's case, and suggest alternative solutions to resolving their disputes. A mediator is not a judge or arbitrator. A mediator has no authority to render a judgment or an award. A mediator is not a legal representative or advocate for any party. A mediator does not counsel. Instead, a mediator is a neutral party who facilitates discussion between parties to a dispute, unrestrained by legal or evidentiary rules. The mediator's ability to assist the parties in reaching an agreement is largely based on trust. A mediator should attempt to do the following:

- Make the proceedings manageable
- Develop an atmosphere conducive to problem-solving negotiations
- Gather all information available about the parties' interests
- Help the parties create options
- Help the parties narrow the options and move toward an agreement
- Help the parties make rational decisions between forging an agreement and pursuing a claim

In the course of a mediation session, a mediator may assume a number of different roles, including the following:

1. *Facilitator.* The mediator facilitates the mediation process by keeping the discussion moving, by directing conflict so that it becomes an impetus for movement rather than a factor in hardening positions, and by phrasing and rephrasing areas of possible agreement.

2. *Opener of communication channels.* When the parties have reached a communication impasse, the mediator intervenes to reestablish communication channels.

3. *Translator and transmitter of information.* Sometimes, when parties talk they do not hear or understand each other. The mediator can act as a transmitter and a translator of information; both are important functions in the process.

4. *Distinguisher of positions and interests.* The mediator knows that bargaining positions may not represent the party's true intent, but rather be a guise for hurt, anger, or desire to punish. Parties cannot usually reach a settlement without modifying either the form or content of their original demands. The mediator helps them distinguish their true underlying needs

(those things that must occur for the dispute to be resolved) from their original desires.

5. *Creator of options.* The mediator can actively participate in the development of options for the parties to consider. This service is one of the most creative aspects of mediation and often helps to overcome impasses between parties.

6. *Agent of reality.* The mediator is an agent of reality in helping each party reach an agreement and understand the other's needs so that a realistic framework can be established to assess the costs and benefits of continuing or resolving the conflict.

Q 12:22   What qualities are desirable in a mediator?

A mediator should (1) be impartial, (2) be personable, (3) be inventive with solutions, (4) have mediation training and experience, (5) have the ability to engender trust in both sides, and (6) have excellent communication skills. A mediator does not have to be an attorney or judge but should be sensitive to human nature. "Truisms" relating to human behavior include the following:

1. People will rarely make a decision if they can avoid it.
2. People may agree on the facts but often disagree on their interpretation.
3. People usually act out of self-interest.
4. When two people have a dispute, it cannot be resolved until they want to resolve it.
5. People do not like to be told what to do.
6. People do not like to apologize.
7. People tend to carry out decisions they have helped to reach.
8. People are more important than their disputes.
9. Disputes will not e resolved by dwelling on them, but rather by dealing with them.
10. No settlement is reached without some doubt along the way.

Q 12:23   What can a mediator add to the negotiating process?

As discussed in Q 12:20, in the context of conflict resolution in contract negotiations, a mediator can bring much to the negotiating process, including the following:

- Enhancing and opening communication among parties
- Identifying and understanding the interests among parties
- Dealing with emotions
- Helping parties focus on their future relationship
- Helping to generate creative solutions
- Helping to overcome reactive devaluation of goals and objectives
- Helping to discover mutually acceptable standards
- Helping the parties understand negotiating constraints
- Maintaining an atmosphere of optimism in achieving a solution or settlement
- Helping to assess the alternatives to an agreement
- Bringing closure and focusing on timing
- Framing and confirming the agreement
- Helping attain ratification of the agreement

Q 12:24 Is mediation always voluntary?

No. Mediation may be compulsory, under the terms of laws or court rules, or may be voluntary, by agreement of the parties. Some jurisdictions have rules requiring mediation of disputes at some point in the litigation process. Voluntary mediation may be undertaken under terms of a mediation clause by which parties to an agreement agree in advance to submit any disputes to mediation. Such mediation clauses are common in agreements in which the parties seek to resolve their disputes in a manner that avoids hostility and preserves an ongoing relationship. Mediation agreements may also be made at the time a dispute arises.

Q 12:25 Is there a standard approach to the mediation process?

No. Mediation may differ depending on the mediator selected. Some mediators view their role as passive; they believe they are responsible only for assisting the parties in negotiating their own resolution to their disputes. Others take a more active role. Some mediators provide evaluations of each party's position; others assist the parties in determining their genuine interests and in understanding the other party's genuine interests so that rational settlement proposals can then be generated and exchanged. Parties considering mediation would do well to inquire from a prospective mediator how that mediator would structure the mediation session and how the mediator views his or her role in the mediation process. Mediation generally progresses according to the following steps:

1. Introducing the process;
2. Gathering information on the dispute and the parties' interests;
3. Developing options;
4. Narrowing the options through discussion of negotiation constraints and alternatives to an agreement; and
5. Closing the process and ending with either an agreement or another process.

A typical mediation might involve allowing each party to submit premediation briefs that succinctly set forth the essence of the dispute and each party's position. At mediation, the mediator will typically conduct introductions, explain the mediation process, provide assurances of confidentiality, and give each party an opportunity to explain the dispute and the reasons behind the party's position. Many mediators will then meet privately with each party and provide an evaluation of the dispute, pointing out the strengths and weaknesses of each party's position. The mediator may then, again in private, assist each party to determine both parties' genuine interests and encourage each party to identify settlement proposals intended to address those interests. Typically, the mediator communicates settlement proposals to each party and helps each party determine how best to respond to a settlement proposal.

Q 12:26   Who provides mediation services?

Mediation services may be provided by an organized tribunal. In some jurisdictions, bar associations and institutes may offer mediation services provided by mediators who undergo mediation training and so earn the privilege of becoming a member of the tribunal's panel of mediators. Private organizations, both profit and nonprofit, may maintain mediation tribunals. These tribunals may maintain panels of mediators and may have rules governing the conduct of mediation proceedings. Parties to disputes may find it desirable to select a mediator with experience in the subject matter of the dispute, or with a background in the industry involved in the dispute. Others may prefer to use the services of mediation organizations whose panels of mediators comprise former jurists. Some jurisdictions maintain government mediation services that provide skilled mediators at no charge to parties involved in certain types of disputes. For example, in the United States the Federal Mediation and Conciliation Service provides mediators to assist in the resolution of significant disputes between management and labor.

Health Care Disputes

Q 12:27 For which types of health care disputes is ADR used?

The types of health care disputes for which ADR is used include the following:

- Commercial disputes with vendors
- Contract disputes within physician groups
- Joint venture disputes
- Medical staff or peer review disputes
- Managed care contract disputes between providers and payers
- Employment contract disputes (physician, executive, supervisor, or employee)
- National Practitioner Data Bank (NPDB) disputes
- Disputes between health care providers
- Disputes between health care providers and their members
- Disputes with government agencies
- Disputes between medical staff departments

Q 12:28 What are the advantages of using ADR in the health care industry?

The advantages of using ADR in the health care industry include the following:

- Expedited process outside of court
- Maintenance of control over the proceedings
- Confidentiality of the process

Managed Care Disputes

Q 12:29 What are the most common areas of dispute in managed care arrangements?

The most common areas of dispute in managed care arrangements involve the following:

- Failure to charge a lower, negotiated contract rate against the risk pool or capitation account

- Failure to credit coordination of benefits and subrogation recoveries

- Failure to credit stop-loss recoveries or failure to hold charges against the risk pool or capitation account for catastrophic cases

- Failure to report utilization data adequately

- Incorrect, lower member counts

- Charging nonassigned members' claims against the risk pool or capitation account

- Excessive incurred but not reported (IBNR) estimates

- Failure to "true up" IBNR estimates retroactively

- Unauthorized additions of unaffiliated providers to the risk pool or capitation account

- Incorrect authorizations

Other disputes involve coverage questions and claims or payment disagreements. Disputes relating to claims or payment disagreements are the most common disputes. Because of the different methods used to calculate payments to providers for services, many disputes involve the amount of payment a provider is entitled to receive under the terms of the provider agreement. In addition, payers sometimes dispute the coordination of benefits. Coverage disputes usually involve whether particular individuals are beneficiaries under a contract, whether a particular service is covered under the terms of an agreement and there was proper notification of such coverage, whether a particular situation constitutes an emergency and the terms of reimbursing a nonparticipating provider, and whether a particular service is "medically necessary" or "medically appropriate."

Other situations appropriate for ADR include contractual interpretation, contractual modification, exclusion of providers, legality of particular arrangements, selection of providers, termination of providers, and utilization review.

Q 12:30 What should be considered in deciding whether to use ADR in a managed care dispute?

Not all disputes are amenable to ADR techniques. First, the parties should consider the level of expense they can afford in connection with the resolution of a particular dispute. Litigation is generally a costlier and more time-consuming process than ADR. Second, to the extent the parties anticipate continuing any working relationship, ADR may offer a less acrimonious approach to resolving the dispute. Certain types of ADR, such as mediation, are not adversarial. Whether the matter at issue is appropriate for compromise is important in the selection of the most applicable ADR technique. For example, arbitration, mini-trial, private adjudication, or summary jury trial may be appropriate for a question that has only one possible answer. Conversely, a dispute relating to the interpretation of a contract rate may be resolved through fact finding, mediation, or negotiation. Third, the parties should determine whether the disputed matter must be kept confidential. Litigation proceedings are matters of public record. It is easier to protect the confidentiality of a dispute by using ADR. Fourth, the parties should consider the remedies that may be needed to resolve the dispute. If the remedy is to reach an agreement, ADR can allow the parties to create unique agreements to accomplish their objectives. Fifth, the parties should decide whether the dispute resolver should have certain qualifications. There is greater flexibility in ADR to use experts as arbitrators or mediators.

ADR does not usually provide a mechanism for discovery of information, and to the extent it is important to the resolution of a dispute, litigation may be a desirable alternative because it provides for discovery as part of the judicial process. In addition, ADR mechanisms usually do not provide for an appeal. To the extent a dispute involves a complicated statutory interpretation, for example, the parties may want to allow for review. Appellate review may be available with ADR.

Q 12:31   Under what circumstances is ADR desirable in resolving disputes arising under managed care arrangements?

Judicial resolution of disputes has traditionally been marked by long delays, uninformed judges and juries, strict rules of evidence, costly discovery, publicity, lengthy appeals, and the use of attorneys. This process is more familiar to the parties and to the public, and it may be more desirable for certain types of disputes for the reasons discussed in Qs 12:10, 12:19, and 12:30.

ADR, on the other hand, is an excellent forum for resolving disputes provided that the dispute resolvers and the method used are selected with care. Nonbinding ADR is widely accepted and has well-defined procedures that are frequently used by managed care organizations (MCOs) to resolve disputes with vendors, providers, and consumers. The use of binding ADR in managed care is more complex. Using binding arbitration in consumer disputes is problematic because there are substantial differences among the states in the enforceability of binding arbitration agreements. The Federal Arbitration Act [9 USC § 1] and the California Civil Procedure Code [Cal Civ Proc Code § 1280] provide for enforcement of arbitration agreements for all matters, whether they involve consumer or vendor disputes. In other states, however, binding arbitration may not be used for personal injury claims. Even when state law and precedent allow binding arbitration, there may be other factors, such as rights reserved to providers under provider agreements, that impede the use of binding arbitration in all disputes arising under a managed care plan. Some states provide for judicially ordered dispute resolution as a means of expediting litigation.

To appreciate the advantages of ADR, one need only review *Fox v. Health Net of California* [No 219692 (Cal Super Ct Dec 23, 1992)], in which a jury awarded $89 million in damages for a health maintenance organization's (HMO's) failure to cover a bone marrow transplant. This decision prompted many MCOs to include binding arbitration provisions in their plan documents and implement these provisions to the fullest extent possible.

Q 12:32   What are the advantages of using ADR in managed care contract dispute resolution?

There are a number of advantages to using ADR techniques to resolve managed care contract disputes. As outlined in the American Health Lawyers Association *Attorney's Managed Care Handbook,* one important advantage is that ADR is inherently less acrimonious and may save the relationship between the parties.[4] This is particularly true when mediation is used. Another advantage is that the binding resolutions reached through binding arbitration are not easily appealed to the courts. This avoids long, costly appeals and protracted litigation. The degree of confidentiality that can be achieved through a mediated settlement, which is protected under a number of state statutes, is another advantage. Even arbitration proceedings take place off the public record and away from potentially adverse publicity. Yet another advantage is the flexibility of an individually designed dispute resolution process, which can be structured to allow for either simple or complex disputes, minimal or extensive discovery, and inclusion or exclusion of certain rules of evidence. Parties can establish in advance certain remedies for certain kinds of disputes, limit or expand the damages available, carve out the ability to get injunctive relief, and take into account the expenses involved in these kinds of options.

Q 12:33   What are the disadvantages of using ADR in managed care contract dispute resolution?

Some argue that precluding access to judicial resolution is not in either party's best interest. This concern can be addressed through use of a nonbinding, conciliatory dispute resolution process such as mediation. Depending, however, on the subject matter and complexity of the issue in dispute, the amount of damages involved, or the relationship of the parties, using all or some of the methods of dispute resolution may be effective without absolutely precluding access to the courts. Most contract disputes should be subject to resolution using a combination of voluntary mediation and arbitration, with only the matters not subject to a mediated agreement being submitted to arbitration. Depending on the issue being arbitrated, the decision of the arbitrator may or may not be subject to judicial review. In *Seller v. Salem Women's Clinic, Inc.* [963 P 2d 56 (Ore Ct App 1998)], the court upheld an arbitrator's award despite finding that the arbitrator was wrong on both facts and law because there was a requirement that binding arbitration be used.[5]

Q 12:34 What is the most effective way to use ADR in managed care?

ADR is appropriate in reviewing payer determinations that are subject to immediate appeal to a neutral decision maker as an interim step to maintain good payer-provider relations. This allows early intervention in areas that could create serious conflict later. Examples of such determinations include enrollee eligibility, coverage, and whether a claim is clean.

ADR can also be used to reach an agreement through consensus rather than through adjudication. The simplest approach is to require the parties to meet informally to attempt to resolve their differences. Failing that, a third-party mediator, with formal opening statements, private caucuses, and direct discussion in a controlled setting, may be effective. Other approaches that can be used with the mediation process include the mini-trial and nonbinding arbitration, which allow the parties to determine, in a no-lose setting, whether their position has any merit. Decisions reached through these methods can be used in an advisory manner to help the parties assess settlement options. If either party refuses to accept the result, the matter can then be submitted to binding arbitration or can proceed to litigation. In this case, however, there should be some agreement that will allow recovery by the winning party of all costs, and possibly assessment of punitive damages.

Q 12:35 How are managed care disputes channeled into ADR?

There are several ways in which managed care disputes can be channeled into an ADR format in lieu of going directly to court. The most common method is to include in the managed care contract a requirement that all disputes be submitted to voluntary mediation and/or arbitration. Whether the decision is to be final and binding will depend on the circumstances of the contract subject matter. In managed care, it is common to include binding arbitration provisions in the policy agreement between the plan and the enrollee. It is also common to include ADR clauses in payer-provider agreements to facilitate the rapid and economical resolution of contract disputes.

The American Health Lawyers Association Alternative Dispute Resolution Service trains and supplies mediators and arbitrators for the resolution of health care disputes. Included in its published code of ethics is a section called "Sample Contractual Mediation/Arbitration Provisions."[6] These provisions are designed to define an ADR process for addressing issues and reforming agreements or resolving disputes that may arise as a result of anticipated legal violations (e.g., fraud and abuse), differences in price or value, or rate modifications.

The following are sample contract clauses:[7]

> **Arbitration.** Any controversy, dispute or disagreement arising out of or relating to this agreement, or the breach thereof, shall be settled by arbitration, which shall be conducted in (City, State) in accordance with the American Health Lawyers Association Alternative Dispute Resolution Service Rules of Procedures for Arbitration, and judgment on the award rendered by the arbitrator may be entered in any court having jurisdiction thereof.
>
> **Mediation.** The parties shall in good faith attempt to resolve any controversy, dispute or disagreement arising out of or relating to this Agreement, or the breach thereof, by negotiation. If any such controversy, dispute or disagreement is not resolved by (Date or Time), that controversy, dispute or disagreement shall be submitted to mediation, which shall be conducted in (City, State) in accordance with the AHLA Alternative Dispute Resolution Service Rules of Procedures for Mediation.
>
> **Mediation/Arbitration.** Resolution of Dispute. The parties hereby agree to submit any dispute arising under this Agreement to mediation under the AHLA Alternative Dispute Resolution Service Rules of Procedures for Mediation. If any dispute is not resolved by mediation no later than (Date, Time), the dispute shall be submitted to arbitration in accordance with the AHLA Alternative Dispute Resolution Service Rules of Procedures for Arbitration. [The same person shall serve as both the mediator and as the arbitrator.] [The same person shall not serve as both the mediator and the arbitrator.]
>
> **Arbitration/Mediation.** Resolution of Dispute. The parties hereby agree to submit any dispute arising under this Agreement to arbitration in accordance with the American Health Lawyers Association Alternative Dispute Resolution Service Rules of Procedures for Arbitration; provided, however, that the decision of the arbitrator shall be maintained in confidence

by the arbitrator without disclosure of the parties or any other person while the parties engage in mediation in accordance with the American Health Lawyers Association Alternative Dispute Resolution Service Rules of Procedures for Mediation for a period of [hours/days/weeks]. If the dispute is not resolved by mediation by the conclusion of such time period, the arbitrator shall render the award as maintained in confidence since the conclusion of the arbitration proceeding, and judgment on this award rendered by the arbitrator may be entered in any court having jurisdiction thereof. The same person shall serve both as the mediator and as the arbitrator in such a proceeding.

Several other ADR provisions may be appropriate in a managed care contract:[8]

1. *Forum law.* Which state's laws will govern the actions of the arbitrator and standards of judicial review?
2. *Award of the arbitrator.* What relief will the arbitrator be allowed to grant? Equitable? Specific performance? Compensatory damages? Punitive damages?
3. *Process.* What procedural rules govern?
4. *Standards of evidence.* Is it necessary to spell out the evidentiary rules for rendering a decision?
5. *Award.* Do the parties want a simple decision or do they want a memorandum that outlines the legal and factual bases for that decision?
6. *Right to injunctive relief.* Do the parties need to have the ability to seek an interim order of the arbitrator?

Q 12:36   When is arbitration appropriate in managed care contract disputes?

If managed care contract disputes cannot be settled using the internal grievance procedure, and the parties do not want to use a formal, nonbinding conciliatory process, arbitration is a viable alternative to litigation. Arbitration clauses need to be carefully drafted to ensure that consistent procedures are used and that the selection of arbitrators is fair in determining where the proceeding will take place. Many contracts will reference private arbitration services and their rules as a guide (e.g., American Arbitration Association or American Health Lawyers Association dispute resolution procedures). Many states have adopted ADR legislation with specific procedures relating to both mediation and arbitration. These can be referenced in the contract as authoritative for the proceeding.

The steps for resolving a managed care contract dispute through ADR are as follows:

1. Review the provisions of the contract relating to the areas of dispute (coverage, claims, payment, etc.).
2. Identify dispute resolution mechanisms.
3. Make an interim determination:
    *   Identify disputes to be referred to interim determinations
    *   Identify decision makers
    *   Describe the determination process and appeal rights
    *   Set time frames
    *   Allocate responsibility for costs
4. Work out arbitration principles:
    *   Identify disputes to be arbitrated
    *   Identify arbitrators or the selection process
    *   Describe the arbitration process
    *   Consider whether arbitration will be binding
    *   Set time frames if necessary
    *   Allocate responsibility for costs

Q 12:38 What has been the experience with the use of ADR in managed care disputes?

The use of ADR in resolving managed care disputes has grown in proportion to the use of managed care as a form of health care delivery. Provider-payer disputes are often submitted to mediation and/or arbitration in order to avoid the time-consuming and costly process of litigation. As many states adopt managed care reform legislation, the appointment of an independent review body to hear disputes has become more common.

The use of ADR in dealing with disputes involving patient care has come under increasing legal scrutiny as member-plaintiffs seek to break the mandatory arbitration clauses in their contracts and have their malpractice claims heard in court. As arbitration ventures from merchant-to-merchant (vendor-based) transactions to consumer transactions, there is a greater risk of inequity and abuse. In May 1991, a 51-year-old patient, Wilfredo Engella, brought a malpractice action against Kaiser Health Plans based on its delay in diagnosing his lung cancer. After Engella filed a claim under the plan's mandatory arbitration clause, Kaiser delayed scheduling the depositions, appointing the arbitrators, and hearing this case until Engella's condition deteriorated to the extent that he died the day after Kaiser finally appointed its third arbitrator. In its ruling, the California Supreme Court noted that Kaiser had failed to meet its own 60-day deadline for setting up arbitration panels in 99 percent of its cases and that Kaiser usually took over 23 months to name the panel and two and one-half years to conduct the arbitration; these time periods went far beyond the average time for disposition in court.[9]

In its first report since it began administering the arbitration process for Kaiser Permanente plan members, the Office of the Independent Administrator (OIA) said that independent arbitrators are appointed 16 times faster than they were when the nation's largest nonprofit HMO administered its own system. The report covered the independent administrator's first year overseeing the arbitration process (March 29, 1999, to March 28, 2000) and outlined the successes of the OIA, including

1. More efficient scheduling and resolution of disputes;
2. The ability to manage an increased volume of requests for ADR; and
3. More settlements using ADR.

The OIA evolved as a result of the *Engella* decision. Since then, the OIA has recruited 323 neutral arbitrators to hear complaints, about 27 percent of whom are retired judges. The OIA continues to accept applications and admit more arbitrators to the pool. The new arbitration system was designed to ensure that Kaiser Permanente members have access to an arbitration process that is fair, timely, and less costly than a court case and that protects the privacy interests of all parties. The full report is available on the OIA's Web site at www.slhartmann.com/oia/annrptyr2.pdf.

Q 12:39   Are mandatory arbitration clauses always enforceable?

No. Despite the judicial favor shown toward ADR in managed care, the courts have begun to scrutinize the appropriateness and fairness of mandatory arbitration. In California, this scrutiny has resulted in the creation of an independent organization for the management and processing of member disputes against Kaiser Permanente (see Q 12:38). Several other cases out of California, a state that has strongly supported mandatory arbitration for managed care arrangements, have focused on the fairness of the requirement and its potential for abuse by the health plan. In *Berman v. Health Net* [129 Cal App 3d 723, 79-30], the California appellate court found that a health plan that had engaged in extensive discovery as part of a disputed claim with an enrollee waived its right to compel arbitration thereafter, even though the enrollee signed an enrollment agreement that included a binding arbitration clause. The court noted that Health Net did nothing to bring about arbitration for about six months; moreover, in the interim, the company used court discovery procedures to obtain 1,600 pages of documents and a two-day, 410-page deposition.

Q 12:40   How else can consumers be protected from an unfair ADR process?

In recognition of the potential for abuse in mandating ADR in consumer-related matters, several organizations have taken a leadership role in addressing the issue of consumer protection. In 1997, the American Bar Association, the American Medical Association, and the American Arbitration Association formed the Commission on Health Care Dispute Resolution to advise on ADR in the managed care industry. In a 1998 report, the commission set forth due process standards and model processes for mediation, arbitration, and ombudsperson programs in which independent consumer advocates work within companies or institutions to resolve disputes. The proposed safeguards for consumers include the following:

- Full, accurate disclosure of information on procedures, rules of conduct, methods of selecting neutral parties, and fees and expenses

- Guarantees of neutrality and independence for ADR services

- Entitlement to competent, qualified neutral parties to handle health care disputes

- Reasonable time limits for conducting ADR proceedings

- Knowing and voluntary consent to ADR, with limits on binding use of ADR and prohibitions against consent as a requirement for receiving emergency treatment

ADR and ERISA Plans

Q 12:41 What are the most common areas of potential dispute under ERISA plans?

Under certain circumstances, because of the fiduciary role of the employer under the Employee Retirement Income Security Act of 1974 (ERISA), employers can become embroiled in disputes between their employees and employees' dependents and the managed care plan. These conflicts commonly include disputes relating to benefit coverage, individual eligibility, provider selection, medical care, and provider monitoring.

Disputes relating to benefit coverage often involve (1) situations in which the patient deemed the need for services an emergency but the plan denied coverage because the patient failed to obtain preauthorization and (2) determining whether treatment is experimental.

Disputes relating to eligibility arise when an employee or his or her dependent may not have met plan eligibility requirements and there is a layoff, termination, or other interruption in employment that affects eligibility and coverage.

Under ERISA, there is employer liability for the negligent selection and monitoring of service providers. These service providers can include the insurers and HMOs, the health care providers in direct contract situations, preferred provider organizations, and third-party administrators.

Q 12:42 What ADR methods are commonly used by ERISA plans?

Instead of resorting to litigation, many ERISA plans provide for a range of dispute resolution opportunities, including grievance procedures; arbitration; mediation, conciliation, or facilitation; early neutral evaluation; fact finding; permanent umpires; mini-trials; summary jury trials; and private judicial tribunals.

Many employee health benefit plans include as a part of their design some form of review, appeal, and grievance procedure in response to the statutory requirement that every employee benefit plan afford any participant whose claim for benefits has been denied a reasonable opportunity for a full and fair review by the appropriate named fiduciary of the decision denying the claim. [29 USC § 1133]

Arbitration is an effective means of dispute resolution in situations involving service providers and can be an effective alternative to litigation in cases involving issues arising outside the scope of ERISA. Arbitration can be an alternative to the judicial process when it is agreed that the determination is binding and not subject to judicial review or when the agreement requires use of permanent umpires. Early neutral evaluation is usually initiated after litigation has begun and involves the use of mediation to determine whether the dispute is subject to resolution or settlement by agreement of the parties.

Sometimes, parties will select a neutral individual in advance of any controversy to serve as an arbiter of disputes involving the contract. Use of an umpire to resolve issues involving benefit coverage, eligibility, and liability claims may be problematic when this person has been selected prior to the occurrence of the event in dispute because the prior selection forecloses the affected party's rights and interests. Further, for ERISA plans, the permanent umpire may be deemed a fiduciary with respect to the ERISA plan in question. An umpire may be appropriate in disputes between an employer and a service provider when each has agreed on the person, but this does not remove the possibility that the umpire may be deemed an ERISA fiduciary.

Mini-trials use aspects of the trial experience to achieve negotiated settlements after litigation has been initiated. The attorneys for the parties argue their cases without presentation of evidence before a neutral third party selected by the court. At the conclusion of the arguments, the parties engage in negotiations with or without the third party. This is not the most effective means of dispute resolution but has the advantage of initiating the negotiated settlement process.

Summary jury trials involve an abbreviated trial in the courtroom using a six-person jury and a judge. There are no witnesses, although the attorneys can put forward documentary and testimony (deposition) evidence. Following closing arguments, the jury renders a decision. This is not a cost-effective process.

Private judicial tribunals are available through organizations such as the Judicial Arbitration and Mediation Service. These groups are private dispute resolution firms through which retired judges and other qualified officials serve as arbiters or mediators in the private trial of disputes outside the public judicial system.

Government Rules

Q 12:43 What government rules govern the resolution of grievances in managed care arrangements?

State and federal rules often govern the resolution of grievances in managed care arrangements. The rules to be applied depend on (1) the sponsor of the health plan and (2) the nature of the dispute.

Sponsor of the Plan. If the plan sponsor is the state or federal government, the procedural due process guarantees of the U.S. Constitution apply. For Medicare, there are mandated hearing procedures for patient disputes. The Centers for Medicare and Medicaid Services (CMMS) is reviewing HMO grievances and appeals in light of *Grijalva v. Shalala.* [152 F 3d 1115 (9th Cir 1998)] For Medicaid, the states are responsible for affording fair hearings to aggrieved members. If the plan sponsor is a private entity, grievances are affected by state tort and contract law and by ERISA. States regulate HMOs, and most state statutes require HMOs to maintain certain grievance procedures for consumers.

Nature of the Dispute. Disputes between consumers and their providers and payers fall into four general areas:

1. Eligibility for services;
2. Amount of payment for services;
3. Coverage of services; and
4. Quality issues.

Bad Deals and Salvage Strategies

Q 12:44 What are the indicators that a deal has gone bad?

The most obvious indicator that a deal has gone bad is a change in the financial benefits to the parties. Rarely do parties end a relationship that is economically satisfactory to all concerned. Often parties affiliate and form integrated delivery systems to gain economic and contracting advantages. Individual participants in such a system may have their financial problems magnified as a result of the new relationship.

Q 12:45　What options are available to salvage the parties to a bad deal?

The techniques described in this chapter are intended to be used to reach agreements and resolve disputes. In addition, in drafting an agreement careful attention should be paid to the ability to "unwind" the relationship without undue difficulty, which is often stated in terms of dissolution or buyout of the disgruntled parties. The more integrated the delivery system is financially, the more difficult it will be to unwind it in a way that will place the parties back in their previous positions.

As discussed in chapter 6, an unattractive option available in the event of financial insolvency is to seek protection of a bankruptcy court under either a Chapter 11 reorganization or a Chapter 7 dissolution. These are discussed in chapter 8.

Q 12:46　What are the major risks to an integrated delivery system when the deal has gone bad?

The greatest single concern is the potential for any one party's economic distress to spill over and adversely affect the other parties. To the extent it is possible to build into any prospective affiliation relationship a review of each party's financial condition, this is one way to identify potential problems. Another is to build into the agreement language that allows termination of the relationship before the "spill-over" liability occurs. Avoiding bankruptcy is important because once application is made and a receiver is appointed, the parties lose all control over their business assets.

References

1. E. Kent, "ADR and Your Lawsuit: How Do They Mesh?" *Findlaw Library,* Oct. 6, 1997 (electronic publication, Hawaii

State Bar Ass'n) http://www.hsba.hostme.com/ADR/mesh. htm.

2. 12 Vt. Stat. Ann. § 5652(b) (Supp. 1996).

3. American Health Lawyers Association, *Alternative Dispute Resolution Code of Ethics and Rules of Procedures,* as reported in the presentation of Gordon J. Apple and Eileen M. Bantel, "ADR in Healthcare: Perspectives, Process and Promotion," AHLA Annual Meeting, June 27–30, 1999, Chicago. The complete code and rules are available online at www.ahla.org.

4. Id.

5. *See* "California Appeals Court Holds that Insurer Cannot Compel Insured to Arbitrate Claim for Misrepresentation of Quality of Services Filed Under State Consumer Legal Remedies Act," *Health L. Dig.,* 26(8):19–20, 1998.

6. American Health Lawyers Association, *Alternative Dispute Resolution Code of Ethics and Rules of Procedures* (American Health Lawyers Ass'n Alternative Dispute Resolution Service 1999). The American Health Lawyers Association can be reached at 1120 Connecticut Ave., NW, Suite 950, Washington, DC 20036-3902.

7. *See* Gordon J. Apple and Eileen M. Bantel, "ADR in Healthcare: Perspectives, Process and Promotion," AHLA Annual Meeting, June 27–30, 1999, Chicago. The complete code and rules are available online at www.healthlawyers.org, or by e-mail from adn@healthlawyers.org.

8. See chapter 13 of the *Managed Care Answer Book,* 5th ed., for more details on the ADR provisions that may be appropriate in managed care contracts.

9. *See* Engella v. Permanente Med. Group, Inc., 938 P.2d 903 (Cal. 1997).

Chapter 13

Health Care Information Systems

Few areas of health care are untouched by advances in the processing of information. To meet the challenge of measuring and accounting for real costs rather than charges, health care information technology advanced rapidly, concomitant with the processing power of the hardware. Even in the early days of managed care it was axiomatic that the one that controlled the information flow controlled the revenue. Cognizant of this, payers were quick to offer cost reporting in contracts with physicians and medical groups. First using mainframe systems that the providers could not afford, and then requiring elaborate reporting of data, payers compelled sophistication in medical care provision.

Technology finally allowed the smaller groups to manage their own information flow by returning control to the provider. The resulting diffusion of health care information and its ready accessibility mean that the security and confidentiality of health care information have become more acute problems that are more difficult to solve. The use of electronic communications in the health care industry also raises important concerns about the privacy, confidentiality, and security of health care information, as well as concerns about liability associated with the use of the information and how to regulate such communications under state and federal laws. In addition, the issue of disclosure of medical records is now more complicated than ever as information flows back and forth between payers, providers, and regulators, and is a major concern in distance medicine, also known as telemedicine. All of these issues are discussed in this chapter.

The fundamental concepts of database development and management in health care were developed by a blue-ribbon committee study conducted by the Institute of Medicine and published in *Health Data in the Information Age: Use, Disclosure, and Privacy.*[1] That study contemplated the establishment of a centralized data storage and clearinghouse entity called a health database organization (HDO). Such a data warehouse was included in the concept of a community health information network (CHIN), which would have linked health care networks and shared outcomes data for improved managed care strategies in a defined user community. The HDO and the CHIN are now only of historical interest, but the principles and problems identified in those concepts are still relevant to the use of information systems and electronic communications and therefore are discussed herein.

Electronic analysis of health care information allows an unprecedented ability to understand patterns in health care delivery as well as quality of care issues; however, the early optimism of the value of the electronic medical record (EMR) and rapid transfer and portability of medical information has faded with the dot-com bubble. Disease management and EMRs are discussed in this chapter.

Application of Information Technology to Managed Care

Q 13:1   What are managed care's priorities for information technology?

Information technology applicable to managed care can improve a range of managed care capabilities, support clinical decision making and disease management, and allow monitoring of quality to measure outcomes. Specific goals include the following:

- Improving ambulatory and outpatient capabilities
- Improving patient care capabilities
- Improving productivity and reducing costs
- Tying costs of care to outcomes
- Using local area networks and connectivity
- Integrating databases
- Using emerging technologies, including hand-held and wireless devices
- Justifying the benefits of technology
- Improving cash flow and collections
- Improving patient accounting capabilities
- Adapting to changes in the requirements of the Joint Commission on the Accreditation of Healthcare Organizations (JCAHO) requirements and to changes in government
- Improving general accounting capabilities

Q 13:2   Why is the ability to warehouse and access information critical for health care organizations that participate in managed care?

Most health care organizations have a wealth of data collected from many sources but are unable to use the data effectively because the data exist in disjointed and, in many cases, nonsystematized formats (i.e., on paper). To survive, all businesses, including health care organizations, need to transform data into usable and intelligible information and to access it when needed. Data warehousing is one way to address this need. Data warehousing is a method of collecting, maintaining, and managing data. In data warehousing, disparate pieces of information are stored and tagged for future needs. This technique is particularly useful in industries, such as health care, where large amounts of information are collected but the ultimate use of the information is not known until later.

Many health care providers have already adopted interface engines as a means of enabling their warehoused information and somewhat vertically oriented operational systems to communicate. This has been one step along the way to effective information management in the health care provider segment of the health care industry. Additionally, large health care application vendors have developed and installed clinical data repositories as a part of their overall clinical information system solutions. Enterprise Resource Planning (ERP) vendors are deploying their package solutions for the human resources, financial, and materials management side of the health care industry. Although these new packages for the health care industry move health care providers much closer to integrated information technology, they do not provide the optimal solution for technology integration in the health care entity. The next step is understanding what information the health care organization needs to make its business successful; this often involves upgrading the technology infrastructure to support the new layer of information applications, and building and executing a plan that will take the health care organization to the right information at the right time for the right users.

There is a void in the integration of managed care organization (MCO) information, clinical information, and population trends and demographics. When this information can be coupled with algorithms and probability tools, all in a way consistent with the Health Insurance Portability and Accountability Act of 1996 (HIPAA) [Pub L No 104-191], great strides will have been made.

Q 13:3 What is the vision of the effect of information technology on the routine practice of medicine?

The Internet is a major component of the medical care of the future. It provides access to an almost infinite amount of information at a negligible unit cost.[2] Bill Gates, the chairman of Microsoft, offers a tantalizing vision of a medical system driven by information technology:

An intelligent, adaptive emergency system gets you to the hospital quickly, and all critical information on your medical history and the current medical situation feeds immediately into the hospital's computers. A doctor uses a touch screen, keyboard, pen, or (fairly soon) voice recognition system to order your treatment. Digital instructions are fired off to the labs and pharmacy. PC-based instruments post lab results automatically. These and other reports are online for review by any physician onsite or off. Alerts pop up automatically for any treatment conflicts or deviations from the approved clinical pathway. Inventory and billing are handled automatically. Transaction-processing systems detect fraud or unusual use and, over time, learn appropriate countermeasures. Instead of spending half their time on paperwork, doctors and nurses spend virtually all their time treating you and their other patients. Test results and bills reach you in a simple understandable language. All your treatment and medication information is evaluated automatically over a longer term to help prevent adverse reactions. Your follow-up care is also scheduled automatically. You research medical information on the Internet and have more informed engaged interactions with the caregivers, whether you communicate with them over the Internet or e-mail or you go in for an appointment. You use e-mail to ask routine questions of your caregiver and to receive reminders about ongoing health programs or medication that's about to expire. When you change health plans, all your medical history goes with you instead of being lost or trailing after you several months later. It stays with you throughout your life. Doctors use your history to identify trends in blood pressure, cholesterol levels, and other factors to look for patterns that might reveal a serious developing problem.[3]

This vision of the near future does not manifestly change the physician-patient relationship or the manner in which health care is provided. Other visions, however, do have that capacity. These visions include the following approaches to health care in the Internet age:

- Consumer-based health care communication, often based in the commercial sector (e.g., Web sites designed to promote specific interventions or pharmaceuticals)

- Health care organization Web sites allowing consumers to schedule physician visits, tests, prescription refills, and other retail medical services

- Prevention, risk assessment, and wellness, including health risk assessments
- Access to information about complementary or alternative medicine
- Fulfillment and product sales
- Disease management linked to outcomes and fulfillment (e.g., Surecare, which allows chronic disease management and product fulfillment online)
- Direct sales of medical equipment and pharmaceuticals (e.g., various contact lens providers and online pharmacies)

Since the dot-com collapse, pure Internet enterprises have generally fared badly, while medical-related Internet enterprises that augment retail outlets such as medical clinics and retail pharmacies find the tie-in salutary. Naturally, there is a dark side to the potential of the Internet, including the following:

- Violation of confidentiality
- Surveillance
- Conflict of interest by commercial information providers
- Lack of editorial control
- Unsubstantiated claims
- Unmonitored prescribing
- Misleading recommendations based on incomplete or inaccurate data
- Problems of system integrity and security
- Unorganized information overload

Q 13:4   What types of health information do consumers want?

There is no way to poll consumers on what information they want from the Internet. Using Web site "hits" as a proxy for interest or need has proven to be highly misleading. Information sources for the general public, such as drKoop.com, WebMD, and Medem, have fared poorly, while "pay sites" directed at specific markets, such as MDconsult (directed at physicians), seem to have staying power. Consumers are unwilling to pay for what they can get for free. Publicly available data sources such as the National Library of Medicine are being used by consumers to assess their medical care. Disease-specific Web sites such as those of the American Heart Association and the American Diabetes Association provide reliable information that is serving as a basis for consumer self-education. These Web sites are supported by the philanthropy directed toward these organizations.

Presumably, consumers want authoritative, nonbiased analysis of medical therapies and interventions. Major medical and scientific journals such as the *Annals of Internal Medicine, New England Journal of Medicine,* and *Science* have added consumer-focused abstracts of their articles that appear both in print and on their Web sites.

Q 13:5   What are the issues affecting provider Internet and e-mail communications with consumers?

A number of legal, practical, and operational issues must be considered in using any form of electronic communication between providers and consumers:

- Whether a physician-patient relationship is established by the communication
- The potential duty to the consumer even if no physician-patient relationship is established
- Giving medical advice or diagnosis to unknown patients
- Giving medical advice or a diagnosis across state lines
- The potential applicability of physician advertising restrictions and requirements
- Implications of links to other Web sites
- Responsibility for accuracy and quality of information

Q 13:6   What are the major advantages and disadvantages of e-mail communication between providers and patients?

Many physicians who have embraced e-mail communication with patients find the method to be a useful adjunct to other forms of communication. The major reason for this is the asynchronous nature of the communication. Unlike the telephone, which requires the patient and the physician to be at a defined location simultaneously, e-mail allows a patient to pose a question or supply information at one time and the physician to respond at another time.

The disadvantages of e-mail communication between providers and patients include the following:

- Lack of confidentiality and security
- Unsuitability for sensitive communications
- Unsuitability for emergency situations
- Difficulty in verifying the identity of the patient

E-mail communication between providers and patients also raises questions with regard to the following:

- Prescribing in response to e-mail communications
- Treating e-mail communications as part of the patient's medical record
- Communicating across state lines

Guidelines for using the e-mail in communications between physicians and patients have been published in the *Journal of the American Medical Informatics Association* (*JAMIA*) and can be found on the Internet at www.amia.org/pubs/pospaper/positio2/htm.

Q 13:7   What are the issues raised by e-mail communications among providers?

A number of important issues are raised when providers use e-mail to communicate with each other about patients and other health care matters:

- Because e-mail is asynchronous, it should be not be used for urgent requests for consultation
- Communicating and authenticating orders and prescriptions
- Verifying the identity of the physician or other provider
- Failure to protect patient privacy
- Inappropriate e-mail comments about patients
- Unprivileged "peer review" information sent in e-mail
- Transfer or sharing of clinical data
- Transfer or sharing of financial or administrative information

Q 13:8   What are the important issues raised by electronic communications between providers and payers?

When payers communicate with providers, certain types of information may be subject to HIPAA and its regulations. Payers and providers that communicate over the Internet must take reasonable precautions to protect confidential patient information, particularly information that is patient identifiable. To the extent that electronic data interchange (EDI) is used, there should be appropriate agreements with the electronic trading partner. Sometimes, there will have to be multilateral EDI agreements.

Q 13:9   Should health care organizations that use the Internet and e-mail for communications have policies relating to issues of confidentiality and privacy?

Yes. Health care organizations that use the Internet and e-mail for communications with consumers, patients, and other providers should have policies and procedures in place to manage and monitor that use. Organizations should adopt policies relating to their employees' use of the Internet, the content of communications, and security measures.

Employee Privacy Issues. Policies are important if employers are to have the ability to regulate the use of e-mail by their employees. There are laws that regulate the interception of electronic communications that may affect the manner in which an organization's employees use the Internet or e-mail and the employer's ability to monitor such use. The Electronic Communications Privacy Act (ECPA) [18 USC §§ 2510–2522, 2701–2711, 3121–3127] prohibits the intentional interception, use, and disclosure of oral, wire, or electronic communications. There are some exceptions that apply in the workplace, where employers may monitor employee e-mail if the employee has given consent or if the employer has a business-related reason for such monitoring. The existence of a policy on the subject can allow the employer to satisfy the exception to the ECPA.

Message Content. Health care organizations may be liable for the content of their employees' electronic communications. Areas of liability include sexual harassment, employment discrimination, defamation, and violation of a third party's intellectual property rights.

Policies can be drafted to expressly prohibit conduct that may result in employer liability.

Security Issues. E-mail policies should include security guidelines that mandate use of passwords and prohibit the disclosure or sharing of passwords. Organizations should implement virus-scanning software that will protect the system by detecting viruses and removing them before they can spread.

Q 13:10   What is the effect of HIPAA on medical records confidentiality?

The HIPAA privacy regulations are fully discussed in chapter 8. The guiding principles relating to electronic communication of medical records include the following:

1. *Boundaries.* An individual's health information should be used only for health care, with very carefully defined exceptions. One exception may be for research when information is made anonymous and protocols are reviewed and approved by an appropriate institutional review board.

2. *Security.* Organizations must protect health information against deliberate or even inadvertent disclosure or misuse. A major source of vulnerability is an organization's employees, who may have access to records for reasons other than patient care.

3. *Consumer access.* Patients should be able to access their records, examine them, obtain a copy of them, correct errors, and find out who else has seen them.

4. *Accountability.* Misuses of information should be penalized.

5. *Benefits.* There is an important public and social good derived from the use of medical information with the understanding that this information will be used with respect and care.

Q 13:11   What entities are subject to the security standards of HIPAA?

The HIPAA security standards apply, in general, to any person or entity that transmits health information in an electronic form. This may be a health plan, a health care clearinghouse, or a health care provider. The National Center for Vital and Health Statistics

(NCVHS) is responsible for advice concerning HIPAA and recommends the following for security in health care transactions:

- Individual authentication of users
- Access controls
- Monitoring access
- Physical security and disaster recovery
- Protecting remote access points
- Protecting external electronic communications
- Software discipline
- System assessment
- Monitoring the integrity of data

To accomplish these goals, NCVHS lists the following security practices as required:

- Scalable confidentiality and security policies and procedures
- Security and confidentiality committees
- Designation of an information security officer in health care organizations
- Education and training for all employees, medical staff, agents, and contractors
- Organizational sanctions for violations of policies and procedures
- Improved patient authorization forms for disclosure of health information
- Patient access to audit logs[4]

Q 13:12   Is Medicaid subject to the HIPAA regulations?

Yes. HIPAA defines state Medicaid programs as health plans, and they are therefore required to comply with the HIPAA regulations.

Q 13:13   Why has the health care industry lagged behind other industries in its use of information technology?

One of the major reasons the health care industry has lagged behind other industries, such as financial services and air travel, in the design and application of information technology is that health care, for a very long time, did not have the impetus to manage itself as a business focused on profit and loss. Managed care has created a totally new environment; now the health care industry is forced to apply technology as a strategic business enabler or to accept the consequences of having not done so.

Additionally, consumers have not, until recently, driven the health care industry to the same extent as they have driven other industries. Consumers now exert greater control as they demand choice. Thus, they are "shopping" for health care in much the same way as they shop for other consumer services. They want the highest quality of care, with the greatest convenience, at the lowest cost. One of the ways the health care provider or MCO can compete in the consumer-driven market is by exploiting and leveraging leading-edge information technology.

Another reason the health care industry has lagged behind other industries in the design and application of information technology is its extensive use of proprietary systems that do not communicate with one another. Often, departments within the same hospital or clinic cannot communicate with one another because of the incompatibility of their systems. This problem has caused many organizations to face the expense of obtaining new systems or upgrading existing systems to allow for expanded capabilities. In general, incompatibility is more a problem with legacy systems than with integrated packages.

Q 13:14 What are the key issues for future health care information technology systems?

Several areas deserve special attention in the development of effective health care information technology systems. The first area concerns the linkages among physicians within a common clinic and between the clinic and other health care facilities and providers. This facilitates the timely communication of important health care information with a focus on the patient and quality.

The second area involves the use of the Internet as a means of communicating health care data and information among providers and as a means of communicating and consulting with patients. Web sites are developing as sites for the public to access medical information. Some Web sites include information about physicians and other providers. This information can include both marketing and health care information. Current medical practice indicates that persons making the health care decision are increasingly using the Internet with the full knowledge that it is unedited, unscreened, and anarchic. Experience is accumulating to suggest that this type of information is compelling consumer inquiries and maybe even decision making. The Internet is also bringing down international boundaries in health care (see chapter 2). Web sites useful for the exchange of professional information include the following:

- Government health care sites that include the rules of Medicare, Medicaid, and the Department of Veterans Affairs (DVA)
- Sites maintained by various professional organizations (e.g., American College of Pediatrics, American College of Physicians, American College of Surgeons) and the Agency for Healthcare Research and Quality (AHRQ) for the dissemination of health care standards and guidelines.
- Numerous portals to the National Library of Medicine (e.g., Medline)
- Sites providing access to university card catalogs
- Journal (some exclusively online) sites
- Sites that include standard textbooks of medicine
- Interest-group sites

The third area that deserves attention is the high cost of the technology, including the cumbersome process of upgrading and maintaining systems. System conversions are nightmares to most users, and in the health care industry, glitches can have disastrous consequences. Problems attendant to conversions include the following:

- Loss of accounts receivable recording
- Delay in collecting accounts receivable
- Conflicts and duplications in registration data
- Expense of retraining staff and other users
- Delays in service caused by unfamiliarity with screen sequences
- Decreases in productivity while the system is being installed and while users become proficient at it

- Changes in government or managed care billing numbers resulting from consolidation

- Inaccuracies and delays resulting from unfamiliar reporting formats

- Change in access to accounts

- Monitoring and quality control expenses resulting from unfamiliarity with the new system

Employers and Managed Care Information

Q 13:15   From the employer's perspective, what type of managed care information is important?

The employer's primary concern is the cost-effective management of a health plan with high-quality outcomes. Therefore, utilization and cost data are most important. To ensure that the employer's needs are met, the MCO typically supplies the following types of reports:

- Demographics and current covered lives

- Spectrum of illness and encounters by ICD (International Classification of Diseases) code

- Services rendered by CPT (Current Procedural Terminology) code

- True cost of service

- Referrals and hospitalizations

- Payments and charges per codable encounter

- Utilization review activities (claims denied; claims modified)

These reports can include clinical information traditionally reserved for the patient's physician. Widespread dissemination of these reports, even when "sanitized" by concealing individual patient identity, can provide the opportunity for a serious breach of confidence. Privacy is only one of the many confidentiality issues raised by electronic interfaces in health care.

Q 13:16   What types of data analyses should employers be performing for future health plan development?

These analyses are becoming increasingly complex. Employers should therefore focus on the following core elements:

1. *Emphasis on quality of care assessments.* Quality of care becomes more critical as adoption of managed care plans influences provider selection by employees. Quality metrics need to be as accessible to the employee as they are to the purchaser. Health Plan Employer Data and Information Set (HEDIS) measures are available to purchasers of health information; other, similar assessments can be expected to become more widely available in the future.

2. *Measuring value in health maintenance organization (HMO) plans.* The increase in HMOs and HMO plan options requires employers to measure the relative values of the various plans to their employees. Employers need more data and better information from their health care program administrators to allow them and their employees to make the purchasing decision. The challenge of rationalizing a large number of plans and a single payer requires substantial computing.

3. *Improved reporting and analysis.* Because HMOs rate by experience, information on utilization of services and costs per employee has become more important to the employer.

4. *Provider reimbursement.* As managed care evolves, different methods of provider reimbursement, requiring more detailed tracking of utilization and comparisons with standard treatment protocols, become important. Paperless claims are required by many plans and urged by virtually all.

5. *Outpatient review.* As services continue to shift from inpatient to outpatient settings, employers want to be able to evaluate the utilization and cost information from these settings. This requires more sophisticated data capture diagnosis coding, and relative value unit (RVU) analysis.

Q 13:17   Who owns health care information?

Employers and providers may have competing interests in the ownership of health care information. Ownership and control of information raise issues under intellectual property law, particularly when the raw data are analyzed using proprietary technology and multiple parties have conflicting interests and claims to the analyzed data. These issues should be raised at the outset of any contract arrangement and addressed in written agreements between the employers or payers, the insurers, and the providers. Of course, the rights and interests of the employees, as patients concerned about privacy and confidentiality, must be respected.

The likelihood of violation of confidentiality increases with the number of people and institutions that have access to health care data. The existence of master patient indices and integrated health information data sets and the requirements for delivering health care across the continuum of illness and geographic locales require close examination of the question. Waller and Alcantara[5] break down the question of ownership and proprietary rights as follows:

1. Who may access data?
2. Who may move or manipulate data?
3. Who may use data and for what purpose?
4. Who may sell data?
5. Who may disclose or publish data?
6. Who must pay to access, use, publish, or sell data?
7. Who is required to disclose data in response to subpoenas or court orders?

Health Plans and Managed Care Information

Q 13:18 What types of data are collected by health plans?

Data are collected for internal purposes such as utilization management, payment of providers, premium setting, and quality improvement. Many plans collect HEDIS-type data to meet demands for information about performance and costs. The types of data collected by health plans include enrollment, survey, encounter and claims, and clinical data. Each type has multiple uses, which may require different data elements and quality of data.

Enrollment Data. Most health plans have basic information on enrollment and disenrollment, benefits, and purchase of care. Often they are required to collect these data for use by regulators. Particularly in Medicare and Medicaid HMOs, disenrollment becomes a quality metric, albeit a very crude one. Some plans have information only on subscribers and not other family members. Demographic data are collected routinely but usually only at the time of enrollment or annual renewal. These items may include employment status, ethnicity, and family status.

Survey Data. Surveys are used to query patients on their perceptions of their health status, the quality of care received, their access to care, their functional status, their symptoms, their knowledge of healing, their satisfaction with the care received, and their health-related behavior (e.g., diet). HEDIS requires plans to survey a sample of their enrollees to determine health status and patient satisfaction with care. Health risk questionnaires are an integral part of managed care. They serve several purposes:

- Allowing patients to assess their risk of developing chronic diseases
- Preparing MCOs for their downstream costs
- Facilitating planning for self-insured corporations
- Assessing population health (e.g., the National Health Information Survey)

Encounter and Claims Data. Encounter and claims data document processes of care—such as the number of visits, the purpose of the visit, and the procedures performed or care given—and such other information as date and site of service, name of patient, provider, and diagnosis necessitating the service. Providers must generate all encounter data before they are transmitted to health plans even when services are provided under capitation. Because there are differences between encounter data for fee-for-service providers and encounter data for various types of capitated providers, as well as between encounter data for physicians and encounter data for hospitals, the quality of the captured data is highly variable.

Clinical Data. Clinical data include signs and symptoms, diagnoses, functional status, and results of tests and procedures as well as ultimate outcomes such as death, ongoing or associated illness, complications, and complete recovery. Some types of data are available in automated form, such as results of laboratory, radiological, and pathologic tests, but most data must be obtained from the patient medical record. Virtually no provider has an information system sophisticated enough to capture these highly specific and sensitive data.

Q 13:19   What are the considerations for external reporting of health plan data?

First, there is a finite risk to an organization to possess the data without reducing them to a reportable form. The organization may be accused of concealment and deception, and there is the opportunity cost of having collected data and not using them to change processes. Second, data should be accurate, complete, standardized, and comparable across plans (but rarely are). Third, cost and confidentiality must be considered.

The accuracy and completeness of data are important to the ultimate purchasers of the product. Because the majority of information is in the hands of the providers, many health plans have incorporated both economic and noneconomic incentives for providers to report this information. The economic incentives can be punitive, such as the use of penalties and withholds for not reporting, or positive, such as being part of the bonus methodology. Noneconomic incentives include giving the providers access to the analyzed data for their own internal use.

Standardization of data is essential if the data are to be useful and credible. Data must be standardized as to format and definitions. An important development in the area of standardization occurred with the passage of HIPAA, which requires the Secretary of Health and Human Services (DHHS) to adopt, with respect to various health care transactions (including claims and encounters), uniform standards and definitions for data elements, and technical standards for transmission of the data. The intent of the law is to promote administrative efficiency by enabling health care entities to communicate in a common language. Health plans and providers are required to report data in the standardized format if so requested by the recipient of the data. Such reporting is not mandatory, but rather a right of access and transmission.

Issues of privacy and confidentiality always arise when patient-specific identifying information is being collected for external use. Particularly sensitive items include mental health conditions, AIDS testing and treatment, and genetic testing. Legislation has attempted to address not only the confidentiality of this information but also its use in a nondiscriminatory manner.[6]

Q 13:20   What is the reason for disparities among health plans in the collection and use of information?

There are many reasons for these disparities. Some providers are unwilling or unable to furnish information to health plans. Data from different sources may be incompatible. Valid data are costly to obtain, and incorrect or misinterpreted data can do more harm than good. Finally, external reporting of data by health plans requires standardization, comparability of data across plans, and confidentiality of medical information.

Health Database Organizations and Community Health Information Networks

Q 13:21   What is a health database organization?

HDOs never developed as envisioned,[7] but it is instructive to examine the HDO vision for what it teaches about the need for standardization.

A health database was to be a large collection of demographic, health, and related data captured in computer-readable format, which could be expanded, updated, and retrieved rapidly for various uses. Although future databases may be derived from primary medical record information held by health care practitioners, the HDO's capability was to be for secondary data sources.

A health database was envisioned to be comprehensive in its tracking of patient care events. It was also to be inclusive of large populations in the relevant geographic area.

Q 13:22   Who would have used health care data from an HDO?

The most likely users of this information would have been health care provider organizations and practitioners, patients and their families, academic and research institutions, payers and purchasers, employers, and health agencies.

Q 13:23 Who should have had access to person-identifiable data?

This question has no easy answer. Possible answers from a variety of authorities include the following:

- Individuals for information about themselves
- Parents for information about a minor child, except when such releases were prohibited by law
- Legal representatives of an incompetent patient for information about the patient
- Researchers with approval from their institution's properly constituted institutional review board
- Licensed practitioners with a need to know when treating patients in life-threatening situations who are unable to consent at the time care is rendered
- Licensed practitioners when treating patients in all other (non-life-threatening) situations, but only with the informed consent of the patient

Employers or those with divided loyalty to the individual must not be allowed access to person-specific information.

Q 13:24 How realistic was the possibility that HDOs would be developed?

If the Health Security Act of 1993 ("Clintoncare") had been passed, HDOs would have been required. It is not clear that HIPAA and its national EDI standards will provide the structure necessary for a nationwide ability to exchange electronic health care information.

Q 13:25 What are the major sources of health care data?

The following organizations and databases have accumulated much individual data from patient encounters and other sources:

- The VA, which operates the largest centralized health system in the country (Although the format of its database is an outgrowth of legacy systems, the VA has invested heavily in outcomes research through its field program.)

- The Minnesota Clinical Comparison and Assessment Project, which is a coalition of provider institutions, professional societies, and other entities coordinated by the Healthcare Education and Research Foundation

- The Greater Cleveland Health Quality Choice, which is a joint effort of the local business coalition, the Greater Cleveland Hospital Association and 32 of Cleveland's hospitals, and the county medical society

- The Manitoba Provincial Health Database, which is a comprehensive database whose claims information is complete and reliable

- The Cardiac Surgery Reporting System, which is under the New York State Department of Health and has collected information on coronary procedures

- The National Trauma Registry of the American College of Surgeons, which includes 152 standardized data elements on patients treated for trauma at 19 trauma centers

- Integrated Medical Systems, Inc., which is a vendor that has developed a database designed to provide administrative information and help in medical management through the provision of information

- The Medicare National Claims History and Beneficiary Health Status Registry, which contains files that include 96 percent of the U.S. population receiving some form of federal benefit (over age 65, disabled, end-stage renal disease)

- AHRQ, which collects information on best practices

Q 13:26   What is a community health information network?

CHINs were to have been in the vanguard of integration in health information technology. Although few CHINs have survived in their original incarnations, the concept of information systems as the backbone of an integrated system is useful to revisit.

A CHIN was a concept for a data highway connecting networks of health care entities to data networks to permit the exchange of clinical and financial information between participating hospitals, physicians, insurers, and other providers such as pharmacies and durable medical equipment suppliers. Unlike the HDO, which would have functioned at a regional or national level for a clearly public purpose, the CHIN was to function at the community level as either a private or public enterprise or some combination thereof. The CHIN would have facilitated patient care by allowing a master patient index to serve all components of the CHIN.

The Aurora Health System and Ameritech started the first functioning CHIN in 1993. It was called the Wisconsin Health Information Network (WHIN), and it linked 16 hospitals, 8 clinics, 3 nursing homes, 7 insurers, 4 billing services, and more than 1,300 physicians.[8] In addition to transmitting claims and other administrative data, the system had the ability to allow physicians to check on the inpatient status of their patients, including laboratory results.[9] The WHIN model is available at *http://www.whin.net/about_us/glance.html.*

Another successful CHIN operated on a voluntary basis in Utah. The Utah Health Information Network (UHIN) was a public-private partnership that included the Utah Department of Health, all hospitals in the state and more than 85 percent of their physicians, 80 percent of all other practitioners, and all but one of the major payers.

The largest CHIN was in California and was run by the Health Data Information Corporation, a nonprofit group made up of more than 40 members covering more than half of the insured population of California. Although it was a good idea, the CHIN required too much voluntary cooperation among competitors to be widely accepted at the current stage of managed care development.

Role of Government

Q 13:27 How have state government entities used health care information technology systems?

Information technology has allowed many state governments to enhance their ability to monitor, purchase, and provide health care services in the interest of public health and welfare. Federal legislation, such as HIPAA, has increased state and private sector attention to electronic communication capabilities. The efforts most commonly undertaken by states include providing meaningful data to state decision makers, disseminating information collected by state governments, coordinating services delivered by government health care providers, creating transactions systems for the public and private sectors, and supporting telemedicine services.

Providing Data. Collection of data has been a long-standing role of state government. Unfortunately, dissemination of collected data was often fragmented and poorly done. Many states have developed improved information systems and communication tools to streamline dissemination of health care information.

Disseminating Public Information. States have always functioned as a repository of public information from such sources as hospital discharges, vital statistics, and communicable disease records. Some state government agencies have taken on a more expanded customer base and seek to share this internal public health information with external audiences. Prospective users of this information include purchasers, consumers, providers, and researchers.

Better Coordination of Government Services. One of the advantages of improved information technology is the states' ability to manage information across different agencies through an integrated information system. Texas centralized and integrated its information management within the agencies under the Texas Commissioner of Health. This change will allow the state to better monitor and integrate welfare recipients with its Medicaid program in order to reduce fraud and abuse by individuals who misrepresent their eligibility status and providers who abuse the Medicaid system.

Supporting Health Transactions. HIPAA calls for the development of data standards at the national level and will require coordination and standardization at the state level. Despite the use of capitation, health care claims and encounter submission will remain a dominant means for reimbursement for services and is a major area of inefficiency. Some states have encouraged efficiencies by requiring insurers and health plans to rely on electronic communications. For example, Texas has established an EDI between providers, payers, and the Texas Department of Health using a Medicaid management information system (MMIS) called TexMedNet.[10] This program includes electronic eligibility verification and claims processing, electronic appeals, electronic claims submission and editing, electronic remittance and status reports, electronic files transfer, an electronic bulletin board system, e-mail, and software to allow access. Users include businesses (e.g., billing companies, vendors, and clearinghouses) and providers (who pay no fee). TexMedNet also provides a list of its EDI standards, which is useful for other EDIs and is shown in Table 13-1.

Telemedicine and Telehealth Services. The ability to use telecommunications in medical education and in the delivery of health care services offers significant benefits to underserved areas. Several states have passed legislation enabling such technology and allowing reimbursement for its use.

Table 13-1   TexMedNet EDI Standards[11]

Transaction Mode	Standard	Standard Title	Version	Notes
Interactive	EDIFACT	Health Care Benefit Inquiry and Response	3050	ANSI-approved interactive format. Ability to initiate search by using several data element combinations and span dates. Returns complete eligibility information, including Medicare, lock-in HMO, prior authorization, other insurance, managed care, Chronically Ill and Disabled Children (CIDC), and service limitations.
Batch	ANSI 270	Health Care/ Benefit Inquiry	3050	Ability to initiate search by using several data element combinations and span dates.
Batch	ANSI 271	Health Care/ Benefit Response	3050	Returns complete eligibility information, including Medicare, lock-in HMO, prior authorization, other insurance, managed care, CIDC, and service limitations.
Batch	Internal	Appeal Submission	N/A	Batch format to submit request for review and reconsideration of previously dispositioned claims.
Batch	ANSI 837	Health Care Claim	3050	All claim types.
Batch	ANSI 277	Health Care Claim Status Notification	3040	Each processed claim submitted via ANSI 837 format receives a 277 response. Rejection codes may be internal Texas Medicaid codes.
Batch	UB92	Institutional Health Care Claim	4	Uses current Texas Medicaid UB92 data set. Continued use of modified record type 61. Additional codes added for other insurance information.

Table 13-1   Continued

Transaction Mode	Standard	Standard Title	Version	Notes
Batch	Internal	Health Care Claim Response	0001	Each processed claim submitted via UB92 format receives a TexMedNet internal accepted or rejected response.
Batch	NSF	Professional Health Care Claim	1.04	All professional claims, including EPSDT Medical, EPSDT Dental and Eyeglass. Some claim restrictions still apply, such as ambulance claims. Additional fields added for Texas Medicaid-specific policy and other insurance requirements.
Batch	Internal	Health Care Claim Response	0001	Each processed claim submitted via NSF format receives a TexMedNet internal accepted or rejected response.
Batch	ANSI 835	Health Care Claim Payment/Advice	3041	Format used for paid or denied claims. Weekly distribution. Uses internal Texas Medicaid explanation of benefit (EOB) codes.
Batch	ANSI 277	Health Care Claim Status Notification	3040	Format used for pended claims. Weekly distribution. Uses internal Texas Medicaid explanation of pending status (EOPS) codes.
Batch	ANSI 997	Functional Acknowledgment	3050	Trading partner relationship establishes use. Only used for ANSI submissions.

Discontinued EDI Formats:

- Texas Local Format—110 byte records
- UB82—192 byte records

Q 13:28   What are the major challenges faced by states in facilitating information technology initiatives in health care?

There are many challenges to pursuing information-based solutions to enhanced health care capabilities: How should states regulate these activities? What type of management is necessary to ensure their success? Where will they get funding? How will personal records be kept confidential and secure? The answers to these questions are evolving as technology becomes more sophisticated.

Q 13:29   What are the lessons learned from different states' involvement in information technology?

In a study of state initiatives relating to health information systems, Daniel Mendelson and Eileen Salinsky developed several guiding principles for system and organizational design:[12]

1. Broad public and private participation is essential.

2. Demand must exist for administrative savings.

3. State government needs to be organized and actively involved.

4. Systems should maximize use of existing data, technology, and expertise.

5. States should support efforts to obtain outside funding.

6. Shared governance between public and private interests is important.

7. Efforts should be made to collaborate rather than compete with existing private networks.

8. Access should be available to the greatest possible number of users through use of low-cost platforms.

9. Training should be made available in the use of the system.

10. Communications capabilities should be sufficiently flexible to evolve as technology advances.

11. All data should be encrypted for security and confidentiality.

12. Goals and objectives should be focused and realistic.

13. Communication solutions should follow widely accepted technical standards.

Confidentiality of Information

Q 13:30   What underlies the need to maintain the confidentiality of health information?

Concerns about the confidentiality of protecting health information evolved from the confidential nature of the physician-patient relationship, which is premised on the theory that a relationship of trust and confidentiality encourages open communication of information that helps the physician in diagnosing a patient's problem. The following legal and ethical precepts reflect the historical and statutory recognition of this relationship:

- Hippocratic oath
- American Medical Association (AMA) Code of Medical Ethics[13]
- American Hospital Association (AHA) Patient Bill of Rights
- Constitutional right to privacy[14]
- State health information statutes[15]
- State licensure laws
- Laws regulating HMOs
- Laws regulating insurance companies and support organizations
- Laws regulating private utilization review organizations
- Federal privacy acts[16]
- State HIV and AIDS testing statutes
- JCAHO standards
- Miscellaneous state peer review and privilege statutes

Q 13:31   What are the exceptions to the general principle of confidentiality?

Most laws and regulations recognize several defined circumstances as permitting disclosure of otherwise confidential information. These circumstances include disclosure with patient consent; disclosure to third-party payers; disclosure for utilization review, quality assurance, and peer review; and statutory exceptions founded in federal and state laws such as mandatory disclosure laws relating to child abuse, disease, and injury reporting.

Q 13:32   What are the elements of a secure computer system?

According to the report of the Workgroup for Electronic Data Interchange (WEDI),[17] a secure computer system does not permit access to information by any unauthorized user; maintains the continuing integrity of the information stored in it by preventing alteration or loss of data; ensures the authenticity of data by verifying the data's source and by retaining a record of communications to and from the system; and is available to its users through efficiently maintained hardware and software and by complete, rapid, and effective recovery from unanticipated disruption.

Q 13:33   What steps can be taken to maintain a secure computer system?

Use of Internet and intranet technologies, with their open architecture and easy access, makes the balance of security and access delicate. The following measures can be taken to maintain the security of a provider's computer system:

- Limiting access to authorized users through methods such as passwords or key cards

- Establishing policies regarding unauthorized disclosure or sharing of passwords, key cards, and so forth

- Restricting each user's access to portions of the data that are relevant to the user's functions

- Tracking access to records by user

- Recording and monitoring attempts to access the system

- Restricting use of software functions that permit certain data-copying capabilities and installing antivirus software

- Using encryption technology

Because a provider may be held liable for improper disclosure of confidential health care information unless all reasonable precautions were taken, the provider should consider taking at least the following steps to minimize the risk of improper disclosure:

- Obtaining express, written patient authorization for disclosure

- Clearly delineating ownership rights in the data

- Delineating the purpose for which a third party is being given access to the data and the extent to which that party may disclose or distribute the data to others

- Limiting access to patient-identifying information and requiring written confidentiality agreements of all who will access identifying information

- Controlling the risk of improper disclosure through control of data content and format

- Requiring compliance with all applicable security policies and procedures

- Clearly outlining data quality standards and procedures for attaining those standards and auditing data quality

Electronic Medical Records

Q 13:34 What is an electronic medical record?

The EMR, or computerized patient record (see Q 13:42), emerged from work done to develop a uniform data entry protocol for clinical research. The problem-oriented medical record (POMR) developed by Dr. Lawrence Weed[18] organized a haphazard format of medical record keeping into a stereotyped form. Although it caught on slowly, the POMR and its variations can now be built into an electronic format to allow data elements such as roentgenograms, scans, graphics, and laboratory results to be tied to a specific problem or clinical event. Further, the EMR allows access by a wide variety of professionals who may have a role to play in a patient's clinical episode.

EMRs have evolved slowly from the original Weed concept because the problem of computerizing medical care information in a form to allow rapid retrieval yet maintain ease of entry has proved daunting. An additional problem has been the lack of an industry standard to allow easy sharing of data across institutional and corporate lines. Finally, physician skepticism that the EMR will improve medical record keeping has not been well challenged until recently.

Certain integrated delivery systems, notably the Veterans Affairs Medical Centers, have had a fully functioning EMR for years. Although in the public domain, this system has not been used widely because it is essentially a legacy system and difficult to modify for the commercial sector. Additionally, in the VA, most patients get their entire spectrum of care, including pharmacy services and durable medical equipment, from the same system, so the EMR is likely to be complete. Few other American systems can make this claim.

Q 13:35 What is the impetus for implementation of the EMR?

Managed care is the major driver for implementation of the EMR. In addition, some hospital systems have used the EMR as a device to cement physician loyalty. A pioneer in the use of the EMR to manage the continuum of care has been Vencor (now Kindred), where an EMR is widely accessible.

Other drivers for implementation of the EMR are payers, which are demanding more integrated information systems and more consistent data about therapies, efficacy, and utilization; providers, who want efficient ways of storing and exchanging information; and health care professionals, who want access to current databases.

Q 13:36 What are the barriers to the widespread use of the EMR?

Perhaps the major barrier to the widespread use of the EMR is the state of the art of voice recognition technology. The EMR still requires the manual input of clinical information, and this limits its broad use. Another barrier is the cost of setting up an EMR. As demand for standardization of records, electronic filing, and billing compliance grows, the EMR can be expected to become the standard of the industry, but it will also require the development of an industry standard. Pundits are confidently predicting the imminent demise of the paper record and have been doing so for years.

Telehealth and Telemedicine

Q 13:37 What are telehealth and telemedicine?

Telemedicine is the use of medical information exchanged from one site to another via electronic communications for the health and education of the patient or health care provider and for the purpose of improving patient care.[19] Telehealth has one or more of these four attributes:

1. Remote settings;

2. Health information and management by non-health care professionals;

3. Dissemination of information from one care site to another; and

4. Integration of medical information.

In remote rural areas, where a patient and the closest health professional can be hundreds of miles apart, telemedicine can mean access to health care where little had been available before. In emergency cases, this access can mean the difference between life and death. In particular, when fast medical response time and specialty care are needed, the availability of telemedicine can be critical. For example, a specialist at a North Carolina university hospital was able to diagnose a rural patient's hairline spinal fracture at a distance, using telemedicine video imaging. The patient's life was saved because treatment was done on-site without physically transporting the patient to the specialist, who was located a great distance away.

Telemedicine also has the potential to improve the delivery of health care in the United States by bringing a wider range of services such as radiology, mental health services, and dermatology to underserved communities and individuals in both urban and rural areas. In addition, telemedicine can help attract and retain health professionals in rural areas by providing ongoing training and collaboration with other health professionals.

Q 13:38   What are the barriers to the widespread use of telemedicine and telehealth?

There are several barriers to the use of telehealth. Reimbursement is uncertain. Liability and licensure issues have not been settled. Questions of "turf" arise when unacquainted specialists consult. Patient and record confidentiality issues have to be addressed. Finally, quality standards are not yet in place. There are obstacles to establishing standards—obstacles in the form of uncertain payment policies, inadequate resources, state licensure requirements, and medical practice issues and training.

The Centers for Medicare and Medicaid Services (CMS) has chosen to define teleconsultation for reimbursement as real-time communication, thus effectively blocking reimbursement for the store-and-forward technology that is becoming more widespread. Additionally, the proposed reimbursement rates are not favorable to substituting telecommunication for on-site consultation. Until the rules, definitions, and schedules are settled, telemedicine and payment for it remain a work in progress.

Physician acceptance of telemedicine is spotty. Several institutions have embraced telemedicine, including Baylor College of Medicine and Texas Children's Hospital, which has a long-standing distance consultation link; University of Texas Medical Branch, which has a contract with the Texas Department of Corrections; Partners HealthCare System in Boston; and Texas Tech University Medical Center.

Q 13:39   What are possible solutions to the problem of reimbursement?

The Council on Competitiveness has analyzed telemedicine and telehealth issues in depth and has proposed the following solutions:[20]

The CMS should base its reimbursement policies on data collected from telemedicine projects for which reimbursement is provided so that the cost-benefit data collected will be realistic. CMS is not yet convinced of telemedicine's clinical and cost effectiveness and does not provide reimbursement for Medicare patients who receive care through telemedicine (except for radiology, pathology, and other diagnostic procedures that do not require face-to-face contact). Because CMS will not provide reimbursement, most private insurers will not either.

To assist CMS in its decision-making process, many health care delivery organizations are conducting demonstration projects to test telemedicine's clinical and cost effectiveness. Most of these efforts, however, were not framed in a competitive market in which telemedicine services would be supported by the operating budgets of health care delivery organizations and health care practitioners would be paid for their work. Instead, they are operating in an artificial environment, supported by government grants that often do not permit reimbursement for physician consultations. As CMS considers whether to reimburse for telemedicine consultations, it needs realistic cost-benefit data that can be measured against the real world, where medical services are routinely reimbursed. The federal government, through the Office of Rural Health Policy, and state governments should therefore fund demonstration projects that are coordinated with CMS, and CMS should ensure reimbursement for their duration. These projects should include telemedicine linkages into the home. CMS should also draw on outcomes data from projects that were designed to be self-sustaining and for which reimbursement is provided, such as in a managed care environment. It should not overlook cost-benefit data available from specialized market activities such as telemedicine in correctional facilities and in the international arena, where cost containment and/or profitability, coupled with increased access to quality care, are the drivers.

Q 13:40   What are the potential legal issues associated with telemedicine?

Legal issues associated with telemedicine include the following:

- Licensing and credentialing
- Financial reimbursement
- Malpractice liability
- Privacy and confidentiality
- Intellectual property rights
- Food and drug regulation
- Fraud and abuse

Questions that arise in the context of licensure relate to interprofessional consultations and use of the technology. Each state regulates health care as part of its public health and consumer protection policies. When a physician in Texas is providing services to a patient in New Mexico, the regulators become concerned. Many states have initiated efforts to address these concerns through statutes. Others, however, retain restrictive practice and licensing statutes that make the use of telemedicine challenging. These issues are discussed in more detail in chapter 8.

R.F. Pendrak and R.P. Ericson observed the following:[21]

> The cause of much of the uncertainty with regard to liability related to telemedicine is a lack of relevant legal precedents.

Much telemedicine technology is so new that telemedicine malpractice cases have not made their way through the legal system yet. . . . It is likely that the courts will continue to apply existing malpractice tests in telemedicine cases, which currently hinge on two legal questions:

- Whether a doctor-patient relationship existed, and
- Whether the physician breached his or her duty of care

Both of these issues present difficulties in the realm of telemedicine. For example, a physician's review of a patient's medical records could be interpreted as either an informal consultation between two doctors or the establishment of a doctor-patient relationship. Moreover, the legal system currently relies on professional standards to determine appropriate levels of care in malpractice cases; because there are few existing telemedicine standards, the courts will face a challenge in determining whether the physician breached his or her duty of care.[22]

Q 13:41   What is the role of the Internet in telehealth?

The National Academy of Science has studied the role of the Internet in telehealth and writes:

Many health-related processes stand to be reshaped by the Internet. In clinical settings, the Internet enables care providers to gain rapid access to information that can aid in the diagnosis of health conditions or the development of suitable treatment plans. It can make patient records, test results, and practice guidelines accessible from the examination room. It can also allow care providers to consult with each other electronically to discuss treatment plans or operative procedures. At the same time, the Internet supports a shift toward more patient-centered care, enabling consumers to gather health-related information themselves; to communicate with care providers, health plan administrators, and other consumers electronically; and even to receive care in the home. The Internet can also support numerous health-related activities beyond the direct provision of care. By supporting financial and administrative transactions, public health surveillance, professional education, and biomedical research, the Internet can streamline the administrative overhead associated with health care, improve the health of the nation's population, better train health care providers, and lead to new insights into the nature of disease.[23]

Notwithstanding the large number of possible applications of Internet technology to medicine, relatively few of these have become widespread in clinical medicine. Physicians and patients use the information-gathering function alike; the recordkeeping function has major HIPAA concerns and has yet to find widespread use.

Technical challenges have, to a certain extent, forestalled the dissemination of the Internet-based health applications. Broadband, now ubiquitous in the United States, is likely to remove some of the limitations. Store-and-forward technology for telehealth is possible on a desktop, obviating the need for a telehealth studio. Another critical problem in the development of telehealth is reliable Internet security.

Nonetheless, the Internet as a tool for managing care is in its infancy. Technological advances to look for include the following:

- Advanced encryption technology
- Advanced data compression
- Expansion of broadband availability
- Self-monitoring devices

The challenge of how to pay for physician services provided through the Internet has not been met.

Q 13:42 What is a Web-based computerized patient record?

A computerized patient record (CPR) is similar to an electronic medical record (EMR) (see Q 13:34), but CPRs are Web-based and EMRs are server-based.

As managed care is becoming more population-based, the computerized patient record takes on uses other than simply transmitting medical information about an individual patient to an individual physician. Other applications include a population-based record for care management and public health purposes.

The National Academy of Science reports:

> At present, most online medical records consist primarily of
> text and demand little bandwidth for fairly rapid downloading.
> If such records begin to include medical images (e.g., X rays,
> computed tomography (CT) scans, and mammograms), then
> much higher bandwidth would be needed for timely download-
> ing. . . . Similarly, reliability requirements are not high because
> online records are still supplements to, as opposed to replace-
> ments for, the records maintained by provider organizations;
> an inability to access an online record is unlikely to interfere
> with the provision of care. If online records become more
> widely used and more complete than providers' records, then
> reliability could become more of a concern. Scalability is not
> an issue, either, because records are not needed simultaneously
> by multiple users.[24]

Disease Management and Information Technology

Q 13:43 What is the role of information technology in disease management?

Disease management requires a number of steps that depend on
the rapid flow and direction of information. Patients whose disease
processes are amenable to a management process must first be
flagged. This can be accomplished by:

1. A health risk assessment (HRA) tool that can be administered
   to a group of employees or subscribers, or self-administered
   using inexpensive terminals;

2. Analysis of screening laboratory tests for indicators such as
   elevated blood sugar (diabetes mellitus), elevated low-density
   lipoprotein (LDL) cholesterol (coronary risk), or abnormal
   urinalysis (kidney disease);

3. Patient self-identification;

4. Participation of the patient in monitoring and therapy modification; or

5. Auditing of pharmaceutical use.

Further, information technology can identify patterns of utilization such as emergency room visits, after-hours calls, and medication use to specify those who would benefit by disease management.

Q 13:44 Is an EMR required for effective disease management?

No. Although an EMR is useful for effective disease management, it is not necessary. Disease management can be accomplished by developing the capacity in the health care organization and showing added value to patients to encourage participation; however, when disease management involves placing a patient or a member in a continuum of medical care, an EMR can make the transfer of information between facilities and providers easier than it would be with paper records. Commercial disease management firms have successfully used nonmedical personnel armed with protocols to staff call centers.

Interactive Health Communication

Q 13:45 What is interactivity?

Interactivity is the exchange of information between an information user and an information provider, often a physician and an information source such as a library or journal, but also a physician or health care provider and a patient or end-user. Media involved can include combinations of the following:

- Radio
- Television
- Printed materials
- Audio communications (e.g., tapes and compact discs)
- Internet and World Wide Web
- Web television
- Video at the point of service (e.g., physician's office, clinic, pharmacy)

T.N. Robinson and others[25] have identified six advantages of new media such as the Internet for health communications:

1. Improved opportunity to find information tailored to the specific needs or characteristics of individuals or groups of users;
2. Improved capabilities of various media to be combined with text, audio, and visuals and of matching specific media to the particular purposes of the learning styles of users;
3. Increased possibility for users to remain anonymous by providing access to sensitive information that people may be uncomfortable in acquiring in a public forum or during a face-to-face discussion;
4. Increased access to information and support on demand;
5. Increased opportunity for users to interact with health professionals or to find support from those similarly situated; and
6. Enhanced ability for widespread dissemination and for keeping content or functions current. . . . As technologies become pervasive in both public and private settings, more people, including traditionally underserved persons (e.g., rural, poor, disabled), may gain access to information that has been out of reach.

Q 13:46   What are the possibilities for harm in interactive technologies?

The fundamental principle of the Internet is availability of uncensored information. Thus, any person or organization can place on the Internet information that is not authoritative. Unverified health claims can cause patients to forgo meaningful treatment or select a harmful treatment modality. Because people place value on computer-generated information over information from television and many other media, they can be misled. This decreases the efficacy of authoritative health information. The growth of health-related Web sites is so rapid that it is impossible to verify or control their content. Authoritative sources such as academic medical centers, professional organizations, and disease-specific not-for-profit entities have assumed some editorial responsibility by reviewing the links that they place on their Web sites.

The Science Panel on Interactive Communication and Health (SciPICH) has published a template that is available on its Web site, http://www.scipich.org, and that will allow evaluation and reporting of interactive health communication without making judgments as to the appropriateness of the outcomes being assessed.

Q 13:47   How can a practice be made "information-friendly"?

SciPICH offers the following guide to making a health care setting accessible for patients:[26]

- Familiarize yourself with the spectrum and functions of interactive health communication (IHC) technologies. Educate yourself about ways to evaluate their quality and impact, especially health information on the Internet. Attend seminars and meetings in this emerging area. Consult with knowledgeable colleagues.

- Learn how to use Web search engines to locate health information. Start by learning how to use popular search mechanisms, such as healthfinder (http://www.healthfinder.gov/) and Medline (http://www.nlm.nih.gov/). Consult with medical librarians about search strategies.

- Encourage patients to be active participants in their health care and share clinical decisions by enlisting them to learn more about their condition. Provide standard written guidance about how to find high-quality and relevant information resources and how to be an informed consumer of IHC. When giving a patient or family members information about a diagnosis, test, or other health issue, providing some keywords on an "information prescription" may help them to find additional information on Web sites and in journals, books, and other resources. Health care professionals can invite patients to bring in information that they have found and may survey patients to learn how a practice can become more "information-friendly."

- Develop and implement information technology (including Web site) policies, standards, and practices that promote quality, privacy, and confidentiality. These should address who can access, add to, or modify Web sites; security measures to protect against external tampering; and encryption for e-mail containing medical records and other patient information.

- Create a Web site for your practice that may include office information and links to Web sites that you judge to be appropriate. Encourage patients to communicate with you and your staff by e-mail. Sponsor or host a listserv, Web forum, or newsletter to allow patients to support each other and share useful information resources on a regular basis. Participate in online discussion groups to learn about the needs of patients.

- Provide patient access to the Internet in your office or waiting area, and place terminals in locations that are accessible while maintaining privacy and confidentiality. "Bookmark" high-quality and relevant sites on the Web browser.

- Designate a staff member to serve as the leader and coordinator for information technology issues (much like an information technology specialist or chief information officer in a business or organization). He or she should regularly surf the Web and peruse reviews of IHC applications for information relevant to the clinicians and patients in the practice, such as late-breaking research from news sites and online journals. This person also could identify and monitor major Web sites, list-servs, and online support groups that are most relevant to the practice. This person does not have to be a health professional, but should be someone with an interest in technology and some training.

- Advocate for evaluation of IHC applications before you endorse them to your patients. Health care professionals should demand evidence of efficacy and safety, just as they do for other health interventions.

Q 13:48   What are some of the major policy issues in interactive health communication?

K. Patrick[27] and others identify several important areas for policy discussion and development:

1. *Privacy and confidentiality.* Despite the convenience of interactive health communication for the physician and the patient, issues of privacy are unresolved. E-mail without suitable encryption should be viewed as being no more private than analog cellular phones.

2. *Oversight and regulation.* The role of government in the exchange of information is hotly contested. Attempts at regulation, such as the Communications Decency Act, have been found to be unconstitutional.

3. *Liability.* The provision of medical advice by nonphysicians and prescription across state lines are hotly contested issues.

4. *Accreditation.* The Internet has no safeguards against unedited and unauthoritative Web sites, some operating under the guise of medical licenses. Authoritative Web sites have been established by many professional organizations, but there is no central accrediting body for interactive health care communication.

5. *Responsibility for research.* It is tempting to allow research and development costs to be borne by other than the end-user. This generally means grant-sponsored research and targeted industry research. The growth of dot-coms and their extensive market capitalizations should continue to pump research and development money into interactive health care communications as companies continue to search for niche markets.

6. *Payment and reimbursement.* In mid-1999, HCFA approved Medicare payment for specific telemedicine services to rural and underserved populations. CMS has no payment mechanism for interactive health communications, although at least 18 states allow for Medicaid payments for telehealth services. Table 13-2 details state initiatives in telehealth reimbursement for Medicaid.[28]

7. *Access to interactive health care.* A disproportionate number of wealthy and urban homes are online as compared to poor and rural homes. Data show that lower-income families, rural households, African-Americans, and Hispanics are less likely to own a computer or have Internet access than other groups. For example, in 1998, only 2.1 percent of rural U.S. households with incomes between $5,000 and $10,000 had access to online services, compared to 50 percent of families with incomes greater than $75,000.[29] Countries in Western Europe are frequently more "wired" than the United States. It is expected that increasing information flow and decreasing cost will promote greater availability.

Table 13-2   States Where Medicaid Reimbursement of Services
Utilizing Telemedicine Is Available

Arkansas	The Medicaid agency recognizes physician consultations when furnished using interactive video teleconferencing.
	Payment is on a fee-for-service basis, which is the same as the reimbursement for covered services furnished in the conventional, face-to-face manner. Reimbursement is made at both ends (hub and spoke sites) for the telemedicine services.
	The state uses specific codes to identify telemedicine services. The state contact is Will Taylor, (501) 682-8362.
California	The Medicaid agency recognizes physician consultations (medical and mental health) when furnished using interactive video teleconferencing.
	Payment is on a fee-for-service basis, which is the same as the reimbursement for covered services furnished in the conventional, face-to-face manner. Reimbursement is made at both ends (hub and spoke sites) for telemedicine services.
	The state uses consultative CPT codes with the modifier "TM" to identify telemedicine services. The state contact is Dr. Michael Farber, (916) 657-0548.
Georgia	The Medicaid agency recognizes physician consultations when furnished using interactive video teleconferencing.
	Payment is on a fee-for-service basis, which is the same as the reimbursement for covered services furnished in the conventional, face-to-face manner. Reimbursement is made at both ends (hub and spoke sites) for telemedicine services.
	The state uses specific local codes to identify the consultation furnished at the hub site. No special codes or modifier is used at the spoke site. The state contact is Sherley Benson, (404) 657-7213.
Illinois	The Medicaid agency recognizes physician consultations when furnished using interactive video teleconferencing.
	Payment is on a fee-for-service basis, which is the same as the reimbursement for covered services furnished in the conventional, face-to-face manner. Reimbursement is made at both ends (hub and spoke sites) for telemedicine services.
	The state uses specific codes to identify telemedicine services. The state contact is R. Calluza or Maryann Daily, (217) 782-2570.
Iowa	The Medicaid agency recognizes physician consultations when furnished using interactive video teleconferencing.
	Payment is based on the state's fee-for-service rates for covered services furnished in the conventional, face-to-face manner. Reimbursement is made at both ends (hub and spoke sites) for telemedicine services.
	Specific local codes are used for the add-on payment and CPT codes with the modifier "TM" are used to identify the consultations. The state contact is Marty Swartz, (515) 281-5147.

Table 13-2   States Where Medicaid Reimbursement of Services
Utilizing Telemedicine Is Available (cont'd)

Kansas	The Medicaid agency recognizes home health care and mental health services already covered by the state plan when furnished using video equipment. Home health is limited to certain services.
	Payment is on a fee-for-service basis for the mental health services, which is the same as the reimbursement for covered services furnished in the conventional manner. Compensation for home health care via telemedicine is made at a reduced rate. Reimbursement is made only for the service furnished at the hub site.
	Local codes have been established to specifically identify home health services furnished using visual communication equipment. No special modifiers are used for mental health services. The state contact is Ms. Fran Seymour-Hunter, (785) 296-3386.
Louisiana	The Medicaid agency recognizes physician consultations when furnished using interactive video teleconferencing.
	Payment is on a fee-for-service basis, which is the same as the reimbursement for covered services furnished in the conventional, face-to-face manner. Reimbursement is made at both ends (hub and spoke site) for the telemedicine services. Physician assistants are allowed to perform the service using telemedicine if they are authorized by a primary physician, who is the only one that is authorized to bill.
	The state uses consultative CPT codes. The state contact is Ms. Kandice McDaniels, (504) 342-3891, Kmcdanie@ dhhmail.dhh.state.la.us.
Minnesota	The Medicaid agency recognizes physician consultations (medical and mental health) when furnished using interactive video or store-and-forward technology. Interactive video consultations may be billed when there is no physician present in the emergency room and the nursing staff requests a consultation from a physician in a hub site. Coverage is limited to three consultations per beneficiary per calendar week.
	Payment is on a fee-for-service basis, using the same payment rate as that used for covered services furnished in a conventional, face-to-face manner. Payment is made at both the hub and spoke sites. No payment is made for transmission fees.
	Minnesota uses consultation CPT codes with the modifier "CT" for interactive video services and the modifier "WT" for consultations provided through store-and-forward technology. Emergency room CPT codes are used with a "GT" modifier for interactive video consultations done between emergency rooms. The state contact is Christine Reisdorf, (651) 296-8822.

Table 13-2   **States Where Medicaid Reimbursement of Services Utilizing Telemedicine Is Available (cont'd)**

Montana	The Medicaid agency recognizes any medical or psychiatric service already covered by the state plan when furnished using interactive video teleconferencing. Payment is on a fee-for-service basis, which is the same as the reimbursement for covered services furnished in the conventional, face-to-face manner. Reimbursement is made at both ends (hub and spoke sites) for the telemedicine service. No special codes have been developed. Providers use codes from the existing CPT. State contact is Dave Thorsen, (406) 444-3634.
Nebraska	The Medicaid agency recognizes most state plan services when furnished using interactive video teleconferencing. In general, services are covered as long as a comparable service is not available to a client within a 30-mile radius of his or her home. Services specifically excluded include medical equipment and supplies; orthotics and prosthetics; personal care aide services; pharmacy services; medical transportation services; and mental health and substance abuse services and home and community-based waiver services provided by persons who do not meet practitioner standards for coverage. Payment is on a fee-for-service basis, which is the same as reimbursement for covered services furnished in the conventional, face-to-face manner. Reimbursement is made at both the hub and spoke sites. Payment for transmission costs is set at the lower of the billed charge or the state's maximum allowable amount. Billing and coding requirements will vary depending on who bills for the service and which claim form is used. The state contact is Dr. Chris Wright, (402) 471-9136.
North Carolina	The Medicaid agency recognizes initial, follow-up, or confirming consultations in hospitals and outpatient facilities when furnished using real-time interactive video teleconferencing. The patient must be present during the teleconsultation. Payment is on a fee-for-service basis. The consulting practitioner at the hub site receives 75 percent of the fee schedule amount for the consultation code. The referring practitioner at the spoke site receives 25 percent of the applicable fee. Teleconsultations are billed with modifiers to identify which portion of the teleconsult visit is billed. The consulting practitioner at the hub site uses a "GT" modifier and the referring practioner at the spoke site uses a "YS" modifier. The state contact is Janet Tudor, (919)-857-4049.

Table 13-2   States Where Medicaid Reimbursement of Services Utilizing Telemedicine Is Available (cont'd)

North Dakota	The Medicaid agency recognizes speciality physician consultations when furnished using interactive video teleconferencing.
	Payment is on a fee-for-service basis, which is the same as the reimbursement for covered services furnished in the conventional, face-to-face manner. Reimbursement is made at both ends (hub and spoke sites) for the telemedicine services.
	Current CPT codes for consultative services are used with a "TM" modifier to specifically identify covered services that are furnished by using audiovisual communication equipment. State contact is David Zetner, (701) 328-3194.
Oklahoma	The Medicaid agency recognizes physician consultations when furnished using interactive video teleconferencing.
	Payment is on a fee-for-service basis, which is the same as the reimbursement for covered services furnished in the conventional, face-to-face manner. Reimbursement is made at both ends (hub and spoke site) for the telemedicine services.
	The state uses consultative CPT codes. The state contact is Ms. Nelda Paden, (405) 530-3398, Padenn@ohca.state.ok.us.
South Dakota	The Medicaid agency recognizes physician consultations when furnished using (interactive and noninteractive) video equipment.
	Payment is on a fee-for-service basis, which is the same as the reimbursement for covered services furnished in the conventional, face-to-face manner. Reimbursement is made at both ends (hub and spoke sites) for the telemedicine services.
	The state uses consultative CPT codes with a "TM" modifier to identify telemedicine services. The state contact is Linda Waldman, (605) 773-3495.
Texas	The Medicaid agency recognizes physician consultations (teleconsultations) when furnished using interactive video teleconferencing.
	Payment is on a fee-for-service basis, which is the same as the reimbursement for covered services furnished in the conventional, face-to-face manner. Reimbursement is made at both ends (hub and spoke site) for the telemedicine services.
	Other health care providers, such as advanced nurse practitioners and certified nurse midwives, are allowed to bill, as are rural health clinics and federally qualified health centers.
	The state uses consultative CPT codes with the modifier "TM" to identify telemedicine services. The state contact is Nora Cox Taylor, (512) 424-6669, nora.taylor@hhsc.state.tx.us.

**Table 13-2   States Where Medicaid Reimbursement of Services
Utilizing Telemedicine Is Available (cont'd)**

Utah	The Medicaid agency recognizes the following services when furnished using interactive video teleconferencing: mental health consultations provided by psychiatrists, psychologists, social workers, psychiatric registered nurses, and certified marriage or family therapists; diabetes self-management training provided by qualified registered nurses or dietitians; and services provided to children with special health care needs by physician specialists, dietitians, and pediatricians when those children reside in rural areas.
	Payment is on a fee-for-service basis, which is the same as the reimbursement for covered services furnished in the conventional, face-to-face manner. Reimbursement is made at both the hub and spoke sites for diabetes self-management training services and services provided to children with special health care needs. Reimbursement is made only to the consulting professional for mental health services. Payment is made for transmission fees.
	The state uses CPT codes with "GT" and "TR" modifiers to identify telehealth services. The state contact is Mr. Blake Anderson, (801) 538-9925.
Virginia	The Medicaid agency recognizes, as a pilot project, medical and mental health services already covered by the state plan when furnished using interactive video teleconferencing.
	Payment is on a fee-for-service basis, which is the same as the reimbursement for covered services furnished in the conventional, face-to-face manner. Reimbursement is made at both ends (hub and spoke sites) only for medical services.
	The state uses specific local codes to identify telemedicine services. The state contact is Jeff Nelson, (804) 371-8857.
West Virginia	The Medicaid Agency recognizes physician consultations when furnished using interactive video teleconferencing.
	Payment is on a fee-for-service basis, which is the same as the reimbursement for covered services furnished in the conventional, face-to-face manner. Reimbursement is made at both ends (hub and spoke sites) for the telemedicine services.
	The state uses consultative CPT codes with the modifier "TV" to identify telemedicine services. The state contact is Laure L. Harbert, (304) 926-1718.

References

1. Committee on Regional Health Data Networks, Division of Health Care Services, Institute of Medicine, *Health Data in the Information Age: Use, Disclosure and Privacy*, M.S. Donaldson and K.N. Lahore, eds. (Washington, DC: National Academy Press, 1994).

2. The economics of the Internet are beyond the scope of this discussion, although it should be noted that nothing is free. The cost of posting information on the Web and managing it is borne by some party that derives value from it. Thus, in the commercial world, the user is, in some form, paying for the use of the information with an incremental price.

3. B. Gates with C. Hemingway, *Business @ the Speed of Thought: Using a Digital Nervous System* (New York: Warner Books, 1999).

4. National Research Council, *For the Record: Protecting Electronic Health Information* (Washington, DC: National Academy Press, 1997).

5. A.A. Waller and O.L. Alcantara, "Ownership of Health Information in the Information Age," *JAHIMA,* 69(3):28–38, 1998.

6. HIPAA looks to Congress or the Secretary of HSS to Develop measures to protect the security of medical information in July 1997, legislation was signed into law prohibiting insurers from using genetic information to deny insurance to individuals with a genetic predisposition to a particular condition. Pub L No 104-191.

7. P. Starr, "Smart Technology, Stunted Policy: Developing Health Information Networks," *Health Affairs,* 16(3):91–105, May–June 1997.

8. C. Appleby, "The Trouble with CHINs," *Hosps. & Health Networks,* May 5, 1995, at 42.

9. J. Ziegler, "Health Care's Search for an Information Injection," *Bus. & Health* 14(4):33–34, 36, 38, 1996.

10. *See* http://www.tdh.state.tx.us/hcf/tmn/default.htm (last accessed Nov. 29, 2001).

11. *See* http://www.tdh.state.tx.us/hcf/tmn/tmnedist.htm (last accessed Nov. 29, 2001).

12. D.N. Mendelson and E.M. Salinsky, "Health Information Systems and the Role of State Government," *Health Affairs*, 16(3):106–119, May–June 1997.

13. American Medical Association, Code of Medical Ethics, Principles of Medical Ethics, IV (1992).

14. Whalen v. Roe, 429 U.S. 589 (1977).

15. Montana and Washington have adopted the Uniform Health Information Act, which limits permissible disclosure of health care information about a patient without a patient's express authorization. California's Confidentiality of Medical Information Act, Cal. Civ. Code § 56, defines the circumstances under which a provider, employer, or third-party administrator may release individually identifiable health information to third parties.

16. Several important federal laws include the Federal Privacy Act, 5 USC § 552a, which provides limited privacy protection. Despite the disclosure requirement under the Freedom of Information Act, 5 USC § 552, there are numerous exceptions to the disclosure permitted under the Act. Under Section 1106 of the Social Security Act, files, records, and information obtained by officers or employees of the Department of Health and Human Services may not be disclosed except as prescribed by regulation. The strictest of all federal statutes are the federal alcohol and drug abuse confidentiality laws, 42 USC §§ 290dd-3, 290ee-3, which impose strict confidentiality requirements with respect to drug and alcohol abuse records.

17. WEDI is a group of industry leaders seeking to reduce administrative costs in the U.S. health care system. This group has set a goal of establishing and processing all financial and clinical information across the health care industry.

18. L.L. Weed, "Medical Records That Guide and Teach," *New Eng. J. Med.*, 278(11):593–600, 1968, and 278(12): 652–657, 1968.

19. Office of Rural Health Policy, Health Resources and Service Administration, Department of Health and Human Services, Telemedicine Report to Congress, 1998.

20. Council on Competitiveness, *Highway to Health: Transforming U.S. Health Care in the Information Age* (Washington, DC: Council on Competitiveness, 1996), 28.

21. R.F. Pendrak and R.P. Ericson, "Telemedicine and the Law," *Healthcare Fin. Mgmt. J.*, 50(12):46, 1996, cited in K.M. Saltzman, "Health Care Technology and the Law," *Med. Group Mgmt. J.*, July/Aug. 1998.

22. Id. at 68–74.

23. National Academy of Science, *Networking Health: Prescriptions for the Internet (2000)*, http://books.nap.edu/html/networking_health/.

24. Id. at 65.

25. T.N. Robinson, K. Patrick, T.R. Eng, et al., "An Evidence-Based Approach to Interactive Health Communication," 280(14):1264–1269, 1998.

26. Science Panel on Interactive Communication and Health, *Wired for Health and Well-Being: The Emergence of Interactive Health Communication* (Washington, DC: U.S. Department of Health and Human Services, U.S. Government Printing Office, April 1999), Appendix F.

27. K. Patrick, T.N. Robinson, F. Alemi, and T. R. Eng, for the Science Panel on Interactive Communication and Health, "Policy Issues Relevant to the Evaluation of Interactive Health Communication Applications," *Am. J. Prev. Med.*, 16: 35–42, 1999.

28. *See* http://www.hcfa.gov/medicaid/telelist.htm.

29. *Falling Through the Net: Defining the Digital Divide: A Report on the Telecommunications and Information Technology Gap in America* (Washington, DC: U.S. Department of Commerce, National Telecommunications and Information Administration, 1999).

Chapter 14

The Future of Managed Care

Managed care has gone from managing medical care for the best interest of the patient to managing costs for the best interest of the payer. This inherent conflict of interest—the payment transaction and the service transaction are not between the same people—is being changed. This is not necessarily best for the consumer, but it makes more sense than the current practice and is the reason for the rise of consumerism.

Health plans continue to use alternative pricing schemes such as point-of-service (POS) plans to shift costs to the consumer. Now, defined contribution plans make the consumer the decision point. Health maintenance organizations (HMOs) continue to merge and consolidate under premium pressure and rising direct costs.

The political winds remain uncertain after the "Clinton care" disaster. In the wake of September 11, 2001, little has emerged from the 107th Congress, other than patient protection legislation. The rise of consumerism in health care will demand protection and more. Access to information and the ability to make sense of it will remain a paramount challenge that has to be facilitated by regulation.

Employers continue to look for risk-sharing opportunities with plans, and to look for ways to put more of the risk and responsibility for health care decisions on employees. Premium contribution plans, demand management programs, and medical savings accounts will test the theories of individual empowerment. Even the government-sponsored programs appear to be moving from a defined benefit to a defined contribution format.

Prophecy is always risky. Ginzberg and Ostow opined in the *New England Journal of Medicine* that physicians were reasserting their power in health care by forming large groups devoted to direct contracting. They wrote, "Such arrangements point to strengthened bargaining power in the future for physicians, whose influence was seriously undermined by the recent rapid changes in the health care sector. Especially notable is the success that the giant merged groups of physicians, such as Mullikan, Med-Partners, and Caremark in California, have had in competing with managed-care plans."[1] None of those organizations existed in their previous forms as of the end of 1999.

Trends

Q 14:1   Is the growth rate of medical care costs slowing down?

Yes. Several studies have suggested there has been a leveling off of, or even a slight decline in the rate of increase of medical care costs. This is presumed to be in response to the increase in health care competition over the past 17 years. As described in chapter 1, the rate of increase in the consumer price index for medical care is once again exceeding that for the general economy.

The promising new models of health care delivery that were intended to manage care and cost better have not met expectations. The provider-sponsored organizations (PSOs) envisioned in the Balanced Budget Act of 1997 (BBA) never got started. Health care premiums continue their upward trend, rising dramatically in 1998 and continuïng to rise in the new century. This supports the hypothesis that the managed care savings may be a "one shot" event, as costs are stripped out of the health care market. Further, deferral of technological investment and infrastructure maintenance and the appearance of new technologies in genetics are likely to accelerate the increase in health care premiums as payers struggle to cover costs and maintain their profit margins.

Altman and Levitt[2] provide an interesting perspective, shown in Figure 14-1. There is a remarkable consistency in health care costs when those costs are corrected for inflation.

Q 14:2   What happened to managed competition?

Managed competition is the idea that purchasers of health care can form purchasing alliances to exert price pressure on health care delivery systems. It is a macroeconomic principle propounded by Alain Enthoven and later adopted by the Jackson Hole Group as a way of allowing economies of scale to be applied to the health care industry. This principle was incorporated into President Bill Clinton's unsuccessful health care reform package of 1994. Today, the concept of managed competition exists in various forms.

Purchasing coalitions (see chapter 4) are the surviving privatized version of the health insurance purchasing cooperatives (HICPs) of the failed Clinton health care reform package. In addition to bringing purchasing power to bear on health care, they have become, in some cases, lobbyists, and in others, policy groups. An example of the latter is the Washington Business Group on Health.

Managed competition seems to have taken root outside the United States. In Eastern Europe multiple payment organizations are superseding the monolithic state-run enterprises. The *kupat holim* (sick funds) in Israel bear more than a passing resemblance to HIPCs, although they also strongly resemble HMOs in that they directly care for their subscribers in addition to being payers.

Figure 14-1.　Annual Change in Private Health Spending per Capita (Adjusted for Inflation), 1961–2001

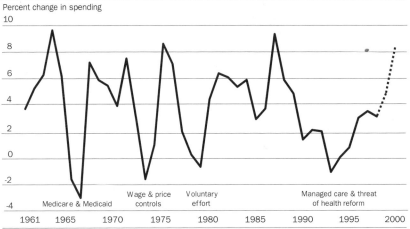

SOURCES: Henry J. Kaiser Family Foundation analysis. Private health expenditures per capita, 1960–1999, are from the Centers for Medicare and Medicaid Services (CMS). Change in private spending per capita, 2000–2001, is estimated based on average premium increases for employer-sponsored coverage from the Kaiser/HRET Survey of Employer-Sponsored Health Benefits. NOTES: Real change in spending is calculated using the Consumer Price Index (CPI-U) all items, average annual change for 1961–2000 and July-to-July change for 2001. This analysis was inspired by an analysis done by Jeff Merrill and Richard Wassermann more than fifteen years ago. See J.C. Merrill and R.J. Wassermann, "Growth in National Expenditures: Additional Analyses," *Health Affairs* (Winter 1985): 91–98.

Source: http://healthaffairs.org/WebExclusives/2101Altman.pdf.

Q 14:3　What are the trends in health care?

In 1997, the authors of *Redesigning Health Care for the Millennium, An Assessment of the Health Care Environment in the United States,* identified eight health care trends:[3]

1. Continued expansion of managed care;

2. Evolving role of government in health care;

3. Cost containment;

4. Continued industry consolidation;

5. Increased consumer demand;

6. Evolving physician roles;

7. Quality improvement and outcomes; and

8. Use of information technology.

Q 14:4   What is the status of health care trends identified in 1997?

An examination of the health care trends identified in 1997 shows the perils of punditry:

1. *Continued expansion of managed care.* As discussed in chapter 1, managed care has become ubiquitous but dilute. There is only a slight resemblance between the managed care of the early twenty-first century and its illustrious predecessor of 60 years ago, Kaiser Permanente. As managed care continues to work on the margins, cutting costs and seeking value for the purchaser, it has ceased to be a viable tool for revolution in the health care market.

2. *Evolving role of government in health care.* The 107th Congress is not taking a leadership role in health care reform. Public, and thus congressional, attention is focused on prescription benefit payment. Although this is a huge economic problem, it is not a pivotal issue in health care delivery. The government, through the Centers for Medicare and Medicaid Services (CMS) and the Agency for Healthcare Research and Quality (AHRQ), has taken a position on quality monitoring and regulation, and the National Academy of Sciences, through the Institute of Medicine, has brought the issue of medical errors to the public forum. Nonetheless, crucial issues—medical staffing, payment for graduate medical education, infant mortality, technology, and genetics—are being handled on a piecemeal basis, without an overarching philosophy or goal.

3. *Cost containment.* Cost containment has been notably unsuccessful in the past several years, with restrictions on utilization and decreasing physician and hospital reimbursements continuing in the face of dramatically rising premiums. Thus, the strategy of shifting the burden of decision making to the consumer is supplanting managed care systems in which third parties make the decisions. Although this may appear to be draconian, it is aligning the service transaction with the payment transaction.

4. *Continued industry consolidation.* Industry consolidation is continuing in the managed care market in general, although many payers are just exiting the market entirely. Consolidators of physician services, such as PhyCor, no longer exist or are bankrupt. Hospitals that spent their treasure on owning

networks of primary care physicians (PCPs) to "feed" specialists and fill beds are finding the losses inherent in that strategy
unsupportable and have divested such practices, usually back
to the physicians themselves.

5. *Increased consumer demand.* Consumer demand is emerging
as one of the primary drivers of change in health care. The
consumer, now being asked to spend his or her own money,
is looking for value and access to "the best." In some cases
the best is defined as the glitziest technology and biggest ma-
chines; in other cases it is defined as the high-class service of
boutique medical practices. Consumers are also expressing a
desire for knowledge and the ability to make their own health
care decisions. Although Web sites such as DrKoop.com were
disasters, the reason for their emergence still exists. People
spending their own money are looking for ways to become
educated consumers, and the Internet promises the most dem-
ocratic and accessible way to do that. The Holy Grail of consumerism on the Internet is the ability to manage the information and stratify it in a meaningful way.

In 2002, several insurance companies agreed to pay physicians for e-mail consultations. This is another example of the
market being driven by the consumer, who will become the
ultimate payer.

6. *Evolving physician roles.* Payers were able to cut physician
compensation radically in the 1990s because of the perception
that the market was glutted with physicians and that managed
care, physician extenders, and nonphysician professionals
would assume the role of provider. The decrease in physician
compensation, coupled with the increased cost of medical education, has caused a progressive decline in applications to
medical school since 1997. Medical journals are beginning to
speculate on a physician shortage, particularly in the specialties where training periods may last as long as eight years following attainment of the M.D. degree. For a doctor who is age
34 at the beginning of his or her career and faces $200,000 or
more in debt, medicine does not look as financially attractive
as it once may have. It is quite reasonable to view the physician's role as being divided once again into technical skills
and information processing skills. Once again, the consumer
is in control and will decide what services he or she is willing

to pay for. The final variable will be physician liability and the extent to which a physician can be held responsible for the decisions his or her patient makes.

7. *Quality improvement and outcomes.* Medical care has traditionally been held to a higher standard than value given for value received. The pervasiveness of information and the easier access to information can be expected to increase the transparency of medical care. For consumerism to prevail, the consumer must have access to enough information of sufficient quality and objectivity to make buying decisions. Government agencies, lead by the AHRQ and the Centers for Disease Control and Prevention (CDCP), have taken up the challenge of accumulating this information at a high level. At the retail level, advertising substitutes for information; advertising does not, obviously, supply the basis for judgment.

8. *Information technology.* Health care organizations of the future will be driven by information technology. Electronic medical records, integrated health information systems, and telemedicine will expand the scope of and enhance efficiencies in the industry. By providing real-time and accurate information about outcomes and quality, information technology can be used by the consumer to make buying decisions. Real-time information, or at least current information, can be used to decrease variation in medical processes and allows medical processes to achieve a higher degree of quality at lower cost.

Q 14:5 What are the trends in health insurance coverage?

As the burden of health insurance decreases profit margins, increased cost sharing by employees is inevitable. Medicare continues to be at risk as the population ages. Perhaps the most important trend, however, is the progress toward universal coverage envisioned by the failed Clinton health care reform efforts of 1994. Although the number of uninsured Americans continues to be a disgrace, the expansion of qualification for children under the State Children's Health Insurance Program (SCHIP) is an important step.

The health care effects of the 2001–2002 recession are not clear at the time of this writing. Because of the fragility of the health care financing industry, however, one can reasonably expect that industry cost cutting will have a degree of permanence not seen in previous economic downturns.

Hospitals and Physician Groups

Q 14:6 What challenges do investor-owned hospitals face?

Challenges faced by investor-owned hospitals include unwinding the physician and network arrangements that they spent so much money building over the past decade. Few, if any, of these arrangements have been successful enough to justify their high cost of maintenance. Hospital admissions will continue to increase as acute exacerbations of chronic illness affect admissions. Technology costs will continue to make each admission more expensive.

Medical staffing in hospitals—especially nurses and hands-on care personnel—is a major problem facing not only the investor-owned sector but all of health care. Many hospitals are operating with a 5 to 25 percent shortage in registered nurses and nurse specialists.

Q 14:7 How might nonprofit hospitals respond to the challenge presented by for-profit hospitals?

Nonprofit hospitals have traditionally held themselves out as more responsive to the needs of the community. In return for their tax-exempt status, they were to care for the indigent and provide public service. The advent of Medicare in 1965 was a watershed because community hospitals finally got paid for the care of the indigent and elderly. Another watershed was the enactment of prospective reimbursement to hospitals in 1983. This put the voluntary hospitals on the same footing as the for-profit hospitals and at risk for health care costs. Payment based on the diagnosis-related group (DRG) standard rewarded cost cutting and was blind to the nonprofits' community service.

A landmark study by N.M. Kane examined the financial returns of the for-profit and the nonprofit institutions and found that nonprofit status provided no compelling benefit to society, although for-profits contributed essentially nothing to medical education other than their taxes.[4] This harsh judgment has been tempered since that report was written, but the question of who pays for community service and medical education remains a difficult one. Consolidation in the hospital industry, as a whole, has decreased. Successful hospital corporations, such as Tenet, have recognized that health care is local and not all processes can be centralized or standardized. Obviously, the nonprofits, with their explicit community service mission, already knew this. Nonetheless, rate contraction, burgeoning technology, and maintenance forgone create evolving challenges for the nonprofits.

The so-called safety-net hospitals face even greater challenges, since they often operate at the whim of state and local governments.

Q 14:8 What will be community hospitals' strategies for survival?

Even as Medicaid becomes a more demanding payer, community hospitals will be better positioned to assume the risk for their patients. Commercial hospitals are unlikely to be preparing in large numbers to care for burns, trauma, neonatal complications, or social illnesses such as drug abuse and alcoholism. Community hospitals know these populations and are better positioned to care for them.

Public and private partnerships are likely to be another strategy. As the number of World War II veterans declines, the Department of Veterans Affairs medical centers will be looking for partners to use their enormous bed and clinic capacity. The community hospitals are most likely to fill this role. Similarly, if Medicaid becomes, like welfare, a system of block grants to the states, the public and nonprofit institutions are likely partners for a delivery system to integrate Medicaid and indigent care.

Medical education is another arena for change. Community and voluntary hospitals are key locales for medical education. This relationship will continue to be jeopardized, however, as the voluntary hospitals become more like the for-profit hospitals and the medical schools adopt the practice dynamics of the physician management corporations.

Emulating the for-profits is another possibility. Many nonprofit and public hospitals are seeking their own HMO certificates of authority to be able to take global risk. It is unlikely, however, that the market will allow a premium for the nonprofits' status. Therefore, the key is whether they can measure and manage costs to compete with the commercial hospitals for a portion of their traditional clientele with payment capability.

Academic medical centers face an additional challenge from the BBA. Direct and indirect medical education payments are in jeopardy. Decreases in these payments will further enhance the stimulus to enact some form of the suggestion that all payers contribute to the expense of medical education.

Q 14:9 What impact have investor-owned physician groups had on managed care?

Investor-owned physician corporations (also referred to as physician practice management companies, or PPMCs) once grew rapidly, fueled by Wall Street enthusiasm. That growth has ended and most PPMCs are struggling or have succumbed.

Academic Medicine

Q 14:10 What is an academic medical center, and what role does the medical school play?

Generally, an academic medical center is a group of related institutions including a teaching hospital or hospitals, a medical school and its affiliated faculty practice plan, and other health professional schools. This description should not be considered a strict definition because there are many differences in composition, number, and structure across centers.

The medical school fulfills several roles in an academic medical center, including hiring faculty, setting faculty base salary and bonuses, granting tenure, operating a medical library, providing facilities for research, and performing numerous administrative functions. Medical schools are financed by a variety of sources, including research grants, tax funds allocated to teaching, and money derived from clinical practice. These sources vary, depending on whether the school is private or state supported, whether it has a health care system or a single hospital, where it is located, the competitive nature of its environment, and the type of research it conducts. Industry-sponsored research is an important source of medical school financing, with some academic medical centers forming medical

Figure 14-2.   Sources of Medical School Revenues, Selected Years

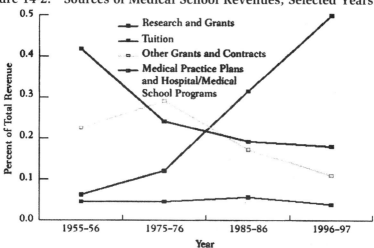

Source: H. Aaron, Academic Medicine, Policy Brief No. 59
(Washington, D.C.: Brookings Institution, May 2000).

research organizations to compete for private research grants. Clinical practice is dramatically increasing as a source of revenue for medical schools, as demonstrated in Figure 14-2.

Q 14:11   What will be the fate of the academic medical centers?

Academic medical centers are under tremendous pressure as the
market consolidates. Traditional rivals have either announced mergers or taken serious steps toward consolidation of their hospitals in
an attempt to compete with the investor-owned, for-profit institutions. Other academic medical centers, such as Tulane University,
have entered into agreements with for-profits that devolve a varying
amount of control to the investor-owned corporation. Even Catholic
health care has been involved in the management agreement between the hospital of St. Louis University and Tenet. Medical schools
themselves have not been exempt from market forces. The merger
of Hahnemann and Pennsylvania Medical College into the Allegheny
system almost forced the closure of both schools when Allegheny
collapsed. Only the timely intervention of Tenet and Drexel University saved the school.

The rapid expansion and multiplication of medical schools in the 1960s and 1970s placed a great deal of pressure on the health care market as it shrank. The funding priorities of the 1970s generally promoted the establishment of a high-overhead research establishment that required the training of large numbers of medical scientists and narrow subspecialists. These physicians are now in their peak productive years in a shrinking market. Simultaneously, many of the new medical schools failed to develop intensive primary care programs or practices and are now left without a strong base. Others invested very heavily in primary care to the point of setting up their own PPMCs and lost heavily, as did their commercial counterparts.

Academic medical centers find that the market is, in some cases, willing to pay a small premium, but this is not enough to offset the costs inherent in teaching and in the indigent-care burden they traditionally assume. The question is not, can academic medical centers compete? but rather, who will pay for their services? The health care industry will ultimately bear the cost, either through cross-subsidization or direct support via a special tax or contribution. In return, the academic medical centers can expect to be held to a standard of market responsiveness blended with innovation and originality. Demanding complete market responsiveness to the exclusion of pure research is unreasonable. Pure research is critical to society and must be supported.

Academic medical centers have adopted a number of strategies in response to the market challenge, including the following:

- Partnering with for-profit institutions
- Expanding into the international market
- Developing primary care networks
- Acquiring, developing, or partnering with HMOs
- Differentiating the product by measurable quality or excellence
- Capitalizing on a well-known brand name
- Marketing consumer education and health care information
- Marketing continuing medical education

Q 14:12 What impact has managed care had on the labor market for physicians?

The change in the financing and delivery of health care services has raised four issues with respect to the physician labor market.

The first issue is supply and the second is specialty mix. There are two market-related concerns as well. The first is the effect of the changing market for physicians' services, and the second is the physician training pipeline. Unfortunately, these market forces are not working together: Market pressure to reduce physician supply may increase academic medical centers' and teaching hospitals' dependence on residents to meet service needs. It is also expected that because of the length of time physicians spend in training, short-term increases and incentives to increase numbers of PCPs will not begin to be realized for several years. In the short term, it is unlikely that changes in physician training will have an effect on the market.

Several initiatives have had a major effect on physician supply, including the following:

- Mandated reductions in specialty training
- Reliance on specialty board certification as a *sine qua non* for credentialing
- Demonstration projects by CMS to reduce the number of residency slots
- Increasing restrictions on foreign medical school graduates seeking postgraduate training in the United States
- Changes in compensation structures for physicians

Physicians continue to be seen as advocates for patients against restrictions imposed by managed care. Robert Blendon, professor of health policy at Harvard University, says, "The backlash against insurance makes doctors by comparison look like the people's representatives."[5]

Q 14:13 What effect has managed care had on physician income?

It is difficult to obtain accurate figures on physician income. The American Medical Association (AMA) and managed care organizations (MCOs) do surveys, as do physician recruiters; however, each has biases or flaws.

For the past several years, the Massachusetts Medical Society (MMS) has been calculating an index called the Physician Practice Environment Index. The index contains nine items grouped into three categories:

1. Patient access to physicians—
   - Medical school applicants
   - Percentage of practicing physicians over age 55
   - Number of Massachusetts employment ads appearing in the *New England Journal of Medicine*
2. Practice financial conditions—
   - Median physician income
   - Ratio of housing prices to physician income
   - Malpractice costs
3. Physicians' work environment—
   - Costs of maintaining a professional practice
   - Mean weekly hours spent in patient care
   - Visits to emergency departments[6]

Of course, the index represents conditions in Massachusetts, which is a unique state medically, but the index is instructive because it describes the work life of a physician, not merely a physician's compensation. Since 1992, there has been a marked deterioration in the index, as shown in Figure 14-3.

Managing Transition

Q 14:14   What is the status of the transition to managed care?

At one time, the transition steps to managed care seemed clear. First came the PPOs and discounted fees in exchange for volume. Next, there were some tentative steps toward capitation and HMOs. With capitation came consolidation in the physician market, with large groups being necessary to take contracts. Hospitals also consolidated and closed as commercial health care systems entered the market and threatened the hegemony of the community hospitals. Consolidation likewise occurred at the level of the insurance companies, as only the large ones had networks of physicians and hospitals sufficient to manage contracts for lives. In the final stages, there were to be a few insurance companies and a few networks managing medical care with some form of prospective payment. Physicians, mean-

Figure 14-3.   MMS Practice Environment Index

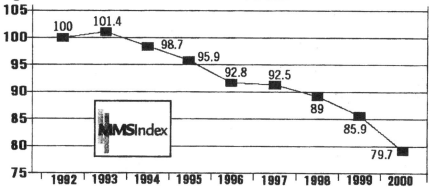

Source: http://www2.mms.org/mmsindex/index.htm (accessed Feb. 2002).

while, went through the stages of denial, rage, bargaining, and, finally, acceptance.

The problem is that the transition has not been quite as tidy as the pundits predicted. The spread of managed care throughout the country has been marked by so many patterns that it can fairly be said that there is no pattern at all. Managed care seems to be evolving differently in different communities. Major influences on the transition seem to be the impact of government programs, the capacity of systems within the community to handle managed care, the influence of employers, and the culture of the medical community and its entrepreneurial spirit. The advent of strictly fee-for-service boutique practices can be seen as a sign that traditional managed care may be at an end.

Q 14:15   How has the transition to managed care affected patient relationships?

For patients, the transition to managed care poses a number of problems, most significantly, the reasonable possibility that their personal physicians will no longer be accessible. In that situation, the patient has the option of either changing physicians to one on the panel or paying cash for the personal physician's services. The number of people doing the latter has not been quantified, but subjectively it seems significant. From the point of view of the coverage provider, this is an ideal circumstance: the patient (or his or her employer) pays for medical care that is never used. This is also beneficial for HMOs, because they are paid prospectively for medical care they never deliver. For the patient, it may not be too bad either, depending on the degree to which the employer contributes to his or her medical coverage. This situation, however, adds to the aggregate of medical costs because of multiple payments and inefficient utilization.

The industry has faced this problem in two ways. First, it has promoted the POS product with limited out-of-network benefits. More important, there appears to be a move to increase the size of primary care networks while controlling the access to specialists and expensive procedures. Thus, diversity and choice are seen by MCOs as value added in the competitive environment.

A recession is not a good time to look for indicators of change in the market. When the business cycle progresses to a tighter labor market, the stresses on health care benefits can be expected to increase as health care benefits are used once more to attract desirable workers.

Q 14:16　What factors have marked the managed care practice?

Having either survived or accepted managed care, physicians are facing new challenges regarding quality, variation in clinical practice, the educated consumer, and the burgeoning of medical knowledge. The decline in payment, coupled with increasing training demands, is making medical school simply "not worth it" for many college graduates. Nonetheless, the quality of medical school graduates remains just as high, suggesting that qualified people are still seeking careers in medicine, perhaps now for the "right" reasons.

For the PCP, managed care promised a golden age. Of great interest to PCPs is emerging rejection of the gatekeeper model. There is a split among MCOs as to how tightly they regulate the therapeutic options of PCPs. Many organizations shall have massive enterprises dedicated to monitoring PCPs. The hospitalist profession, where a physician cares exclusively for hospitalized patients and returns them to the outpatient physician when their acute episode has resolved, appears to be gaining ground. The PCP may thus become an "officist," responsible for the ambulatory and chronically ill patient. For many physicians, this split would be a highly desirable resolution to the skill demands of the two different styles of practice.

As managed care matures in the United States, choice will probably be extended to physicians. As consumers of health care continue to be more demanding, the successful and popular physician groups will be able to negotiate more stringent terms with payers and reject some plans in which they do not wish to participate. Even some physician management companies have recognized that the practice of medicine is best left to medical practitioners with capable administrators. Of course, this places hospitals in the position of vendors instead of partners, with all the risk of misalignment attendant to that status.

Carve-out strategies, once aggressively pursued, have proven to be very frustrating to physicians and patients alike and are dwindling in number.

Q 14:17 Is the role of the payer affected by managed care?

Yes. Heretofore, *payer* was synonymous with *insurance company.* The insurance company was a large company that accepted risk and spread it over a population. Now, the payer may be a third-party administrator (TPA) for a corporation or even a "private label" HMO. In some cases, the payer provides no insurance function at all except perhaps to provide stop-loss insurance.

Q 14:18 How are purchasers of health care benefits and services dealing with managed care?

Purchasers have different responses to managed care depending on whether the purchaser is considered to be the enrollee. Enrollees are sharing more financial responsibility for the cost of medical care through copayments, deductibles, and coinsurance. They are accepting controlled access to providers and limitations on freedom of choice and assuming increasing responsibility for compliance and wellness programs. This transition is difficult for the enrollee. Because much of managed care still restricts provider number and access, the enrollee must learn to navigate physician and provider choice from a list of available options, not from personal or professional recommendations. Financial schemes such as medical savings accounts will also affect consumers in that, for the first time in 50 years, they will be spending their own money on health care. Whether they will do this wisely, keeping in mind the long-term benefits of prevention and screening, remains to be seen. One can foresee full-scale marketing by health care providers promoting their high-margin screening and prevention programs with the same techniques used so successfully to create demand for other commercial products. The future of these savings account instruments is cloudier than in the past. Although many jurisdictions allow them, they have not found wide popularity.

Employers continue to look for ways to cut their exposure to unpredictable health care costs by moving to defined contribution benefit plans.

New Products and New Approaches

Q 14:19 What is happening to existing managed care products?

The lines separating indemnity, HMO, and preferred provider organization (PPO) plans are blurring. Insurers are developing HMO look-alike products such as exclusive provider organizations (EPOs), as well as HMOs with high- and low-benefit options. HMOs are also developing POS products and indemnity opt-outs to compete with insurers and PPOs. PPOs are developing EPOs to compete with HMOs. HMOs and PPOs are being offered as local in-network providers, while insurers or TPAs are administering out-of-network benefits.

This array is creating a dilemma for purchasers of plans and services as they struggle to decide what to buy, from whom to buy it, and what is actually contained in the program called managed care. One of the fallouts of this confusion and profusion of acronyms is the inability of the consumer to define the product that is being offered by the employer. Masquerading under the title of HMO can be a wide variety of plans and regulations. The definitions and regulations are state specific and are often impenetrable to consumers.

Centers of Excellence

Q 14:20 What is a center of excellence?

A center of excellence is created when a health care system, sponsored by either a provider or a payer, centralizes highly technical or complex medical care for its providers. Alternatively, a tertiary care institution or academic medical center can create a center of excellence by bringing together a team of physicians, services, and hospital facilities to provide highly specialized care for a disease, procedure, or set of conditions. All patients with the problem cared for by the center of excellence are generally moved there. The concept is that procedures that are rare or costly can be done best by an experienced team.

Centers of excellence answer the following strategic questions for large and tertiary care institutions:

1. What is the best way for us to use specialists? An early reason for centers of excellence was the perceived glut of subspecialists and the need to keep them employed. Since the workforce issue has become more cloudy, centers of excellence may serve to leverage specialist skills.

2. How can we do disease-specific research? A center of excellence creates a concentration of patients with a particular disease or condition, allowing clinical research and pharmaceutical development.

3. How can we compete with community hospitals, particularly the chains? For the chain hospitals—for which the motto is faster, cheaper, and, if possible, better—diseases and conditions treated at centers of excellence, such as AIDS and leukemia, organ transplants, are a major problem. Particularly if they participate in risk, the hospitals have to ensure that the specialized coverage is available. It is clearly impossible for the community hospitals to provide such coverage. The tertiary care institutions thus turn the chains' problem into an improved strategic position. With telemedicine, electronic communication, and the Internet, competition among centers of excellence can become stiff.

4. How can we exploit the international market? The services of centers of excellence are attractive to countries that are unable to provide needed services in an economical way for their citizens. Electronic communications media can be the key to success as well as differentiation within the international market.

5. How can we become knowledge merchants and get out of the retail medicine business where the margins are becoming in-

creasingly tight and the market is beginning to behave like a commodity exchange?

What requires a center of excellence is evolving. Only 25 years ago, coronary surgery was a highly specialized procedure that a few centers could perform competently. Today, open heart surgery occurs in most major institutions.

Q 14:21   How is a center of excellence evaluated?

To evaluate a center of excellence, the following questions must be asked:

1. *Is it really excellent?* There is no registration or specific qualification required for a health care institution to be called a *center of excellence.* The proliferation of such centers is akin to the widespread use of the term *cancer center* by institutions seeking to capitalize on the few National Cancer Institute–designated cancer centers. A center of excellence should have assembled a team of physicians and ancillary personnel specifically to perform the service it claims it provides, should be able to demonstrate that it performs the service better and at lower cost than a routine hospital or institute, and should have a repertoire of quality metrics to allow comparison among centers. The metrics should use established tools and data management techniques. The *center of excellence* designation often is nothing more than a marketing tool and represents neither a center nor excellence.

2. *Does the center of excellence really improve the care of patients with the cited disease?* When rehabilitation hospitals were profitable because of their DRG exemption, wound care centers of excellence sprang up all over the country. These centers purported to be able to take care of difficult and nonhealing wounds better than routine hospital or medical care. Often they included technology such as hyperbaric oxygen treatment, for which there is conflicting scientific evidence of improved outcome. Hyperbaric oxygen is, however, expensive and produces a high cash flow. A good retrospective method of analyzing the necessity of a center of excellence is whether it remains open after reimbursement profiles change.

3. *Does the center of excellence work to refine its specialty technique or procedure?* One of the characteristics of a center of excellence should be the advancement of knowledge in its

specialty technique or procedure. Otherwise, there is no advantage other than economies of scale to lead a payer to contract with such a center.

4. *Is it practical?* Several payers have established centers of excellence throughout the country and even the world. They propose to ship patients and their families many miles, perform the procedures, and return them to their communities. Sometimes this is the best available option; sometimes it is only to the advantage of the payer.

Q 14:22   How does disease management affect what will be expected from centers of excellence?

Disease management is a technique used by care managers to ensure that protocols are followed in the care of patients with certain high-cost, complex conditions. Disease management usually involves assigning a case manager to a patient. The next step for the acutely ill is the center of excellence, where all aspects of the patient's care are assumed for the episode of care. Of course, centers of excellence do not supplant disease-state management in the case of chronic illnesses that require continuity of care.

It is intriguing to speculate how the burgeoning knowledge transfer industry will affect disease management. Commercial enterprises that invested in large, computer-based disease management systems are now frustrated by the inability of those systems to change rapidly with changes in the knowledge base. Many of these systems, directed at payers and third parties, ignored the "last mile," the ability to motivate patients to make significant changes that could determine the success of disease management.

Predictions

Q 14:23   As different forms of managed care spread throughout the country, what developments are likely?

As managed care strategies spread throughout the country, there are few data to suggest that managed care progresses in defined stages, one stage leading to another. In fact, it appears that the evolution of managed care is almost anarchical, with the product changing to fit local economic conditions and mores.

Any form of prepayment for enrollees requires integration because management of the capitated dollar requires alignment of goals among physicians, hospitals, and payers. In large cities, the trend toward integration is likely to persist, with health care systems assuming an increasing proportion of risk and ultimately becoming the payers; however, this integration will be tempered by the desire of physicians and other providers to control the market and negotiate as a block.

In smaller communities, the fee-for-service system is likely to persist, because the actuarial resources required to assume risk will not be operative. Small community hospitals, previously the bulwark of philanthropy in towns, are being swallowed by the conglomerates or forced out of business.

There is some possibility that the HIPCs envisioned in the failed Clinton health reform package will find a home in the less densely populated parts of the country. To be competitive, the HIPCs will have to be subsidized, either by the government or by a consortium of payers, in a system somewhat akin to the risk pools in states where automobile insurance is mandatory. Business alliances and small-employer pools may allow rural areas to participate in managed care savings without crippling the delivery system.

HMOs are at risk as a result of their increasing visibility. Regulation of the industry is increasing, with many states proposing patient protection legislation, physician protections limiting the HMOs' ability to deselect, and increased financial security provisions. In a similar vein, continued pressure on prices will drive the HMOs to their limit in squeezing concessions from providers.

There will continue to be mergers among insurance companies and HMOs, and among health plans and payers. The large pharmaceutical companies have acquired or merged with distributors to ensure sales channels for their products, although the divestiture of Medco by Merck, announced as this chapter is being written, may be a harbinger of the ultimate divorce of managed pharmacy benefits and manufacturing. Tying distribution of supplies and drugs to disease management does seem to be a viable long-term strategy.

The varieties of risk sharing are proliferating, so traditional lock-in capitation will not be the only risk-sharing vehicle. Lock-in capitation is too restrictive for both consumers and providers, and there is a backlash. Lock-in capitation may, however, continue to be the risk-sharing vehicle for care of the Medicaid population and the indigent.

Q 14:24 What strategies might be used to reform basic health benefits?

Basic health benefits are a core of services covered under any health plan. Strategies focused on reform of basic benefits can take two main paths.

In one, a broad menu of benefits can be provided, but with a very high deductible under this arrangement, basic services are essentially fee for service and insurance is used for catastrophic coverage. Although this strategy has historical appeal (remember major medical), it is unlikely, after the battering Congress took on catastrophic coverage for Medicare, that it will form the cornerstone of health care reform. Medical savings accounts, or medical IRAs, have been incorporated into recently enacted federal legislation as a pilot project and have a great deal of support from conservative legislators and indemnity payers. The evidence for the success of medical savings accounts is not yet in.

Thse second strategy is to broaden the availability of high-volume, low-cost benefits that have been proved to be effective. These include immunizations for children, breast cancer screening and Pap smears for women, and colon cancer screening for all at risk.

The major problems for reform of basic benefits are likely to be mental health care, prescription drugs, and long-term care.

Q 14:25 What new technologies can be expected to influence the cost of health care in the near future?

Because major breakthroughs in medicine can arise from the most obscure discovery, it is a bit risky to foretell trends in medicine and medical care delivery. The following emerging technologies, however, are likely to prove groundbreaking:

Gene Therapy. This technology relies on the ability to insert genes into human chromosomes to replace or repair defective genetic material that is causing disease. Illnesses amenable to gene therapy range from rare inborn errors of metabolism such as Tay-Sachs disease in children to common conditions such as diabetes and certain malignancies. Clinical trials of some of this technology is under way, and there is intense interest in this research from both the academic and business communities. The completion of the human genome project will contribute to the knowledge necessary to advance gene therapy. Gene therapy can be expected to be effective, widespread, and fabulously expensive. Of interest is the competition that has emerged between the government-sponsored Human Genome Project and a commercial rival largely funded by Perkin-Elmer Corp., a maker of scientific instruments. This competition is a tribute to the ultimate market of gene therapy.

Immunotherapy. Elucidation of the mechanisms of inflammation will have a major impact on the treatment of a wide variety of illnesses, including asthma, arthritis, and malignancies.

Joint Replacement Therapy. Advances in materials and surgical techniques will allow the replacement of joints with greater facility and fewer complications.

Organ Transplants. Advances in immunomodulation, surgical techniques, and organ preservation will allow the transplantation of more organs to replace diseased and worn-out organs. Even metabolic illnesses such as diabetes and Parkinson's disease can be expected to be treated successfully with organ and tissue transplantation.

Imaging. Radiologic and other techniques continue to advance in sophistication. As they do, exploratory surgery can be expected to continue to decline, because noninvasive techniques that allow physicians to examine specific organs and metabolic processes will be available.

Minimally Invasive Surgery. Advances in surgical and anesthesia techniques will allow the continued advancement of laparoscopic surgery. This technique can be expected to advance in the exploration of the abdomen, pelvis, sinuses, and joints, and eventually the chest and the brain. The result will be a decrease in complications, length of hospital stay, and costs.

Prenatal Diagnosis. Advances in diagnosis of genetic and metabolic abnormalities in the fetus continue. Advances in the field are beginning to allow detection of the same abnormalities from maternal blood without invading the uterus or the fetus. Early detection of abnormalities can be expected to allow in utero therapy.

Novel Cancer Therapies. Combinations of the preceding modalities can be expected to influence cancer treatment, particularly in cancer centers of excellence.

Molecular Medicine. The field of targeted intervention such as receptor-specific drugs can be expected to burgeon, adding specificity and accuracy to therapy. Receptor-specific drugs have emerged in psychiatry with the selective serotonin reuptake inhibitors, such as Prozac, and the so-called designer estrogens, such as raloxifene (Evista).

Women's Health. There is increasing recognition of the unique health care needs of women and the unique biologic responsivity of women. Women traditionally make over three quarters of the health care purchasing decisions for the family, and thus commercial health care providers have a great interest in satisfying this population.

Prosthetics. Reintroduction of the totally implantable artificial heart and sophistication in insulin pumps are laying the groundwork for organ and function-specific substitution.

References

1. E. Ginzberg and M. Ostow, "Managed Care: A Look Back and a Look Ahead," *New Eng. J. Med.,* 336:1018–1020, 1997.

2. D.E. Altman and L. Levitt, "The Sad History of Health Care Cost Containment As Told in One Chart," *Health Affairs,* Jan. 23, 2002.

3. VHA, Inc. and Deloitte & Touche, LLP, *Environmental Assessment, Redesigning Health Care for the Millenium, An Assessment of the Health Care Environment in the United States* (1997).

4. N.M. Kane, *Nonprofit Hospital Status: What Is It Worth?* (Boston: Harvard School of Public Health, 1994).

5. J. Calmes, "Images of Industry Players Shape Debates Nation-wide," *W.S.J. Interactive Edition,* June 25, 1998.

6. MMS Physician Practice Environment Index Report—July 2001, Health Policy, Massachusetts Medical Society, July 23, 2001.

Glossary

For the convenience of the reader, commonly used acronyms are defined in the "Acronyms" section, then further defined in the "Terms" section.

Acronyms

AAHC: Association of Academic Health Centers

AAHP: American Association of Health Plans

AAMC: Association of American Medical Colleges

AAPCC: Adjusted Average Per Capita Cost (Medicare)

AARP: American Association of Retired Persons

ABMS: American Board of Medical Specialties

ACE: Accelerated-Compensation Event

ACG: Ambulatory Care Group

ASC: Administrative Services Contract

ADA: Americans with Disabilities Act

ADL: Activity of Daily Living

ADR: Alternative Dispute Resolution

AFDC: Aid to Families with Dependent Children *(see TANF)*

AFDS: Alternative Financing and Delivery System

AHA: American Hospital Association

AHCPR: Agency for Health Care Policy Research (now known as the Agency for Healthcare Research and Quality (AHRQ))

AHP: Accountable Health Plan

AHPB: Adjusted Historical Payment Basis

AHRQ: Agency for Healthcare Research and Quality

ALOS: Average Length of Stay

AMA: American Medical Association

AMC: Academic Medical Center

APR: Average Payment Rate

ASC: Ambulatory Surgery Center

BBA: Balanced Budget Act

Ca: Cancer

CABG: Coronary Artery Bypass Graft

CAGR: Cumulative Annual Growth Rate

CalPERS: California Public Employees Retirement System

CAT (scan): Computerized Axial Tomography

CHAMPUS: Civilian Health and Medical Program of the United States

CHIN: Community Health Information Network

CISN: Community Integrated Service Network

CLEAR: Consolidated Licensure for Entities Assuming Risk

CLIA: Clinical Laboratory Improvement Act

CM: Case Management

CMI: Case-Mix Index

CMP: Competitive Medical Plan

CMS: Centers for Medicare and Medicaid Services (formerly Health Care Financing Administration (HCFA))

CMSA: Consolidated Metropolitan Statistical Area

COBRA: Consolidated Omnibus Budget Reconciliation Act

CON: Certificate of Need

CPEP: Clinical Practice Expert Panel

CPI-U: Consumer Price Index for Urban Consumers

CPS: Current Population Survey

CPT-4: Current Procedural Terminology, 4th edition

CT: Computerized Tomography (the same as CAT scan)

CY: Calendar Year

DCG: Diagnostic Cost Group

DHHS: Department of Health and Human Services

DOD: U.S. Department of Defense

DOJ: U.S. Department of Justice

DRG: Diagnosis-Related Group

DSH: Disproportionate Share Hospital

DUR: Drug Utilization Review

EBRI: Employee Benefit Research Institute

EC: Emergency Center

ECI: Employee Cost Index

ED: Emergency Department

E/M: Evaluation and Management

EMR: Electronic Medical Record

EMT: Emergency Medicine Technician

ENT: Ear, Nose, Throat (Otorhinolaryngology)

EOB: Explanation of Benefits

EPSDT: Early and Periodic Screening, Diagnosis, and Treatment

ER: Emergency Room

ERISA: Employee Retirement Income Security Act of 1974

ESRD: End-Stage Renal Disease

FAS: Financial Accounting Standard

FCA: Fraudulent Claims Act

FDA: Food and Drug Administration

FEHBP: Federal Employees Health Benefits Program

FFS: Fee for Service

FNP: Family Nurse Practitioner

FP: Family Practitioner

FPL: Federal Poverty Level

FY: Fiscal Year

GAF: Geographic Adjustment Factor

GAO: General Accounting Office

GDP: Gross Domestic Product

GI: Gastrointestinal

GPCI: Geographic Practice Cost Index

GPWW: Group Practice Without Walls

H&P: History and Physical Examination

HCC: Hierarchical Coexisting Conditions

HCFA: Health Care Financing Administration (now known as Centers for Medicare and Medicaid Services (CMS))

HCQIA: Health Care Quality Improvement Act

HEDIS: Health Plan Employer Data and Information Set

HER: Health Economics Research, Inc.

HI: Hospital Insurance

HIAA: Health Insurance Association of America

HIPAA: Health Insurance Portability and Accountability Act

HIV: Human Immunodeficiency Virus

HMO: Health Maintenance Organization

HPSA: Health Professional Shortage Area

IBNR: Incurred But Not Reported

ICD-9-CM: International Classification of Diseases, Ninth Revision, Clinical Modification

ICF: Intermediate Care Facility

ICU: Intensive Care Unit

IDN: Integrated Delivery Network

IDS: Integrated Delivery System

IMG: International Medical Graduate

IOM: Institute of Medicine of the National Academy of Science

IPA: Independent Practice Association

IRS: Internal Revenue Service

ISN: Integrated Service Network

JCAHO: Joint Commission on the Accreditation of Healthcare Organizations

LOS: Length of Stay

M + C: Medicare + Choice

MCBS: Medicare Current Beneficiary Survey

MCO: Managed Care Organization

MedPAR: Medicare Provider Analysis and Review

MEI: Medicare Economic Index

MGCRB: Medicare Geographic Classification Review Board

MIG: Medicare Insured Group

MOB: Medical Office Building or Maintenance of Benefits

MPCC: Medicare Per Capita Cost

MPR: Mathematica Policy Research, Inc.

MRI: Magnetic Resonance Image

MSA: Medical Savings Account or Metropolitan Statistical Area

MSO: Medical Service Organization

MTS: Medicare Transaction System

NASHP: National Academy for State Health Policy

NCHS: National Center for Health Statistics

NCI: National Cancer Institute

NCQA: National Committee for Quality Assurance

NHIS: National Health Interview Survey

NIH: National Institutes of Health, DHHS

NMES: National Medical Expenditure Survey

NP: Nurse Practitioner

NPDB: National Practitioner Data Bank

OBG, OB-GYN: Obstetrics/Gynecology

OBRA: Omnibus Budget Reconciliation Act

ODS: Organized Delivery System

OIG: Office of the Inspector General

OMB: Office of Management and Budget

OPHC: Office of Prepaid Health Care

OPM: Office of Personnel Management

OR: Operating Room

OSHA: Occupational Safety and Health Act

PA: Physician Assistant

PACE: Program of All-Inclusive Care for the Elderly

PAR: Preadmission Review

PCCM: Primary Care Case Management

PCP: Primary Care Provider

PHO: Physician-Hospital Organization

PHP: Prepaid Health Plan

PMPM: Per Member Per Month

PMPY: Per Member Per Year

PMSA: Primary Metropolitan Statistical Area

POS: Point of Service

PPMC: Physician Practice Management Corporation

PPO: Preferred Provider Organization

PPRC: Physician Payment Review Commission

PPS: Prospective Payment System

ProPAC: Prospective Payment Assessment Commission

PSN: Provider-Sponsored Network

PSO: Provider-Sponsored Organization

PTCA: Percutaneous Transluminal Coronary Angioplasty

QDWI: Qualified Disabled and Working Individual

QI: Quality Improvement

QIO: Quality Improvement Organization

QM: Quality Management

QMB: Qualified Medicare Beneficiary

RAPs: Radiologists, Anesthesiologists, and Pathologists

RBRVS: Resource-Based Relative Value Scale

R&C: Reasonable and Customary Charge

RTI: Research Triangle Institute

RUC: RVS Update Committee

RVS: Relative Value Scale

RVU: Relative Value Unit

SAF: Standard Analytical Files (Medicare)

SLMB: Specified Low-Income Medicare Beneficiary

SMI: Supplementary Medical Insurance

SNF: Skilled Nursing Facility

SSA: Social Security Administration

SSI: Supplemental Security Income

TANF: Temporary Assistance for Needy Families (formerly AFDC)

TEFRA: Tax Equity and Fiscal Responsibility Act

TPA: Third-Party Administrator

TQM: Total Quality Management

TURP: Transurethral Resection of the Prostate

UB-92: Uniform Billing Code of 1992

UCR: Usual, Customary, and Reasonable

UM: Utilization Management

UR: Utilization Review

USPCC: United States Per Capita Cost

VA: Department of Veterans Affairs

Terms

Academic Medical Center: A group of related institutions including a teaching hospital or hospitals, a medical school and its affiliated faculty practice plan, and other health professional schools.

Accelerated-Compensation Event (ACE): A medically caused injury determined by experts to be normally avoidable if patients are given good care. Under a proposed alternative standard of liability for medical malpractice, a patient would receive compensation if an ACE occurred, without a determination of whether fault or negligence was involved in that particular case.

Access: The ability to obtain needed health care services.

Accountable Health Plan (AHP): An organization proposed under various health care reform proposals that combines health insurance and caregiving functions; it would function much like an HMO but could also be a more loosely organized network.

Activity of Daily Living (ADL): Activities such as bathing, dressing, and toileting that are needed for self-care. ADLs are measured to evaluate the continued feasibility of self-care.

Adjusted Average Per Capita Cost (AAPCC): The CMS's best estimate of the amount of money it costs to care for Medicare recipients under fee-for-service Medicare in a specific geographic region. *See also* Average Payment Rate.

Adjusted Community Rate (ACR): A rate-setting methodology used by managed care plans to set rates based on expected use of health care services by a group; includes the normal profit of a for-profit HMO or CMP; may be equal to or lower than the APR, but can never exceed it.

Adjusted Historical Payment Basis (AHPB): The average payment for a service in a locality in a given year.

Administrative Services Contract (ASC): A contract between an insurance company and a self-funded plan under which the insurance company performs administrative services only and does not assume any risk; services usually include claims processing, but may include other services such as actuarial analysis, and utilization review, also called administrative services only (ASO) contract.

Adverse Selection: Adverse selection occurs when a larger proportion of persons with poorer health status enroll in specific plans or insurance options, while a larger proportion of persons with better health status enroll in other plans or insurance options. Plans with a subpopulation with higher than average costs are adversely selected. Plans with a subpopulation with lower than average costs are favorably selected.

Age Discrimination in Employment Act of 1967 (ADEA): As amended in 1978, requires employer with 20 or more employees to offer active employees over age 40 (and their spouses) the same health insurance coverage that is provided to younger employees.

Agency for Health Care Research and Quality (AHCRQ): An agency of the U.S. Public Health Service, Department of Health and Human Services, that conducts scientific research, assesses health care technologies, and supports clinical practice guideline development.

Aid to Families with Dependent Children (AFDC): A program established by the Social Security Act of 1935 and eliminated by welfare reform legislation in 1996. AFDC provided cash payments to needy children (and their caretakers) who lacked support because at least one parent was unavailable. Families had to meet income and resource criteria specified by the state to be eligible. AFDC has been replaced by a new block grant program, but AFDC standards are retained for use in Medicaid. *See* TANF.

Allowed Charge: The amount Medicare approves for payment to a physician. Typically, Medicare pays 80 percent of the allowed charge, and the beneficiary pays the remaining 20 percent. The allowed charge for a nonparticipating physician is 95 percent of that for a participating physician. Nonparticipating physicians may bill beneficiaries for an additional amount above the allowed charge.

Alternative Delivery Systems (ADS): Nontraditional methods of providing health care services such as ambulatory surgery and transitional care.

Alternative Dispute Resolution (ADR): Methods of resolving disputes, claims, and disagreements other than by the traditional method of a lawsuit.

Ambulatory Patient Group (APG): A modification of an ambulatory visit group, developed as an outpatient classification scheme for CMS. The reimbursement methodology for outpatient procedures provides for a fixed reimbursement to an institution for outpatient procedures or visits, incorporates data regarding the reason for the visit and patient data, and prevents unbundling of ancillary services.

Ambulatory Surgery Center (ASC): Setting for surgery of an uncomplicated nature that has traditionally been done in the more expensive inpatient setting but that can be done with equal efficiency without hospital admission. Centers may be hospital based or hospital sponsored or independently owned in competition with hospitals; also called same-day surgery center.

American Association of Health Plans (AAHP): A trade association serving nearly 1,000 HMOs, PPOs, and other managed care organizations representing nearly 100 million enrollees, created with the merger of the Group Health Association of America, Inc. and the American Managed Care and Review Association.

American Association of Physician-Hospital Organizations (AAPHO): A resource of PHOs, established in 1993 (P.O. Box 4913, Glen Allen, VA 23058-4913).

American Association of Preferred Provider Organizations (AAPPO): A trade association of preferred provider organizations (1101 Connecticut Avenue, Suite 700, Washington, D.C. 20036).

American Managed Care and Review Association (AMCRA): A national trade association of managed care organizations such as HMOs, PPOs, IPAs, and UROs (1227 25th St., N.W., Suite 610, Washington, D.C. 20037).

American Medical Peer Review Association (AMPRA): A national trade association representing federally designated PROs (810 First St., N.E., Suite 410, Washington, D.C. 20002).

Americans with Disabilities Act (ADA): A federal law enacted in 1990 that prohibits discrimination against persons with disabilities in such areas as public accommodations and terms and conditions of employment.

Ancillary Outpatient: Services to support diagnostic workup of the patient or supplemental services needed as part of providing other care; includes anesthesia, laboratory, radiology, or pharmacy, but not room, board, medical, or nursing services.

Any Willing Provider Laws: State laws that challenge and establish policy governing managed care organizations. They require the granting of network enrollment to any provider who is willing to join, as long as it meets provisions outlined in the plan. The central issue is the fairness of physician deselection by a plan, and, conversely, the plan's ability to reduce medical costs by eliminating overusing physicians.

Assignment (Medicare): A process under which Medicare pays its share of the allowed charge directly to the physician or supplier. Medicare will do this only if the physician accepts Medicare's allowed charge as payment in full (guarantees not to balance bill). Medicare provides other incentives to physicians who accept assignment for all patients under the Participating Physician and Supplier Program.

Average Length of Stay (ALOS): The average number of patient days of hospitalization for each admission, expressed as an average of the population within the plan for a given period of time.

Average Payment Rate (APR): The amount of money that the CMS could conceivably pay an HMO or CMP for services to Medicare recipients under a risk contract. The figure is derived from the AAPCC for the service area, adjusted for the enrollment characteristics the plan would expect to have. The payment to the plan, the ACR, can never be higher than the APR but may be less.

Balance Billing: In Medicare and private fee-for-service health insurance, the practice of billing patients in excess of the amount approved by the health plan. In Medicare, a balance bill cannot exceed 15 percent of the allowed charge for nonparticipating physicians.

Behavioral Offset: *See* Volume Offset.

Beneficiary: Someone who is eligible for or receiving benefits under an insurance policy or plan. The term is commonly applied to people receiving benefits under the Medicare or Medicaid programs.

Benefit Package: Services covered by a health insurance plan and the financial terms of such coverage, including cost sharing and limitations on amounts of services.

Block Grant: Federal funds provided to the states as a nucleus of support for Medicaid payments by the state to its beneficiaries.

Blue Cross/Blue Shield: An umbrella term for independent Blue Cross/Blue Shield health plans across the country, also called "The Blues."

Board Certified: A term applied to a physician or other health professional who has passed an examination from a recognized medical specialty board and is thereby certified to provide care within that specialty.

Bonus Payment: An additional amount paid by Medicare for services provided by physicians in health professional shortage areas. Currently, the bonus payment is 10 percent of the Medicare share of allowed charges.

Budget Neutrality: For the Medicare program, adjustment of payment rates when policies change so that total spending under the new rules is expected to be the same as it would have been under the previous payment rules.

Bundled Payment: A single, comprehensive payment for a group of related services.

Buy-In: Refers to the arrangements states make for paying Medicare premiums on behalf of those they are required or choose to cover.

Capitation (CAP): A payment arrangement on a per member basis for a given number of patients under a provider's care; a set amount of money received or paid out, based on a prepaid agreement rather than on actual cost of separate episodes of care and services delivered, usually expressed in units of PMPM; may be varied by such factors as age, sex, and benefit plan of the enrolled member.

Carrier: A private contractor that administers claims processing and payment for Medicare Part B services.

Carve-Out: A category of health care not covered as a benefit under the contract; usually an area of high cost or requiring special expertise, such as behavioral, subacute, podiatry, chiropractic, x-ray, and transplants, that is not subject to discretionary utilization and not included within the capitation rate.

Case Management (CM): The control of health care services, including either medical or ancillary health care resources, for efficiency and medical appropriateness for enrolled members; designed to achieve the optimal patient outcome in the most cost-effective manner.

Case Manager: A nurse, doctor, or social worker who works with patients, providers, and insurers to coordinate all services to provide a patient with medically necessary and appropriate care.

Case Mix: The frequency and intensity of hospital admissions or services reflecting different needs and uses of hospital resources; can be measured based on patients' diagnoses or the severity of their illnesses, the utilization of services, and the characteristics of a hospital; influences ALOS, cost, and scope of services provided by a hospital.

Case Rate: Reimbursement model used by hospitals to establish a flat rate per admission based on an assumed ALOS per admission; the HMO is charged this rate for each member admitted; unique rates may be set or grouped by diagnosis type or categories of medical-surgical, obstetrical, critical care, cardiac, and so on; other elements may include sliding scale volume, ALOS by type, volume of ancillary per patient, and contribution margin.

Categorically Needy (CN): Aged, blind, or disabled persons or families and children under established financial thresholds of eligibility for AFDC, SSI, or an optional state supplement.

Center of Excellence: Health care institution that has been credentialed and through clinical expertise and capital equipment improvements has proven its ability to provide a major resource-intensive procedure such as an organ or bone marrow transplant, open heart surgery, high-risk obstetrics, or neonatal intensive care in a more effective and efficient manner than possible anywhere else within a specific geographic region; centers of excellence are listed in the Federal Register.

Center for Medicare and Medicaid Services (CMS): The federal agency responsible for administering Medicare and overseeing states' administration of Medicaid; manages HMO qualification and other utilization and quality review programs. Until 2001, known as Health Care Financing Administration (HCFA).

Certificate of Authority (COA): The state-issued operating license for an HMO.

Certificate of Coverage (COC): A document provided to covered employees by the insurance carrier or managed care plan that outlines the benefits, covered services, and principal provisions of the group health plan provided under contract by the insurer or managed care organization.

Certificate of Need (CON): The requirement that a health care organization obtain permission from an oversight agency before making changes (federally qualified HMOs are exempt).

Chemical Dependency Services: Services in support of patients who are addicted to various chemicals, drugs, or alcohol, as classified by the U.S. Department of Health and Human Services.

Civilian Health and Medical Program of the United States (CHAMPUS): A health benefit program that provides coverage for armed forces personnel receiving care outside a military treatment facility.

Claims Services Only (CSO): A contract designed for fully self-insured employers that need little administrative assistance. Under a CSO arrangement, the insurer administers only the claims portion of the plan. *See also* Administrative Services Contract.

Clinic Without Walls: A centralized business operation serving medical groups in a network while the delivery of care remains decentralized, usually involving professional management services, group purchasing and support systems, centralized billing and accounting, a uniform fee schedule, and the employment of all nonphysician staff.

Closed Panel: A managed care plan that contracts with physicians on an exclusive basis for services and does not allow those physicians to see patients for another managed care organization (e.g., staff- and group-model HMOs or a large private medical group that contracts with an HMO); a physician must normally meet strict criteria to join the closed panel of a plan's providers.

Closed PHO: A closed physician-hospital organization limited to providers that have expertise in managing utilization and are continually approved as meeting certain standards; similar governance to open PHO but more attractive to payers because of demonstrated cost reductions; increased feedbacks to providers of personal and peer practice utilization. This model does not contain the more advanced incentives of equity sharing from venture profits.

CMS 1500: A standardized claim form developed by the CMS and used by providers to bill health carriers.

Coding: A mechanism for identifying and defining providers' services.

Coinsurance: A type of cost sharing in which the insured party and insurer share payment of the approved charge for covered services in a specified ratio after payment of the deductible by the insured. Under Medicare Part B, the insured pays coinsurance of 20 percent of allowed charges.

Community Health Information Network (CHIN): A system that electronically links providers, payers, employers, and consumers in communities to improve health care quality and promote community wellness.

Community Health Purchasing Alliance (CHPA): A purchaser of health care benefits on behalf of employer groups.

Community Rating: The method of establishing a premium level that does not take into account the actual claims experience of a group (as in experience rating), but predicts the utilization of the entire community; required it for any federally qualified HMO; many states require it for HMOs or even for some indemnity plans.

Community Rating by Class: A form of community rating in which separate groups of enrollees can have different actuarial premium rates depending on the age, sex, marital status, and industry component; not equivalent to experience rating because no actual cost experience is used for the specific group of patients under review.

Competitive Bidding: A pricing method that elicits information on costs through a bidding process to establish payment rates that reflect the costs of an efficient health plan or health care provider.

Competitive Medical Plan (CMP): A federal designation that allows a health plan to obtain eligibility to receive a Medicare risk contract without having to obtain qualification as an HMO; requirements for eligibility are somewhat less restrictive than those for an HMO.

Concurrent Review: A screening assessment of hospital admissions at the time they occur, performed by a professional managed care support staff during a patient's hospitalization, either by telephone or through a representative's visit to the hospital location; this review ensures that utilization is appropriate.

Consolidated Omnibus Budget Reconciliation Act (COBRA): A federal law that, among other things, requires employers to offer continued health insurance coverage for a certain length of time to certain employees and their beneficiaries whose group health insurance coverage has been terminated.

Continuing Care Retirement Community (CCRC): A community that, in exchange for an entrance fee and a monthly charge, guarantees lifetime housing and nursing care as required.

Continuum of Care: A spectrum of health care options ranging from limited care needs through tertiary care to provide the appropriate expertise for the patient without providing a more expensive setting than necessary; an integrated delivery network can take full advantage of the continuum by ensuring good communication throughout the patient episode and by using step-down, long-term care, rehabilitation, subacute, or assisted living center features as soon as they become an option over more costly hospitalization choices.

Contractual Allowance: A bookkeeping adjustment to reflect the difference between established charges for services rendered to insured persons and rates payable for those services under contracts with third-party payers (similar to a trade discount).

Conversion Factor: The dollar amount of one unit of service rendered; used to convert various medical procedures into an established fee-schedule payment structure in which the conversion factor times the relative value unit equals the payment amount.

Conversion Factor Update: Annual percentage change to the conversion factor. For Medicare, the update is either established by Congress or set by a formula to reflect whether actual expenditure growth from two years earlier fell below or above the target rate.

Coordination of Benefits (COB): A cost-control mechanism used by most insurers and managed care plans to avoid duplication of benefits.

Copayment: A type of cost sharing under which the insured party is responsible for paying a fixed dollar amount per service. Sometimes used more generally as a synonym for cost sharing.

Cost Compression: A marketplace factor in which the amounts of revenue or premium are reduced (perhaps quite quickly) as managed care practices begin to occur; cost compression occurs as a result of pricing, utilization, and premiums.

Cost HMO: One of the three distinct types of managed care contracts with the CMS; paid by Medicare and receives a predetermined monthly amount per beneficiary based on a total estimated budget, with adjustments at year-end for any variations from the budget; does not lock Medicare enrollees into their networks but is structured like a POS program. Medicare will pay its share for nonplan providers (after the member's coinsurance and annual deductible, as in the traditional FFS system), but the cost HMO will not pay anything.

Cost Sharing: A health insurance policy provision that requires the insured party to pay a portion of the costs of covered services. Deductibles, coinsurance, copayment, and balance bills are types of cost sharing.

Cost Shifting: Practice whereby a health care provider charges certain patients or third-party payers more for services in order to subsidize service provided below cost or free to the poor or uninsured.

Covered Lives: The number of persons who are enrolled within a particular health plan or enrolled for coverage by a provider network, including covered dependents.

Covered Services: The services specified in a managed care contract; specific services and supplies for which Medicaid will provide reimbursement; a combination of mandatory and optional services within each state.

CPT-4 (Current Procedural Terminology, 4th edition): Unique sets of five-digit codes established by the AMA that apply to the medical service or procedure performed by providers and used as a standard in the industry; used for billing purposes.

Credentialing: The review process by a hospital or insurer to approve a provider; careful review of documents, medical license, evidence of malpractice insurance (if the insurance is needed or not provided by the supporting hospital or HMO by agreement); history involving actual or alleged malpractice; and educational background of professional providers; may apply to those seeking candidacy on care panels.

Customary, Prevailing, and Reasonable (CPR): Medicare's method of determining approved charges for a Part B service from a specific physician or supplier.

Days Per Thousand: The number of hospital days used in a year for each 1,000 covered lives, derived by first taking the number of bed-days divided by member months, then multiplying by each 1,000 members and by the number of months under consideration; also called bed-days per 1,000.

Deductible: The minimum threshold payment that must be made by an enrollee each year before the plan begins to make payments on a shared or total basis; the amount of loss the plan must sustain for each member in each contract year for each category of coverage before any benefits become payable under the agreement. For example, if an enrollee has a $100 annual deductible, no payment assistance comes from the plan until at least a total of $101 in eligible claims are processed within the calendar or contract year. Plans will typically reduce the deductible if they wish to create an added incentive for patients to enroll, or will use reduced deductibles to get reluctant patients to try some form of managed care.

Defined Benefits Coverage: An approach to providing health benefits whereby employers and other purchasers promise coverage for a specific package of health benefits.

Defined Contribution Coverage: A funding mechanism for health benefits whereby employers make a specific dollar contribution toward the cost of insurance coverage for employees.

Demand Management: Strategies designed to ensure patient care quality while reducing traditional demand on a primary care physician, such as workplace health promotion or wellness programs, lifestyle management (behavioral changes that avoid or reduce health risks), self-management of minor acute conditions, or self-help to manage chronic conditions. Support systems for demand management include telephone hotlines, trained nurse counselors, and educational and psychosocial support for informed choice.

Dental Carve-Out: A carve-out segment of the PMPM or contract pricing that may require that oral surgeons be participating providers if oral surgery is included as a benefit.

Dental Maintenance Organization (DMO): Type of managed dental care plan that provides comprehensive dental services to enrollees for a fixed per capita fee; similar to an HMO; uses a closed panel of dentists.

Dental Service Corporation (DSC): A nonprofit organization that underwrites or administers contracts for managed dental care plans.

Deselection: A process by which an HMO removes a physician from its panel of providers.

Diagnosis-Related Groups (DRGs): A system of classification used by Medicare and many other health care plans for inpatient hospital services based on principal diagnosis, secondary diagnosis, surgical procedures, age, sex, and presence of complications. This system of classification is used as a financing mechanism to reimburse hospitals and selected other providers for services rendered.

Direct Contracting: The practice of providing care under a direct agreement between employers or business coalitions and providers, with no HMO or PPO intermediary. Normally, hospitals offer price discounts and employers agree to limit the number of providers while creating incentives for employees to use in-network providers.

Disability: Physical or mental condition that makes an insured person incapable of performing one or more occupational duties temporarily, long term, or permanently.

Discounted Fee for Service (DFFS): A payment method that is calculated as a certain percentage of discount from fee-for-service charges; among the least risky contracting approaches, second only to billed charges; may include a sliding scale tied to volume, with varying discounts by product line; similar to full FFS except that the HMO agrees to pay billed hospital charges or outpatient services, minus a fixed percentage that is based on the efficiencies of guaranteed payments.

Disenrollment: The termination of coverage. Normally, voluntary disenrollment is not allowed until the patient has remained in the plan for at least 6 to 12 months; a patient can be involuntarily disenrolled because of a change in employment.

Disproportionate Share Hospital (DSH): Hospitals where persons covered by Medicaid or without any health insurance make up a large proportion of all patients served. Federal law authorizes special payments to these hospitals to help them meet the costs of serving patients not covered by other revenue sources.

Downstream Risk: An arrangement by which an entity (typically, a provider group) accepts risk from another entity (typically, a licensed organization, such as an HMO).

Drug Utilization Review (DUR): Quantitative evaluation of prescription drug use, physician prescribing patterns, and patient drug utilization to determine the appropriateness of drug therapy.

Dual Choice: Employee option of joining an HMO or an indemnity insurance plan as a basic entitlement. The employer must give the HMO marketing opportunities at least equal to those given the current indemnity carrier (dual choice does not apply to CMPs). Employers are not required to offer multiple HMOs of the same type unless the second HMO can prove that it has a unique service area. Title 13 of the Public Health Service Act requires employers of 25 or more persons with employees residing in an HMO's service area to pay minimum wage, to offer their employees health benefits to which they contribute, and to offer dual choice of plans.

Dual Eligible: A beneficiary who is eligible for Medicare and Medicaid.

Due Diligence: A review or investigation by a prospective party to a contract, such as a hospital evaluating a contract with a managed care organization or a physician practice to be acquired, in order to ascertain financial stability, proper legal structure, reputation, adequate supplier-provider relationships, and acceptable reimbursement or equity-sharing strategy for the resulting contract.

Durable Medical Equipment: Equipment that can endure repeated use without being subject to disposal (e.g., insulin pumps, wheelchairs, home hospital beds, walkers, glucometers, motor-driven wheelchairs, oxygen equipment).

Early and Periodic Screening, Diagnosis, and Treatment: A Medicaid-funded program to provide comprehensive care for (some) Medicaid-eligible children.

Electronic Data Interchange (EDI): The computer-to-computer exchange of business or other information between organizations; data may be in either a standardized or proprietary format.

Electronic Medical Record (EMR): An automated online medical record that is available to providers, ancillary service departments, pharmacies, and others involved in patient treatment or care. It stores, processes, and retrieves patient clinical and demographic information; eliminates redundance or illegibility; reduces human error; streamlines data entry; and centralizes management of the patient.

Emergency: Life-endangering bodily injury or sudden and unexpected illness that requires an enrollee to seek immediate medical attention under circumstances that effectively preclude seeking care through a plan physician or a plan medical center; injury or illness requiring immediate care needed to preserve life, limb, eyesight, or bodily tissue, or to preclude unnecessary pain and suffering.

Employee Assistance Program (EAP): Services designed to assist employees, their family members, and employers in finding solutions for workplace and personal problems. Services may include assistance for family or marital concerns, legal or financial problems, elder care, child care, substance abuse, emotional or stress issues, violence in the workplace, sexual harassment, dealing with troubled employees, transition in the workplace, and other events that increase the rate of absenteeism or employee turnover, lower productivity, and affect an employer's financial success or employee relations management. An EAP can provide voluntary or mandatory access to behavioral health benefits through an integrated behavioral health program.

Employee Retirement Income Security Act: A federal law enacted in 1974 that allows self-funded plans to avoid paying premium taxes or comply with state-mandated benefits even when insurance companies and managed care plans must do so. Another provision requires that plans and insurance companies provide an EOB to a member or covered insured in the event of a denial of a claim explaining why a claim was denied and informing the individual of his or her rights of appeal.

Employer Group Health Plan (EGHP): A private employment-originated health plan covering an individual who, due to being 65 or over, has Medicare as a secondary payer.

Encounter: A health care visit of any type that warrants payment of services by an enrollee to a provider of care or services.

Encounter Date: Description of the diagnosis made and services provided when a patient visits a health care provider under a managed-care plan. Encounter data provide much of the same information available on the bills submitted by fee-for-service providers.

End-Stage Renal Disease (ESRD): A variety of conditions ending in kidney failure requiring dialysis or transplantation. Those suffering from ESRD are eligible for Medicare benefits.

Enrollee: A covered member of a health care contract who is eligible to receive contract services.

Enrollment: The number of patients who have contracted with a carrier; the process or activity of recruiting and signing up individuals and groups for membership in a plan; a description of the covered lives in a plan.

Evaluation and Management (E/M) Service: A nonprocedural service, such as a visit or consultation, provided by physicians to diagnose and treat diseases and counsel patients.

Exclusive Provider Organization (EPO): A form of managed care plan, similar to an HMO in that it uses primary care physicians as gatekeepers, often capitates providers, has a limited provider panel, and uses an authorization system, yet is generally regulated under insurance statutes rather than HMO regulations (not allowed in many states that maintain that EPOs are really HMOs).

Expenditure Limits: A mechanism that adjusts payment levels downward if spending levels or growth rates exceed predetermined spending caps.

Expenditure Targets: A mechanism that adjusts payment levels upward or downward depending on whether spending levels or growth rates meet prospectively determined targets or standards. Designed to hold spending to a predetermined budget trajectory.

Experience Rating: A system used by insurers to set premium levels based on the insureds' past claims experience. For example, experience rating may be based on service utilization for health insurance or on liability experience for professional liability insurance.

Explanation of Benefits Statement (EOB): A statement mailed to a member or covered insured explaining how reimbursement was determined, why a claim was or was not paid, and the general appeal process.

Faculty Practice Plan: An organization created to bill, collect, and distribute income from professional fees of medical school faculty.

Failsafe Budget Mechanism: An overall limit on Medicare spending proposed in the Balanced Budget Act passed by Congress in November 1995.

Federal Employees Health Benefits Program (FEHBP): The program that provides health benefits to federal employees. *See* Office of Personnel Management.

Federal Qualifications: Designation rendered by the CMS following a methodical review to determine a plan's preparation of an HMO; includes a review of documentation, contracts that are required for support by individual providers or hospital systems, infrastructure systems and facilities, marketing capabilities, and accountant's evidences of financial security.

Federal Trade Commission (FTC): Federal government agency that reviews mergers and acquisitions of HMOs, hospitals, medical groups, and various levels of health networks and combinations thereof to ensure no infringements of antitrust laws.

Federally Qualified HMO: An HMO that has satisfied certain federal qualifications pertaining to organizational structure, provider contracts, health service delivery information, utilization review and quality assurance, grievance procedures, financial status, and marketing information, as specified in Title XIII of the Public Health Service Act.

Fee for Service (FFS): The full rate of charge for a private patient without any type of insurance arrangement or discounted prospective health plan.

Fee Schedule: A list of predetermined payment rates for medical services.

Fee Schedule Payment Area: A geographic area within which payment for a given service under the Medicare Fee Schedule does not vary.

Fiscal Intermediary: An entity, usually an insurance company, that has a contract with the CMS to determine and make Medicare payments for Part A and certain Part B benefits to hospitals and other providers for services and to perform other related functions.

Five-Year Review: A review of the accuracy of the Medicare RVS that the CMS is required to conduct every five years.

Flexible Benefit Plan: A variety of health plan coverage features offered to employees based on their needs or their ability to pay; decisions regarding which plan is needed may be made at the time of need for service.

Foundation Model: A nonprofit physician-hospital entity for markets that do not allow physicians to be directly employed by a hospital; involves more advanced managed care integration than the GPWW, open PHO, or closed PHO; contains MSO centralized support and physician practice procurement features, but MSO costs are paid by the foundation, not physicians; may allow physicians to share in revenue.

Freedom of Choice: Beneficiary's ability to choose which provider will provide care.

Full-Time Equivalent (FTE): The equivalent of one full-time employee. For example, two part-time employees are one-half FTE each, for a total of one FTE.

Generalists: Physicians who are distinguished by their training as not limiting their practice by health condition or organ system, who provide comprehensive and continuous services, and who make decisions about treatment for patients presenting with undifferentiated symptoms; typically family practitioners, general internists, and general pediatricians.

Generic Equivalents: Drug products not protected by a trademark that have the same active chemical ingredients as those sold under proprietary brand names; also generic drugs.

Geographic Adjustment Factor (GAF): The GAF for each service in a particular payment area is the average of the area's three geographic practice cost indexes weighted by the share of the service's total RVUs accounted for by the work, practice expense, and malpractice expense components of the Medicare Fee Schedule.

Geographic Practice Cost Index (GPCI): An index summarizing the prices of resources required to provide physicians' services in each payment area relative to national average prices. There is a GPCI for each component of the Medicare Fee Schedule: physician work, practice expense, and malpractice expense. The indexes are used to adjust RVUs to determine the correct payment in each fee schedule payment.

Global Capitation: A reimbursement mechanism that pays for all care needs for a population of patients, including physicians and hospitals; may involve payment from an HMO to each primary care physician at risk for a contractually determined PMPM amount that is to pay for the costs of all physician services; may involve payment to a provider network or IDS for all physician and hospital care, with other stated commitments or limitations for pharmacy, mental health, or other carve-outs; a portion of the global capitation payment may be withheld in a reserve fund to pay for specialist care referred by the PCP (excess remaining each year is paid out, or shortages are carried forward against future global capitation payments to the PCP).

Global Fee: A reimbursement mechanism used by a provider for a given episode of care; the single fee for the entire charge of all aspects and services surrounding the episode (e.g., $1,600 for a normal vaginal delivery to include a stated amount of prenatal and postnatal care in addition to the delivery), best used with a large number of covered lives to spread risk.

Global Per Diem: A reimbursement mechanism used by a provider to include all costs of care for a day, fixed regardless of case type.

Graduate Medical Education (GME): The period of medical training that follows graduation from medical school; commonly referred to as internship, residency, and fellowship training.

Gross Domestic Product (GDP): The total current market value of all goods and services produced domestically during a given period; differs from the gross national product by excluding net income that residents earn abroad.

Group Health Association of America, Inc. (GHAA): A trade association for HMOs now part of AAHP.

Group-Model HMO: An HMO model in which the physicians, employed by the HMO, are typically paid on a salary basis or fee schedule and may receive incentive payments based on their performance.

Group Practice: A combined practice of three or more physicians or dentists who may share office personnel, expenses, equipment, space, records, and income.

Group Practice Without Walls (GPWW): An early managed care market structure that allows physicians to retain their separate offices, combining centralized business operations with decentralized delivery of care to preserve traditional autonomy; a group of physicians with varying interests and geographical locations, who may or may not have hospital affiliations as primary care or specialty orientations. GPWWs fail to attract meaningful covered lives.

Guaranteed Issue: The requirement that each insurer and health plan accept everyone who applies for coverage and guarantee the renewal of that coverage as long as the applicant pays the premium.

Guaranteed Renewable: The requirement that each insurer and health plan continue to renew health policies purchased by individuals as long as the person continues to pay the premium for the policy.

Health Benefit Organization (HBO): CMS-contracted entities that are required to provide a package of benefits that essentially matches Medicare's benefits without exceeding current program cost-sharing levels. Under the private health plan option, these HBOs might be contracting with CMS. Under the voucher proposals, beneficiaries could present vouchers worth 95 percent of the adjusted average beneficiary costs in an area to the HBO in return for services.

Health Care Financing Administration (HCFA): *See* Center for Medicare and Medicaid Services (CMS).

Health Care Prepayment Plan (HCPP): A health plan with a Medicare cost contract to provide only Medicare Part B benefits. Some administrative requirements for these plans are less stringent than those for risk contracts or other cost contracts.

Health Care Quality Improvement Act of 1986 (HCQIA): A federal law that affords antitrust immunity for good-faith peer review activities. The reporting requirement to the National Practitioner Data Bank (NPDB) is mandatory for settlements, acts involving licensure, and medical staff actions involving a physician's status.

Health Insurance Portability and Accountability Act (HIPAA): Also known as the Kennedy-Kassebaum Act, HIPAA allows people to carry their health coverage from one employer to another. It also expands the government's efforts to fight health care fraud and abuse.

Health Insurance Purchasing Cooperative or Coalition (HIPC): One of many types of purchasing alliances, begun by California in 1992, without premium capitations or state price controls, designed to spread the risk of small group and individual health care members among a broad representation of purchasers and guarantee insurance to small businesses of 3 to 50 employees by acting as the purchasing agent for consumers under a system of managed competition in negotiating the best plan at the lowest cost from networks of doctors and hospitals or HMOs; proposed as part of the national health care reform in 1992 (many reform proposals surrounding President Clinton's Health Security Act also contained HIPC applications of restrictions for preexisting condition limits, portability, guaranteed renewals for groups, and universal access).

Health Insuring Organization (HIO): Usually an organization that contracts with a state or federal agency to ensure the delivery of services to beneficiaries of a state or federal program such as Medicaid or Medicare. The HIO will contract with health services organizations, either on a discounted fee-for-service or a capitated basis, for the provision of hospital and physician services.

Health Maintenance Organization (HMO): An organization that provides comprehensive medical care for a fixed annual fee. Physicians and other health professionals often are on salary or on contract with the HMO to provide services. Patients are assigned to a primary care doctor or nurse practitioner as a gatekeeper, who decides what health services are needed and when. There are four basic models of HMOs: group model, IPA, network model, and staff model.

Health Plan: An organization that acts as insurer for an enrolled population.

Health Plan Employer Data and Information Set (HEDIS): A core set of performance measures to assist employers and other health purchasers in understanding the value of health care purchases and evaluating health plan performance; used by the NCQA to accredit HMOs.

Health Professional Shortage Area (HPSA): An urban or rural geographic area, a population group, or a public or nonprofit private medical facility that the Secretary of Health and Human Services determines is being served by too few health professionals. Physicians who provide services in HPSAs qualify for the Medicare bonus payment.

Hierarchical Coexisting Conditions (HCC): A risk-adjustment model that groups beneficiaries based on their diagnoses.

High Self-Insured Deductible (HSID): A way for employers to improve cash flow by self-funding the first tier of any employee's health care expenses; also known as shared funding. Employers can thus retain funds that would normally be paid to the insurance company to cover current and future claims.

Highly Compensated Employees (HCEs): As defined by Section 414(q) of the Internal Revenue Code, 5 percent owners, employees who earned more than $90,000 (in 2002), and the top-paid 20 percent of employees. HCEs are not permitted to receive benefits disproportionately larger than other employees under the nondiscrimination rules applicable to employee benefits plans; also called highly compensated individuals and highly compensated participants. The definition of HCEs is revised annually to reflect inflation or cost-of-living increases.

HMO Act: A 1973 federal law outlining requirements for federal qualification of HMOs, including legal and organizational structures, financial strength requirements, marketing provisions, and health care delivery; the voluntary status of "federally qualified" is sought by HMOs to gain credibility with employers and to gain covered lives from dual choice mandates, which require employee access to such plans.

Hold-Harmless Clause: A contractual provision that protects enrollees in the event of a health plan failure by prohibiting health care providers from collecting payment from enrollees for services rendered but not paid for by the plan.

Home Health Agency (HHA): A facility or program licensed, certified, or otherwise authorized pursuant to state and federal laws to provide health care services in the home.

Hospital Insurance (HI): The part of the Medicare program that covers the cost of hospital and related posthospital services. Eligibility is normally based on prior payment of payroll taxes. Beneficiaries are responsible for an initial deductible per episode of illness and copayments for some services. Also called Part A coverage or benefits.

Hospital Market Basket Index: An index of the average annual nationwide change in the prices of goods and services that hospitals purchase to provide each unit of service. Also referred to as an input price index.

Incurred But Not Reported (IBNR): A term to describe the amount of money that the plan should accrue for medical expenses that the authorization system has not captured and for which claims have not yet been submitted. Unexpected IBNR expenses have been the major cause of financial insolvency for many managed care plans and providers.

Indemnity: The insurance protection against injury or loss of health. Although this type of traditional system is now being replaced with other forms of insurance that share risk with providers or employers, indemnity programs still exist to provide reimbursement to the enrolled members for benefits under the contract.

Indemnity Insurance: An insurance plan whereby the insurer reimburses the insured for liability incurred.

Independent Living Program (ILP): A program of housing assistance, job retraining, and other types of assistance to help disabled individuals live as independently as possible.

Independent Practice Association (IPA): A health care model that contracts with an entity, which in turn contracts with physicians, to provide health care services in return for a negotiated fee. Physicians continue in their existing individual or group practices and are compensated on a per capita, fee schedule, or fee-for-service basis.

Indigent: Without insufficient income or savings to pay for adequate medical care without depriving oneself or one's dependents of food, clothing, shelter, or other essentials of living.

Indirect Costs: Costs that cannot be easily traced to particular services but that must be assigned using explicit accounting methods; sometimes referred to as common or overhead costs.

Indirect Medical Education (IME): Part of the payment to academic medical centers for the indirect costs associated with educating residents.

Inpatient: An enrollee in a health plan who is admitted to the hospital for treatment or services.

Institute of Medicine (IOM): An organization of the National Academy of Science often called on by Congress to provide objective opinions on health care issues.

Insured: Any person or organization under a contract or policy for benefits that are received in return for payment.

Integrated Delivery System (IDS): A single organization or a group of affiliated organizations that provide the full range of health care services to a population of enrollees within a market area and that consists of physicians, dispersed clinic settings, hospitals, a referral network, and a full continuum of after-care offerings; may obtain an HMO license and retail health services, or may wholesale the provision of health care services and seek to accept risk within components of the system, such as a physician network or its hospitals, or may obtain global risk agreements with HMOs.

Integration: The construction or reorganization of a health care entity by connecting previously independent segments of the care continuum to emphasize economic interactions between segments for the most appropriate care, services, and use of resources (e.g., subacute versus traditional care).

Intermediate Care Facility (ICF): A preferred, lower-cost setting within the managed care environment for patients who require intermediate care, without hospital or skilled nursing facility capabilities but above the care offered by an assisted living center.

International Classification of Diseases, Ninth Revision, Clinical Modification (ICD-9-CM): A statistical classification system of diagnoses and identifying codes for reporting by physicians to ensure accurate and consistent documentation for claims. The codes are revised periodically by the World Health Organization.

Joint Commission on the Accreditation of Healthcare Organizations (JCAHO): A private, not-for-profit organization that evaluates and accredits hospitals and other health care organizations providing home care, mental health care, ambulatory care, and long-term care services.

Joint Venture (JV): Arrangement involving risk and benefit sharing between one or more entities, whose rights and obligations are specified in contractual terms, for a specific purpose. Examples are a hospital JV with a provider group for 50 percent of the group profits or downside risk, a hospital JV with an HMO for 50 percent exposure to the mutual patient business, or a hospital buying a certain percentage of common shares of an HMO to broaden sharing of business.

Length of Stay (LOS): The number of days that a covered person stayed in an inpatient facility. *See also* Average Length of Stay.

Limited Liability Company or Corporation (LLC): A legal entity that provides for partnership agreements and liability protection of the owners; an excellent way to share risk and equity between hospital systems and physician practices.

Limiting Charge: The maximum amount that a nonparticipating physician is permitted to charge a Medicare beneficiary for a service, in effect, a limit on balance billing. Starting in 1993, the limiting charge has been set at 115 percent of the Medicare-allowed charge.

Long-Term Care (LTC): The segment of the health care continuum that consists of maintenance, custodial, and health services for the chronically ill or disabled; may be provided on an inpatient (rehabilitation facility, nursing home, mental hospital) or outpatient basis, or at home.

Loss: Paid claims and incurred claims plus expenses belonging to the contract year; does not include claim administration expenses or salaries paid to employees of the plan, any amount paid by the plan for punitive, exemplary, extracontractual, or compensatory damages awarded or paid to any member arising out of the handling, investigation, litigation, or settlement of any claim or failure to pay, or delay in payment of, plan benefits, or any statutory penalty imposed on the plan on account of any unfair trade practice or any unfair claim practice, or amounts paid by the plan after the three-month period following the contract year without the express written approval of the reinsurer.

Maintenance of Benefits (MOB): A type of coordination of benefits that limits the total reimbursement from all health plans to a given individual for a program of treatment.

Maintenance of Effort (MOE): A requirement that employers increase benefits or provide refunds to employees with Medicare as their primary insurance to compensate for the reduced wraparound plan costs that resulted from the increased Medicare coverages of the Medicare Catastrophic Coverage Act of 1988.

Major Medical Insurance: Insurance with a high or no maximum limit to cover the costs of major illness, usually with substantial cost sharing for initial liability.

Malpractice Expense: The cost of professional liability insurance incurred by physicians; a component of the Medicare RVS.

Managed Behavioral Care: Mental health or chemical dependency treatment that is screened and monitored for meeting utilization criteria, treatment effectiveness, and/or quality.

Managed Behavioral Healthcare Organization (MBHO): Organization that contracts with a larger entity, typically another managed care organization, for the provision of mental health and substance abuse services to plan enrollees. This arrangement, wherein a portion of the benefit package is administered by a separate subcontracting organization, is known as a carve-out.

Managed Care: Any method of health care delivery designed to reduce unnecessary utilization of services, contain costs, and measure performance while providing accessible, quality, effective health care.

Managed Care Organization (MCO): A generic term for any organization that manages and controls medical service. It includes HMOs, PPOs, CMPs, managed indemnity insurance programs, and managed Blue Cross/Blue Shield programs.

Management Information System (MIS): The common term for the computer hardware and software that provides the support for managing a plan.

Management Service Organization (MSO): A legal entity that offers practice management and administrative support to physicians or that purchases physician practices and obtains payer contracts as a PHO. It can be wholly owned, a for-profit subsidiary of a hospital, a hospital-physician joint venture, or a private joint venture with physicians or with hospitals and physicians. It offers a menu of services through shared practice management (group purchasing discounts, consulting, information newsletters and educational seminars, computer and other information systems, marketing, employee leasing for office coverage, and claims processing), creates economies, and allows physicians to delegate management and administration. An MSO is generally intended to make a profit.

Maximum Allowable Charge or Cost (MAC): The maximum that a vendor may charge for something; often used in pharmacy contracting. A related term, used in conjunction with professional fees, is fee maximum.

Medicaid: A medical program of aid provided by the federal government and administered at the state level to provide benefits according to established criteria for the poor, aged, blind and disabled, and dependent children.

Medi-Cal: The California version of the Medicaid federally aided, state-operated and -administered program that provides medical benefits for certain low-income persons in need.

Medical Care Evaluation (MCE): A component of a quality assurance program that looks at the process of medical care.

Medical Group Management Association (MGMA): An association of large medical groups that collects data from its members for the purpose of benchmarking.

Medical Loss Ratio: A ratio of costs to provide health benefits to revenue from premiums (or total medical expenses of paid claims plus the IBNR component, divided by premium revenue); a common way to describe the efficiency of an HMO.

Medical Savings Account (MSA): The Medicare + Choice proposal that offers a medical savings account (MediSave) option to all seniors. A senior choosing MediSave would get a high-deductible insurance policy along with a cash deposit in an MSA that would cover a significant portion of the deductible. The high-deductible policy would have no copayments, so that seniors would be assured a limit on their out-of-pocket costs. This plan is designed to give a patient incentive to save unnecessary care expenses, yet give him or her control to spend for whatever needs may exist, or to purchase long-term insurance. Now incorporated into the Balanced Budget Act.

Medicare: A national program of health insurance that provides benefits primarily to persons over the age of 65 and others eligible for Social Security benefits; covers the cost of hospitalization, medical care, and some related services. Part A includes inpatient costs, and Part B includes outpatient physician costs. It was created by Title XVIII, Health Insurance for the Aged, in 1965 as an amendment to the Social Security Act. It is operated by the CMS (formerly the HCFA).

Medicare Catastrophic Coverage Act of 1988 (MCCA): A federal law that added significant coverage and substantially increased the cost of Medicare; repealed in 1989.

Medicare Choices: With the establishment of Medicare + Choice as the Medicare managed care option for enrollees, Medicare Choices became Medicare policy in 1998.

Medicare Choices Demonstration: A demonstration project designed to offer flexibility in contracting requirements and payment methods for Medicare managed care programs. Participating plans include PSOs and PPOs.

Medicare Cost Contract: A contract between Medicare and a health plan under which the plan is paid on the basis of reasonable costs to provide some or all Medicare-covered services for enrollees.

Medicare Fee Schedule: The resource-based fee schedule currently used by Medicare to pay for physicians' services.

Medicare Part A: An insurance program that provides basic protection against the costs of hospital and related posthospital services for individuals age 65 or over who are eligible for retirement benefits under the Social Security or the Railroad Retirement System; individuals under age 65 entitled for not less than 24 months to benefits under the Social Security or Railroad Retirement System on the basis of disability; and certain other individuals with end-stage renal disease who are covered by the Social Security or Railroad Retirement System. After various cost-sharing requirements are met, Part A pays for inpatient hospital and home health care. It is financed from a separate trust fund maintained by a payroll tax levied on employers, employees, and the self-employed. Also called hospital insurance program.

Medicare Part B: A voluntary portion of Medicare that covers physician costs within various outpatient or ambulatory settings; also called supplementary Medicare insurance.

Medicare Risk Contract: A contract between Medicare and a health plan under which the plan receives monthly capitated payments to provide Medicare-covered services for enrollees, and thereby assumes insurance risk for those enrollees. A plan is eligible for a risk contract if it is a federally qualified HMO or a competitive medical plan.

Medicare SELECT: A demonstration project that allowed Medigap insurers to experiment with the provision of supplemental benefits through a network of providers. Coverage of supplemental benefits was often limited to services furnished by participating network providers and emergency, out-of-area care. The Medicare + Choice program replaced this program for managed care enrollees in 1998.

Medicare Transaction System (MTS): MTS is an electronic claims processing and information management system under development by the CMS. When implemented it will act as a single, standardized repository of information related to fee-for-service Medicare, Medicare managed care plans, and beneficiaries secondary insurance.

Medigap Insurance: Privately purchased individual or group health insurance policies designed to supplement Medicare coverage. Benefits may include payment of Medicare deductibles, coinsurance, and balance bills, as well as payment for services not covered by Medicare. Medigap insurance must conform to one of ten federally standardized benefit packages.

Mental Health Carve-Out: Specified services for mental health or substance abuse that can be provided more efficiently through either a focused effort or separate entity contract—for example, $1.75 to $2.50 PMPM for annual benefits of 30 inpatient days and 20 visits, with varying copayments and deductibles. They may include UM for preauthorization, concurrent review, retrospective review, discharge planning, and CM.

Messenger Model: Nickname for an early model of physician integration, normally fostered by a supporting hospital entity, to help local physicians move toward more sophisticated managed care. This formation signals nonaffiliated physicians and insurers that capabilities are being enhanced to manage care and accept risk. Typically, membership is both easy to obtain and inexpensive.

Mid-Level Practitioner or Provider: Physician assistants, clinical nurse practitioners, nurse midwives, nutritionists, aides, medical technicians, physical therapists, and other health care professionals who deliver medical care as nonphysicians, generally under the supervision of a physician, but often at less cost. This term is sometimes considered pejorative by practitioners.

Mixed Model: A managed care plan that mixes two or more types of delivery systems, such as an HMO and a closed- and open-panel system; also called a hybrid model.

Modified FFS: A reimbursement mechanism that pays providers on a fee-for-service basis but with certain fee maximums established by procedure; distinct from a discounted FFS in that modified FFS may not always be the same percentage discount from the prevailing FFS. This unit-of-service type arrangement is a typical reimbursement mechanism for many arrangements that are considered to involve managed care but have not yet evolved to global risk.

Most Favored Nation (MFN): A status granted to insurers in contracts between insurers or managed care organizations and providers by stating that any time the provider gives a better price to a second or subsequent insurer or patient, it will notify the first insurer and give the same price reductions.

Multiple Employer Trust (MET): A mechanism that allows small employers in the same or a related industry to provide group insurance to their employees under a trust arrangement. *See also* Multiple Employer Welfare Arrangement.

Multiple Employer Welfare Arrangement (MEWA): An employee welfare benefit plan or other arrangement designed to provide benefits to employees of two or more employers that form an association for the purpose of purchasing group health insurance. *See also* Multiple Employer Trust.

Multispecialty Group Practice: A group of providers in which at least one physician is a family practitioner, internist, or general medical officer, and the others practice other specialties.

National Association of Insurance Commissioners (NAIC): A trade organization of state insurance regulators that has addressed the development of uniform standards in the regulation of insurance (120 W. 12th Street, Suite 1100, Kansas City, MO 64105).

National Claims History System: A CMS data reporting system that combines both Part A and Part B Medicare claims in a common file.

National Committee for Quality Assurance (NCQA): An independent, nonprofit group that accredits HMOs (1350 New York Avenue, Suite 700, Washington, DC 20005).

National Practitioner Data Bank (NPDB): A database on physician discipline or malpractice payment experience; queried by HMOs, private and federal hospitals, and health systems; used for credentialing a provider for clinical privileges or granting status as medical director or medical staff positions; requery of NPDB is required at two-year intervals for reappointment.

Network-Model HMO: An HMO that contracts with several different medical groups, often at a capitated rate. Groups may use different methods to pay their physicians.

Nominal Value: Measurement of an economic amount in terms of current prices.

Nonparticipating Physician: A physician who does not sign a participation agreement and therefore is not obligated to accept assignment on all Medicare claims.

Nonphysician Practitioner (NPP): A health care provider, such as a physician assistant, clinical psychologist, nurse midwife, clinical social worker, certified nurse anesthetist, or nurse practitioner, who can be billed under the Medicare program on a fee-for-service basis.

Occupational Safety and Health Act (OSHA): A federal law that provides national standards for health and safety in a workplace.

Office of Personnel Management (OPM): The federal agency that administers the FEHBP; the agency that a managed care plan contracts with to provide coverage for federal employees.

Open Access: Patient access to providers of specialty care without going through a gatekeeper or primary care provider, as long as the specialist participates in the network.

Open Enrollment Period: The time allowed for subscribers to choose a health plan, either by reenrolling in their existing plan or switching to a competitor's plan. Open enrollment periods last at least 30 days and accept members on a first-come, first-served basis to the limit of the plan's capacity, usually without evidence of insurability or waiting periods. Most managed care plans have half of their membership up for open enrollment in the fall, with an effective date of January 1.

Open PHO: An early-stage managed care physician-hospital model with an open and almost nonrestrictive policy for allowing physicians to join, in an attempt to build a network for payer contracts; commonly featuring joint governance between hospital and physician leadership, varying degree of MSO support and centralization. It has shown weak attraction for covered lives, a lack of physician practice behavior modification, and little long-term loyalty from providers.

Other Weird Arrangement (OWA): Any new and bizarre managed care plan or provider arrangement.

Outcome: An indicator of the effectiveness of health care measures on patients; also called health outcome, or the result of a process of prevention, detection, or treatment.

Outliers: Under Medicare, cases with an extremely long length of stay (day outliers) or extraordinarily high costs (cost outliers) when compared with other cases classified in the same DRG.

Out-of-Area: Any area (where health care services or supplies may be received) outside the HMO's service area and where only emergency services are allowed.

Out-of-Pocket Expenditures: Health-related expenditures for which beneficiaries are financially liable. For Medicare beneficiaries, the total amount includes cost sharing for Medicare-covered services (e.g., deductibles, copayments, and balance bills), cost of Medicare Part B and private health insurance premiums, and cost of noncovered services.

Outpatient: An enrollee who receives treatment or services without being admitted to a hospital.

Packaged Pricing: A reimbursement strategy used by hospitals that offers flat fees on a limited number of case types (which may include category-base pricing) in order to offer employers and insurers preferred pricing on DRGs that the hospital can manage well, without setting a fixed fee for all diagnoses.

Paid Amount: The portion of a submitted charge that is actually paid by both third-party payers and the insured, including copayments and balance bills. For Medicare this amount may be less than the allowed charge if the submitted charge is less, or it may be more because of balance billing.

Par Provider: Short for participating provider.

Partial Capitation: An insurance arrangement whereby the payment made to a health plan is a combination of a capitated premium and payment based on actual use of services. The proportions specified for these components determine the insurance risk faced by the plan.

Partial-Risk Contract: A contract between a purchaser and a health plan in which only part of the financial risk is transferred from the purchaser to the plan.

Participating Physician: A physician who signs a participation agreement, agreeing to accept assignment on all Medicare claims for one year.

Participating Physician and Supplier Program: A program that provides financial and administrative incentives for physicians and suppliers to agree in advance to accept assignment on all Medicare claims for a one-year period.

Participating Provider: An individual provider, hospital, integrated delivery network, pharmacist, dentist, optometrist, chiropractor, podiatrist, nurse, group practice, nursing home, behavioral or mental health entity, skilled nursing facility, long-term care facility, or other medical institution agreeing to provide care or services to enrolled members of a particular plan, according to stated rates and conditions. In most prepayment relationships, including CHAMPUS, the participating provider receives payment directly from the plan, but the patient must pay any cost-share or deductible.

Patient Dumping: The practice of refusing services to uninsured indigent patients or of transferring them to a public hospital or a private, non-profit hospital willing to treat indigents.

Patient Self-Determination Act (PSDA): An act passed in 1990 that became effective in December 1991, which requires most hospitals, nursing homes, and other patient care institutions to ask all admitted patients whether they have made advance directives as to their wishes as to the use of medical interventions for themselves in case of the loss of their own decision-making capacity. The institution is required to furnish each patient with written information about advance directives.

Payment Rate: The total amount paid for each unit of service rendered by a health care provider, including both the amount covered by the insurer and the insured person's cost sharing; sometimes referred to as payment level. Also used to refer to capitation payments to health plans.

Peer Review: An evaluation by a group of unbiased practicing physicians of the effectiveness and efficiency of care rendered under a plan's benefits.

Peer Review Organization (PRO): An entity established by the Tax Equity and Fiscal Responsibility Act of 1982 (TEFRA) to review quality of care and appropriateness of admissions, readmissions, and discharges for Medicare and Medicaid. PROs were held responsible for maintaining and lowering admission rates and reducing LOS while insuring against inadequate treatment. Now called quality improvement organization.

Per Member Per Month (PMPM): Revenue or cost for each enrolled member each month.

Per Member Per Year (PMPY): Revenue or cost for each enrolled member per year.

Performance Measure: A specific measure of how well a health plan does in providing health services to its enrolled population; can be used as a measure of quality. Examples include percentage of diabetics receiving annual referrals for eye care, screening mammography rate, and percentage of enrollees indicating satisfaction with care.

Performance Standard: The target rate of expenditure growth set by the Volume Performance Standard System. *See* Volume Performance Standard.

Physician Payment Review Commission (PPRC): A group created by Congress in 1986 to recommend changes in reimbursement procedures for physicians under Medicare; prepares an annual report to Congress.

Physician Work: A measure of the physician's time, physical effort and skill, mental effort and judgment, and stress associated with providing a medical service. A component of the RBRVS.

Physician-Hospital Organization (PHO): A legal entity formed and owned by one or more hospitals and physician groups to obtain payer contracts and to further mutual interests. Physicians maintain ownership of their practices while agreeing to accept managed care patients under the terms of the PHO agreement; the PHO serves as a negotiating, contracting, and marketing unit.

Plan Age: Refers to the number of full years an HMO has been in operation. The operational date is the date when the HMO first offered prepaid medical services to an enrolled population.

Point of Service (POS): A provision that allows patients in managed care plans that limit choice of doctors and hospitals to seek treatment outside of the plans. Patients who use this option typically are required to pay more.

Point-of-Service (POS) Plan: A plan that provides flexibility for an enrollee to choose to receive a service from a participating or nonparticipating provider, with corresponding benefit or penalty of copayments depending on the level of benefit selected, with the goal of encouraging the use of network or participating provider care options. POS plans maintain the popularity of choice by offering the typical HMO provision, PPO, or combinations of both. In many POS plans, enrollees coordinate their care needs through the PCP. HMOs pay nonparticipating providers at an FFS rate. Also called HMO swing-out plan or out-of-plan rider to an HMO.

Portability: The requirement (enacted by HIPAA) that insurers waive any preexisting-condition exclusion for someone who was previously covered through other insurance as recently as 30 to 90 days earlier.

Practice Expense: The cost of nonphysician resources incurred by the physician to provide services. Examples are salaries and fringe benefits received by the physician's employees, and the expenses associated with the purchase and use of medical equipment and supplies in the physician's office. Practice expense is a component of the Medicare RVS.

Practice Expense Relative Value: A value that reflects the average amount of practice expenses incurred in performing a particular service. All values are expressed relative to the practice expenses for a reference service whose value equals one practice expense unit.

Practice Guideline: An explicit statement about the benefits, risks, and costs of particular courses of medical action based on the medical literature and expert judgment that is intended to help practitioners, patients and others make decisions about appropriate health care for specific clinical conditions.

Preadmission Certification: A certification performed before the patient's admission that acute hospitalization or surgery is necessary, based on the judgment of medically appropriate care by a qualified peer.

Preadmission Review (PAR): A UR mechanism used by plans that utilize telephone-based nurses to review cases, assign expected LOS, and issue an authorization number. Also referred to as precertification.

Preauthorization: Sanction by a managed care company that treatment is needed, thereby providing authorization for payment for service provided to beneficiary of contract.

Preexisting Condition: Any single or multiple physical and/or mental impairment or disease of an enrollee that exists before insurance begins. Many plans stipulate a waiting time before an enrollee can begin to receive care for preexisting conditions to establish that his or her health condition is relatively stable (e.g., post-transplant enrollees).

Preferred Provider: Any entity defined as a provider that has agreed to contract for the provision of health services for all enrolled members of a plan.

Preferred Provider Arrangement (PPA): Same as a PPO, but sometimes refers to a somewhat looser type of plan in which the payer (i.e., the employer) makes the arrangements rather than the providers.

Preferred Provider Organization (PPO): A plan or an affiliation of providers seeking contracts with a plan (by virtue of their ability to cover a broad geographical area or provide multispecialty skills). Incentives for providers to participate include quick turnaround of claims payment, a valuable pool of patients, and FFS payment. Payer incentive is negotiated discounts to FFS. Usually a PPO does not prepay physicians. A physician-sponsored PPO increasingly will bear risk when seeking arrangements with insurance companies or self-insured companies. There is great consensus that PPOs are early-stage managed care relationships that are formed in response to HMO pressure or competition, but do not bring the same savings on health care.

Premium: An amount paid periodically to purchase health insurance benefits.

Prevailing Charges: The fees most frequently charged by physicians in a specific geographic area for Medicare, which are 75 percent of the customary charges for similar services in the same locality (the maximum Medicare rate is controlled by an economic index). Other plans may pay a different percentage based on the prevailing charge.

Primary Care Case Management (PCCM): Case management that requires a gatekeeper to coordinate and manage primary care services, referrals, preadmission certification, and other medical or rehabilitative services. The primary advantage of PCCM for Medicaid eligibles is increased access to a PCP, which reduces use of hospital outpatient departments and ERs.

Primary Care Provider (PCP): A physician whose practice is mainly devoted to general internal medicine, family medicine, general practice, or pediatrics.

Primary Care-Sensitive Admission: A hospital admission that might have been avoided through timely and adequate care; typically an admission for conditions where a lack of detection and management leads to more radical treatments.

Privileges: Formal authority by an HMO or hospital-based system to treat patients at a hospital or within a system as granted by a governing authority.

Professional Liability Insurance (PLI): The insurance physicians purchase to help protect themselves from the financial risks associated with medical liability claims.

Peer Review Organization (PRO): A physician-sponsored organization charged with reviewing services provided to patients to determine if the services rendered are medically necessary; are provided in accordance with professional criteria, norms, and standards; and are provided in the appropriate setting.

Professional Standards Review Organization (PSRO): One of 203 physician groups that reviewed the care rendered to Medicare and Medicaid patients pursuant to a 1972 law. The PSRO program was repealed in 1982 and replaced by the PRO program.

Profiling: Expressing a pattern of practice as a rate; some measure of utilization (costs of services) or outcome (functional status, morbidity, or mortality) aggregated over time for a defined population of patients to compare with other practice patterns; may be done for physician practices, health plans, or geographic areas.

Program for All-Inclusive Care for the Elderly (PACE): CMS demonstration using managed care programs to serve frail elderly persons who are, for the most part, dually eligible for Medicare and Medicaid and have been assessed as eligible for nursing home placement. The program provides adult day health care and CM to help the program participants maintain independent living in the community.

Prospective Payment System (PPS): Established by Title VI of the Social Security Amendments of 1983 and developed and implemented by the CMS to pay health care facilities for Medicare patients; replaced the retrospective cost-based method that was begun in 1968. The primary prevention against premature discharge of patients is the presence of sound quality assurance programs.

Provider: A physician, pharmacist, dentist, optometrist, chiropractor, podiatrist, nurse, hospital, group practice, nursing home, behavioral or mental health entity, skilled nursing facility, long-term care facility, pharmacy, other medical institution, or any individual or group of individuals that provides health care services. A distinction between provider and supplier in Medicare policy will determine payment on a charge basis for suppliers and a prospective or retrospective cost-related basis for providers.

Provider-Sponsored Network (PSN): A formal affiliation of health care providers organized and operated to provide a full range of health care services.

Provider-Sponsored Organization (PSO): Any organization created through the formal affiliation of health care providers that seeks to act as an insurer for an enrolled population. PSOs can be physician based, hospital based, or a combination of both. Typically, they are local health delivery systems.

Qualified Medicare Beneficiary (QMB): Medicare beneficiaries whose incomes are at or below 100 percent of the federal poverty level and whose resources do not exceed 200 percent of that allowed under the SSI program in each state. QMBs are entitled under federal law to have their Medicare premiums, coinsurance, and deductibles paid by the state in which they reside.

Quality Assurance: Program activities that are conducted from the perspective of individual hospitals or insurers and reviewed by internal leadership or external entities such as NCQA to ensure that medical care and service meets clinical standards of quality; includes elements of peer review and audits of care, medical protocols, credentialing, and assessment of patient satisfaction.

Quality Improvement (QI): A management-engineering theory applied to the medical industry to effect continuous and incremental improvements through the identification of problems in health care delivery, the testing of solutions to those problems, and the tracking of solutions. QI seeks to identify the optimal process to accomplish a task and then to eliminate process deviation that causes waste or delay. The "clean sheet of paper" approach, a more nonlinear theory of reengineering, allows a team to design a preferred process as if no process were already in place. QI is also called linear improvement.

Quality Improvement Organization (QIO): An organization contracting with CMS to review the medical necessity and quality of care provided to Medicare beneficiaries; previously called peer review organization.

RAPs: DRGs for radiologists, anesthesiologists, and pathologists used by the CMS to reimburse these specialists for care to Medicare recipients.

Real Value: Measurement of an economic amount corrected for change in price over time (inflation), thus expressing a value in terms of constant prices.

Reasonable and Customary Charge (R&C): The amount of money usually billed for individual health care services within a specific geographic region. Sometimes all fees in the 80th or 90th percentile are averaged to determine R&C; other times R&C is synonymous with fee schedule rate ceilings, when the rates are relatively high.

Referral: The request for additional care, usually of a specialty nature, by a PCP or by a specialist needing additional medical information on behalf of the patient. Referrals within the context of managed care are more restricted in that a PCP who accepts financial risk for downstream medical care is more sensitive to the balance between medical necessity and cost. Good information systems are needed to track referral costs to aid physicians in learning more about this factor.

Refinement: The correction of relative values in the Medicare RVS that were initially set incorrectly or have become incorrect as a result of changes in medical practice.

Reinsurance: Insurance procured by an insurance company, provider, or employer to guard against the partial or complete loss of money from medical claims. Typical coverage is purchased for either individual stop-loss, aggregate stop-loss, out-of-area care, or insolvency protection. A larger health plan typically reduces reinsurance coverage as it grows. Also called risk control insurance or stop-loss insurance.

Relative Value Scale (RVS): An index that assigns weights to each medical service. The weights represent the relative amount to be paid for each service. The RVS used in the Medicare Fee Schedule consists of three components: physician work, practice expense, and malpractice expense.

Relative Value Unit (RVU): The building block of the RBRVS. For each service, there are three RVUs to cover work, practice expenses, and the cost of professional liability insurance.

Reserves: Fiscal method of providing a fund for incurred but not reported health services or other financial liabilities; also refers to deposits and/or other financial requirements that must be met by an entity as defined by various state or federal regulatory authorities.

Resource-Based Relative Value Scale (RBRVS): A fee schedule introduced by the CMS to reimburse physicians' Medicare fees based on the amount of time, resources, and expertise expended in selected specific medical procedures. Adjustments are made for regional variations in rents, wages, and other geographic differences. Developed by Dr. William Hsiao and a Harvard research team, it divides Medicare treatments into 7,000 procedures with specific scales.

Respondeat Superior: The legal doctrine of vicarious liability, which may be applied in the case of a suit against a health care provider by a patient, making the employer responsible for the employee's negligent acts because the employer has the responsibility to control that behavior.

Retention: The administrative fee that normally serves as the profit for a plan. Retention funds may be reinvested in the organization that administers the plan, applied toward the cost of medical claims and miscellaneous expenses, or, in the case of for-profit entities, passed to shareholders.

Retrospective Review: A method of determining medical necessity and/or appropriate billing practice for services that have already been rendered.

Revenue Share: The proportion of total revenue devoted to a particular type of expense. For example, the practice expense revenue share is the proportion of revenue used to pay for practice expense.

Risk: The loss foreseen by a provider, IDN, or insurer in providing health care services; also refers to the generic arrangements within managed care that involve a departure from FFS medicine toward prepayment, which focuses on the care of a given population by a PCP or hospital system taking full economic responsibility for that population's care needs.

Risk Adjuster: A measure used to adjust payments in order to compensate for spending that is expected to be lower or higher than average, based on the health status or demographic characteristics of enrollees.

Risk Adjustment: The process used to adjust payments to plans to compensate for differences in health status of enrollees across plans.

Risk Analysis: The methodology for evaluating the expected medical care costs for a prospective group, assuming best application of all available products (with the employer-customer in mind) and benefit levels and prices that best meet the needs of the group under evaluation.

Risk Contract: A contract involving medical claims risk on a prepayment basis between two entities, such as a provider and an HMO, the CMS and a federally qualified HMO, or an IDN and an individual PCP or medical group. It will specify the medical services to be included, together with the associated reimbursement structure, and the amount to be withheld or the physician contingency reserve to be set aside for potential claims above estimates or incremental risk corridors. If claims run above projections, it is the responsibility of the party that bears risk under the contract to pay those excess costs. Any savings are similarly allocated to the party bearing risk.

Risk Corridor: A mechanism to share risk within a stated range of performance, such as where providers are assessed penalties or given financial rewards if their actual claims PMPM fall outside a specific percentage above or below an established claims target. For example, for a 10 percent corridor on a PCP set at $23 PMPM, a physician will be subject to rewards for amounts under $21.70 and penalties over $25.30 for PMPM claims costs.

Risk Selection: Any situation in which health plans differ in the health risk associated with their enrollees because of enrollment choices made by the plans or enrollees. One health plan's expected costs differ from another's expected costs as a result of underlying differences in their enrolled populations.

Risk Sharing: Any mechanism that gives financial incentive to managed care providers for rendering cost-effective, high-quality care.

Rural Area: Any geographic region not listed as having a population of 2,500 or more in Document PC(1)A, Number of Inhabitants, of Table VI, Population of Places, and not listed as an urbanized area in Table XI, Population of Urbanized Areas, of the most recent update of the Bureau of Census, U.S. Department of Commerce.

Scored Savings: Amount of savings expected to result from enacting new legislation. Estimated by the Congressional Budget Office by calculating the difference in spending projected under current law and under the proposed legislation.

Secondary Insurance: Any insurance that supplements Medicare coverage. The three main sources for secondary insurance are employers, privately purchased Medigap plans, and Medicaid.

Selective Contracting: State mechanism used as a cost-control measure for obtaining services for Medicaid patients from fewer than all available providers through a competitive bidding process.

Self-Insurance: A risk strategy that allows the potential profit that an HMO or carrier traditionally receives from funding insurance risk to be experienced instead by an employer or other legal entity, such as a hospital-based delivery network; different from reinsurance in that an external insurance protection is not used as a general format, but certain protection may be sought for a segment such as catastrophic care. Essentially, the health benefits are funded from internal resources without purchasing insurance. Self-insurance entities may obtain outside administrative assistance to manage requirements.

Self-Insured Health Plan: Employer-provided health insurance in which the employer, rather than an insurer, is at risk for its employees' medical expenses.

Sentinel Event: An adverse health event that could have been avoided through appropriate care. An example is hospitalization for uncontrolled hypertension that might have been avoided. *See* Primary Care-Sensitive Admission.

Shared Risk: An arrangement where any two entities, such as a health plan and a provider, agree to share in the risk to some contracted percentage of hospital costs that may come in over budget, as well as share profits for care provided under budget.

Site-of-Service Differential: The difference in the amount paid to the physician when the same service is performed in different practice settings, for example, a colonoscopy in a physician's office or a hospital clinic.

Sixth Omnibus Reconciliation Act of 1985 (OBRA/SOBRA): A federal law, a portion of which created quality review organizations and empowered QROs and peer review organizations (PROs) to monitor quality of care for Medicare recipients enrolled in HMOs or CMPs, provided for civil monetary penalties for plans that failed to provide proper care, and restricted the types of physician incentives that a managed care plan may use when providing care for Medicare recipients; also made disenrollment from HMOs and CMPs far easier for Medicare recipients.

Skilled Nursing Facility (SNF): A facility that provides health and social services to patients on a less than acute basis when ongoing skilled care is required; commonly referred to as a nursing home.

Social Health Maintenance Organization (SHMO): Federally funded demonstration project for the elderly that provides comprehensive health and long-term care benefits to Medicare beneficiaries. Unlike care in other Medicare-enrolling HMOs, care in a social HMO is reimbursed at 100 percent.

Sole Community Provider: A hospital that qualifies for increased PPS or DRG payments.

Specified Low-Income Medicare Beneficiary (SLMB): Medicare beneficiaries who have income below 120 percent of the federal poverty level and whose resources do not exceed 200 percent of that allowed under the SSI program in each state. States are required, under federal law, to pay the Medicare Part B premiums for resident SLMBs.

Spend-Down: A procedure by which income or other assets are spent on health care to qualify for Medicaid coverage.

Staff-Model HMO: An HMO in which physicians practice solely as employees of the HMO and usually are paid a salary.

Standard Benefit Package: A defined set of health insurance benefits that all insurers are required to offer.

Stark I: A section of 1989 OBRA, effective January 1992, that precludes patient referrals by a physician to an entity in which a physician has a financial interest, such as a clinical laboratory owned by a relative; formally called the Ethics in Patient Referrals Act; contains several exceptions to referral relationships or purposes.

Stark II: Legislation, effective August 1993, that strengthened restrictions imposed by Stark I; precludes patient referrals to an expanded list of health care services by a physician having a financial interest in the referral entity.

Stop-Loss Insurance: Insurance that is designed to stop the loss, or limit risk exposure beyond a stated amount, for either the catastrophic loss of individual patients or group claims. Stop-loss insurance is sought by nearly any entity that accepts risk. It is also called "stop-loss" because the more protection, the higher the insurance cost. A point of attachment to stop-loss at $75,000 might cost $2.50 PMPM, whereas an attachment at $100,000 might cost $2.

Subcapitation: Any capitation arrangement at a level subordinate to global capitation, such as a subcapitation between an IDS and PCPs, specialists, or ancillary services.

Submitted Charge: The charge submitted by a provider to the patient or a payer.

Supplemental Security Income (SSI): A program of income support for low-income, aged, blind, and disabled persons established in Title XVI of the Social Security Act.

Supplementary Medical Insurance (SMI): The part of Medicare that covers the costs of physicians' services, outpatient laboratory and x-ray tests, durable medical equipment, outpatient hospital care, and certain other services. This voluntary program requires payment of a monthly premium, which covers 25 percent of program costs, with the rest covered by general revenues. Beneficiaries are responsible for a deductible and coinsurance payments for most covered services. Also called Part B coverage or benefits.

Supplier: A provider of health care services, other than a practitioner, that is permitted to bill under Medicare Part B. Suppliers include independent laboratories, durable medical equipment providers, ambulance services, orthotists, prosthetists, and portable x-ray providers.

Surplus: The funds remaining relative to a risk product or arrangement for payout as bonus or retention, either at the level of an HMO, a hospital withhold pool, an IPA, medical group, or individual PCP under full personal capitation.

Sustainable Growth Rate: The target rate of expenditure growth set by the Sustainable Growth Rate System. Similar to the performance standard under the Volume Performance Standard System, except that the target depends on growth of GDP instead of historical trends.

Sustainable Growth Rate System: A revision to the Volume Performance Standard System; proposed by Congress and the Clinton Administration. This system would provide an alternative mechanism for adjusting fee updates for the Medicare Fee Schedule. The mechanism would use a single conversion factor, base target rates of growth on growth of GDP, and change the method for calculating the conversion factor update to eliminate the two-year delay.

Tail Policy: A policy that covers incidents of medical risk that originated during the policy period but were not reported until after the policy period ended; coverage provided to a physician who leaves a program to retire or join another plan; also known as tail coverage.

Tax Equity and Fiscal Responsibility Act of 1982 (TEFRA): A federal law that created risk and cost contract provisions under which health plans contracted with the CMS and which defined the primary and secondary coverage responsibilities of the Medicare program.

Technical and Miscellaneous Revenue Act of 1988 (TAMRA): A federal law that revised the nondiscrimination rules of Internal Revenue Code Section 89 and amended the penalties for noncompliance with COBRA.

Temporary Assistance for Needy Families (TANF): Block grant program created under federal welfare reform legislation; replaces Aid to Families with Dependent Children (AFDC). Medicaid eligibility is not linked to TANF as it has been to AFDC.

Third-Party Administrator (TPA): Any third-party entity that administers health plan entitlements and is supported by the infrastructure to process claims. A TPA does not underwrite the risk of a contract but performs largely administrative functions that are supported by computer systems. As markets mature, many TPAs are looking to evolve into other lines of business because HMOs and providers are becoming more able to perform the TPA's primary mission.

Tolerable Loss Ratio (TLR): The loss ratio an insurer can fund without losing money on the group.

Total Quality Management (TQM): An organization-wide process of improving the quality of products and services in any organization; also often referred to as CQI (continuous quality improvement) or TQM/CQI.

TriCare: The acronym applied to the DOD program of managed care, which uses a commercial HMO to supplement the health care services the collective military treatment facilities provide; includes a triple option array of HMO (TriCare Prime), PPO (TriCare extra), and indemnity-type coverage (TriCare Standard or traditional CHAMPUS). The coverage for the 50 states, Canada, Europe, and Latin America is divided into 15 regions, which are competitively bid.

Undergraduate Medical Education: The medical training provided to students in medical school.

Underwriting: The process by which an insurer determines whether and on what basis it will accept an application for insurance. Some insurers use medical underwriting to exclude individuals, groups, or coverage for certain health conditions that are expected to incur high costs.

Underwriting Cycle: The cyclical pattern of insurer profitability and premium prices in group health insurance. The underwriting cycle consists of three phases. Phase I is characterized by rapid price increases and rising revenue for insurance companies. Phase II is marked by relatively stable premium prices and an increase in insurers' capital reserves. Phase III consists of increasing premium price competition and the depletion of insurers' capital reserves.

Unified Insurance: Health insurance coverage that is provided through a single insurance policy.

Uniform Billing Code of 1992 (UB-92): The federal directive requiring hospitals to follow specific billing procedures and use a standard billing form for Medicare services.

United States Per Capita Cost (USPCC): The national average cost per Medicare beneficiary, calculated annually by CMS's Office of the Actuary.

Upcode: To bill for a service that is paid more than the service actually provided.

Usual, Customary, and Reasonable (UCR): A method used by private insurers for paying physicians based on charges commonly used by physicians in a local community. Sometimes called customary, prevailing, and reasonable charges or reasonable and customary (R&C) charges.

Utilization Management (UM): The process of evaluating the necessity, appropriateness, and efficiency of health care services. A review coordinator or medical director gathers information about the proposed hospitalization, service, or procedure from the patient and/or provider, then determines whether it meets established guidelines and criteria, which may be written or automated protocols approved by the organization. A provider or IDN that proves it is skilled in UM may negotiate more advantageous pricing if UM is normally performed by the HMO but could be more effectively passed downward at a savings to the HMO.

Utilization Review (UR): A formal assessment of the medical necessity, efficiency, and/or appropriateness of health care services and treatment plans on a prospective, concurrent, or retrospective basis.

Utilization Review Accreditation Commission (URAC): An independent accreditation organization for UR organizations with a goal of encouraging effective and efficient UR processes and providing a method of evaluation and the accreditation for UR programs (1130 Connecticut Avenue, N.W., Suite 450, Washington, DC 20036).

Utilization Review Organization (URO): An organization that conducts UR activities for managed care organizations.

Vision Carve-Out: The specific reference to eye care that is a carve-out segment of the PMPM or contract pricing; may require that ophthalmologists be participating providers in the case that ophthalmology services are included in the coverage.

Volume and Intensity of Services: The quantity of health care services per enrollee, taking into account both the number and the complexity, or mix, of the services provided.

Volume Offset: The change in the number and mix of services that is projected to occur in response to a change in fees. A 50 percent volume offset means that half the savings from fee reductions will be offset by increased volume and intensity of services. Used to estimate budget effects for Medicare payment changes. Also referred to as behavioral offset.

Volume Performance Standard (VPS): The desired growth rate for spending on Medicare Part B physician services, which is set each year by Congress.

Voluntary Employees' Beneficiary Association (VEBA): A means of accumulating tax-free income-producing reserves for life, sick, accident, or other benefits; initially formed and funded by employees but changes in the law have allowed a VEBA to be used as an employee benefits vehicle by employers; also known as a Section 501(c)(9) trust.

Work Relative Value: A value that reflects the average amount of physician work incurred in performing a particular service, relative to that of other services.

Workers' Compensation (WC): A program that provides liability insurance for an employer and benefits to the employees in the case of job-related injury, with added consideration for family members of employees who are killed in the line of duty. The premium is paid by the employer. Rehabilitation entities attempt to reduce health care costs and the costs of lost employment value by speeding recovery and return to work.

Index

A

AAMC. *See* American Association of Medical Colleges (AAMC)

AAPI. *See* American Accreditation Program, Inc. (AAPI)

Academic health center (AHC). *See also* Medical education and training
medical education, 1:31

Academic medical center (AMC). *See also* Medical education and training
defined, 14:10
fate of, 14:11
labor market and, 14:12
sources of revenue, 14:10

Access
direct access laws, consumer protection initiatives, 8:206
fees, network intermediaries, 11:18
health care information, 13:2
person-identifiable data, 13:23
restrictions, liability, 8:181
trends predicted, 3:6

Accountability
employer benefit plan, 4:10
direct contracting, 4:37
quality accountability, key component, 10:6

Accreditation
Accreditation Association for Ambulatory Health Care (AAAHC), 10:36
American Medical Accreditation Program (AMAP), 10:45
defined, 10:23
interactive health communication, 13:48
Joint Committee on Accreditation of Healthcare Organizations (JCAHO), 10:33–10:35
vs licensing and certification, 10:77
National Committee for Quality Assurance (NCQA), 10:25–10:30, 11:63
quality management, 10:23–10:24
utilization management safeguards, 9:6
Utilization Review Accreditation Commission, 10:31–10:32

Accreditation Association for Ambulatory Health Care (AAAHC)
defined, 10:36

Acquisition of physician practice
antitrust law, 8:41

Adjudication
generally, 12:4
mediation, differences, 12:19

mental health care, 4:9
multiple options, 4:9
out-of-pocket maximum, 4:5
penalty provisions, 4:5
percentage-of-pay cost, 4:5
per-confinement deductible, 4:5
POS arrangement
  incentives, 4:14
  use, 4:13
problem areas, 4:6
reasons for managed care products,
  4:10
uniformity of plans and benefits,
  4:9
**Benefits Improvement and
Protection Act of 2000 (BIPA).** *See*
SCHIP Benefits Improvement and
Protection Act of 2000 (BIPA)
Billing fraud, 8:137
Bioterrorism, threat of, 3:7
BIPA. *See* SCHIP Benefits
Improvement and Protection Act of
2000 (BIPA)
Blue Cross/Blue Shield, 3:1, 8:216
history of, 1:2
Board of directors
IDS, bankruptcy and, 8:69
Boren Amendment, repeal of, 1:20
Boycott. *See* Antitrust issues
Breach of fiduciary duty
liability, 8:181
Bundled fee arrangements
risk sharing, 11:61
Bureau of Competition, 8:5
Business health care coalition. *See*
Health care purchasing coalitions
Business-to-business transactions
health care fraud and abuse,
  Internet, 8:156
Business-to-consumer transactions
health care fraud and abuse,
  Internet, 8:156
**Buyers Health Care Action Group of
Minneapolis,** 4:35

C

CAHPS. *See* Consumer Assessment of
Health Plan Study (CAHPS)
**California Managed Care Liability
Provision,** 8:204
**California Public Employees
Retirement System (CalPERS),**
1:21, 4:16
managed competition, 3.4
Canadian health care, special issues
controversial issues, 2:25
generally, 2:24
Cancer therapies, novel, 14:26
Capitated PPO, 3:25
Capitation
compensation provisions, 11:61
defined, 11:15
full-risk, 11:56
global, 11:61
managed care contract, 11:20
  structure of, 11:22
partial risk, 11:57
physician compensation, 10:43
subcapitation, 11:55
Capped fee schedules
managed care contract, 11:20
Captive physician group PPMC,
6:31
Cardiac Surgery Reporting System,
13:25
Cartwright Act, 8:55
Carve-out benefit programs
reducing financial risk in managed
care contracts, 11:27
Case management, 9:24–9:42
assessment, 9:26
care and cost management, 9:25
certification, licensing, regulation,
  9:29
communication, 9:26
components, 9:26
coordination, 9:26
cost-benefit analysis, 9:26

Health maintenance organization (HMO) (*continued*)
  direct contracting for purchasing and evaluation, 4:42
  direct contract model, 3:12
  employer experiences with, 4:1
  enrollment, 1988 to 1998, 1:6
  evaluation, criteria used, 4:2–4:3
  federal tax exemptions, 8:216
  for-profit, 3:13
  fraud, antikickback, and antireferral laws, risk reduction, 8:151
  generally, 1:1, 5:1
  group practice model, 3:12
  growth rate, 1988 to 1998, 1:6
  Health Maintenance Organization Act, 5:26
  hospital use, 3:16
  independent practice association (IPA) model, 3:12
  individual model, 3:12
  largest growth, 1:12
  legal and regulatory issues and trends, 8:213, 8:214
  Medicaid, 7:14
  medical director
    quality perspective, 10:37–10:39
    role, 1:40
  medical service payment arrangements, changes, 3:14
  Medicare
    payment, 7:29
  Medicare+Choice
    pullout of HMOs, 7:38, 7:39
  Medigap policy, use of HMO instead of, 7:52
  MSA and, 3:46
  network model, 3:12
  new products, 14:19
  not-for-profit, 3:13
  number of, 1976-1997, 1:13
  open-access HMO, 3:24
  participation in RCHS, 3:37
  point-of-service HMO, 3:24
  vs PPO, 3:22
  premium costs, increases, 3:15
  regulation of, 6:44
  selection, criteria used, 4:2–4:3
  staff model, 3:12
  state regulatory analysis, direct contracting, 11:70
  traditional models, 3:12
  uninsured population, extension of coverage to, 1:37
Health Plan Employer Data and Information Set (HEDIS)
  characteristics, and future versions, 10:55
  defined, 10:53
  HEDIS 3.0, 10:53–10:55
  performance measurement, 10:54
Health Reform Act of 1996, 3:43
Health Security Act, 3:1
Health status
  vs economic status, 2:9
  international indicators, 2:5
Hill-Burton Act, 1:6
HIP. *See* Health Insurance Plan (HIP) of Greater New York
HIPAA. *See* Health Insurance Portability and Accountability Act of 1996 (HIPAA)
HIPDB. *See* Health Care Integrity and Protection Data Bank (HIPDB)
HMO. *See* Health maintenance organization (HMO)
HMO Act of 1973, 1:3, 5:26
Hold-harmless clauses
  reducing financial risk in managed care contracts, 11:27
Home health care
  Medicare, 7:23
Horizontal merger, 8:36, 8:37
Hospice care
  Medicare, 7:23
Hospital
  affiliation, quality management, 10:49
  antitrust issues
    MCOs, integration strategy, 8:36

protections, 4:26
purchasing groups, 4:26
reinsurance, 4:27
small employer problems in
insurance selection, 4:25
**Social health maintenance
organizations,** 7:69
Social Security Act of 1935
Title II, 7:1
Title XIX, 7:3, 7:9
Social welfare organizations
federal tax exemptions, 8:216
Specialists
certification, 10:47
severity of illness and, 10:48
Specialty care referrals
antikickback law, 8:145
**Specified low-income Medicare
beneficiaries (SLMBs),** 7:2, 7:8
Spillover liability exposure, 1:11
Standards of review
antitrust issues, 8:16
Stark laws, 8:147–8:149
State. See Government
State boards of medical examiners
managed care contract provisions,
11:63
State departments of health
managed care contract provisions,
11:63
State departments of insurance
managed care contract provisions,
11:63
Sterling Option ISM, 7:36
Stop-loss coverage
reducing financial risk in managed
care contracts, 11:27, 11:28
risk sharing, 11:61
Subcapitation, 11:55
Subrogation
cost control and, 5:33
**Subscriber/employer/payer and
intermediary contract.** See
Contracting and negotiation
strategies

Subscriber/insurer contract. See
Contracting and negotiation
strategies
Summary jury trial
alternative dispute resolution
(ADR), 12:4, 12:41
**Suppliers and distributors,
agreements between**
antitrust issues, 8:17
Surgery
minimally invasive, 14:26
**Surrounding circumstances test,
ERISA,** 5:10
Swing beds, rural hospitals, 7:63

T

TANF. See Temporary Assistance for
Needy Families (TANF)
**Tax and Equity and Fiscal
Responsibility Act of 1982 (TEFRA)**
health maintenance organization
(HMO), 3:13
Taxation, 8:216–8:223
exemptions. See also Tax-exempt
organization
charitable organizations, 8:216
commercial-type insurance, 8:216
HMO, 8:216
IDS, 6:44
most often used, 8:216
social welfare organizations,
8:216
federal
incentives behind private health
coverage, 5:4
tax exemptions most used, 8:216
issues most raised in managed care
arrangements, 8:217
managed care arrangements, issues
arising, 8:217
state regulation of coverage, 5:30
tax incentives, managed care, 1:10
unrelated business income